Black Jack

Volume 7

Osamu Tezuka

VERTICAL.

Production—Glen Isip
Akane Ishida
Lawrence Leung
Vivian Ho

Published by Vertical, Inc., New York.

Originally published in Japanese as *Burakku Jakku 7*
by Akita Shoten, Tokyo, 1987.
Burakku Jakku first serialized in *Shukan Shonen Champion*,
Akita Shoten, 1973-83.

ISBN: 978-1-934287-60-6

Manufactured in the United States of America

First Edition

Second Printing

Vertical, Inc.
451 Park Avenue South, 7th Floor
New York, NY 10016
www.vertical-inc.com

CONTENTS

GUYS AND BIRDS

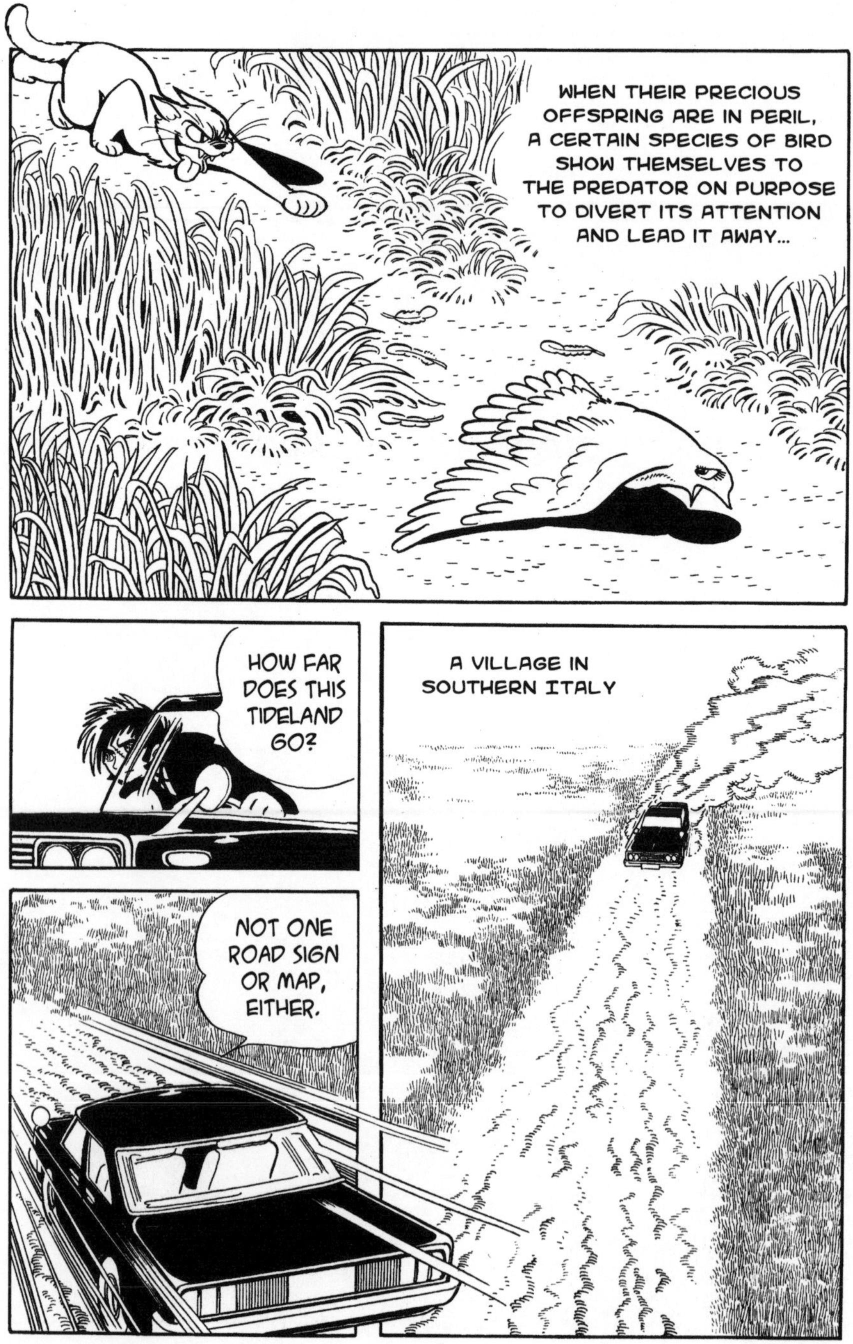
WHEN THEIR PRECIOUS OFFSPRING ARE IN PERIL, A CERTAIN SPECIES OF BIRD SHOW THEMSELVES TO THE PREDATOR ON PURPOSE TO DIVERT ITS ATTENTION AND LEAD IT AWAY...
A VILLAGE IN SOUTHERN ITALY
HOW FAR DOES THIS TIDELAND GO?
NOT ONE ROAD SIGN OR MAP, EITHER.

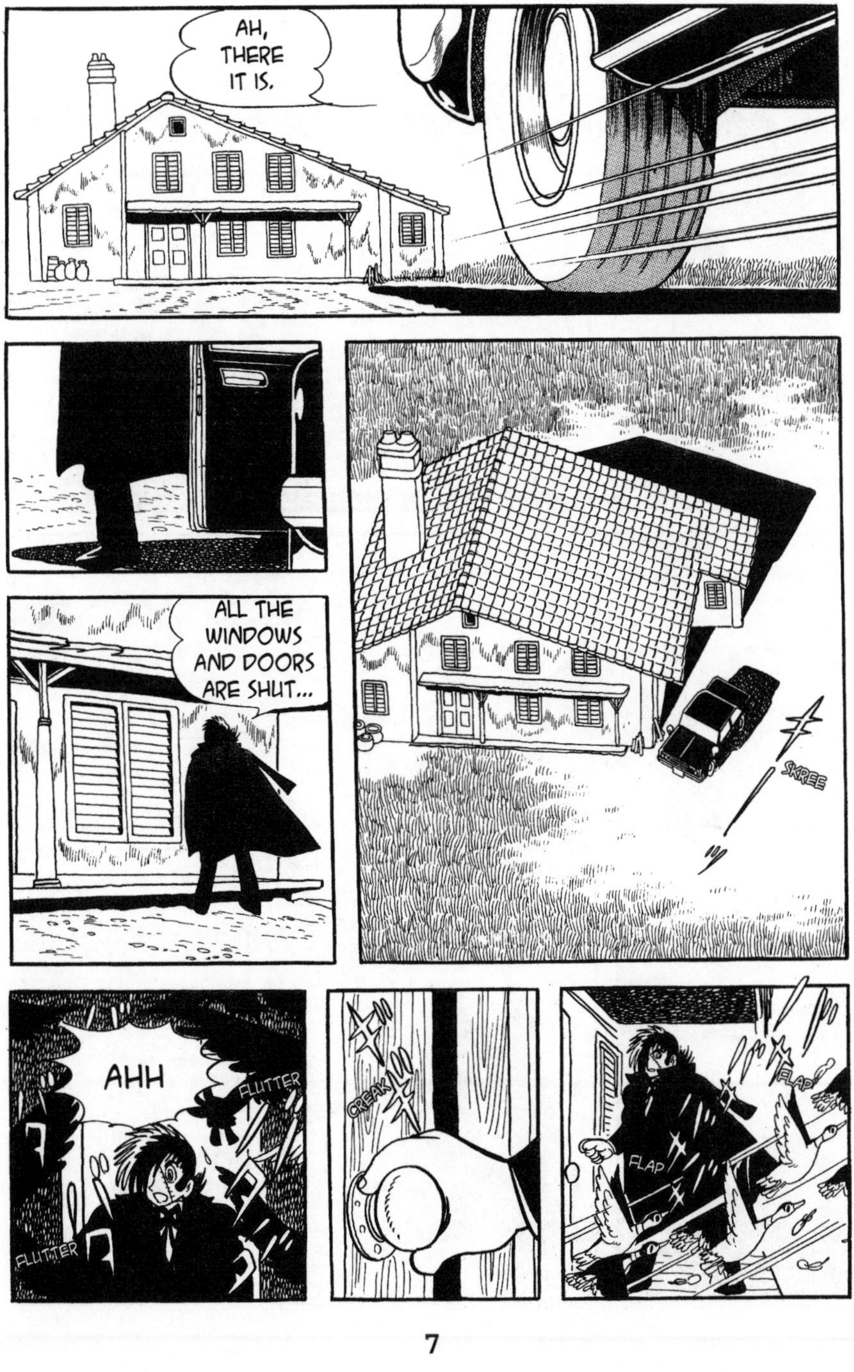
AH, THERE IT IS.
SKREE
ALL THE WINDOWS AND DOORS ARE SHUT...
FLAP
FLAP
CREAK
AHH
FLUTTER
FLUTTER

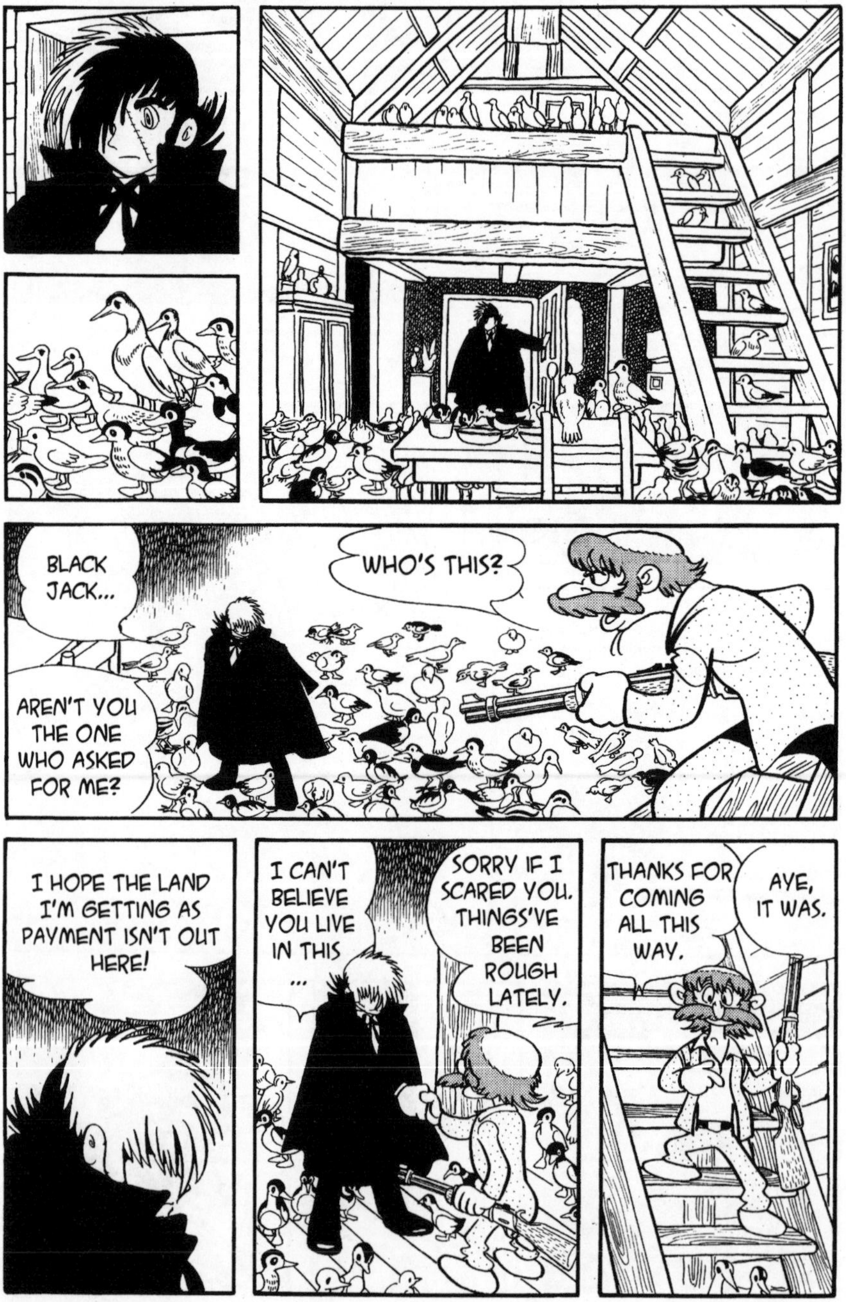
WHO'S THIS?
BLACK JACK...
AREN'T YOU THE ONE WHO ASKED FOR ME?
AYE, IT WAS.
THANKS FOR COMING ALL THIS WAY.
SORRY IF I SCARED YOU. THINGS'VE BEEN ROUGH LATELY.
I CAN'T BELIEVE YOU LIVE IN THIS ...
I HOPE THE LAND I'M GETTING AS PAYMENT ISN'T OUT HERE!

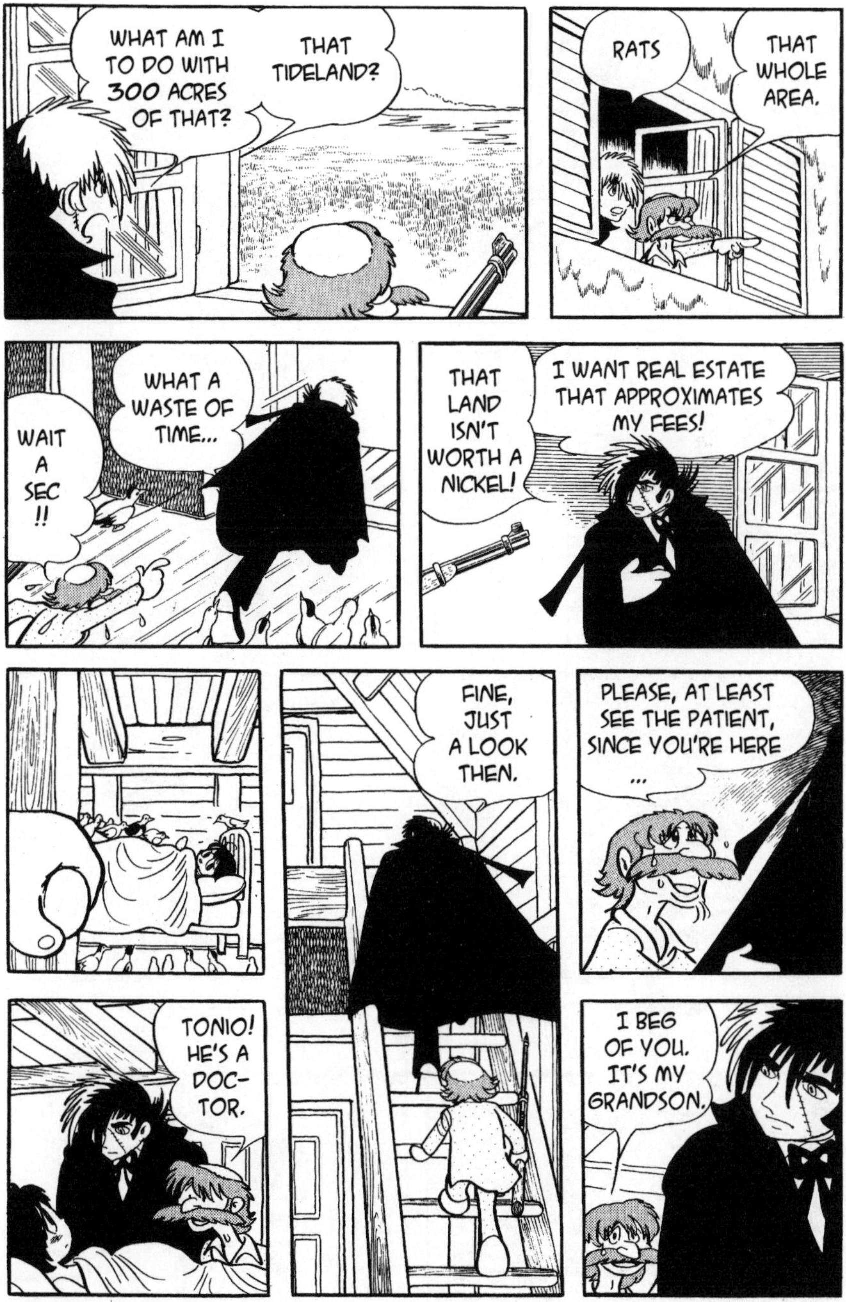
THAT WHOLE AREA.
RATS
THAT TIDELAND?
WHAT AM I TO DO WITH 300 ACRES OF THAT?
I WANT REAL ESTATE THAT APPROXIMATES MY FEES!
THAT LAND ISN'T WORTH A NICKEL!
WHAT A WASTE OF TIME...
WAIT A SEC !!
PLEASE, AT LEAST SEE THE PATIENT, SINCE YOU'RE HERE ...
I BEG OF YOU. IT'S MY GRANDSON.
FINE, JUST A LOOK THEN.
TONIO! HE'S A DOC-TOR.

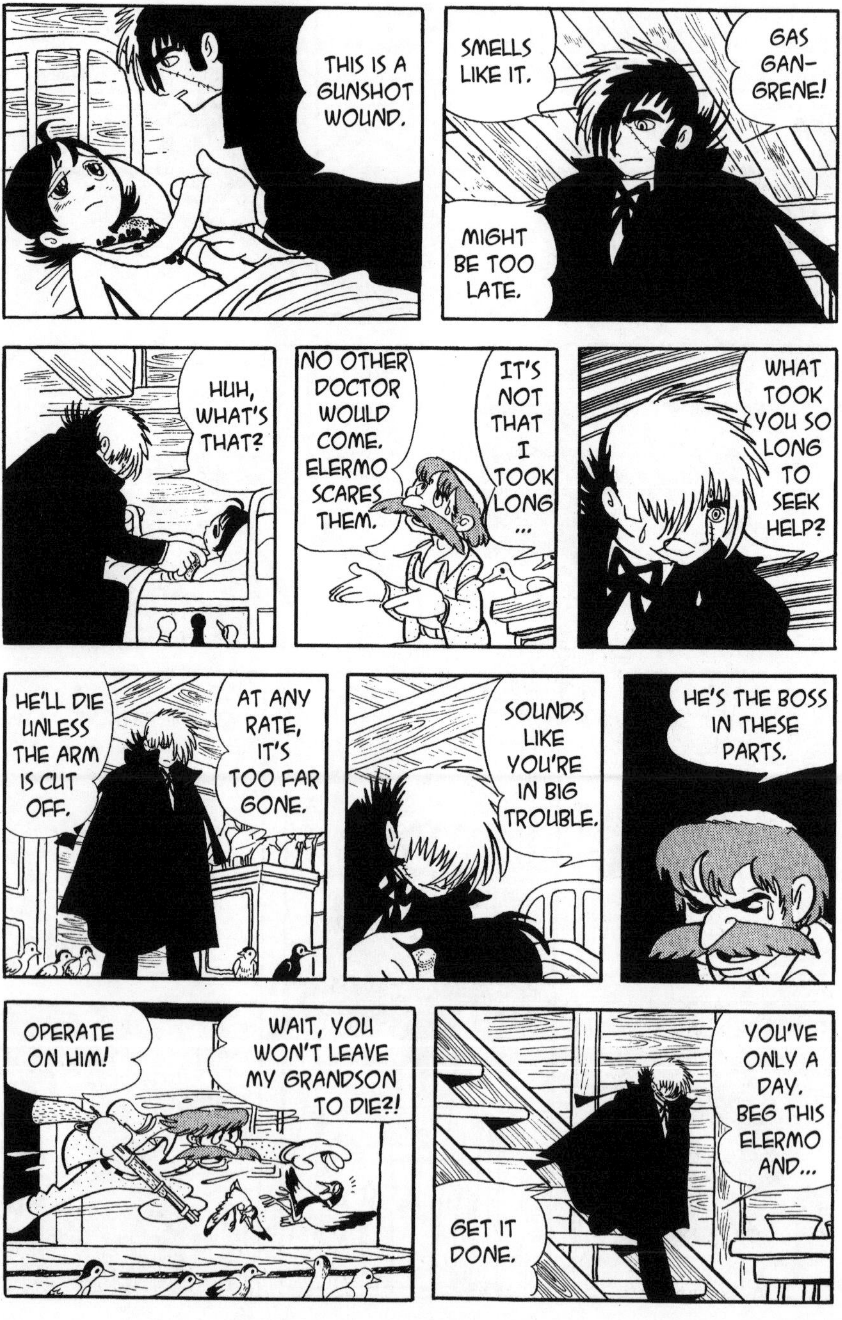
GAS GANGRENE!
SMELLS LIKE IT.
MIGHT BE TOO LATE.
THIS IS A GUNSHOT WOUND.
WHAT TOOK YOU SO LONG TO SEEK HELP?
IT'S NOT THAT I TOOK LONG...
NO OTHER DOCTOR WOULD COME. ELERMO SCARES THEM.
HUH, WHAT'S THAT?
HE'S THE BOSS IN THESE PARTS.
SOUNDS LIKE YOU'RE IN BIG TROUBLE.
AT ANY RATE, IT'S TOO FAR GONE.
HE'LL DIE UNLESS THE ARM IS CUT OFF.
YOU'VE ONLY A DAY. BEG THIS ELERMO AND...
GET IT DONE.
WAIT, YOU WON'T LEAVE MY GRANDSON TO DIE?!
OPERATE ON HIM!

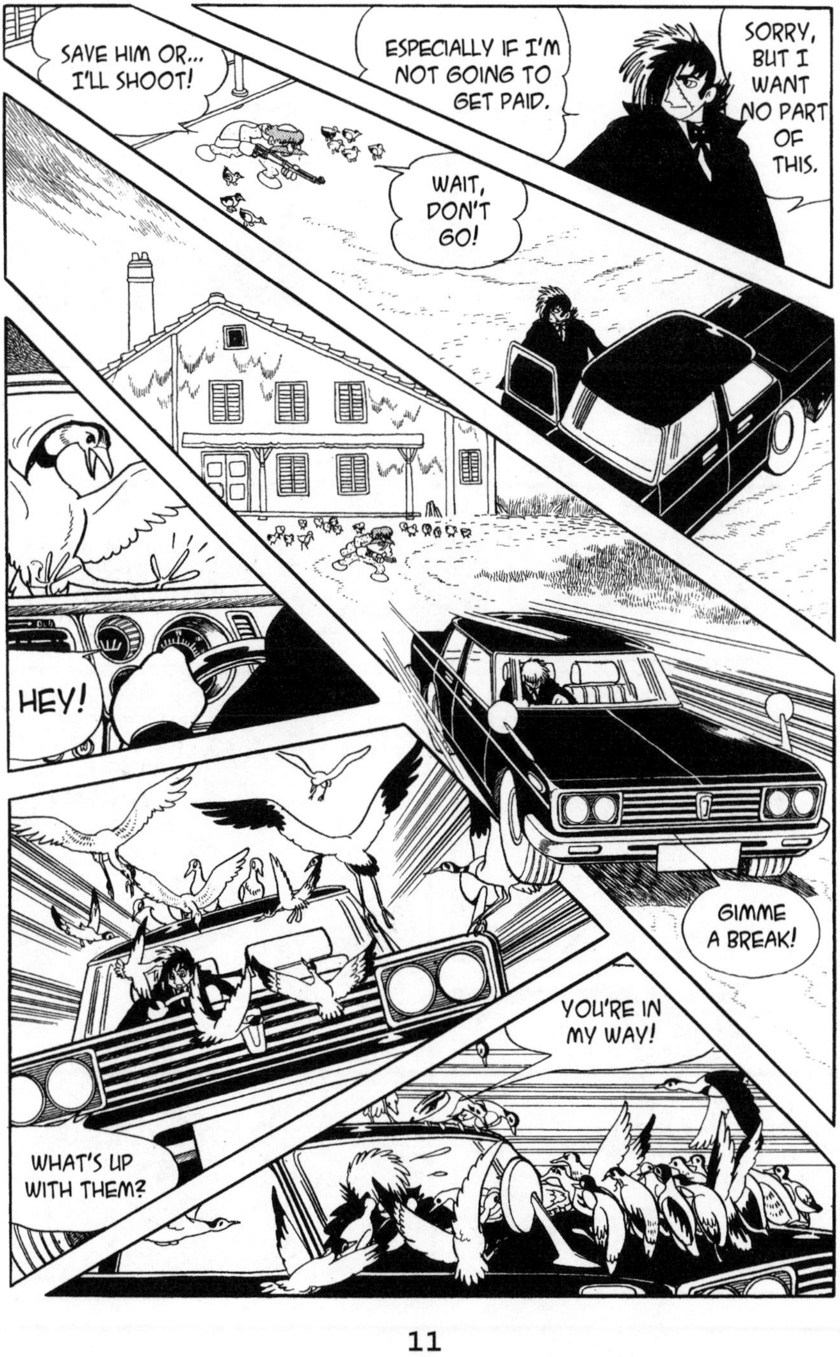
SORRY, BUT I WANT NO PART OF THIS.
ESPECIALLY IF I'M NOT GOING TO GET PAID.
SAVE HIM OR... I'LL SHOOT!
WAIT, DON'T GO!
HEY!
GIMME A BREAK!
YOU'RE IN MY WAY!
WHAT'S UP WITH THEM?

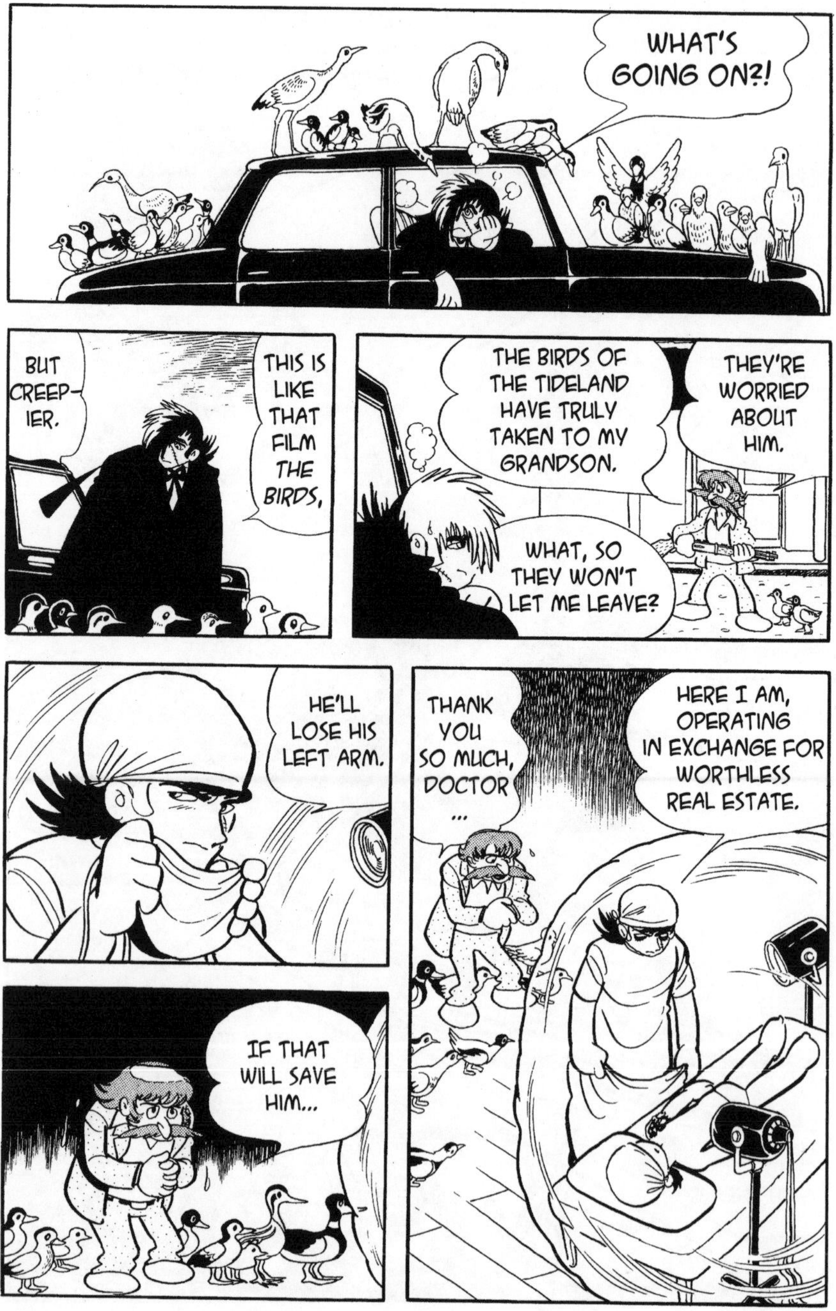
WHAT'S GOING ON?!
THEY'RE WORRIED ABOUT HIM.
THE BIRDS OF THE TIDELAND HAVE TRULY TAKEN TO MY GRANDSON.
WHAT, SO THEY WON'T LET ME LEAVE?
THIS IS LIKE THAT FILM THE BIRDS,
BUT CREEP-IER.
HERE I AM, OPERATING IN EXCHANGE FOR WORTHLESS REAL ESTATE.
THANK YOU SO MUCH, DOCTOR ...
HE'LL LOSE HIS LEFT ARM.
IF THAT WILL SAVE HIM...

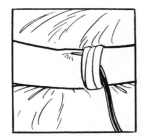

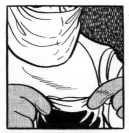

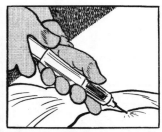

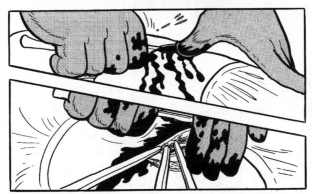

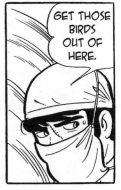

GET THOSE BIRDS OUT OF HERE.
POPS, I CAN'T CONCENTRATE WITH THESE BIRDS STARING AT ME!
BUT THEY'RE WORRIED ABOUT MY GRANDSON.
TONIO'S CARED FOR THEM AS IF FOR HIS OWN LIFE.

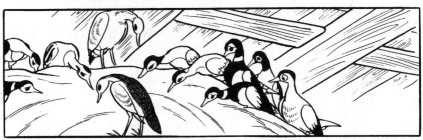

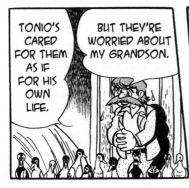

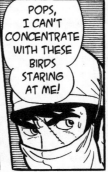

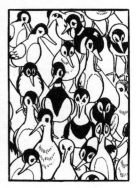

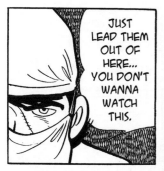

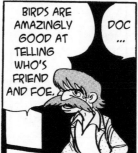

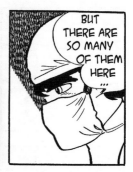

BUT THERE ARE SO MANY OF THEM HERE ...
DOC ...
BIRDS ARE AMAZINGLY GOOD AT TELLING WHO'S FRIEND AND FOE.
JUST LEAD THEM OUT OF HERE... YOU DON'T WANNA WATCH THIS.
KRAK
KREAK
HE NEEDS TO BE TAKEN TO A HOSPITAL AND SOON.

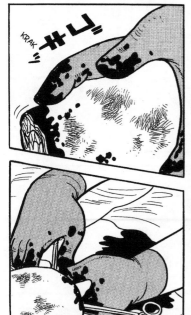

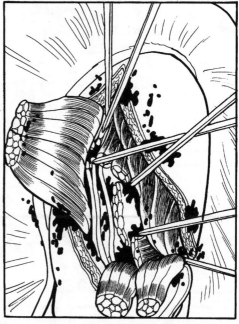

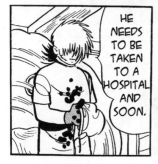

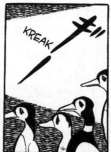

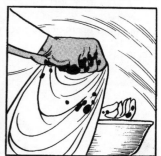

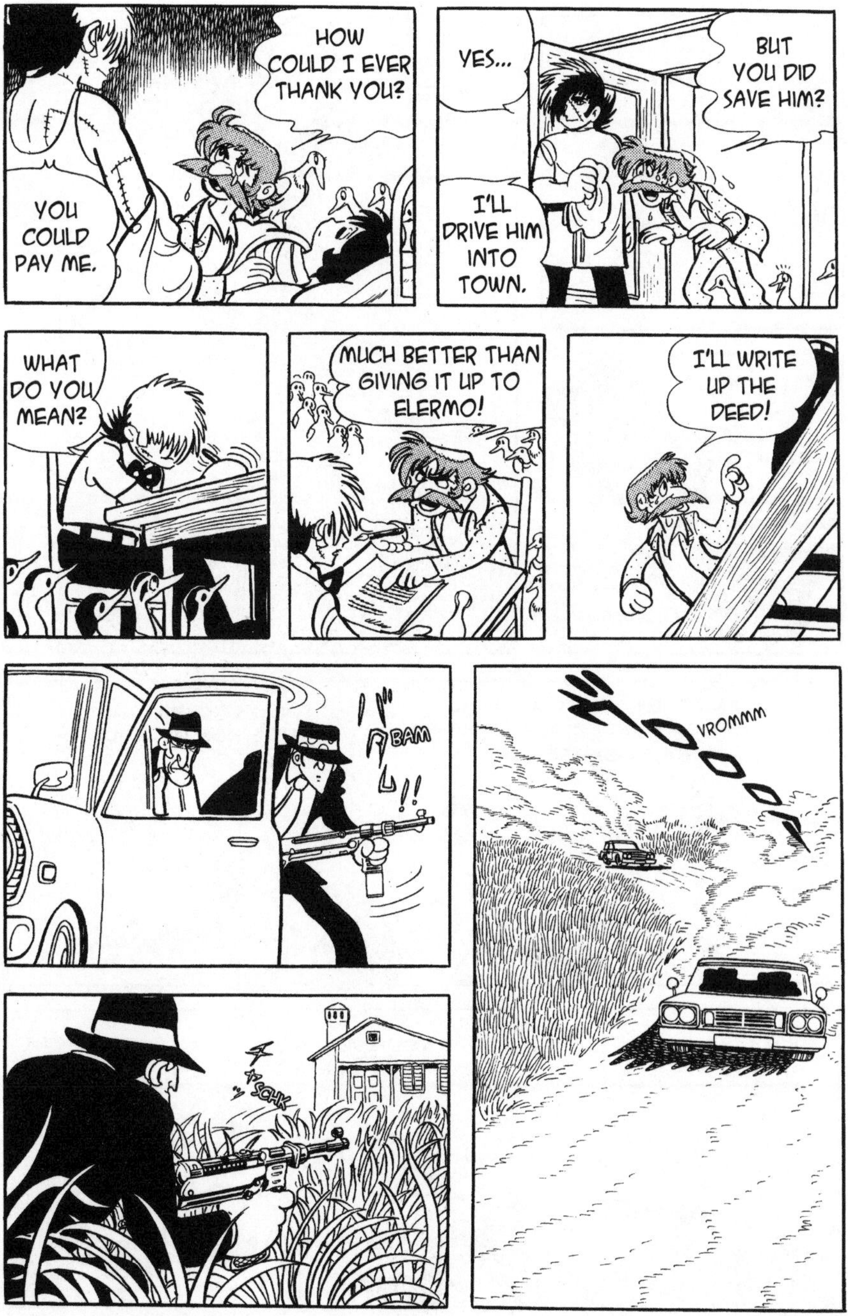
BUT YOU DID SAVE HIM?
YES...
I'LL DRIVE HIM INTO TOWN.
HOW COULD I EVER THANK YOU?
YOU COULD PAY ME.
I'LL WRITE UP THE DEED!
MUCH BETTER THAN GIVING IT UP TO ELERMO!
WHAT DO YOU MEAN?
VROMMM
BAM
SCHK

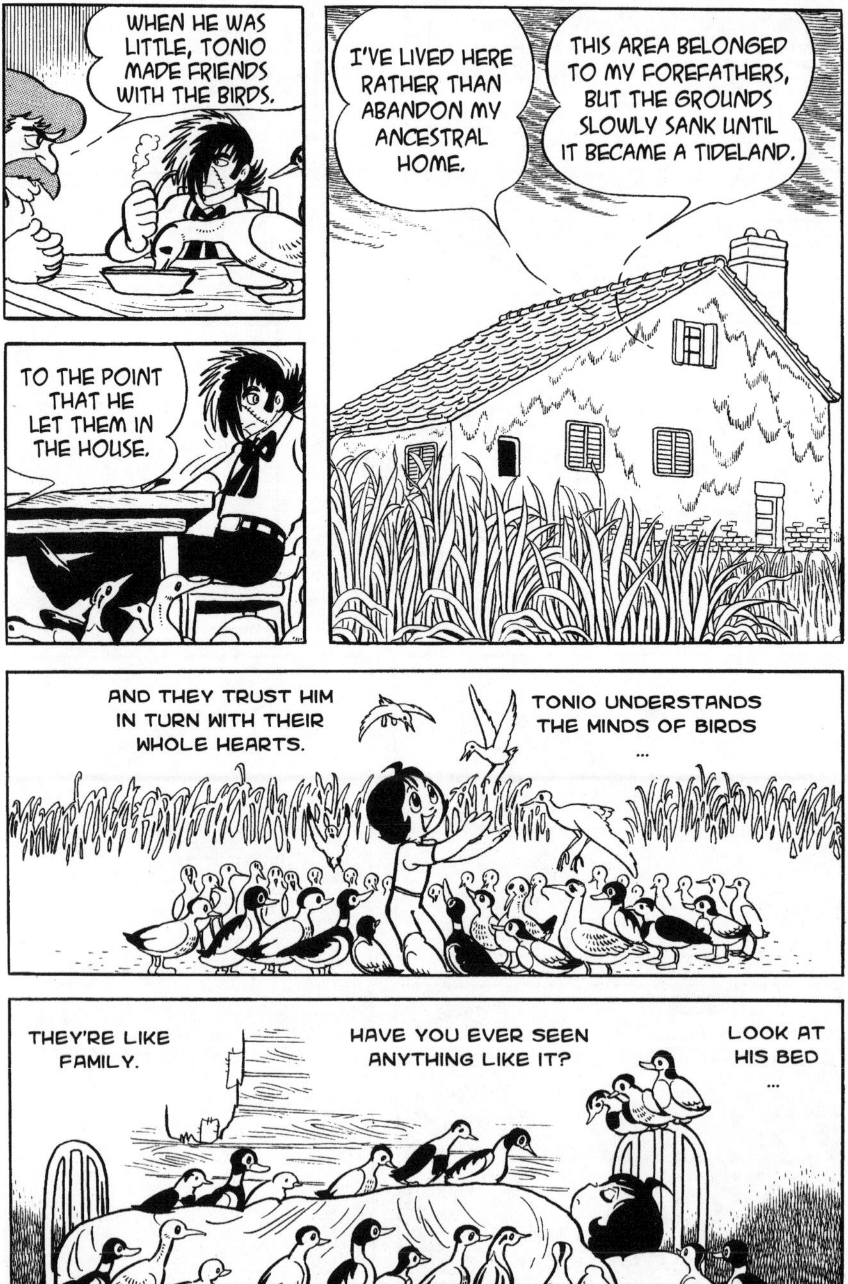
THIS AREA BELONGED TO MY FOREFATHERS, BUT THE GROUNDS SLOWLY SANK UNTIL IT BECAME A TIDELAND.
I'VE LIVED HERE RATHER THAN ABANDON MY ANCESTRAL HOME.
WHEN HE WAS LITTLE, TONIO MADE FRIENDS WITH THE BIRDS.
TO THE POINT THAT HE LET THEM IN THE HOUSE.
TONIO UNDERSTANDS THE MINDS OF BIRDS ...
AND THEY TRUST HIM IN TURN WITH THEIR WHOLE HEARTS.
LOOK AT HIS BED ...
HAVE YOU EVER SEEN ANYTHING LIKE IT?
THEY'RE LIKE FAMILY.

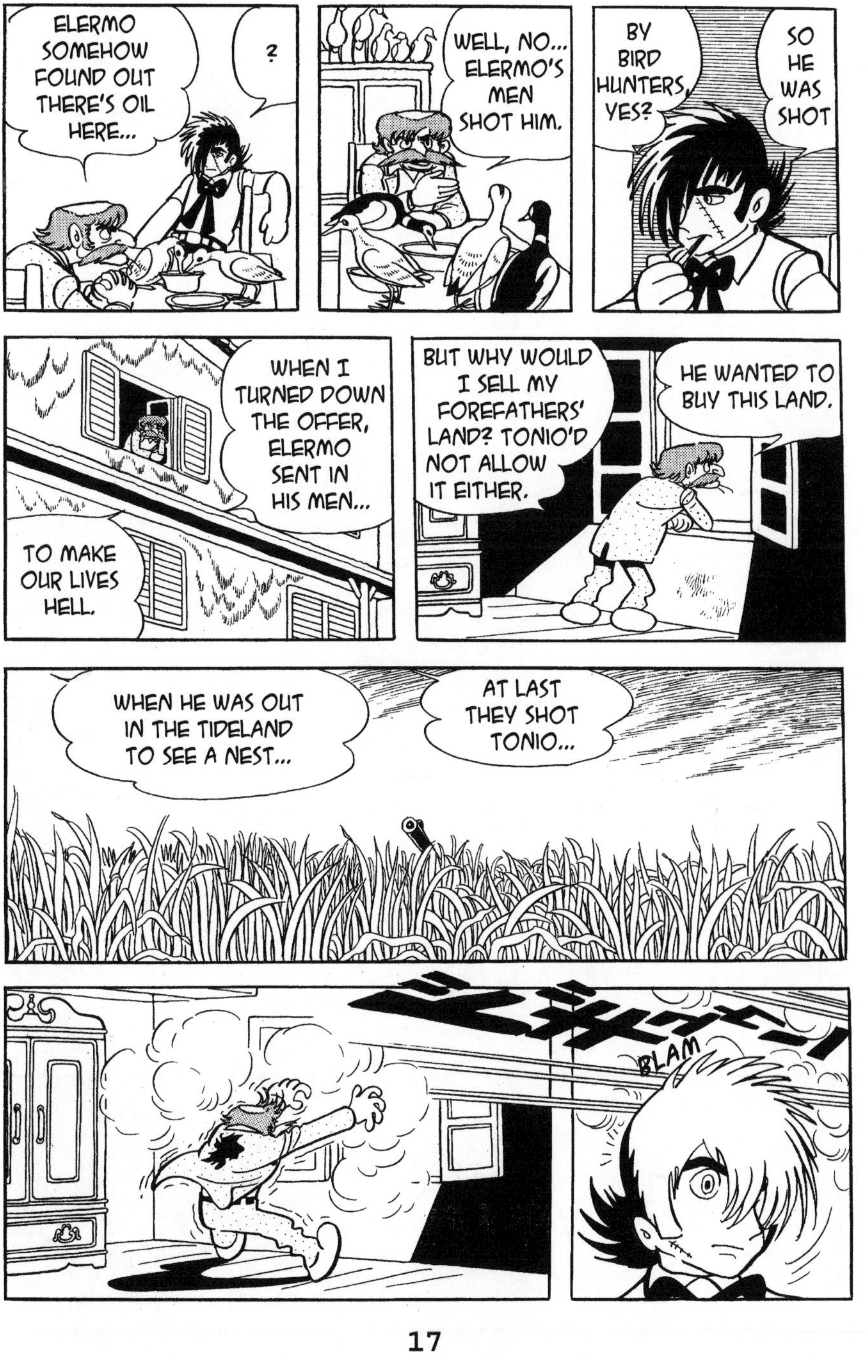
SO HE WAS SHOT
BY BIRD HUNTERS, YES?
WELL, NO... ELERMO'S MEN SHOT HIM.
?
ELERMO SOMEHOW FOUND OUT THERE'S OIL HERE...
HE WANTED TO BUY THIS LAND.
BUT WHY WOULD I SELL MY FOREFATHERS' LAND? TONIO'D NOT ALLOW IT EITHER.
WHEN I TURNED DOWN THE OFFER, ELERMO SENT IN HIS MEN...
TO MAKE OUR LIVES HELL.
AT LAST THEY SHOT TONIO...
WHEN HE WAS OUT IN THE TIDELAND TO SEE A NEST...
BLAM

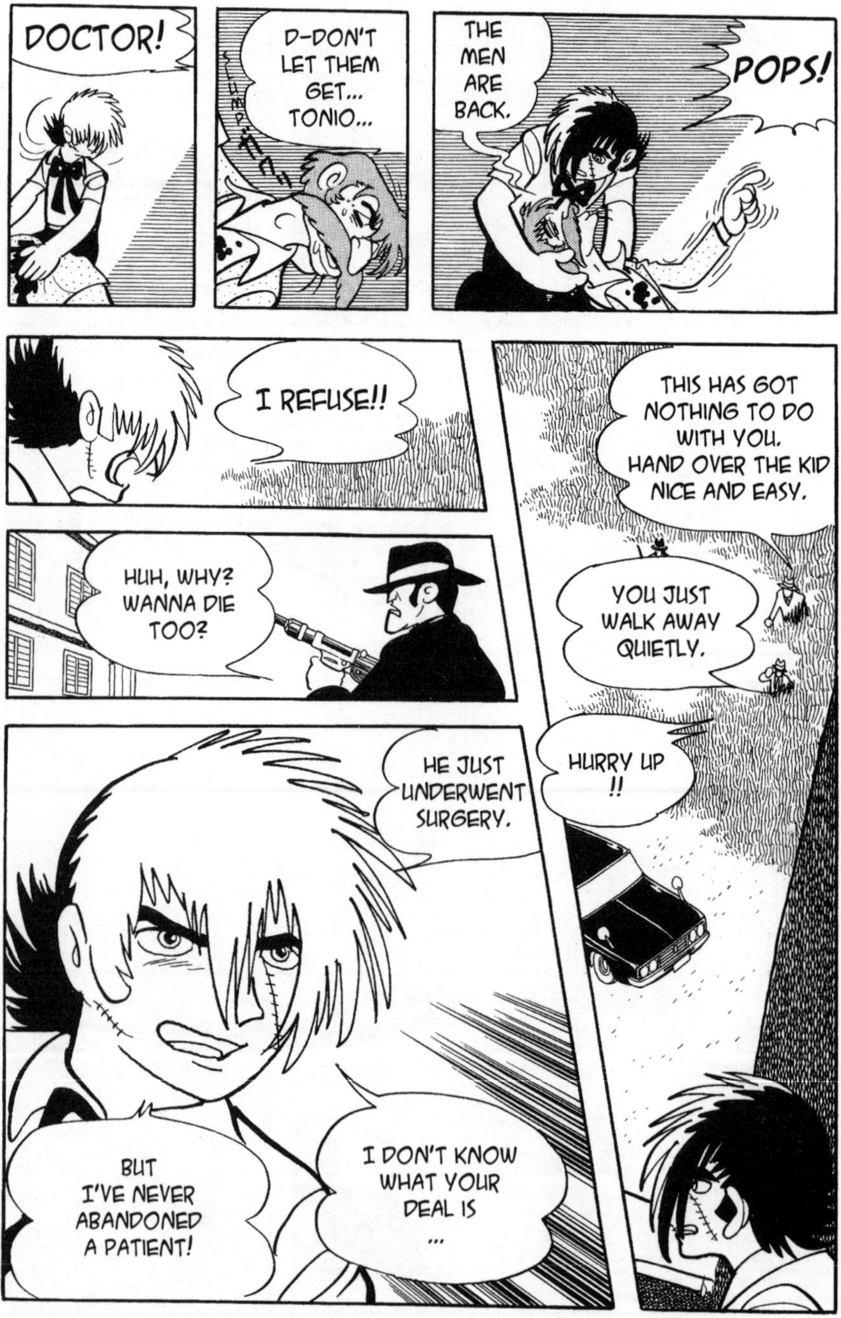
THE MEN ARE BACK.
POPS!
D-DON'T LET THEM GET... TONIO...
SLUMP
DOCTOR!
THIS HAS GOT NOTHING TO DO WITH YOU. HAND OVER THE KID NICE AND EASY.
YOU JUST WALK AWAY QUIETLY.
HURRY UP !!
I REFUSE!!
HUH, WHY? WANNA DIE TOO?
HE JUST UNDERWENT SURGERY.
I DON'T KNOW WHAT YOUR DEAL IS ...
BUT I'VE NEVER ABANDONED A PATIENT!

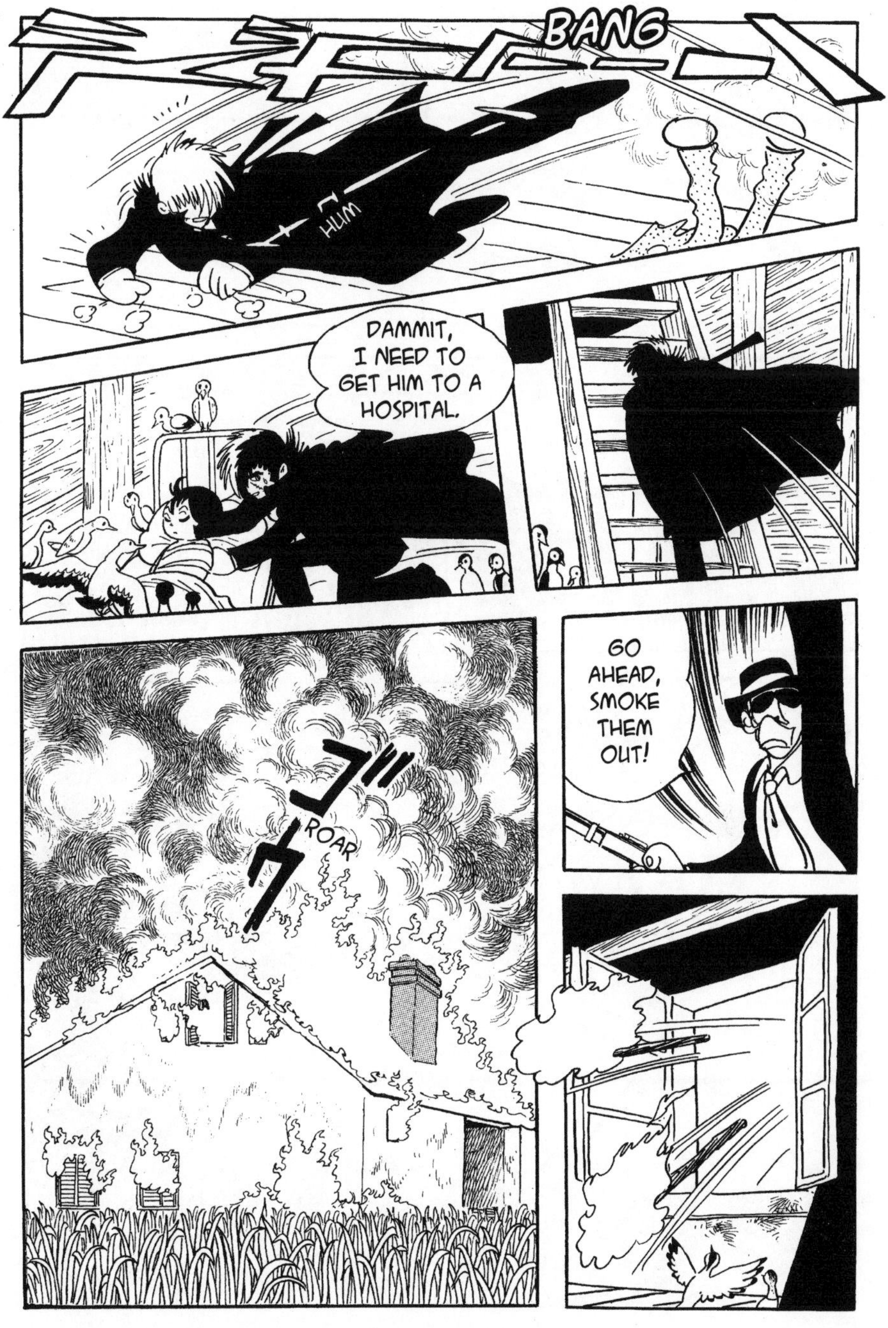
BANG
HUM
DAMMIT, I NEED TO GET HIM TO A HOSPITAL.
GO AHEAD, SMOKE THEM OUT!
ゴウ
ROAR

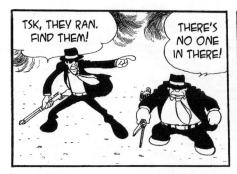

CRACKLE
THERE'S NO ONE IN THERE!
TSK, THEY RAN. FIND THEM!
ZASH
...
BRING US THE KID, AND WE LET YOU GO.
HEY, YA QUACK! YOU WON'T GET AWAY!
OH YEAH? WANNA DIE THAT BAD?
BRO!
HM?

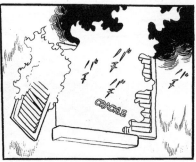

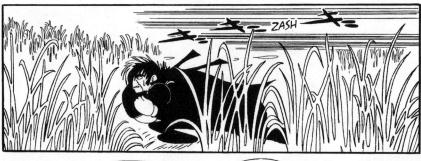

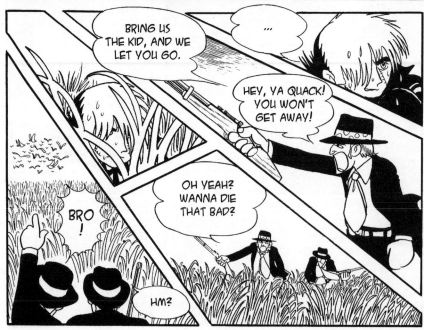

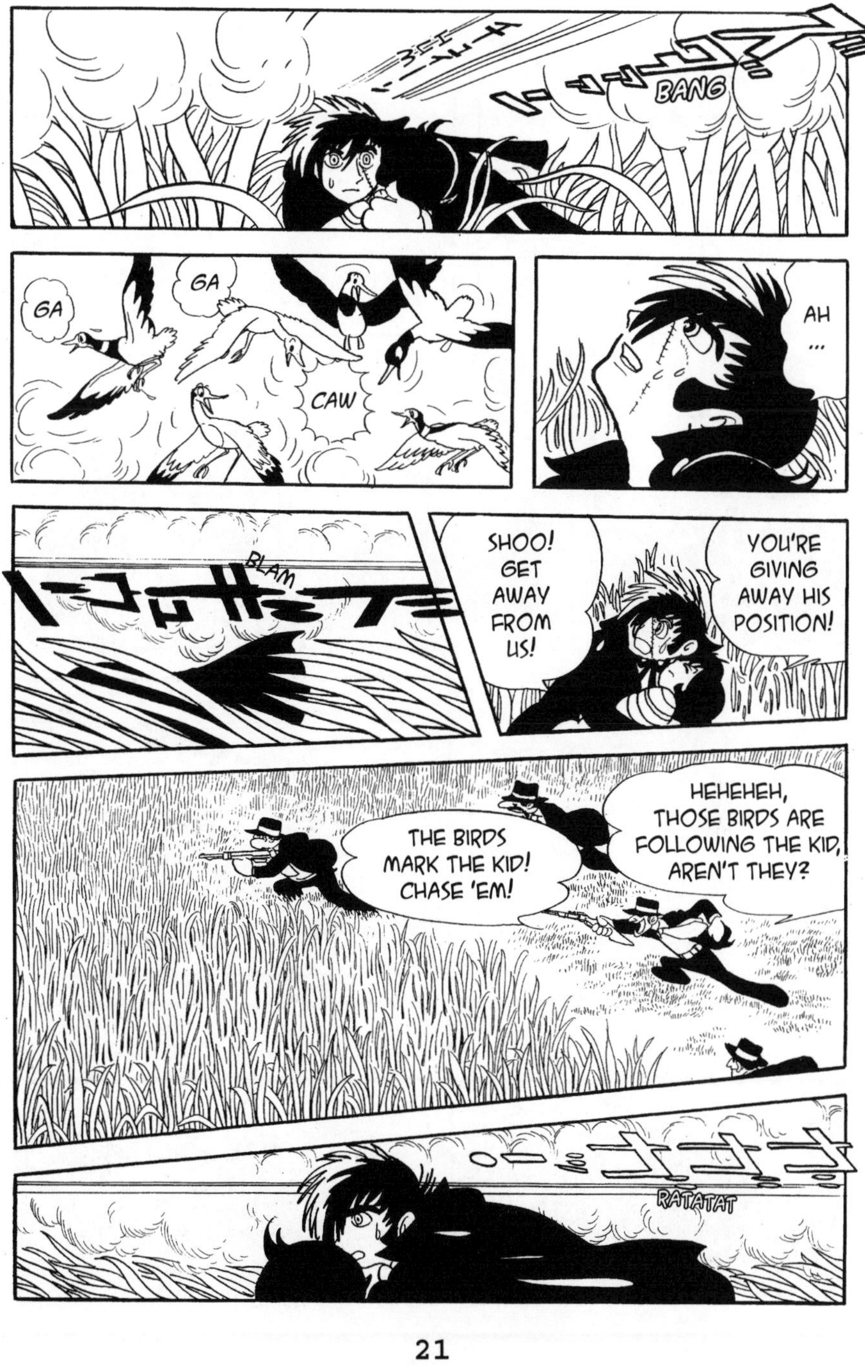
BANG
AH ...
GA
GA
CAW
YOU'RE GIVING AWAY HIS POSITION!
SHOO! GET AWAY FROM US!
BLAM
HEHEHEH, THOSE BIRDS ARE FOLLOWING THE KID, AREN'T THEY?
THE BIRDS MARK THE KID! CHASE 'EM!
RATATAT

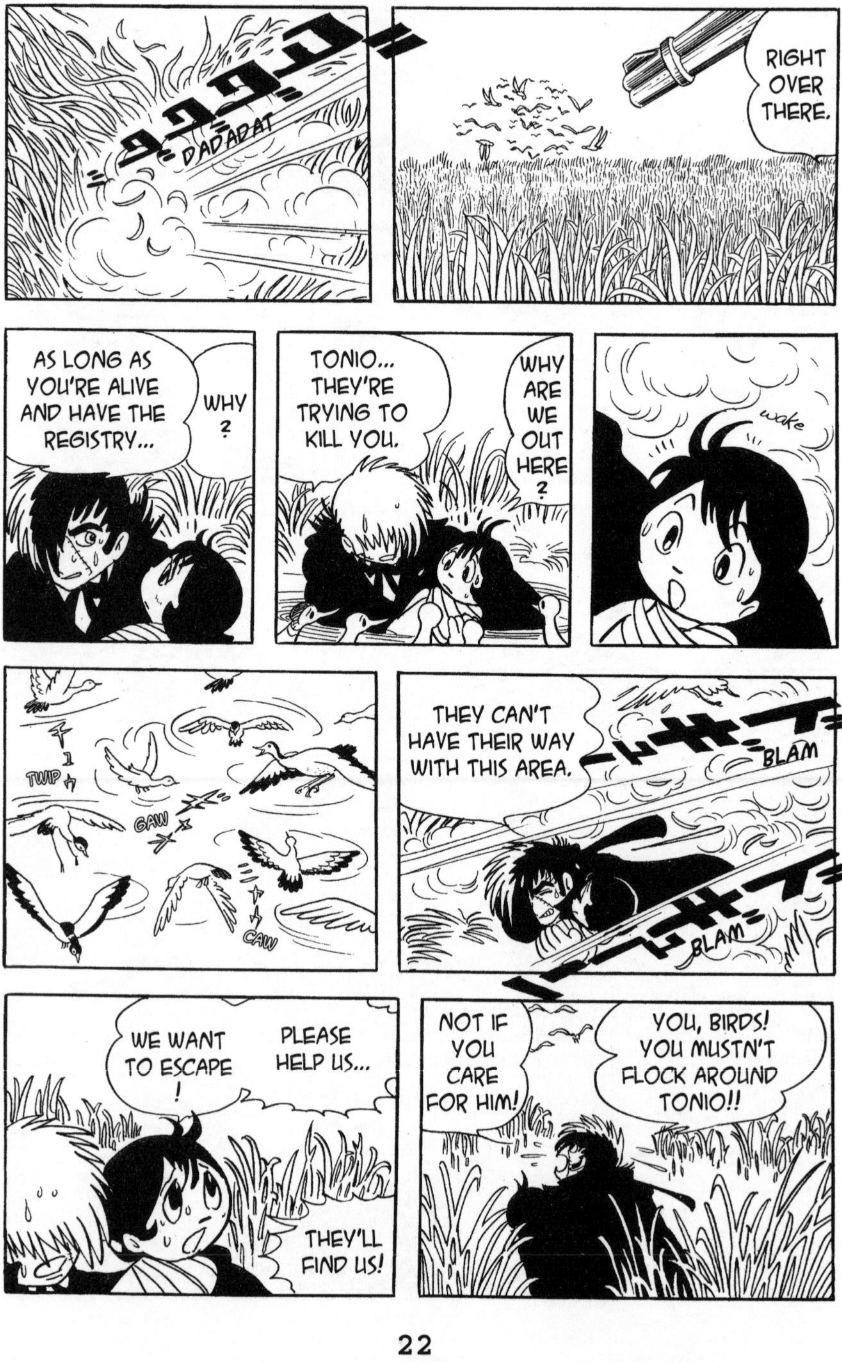
RIGHT OVER THERE.
DADADAT
wake
WHY ARE WE OUT HERE?
TONIO... THEY'RE TRYING TO KILL YOU.
WHY?
AS LONG AS YOU'RE ALIVE AND HAVE THE REGISTRY...
THEY CAN'T HAVE THEIR WAY WITH THIS AREA.
BLAM
BLAM
TWIP
GAW
CAW
YOU, BIRDS! YOU MUSTN'T FLOCK AROUND TONIO!!
NOT IF YOU CARE FOR HIM!
PLEASE HELP US...
WE WANT TO ESCAPE!
THEY'LL FIND US!

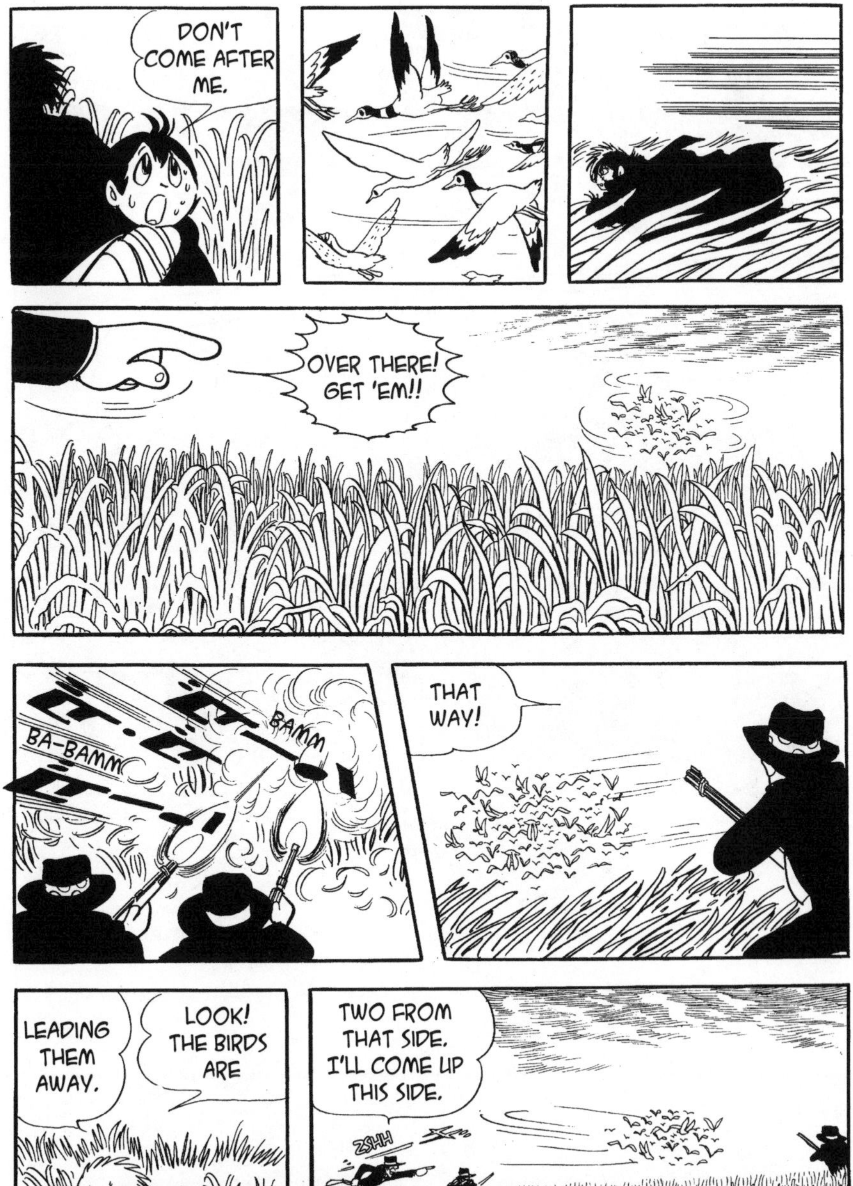
DON'T COME AFTER ME.
OVER THERE! GET 'EM!!
THAT WAY!
BAMM
BA-BAMM
TWO FROM THAT SIDE. I'LL COME UP THIS SIDE.
ZSHH
LOOK! THE BIRDS ARE
LEADING THEM AWAY.
NOW!

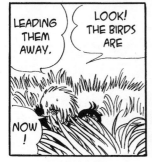

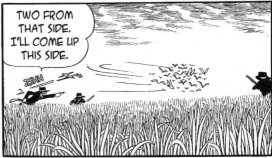

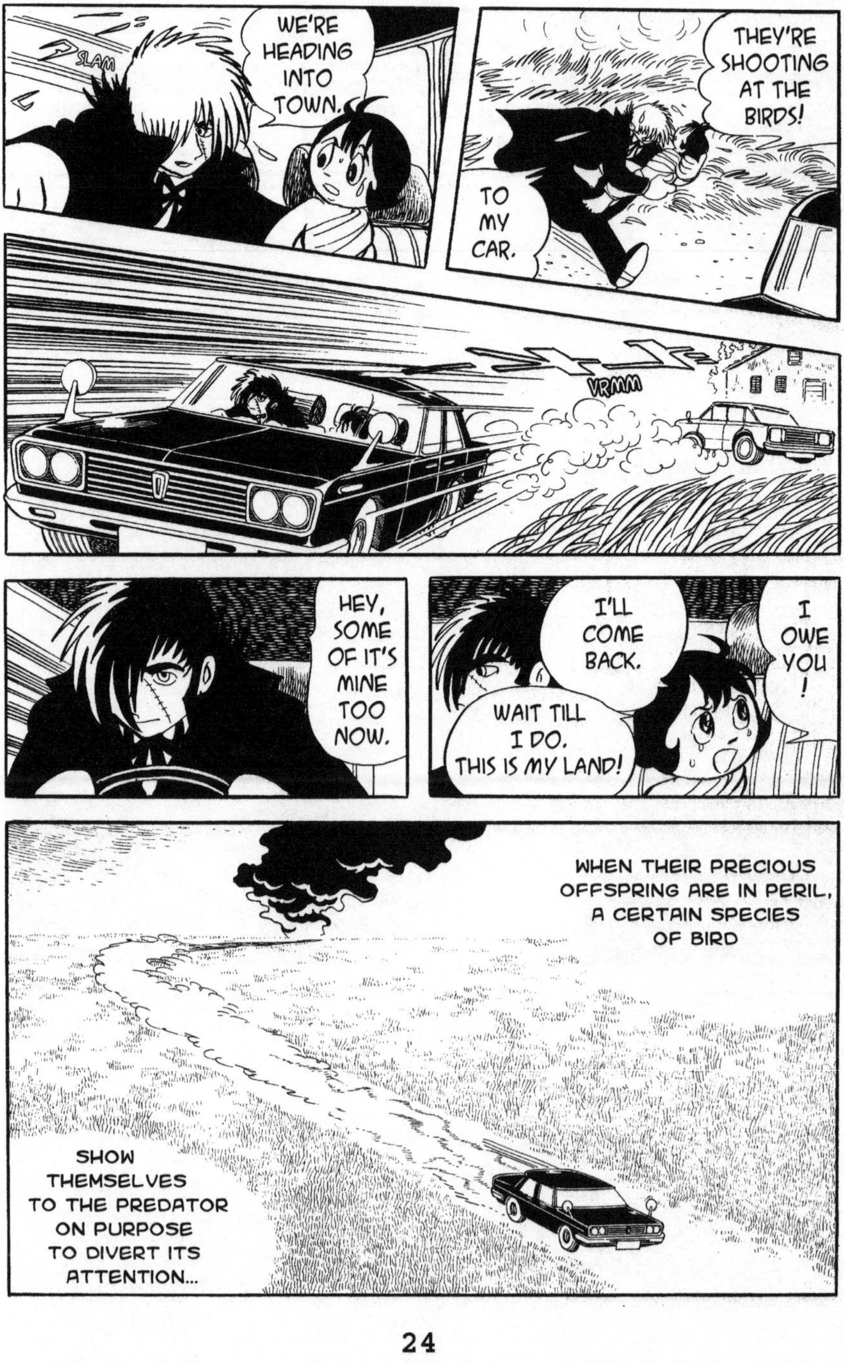
THEY'RE SHOOTING AT THE BIRDS!
TO MY CAR.
SLAM
WE'RE HEADING INTO TOWN.
VRMM
I OWE YOU!
I'LL COME BACK.
WAIT TILL I DO. THIS IS MY LAND!
HEY, SOME OF IT'S MINE TOO NOW.
WHEN THEIR PRECIOUS OFFSPRING ARE IN PERIL, A CERTAIN SPECIES OF BIRD
SHOW THEMSELVES TO THE PREDATOR ON PURPOSE TO DIVERT ITS ATTENTION...

THE GRAY MANSION

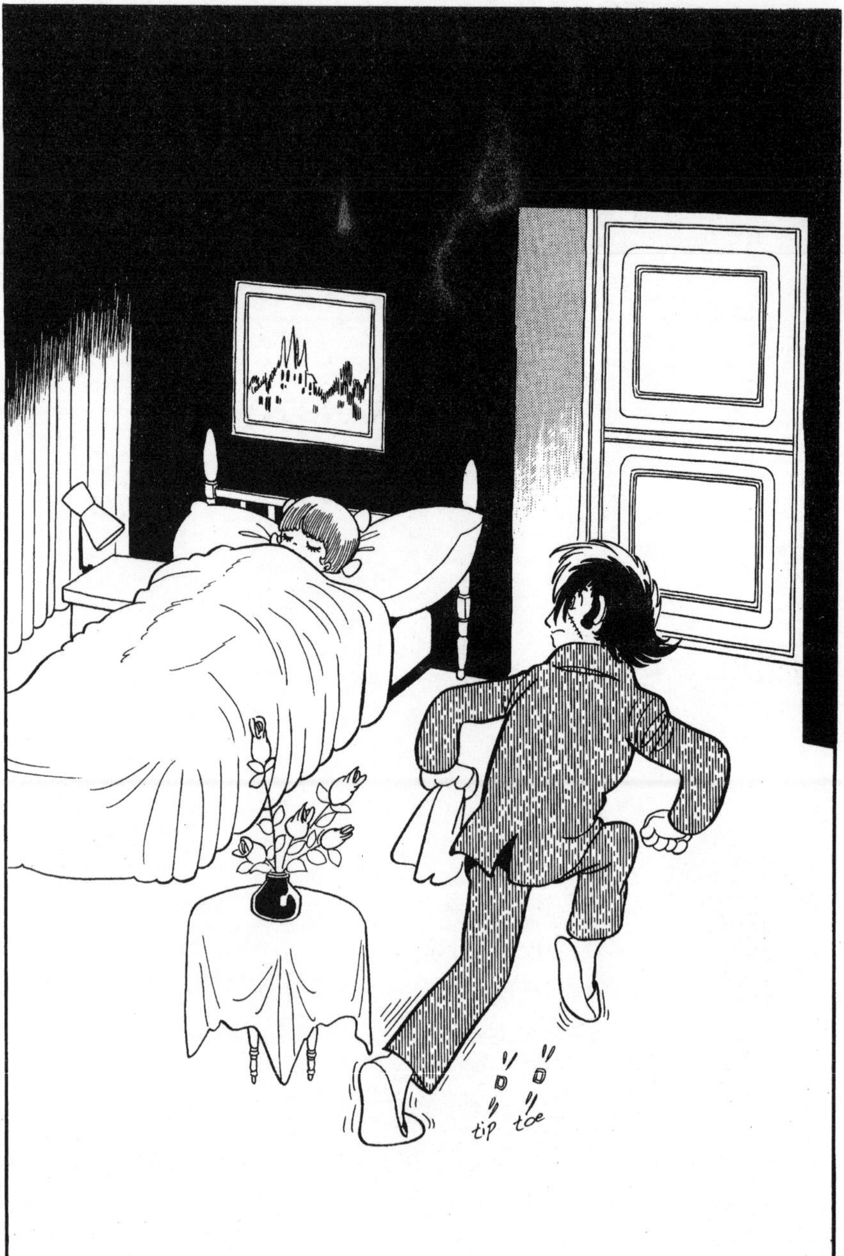
tip toe

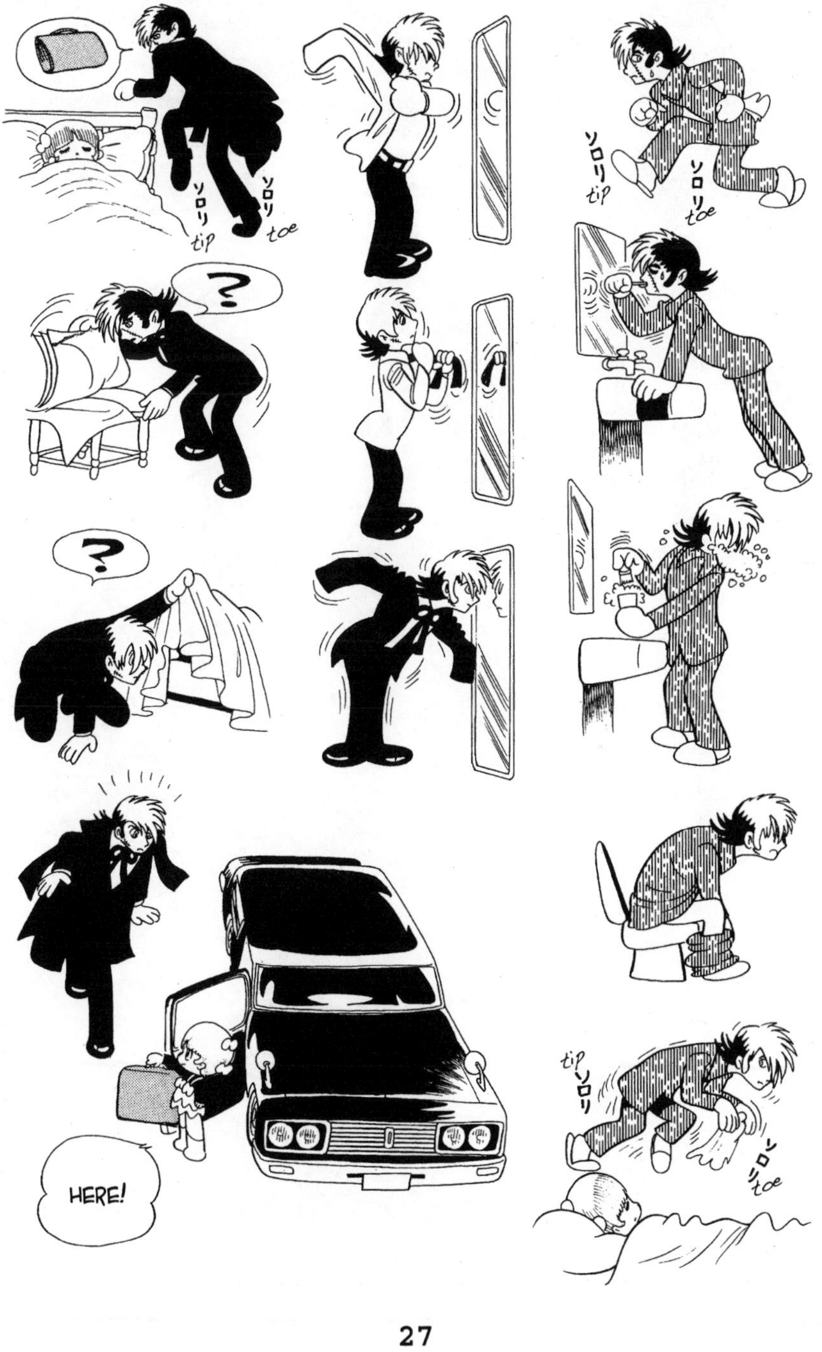
ソロリ tip
ソロリ toe
tip ソロリ
ソロリ toe
ソロリ tip
ソロリ toe
?
?
HERE!

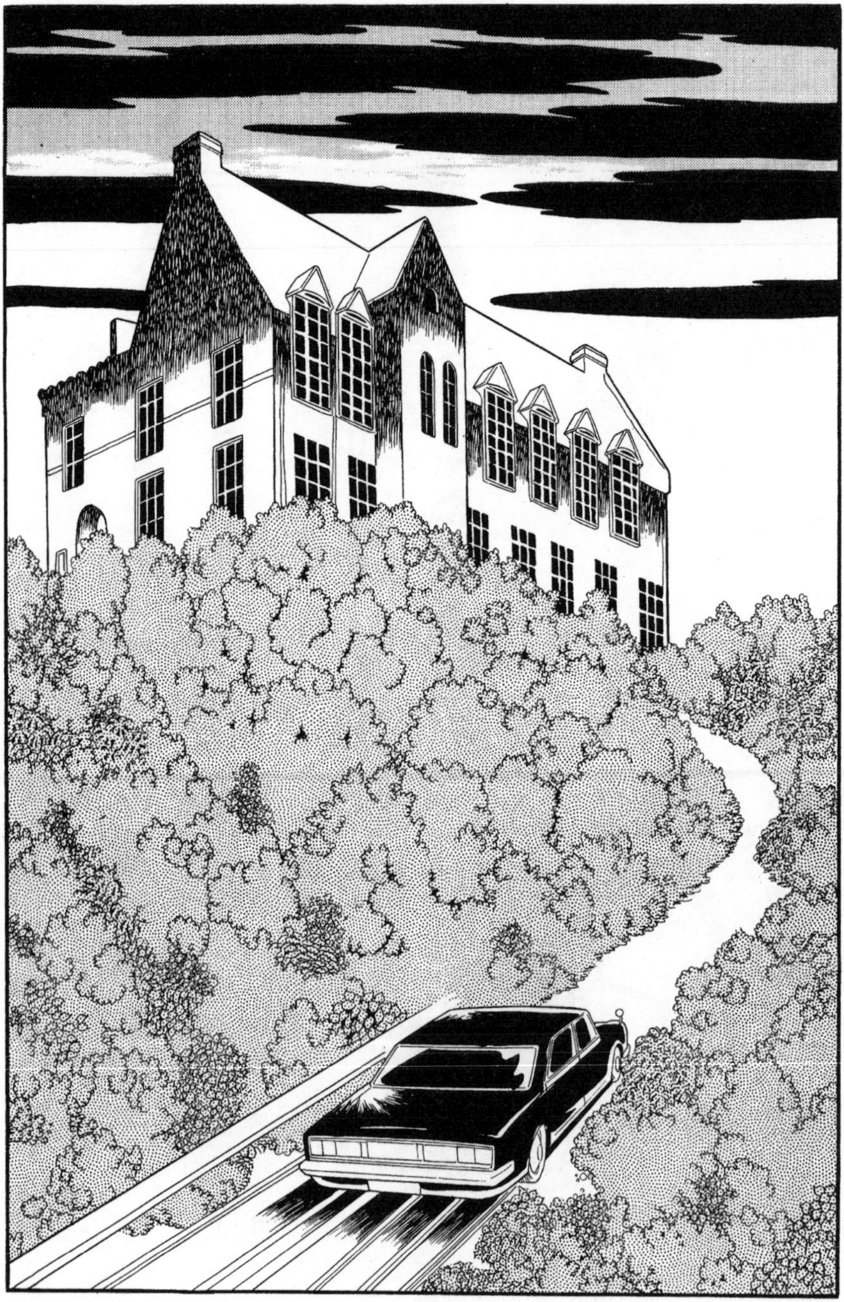

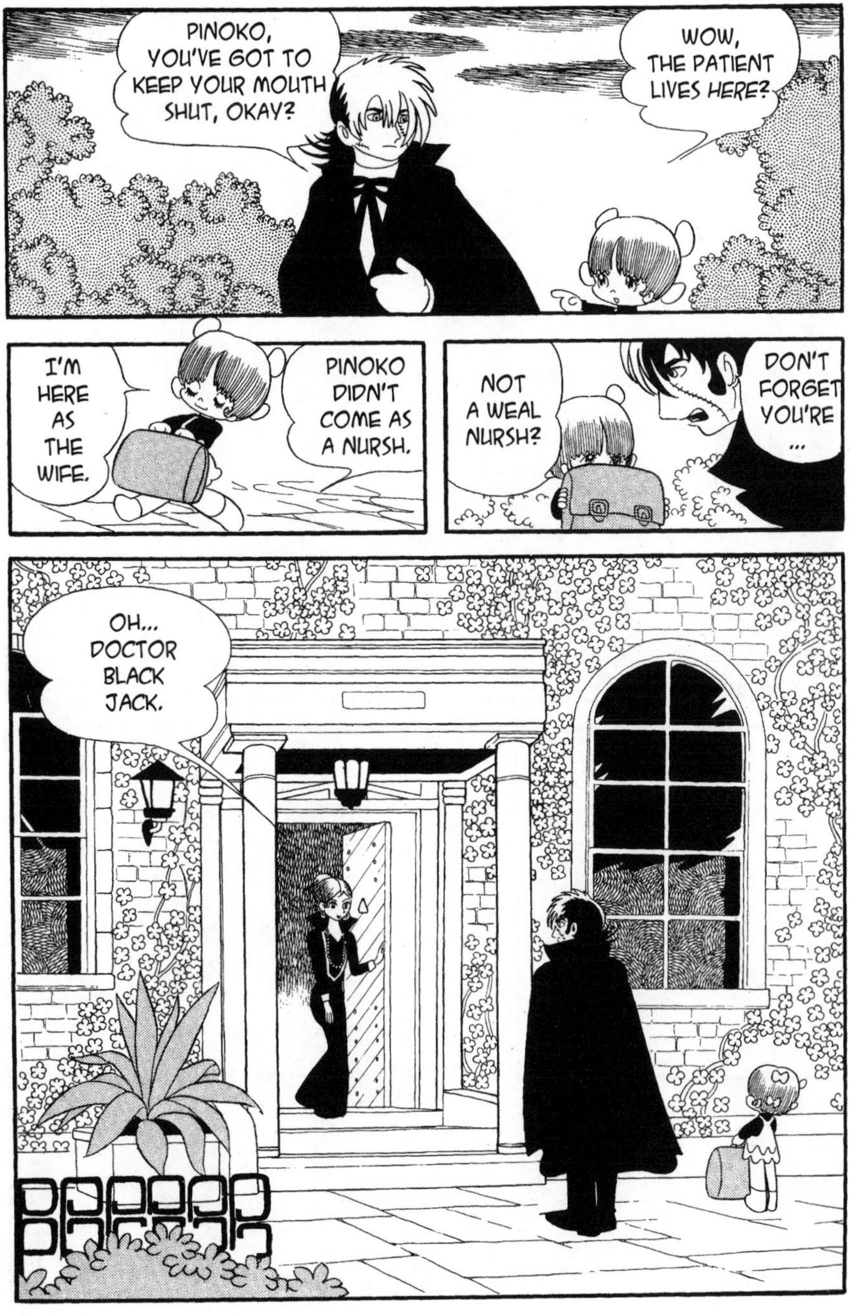
WOW, THE PATIENT LIVES HERE?
PINOKO, YOU'VE GOT TO KEEP YOUR MOUTH SHUT, OKAY?
DON'T FORGET YOU'RE ...
NOT A WEAL NURSH?
PINOKO DIDN'T COME AS A NURSH.
I'M HERE AS THE WIFE.
OH... DOCTOR BLACK JACK.

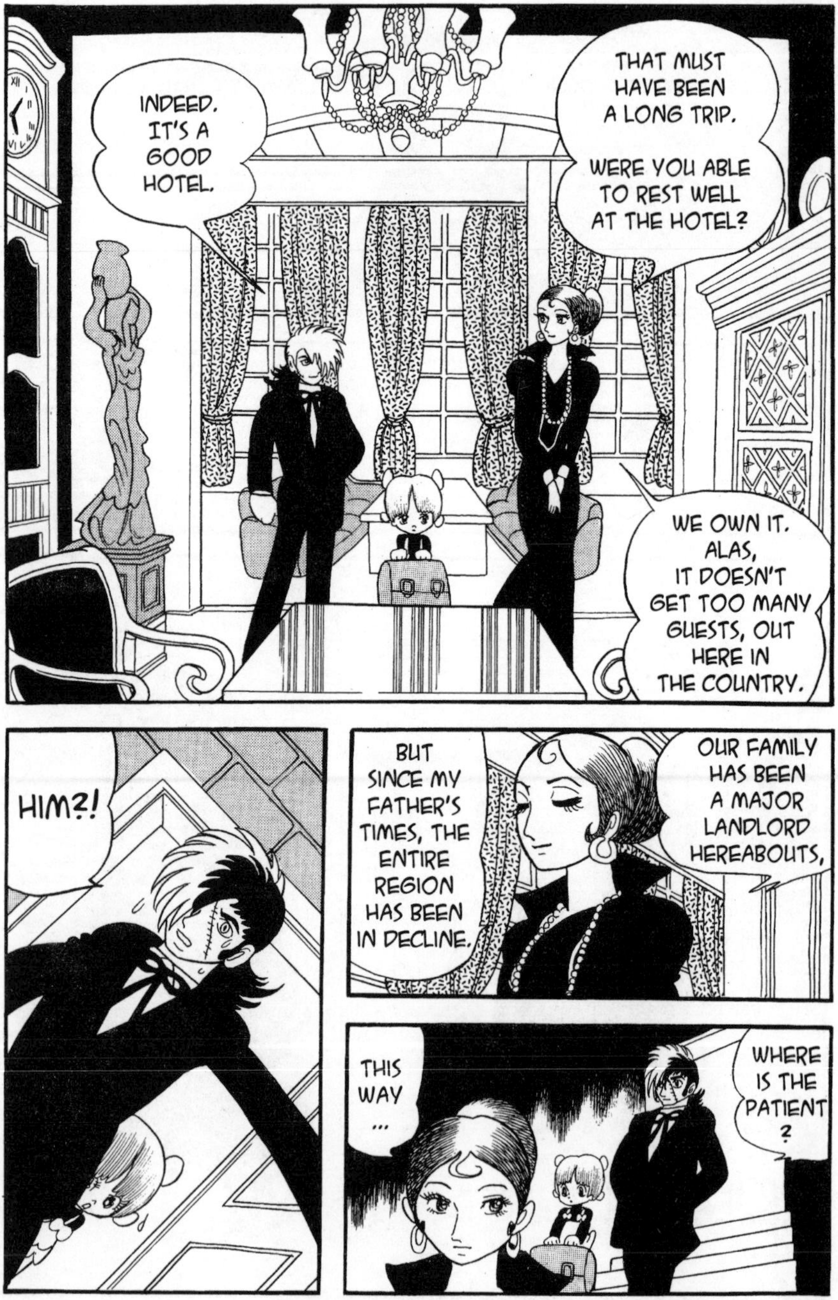
THAT MUST HAVE BEEN A LONG TRIP.
WERE YOU ABLE TO REST WELL AT THE HOTEL?
INDEED. IT'S A GOOD HOTEL.
WE OWN IT. ALAS, IT DOESN'T GET TOO MANY GUESTS, OUT HERE IN THE COUNTRY.
OUR FAMILY HAS BEEN A MAJOR LANDLORD HEREABOUTS,
BUT SINCE MY FATHER'S TIMES, THE ENTIRE REGION HAS BEEN IN DECLINE.
WHERE IS THE PATIENT?
THIS WAY ...
HIM?!

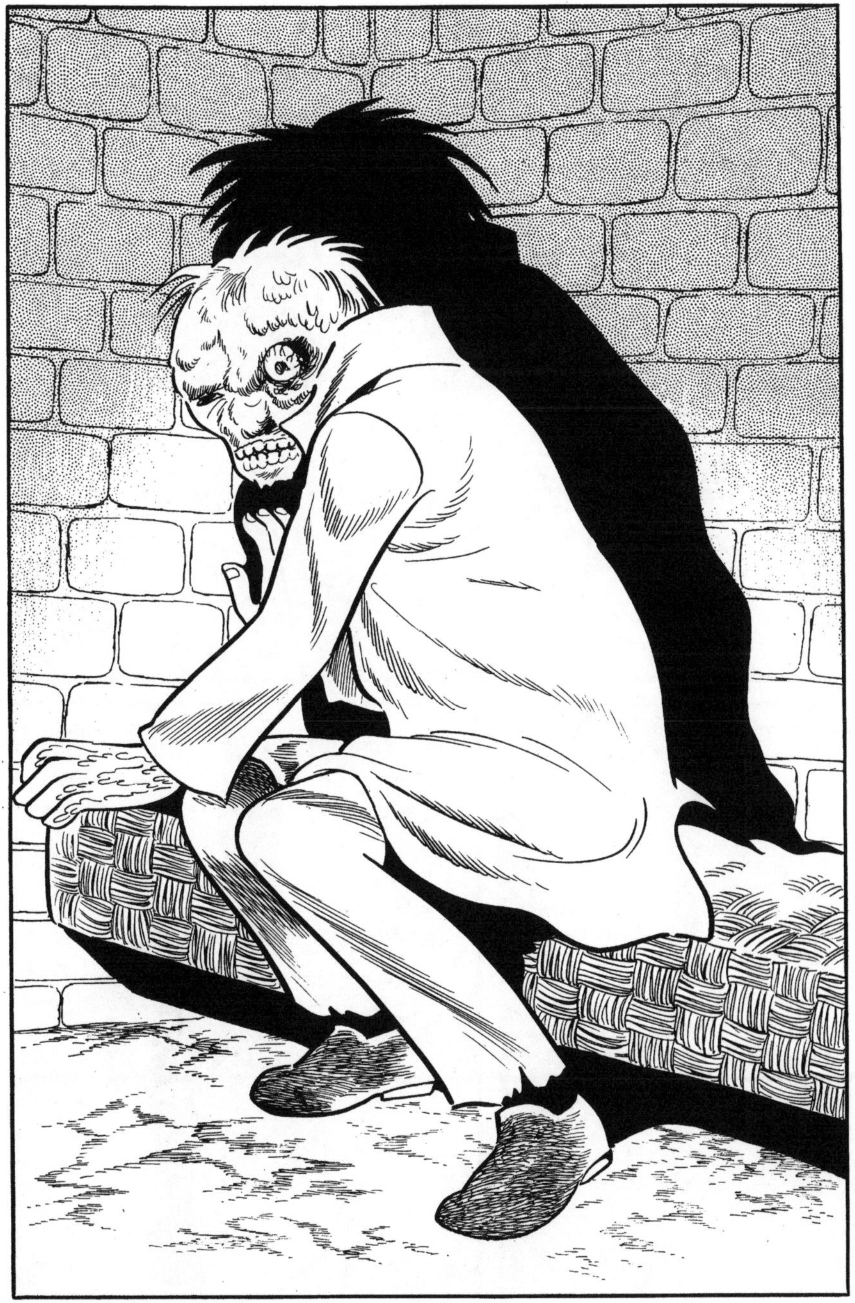

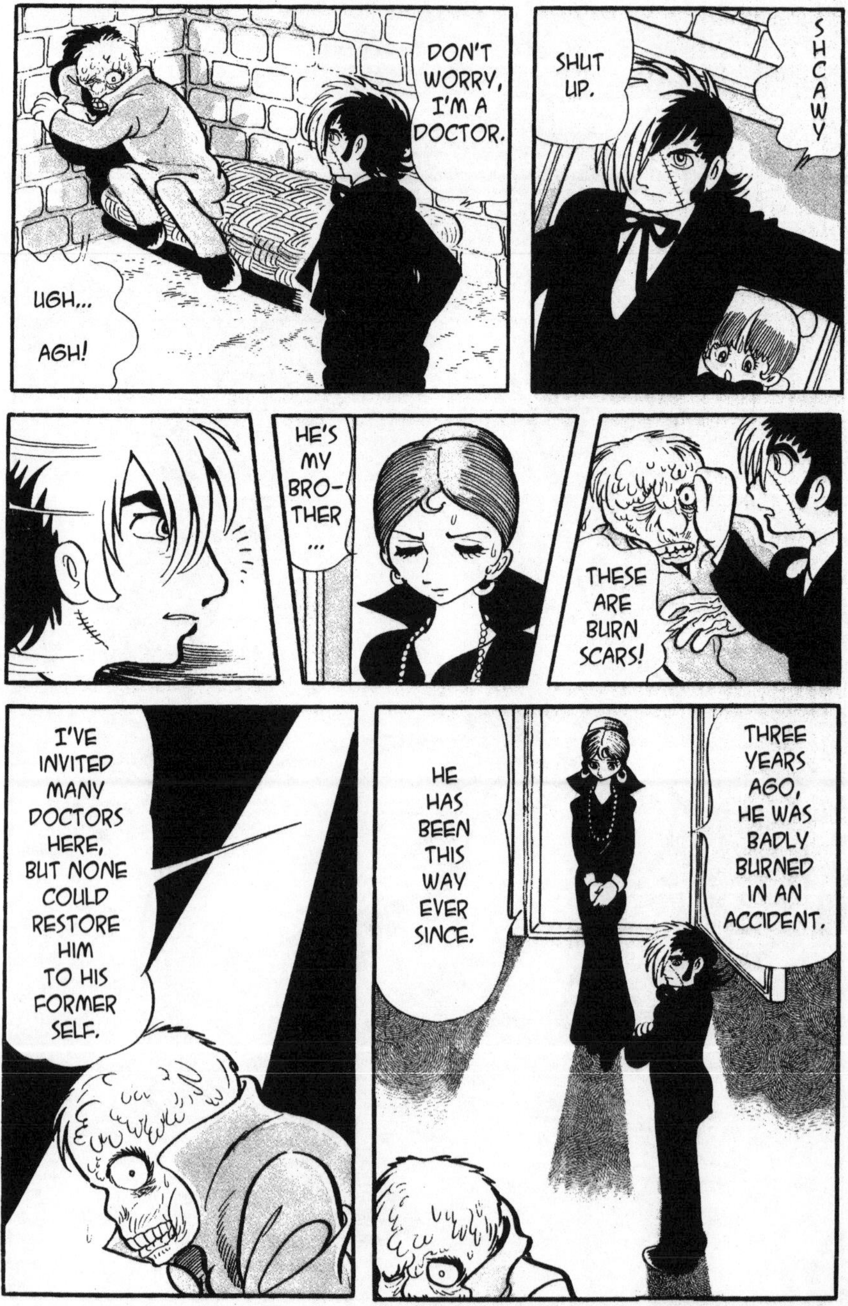
SHUT UP.
SHCAWY
DON'T WORRY, I'M A DOCTOR.
UGH... AGH!
THESE ARE BURN SCARS!
HE'S MY BRO- THER ...
THREE YEARS AGO, HE WAS BADLY BURNED IN AN ACCIDENT.
HE HAS BEEN THIS WAY EVER SINCE.
I'VE INVITED MANY DOCTORS HERE, BUT NONE COULD RESTORE HIM TO HIS FORMER SELF.

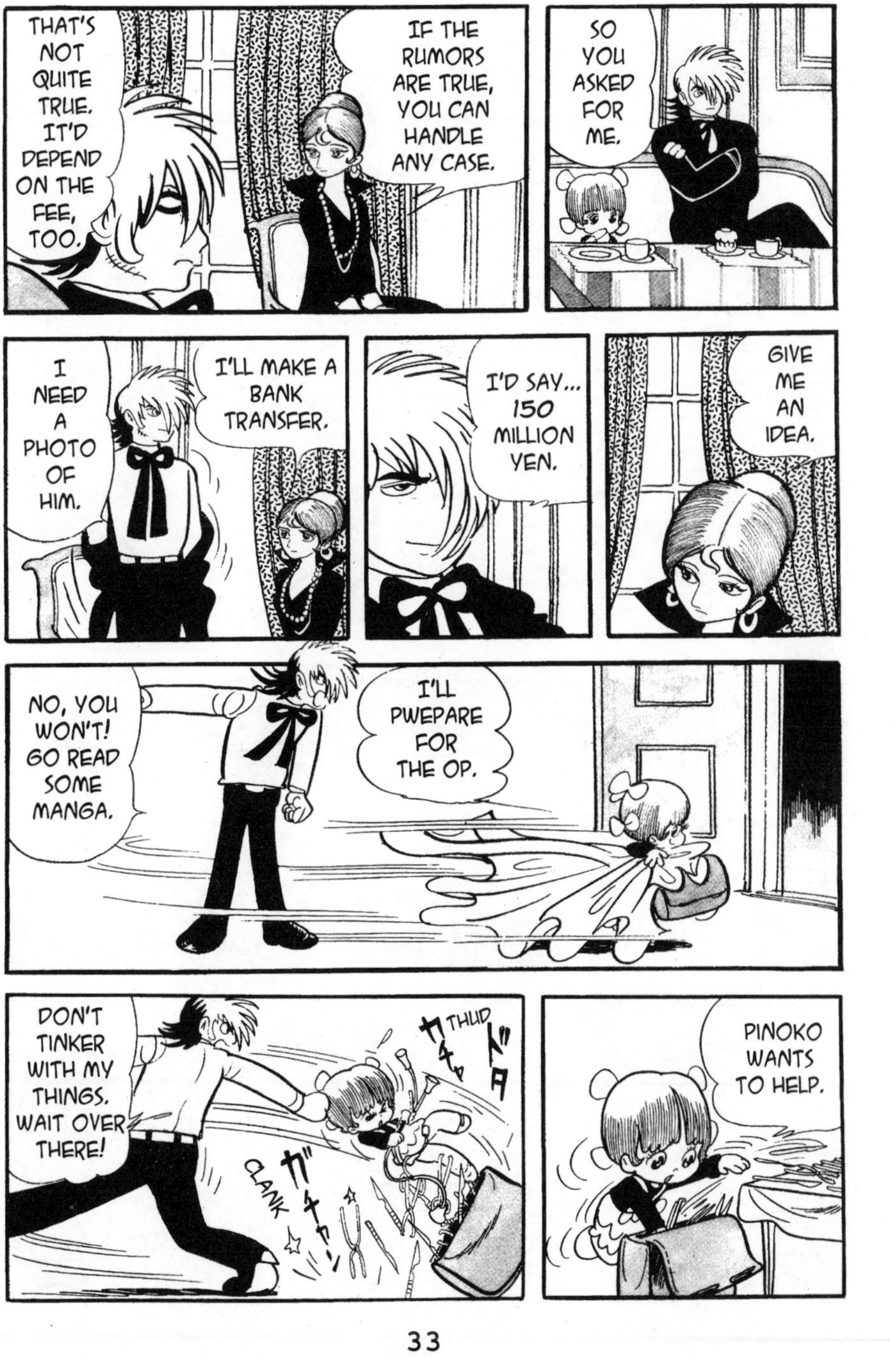
SO YOU ASKED FOR ME.
IF THE RUMORS ARE TRUE, YOU CAN HANDLE ANY CASE.
THAT'S NOT QUITE TRUE. IT'D DEPEND ON THE FEE, TOO.
GIVE ME AN IDEA.
I'D SAY... 150 MILLION YEN.
I'LL MAKE A BANK TRANSFER.
I NEED A PHOTO OF HIM.
I'LL PWEPARE FOR THE OP.
NO, YOU WON'T! GO READ SOME MANGA.
PINOKO WANTS TO HELP.
ドタ
THUD
カチャ
DON'T TINKER WITH MY THINGS. WAIT OVER THERE!
ガチャーン
CLANK

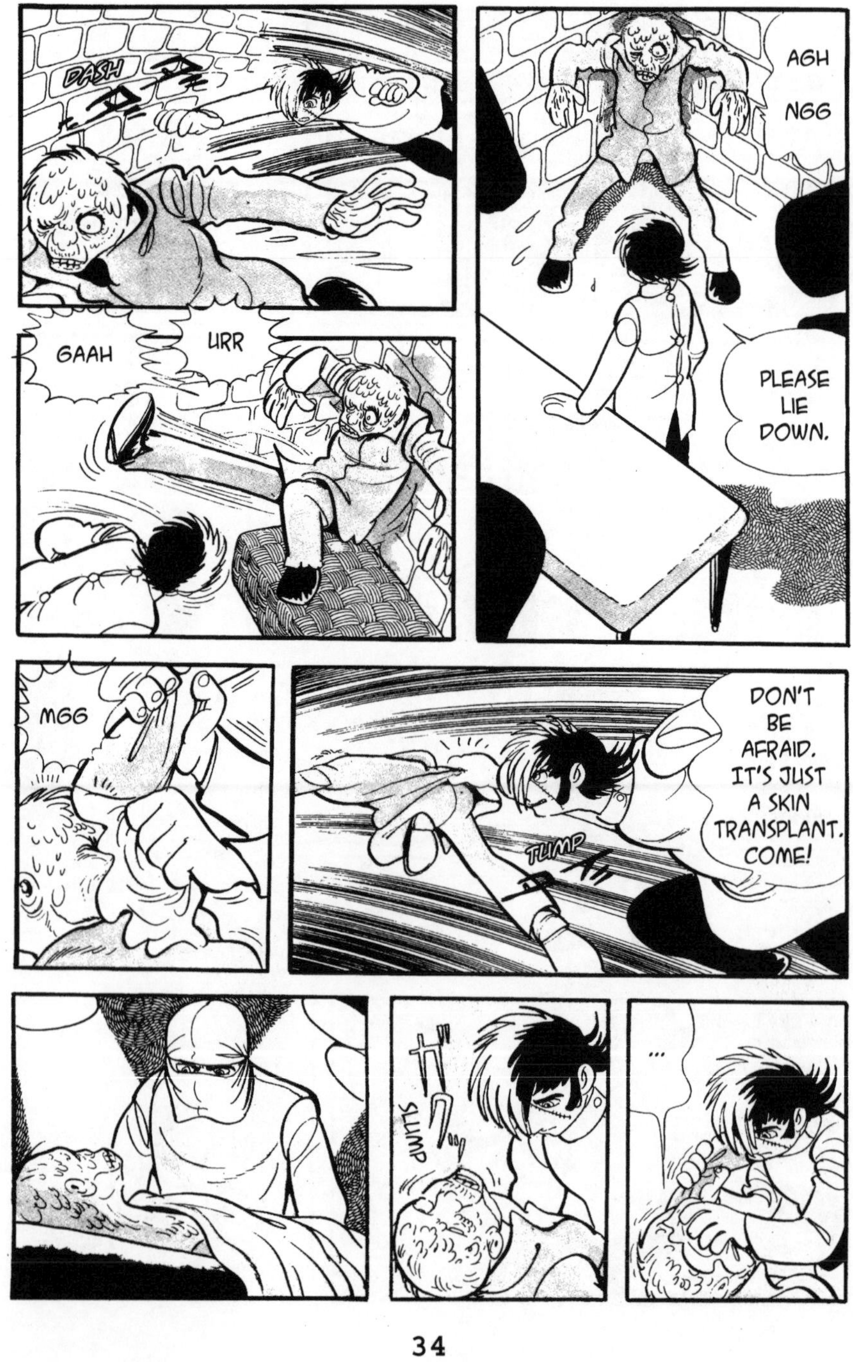
AGH
NGG
PLEASE LIE DOWN.
DASH
GAAH
URR
DON'T BE AFRAID. IT'S JUST A SKIN TRANSPLANT. COME!
TLUMP
MGG
...
SLUMP

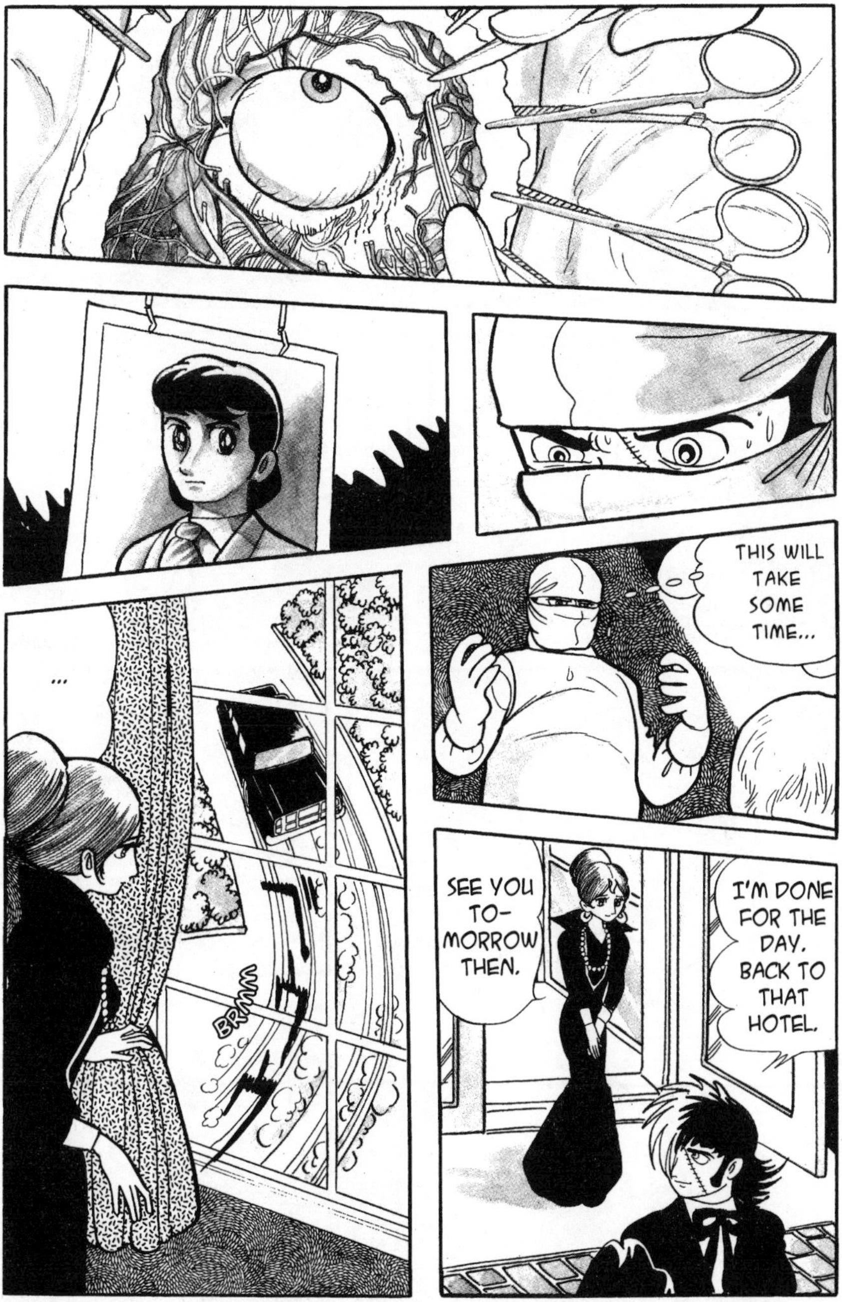
THIS WILL TAKE SOME TIME...
I'M DONE FOR THE DAY. BACK TO THAT HOTEL.
SEE YOU TO-MORROW THEN.
...
BRMM

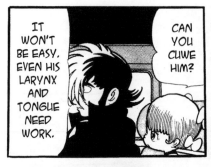

I DON'T LIKE THAT LADY.
SAME HERE. THOSE TWO HAVE SOME SECRET.
CAN YOU CUWE HIM?
IT WON'T BE EASY. EVEN HIS LARYNX AND TONGUE NEED WORK.
HIS FINGERS ARE DRAWN UP, SO HE CAN'T HOLD ANYTHING. HE CAN'T SPEAK OR WRITE...
NO ONE KNOWS WHAT'S IN THAT MAN'S MIND.
HE'S ALL ALONE?
YES, THE POOR FELLOW.
WHAT'S MORE, HE'S BEEN LOCKED IN A CELLAR FOR 3 YEARS. HORRID.
THIS SCAR ON THE HEAD...
IT'S FROM SOME BLUNT OBJECT.

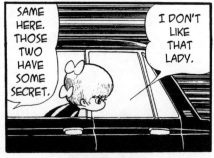

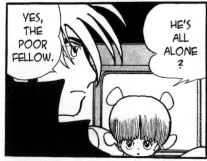

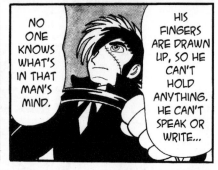

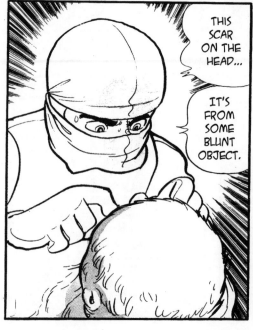

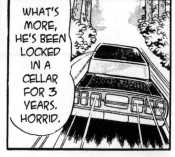

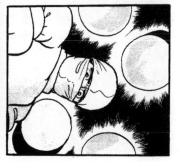

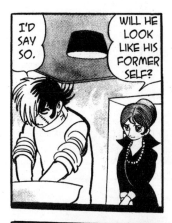

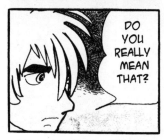

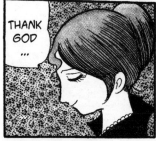

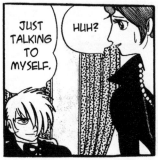

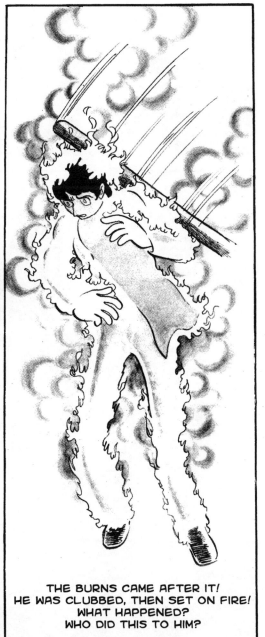

THE BURNS CAME AFTER IT! HE WAS CLUBBED, THEN SET ON FIRE! WHAT HAPPENED? WHO DID THIS TO HIM?
WILL HE LOOK LIKE HIS FORMER SELF?
I'D SAY SO.
THANK GOD ...
DO YOU REALLY MEAN THAT?
HUH?
JUST TALKING TO MYSELF.

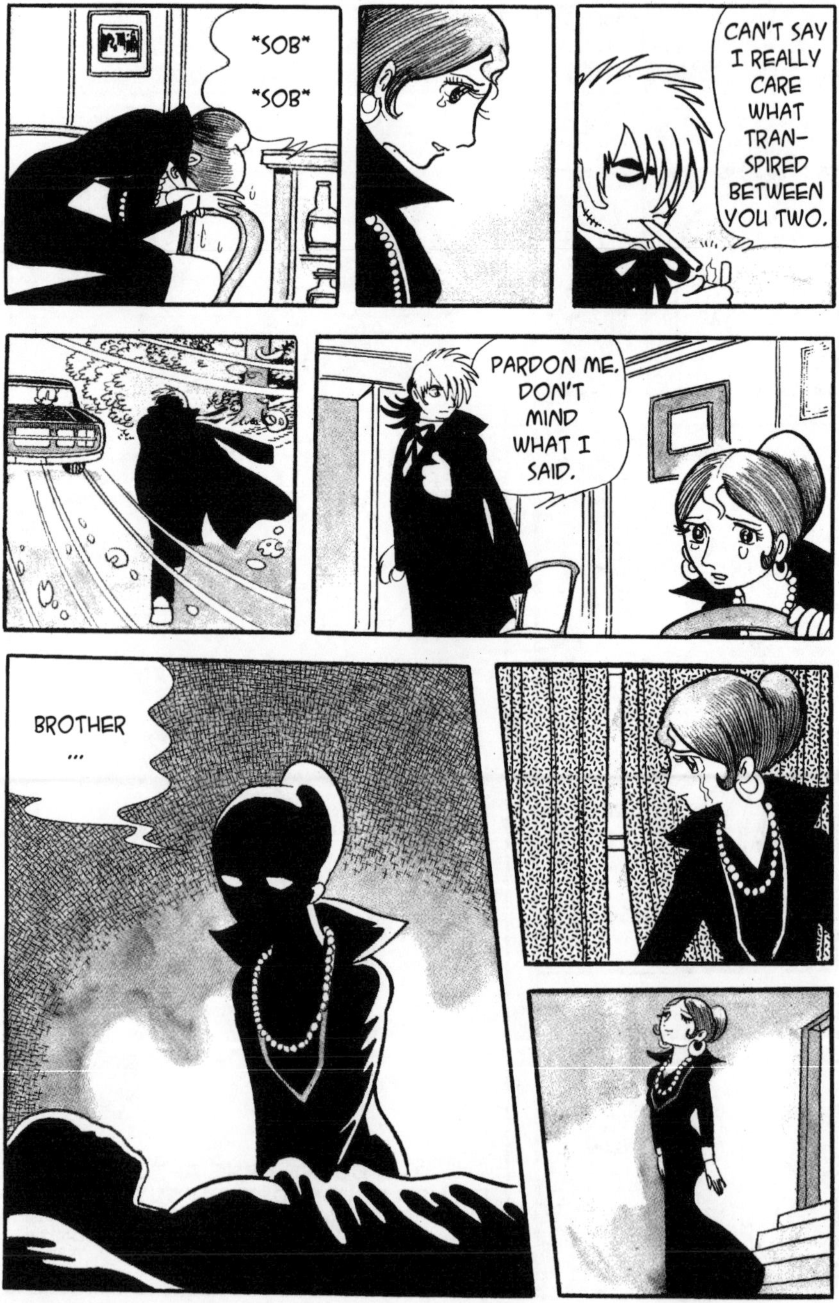
CAN'T SAY I REALLY CARE WHAT TRAN-SPIRED BETWEEN YOU TWO.
SOB *SOB*
PARDON ME. DON'T MIND WHAT I SAID.
BROTHER ...

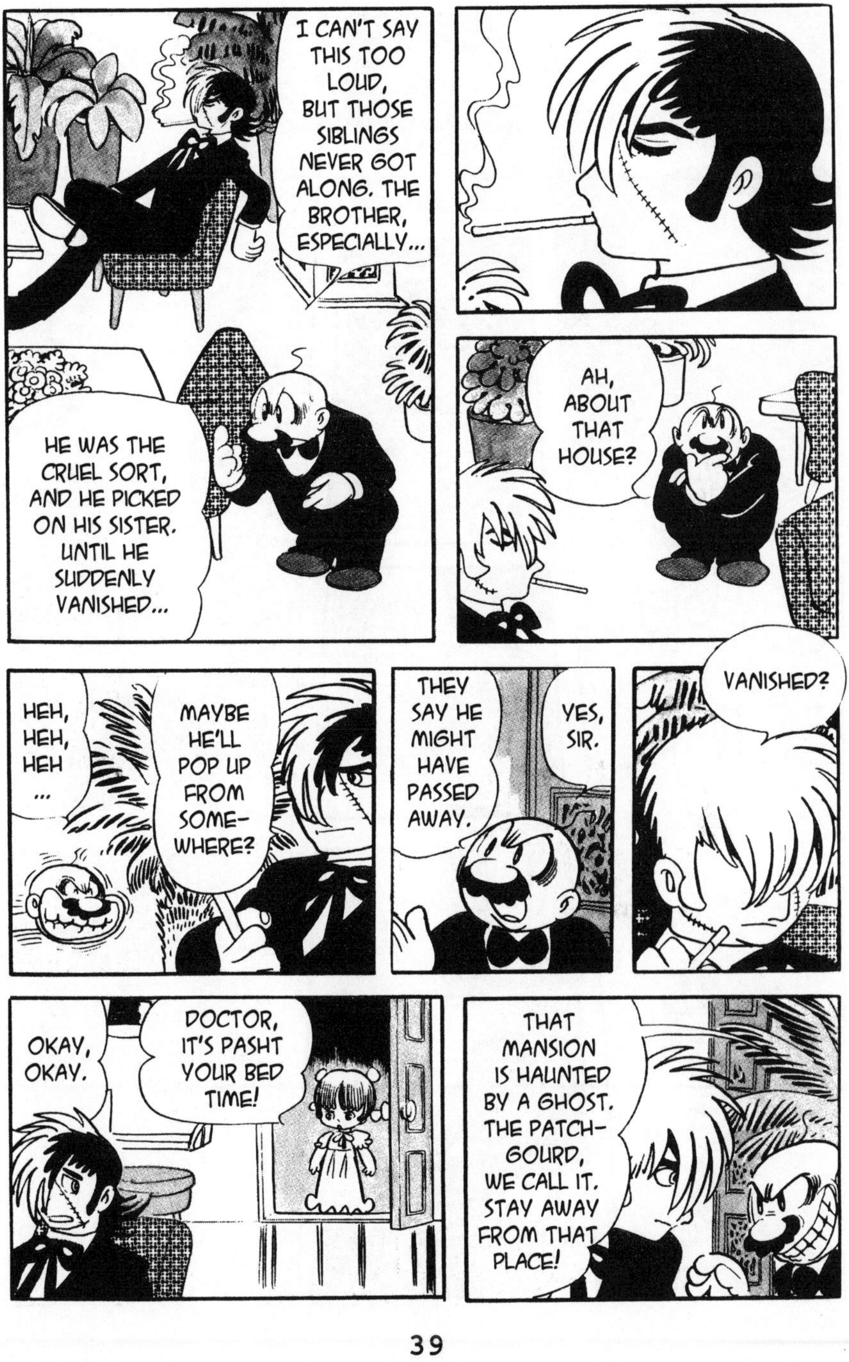
AH, ABOUT THAT HOUSE?
I CAN'T SAY THIS TOO LOUD, BUT THOSE SIBLINGS NEVER GOT ALONG. THE BROTHER, ESPECIALLY...
HE WAS THE CRUEL SORT, AND HE PICKED ON HIS SISTER. UNTIL HE SUDDENLY VANISHED...
VANISHED?
YES, SIR.
THEY SAY HE MIGHT HAVE PASSED AWAY.
MAYBE HE'LL POP UP FROM SOME-WHERE?
HEH, HEH, HEH ...
THAT MANSION IS HAUNTED BY A GHOST. THE PATCH-GOURD, WE CALL IT. STAY AWAY FROM THAT PLACE!
DOCTOR, IT'S PASHT YOUR BED TIME!
OKAY, OKAY.

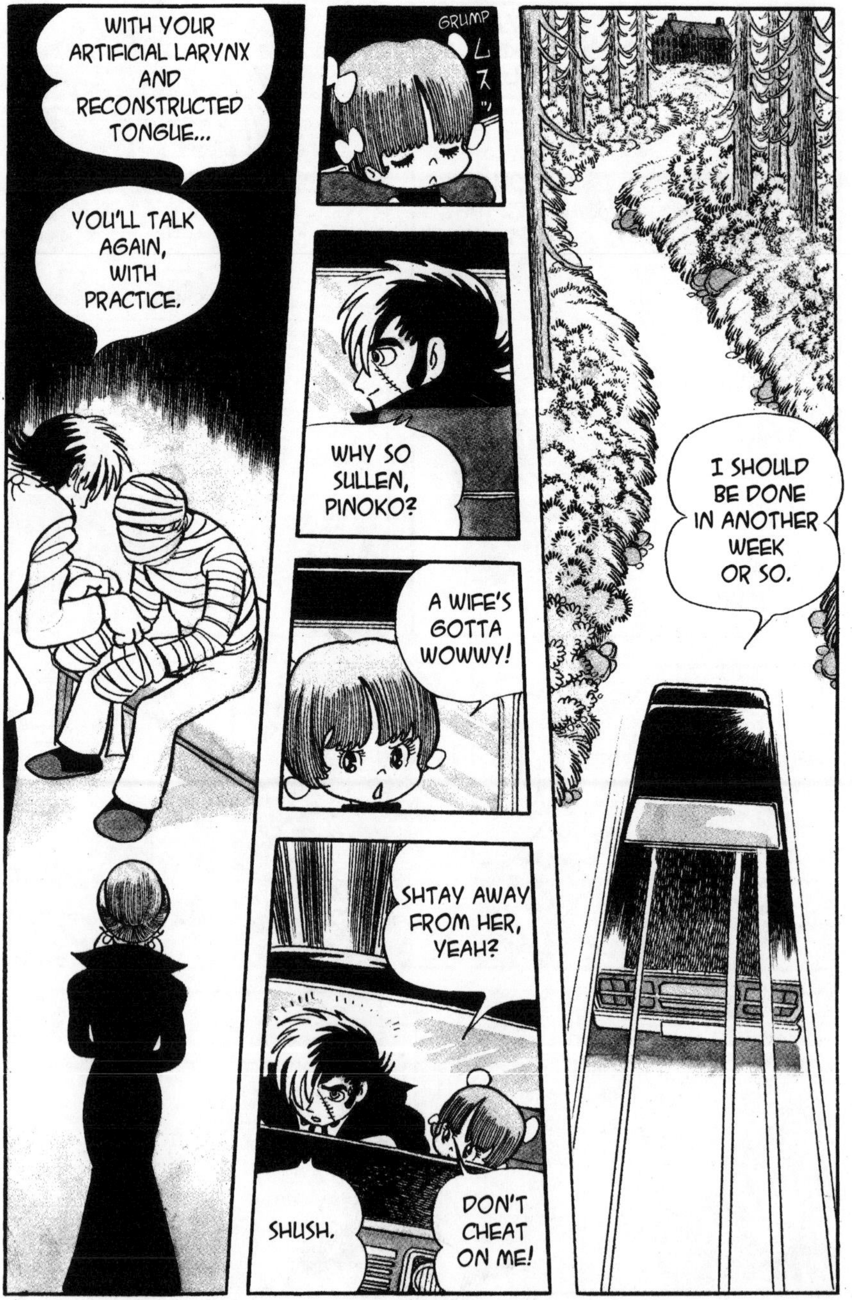
I SHOULD BE DONE IN ANOTHER WEEK OR SO.
GRUMP
ムスッ
WHY SO SULLEN, PINOKO?
A WIFE'S GOTTA WOWWY!
SHTAY AWAY FROM HER, YEAH?
DON'T CHEAT ON ME!
SHUSH.
WITH YOUR ARTIFICIAL LARYNX AND RECONSTRUCTED TONGUE...
YOU'LL TALK AGAIN, WITH PRACTICE.

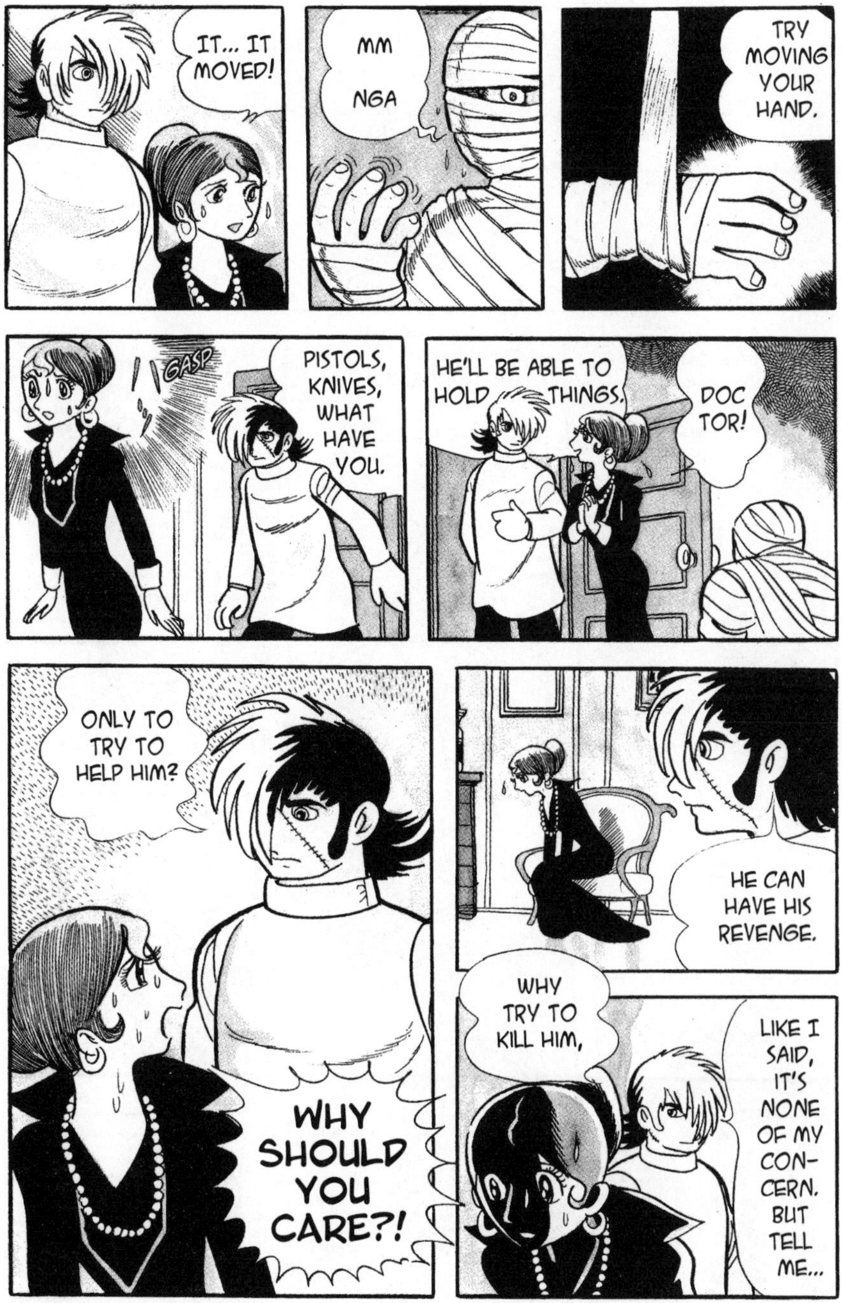
TRY MOVING YOUR HAND.
MM NGA
IT... IT MOVED!
DOC TOR!
HE'LL BE ABLE TO HOLD THINGS.
PISTOLS, KNIVES, WHAT HAVE YOU.
GASP
HE CAN HAVE HIS REVENGE.
LIKE I SAID, IT'S NONE OF MY CON-CERN. BUT TELL ME...
WHY TRY TO KILL HIM,
ONLY TO TRY TO HELP HIM?
WHY SHOULD YOU CARE?!

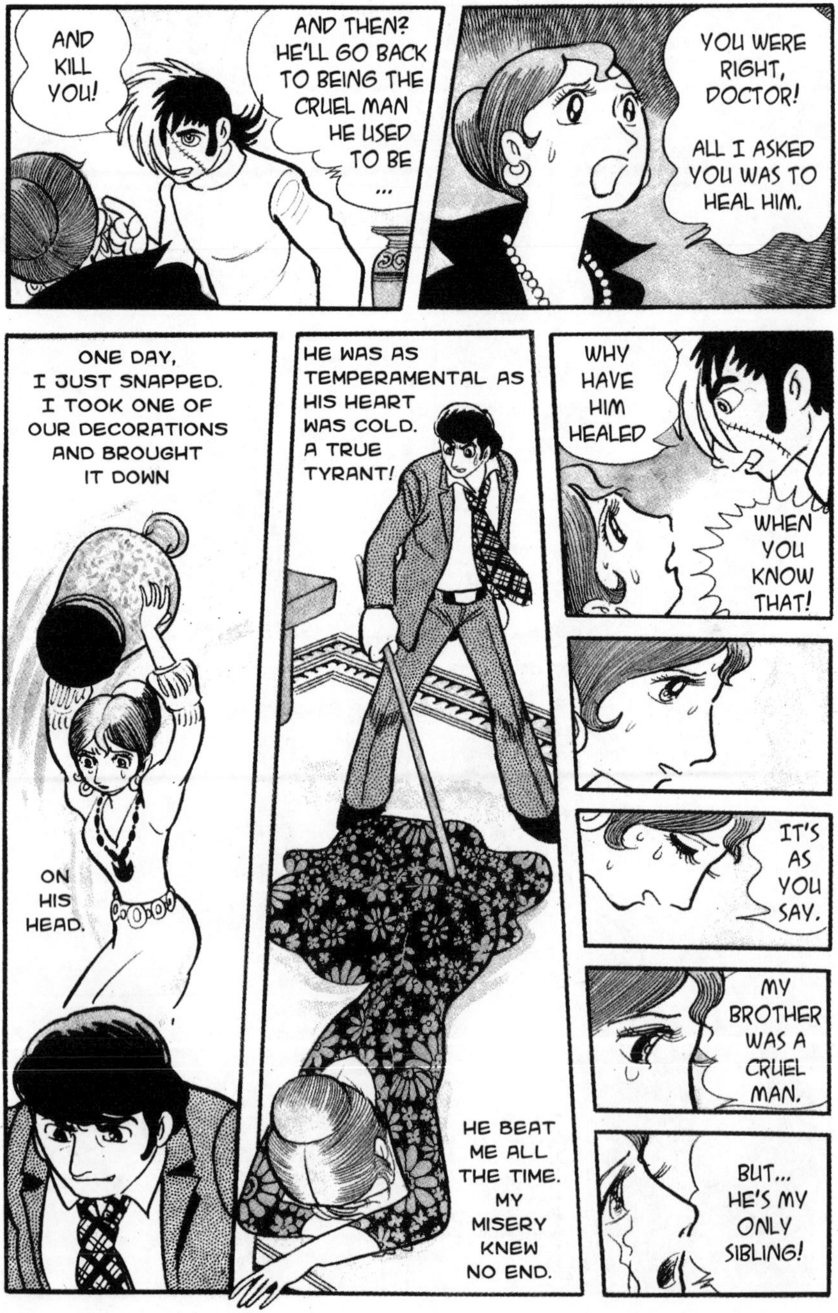

YOU WERE RIGHT, DOCTOR!
ALL I ASKED YOU WAS TO HEAL HIM.
AND THEN? HE'LL GO BACK TO BEING THE CRUEL MAN HE USED TO BE ...
AND KILL YOU!
WHY HAVE HIM HEALED
WHEN YOU KNOW THAT!
IT'S AS YOU SAY.
MY BROTHER WAS A CRUEL MAN.
BUT... HE'S MY ONLY SIBLING!
HE WAS AS TEMPERAMENTAL AS HIS HEART WAS COLD. A TRUE TYRANT!
HE BEAT ME ALL THE TIME. MY MISERY KNEW NO END.
ONE DAY, I JUST SNAPPED. I TOOK ONE OF OUR DECORATIONS AND BROUGHT IT DOWN
ON HIS HEAD.

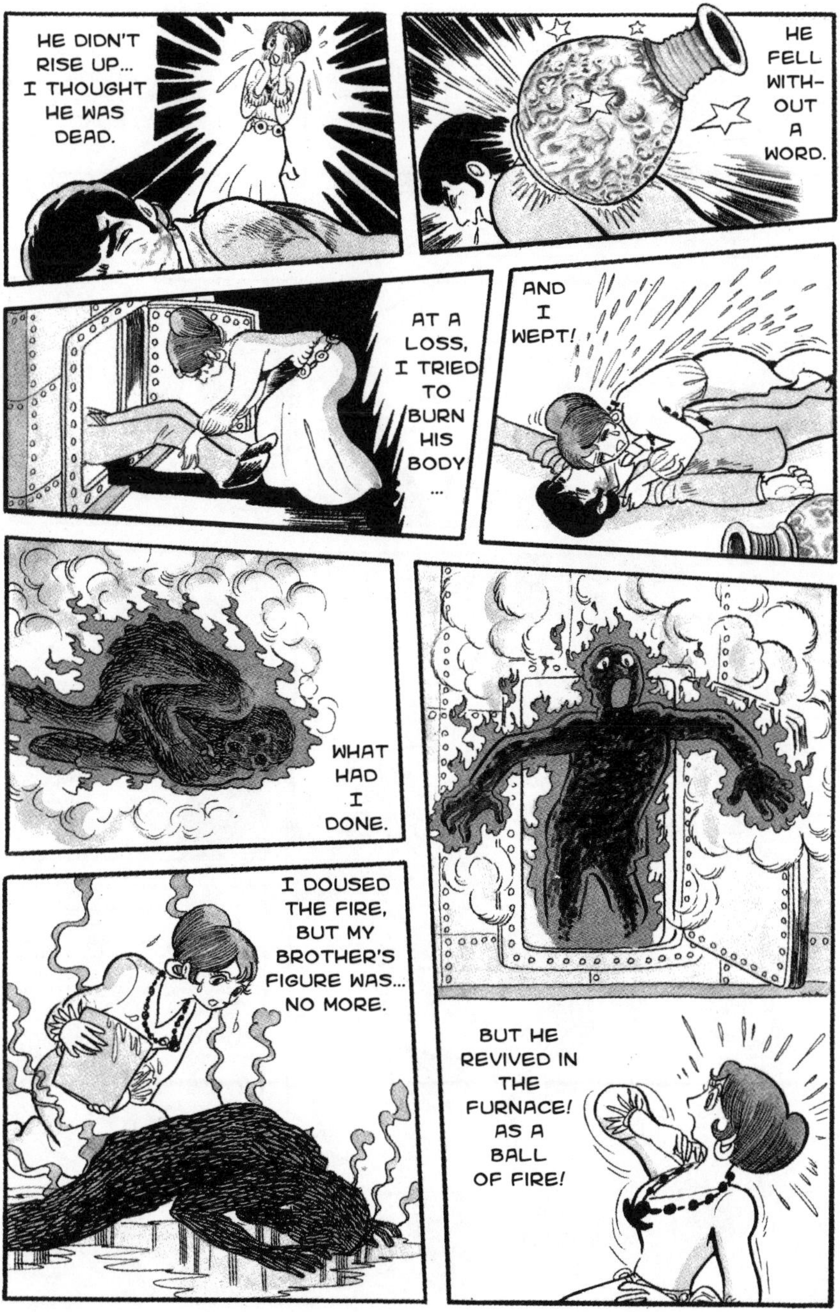
HE FELL WITHOUT A WORD.
HE DIDN'T RISE UP... I THOUGHT HE WAS DEAD.
AND I WEPT!
AT A LOSS, I TRIED TO BURN HIS BODY ...
WHAT HAD I DONE.
I DOUSED THE FIRE, BUT MY BROTHER'S FIGURE WAS... NO MORE.
BUT HE REVIVED IN THE FURNACE! AS A BALL OF FIRE!

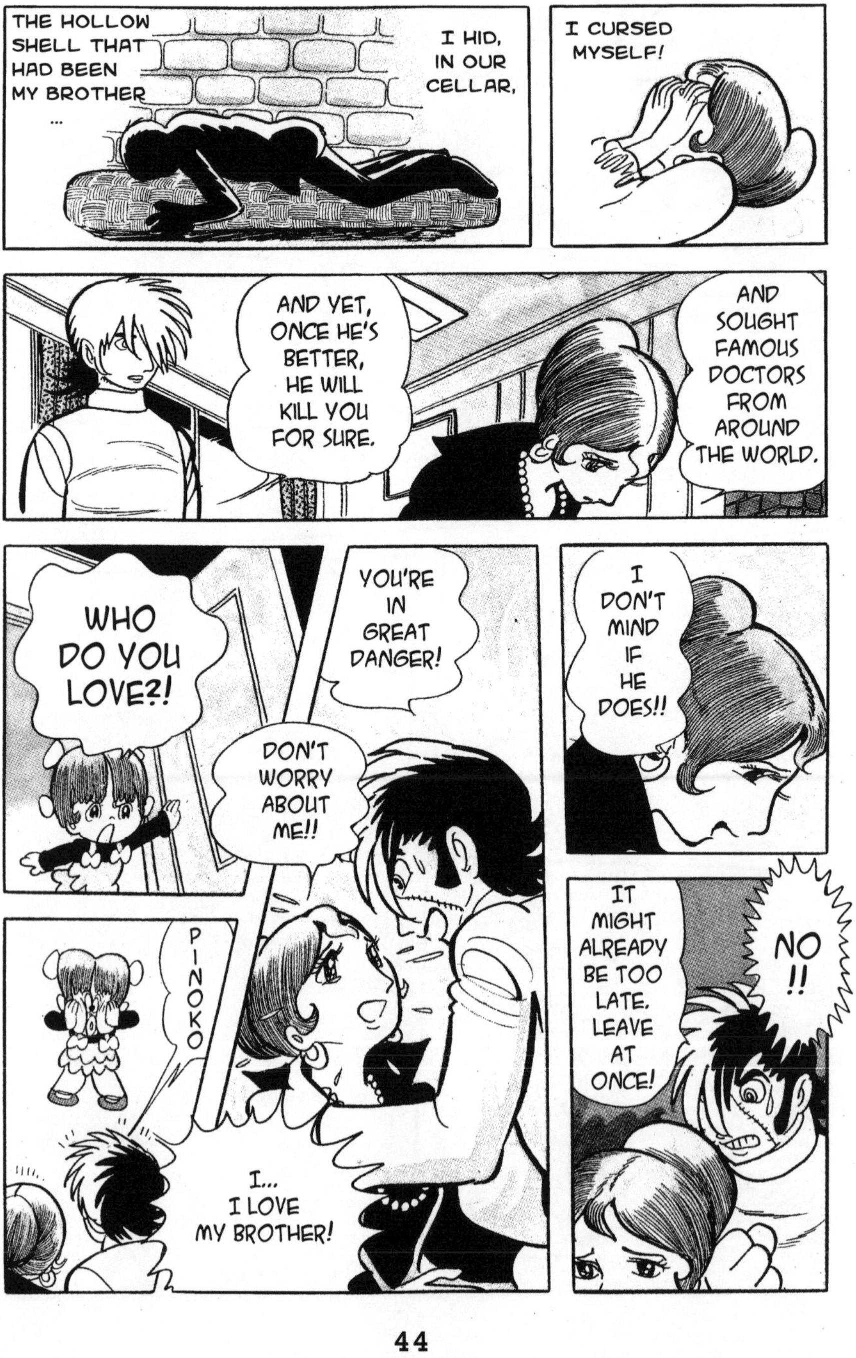
I CURSED MYSELF!
I HID, IN OUR CELLAR,
THE HOLLOW SHELL THAT HAD BEEN MY BROTHER ...
AND SOUGHT FAMOUS DOCTORS FROM AROUND THE WORLD.
AND YET, ONCE HE'S BETTER, HE WILL KILL YOU FOR SURE.
I DON'T MIND IF HE DOES!!
IT MIGHT ALREADY BE TOO LATE. LEAVE AT ONCE!
NO !!
YOU'RE IN GREAT DANGER!
DON'T WORRY ABOUT ME!!
WHO DO YOU LOVE?!
PINOKO
I... I LOVE MY BROTHER!

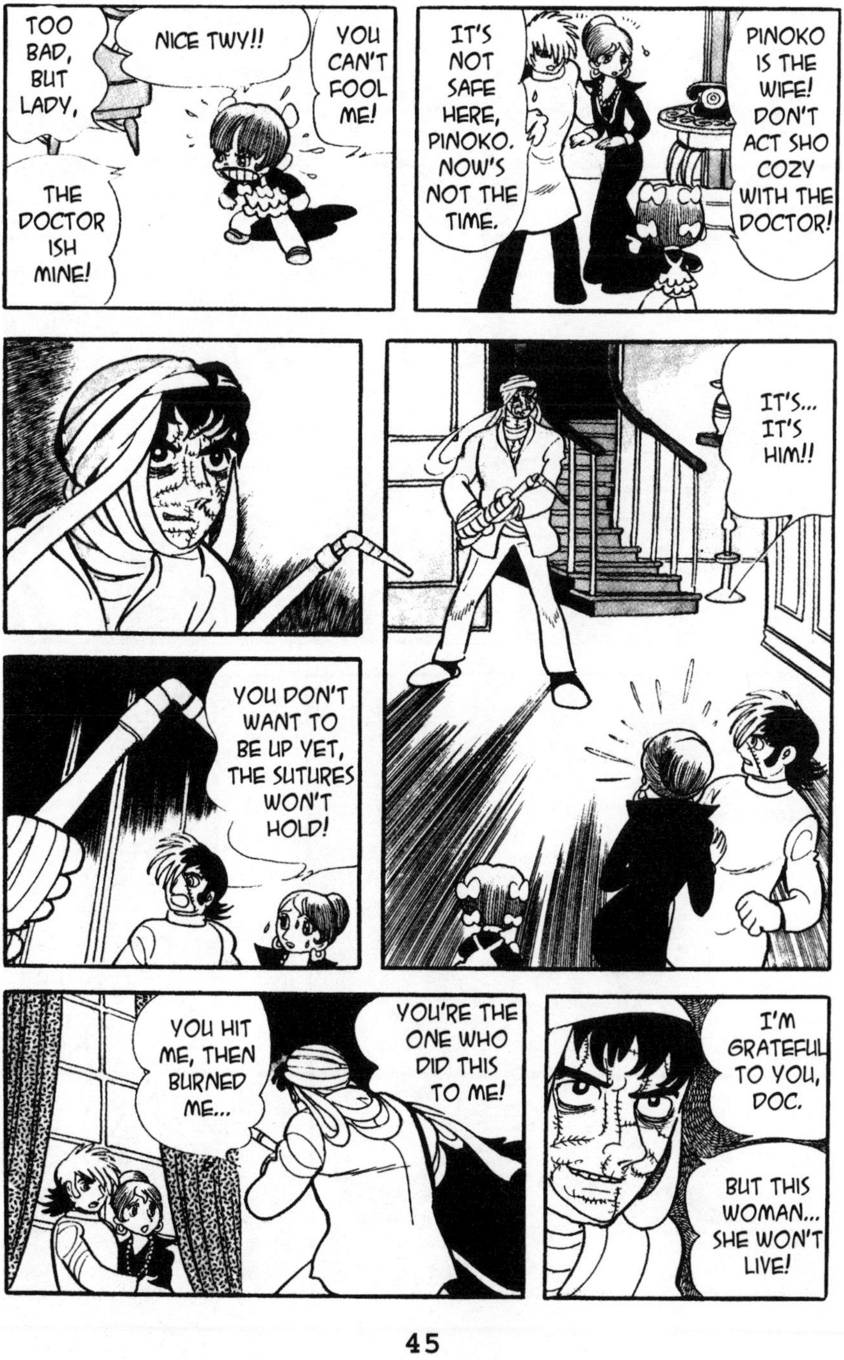
PINOKO IS THE WIFE! DON'T ACT SHO COZY WITH THE DOCTOR!
IT'S NOT SAFE HERE, PINOKO. NOW'S NOT THE TIME.
YOU CAN'T FOOL ME!
NICE TWY!!
TOO BAD, BUT LADY,
THE DOCTOR ISH MINE!
IT'S... IT'S HIM!!
YOU DON'T WANT TO BE UP YET, THE SUTURES WON'T HOLD!
I'M GRATEFUL TO YOU, DOC.
BUT THIS WOMAN... SHE WON'T LIVE!
YOU'RE THE ONE WHO DID THIS TO ME!
YOU HIT ME, THEN BURNED ME...

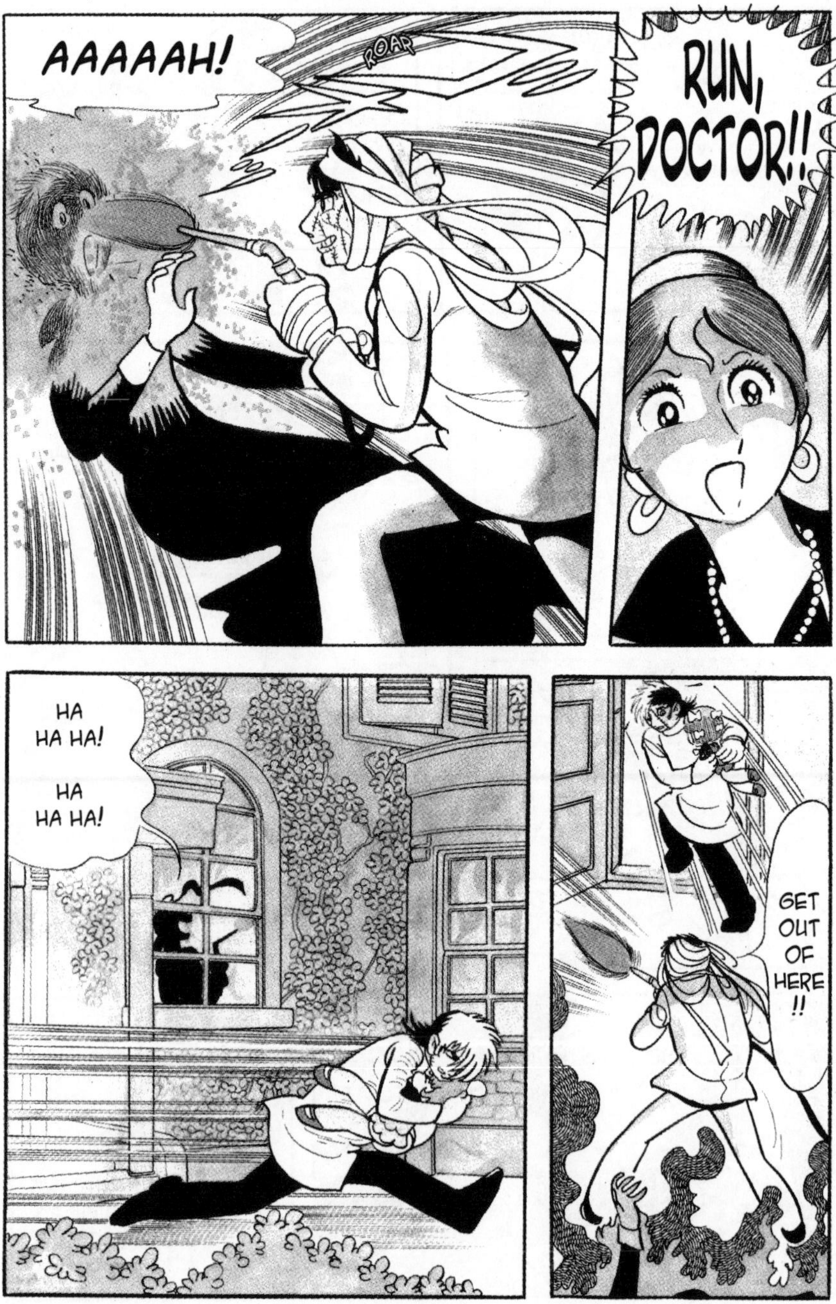
RUN, DOCTOR!!
AAAAAH!
ROAR
GET OUT OF HERE!!
HA HA HA!
HA HA HA!

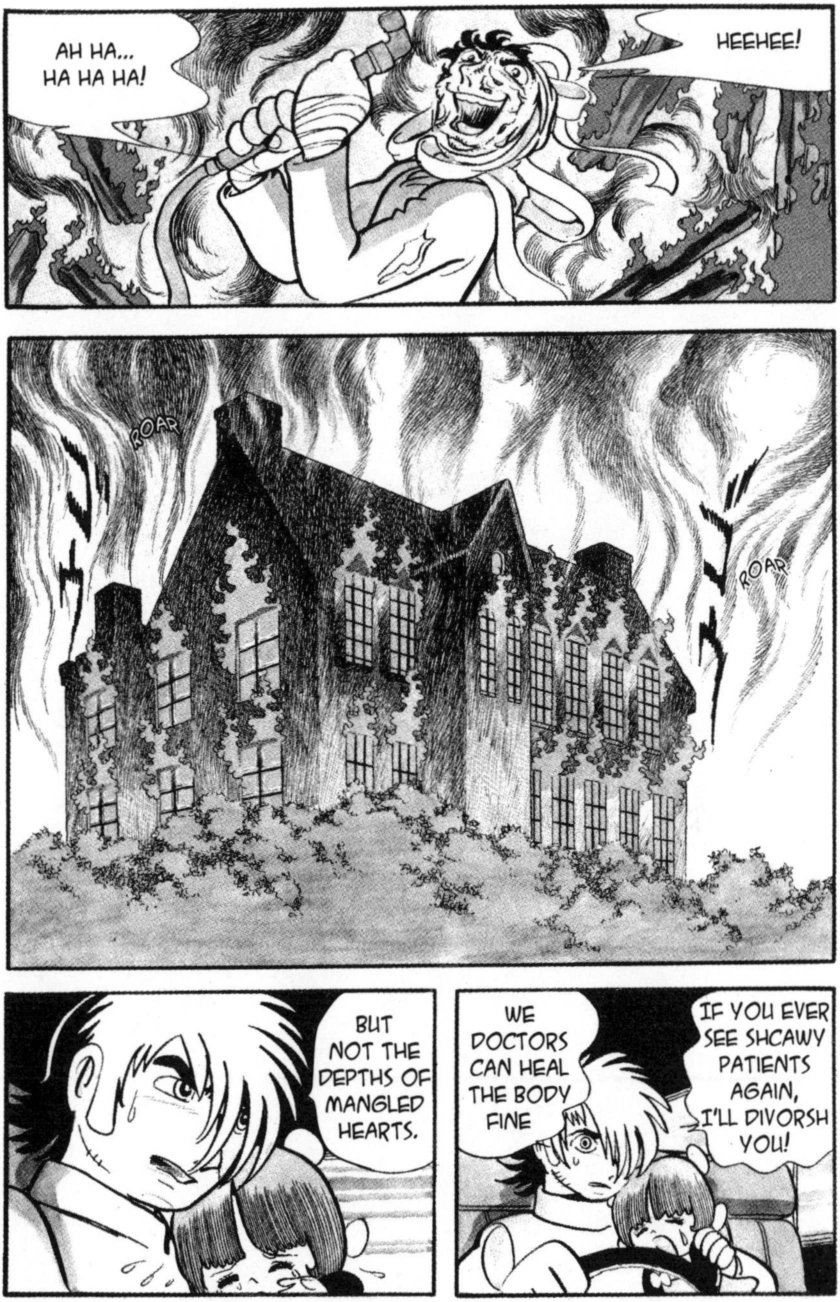
HEEHEE!
AH HA... HA HA HA!
ROAR
ROAR
IF YOU EVER SEE SHCAWY PATIENTS AGAIN, I'LL DIVORSH YOU!
WE DOCTORS CAN HEAL THE BODY FINE
BUT NOT THE DEPTHS OF MANGLED HEARTS.

A CAT AND SHOZO

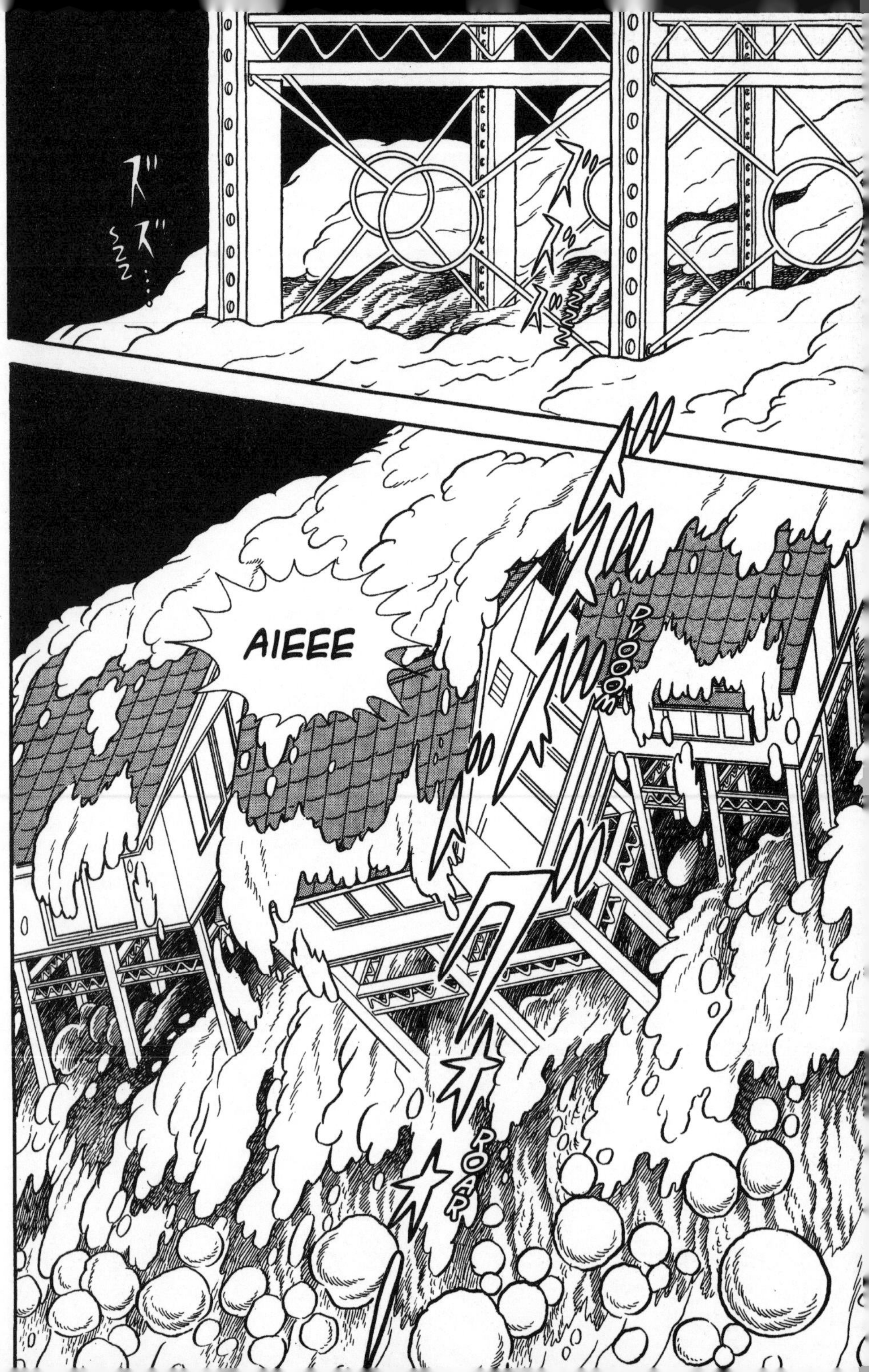
SZZZ
ズズ…
SZZ
DVOOOM
AIEEE
ROAR

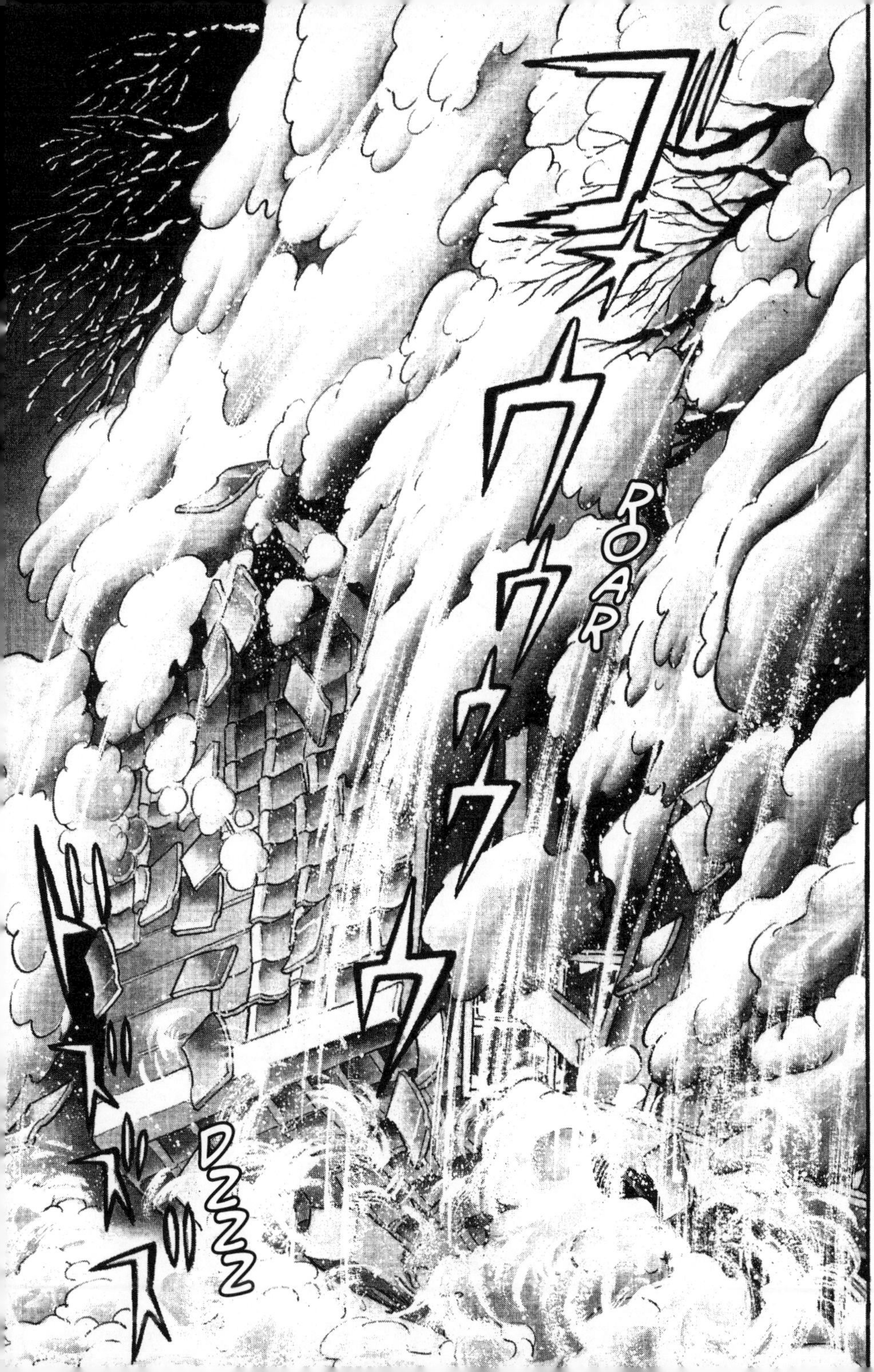
ゴオオオオオ
ROAR
ZZZ

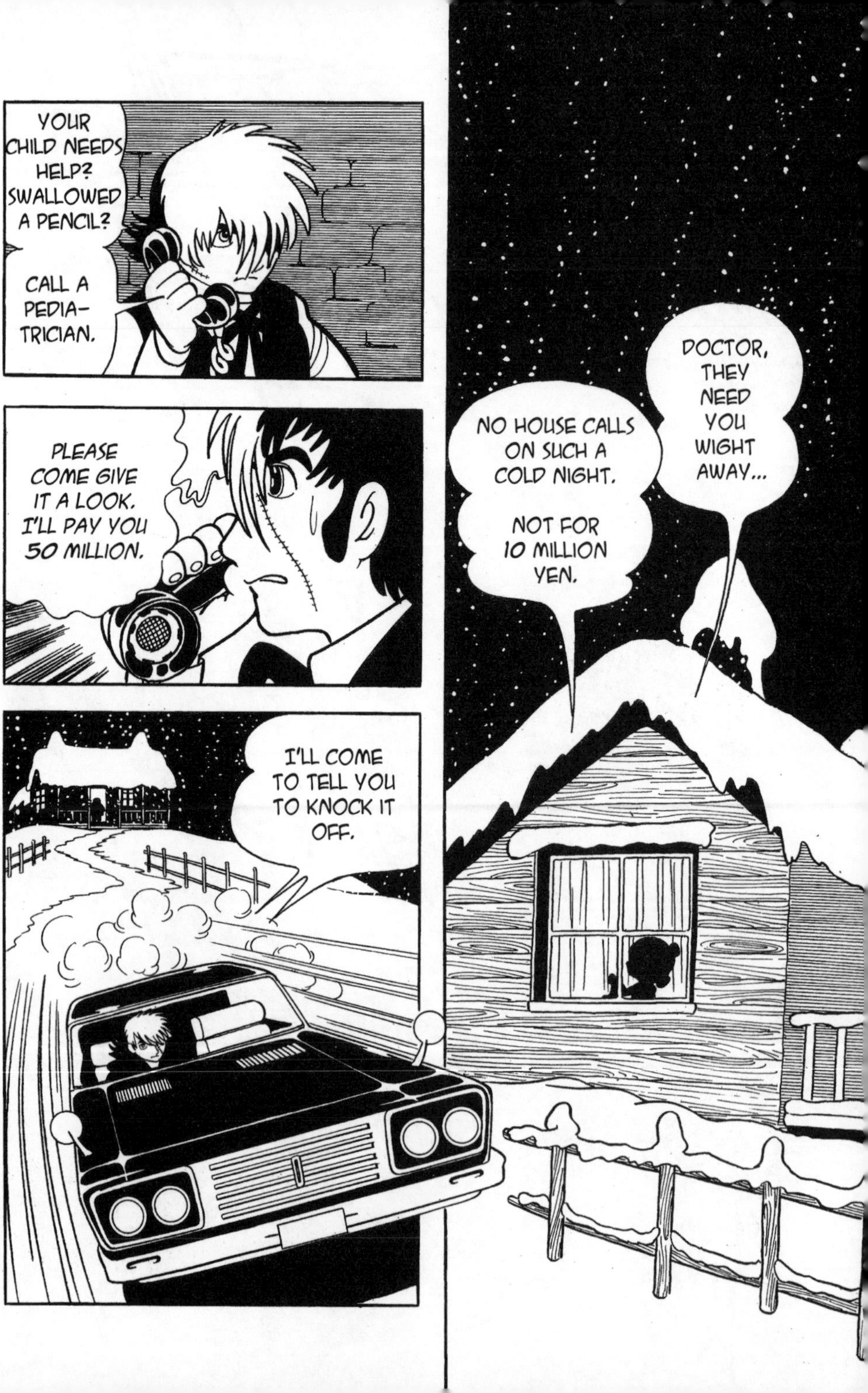
DOCTOR, THEY NEED YOU WIGHT AWAY...
NO HOUSE CALLS ON SUCH A COLD NIGHT.
NOT FOR 10 MILLION YEN.
YOUR CHILD NEEDS HELP? SWALLOWED A PENCIL?
CALL A PEDIA-TRICIAN.
PLEASE COME GIVE IT A LOOK. I'LL PAY YOU 50 MILLION.
I'LL COME TO TELL YOU TO KNOCK IT OFF.

I'M SURE THIS IS THE HOUSE ...

NOT WHAT I EXPECTED.

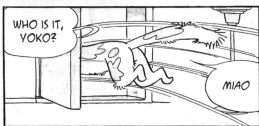

WHO IS IT, YOKO?

MIAO

MIAOW

DOCTOR BLACK JACK!

AH, IT'S YOU.

COME IN.

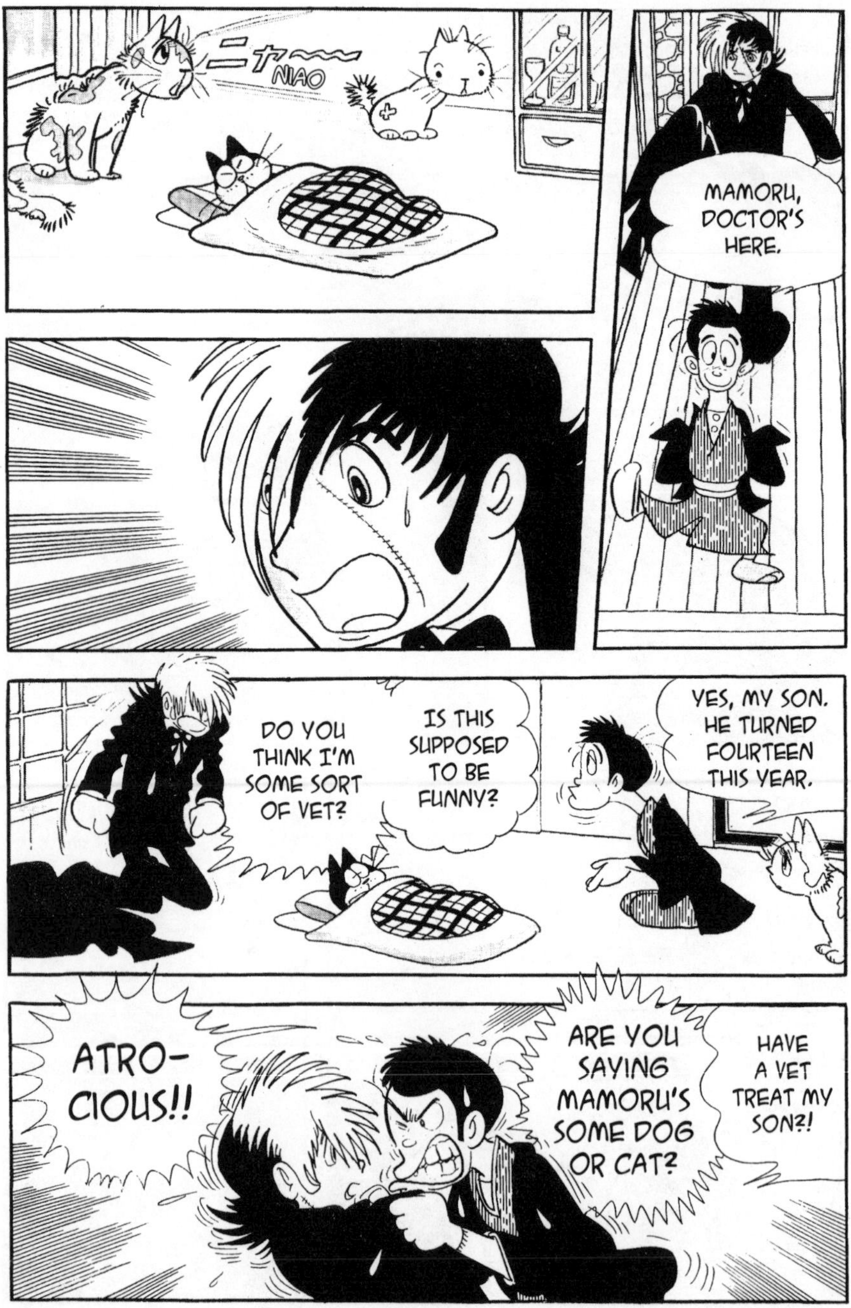
MAMORU, DOCTOR'S HERE.
ニャ〜〜
NIAO
YES, MY SON. HE TURNED FOURTEEN THIS YEAR.
IS THIS SUPPOSED TO BE FUNNY?
DO YOU THINK I'M SOME SORT OF VET?
HAVE A VET TREAT MY SON?!
ARE YOU SAYING MAMORU'S SOME DOG OR CAT?
ATRO-CIOUS!!

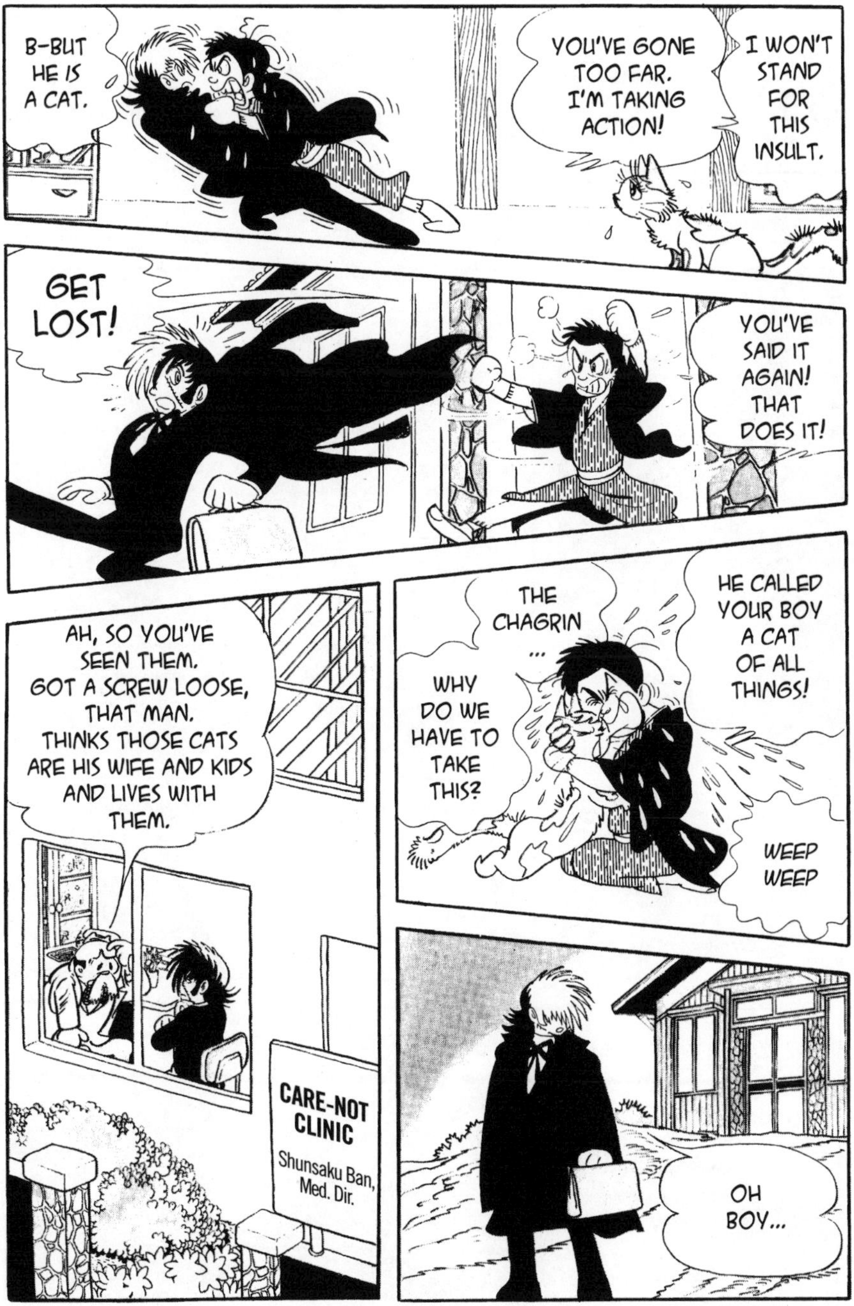
I WON'T STAND FOR THIS INSULT.
YOU'VE GONE TOO FAR. I'M TAKING ACTION!
B-BUT HE IS A CAT.
YOU'VE SAID IT AGAIN! THAT DOES IT!
GET LOST!
HE CALLED YOUR BOY A CAT OF ALL THINGS!
THE CHAGRIN ...
WHY DO WE HAVE TO TAKE THIS?
WEEP WEEP
OH BOY...
AH, SO YOU'VE SEEN THEM. GOT A SCREW LOOSE, THAT MAN. THINKS THOSE CATS ARE HIS WIFE AND KIDS AND LIVES WITH THEM.
CARE-NOT CLINIC
Shunsaku Ban, Med. Dir.

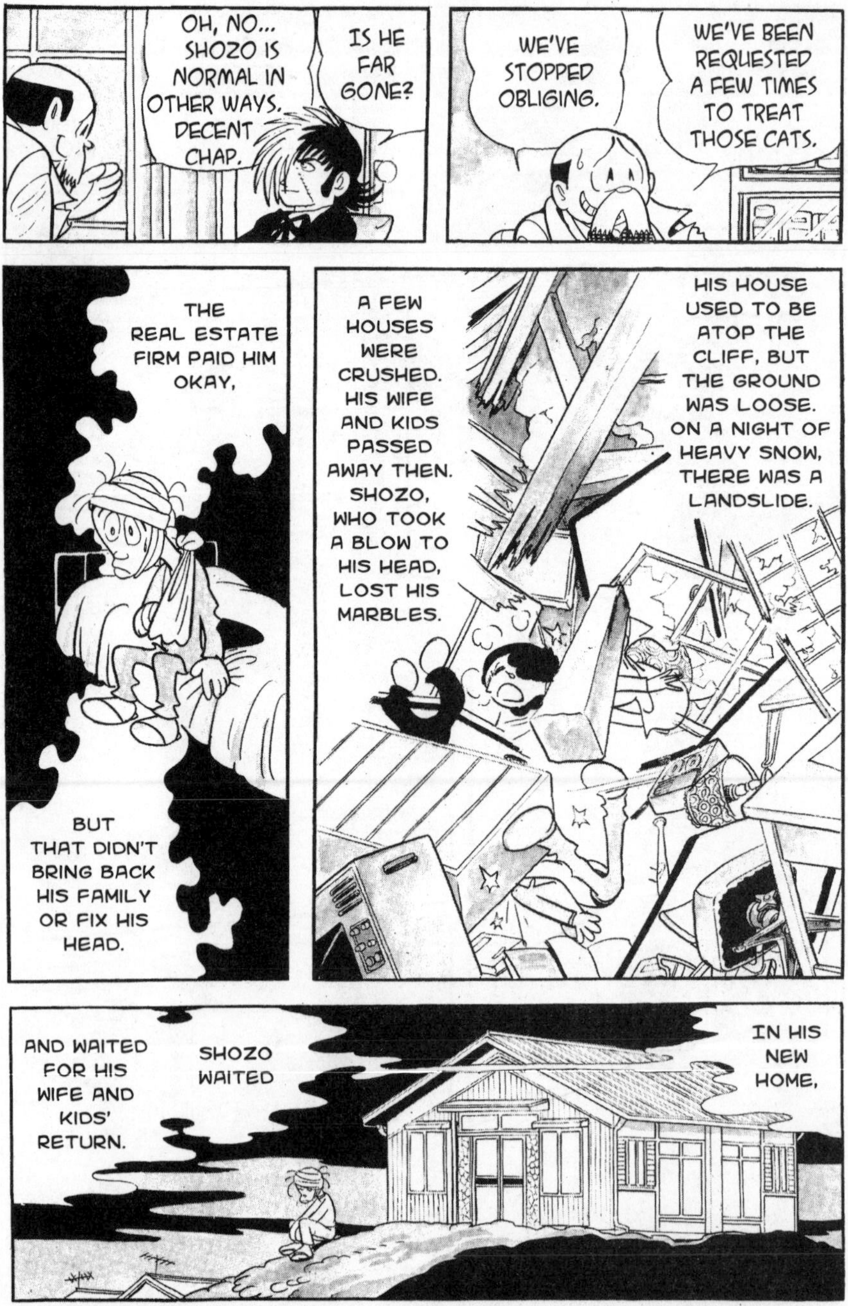
WE'VE BEEN REQUESTED A FEW TIMES TO TREAT THOSE CATS.
WE'VE STOPPED OBLIGING.
IS HE FAR GONE?
OH, NO... SHOZO IS NORMAL IN OTHER WAYS. DECENT CHAP.
HIS HOUSE USED TO BE ATOP THE CLIFF, BUT THE GROUND WAS LOOSE. ON A NIGHT OF HEAVY SNOW, THERE WAS A LANDSLIDE.
A FEW HOUSES WERE CRUSHED. HIS WIFE AND KIDS PASSED AWAY THEN. SHOZO, WHO TOOK A BLOW TO HIS HEAD, LOST HIS MARBLES.
THE REAL ESTATE FIRM PAID HIM OKAY,
BUT THAT DIDN'T BRING BACK HIS FAMILY OR FIX HIS HEAD.
IN HIS NEW HOME,
SHOZO WAITED
AND WAITED FOR HIS WIFE AND KIDS' RETURN.

NOTE: THE TITLE OF THIS STORY ALLUDES TO MASTER PROSE AUTHOR JUN'ICHIRO TANIZAKI'S *A CAT AND SHOZO AND TWO WOMEN*, A 1936 NOVEL ABOUT A CAT-LOVING LADIES' MAN.

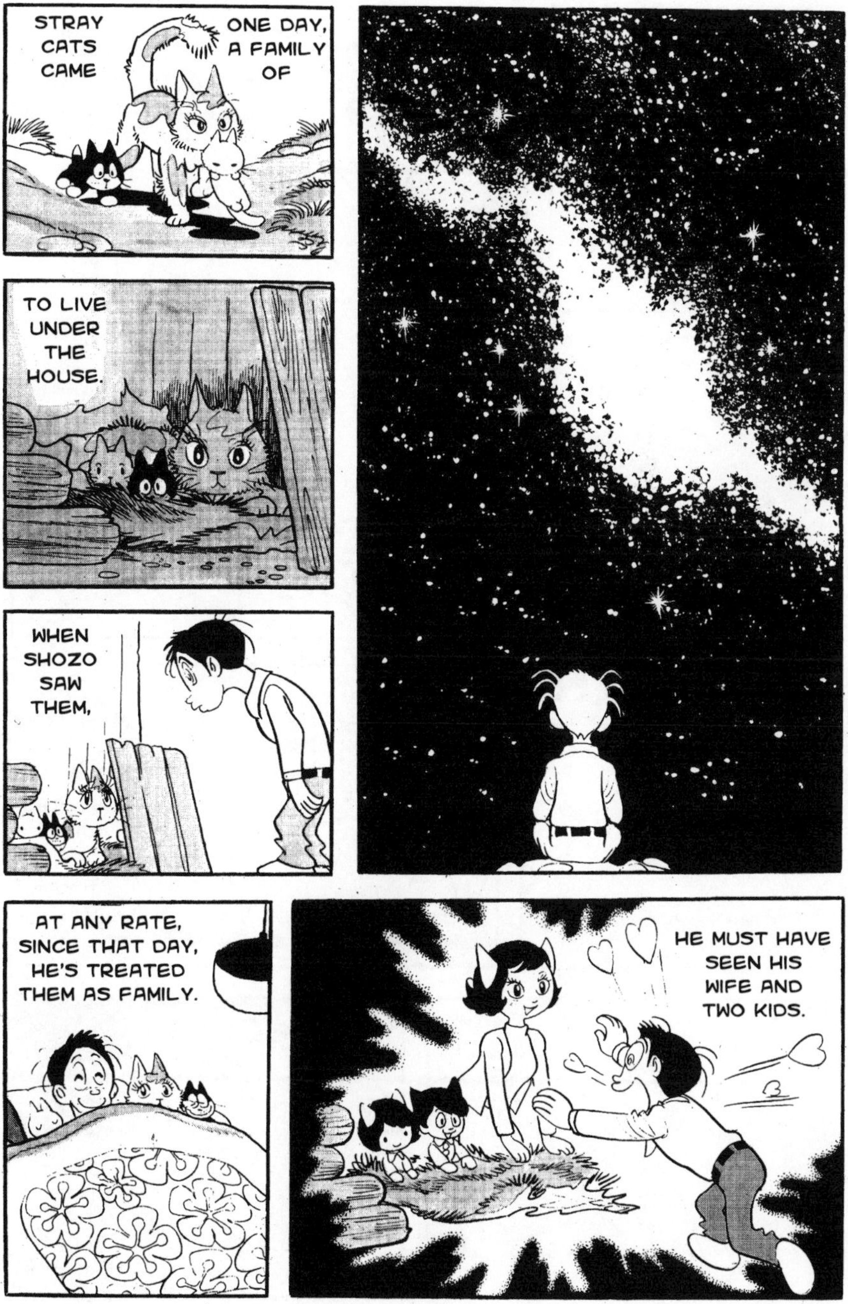
ONE DAY, A FAMILY OF
STRAY CATS CAME
TO LIVE UNDER THE HOUSE.
WHEN SHOZO SAW THEM,
HE MUST HAVE SEEN HIS WIFE AND TWO KIDS.
AT ANY RATE, SINCE THAT DAY, HE'S TREATED THEM AS FAMILY.

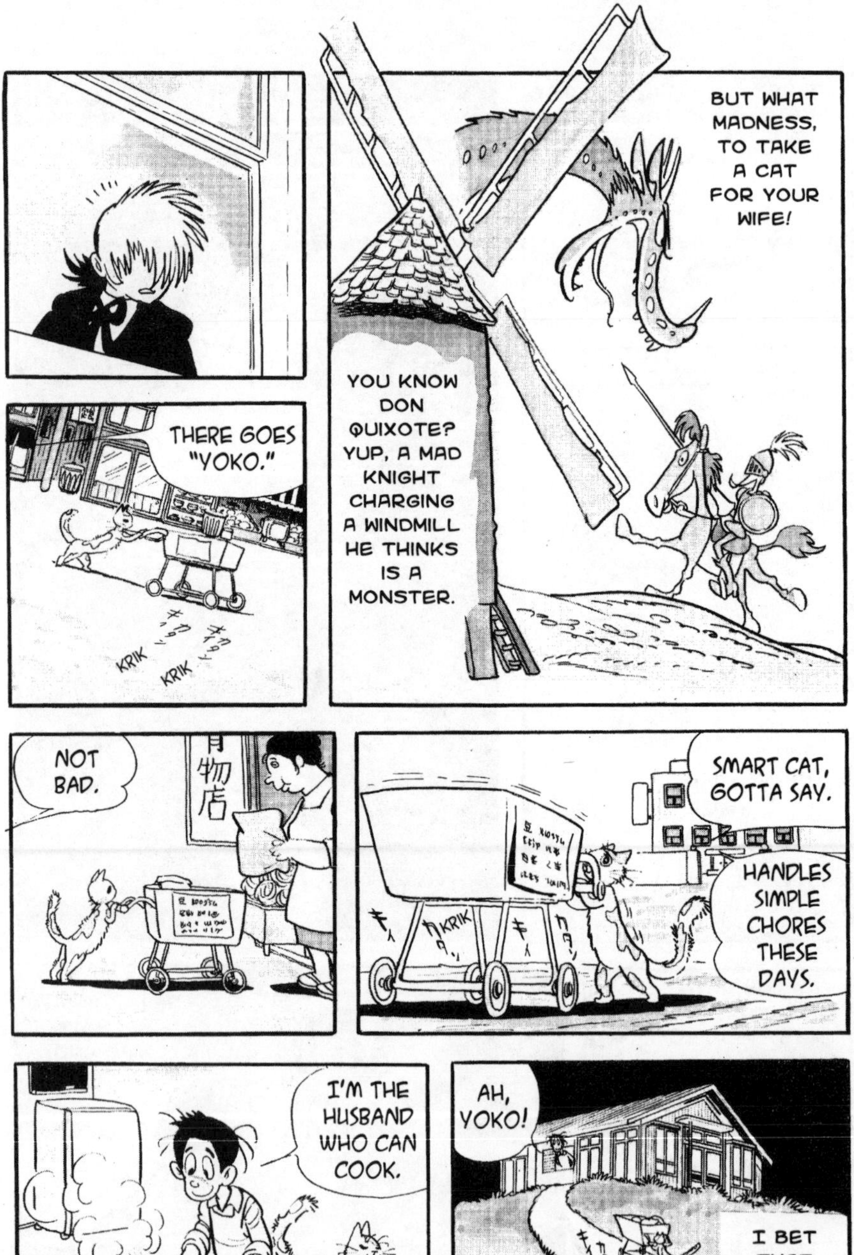
BUT WHAT MADNESS, TO TAKE A CAT FOR YOUR WIFE!
YOU KNOW DON QUIXOTE? YUP, A MAD KNIGHT CHARGING A WINDMILL HE THINKS IS A MONSTER.
THERE GOES "YOKO."
KRIK
KRIK
SMART CAT, GOTTA SAY.
HANDLES SIMPLE CHORES THESE DAYS.
KRIK
NOT BAD.
AH, YOKO!
I BET THAT CAT FEELS HIS LOVE.
KRIK
I'M THE HUSBAND WHO CAN COOK.

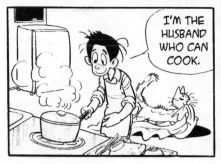

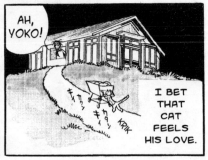

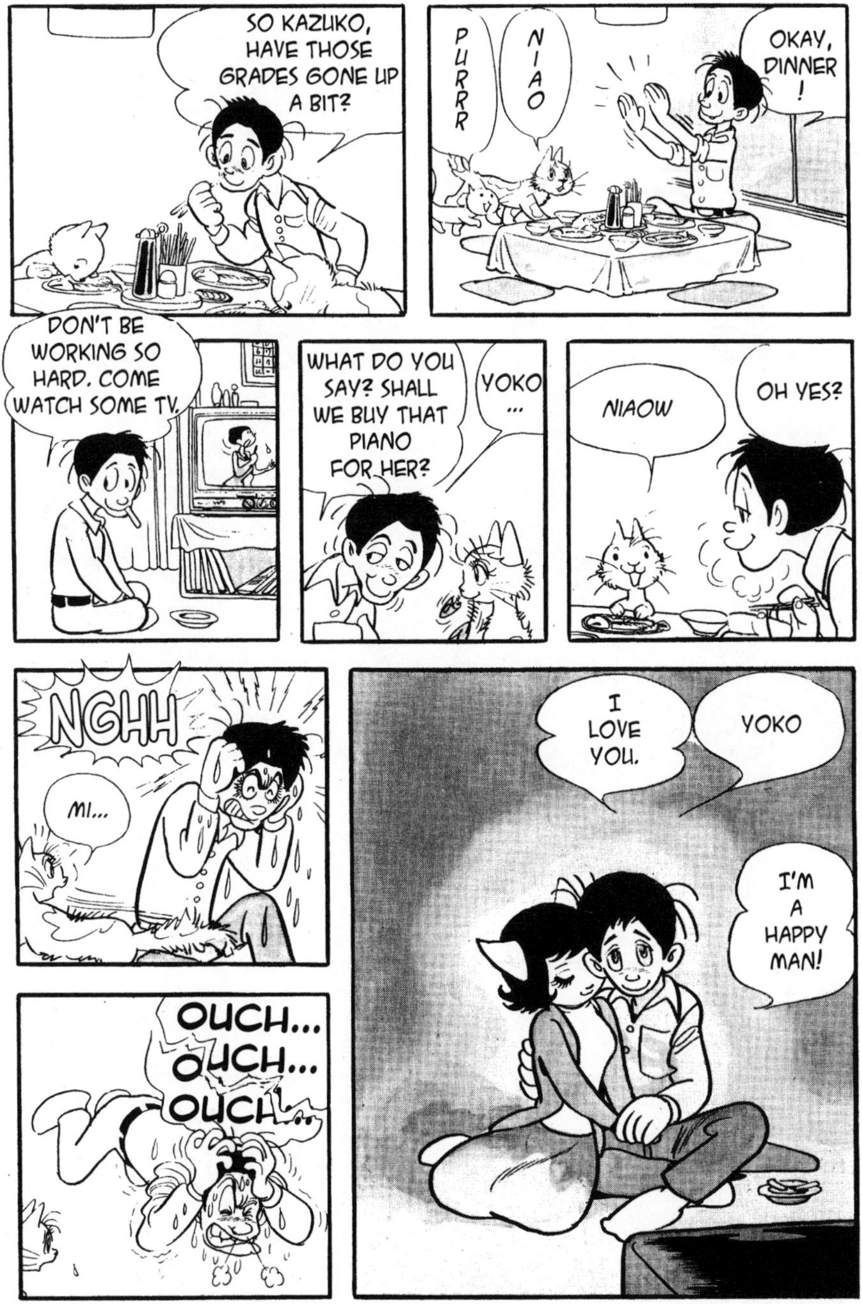
OKAY, DINNER!
NIAO
PURRR
SO KAZUKO, HAVE THOSE GRADES GONE UP A BIT?
OH YES?
NIAOW
YOKO ...
WHAT DO YOU SAY? SHALL WE BUY THAT PIANO FOR HER?
DON'T BE WORKING SO HARD. COME WATCH SOME TV.
YOKO
I LOVE YOU.
I'M A HAPPY MAN!
NGHH
MI...
OUCH... OUCH... OUCH...

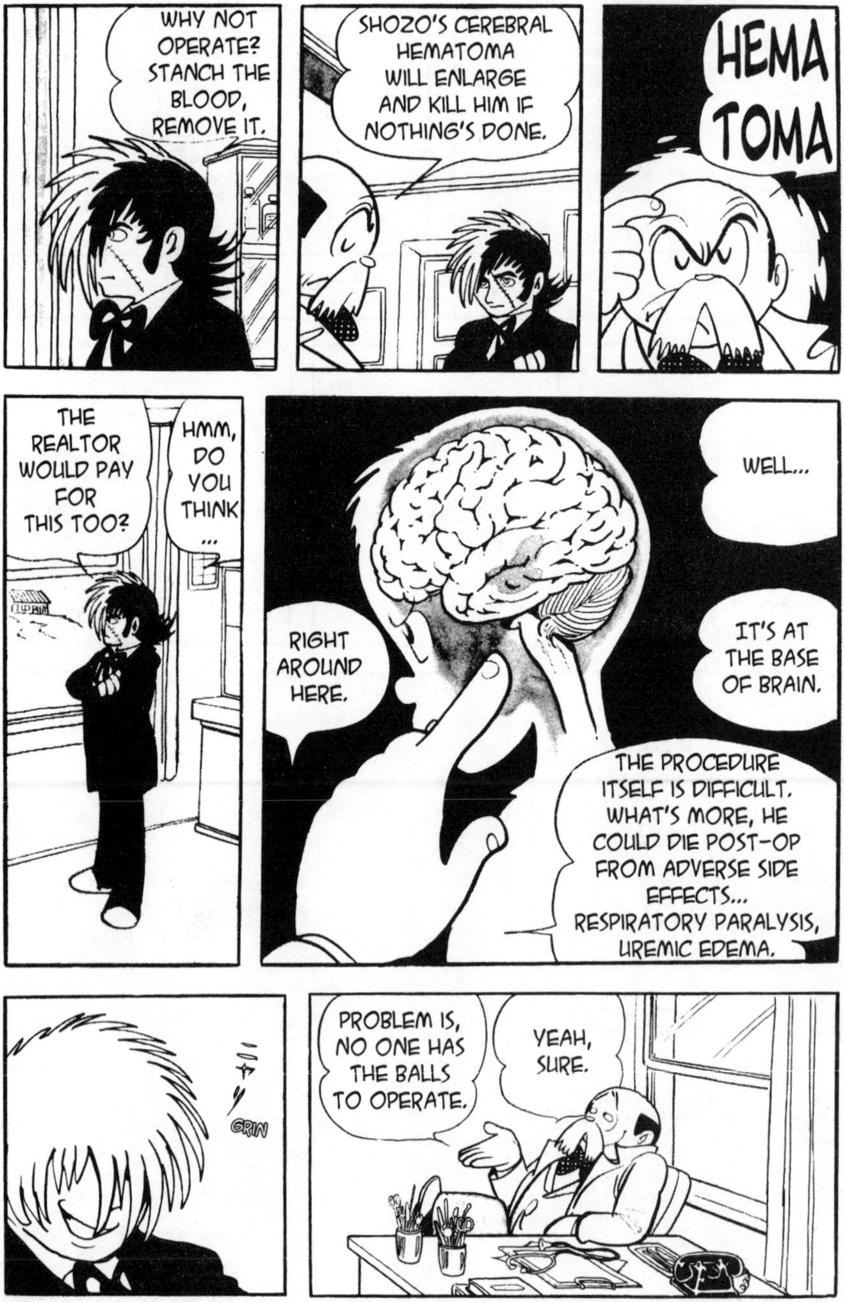
HEMA TOMA
SHOZO'S CEREBRAL HEMATOMA WILL ENLARGE AND KILL HIM IF NOTHING'S DONE.
WHY NOT OPERATE? STANCH THE BLOOD, REMOVE IT.
WELL...
IT'S AT THE BASE OF BRAIN.
RIGHT AROUND HERE.
THE PROCEDURE ITSELF IS DIFFICULT. WHAT'S MORE, HE COULD DIE POST-OP FROM ADVERSE SIDE EFFECTS... RESPIRATORY PARALYSIS, UREMIC EDEMA.
HMM, DO YOU THINK ...
THE REALTOR WOULD PAY FOR THIS TOO?
YEAH, SURE.
PROBLEM IS, NO ONE HAS THE BALLS TO OPERATE.
ニヤッ
GRIN

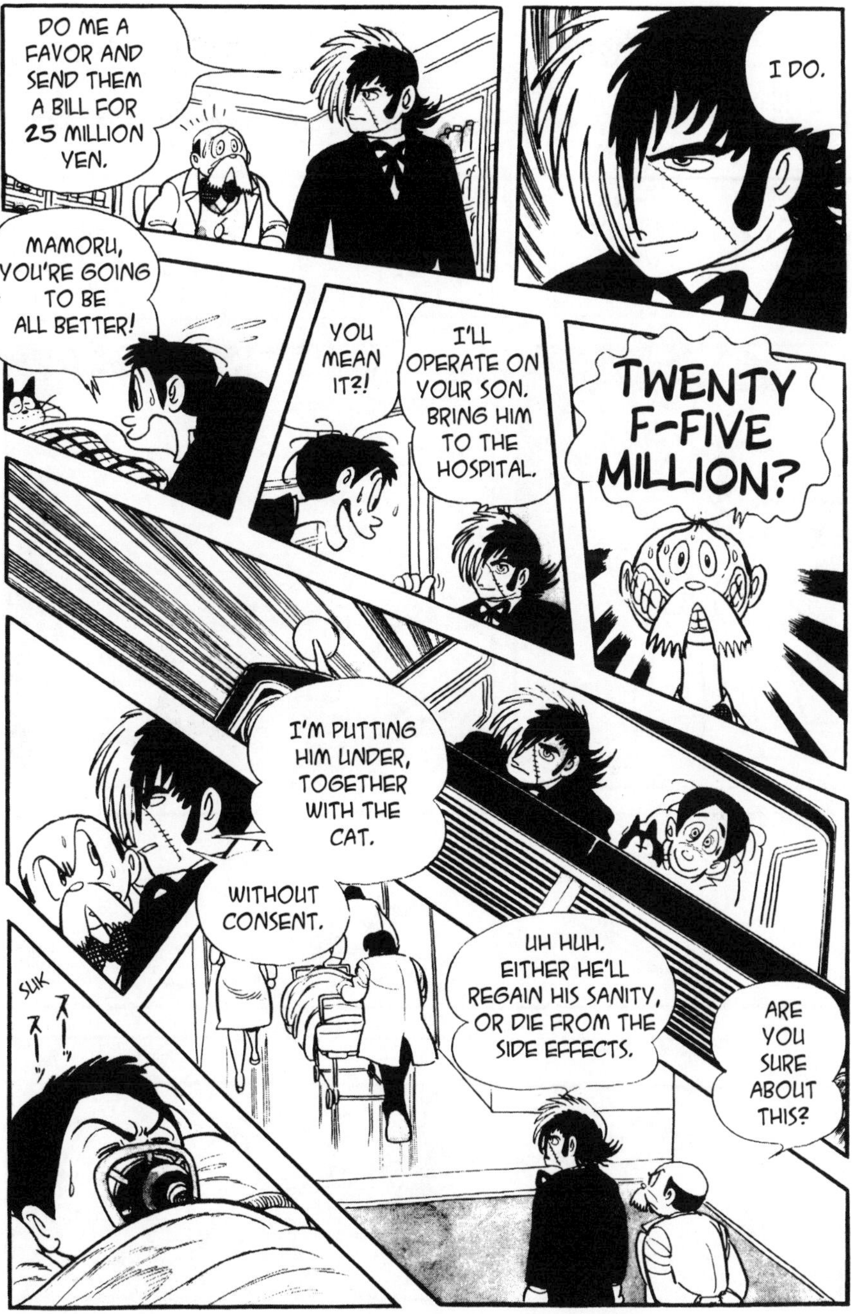

I DO.
DO ME A FAVOR AND SEND THEM A BILL FOR 25 MILLION YEN.
TWENTY F-FIVE MILLION?
I'LL OPERATE ON YOUR SON. BRING HIM TO THE HOSPITAL.
YOU MEAN IT?!
MAMORU, YOU'RE GOING TO BE ALL BETTER!
I'M PUTTING HIM UNDER, TOGETHER WITH THE CAT.
WITHOUT CONSENT.
ARE YOU SURE ABOUT THIS?
UH HUH. EITHER HE'LL REGAIN HIS SANITY, OR DIE FROM THE SIDE EFFECTS.
SUK

PINPOINT THE SITE USING ULTRASONIC WAVES.

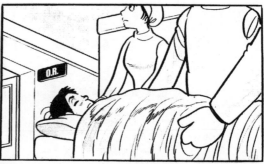

PRIK

DIAGNOSTIC PUNCTURE.

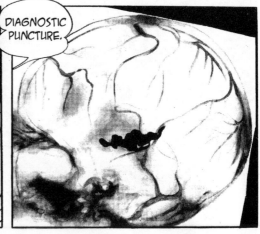

MIAOW

MIAO

MIAOW

MIAO

SHUT UP!

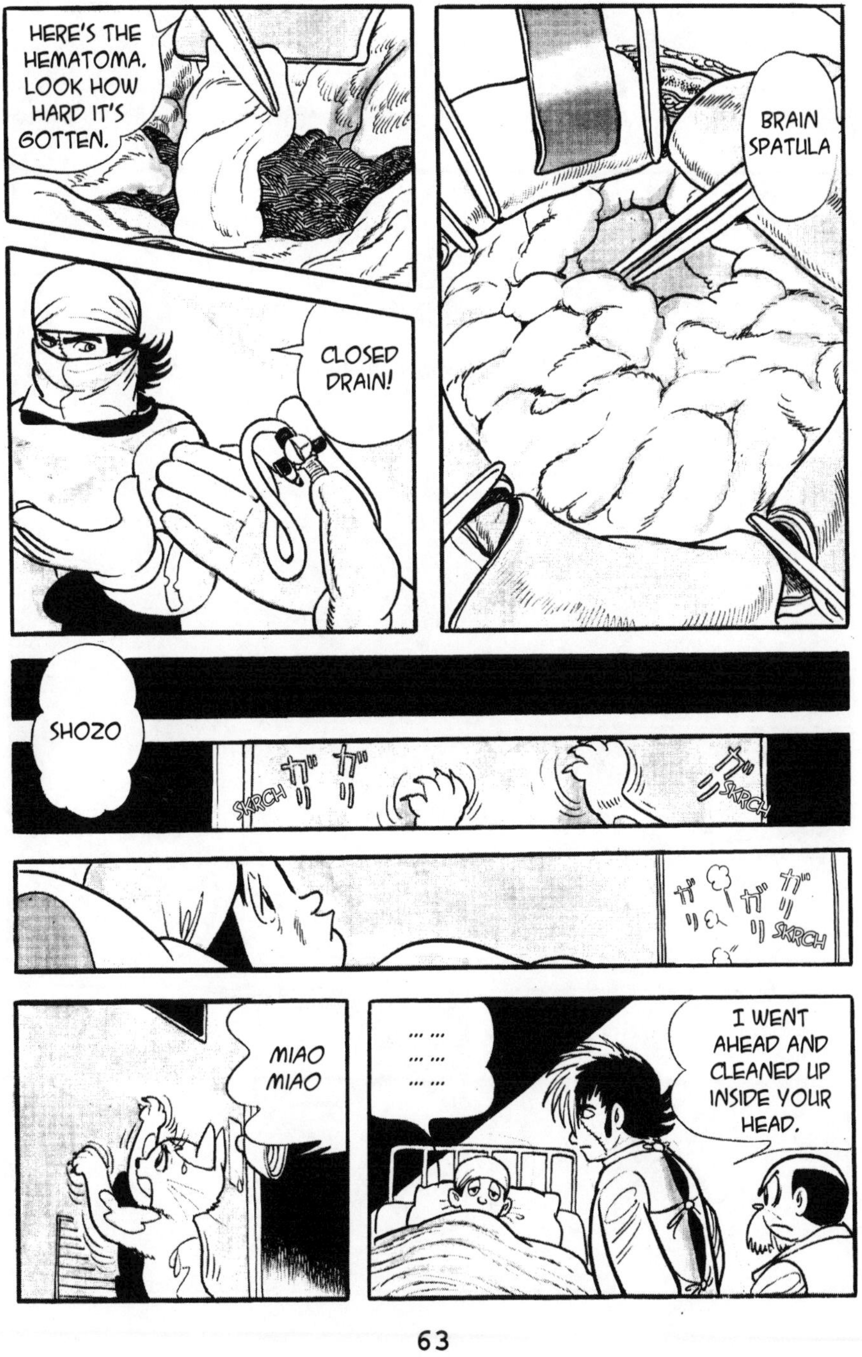
BRAIN SPATULA
HERE'S THE HEMATOMA. LOOK HOW HARD IT'S GOTTEN.
CLOSED DRAIN!
SHOZO
SKRCH
SKRCH
SKRCH
I WENT AHEAD AND CLEANED UP INSIDE YOUR HEAD.
... ...
... ...
... ...
MIAO MIAO

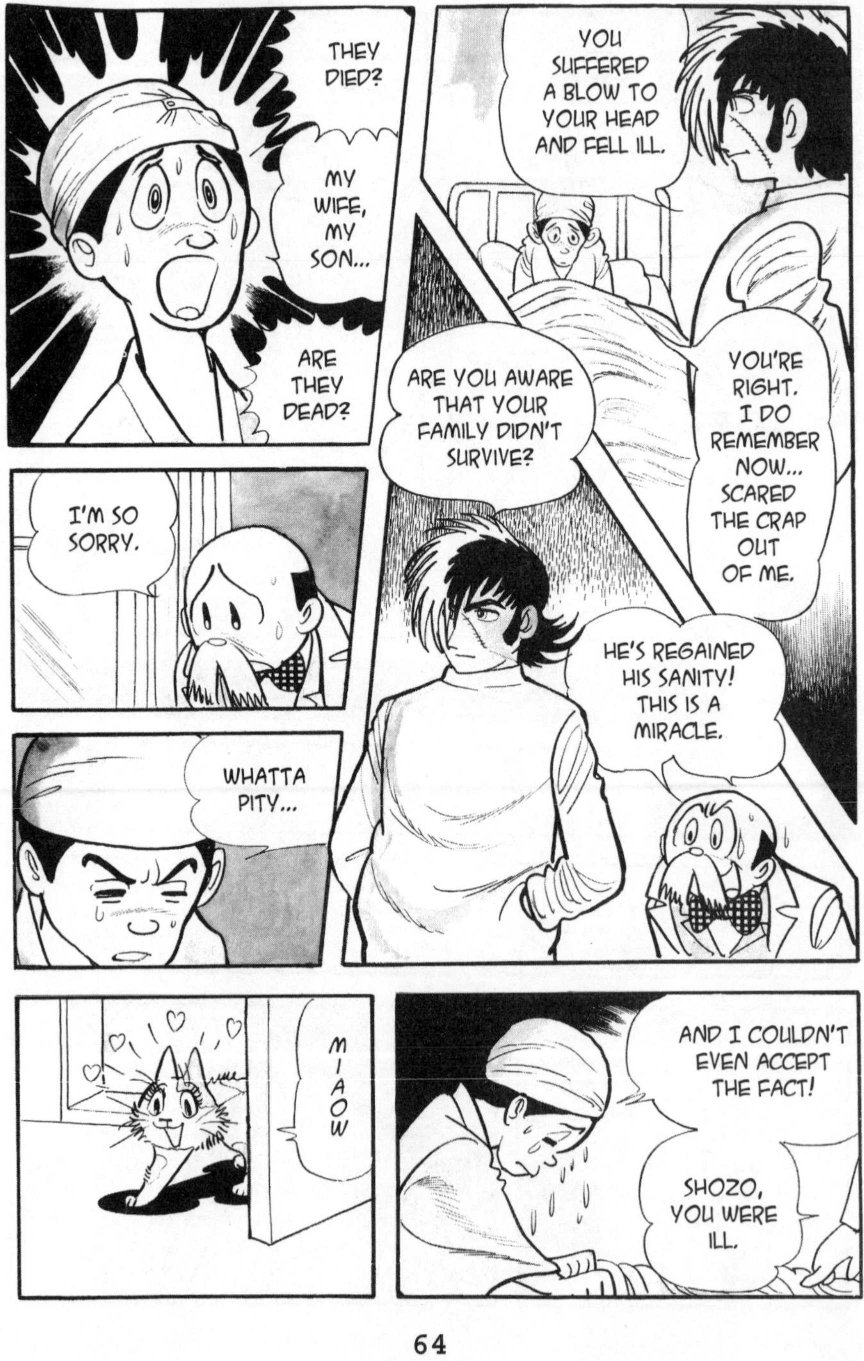
YOU SUFFERED A BLOW TO YOUR HEAD AND FELL ILL.
YOU'RE RIGHT. I DO REMEMBER NOW... SCARED THE CRAP OUT OF ME.
ARE YOU AWARE THAT YOUR FAMILY DIDN'T SURVIVE?
HE'S REGAINED HIS SANITY! THIS IS A MIRACLE.
THEY DIED?
MY WIFE, MY SON...
ARE THEY DEAD?
I'M SO SORRY.
WHATTA PITY...
AND I COULDN'T EVEN ACCEPT THE FACT!
SHOZO, YOU WERE ILL.
MIAOW

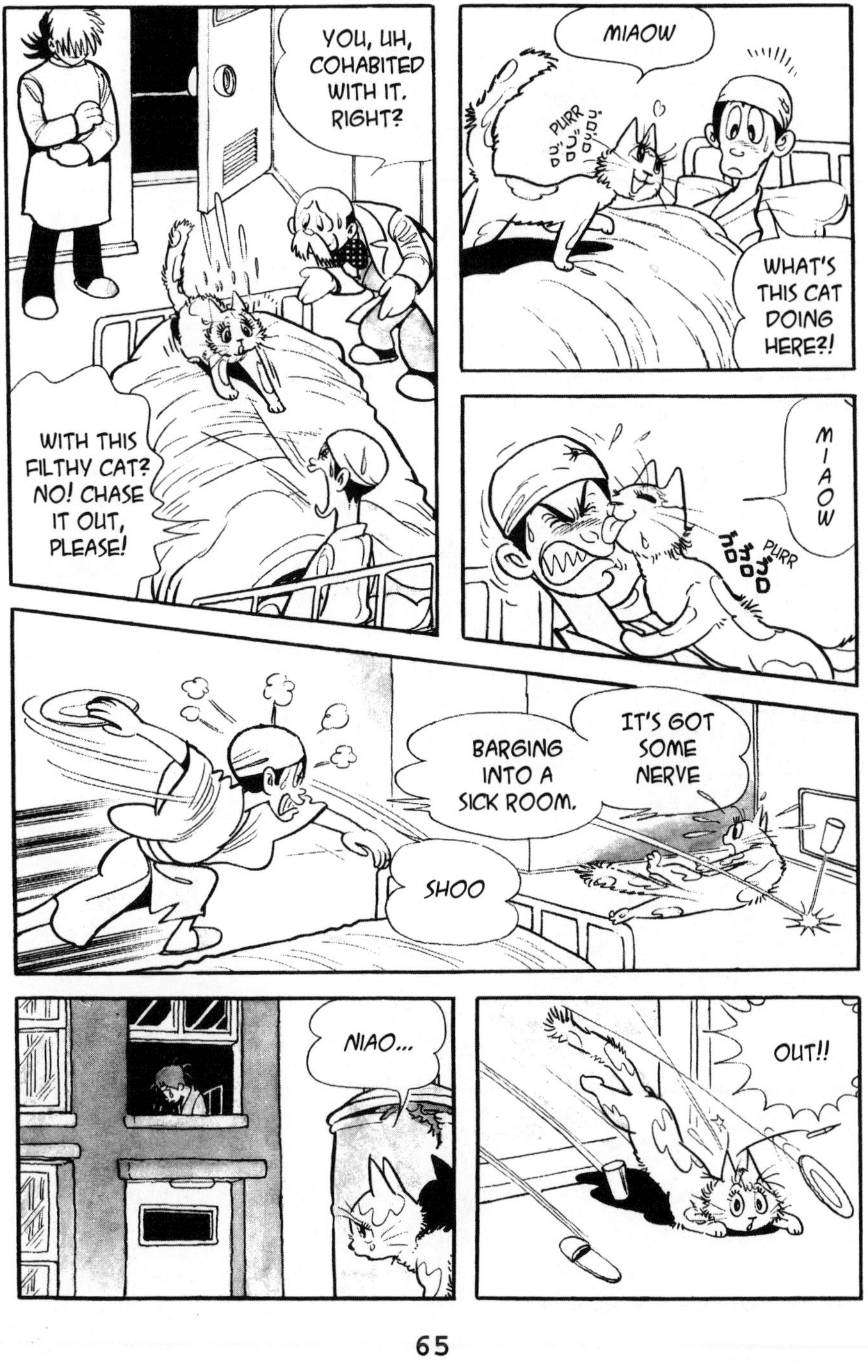
MIAOW
PURR
WHAT'S THIS CAT DOING HERE?!
MIAOW
PURR
YOU, UH, COHABITED WITH IT. RIGHT?
WITH THIS FILTHY CAT? NO! CHASE IT OUT, PLEASE!
IT'S GOT SOME NERVE
BARGING INTO A SICK ROOM.
SHOO
OUT!!
NIAO...

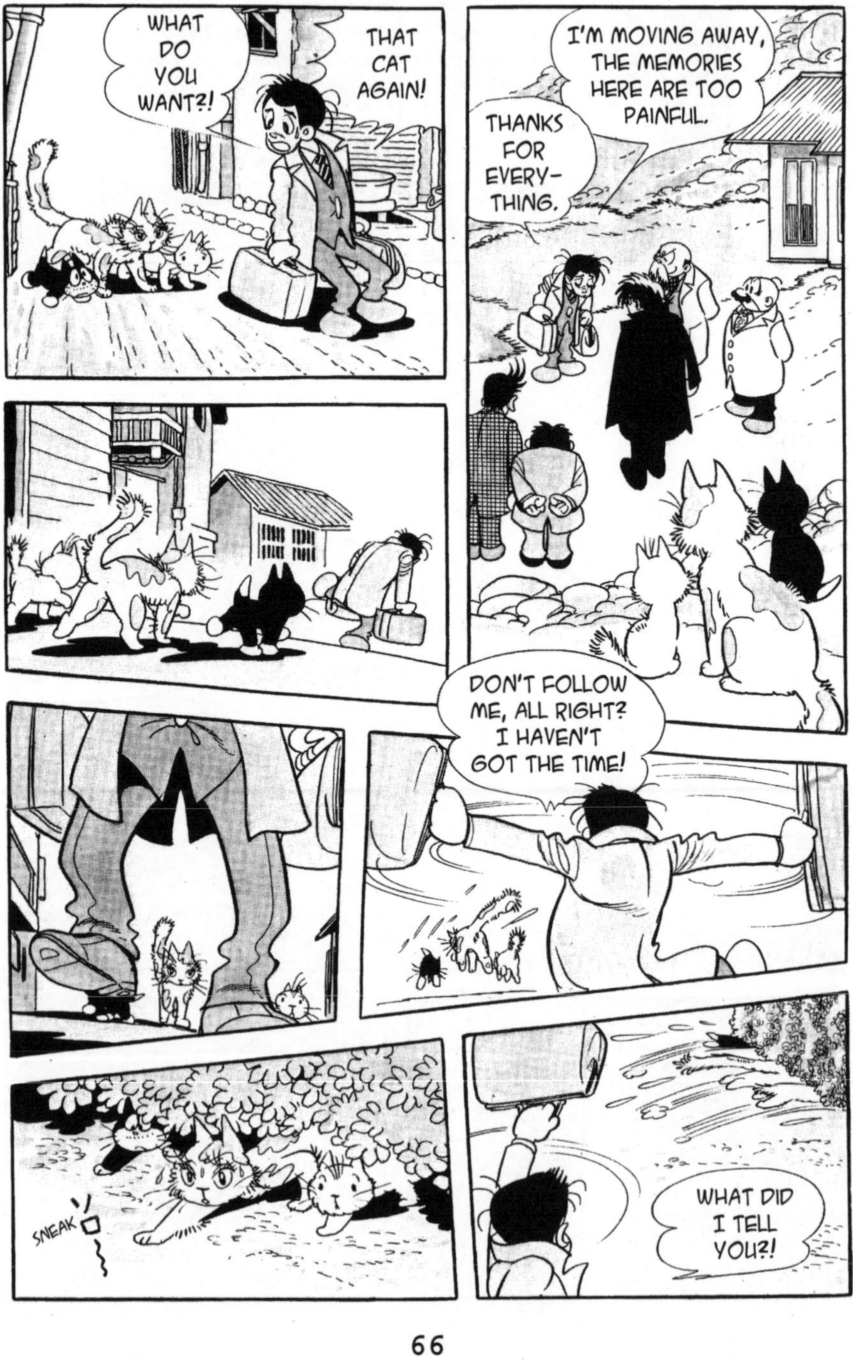
I'M MOVING AWAY, THE MEMORIES HERE ARE TOO PAINFUL.
THANKS FOR EVERY-THING.
THAT CAT AGAIN!
WHAT DO YOU WANT?!
DON'T FOLLOW ME, ALL RIGHT? I HAVEN'T GOT THE TIME!
WHAT DID I TELL YOU?!
SNEAK

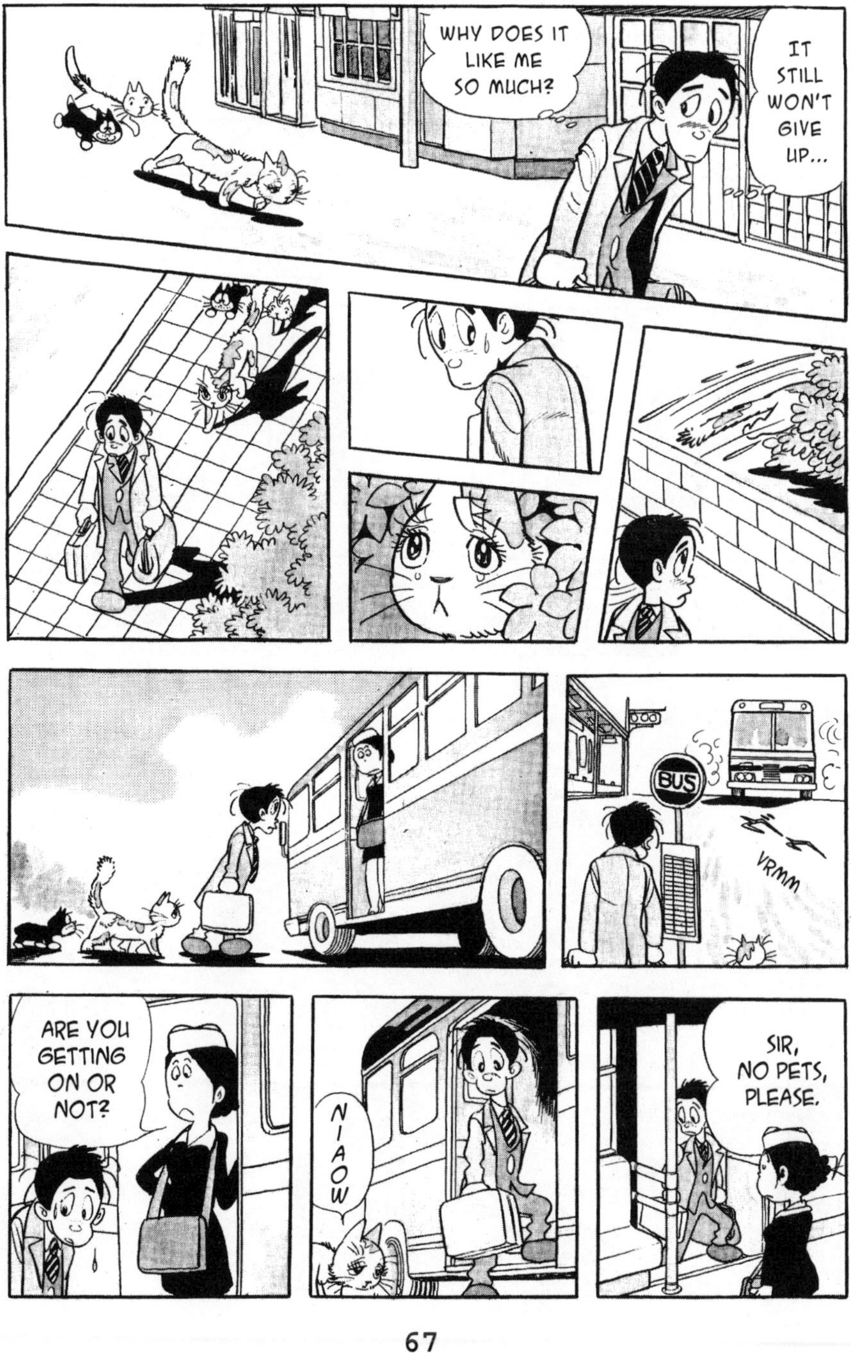
IT STILL WON'T GIVE UP...
WHY DOES IT LIKE ME SO MUCH?
BUS
VRMM
SIR, NO PETS, PLEASE.
NIAOW
ARE YOU GETTING ON OR NOT?

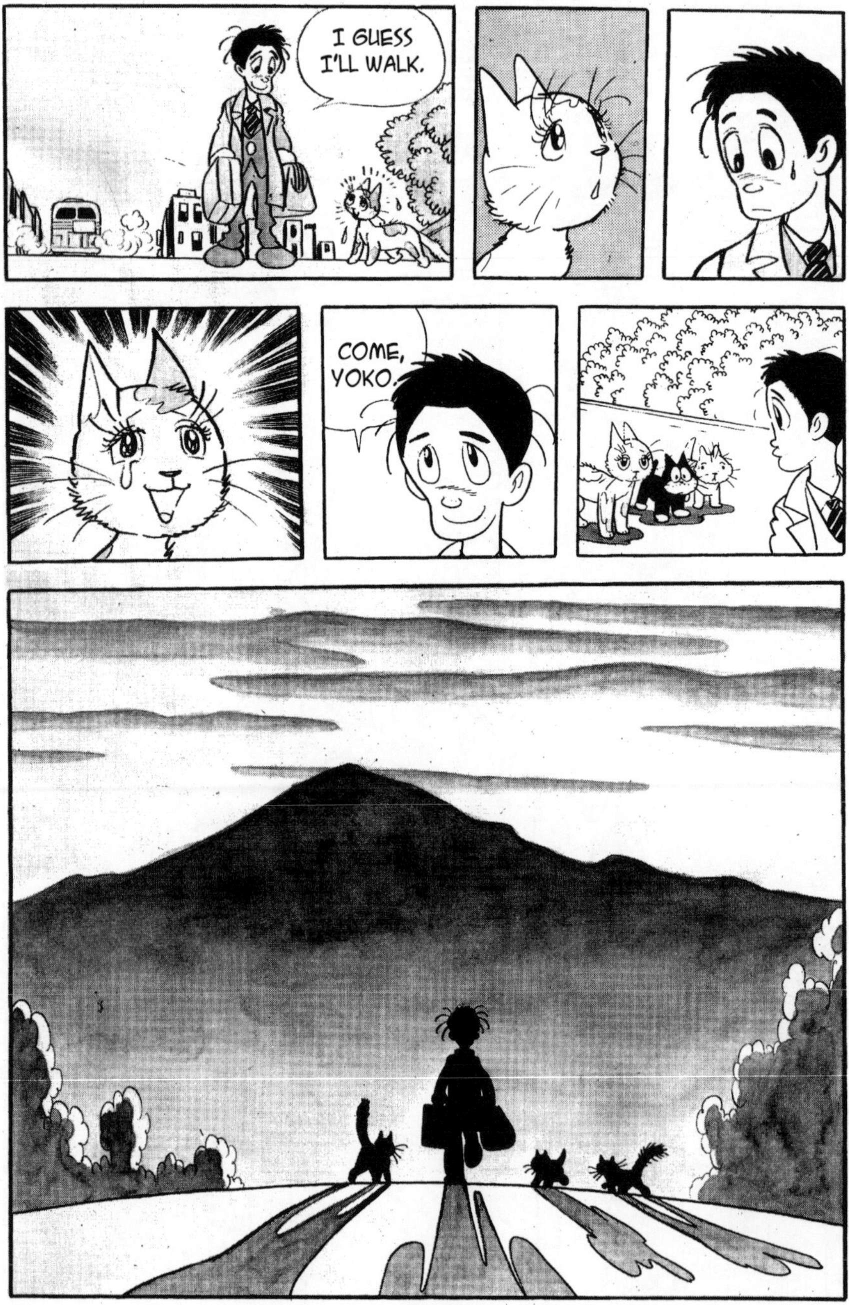
I GUESS I'LL WALK.
COME, YOKO.

THE TWO PINOKOS

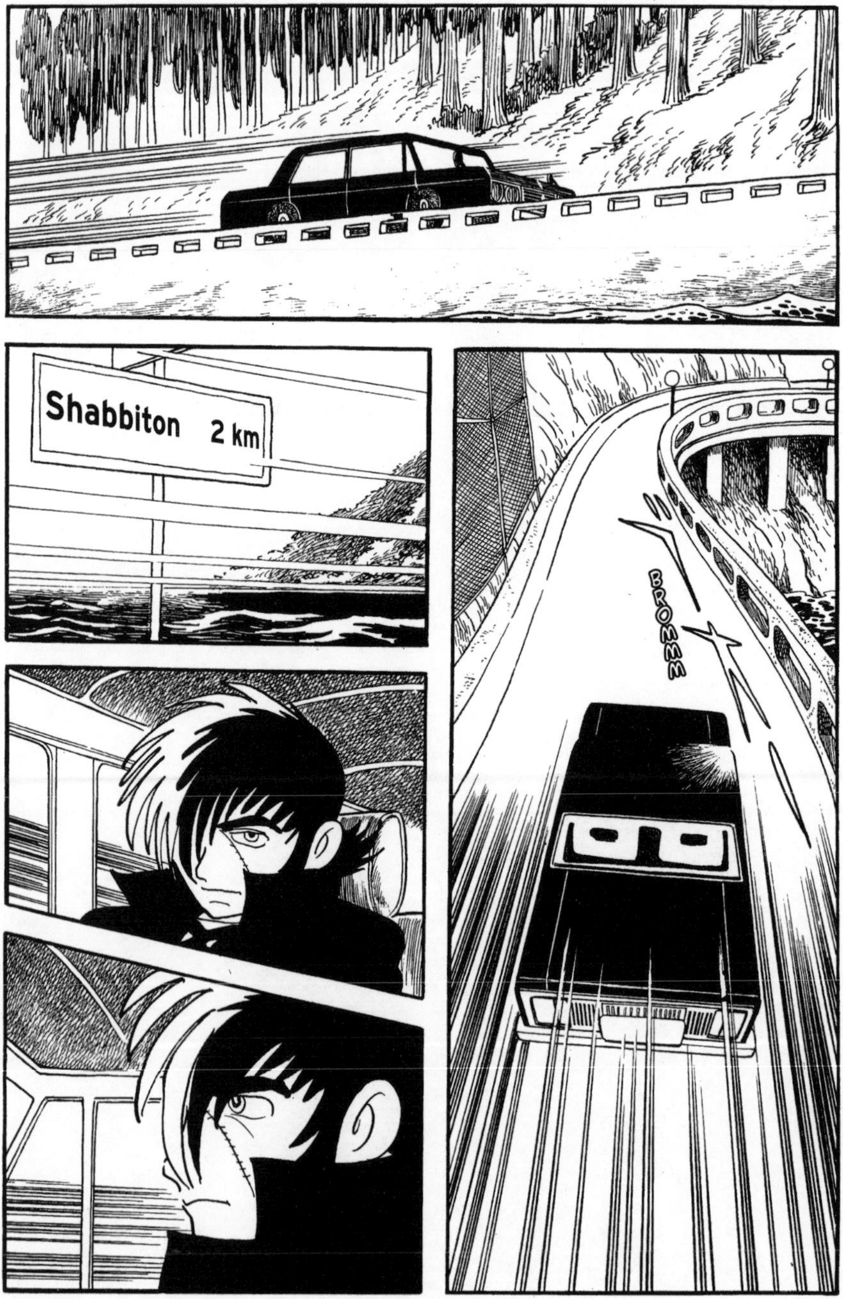
BROMMM
Shabbiton 2 km

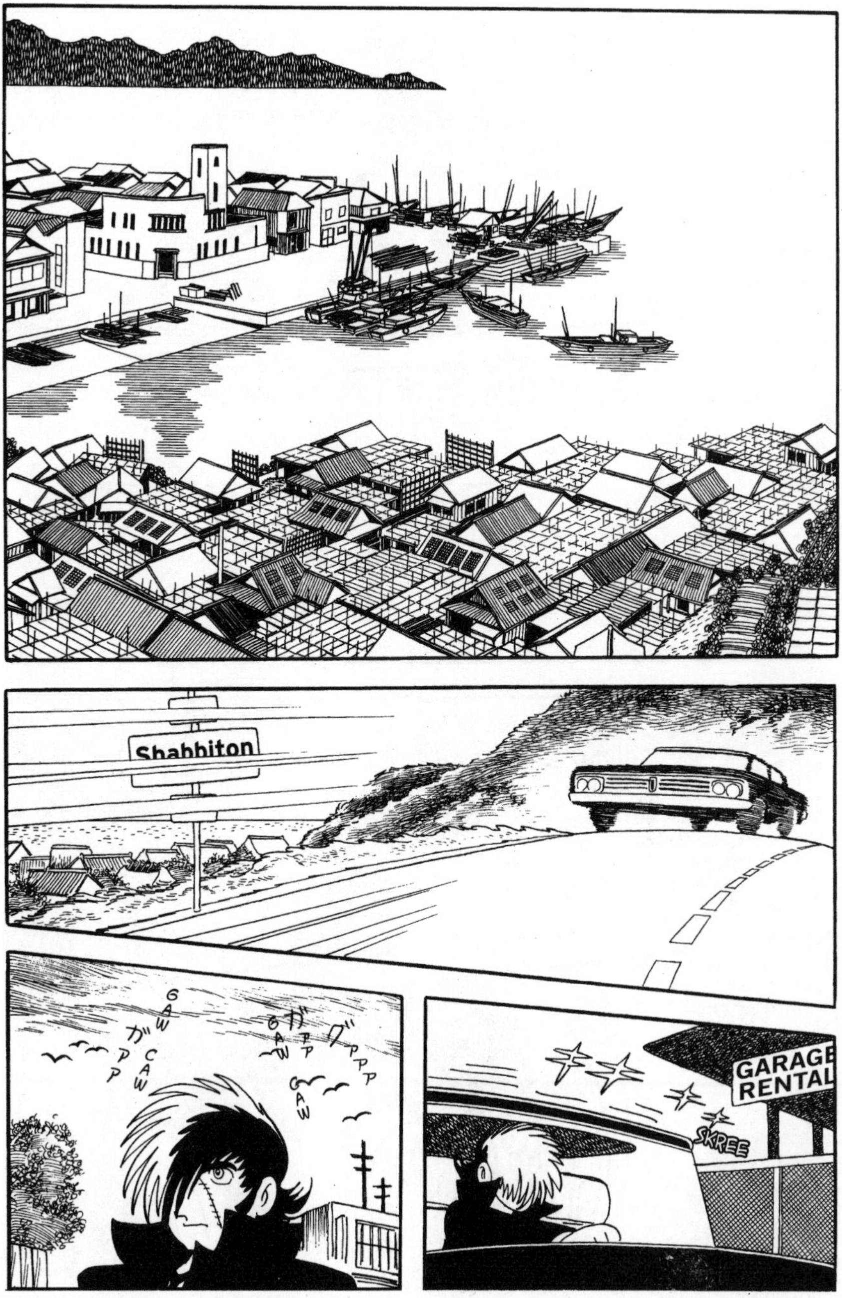
Shabbiton
GARAGE RENTAL
SKREE
グ
PPP
ガ
PP
GAW
GAW
GAW
ガ
PP
CAW

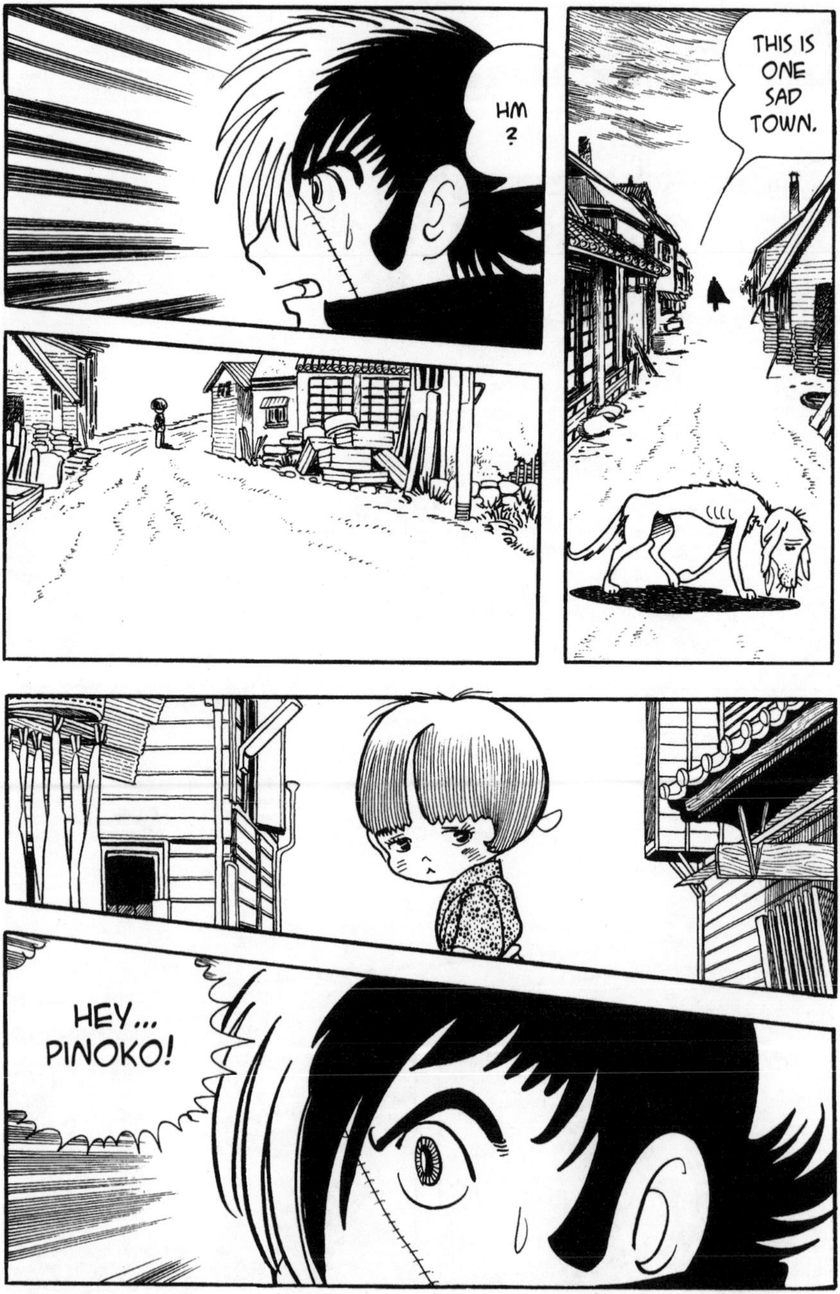
THIS IS ONE SAD TOWN.
HM?
HEY... PINOKO!

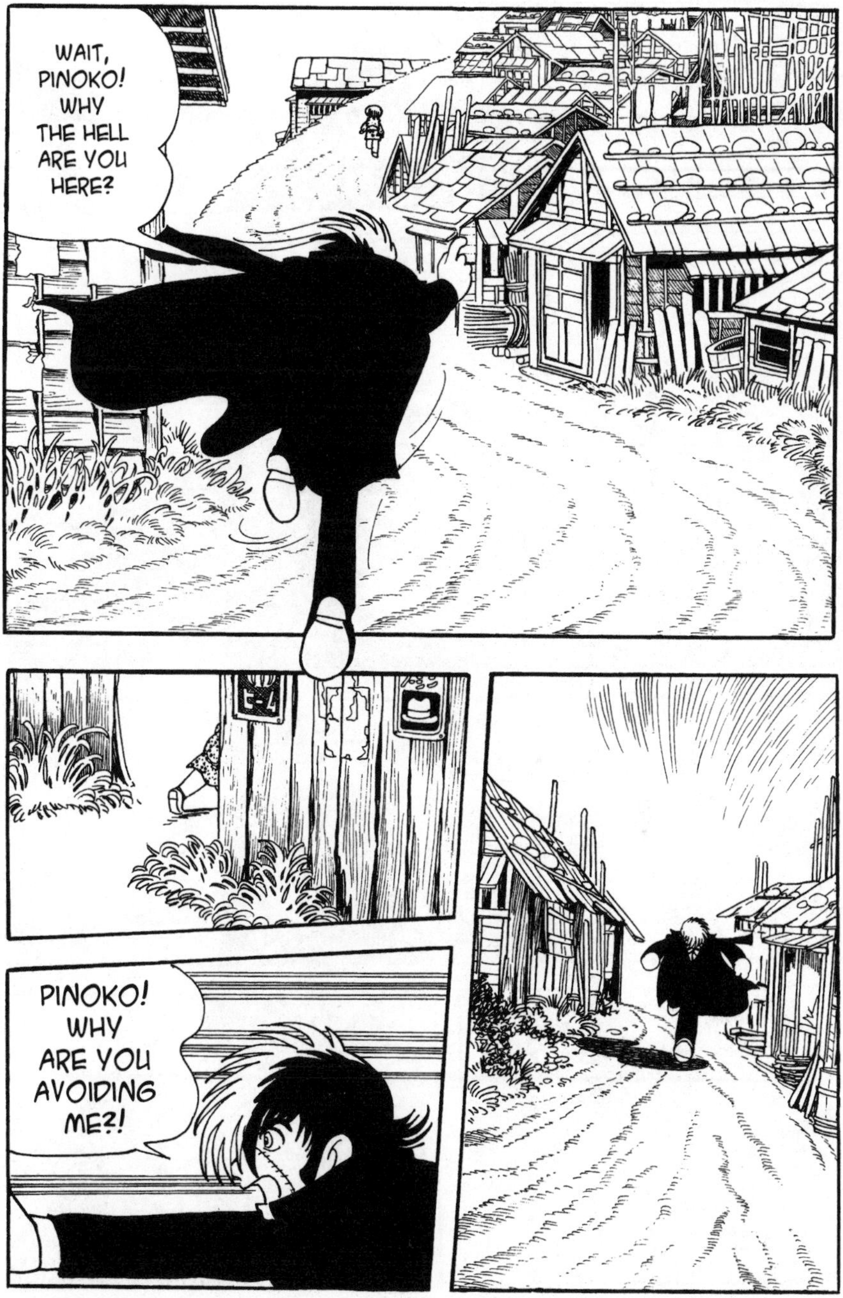
WAIT, PINOKO! WHY THE HELL ARE YOU HERE?
PINOKO! WHY ARE YOU AVOIDING ME?!

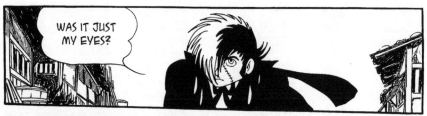

WAS IT JUST MY EYES?
AREN'T YOU DR. BLACK JACK?
コンクリート
下水工事
...
THAT SCAR... DIDN'T YOU OPERATE AT H. UNIV. HOSPITAL LAST YEAR? MY ALMA MATER.
WHAT BRINGS YOU HERE?

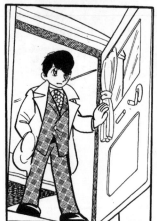

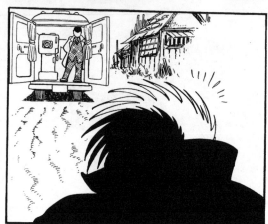

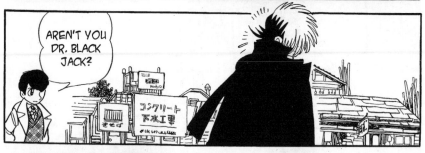

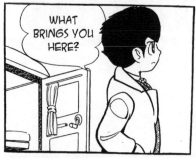

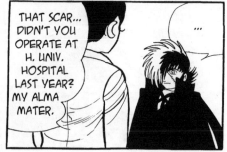

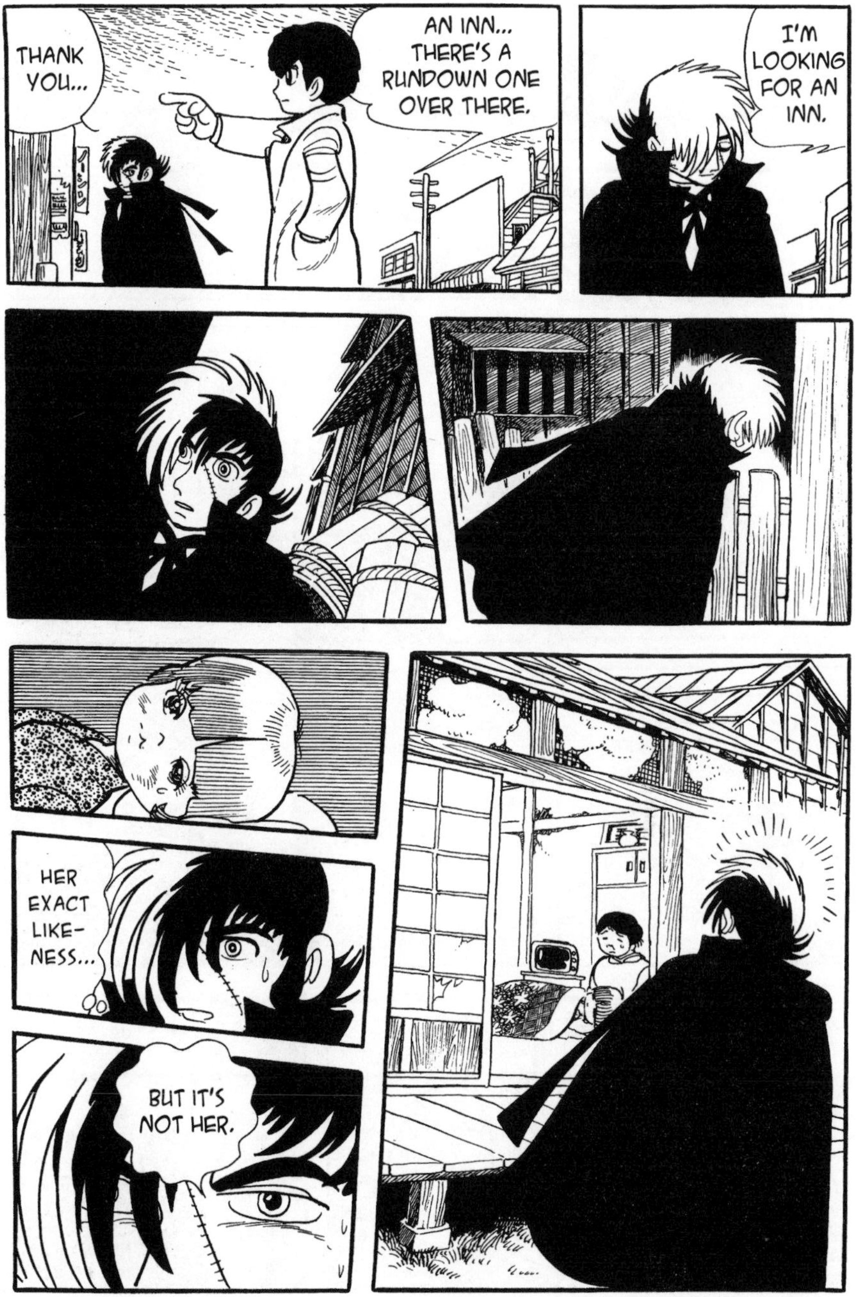
I'M LOOKING FOR AN INN.
AN INN... THERE'S A RUNDOWN ONE OVER THERE.
THANK YOU...
HER EXACT LIKE-NESS...
BUT IT'S NOT HER.

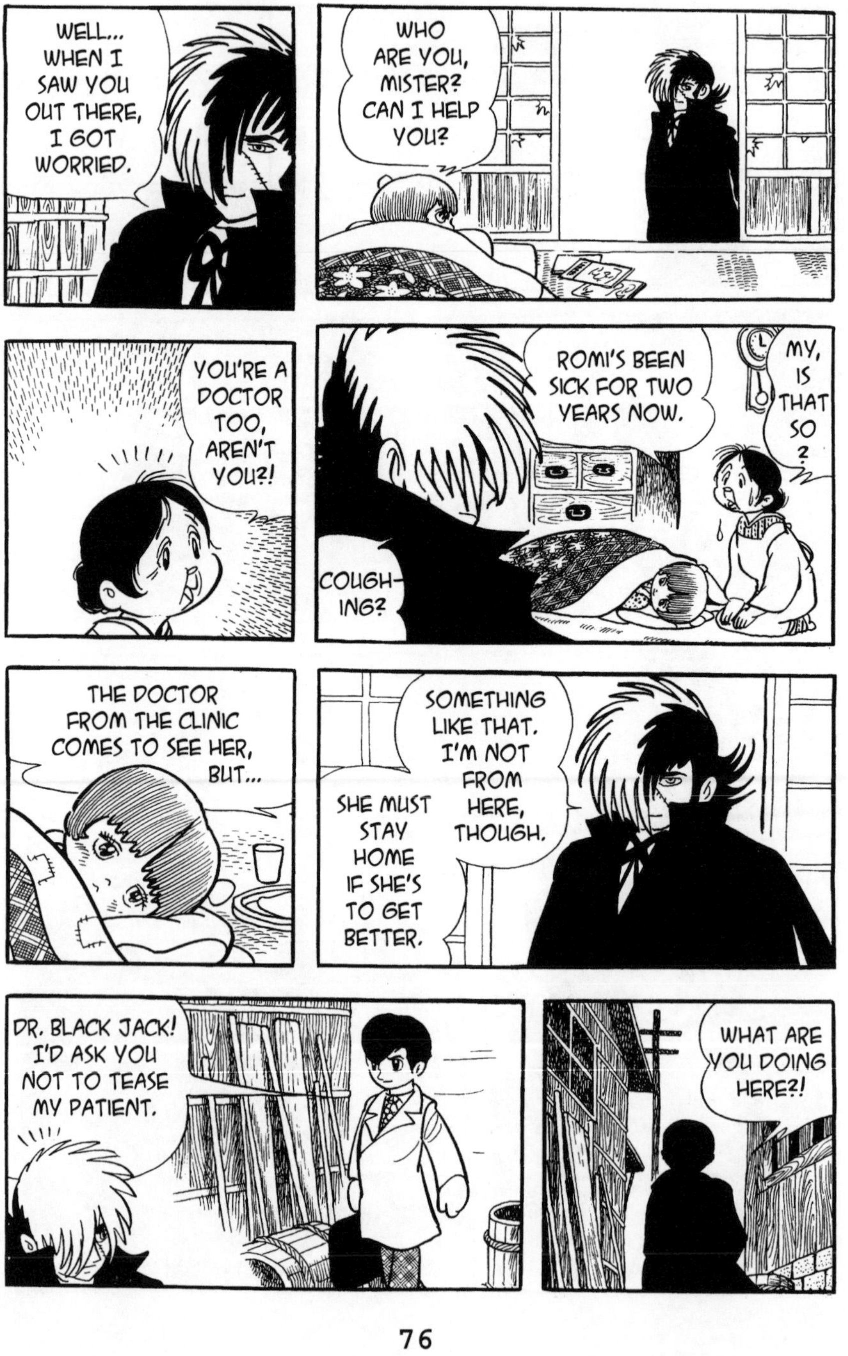
WHO ARE YOU, MISTER? CAN I HELP YOU?
WELL... WHEN I SAW YOU OUT THERE, I GOT WORRIED.
MY, IS THAT SO?
ROMI'S BEEN SICK FOR TWO YEARS NOW.
COUGHING?
YOU'RE A DOCTOR TOO, AREN'T YOU?!
SOMETHING LIKE THAT. I'M NOT FROM HERE, THOUGH.
SHE MUST STAY HOME IF SHE'S TO GET BETTER.
THE DOCTOR FROM THE CLINIC COMES TO SEE HER, BUT...
WHAT ARE YOU DOING HERE?!
DR. BLACK JACK! I'D ASK YOU NOT TO TEASE MY PATIENT.

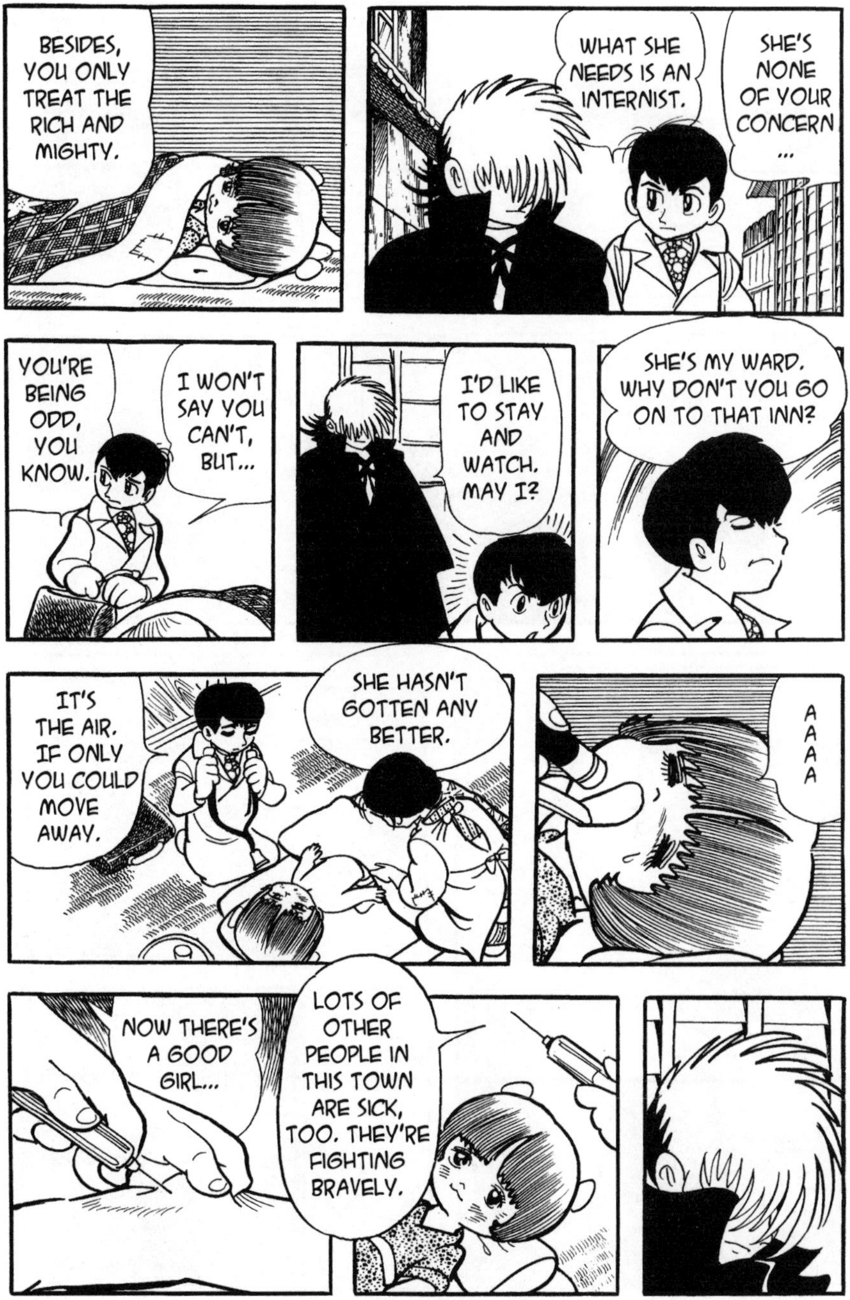
SHE'S NONE OF YOUR CONCERN ...
WHAT SHE NEEDS IS AN INTERNIST.
BESIDES, YOU ONLY TREAT THE RICH AND MIGHTY.
SHE'S MY WARD. WHY DON'T YOU GO ON TO THAT INN?
I'D LIKE TO STAY AND WATCH. MAY I?
I WON'T SAY YOU CAN'T, BUT...
YOU'RE BEING ODD, YOU KNOW.
AAAA
SHE HASN'T GOTTEN ANY BETTER.
IT'S THE AIR. IF ONLY YOU COULD MOVE AWAY.
LOTS OF OTHER PEOPLE IN THIS TOWN ARE SICK, TOO. THEY'RE FIGHTING BRAVELY.
NOW THERE'S A GOOD GIRL...

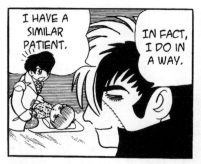

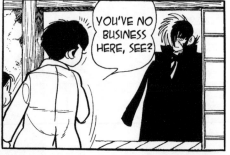

YOU'VE NO BUSINESS HERE, SEE?
IN FACT, I DO IN A WAY.
I HAVE A SIMILAR PATIENT.
YOU MEAN IN THIS TOWN?
NO...
AT A FACTORY JUST SEVERAL MILES AWAY.
THAT PATIENT IS DOING WORSE.
IT'S NOT JUST HIS LUNGS, BUT HIS HEART.
GO! ENOUGH OF THIS USELESS TALK!
SHE'LL GET THERE, TOO.
DON'T MIND WHAT HE SAID.
HE'S NOT LICENSED. TERRIBLE REP.

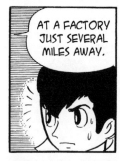

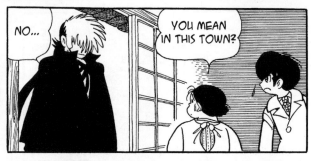

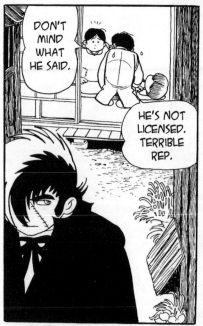

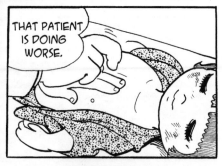

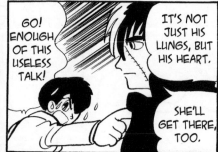

旅館
-TH ST INN
旅館
秋田書
S27年代の
YES... THERE'S BEEN A STRANGE ILLNESS LATELY.
THIS TOWN AND PORT ARE GOIN' DOWN.
WHEN I HAD TO COME UP WITH A FACE FOR PI-NOKO...
I USED AS MY MODEL THE PHOTO OF A CUTE GIRL I'D SEEN IN A MEDICAL JOURNAL. SHE SUFFERED FROM A LUNG AILMENT OF UNKNOWN ORIGIN.
THAT WAS A YEAR AGO... I CHOSE HER CUZ SHE WAS SO CUTE.
IS THIS THE SAME GIRL? NO WONDER SHE LOOKS LIKE PINOKO...

NOTE: THE RIGHTMOST SIGN IN THE FIRST PANEL READS "AKITA SHOTEN" OR AKITA BOOKS. THE SIGNBOARD IS FOR A BOOKSTORE, BUT ITS NAME IS ALSO THAT OF THE SERIES' ORIGINAL PUBLISHER.

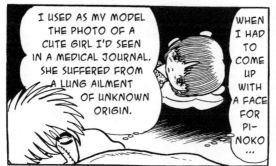

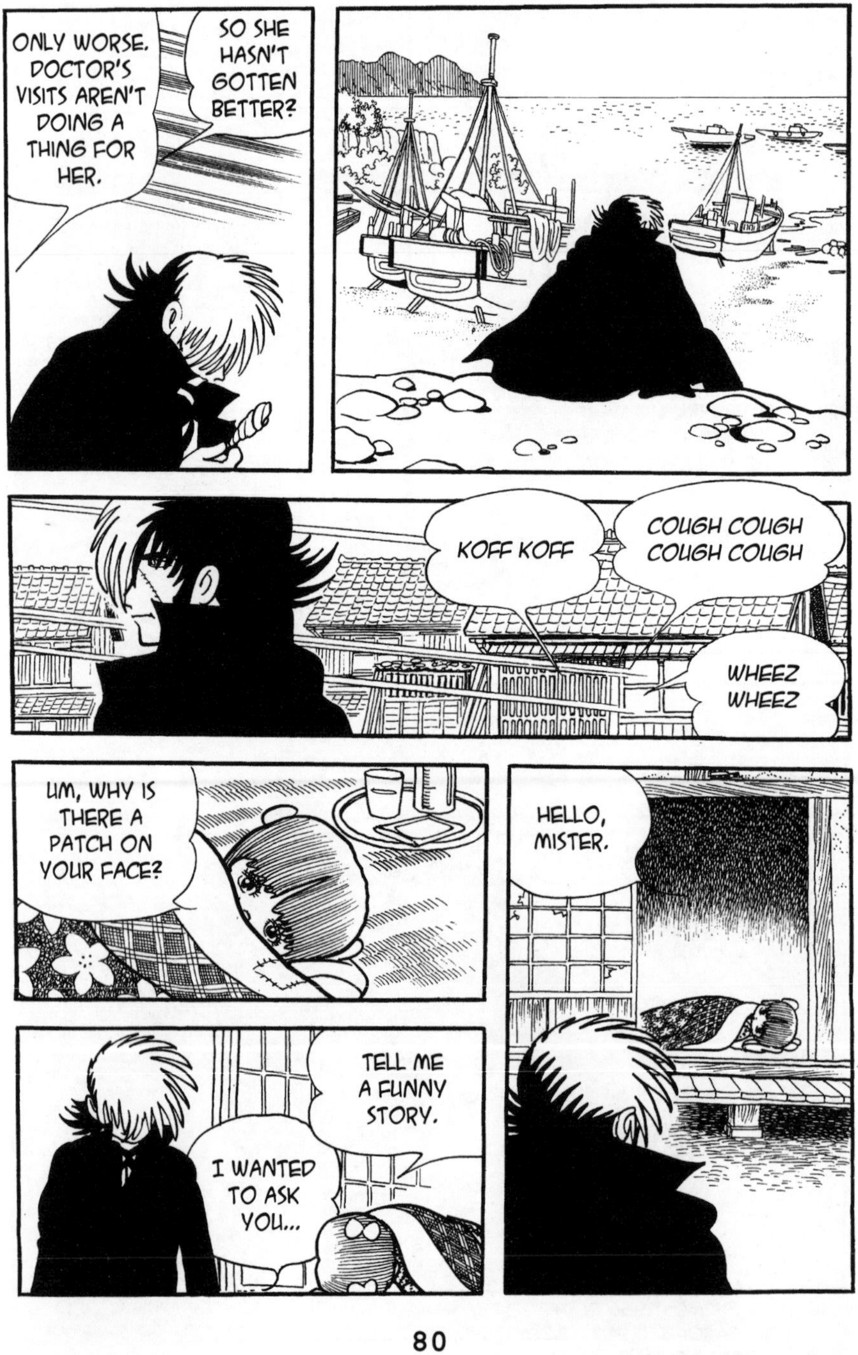
SO SHE HASN'T GOTTEN BETTER?
ONLY WORSE. DOCTOR'S VISITS AREN'T DOING A THING FOR HER.
COUGH COUGH COUGH COUGH
KOFF KOFF
WHEEZ WHEEZ
HELLO, MISTER.
UM, WHY IS THERE A PATCH ON YOUR FACE?
TELL ME A FUNNY STORY.
I WANTED TO ASK YOU...

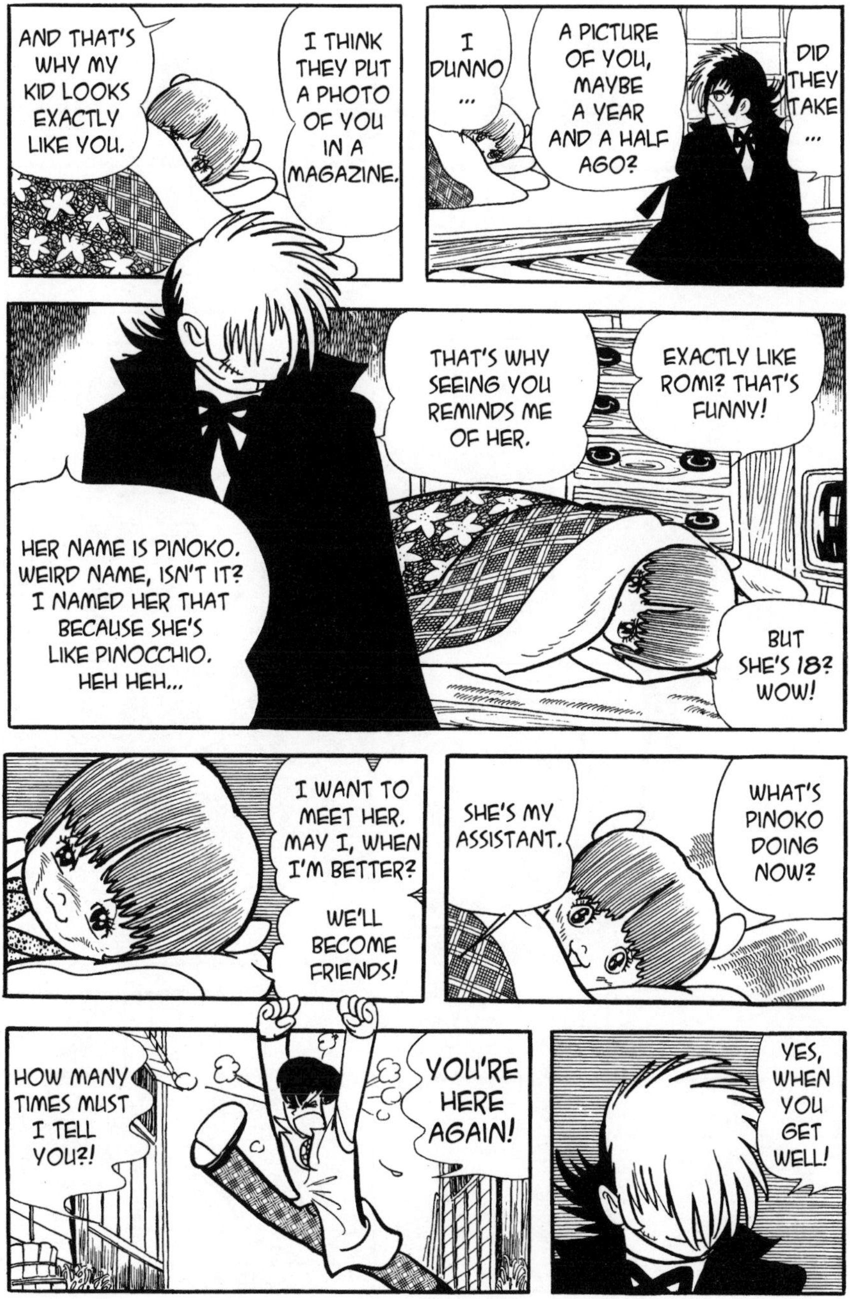
DID THEY TAKE ...
A PICTURE OF YOU, MAYBE A YEAR AND A HALF AGO?
I DUNNO ...
I THINK THEY PUT A PHOTO OF YOU IN A MAGAZINE.
AND THAT'S WHY MY KID LOOKS EXACTLY LIKE YOU.
EXACTLY LIKE ROMI? THAT'S FUNNY!
THAT'S WHY SEEING YOU REMINDS ME OF HER.
HER NAME IS PINOKO. WEIRD NAME, ISN'T IT? I NAMED HER THAT BECAUSE SHE'S LIKE PINOCCHIO. HEH HEH...
BUT SHE'S 18? WOW!
WHAT'S PINOKO DOING NOW?
SHE'S MY ASSISTANT.
I WANT TO MEET HER. MAY I, WHEN I'M BETTER?
WE'LL BECOME FRIENDS!
YES, WHEN YOU GET WELL!
YOU'RE HERE AGAIN!
HOW MANY TIMES MUST I TELL YOU?!

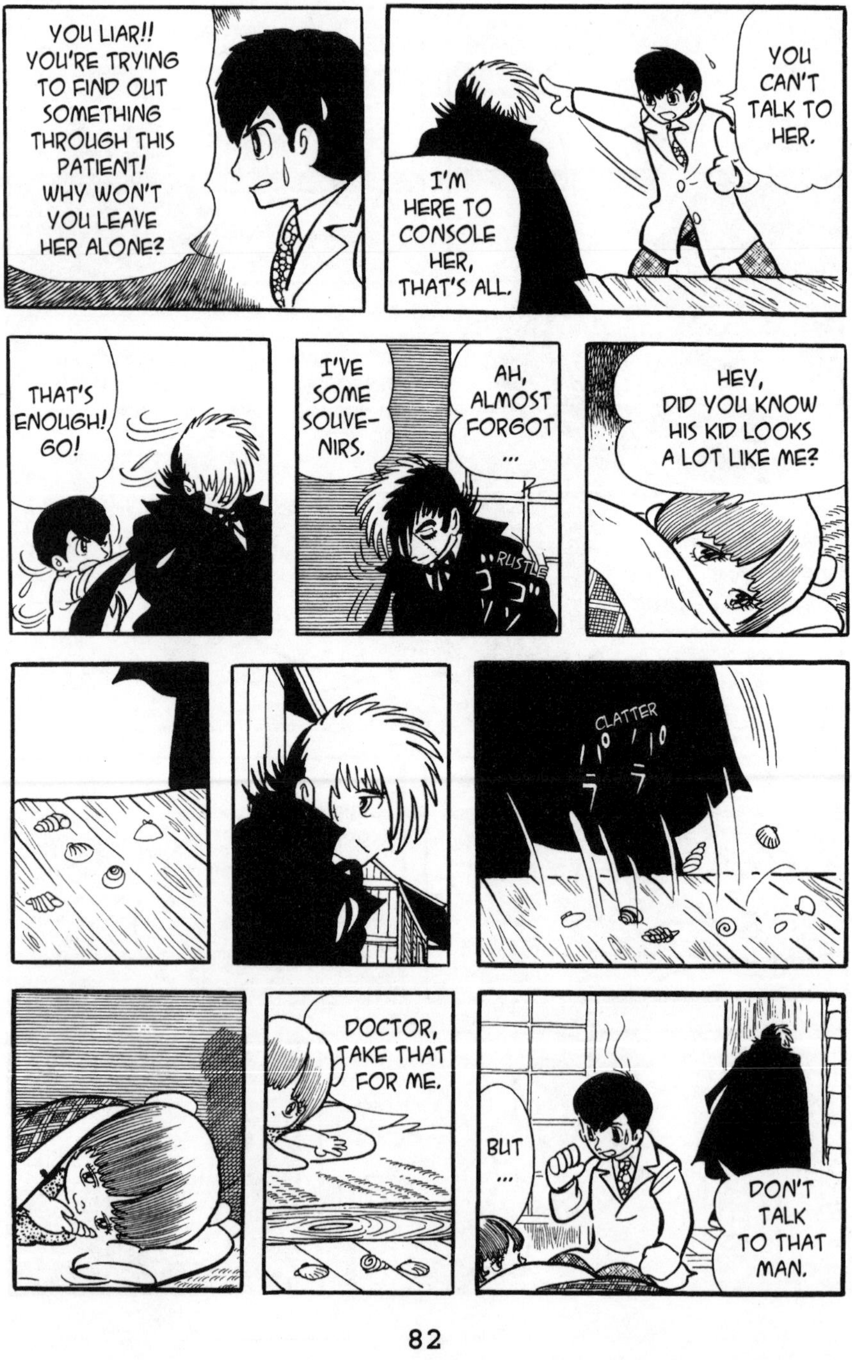
YOU CAN'T TALK TO HER.
I'M HERE TO CONSOLE HER, THAT'S ALL.
YOU LIAR!! YOU'RE TRYING TO FIND OUT SOMETHING THROUGH THIS PATIENT! WHY WON'T YOU LEAVE HER ALONE?
HEY, DID YOU KNOW HIS KID LOOKS A LOT LIKE ME?
AH, ALMOST FORGOT ...
I'VE SOME SOUVE-NIRS.
RUSTLE
THAT'S ENOUGH! GO!
CLATTER
DON'T TALK TO THAT MAN.
BUT ...
DOCTOR, TAKE THAT FOR ME.

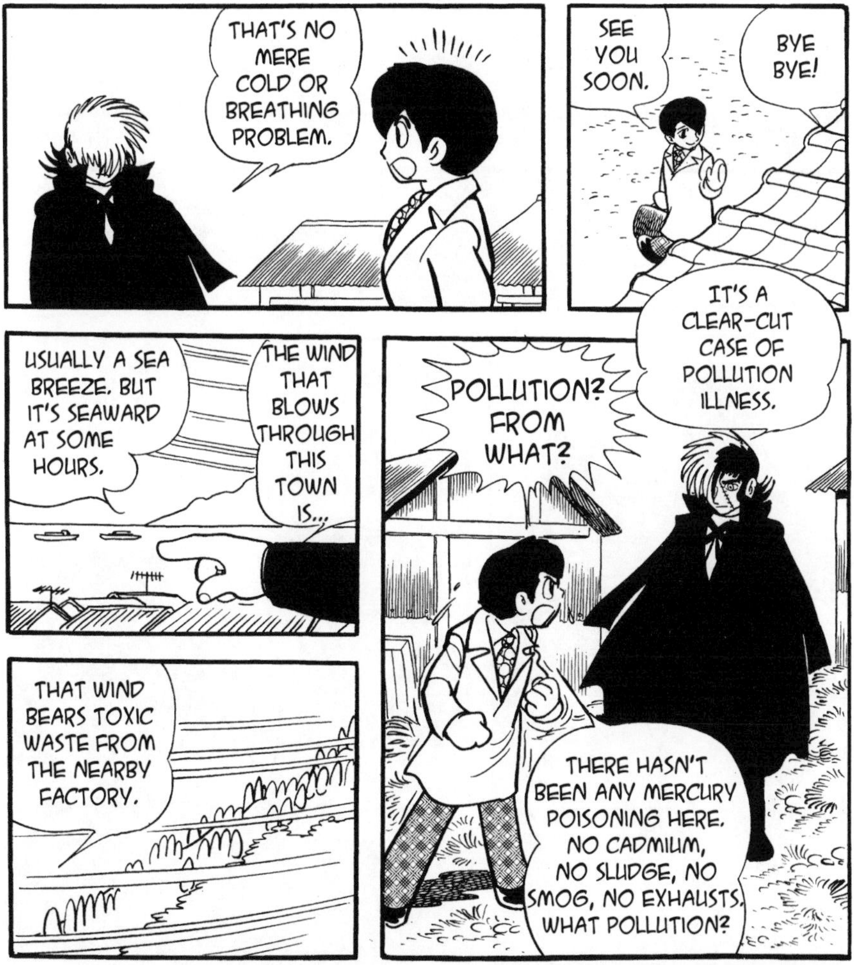
BYE BYE!
SEE YOU SOON.
THAT'S NO MERE COLD OR BREATHING PROBLEM.
IT'S A CLEAR-CUT CASE OF POLLUTION ILLNESS.
POLLUTION? FROM WHAT?
THERE HASN'T BEEN ANY MERCURY POISONING HERE. NO CADMIUM, NO SLUDGE, NO SMOG, NO EXHAUSTS. WHAT POLLUTION?
THE WIND THAT BLOWS THROUGH THIS TOWN IS...
USUALLY A SEA BREEZE. BUT IT'S SEAWARD AT SOME HOURS.
THAT WIND BEARS TOXIC WASTE FROM THE NEARBY FACTORY.
IS THAT HER LUNG X-RAY?
THAT'S PRETTY BAD...
YOU THINK THAT SWELLING'S NORMAL?

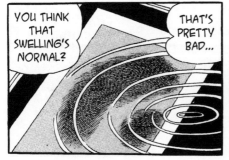

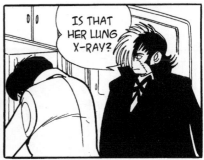

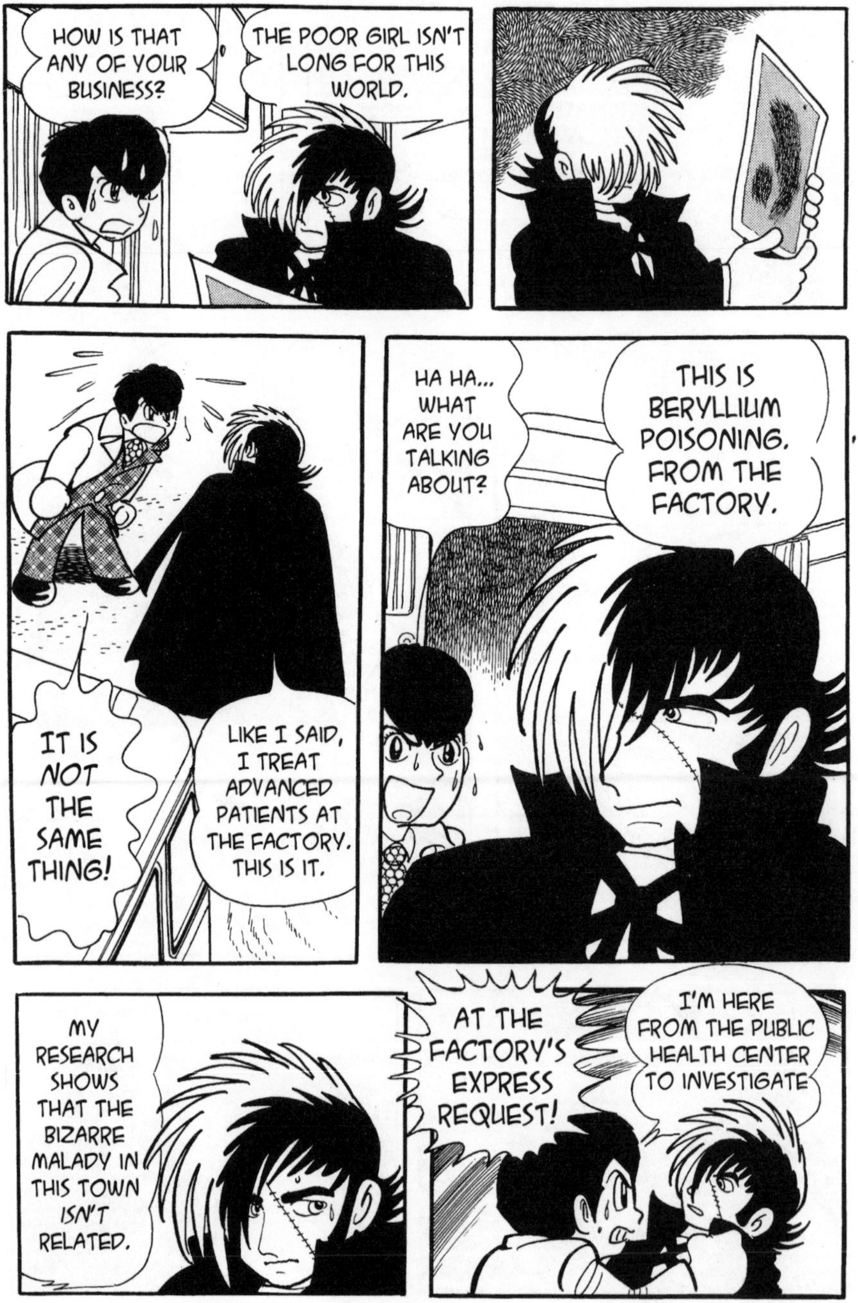
THE POOR GIRL ISN'T LONG FOR THIS WORLD.
HOW IS THAT ANY OF YOUR BUSINESS?
THIS IS BERYLLIUM POISONING. FROM THE FACTORY.
HA HA... WHAT ARE YOU TALKING ABOUT?
LIKE I SAID, I TREAT ADVANCED PATIENTS AT THE FACTORY. THIS IS IT.
IT IS NOT THE SAME THING!
I'M HERE FROM THE PUBLIC HEALTH CENTER TO INVESTIGATE
AT THE FACTORY'S EXPRESS REQUEST!
MY RESEARCH SHOWS THAT THE BIZARRE MALADY IN THIS TOWN ISN'T RELATED.

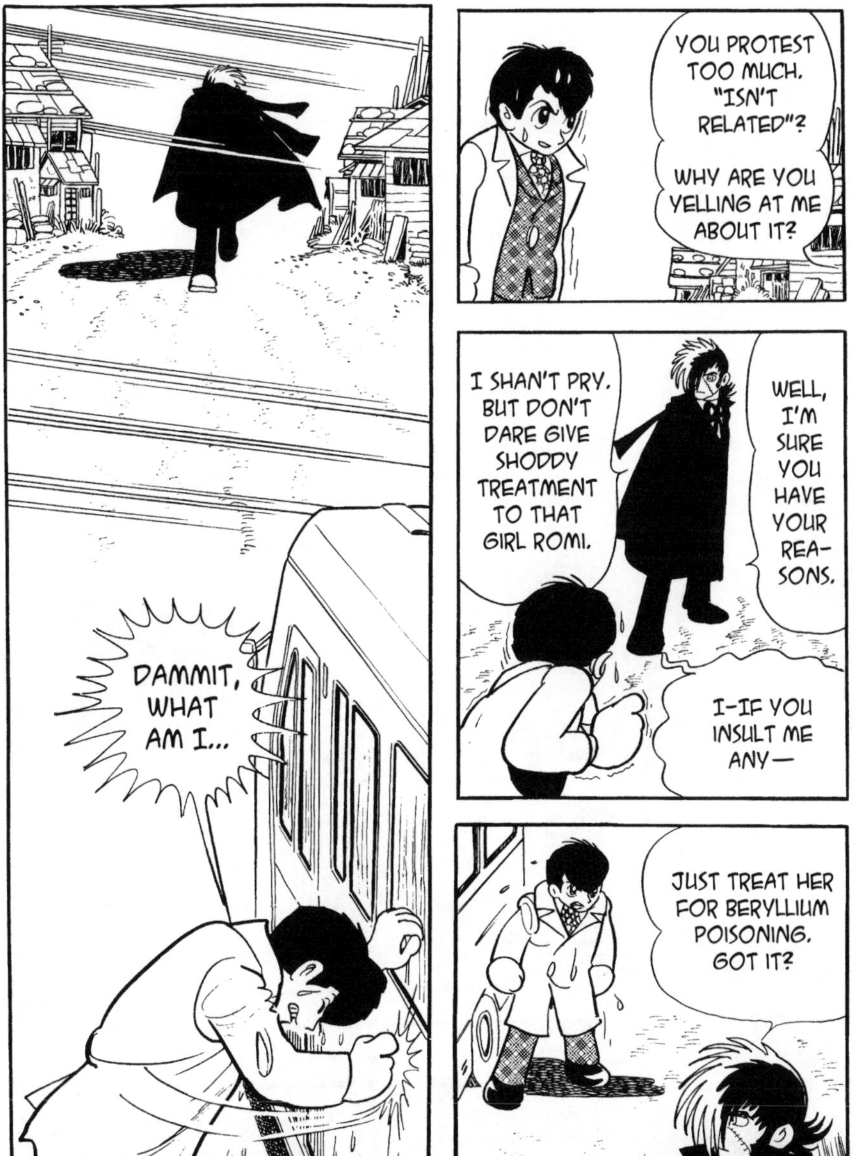
YOU PROTEST TOO MUCH. "ISN'T RELATED"?
WHY ARE YOU YELLING AT ME ABOUT IT?
WELL, I'M SURE YOU HAVE YOUR REA- SONS.
I SHAN'T PRY. BUT DON'T DARE GIVE SHODDY TREATMENT TO THAT GIRL ROMI.
I-IF YOU INSULT ME ANY—
JUST TREAT HER FOR BERYLLIUM POISONING. GOT IT?
DAMMIT, WHAT AM I...

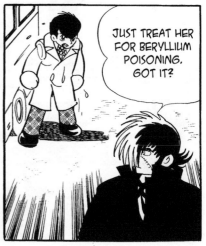

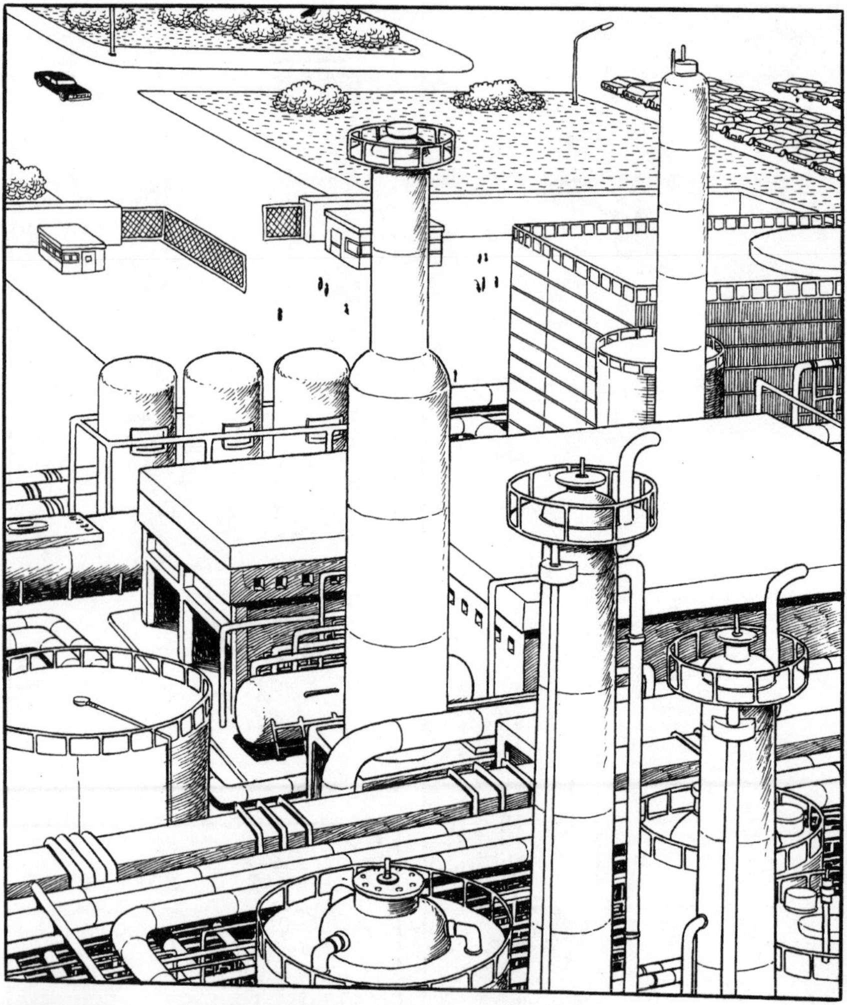

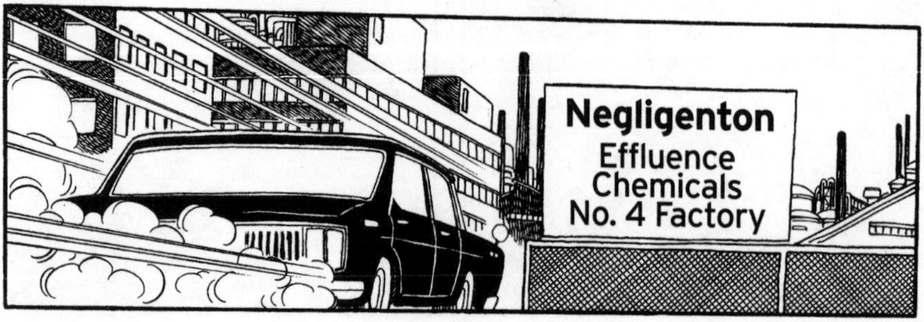
Negligenton
Effluence
Chemicals
No. 4 Factory

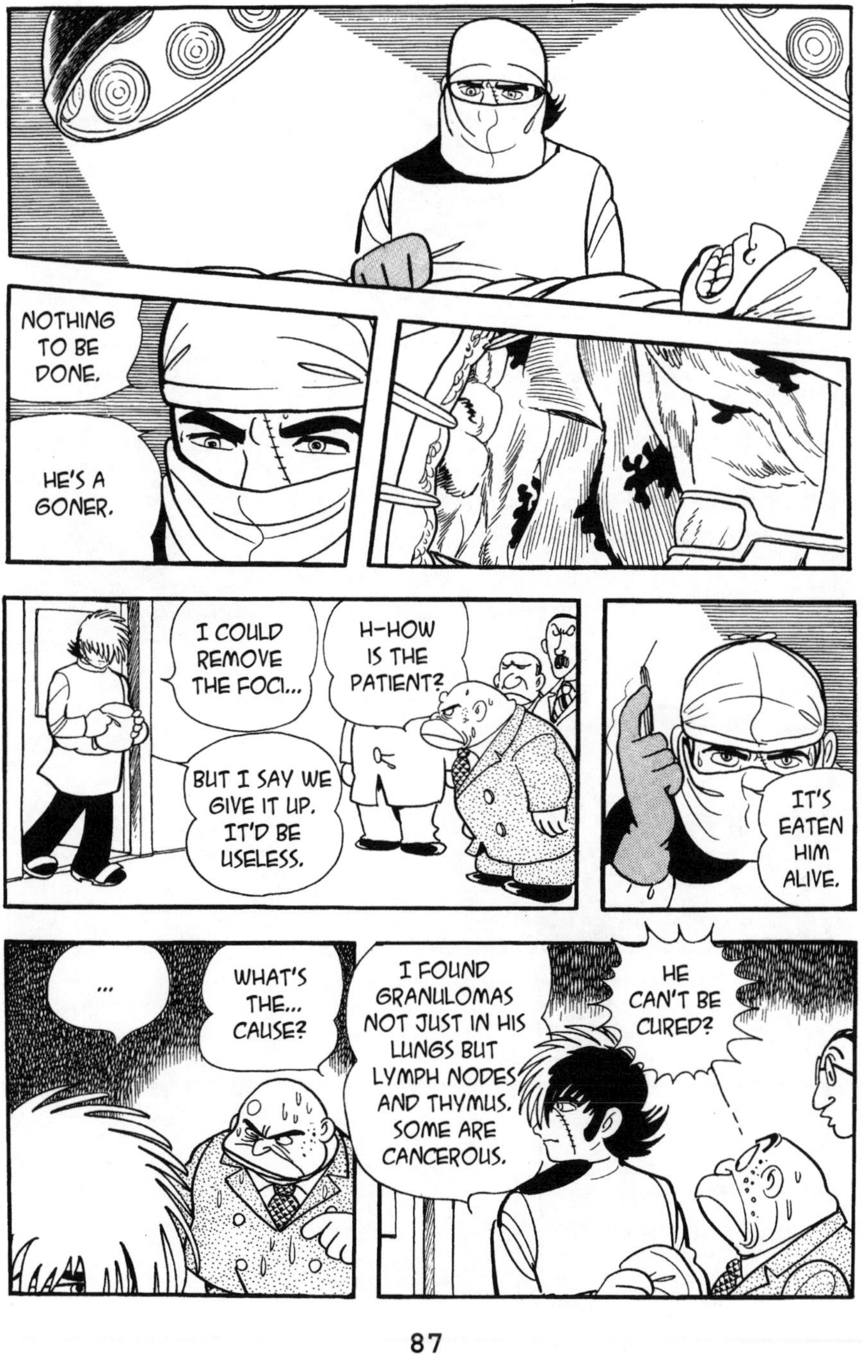
NOTHING TO BE DONE.
HE'S A GONER.
IT'S EATEN HIM ALIVE.
H-HOW IS THE PATIENT?
I COULD REMOVE THE FOCI...
BUT I SAY WE GIVE IT UP. IT'D BE USELESS.
HE CAN'T BE CURED?
I FOUND GRANULOMAS NOT JUST IN HIS LUNGS BUT LYMPH NODES AND THYMUS. SOME ARE CANCEROUS.
WHAT'S THE... CAUSE?
...

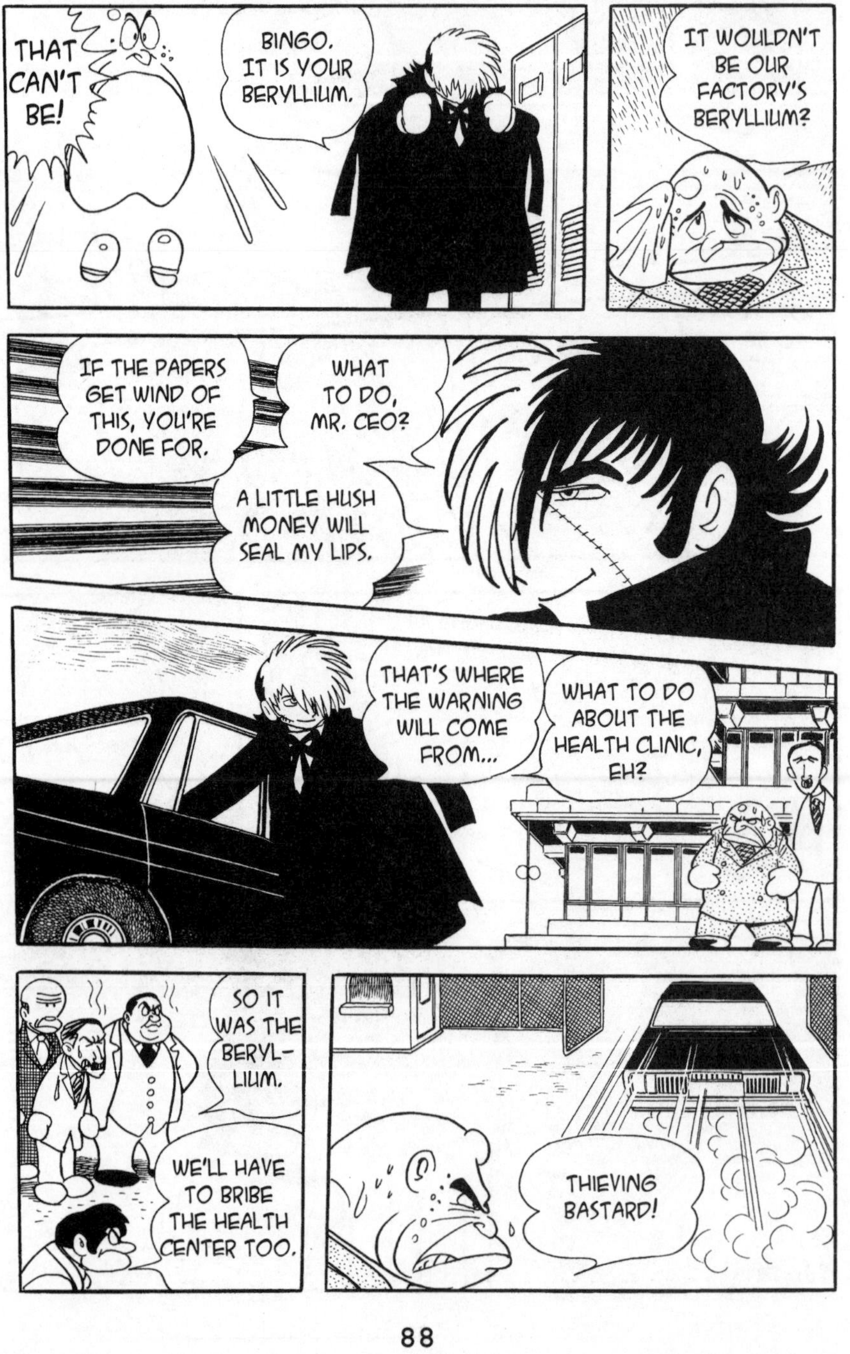
IT WOULDN'T BE OUR FACTORY'S BERYLLIUM?
BINGO. IT IS YOUR BERYLLIUM.
THAT CAN'T BE!
WHAT TO DO, MR. CEO?
IF THE PAPERS GET WIND OF THIS, YOU'RE DONE FOR.
A LITTLE HUSH MONEY WILL SEAL MY LIPS.
WHAT TO DO ABOUT THE HEALTH CLINIC, EH?
THAT'S WHERE THE WARNING WILL COME FROM...
THIEVING BASTARD!
SO IT WAS THE BERYL-LIUM.
WE'LL HAVE TO BRIBE THE HEALTH CENTER TOO.

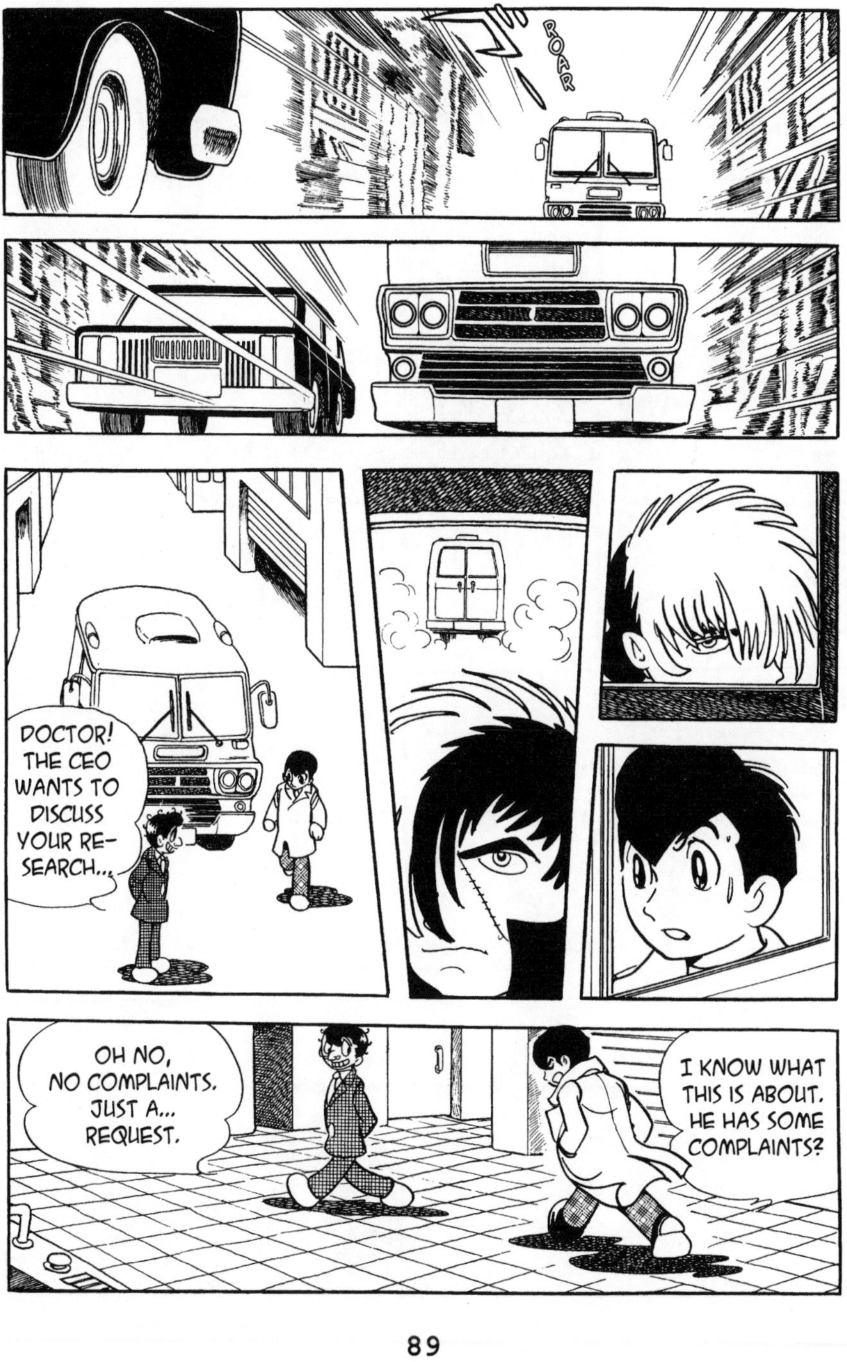
ROAR
DOCTOR! THE CEO WANTS TO DISCUSS YOUR RE-SEARCH...
I KNOW WHAT THIS IS ABOUT. HE HAS SOME COMPLAINTS?
OH NO, NO COMPLAINTS. JUST A... REQUEST.

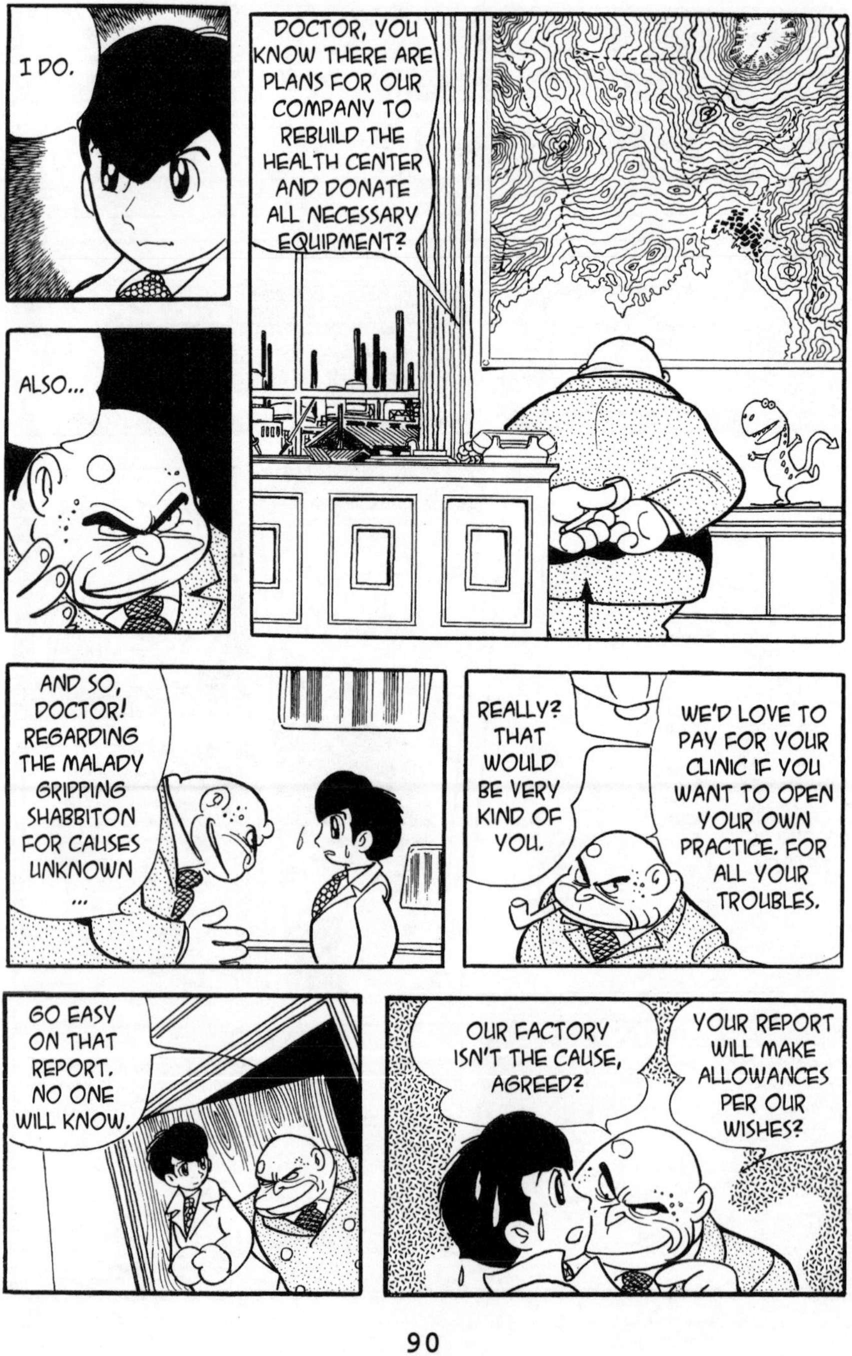
DOCTOR, YOU KNOW THERE ARE PLANS FOR OUR COMPANY TO REBUILD THE HEALTH CENTER AND DONATE ALL NECESSARY EQUIPMENT?
I DO.
ALSO...
WE'D LOVE TO PAY FOR YOUR CLINIC IF YOU WANT TO OPEN YOUR OWN PRACTICE. FOR ALL YOUR TROUBLES.
REALLY? THAT WOULD BE VERY KIND OF YOU.
AND SO, DOCTOR! REGARDING THE MALADY GRIPPING SHABBITON FOR CAUSES UNKNOWN ...
YOUR REPORT WILL MAKE ALLOWANCES PER OUR WISHES?
OUR FACTORY ISN'T THE CAUSE, AGREED?
GO EASY ON THAT REPORT. NO ONE WILL KNOW.

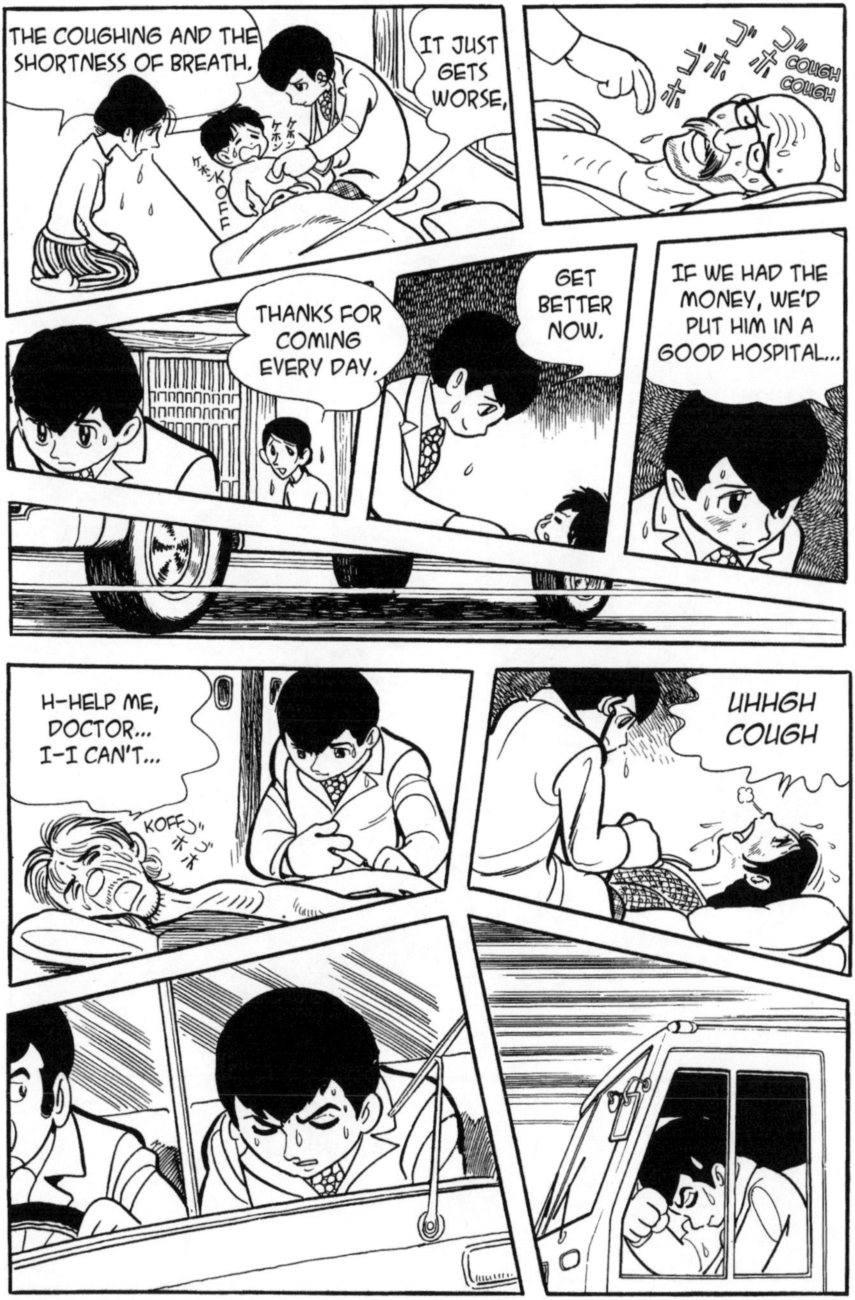
ゴホ ゴホ ゴホ
COUGH COUGH
THE COUGHING AND THE SHORTNESS OF BREATH.
IT JUST GETS WORSE,
ケホン ケホン ケホン
KOFF
IF WE HAD THE MONEY, WE'D PUT HIM IN A GOOD HOSPITAL...
GET BETTER NOW.
THANKS FOR COMING EVERY DAY.
UHHGH COUGH
H-HELP ME, DOCTOR... I-I CAN'T...
KOFF
ゴホゴホ

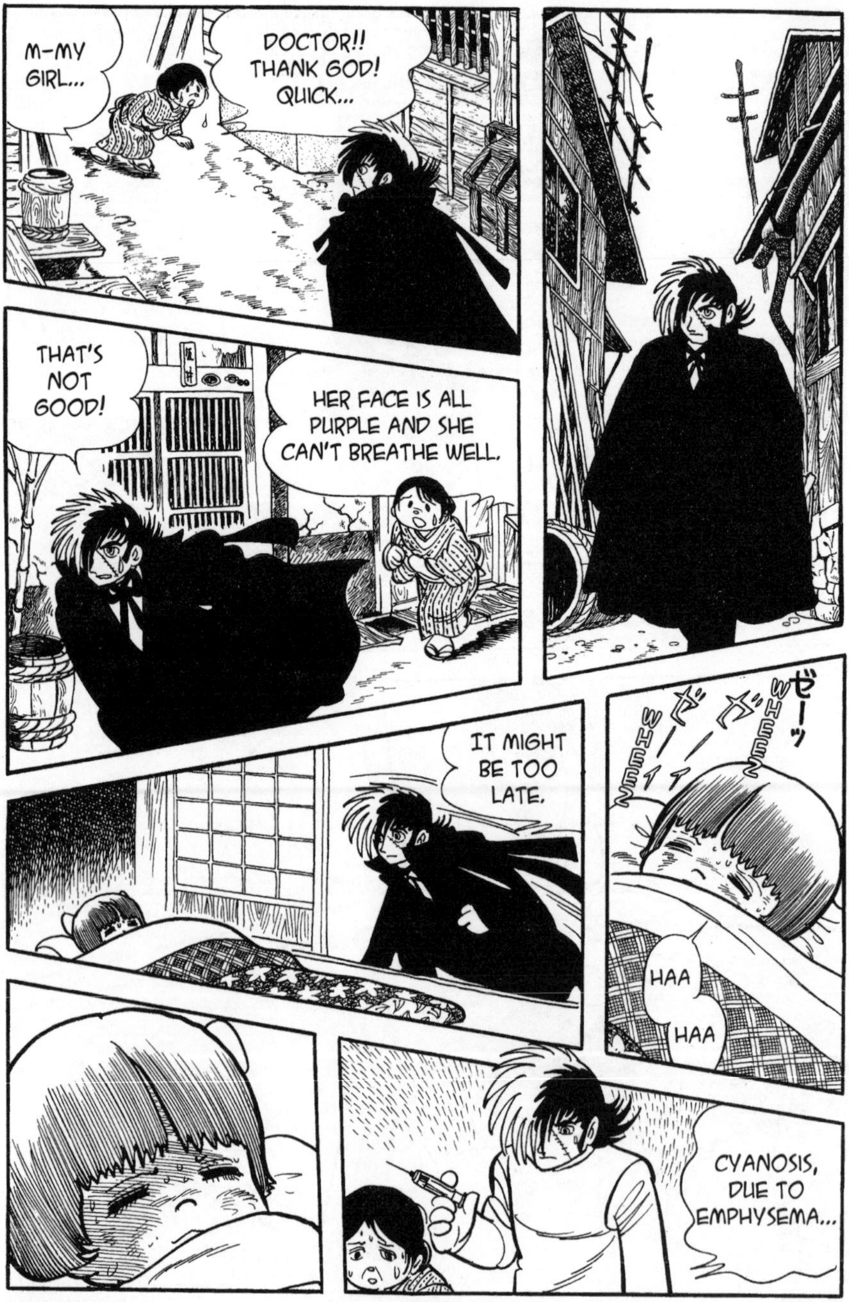
DOCTOR!! THANK GOD! QUICK...
M-MY GIRL...
HER FACE IS ALL PURPLE AND SHE CAN'T BREATHE WELL.
THAT'S NOT GOOD!
ゼーッ
WHEEZ
ゼーィ
WHEEZ
HAA
HAA
IT MIGHT BE TOO LATE.
CYANOSIS, DUE TO EMPHYSEMA...

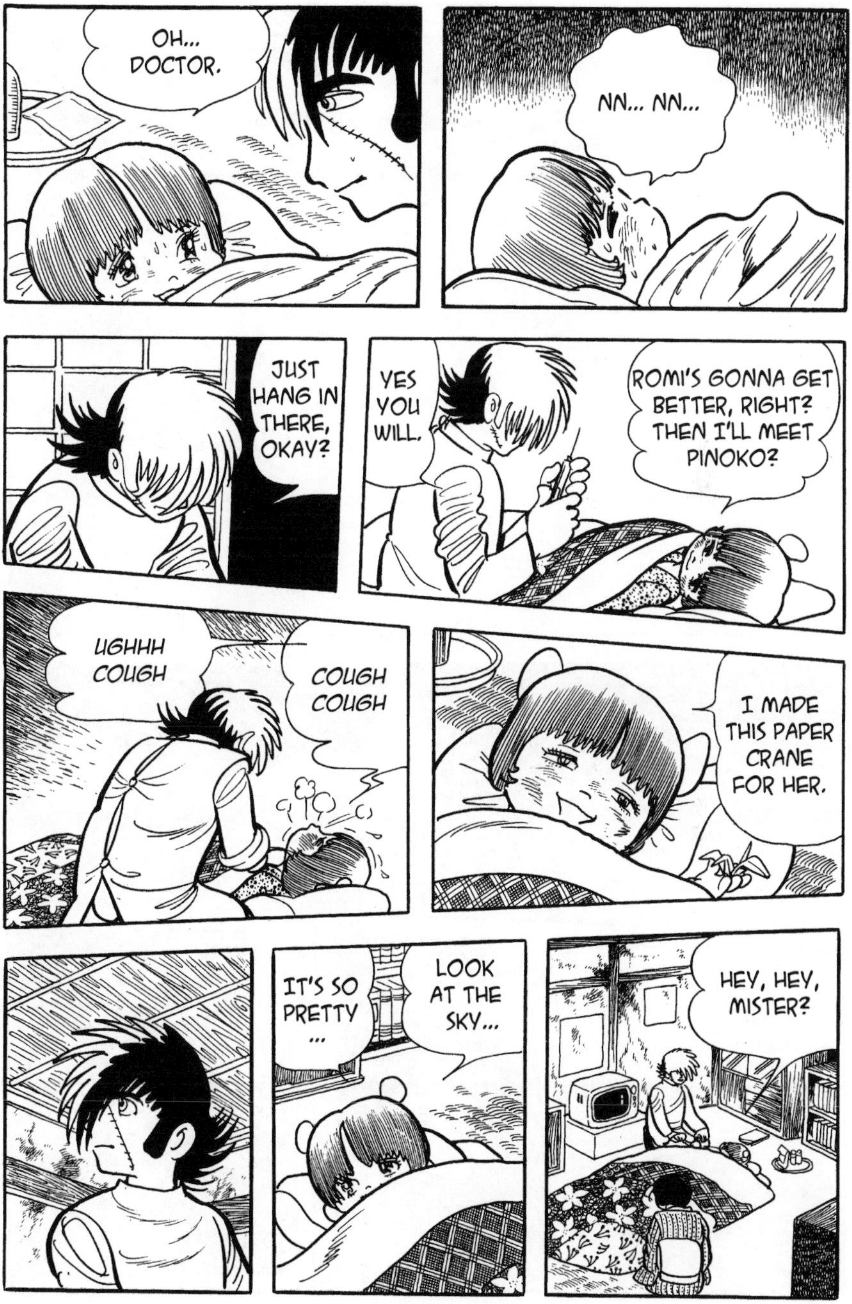
NN... NN...
OH... DOCTOR.
ROMI'S GONNA GET BETTER, RIGHT? THEN I'LL MEET PINOKO?
YES YOU WILL.
JUST HANG IN THERE, OKAY?
I MADE THIS PAPER CRANE FOR HER.
COUGH COUGH
UGHHH COUGH
HEY, HEY, MISTER?
LOOK AT THE SKY...
IT'S SO PRETTY ...

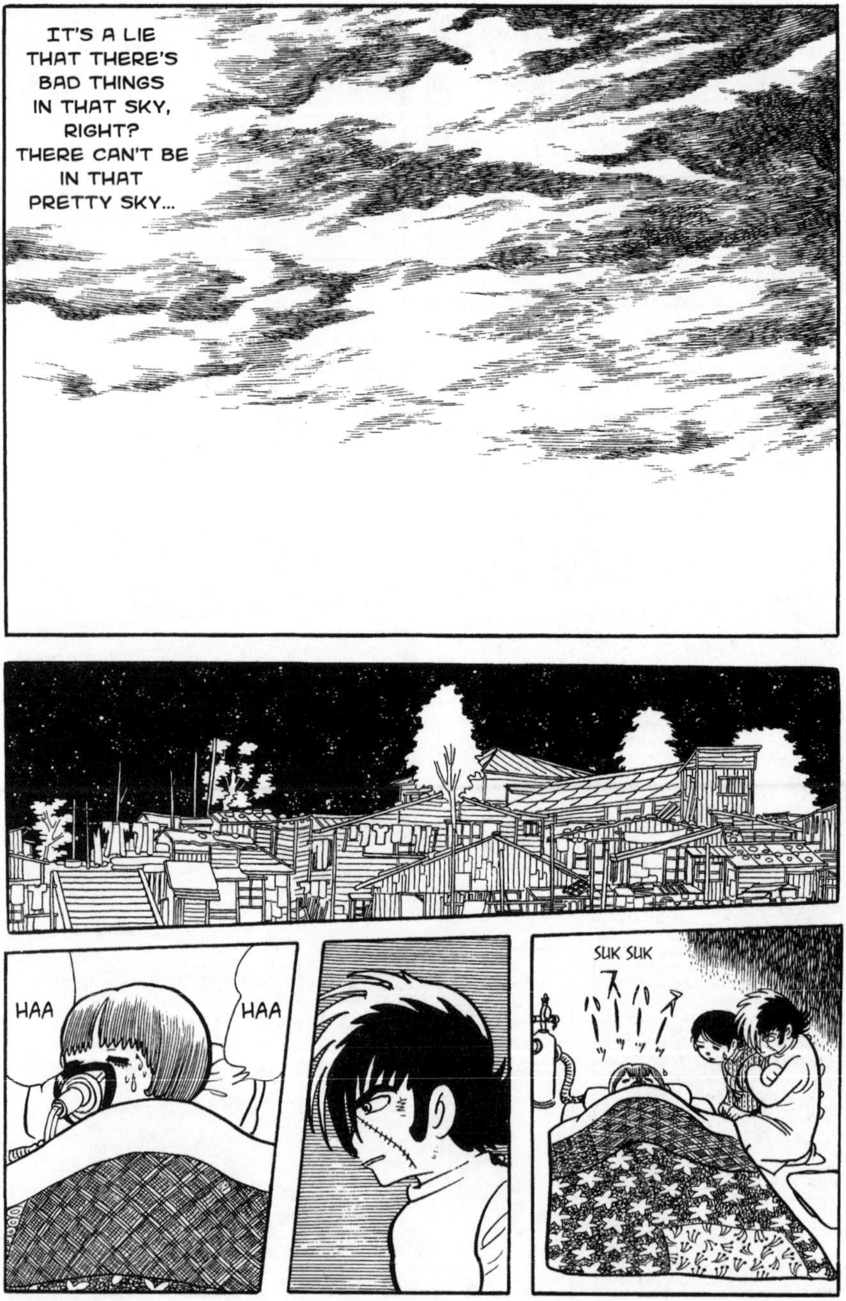
IT'S A LIE THAT THERE'S BAD THINGS IN THAT SKY, RIGHT?
THERE CAN'T BE IN THAT PRETTY SKY...
SUK SUK
HAA
HAA

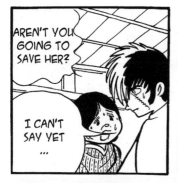

TIC TOC TOC TIC
SUK
AREN'T YOU GOING TO SAVE HER?
I CAN'T SAY YET ...
GAW GAW GAW GAW GAW GAW
MOMMY
SHE'S OPENED HER EYES, DOCTOR!!
I LIKE YOU... MISTER DOCTOR.
ROMI WILL BE A DOCTOR TOO.
THEN WE CAN ALWAYS BE FRIENDS ...

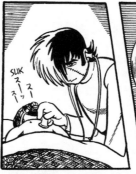

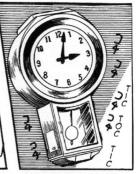

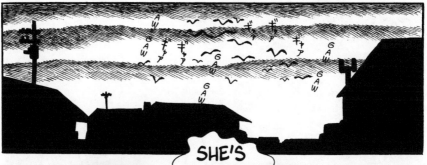

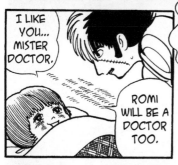

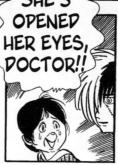

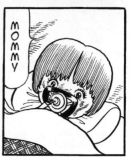

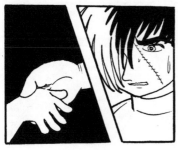

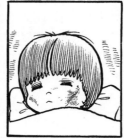

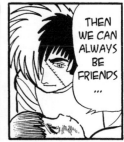

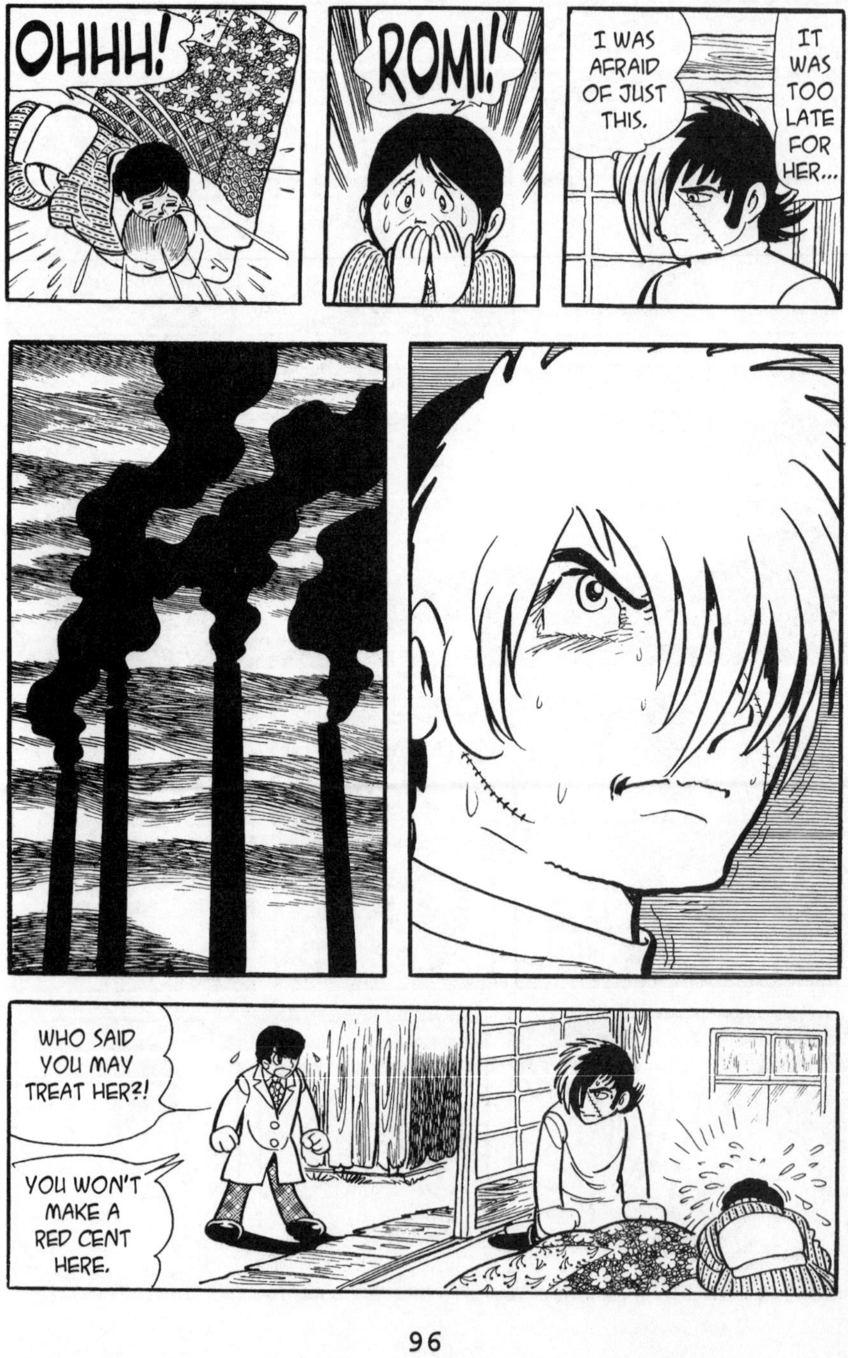

IT WAS TOO LATE FOR HER...
I WAS AFRAID OF JUST THIS.
ROMI!
OHHH!
WHO SAID YOU MAY TREAT HER?!
YOU WON'T MAKE A RED CENT HERE.

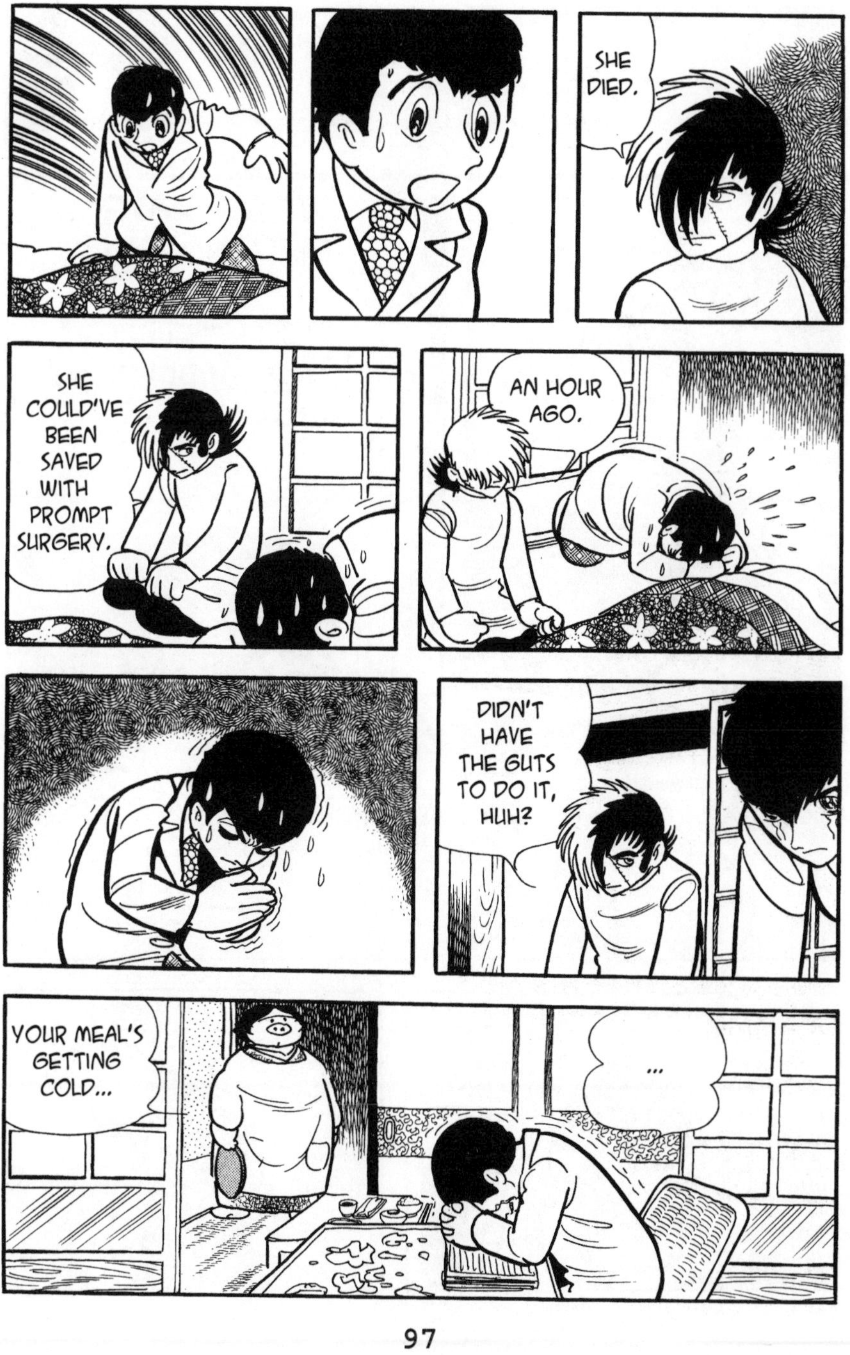
SHE DIED.
AN HOUR AGO.
SHE COULD'VE BEEN SAVED WITH PROMPT SURGERY.
DIDN'T HAVE THE GUTS TO DO IT, HUH?
...
YOUR MEAL'S GETTING COLD...

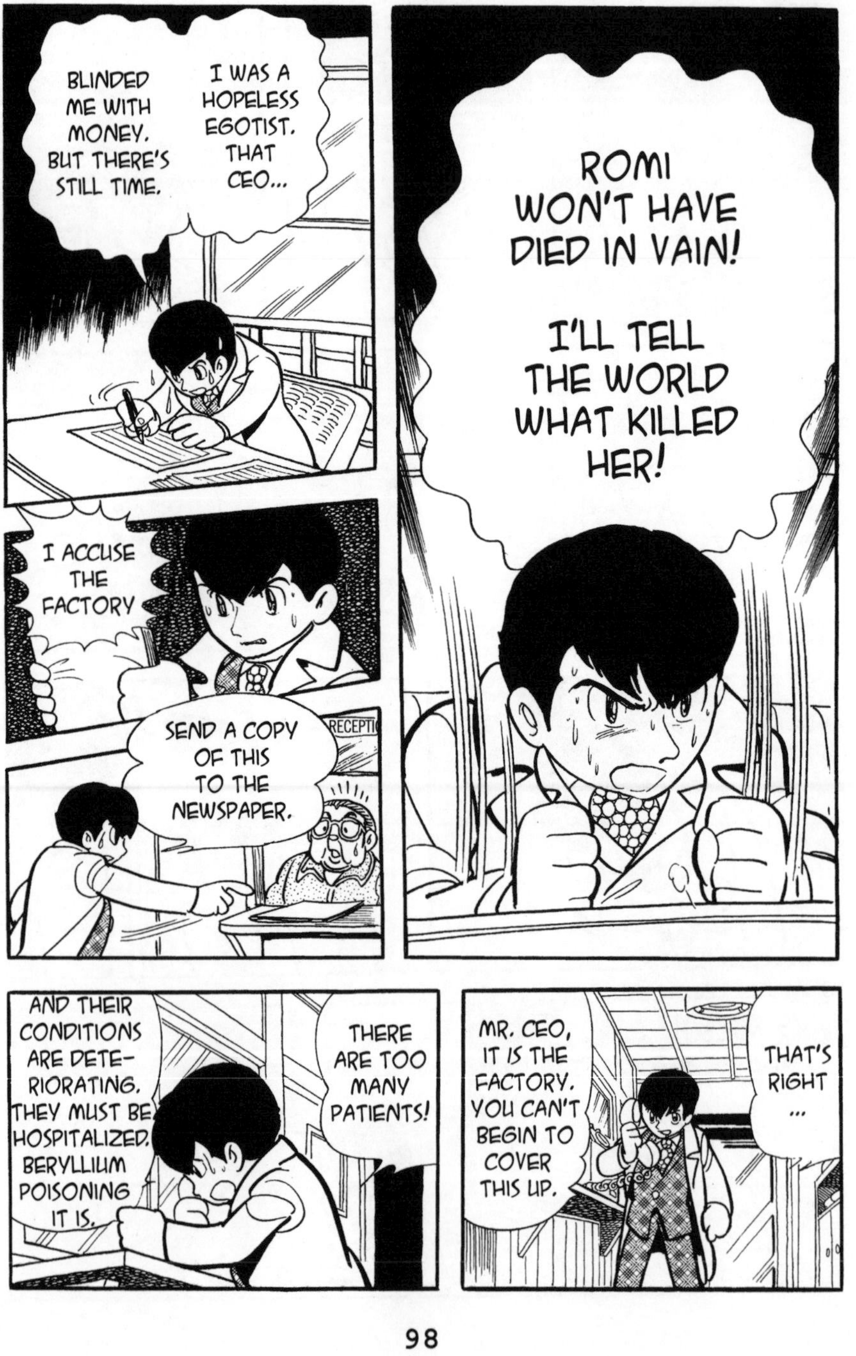
ROMI WON'T HAVE DIED IN VAIN!
I'LL TELL THE WORLD WHAT KILLED HER!
I WAS A HOPELESS EGOTIST. THAT CEO...
BLINDED ME WITH MONEY. BUT THERE'S STILL TIME.
I ACCUSE THE FACTORY
RECEPTI
SEND A COPY OF THIS TO THE NEWSPAPER.
THAT'S RIGHT ...
MR. CEO, IT IS THE FACTORY. YOU CAN'T BEGIN TO COVER THIS UP.
THERE ARE TOO MANY PATIENTS!
AND THEIR CONDITIONS ARE DETE-RIORATING. THEY MUST BE HOSPITALIZED. BERYLLIUM POISONING IT IS.

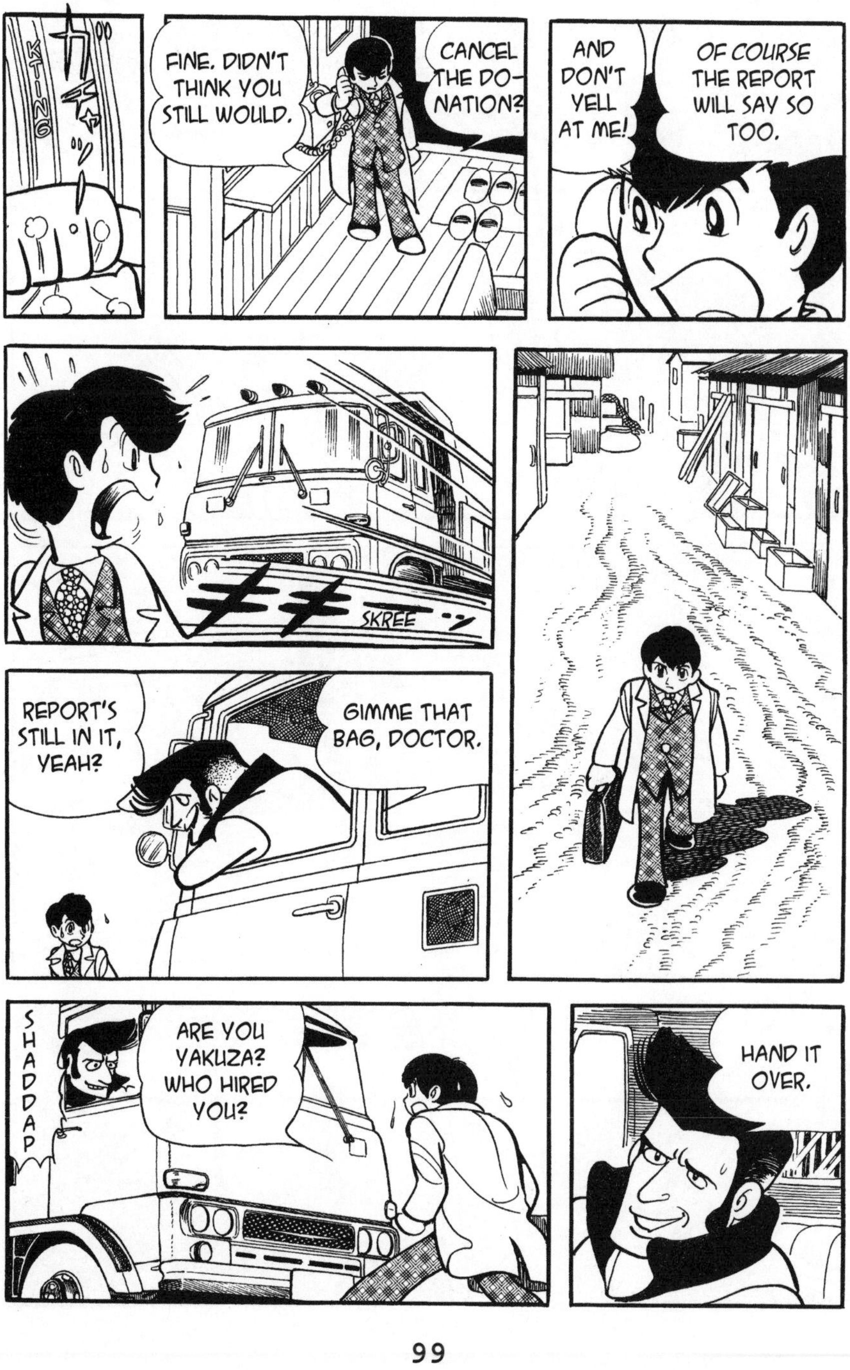
OF COURSE THE REPORT WILL SAY SO TOO.
AND DON'T YELL AT ME!
CANCEL THE DO-NATION?
FINE. DIDN'T THINK YOU STILL WOULD.
KTING
SKREE
GIMME THAT BAG, DOCTOR.
REPORT'S STILL IN IT, YEAH?
HAND IT OVER.
ARE YOU YAKUZA? WHO HIRED YOU?
SHADDAP

BROAMM
BRMM
BROAMM
VRMM
BUMP

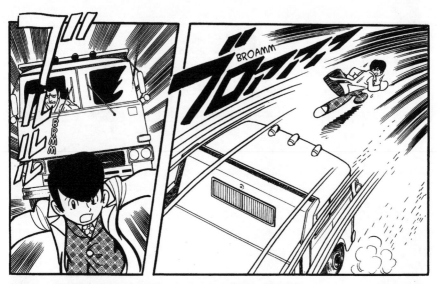

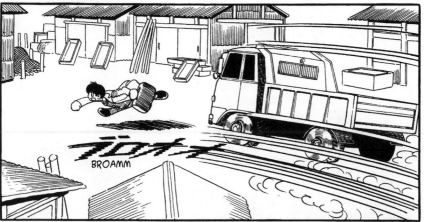

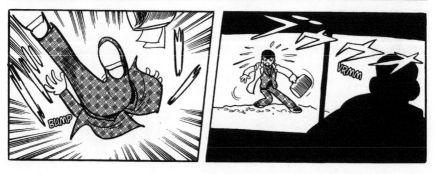

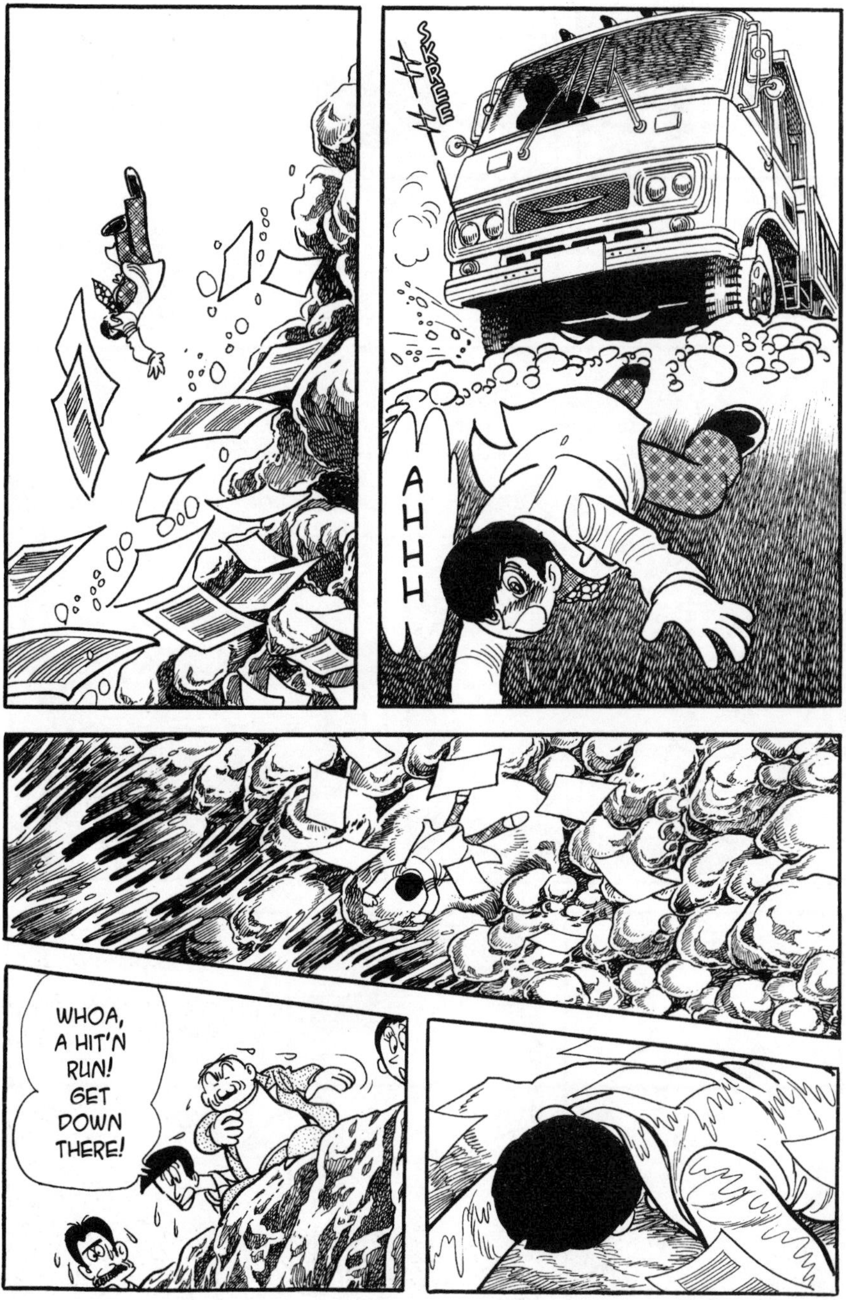
SKREE
AHHH
WHOA, A HIT'N RUN! GET DOWN THERE!

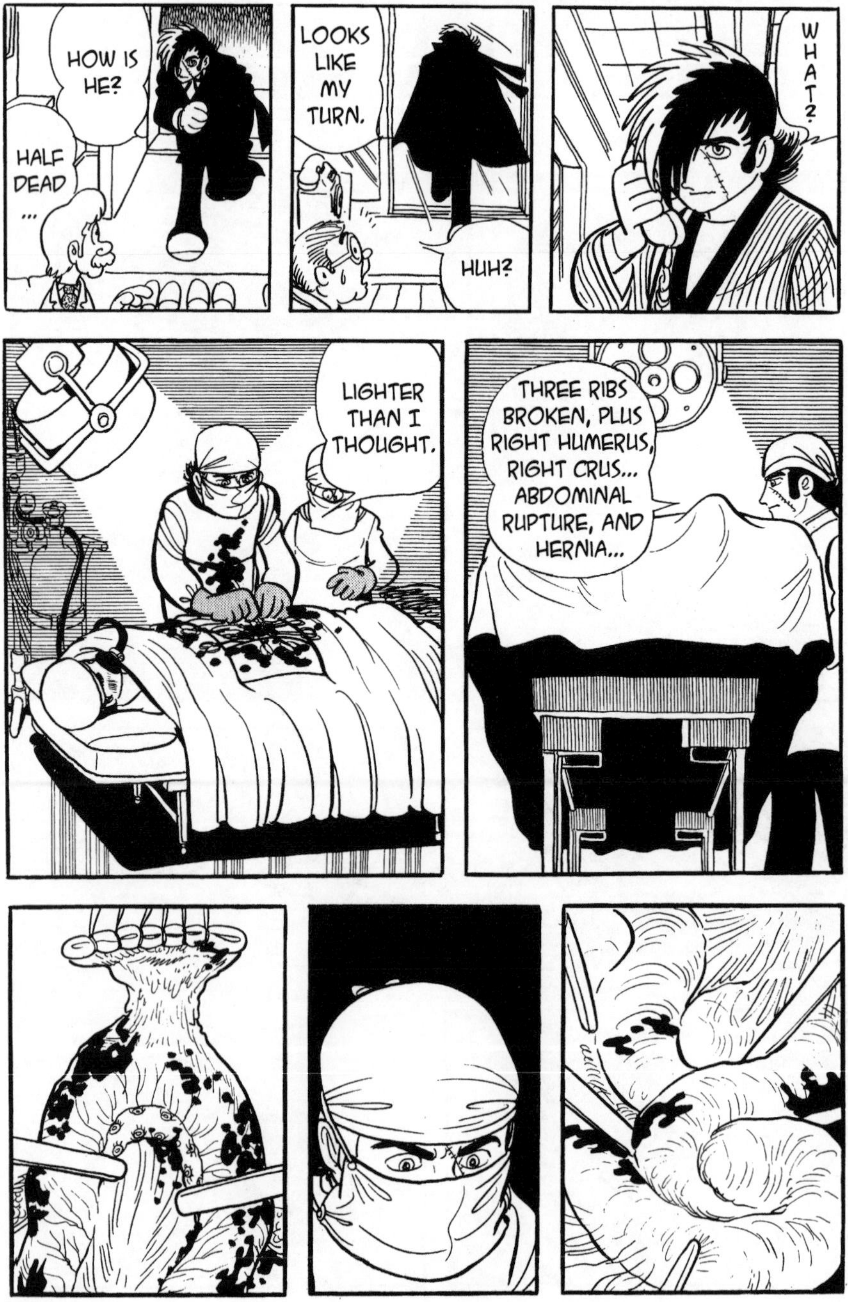
WHAT?
LOOKS LIKE MY TURN.
HUH?
HOW IS HE?
HALF DEAD ...
THREE RIBS BROKEN, PLUS RIGHT HUMERUS, RIGHT CRUS... ABDOMINAL RUPTURE, AND HERNIA...
LIGHTER THAN I THOUGHT.

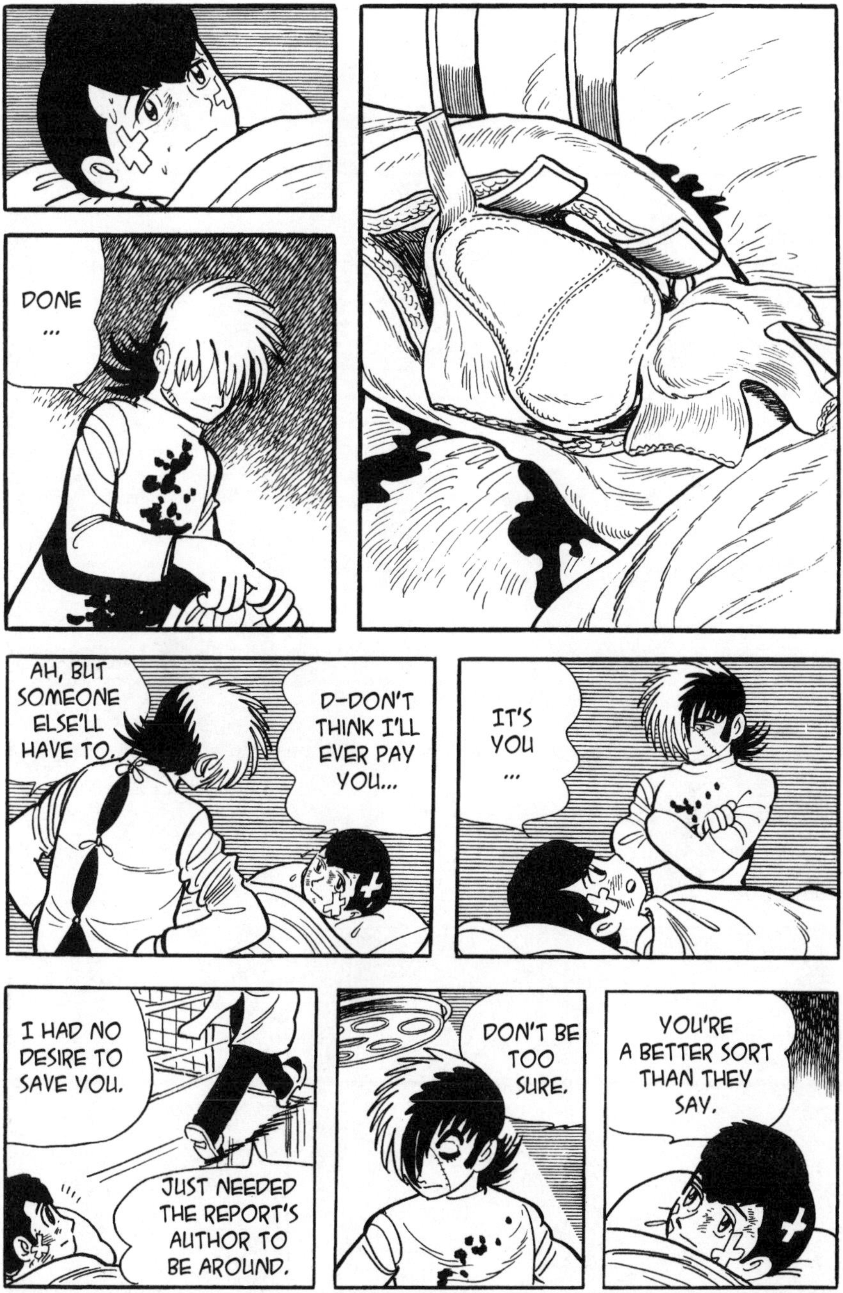
DONE ...
IT'S YOU ...
D-DON'T THINK I'LL EVER PAY YOU...
AH, BUT SOMEONE ELSE'LL HAVE TO.
YOU'RE A BETTER SORT THAN THEY SAY.
DON'T BE TOO SURE.
I HAD NO DESIRE TO SAVE YOU.
JUST NEEDED THE REPORT'S AUTHOR TO BE AROUND.

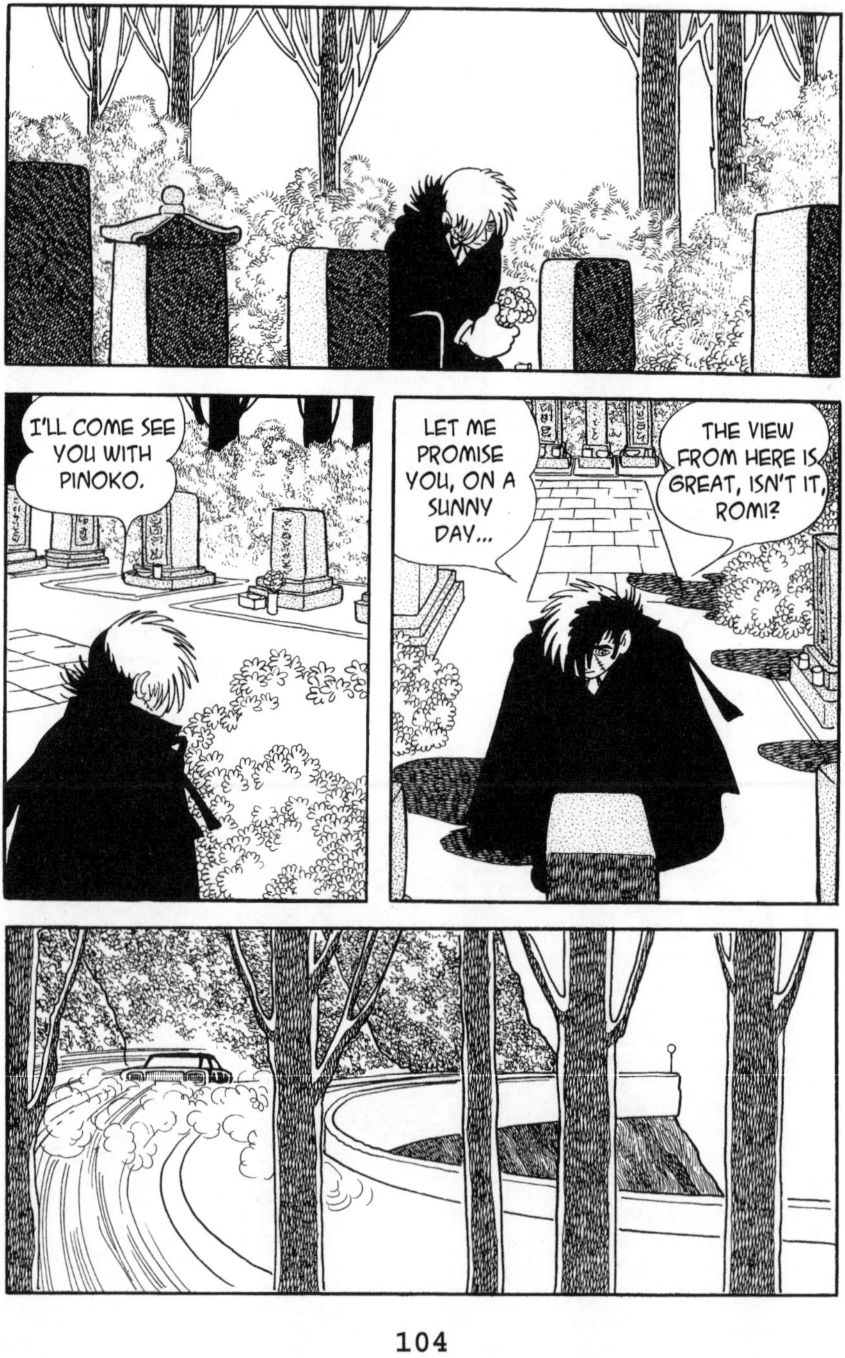
THE VIEW FROM HERE IS GREAT, ISN'T IT, ROMI?
LET ME PROMISE YOU, ON A SUNNY DAY...
I'LL COME SEE YOU WITH PINOKO.

UNEXPLODED BOMB

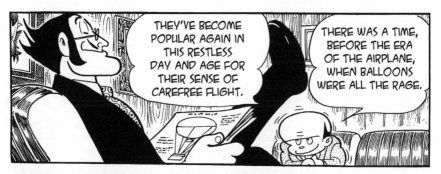

THERE WAS A TIME, BEFORE THE ERA OF THE AIRPLANE, WHEN BALLOONS WERE ALL THE RAGE.
THEY'VE BECOME POPULAR AGAIN IN THIS RESTLESS DAY AND AGE FOR THEIR SENSE OF CAREFREE FLIGHT.
MR. PRESIDENT, I HAVE A SPECIAL INVITATION TICKET HERE FOR YOU SO I SURE DO HOPE YOU TRY IT.
BAL-LOON...
IS THIS IT? WON'T THE BOTTOM FALL OFF OR THE GAS LEAK?
HELLO. YOU'RE TRYING THIS TOO?
SPECIAL INVITEE
FREE
WILL OUR INVITED GUESTS BOARD PLEASE?
SPECIAL INVITEE

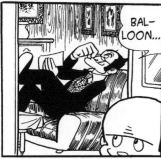

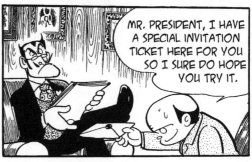

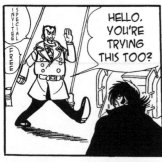

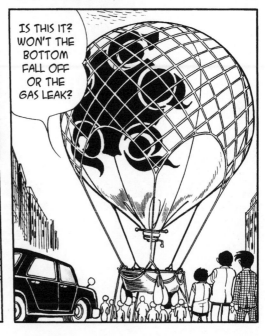

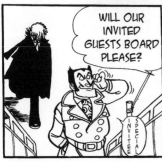

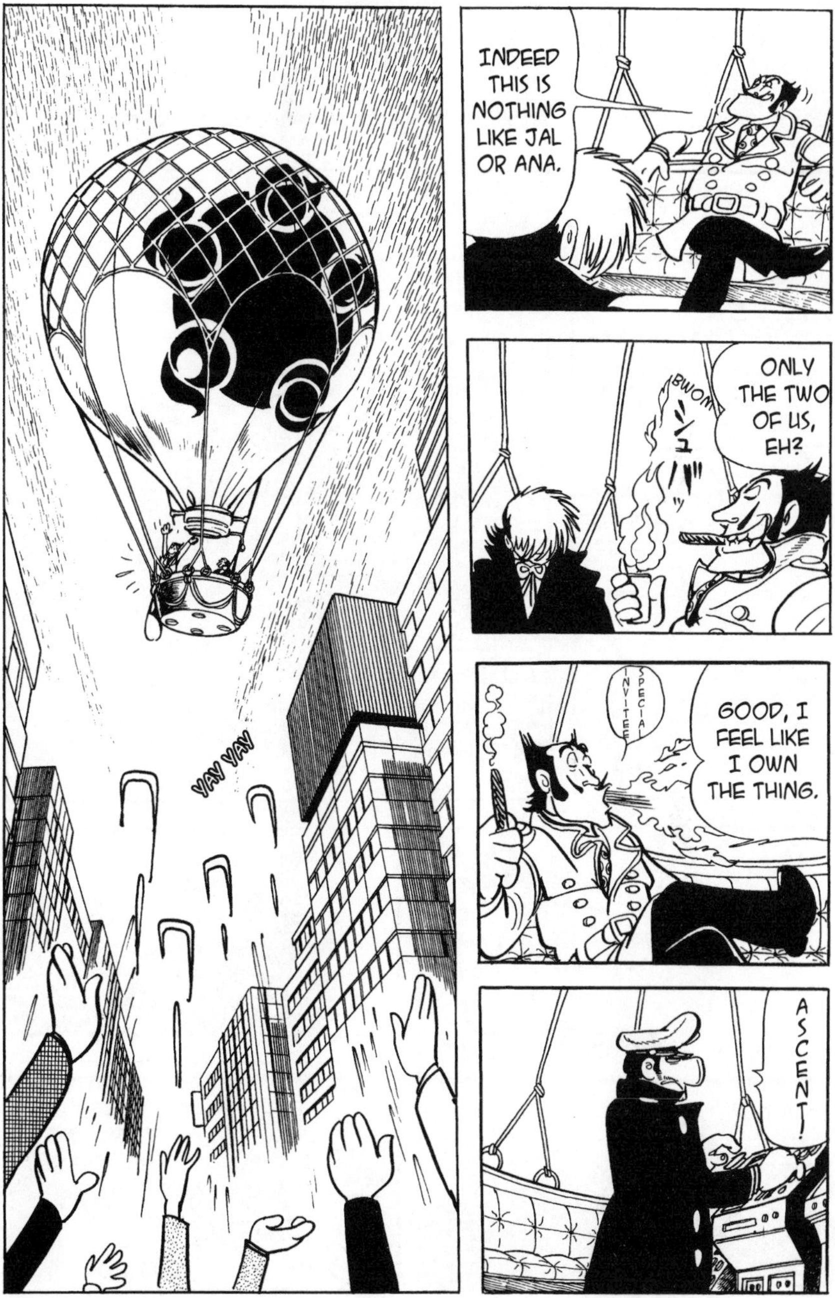
INDEED THIS IS NOTHING LIKE JAL OR ANA.
ONLY THE TWO OF US, EH?
BWOM
SPECIAL INVITEE
GOOD, I FEEL LIKE I OWN THE THING.
ASCENT!
YAY YAY

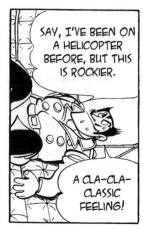

SAY, I'VE BEEN ON A HELICOPTER BEFORE, BUT THIS IS ROCKIER.
A CLA-CLA-CLASSIC FEELING!
ARE WE BEING BLOWN OFF COURSE?
NOT TO WORRY.
NOT TO WORRY?! BUT WHERE ARE WE DRIFTING TO ANYWAY?
HEY, THIS DOESN'T FEEL RIGHT ...
OUT TO SEA?
WE'RE GOING SOUTH, HUH?

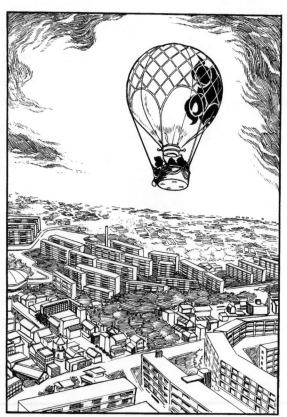

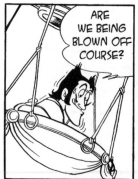

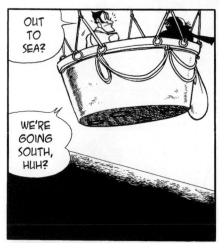

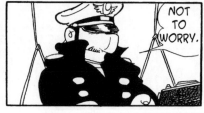

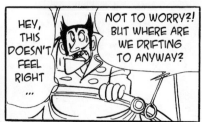

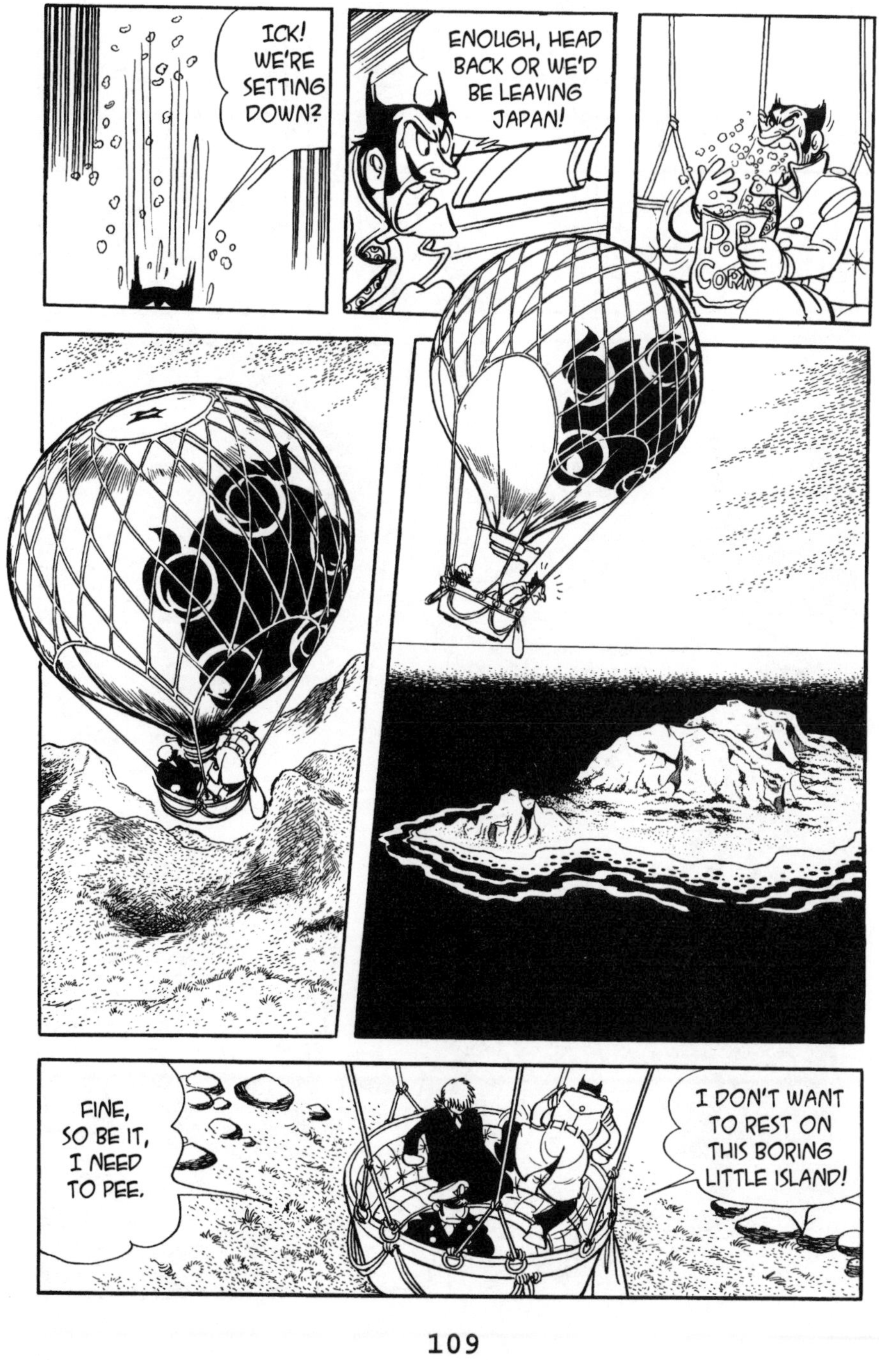
ENOUGH, HEAD BACK OR WE'D BE LEAVING JAPAN!
ICK! WE'RE SETTING DOWN?
I DON'T WANT TO REST ON THIS BORING LITTLE ISLAND!
FINE, SO BE IT, I NEED TO PEE.

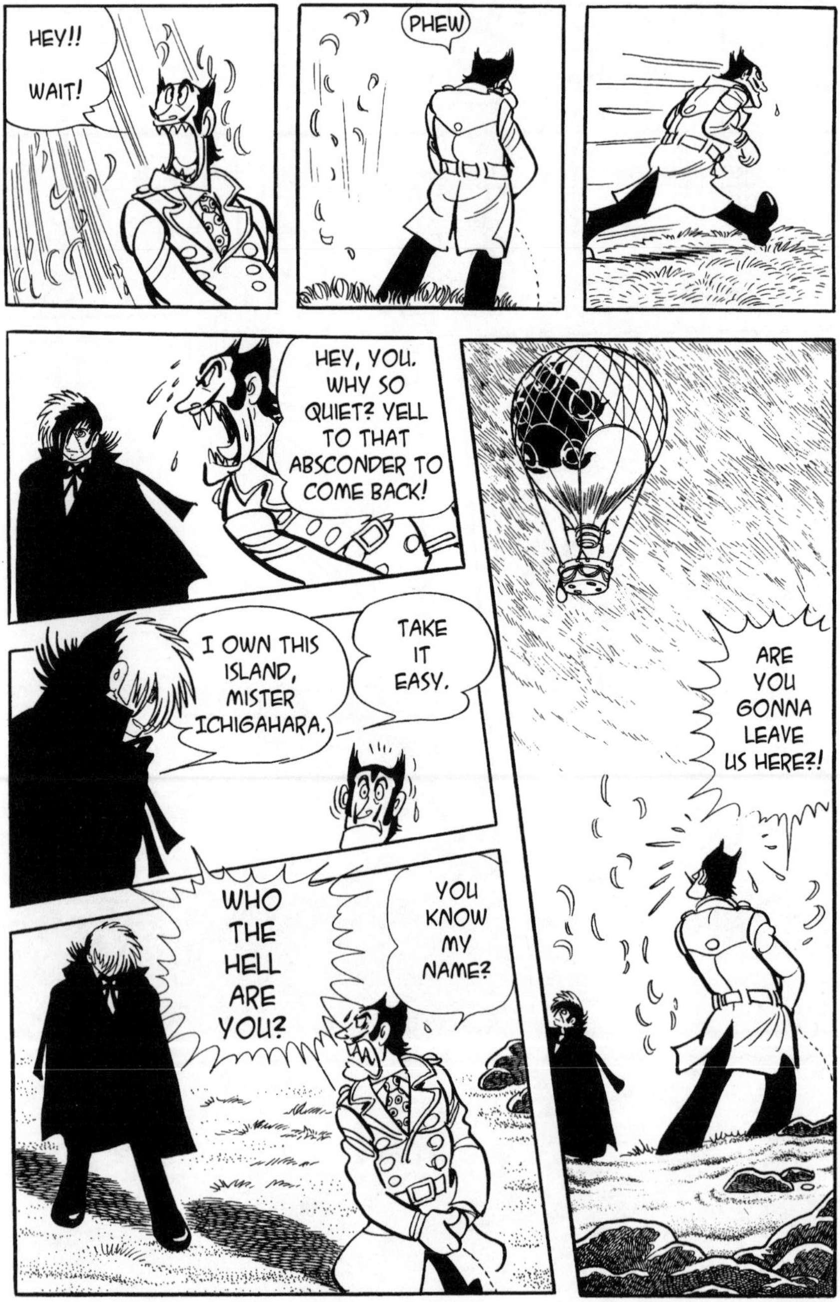
PHEW
HEY!! WAIT!
ARE YOU GONNA LEAVE US HERE?!
HEY, YOU. WHY SO QUIET? YELL TO THAT ABSCONDER TO COME BACK!
TAKE IT EASY.
I OWN THIS ISLAND, MISTER ICHIGAHARA.
YOU KNOW MY NAME?
WHO THE HELL ARE YOU?

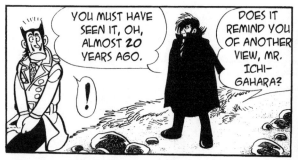

AS YOU SEE, THIS ISLAND HAS...
NOTHING BUT SAND AND SOME GRASS.
DOES IT REMIND YOU OF ANOTHER VIEW, MR. ICHI-GAHARA?
YOU MUST HAVE SEEN IT, OH, ALMOST 20 YEARS AGO.
!
WHO ARE YOU?
WE'RE AT THE EXACT CENTER OF THE ISLAND.
SOMEWHERE ALONG ITS SHORE IS A BOAT. GET TO IT TO ESCAPE WHOLE.
BUT THAT WOULD BE NO GAME. 555 MINES HAVE BEEN LAID ON THIS TINY ISLAND.
DON'T TRY TO SCARE ME.
YOU'RE ONE BIG LIAR!
WHISH

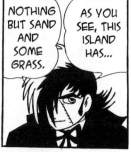

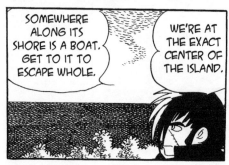

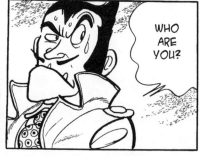

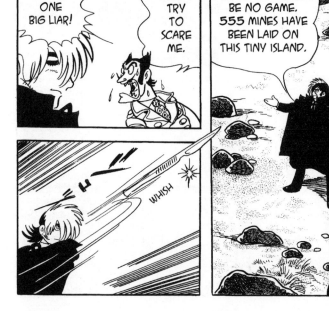

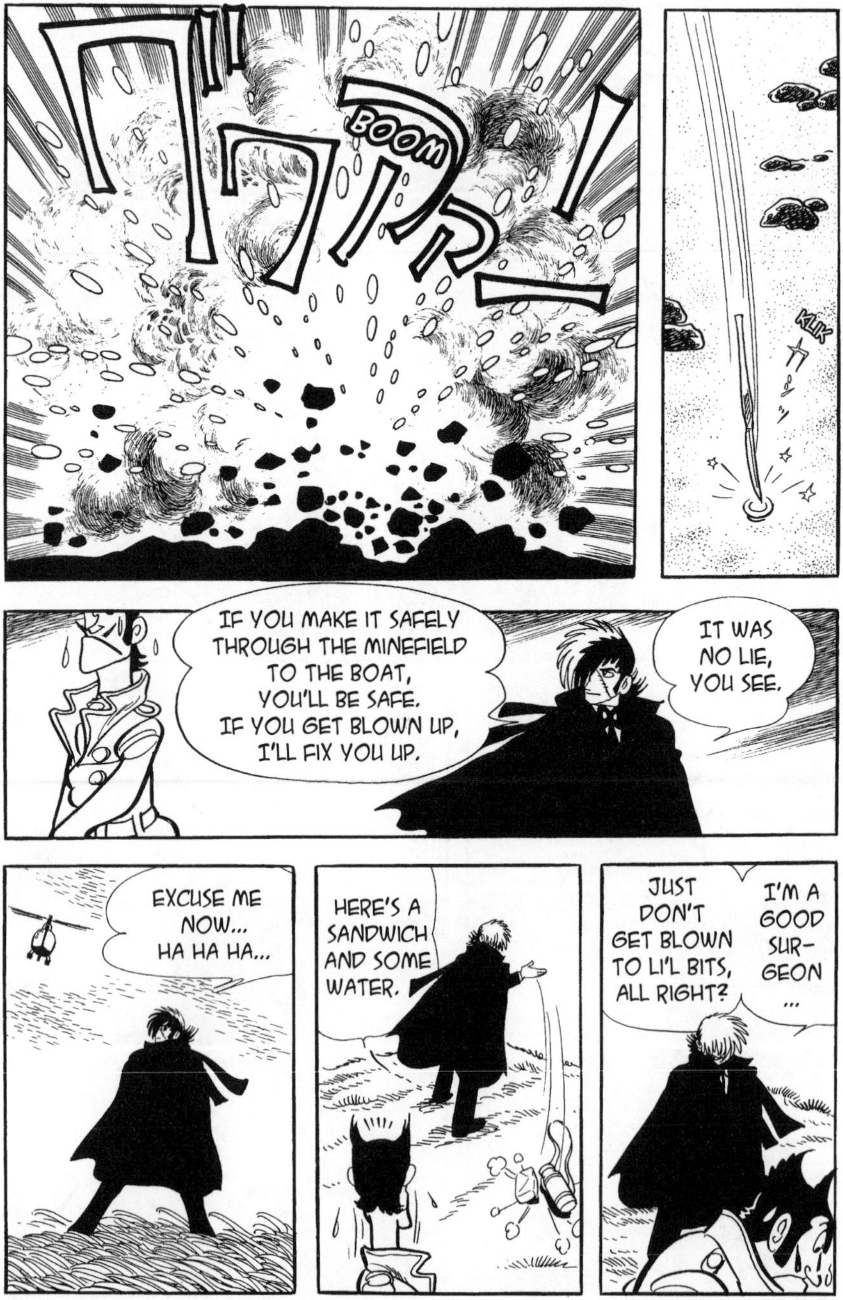
KLIK
BOOM
IT WAS NO LIE, YOU SEE.
IF YOU MAKE IT SAFELY THROUGH THE MINEFIELD TO THE BOAT, YOU'LL BE SAFE. IF YOU GET BLOWN UP, I'LL FIX YOU UP.
I'M A GOOD SURGEON ...
JUST DON'T GET BLOWN TO LI'L BITS, ALL RIGHT?
HERE'S A SANDWICH AND SOME WATER.
EXCUSE ME NOW... HA HA HA...

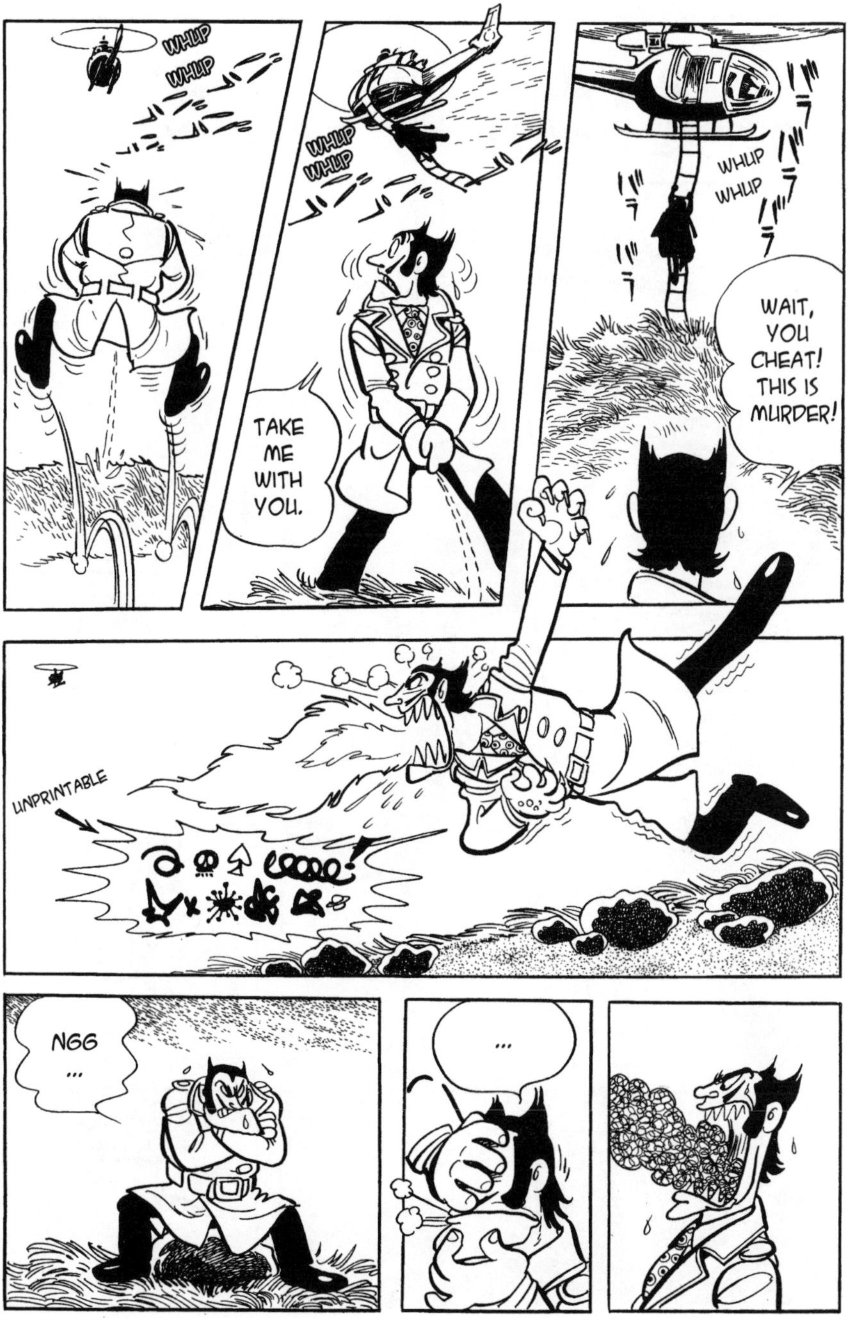
WHUP
WHUP
WAIT, YOU CHEAT! THIS IS MURDER!
WHUP
WHUP
TAKE ME WITH YOU.
WHUP
WHUP
UNPRINTABLE
...
NGG ...

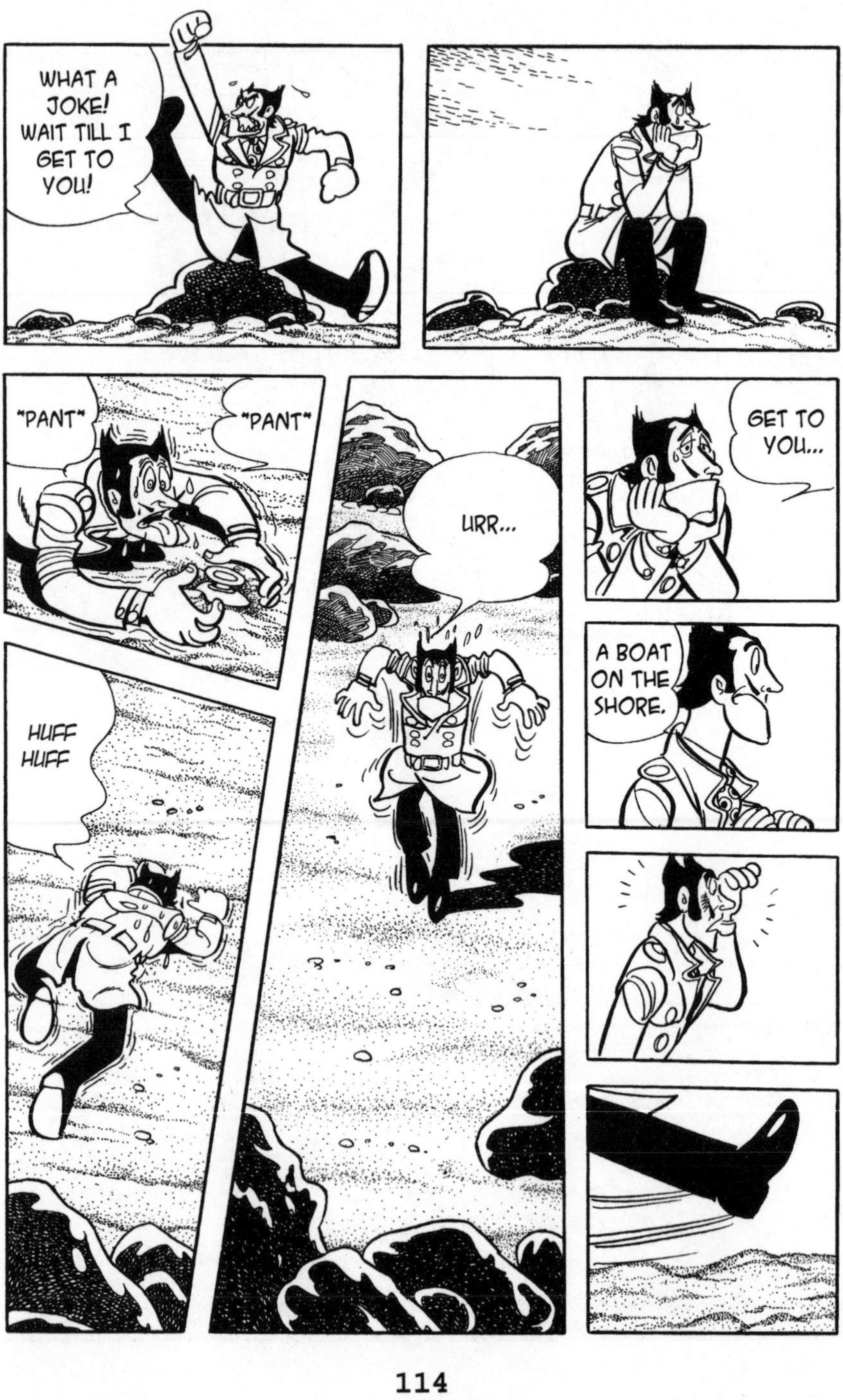
WHAT A JOKE! WAIT TILL I GET TO YOU!
GET TO YOU...
A BOAT ON THE SHORE.
URR...
PANT
PANT
HUFF HUFF

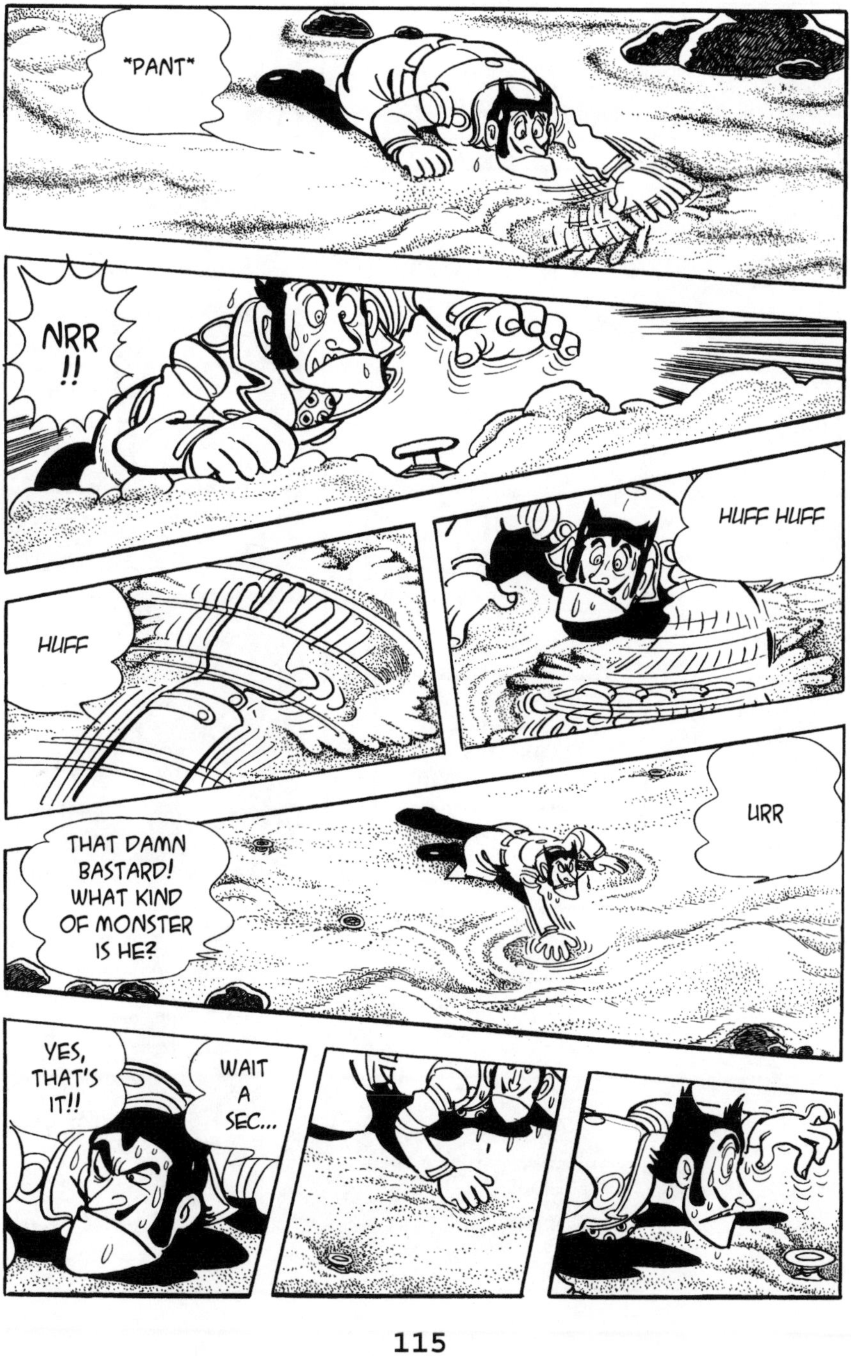
PANT
NRR !!
HUFF HUFF
HUFF
URR
THAT DAMN BASTARD! WHAT KIND OF MONSTER IS HE?
WAIT A SEC...
YES, THAT'S IT!!

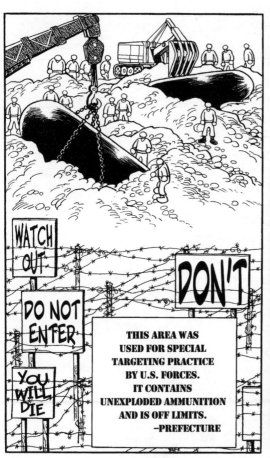

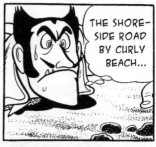

THE SHORE-SIDE ROAD BY CURLY BEACH...
I WAS IN A SPECIAL SQUAD IN THE DEFENSE FORCES
ASSIGNED TO BOMB DISPOSAL.
DON'T
WATCH OUT
DO NOT ENTER
YOU WILL DIE
THIS AREA WAS USED FOR SPECIAL TARGETING PRACTICE BY U.S. FORCES. IT CONTAINS UNEXPLODED AMMUNITION AND IS OFF LIMITS. –PREFECTURE
THIS THE LAST ONE?
YUP, THIS OUGHTA BE IT.

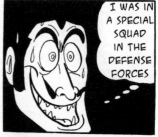

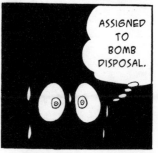

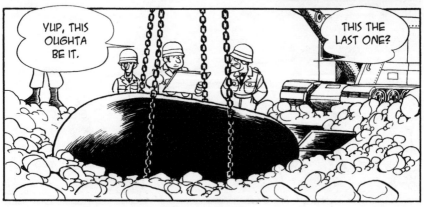

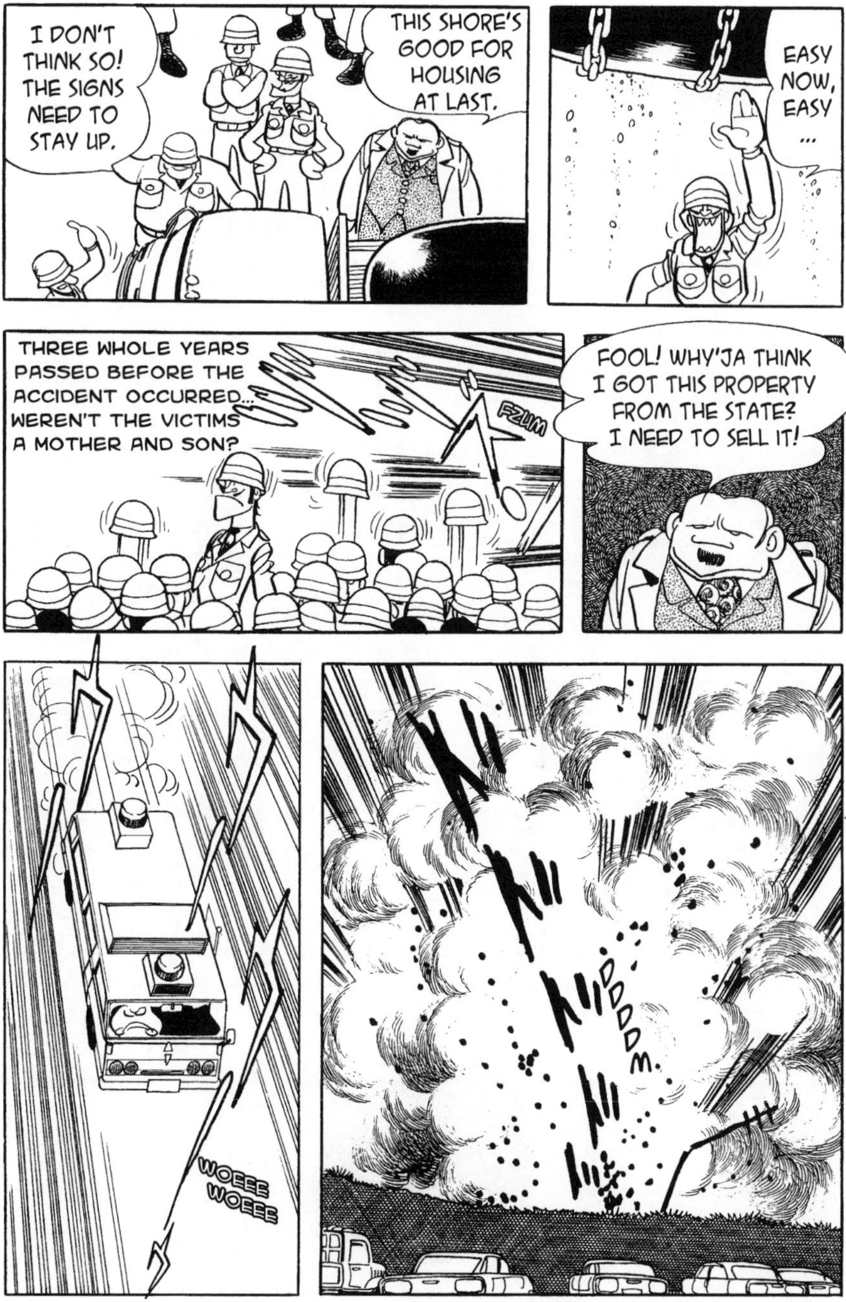
EASY NOW, EASY ...
THIS SHORE'S GOOD FOR HOUSING AT LAST.
I DON'T THINK SO! THE SIGNS NEED TO STAY UP.
FOOL! WHY'JA THINK I GOT THIS PROPERTY FROM THE STATE? I NEED TO SELL IT!
FZUM
THREE WHOLE YEARS PASSED BEFORE THE ACCIDENT OCCURRED... WEREN'T THE VICTIMS A MOTHER AND SON?
DDDDDM.
WOEEE WOEEE

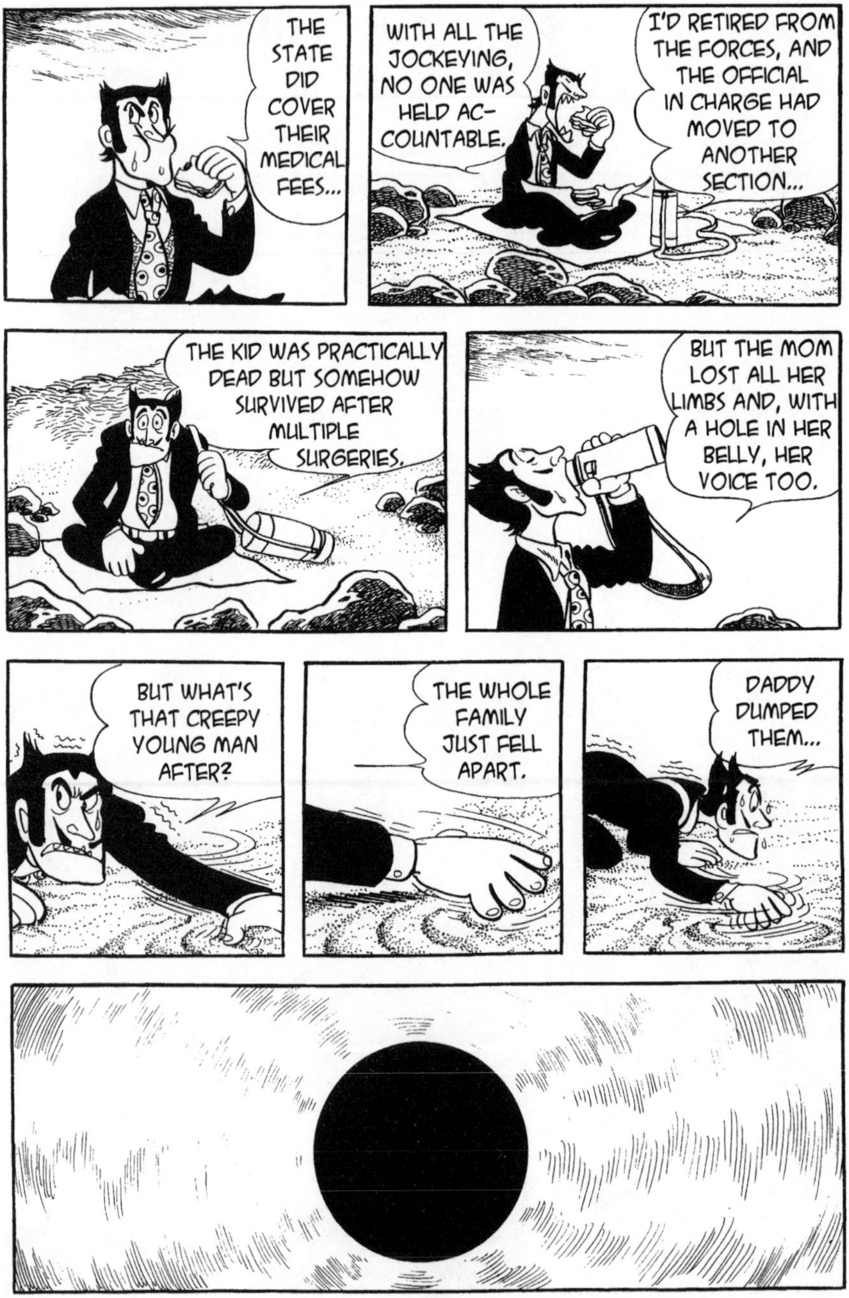
I'D RETIRED FROM THE FORCES, AND THE OFFICIAL IN CHARGE HAD MOVED TO ANOTHER SECTION...
WITH ALL THE JOCKEYING, NO ONE WAS HELD AC-COUNTABLE.
THE STATE DID COVER THEIR MEDICAL FEES...
BUT THE MOM LOST ALL HER LIMBS AND, WITH A HOLE IN HER BELLY, HER VOICE TOO.
THE KID WAS PRACTICALLY DEAD BUT SOMEHOW SURVIVED AFTER MULTIPLE SURGERIES.
DADDY DUMPED THEM...
THE WHOLE FAMILY JUST FELL APART.
BUT WHAT'S THAT CREEPY YOUNG MAN AFTER?

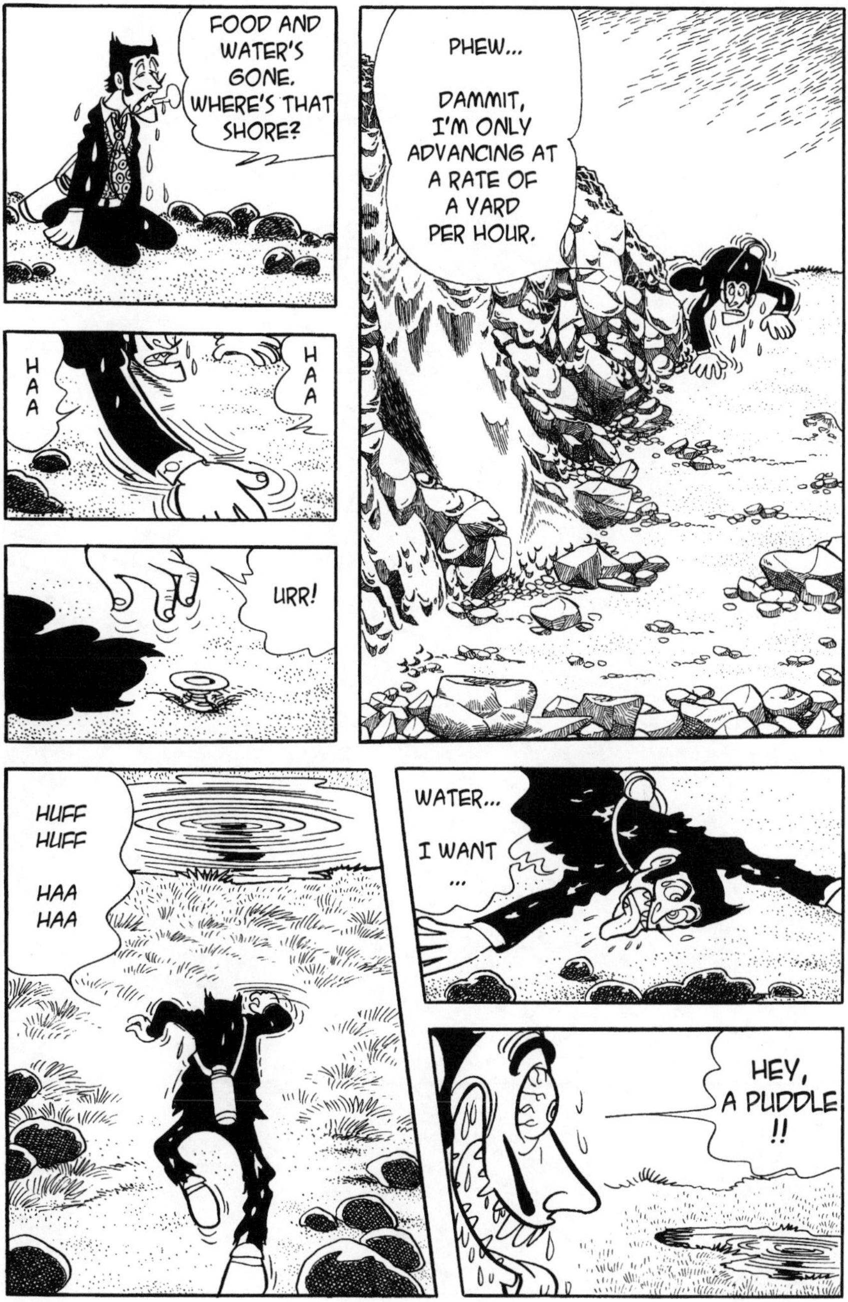
PHEW...
DAMMIT, I'M ONLY ADVANCING AT A RATE OF A YARD PER HOUR.
FOOD AND WATER'S GONE. WHERE'S THAT SHORE?
HAA
HAA
URR!
WATER...
I WANT ...
HEY, A PUDDLE !!
HUFF HUFF
HAA HAA

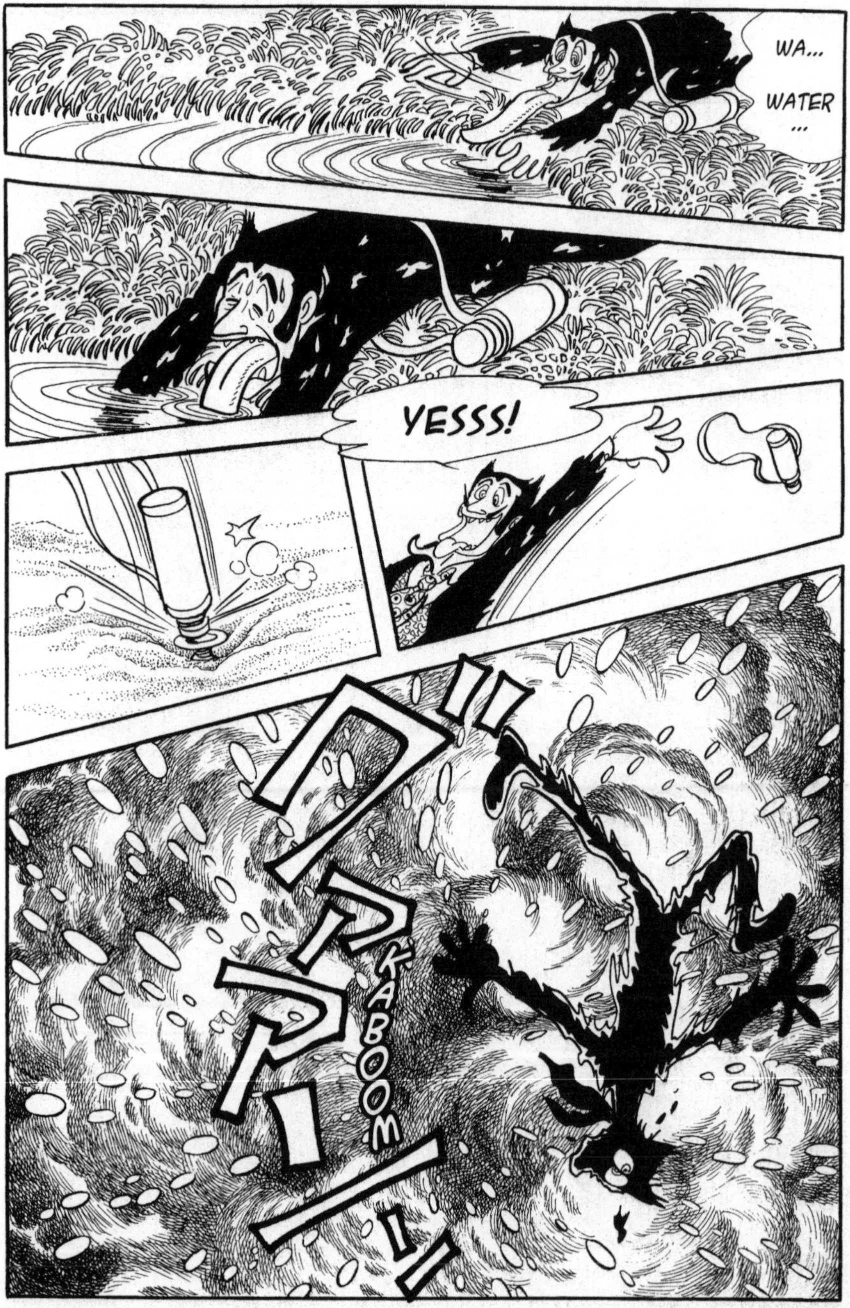
WA...
WATER
...
YESSS!
KABOOM

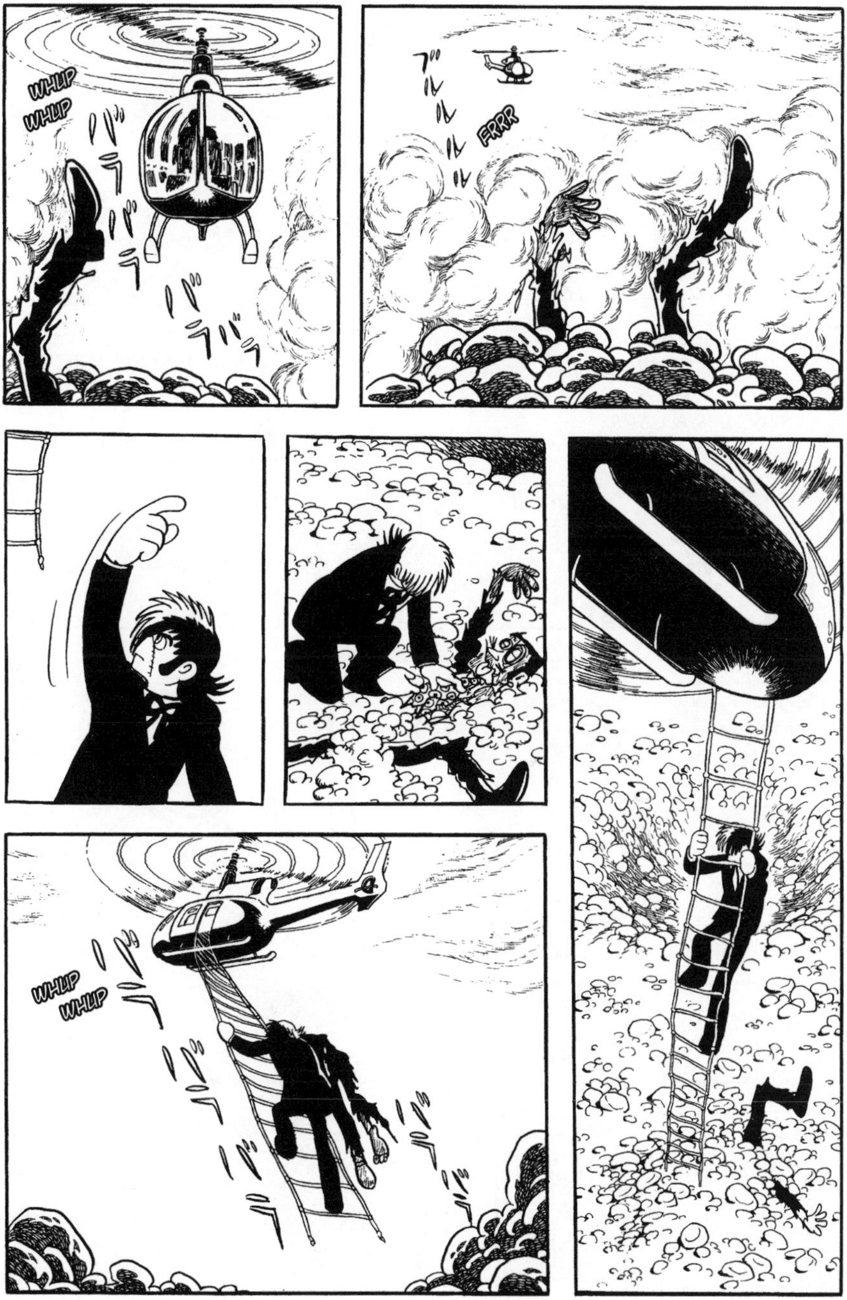
FRRR
WHUP
WHUP
WHUP
WHUP

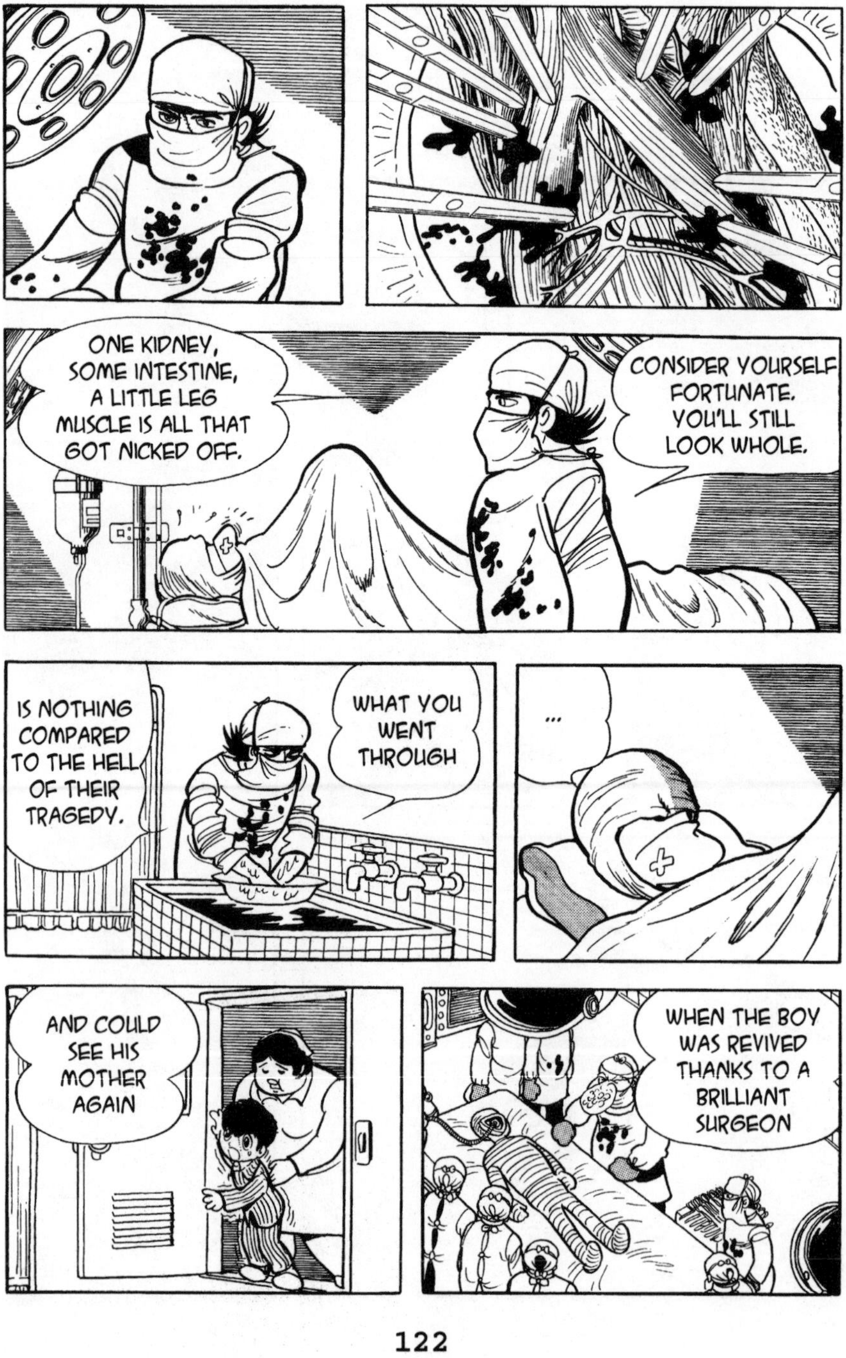
ONE KIDNEY, SOME INTESTINE, A LITTLE LEG MUSCLE IS ALL THAT GOT NICKED OFF.
CONSIDER YOURSELF FORTUNATE. YOU'LL STILL LOOK WHOLE.
...
WHAT YOU WENT THROUGH
IS NOTHING COMPARED TO THE HELL OF THEIR TRAGEDY.
WHEN THE BOY WAS REVIVED THANKS TO A BRILLIANT SURGEON
AND COULD SEE HIS MOTHER AGAIN

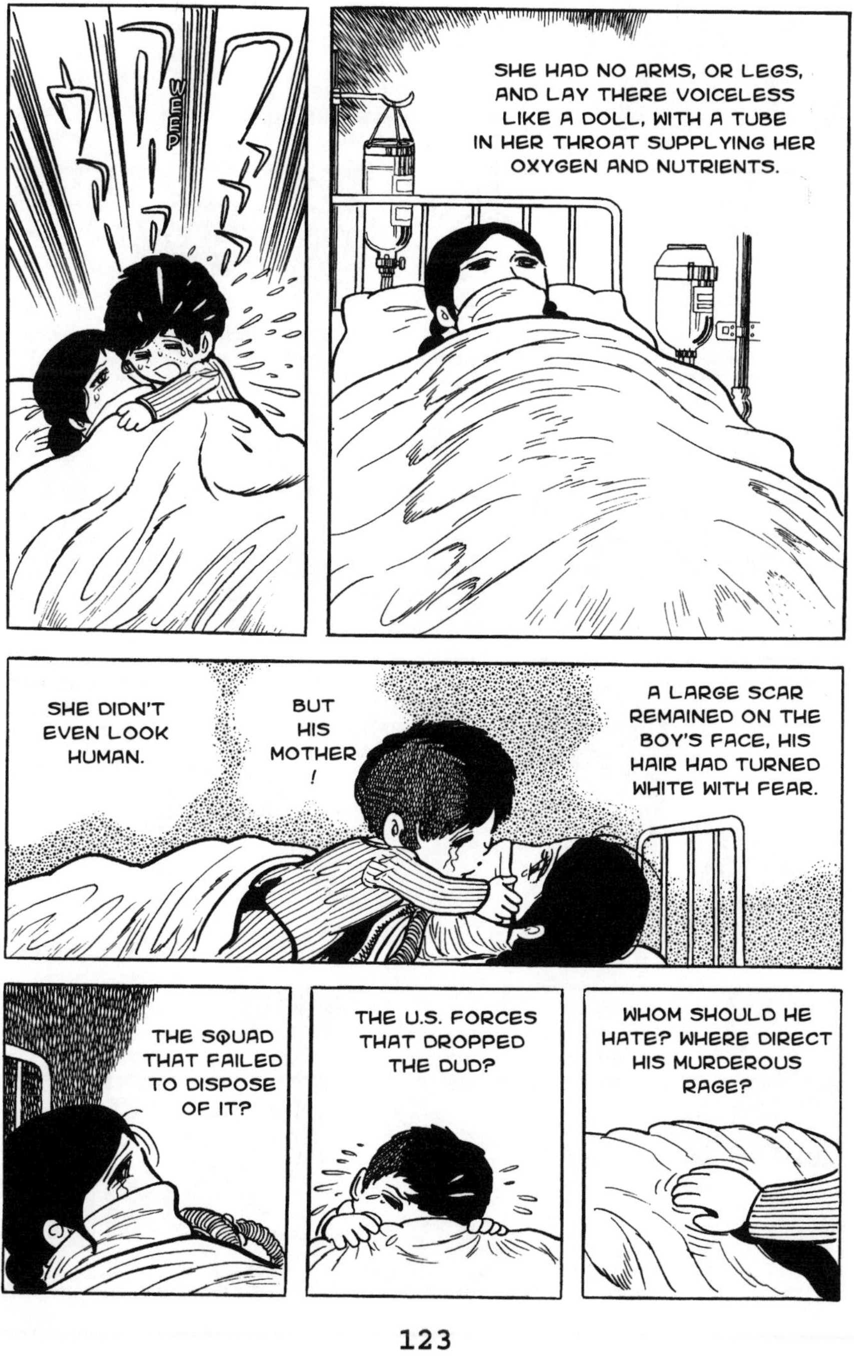
SHE HAD NO ARMS, OR LEGS, AND LAY THERE VOICELESS LIKE A DOLL, WITH A TUBE IN HER THROAT SUPPLYING HER OXYGEN AND NUTRIENTS.
WEEP
A LARGE SCAR REMAINED ON THE BOY'S FACE, HIS HAIR HAD TURNED WHITE WITH FEAR.
BUT HIS MOTHER!
SHE DIDN'T EVEN LOOK HUMAN.
WHOM SHOULD HE HATE? WHERE DIRECT HIS MURDEROUS RAGE?
THE U.S. FORCES THAT DROPPED THE DUD?
THE SQUAD THAT FAILED TO DISPOSE OF IT?

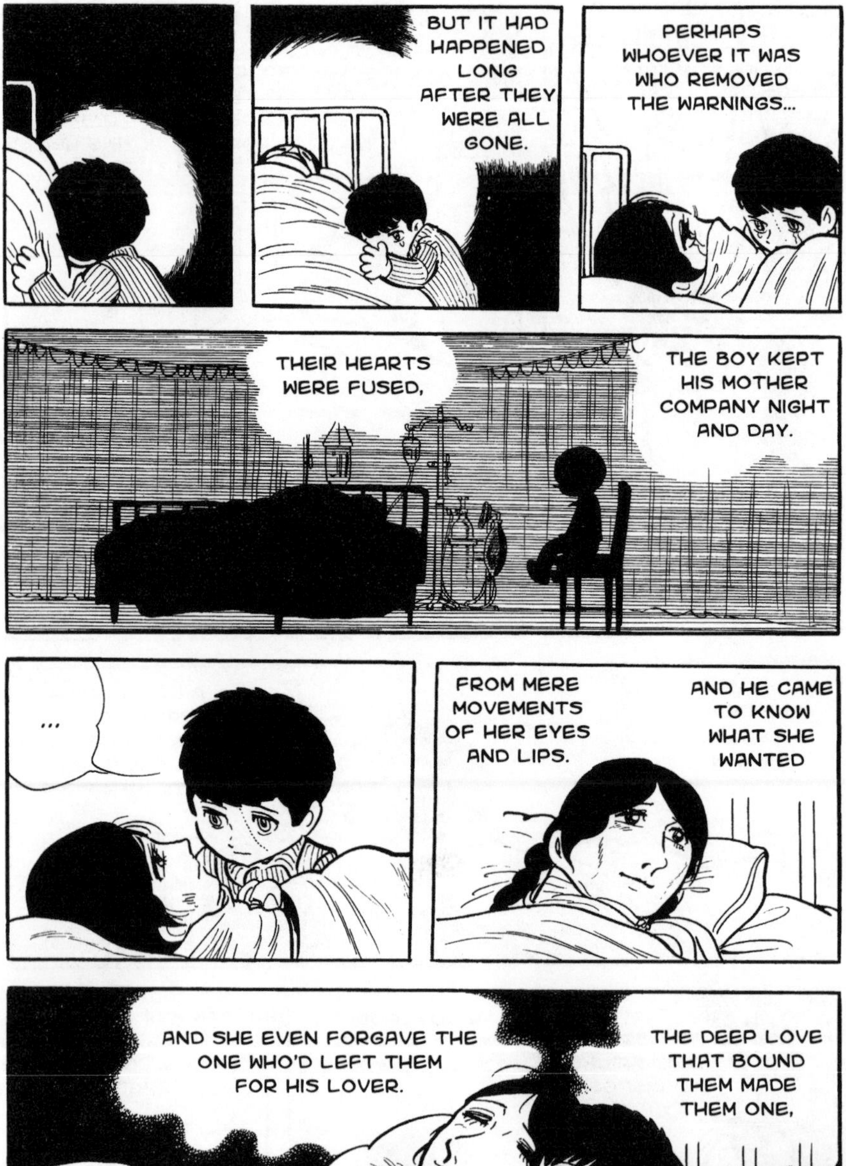
PERHAPS WHOEVER IT WAS WHO REMOVED THE WARNINGS...
BUT IT HAD HAPPENED LONG AFTER THEY WERE ALL GONE.
THE BOY KEPT HIS MOTHER COMPANY NIGHT AND DAY.
THEIR HEARTS WERE FUSED,
AND HE CAME TO KNOW WHAT SHE WANTED
FROM MERE MOVEMENTS OF HER EYES AND LIPS.
...
THE DEEP LOVE THAT BOUND THEM MADE THEM ONE,
AND SHE EVEN FORGAVE THE ONE WHO'D LEFT THEM FOR HIS LOVER.

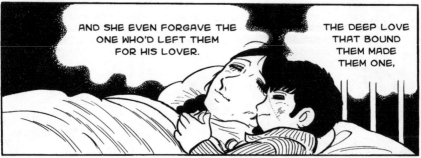

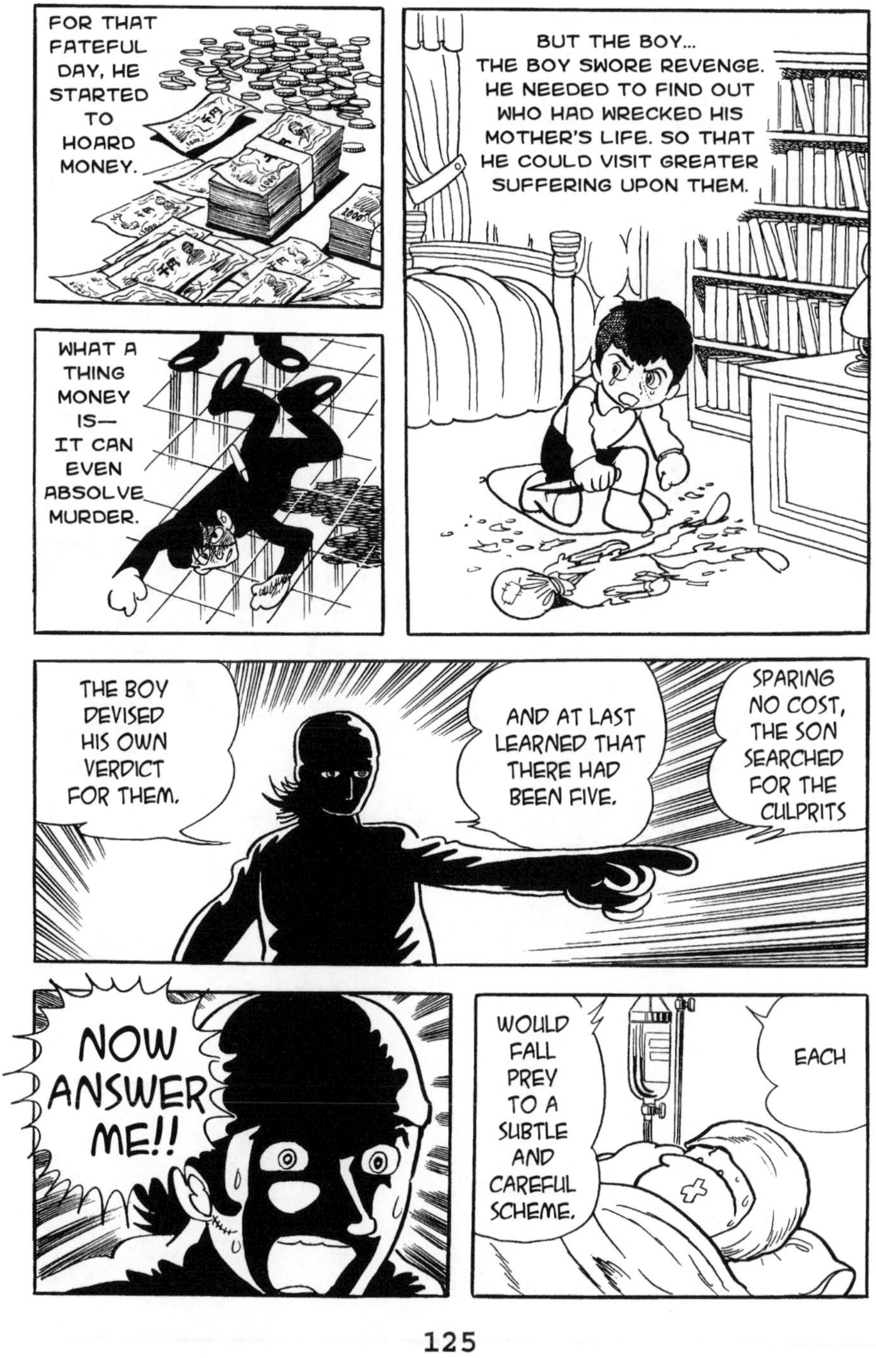
BUT THE BOY... THE BOY SWORE REVENGE. HE NEEDED TO FIND OUT WHO HAD WRECKED HIS MOTHER'S LIFE. SO THAT HE COULD VISIT GREATER SUFFERING UPON THEM.
FOR THAT FATEFUL DAY, HE STARTED TO HOARD MONEY.
WHAT A THING MONEY IS— IT CAN EVEN ABSOLVE MURDER.
SPARING NO COST, THE SON SEARCHED FOR THE CULPRITS
AND AT LAST LEARNED THAT THERE HAD BEEN FIVE.
THE BOY DEVISED HIS OWN VERDICT FOR THEM.
EACH
WOULD FALL PREY TO A SUBTLE AND CAREFUL SCHEME.
NOW ANSWER ME!!

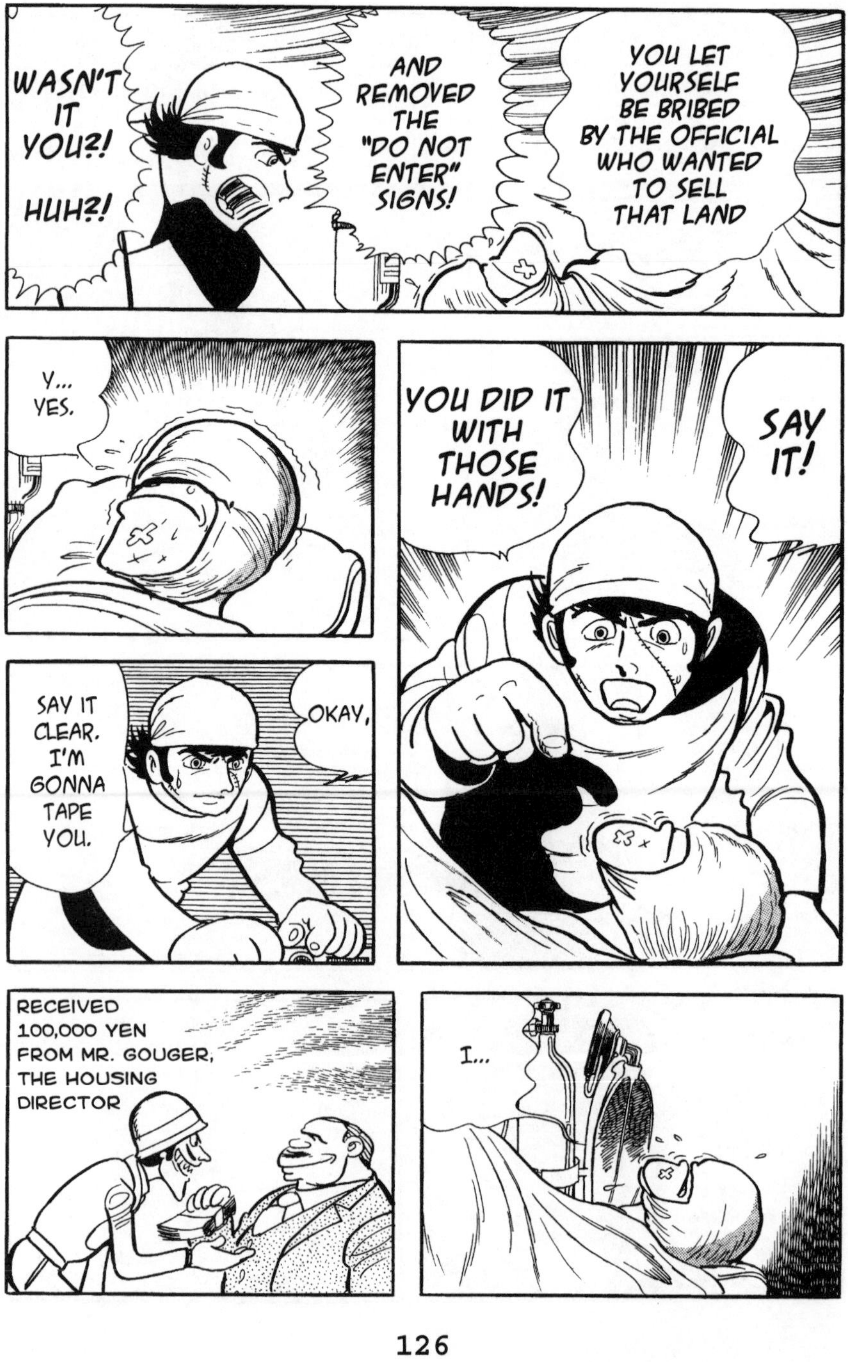
YOU LET YOURSELF BE BRIBED BY THE OFFICIAL WHO WANTED TO SELL THAT LAND
AND REMOVED THE "DO NOT ENTER" SIGNS!
WASN'T IT YOU?!
HUH?!
SAY IT!
YOU DID IT WITH THOSE HANDS!
Y... YES.
OKAY,
SAY IT CLEAR. I'M GONNA TAPE YOU.
I...
RECEIVED 100,000 YEN FROM MR. GOUGER, THE HOUSING DIRECTOR

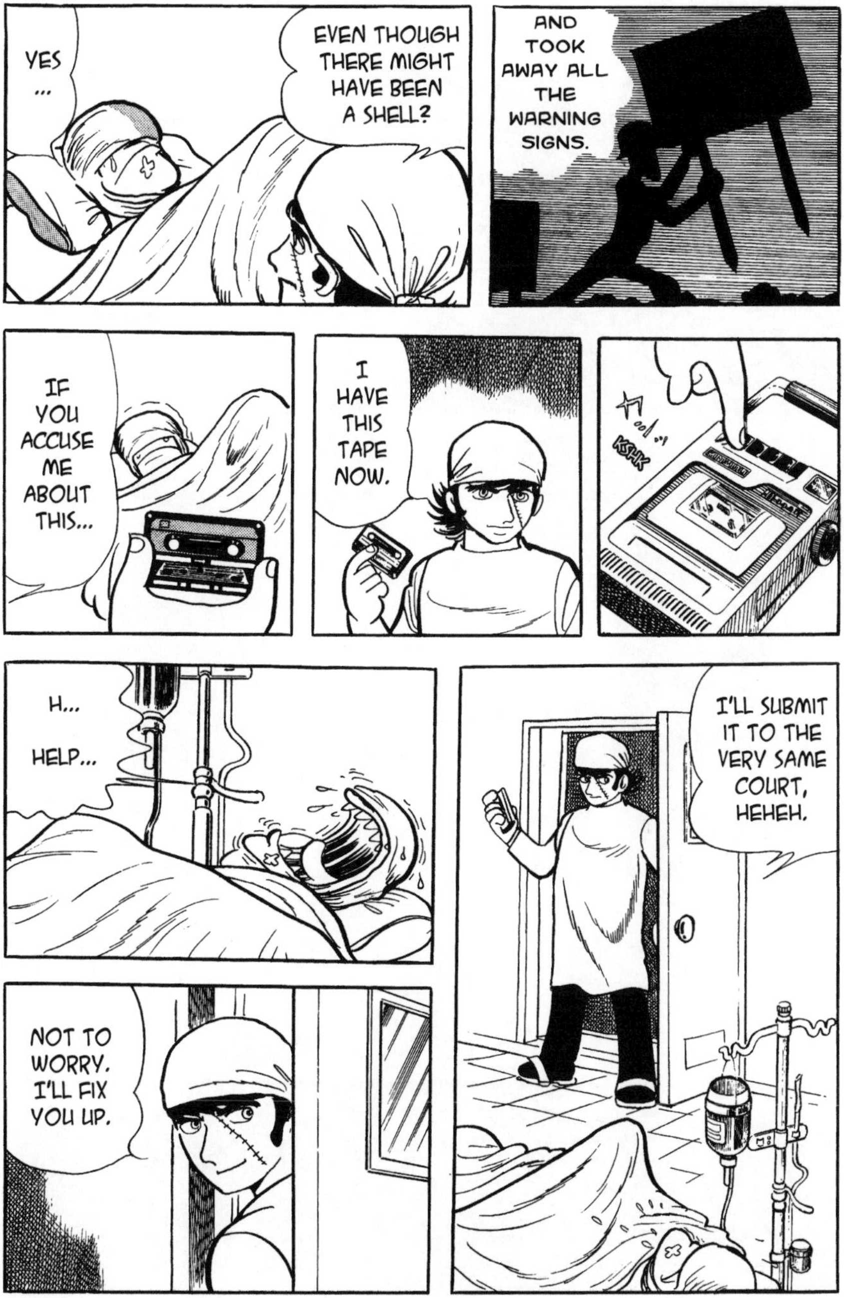
AND TOOK AWAY ALL THE WARNING SIGNS.
EVEN THOUGH THERE MIGHT HAVE BEEN A SHELL?
YES ...
KSHK
I HAVE THIS TAPE NOW.
IF YOU ACCUSE ME ABOUT THIS...
I'LL SUBMIT IT TO THE VERY SAME COURT, HEHEH.
H... HELP...
NOT TO WORRY. I'LL FIX YOU UP.

ZVSHH
ZVSHHH
ZVSH
FOUR MORE!

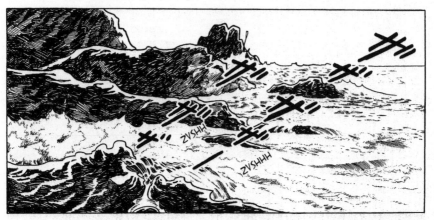

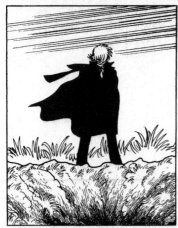

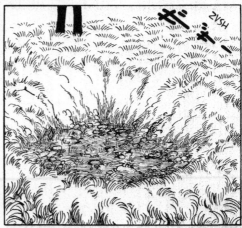

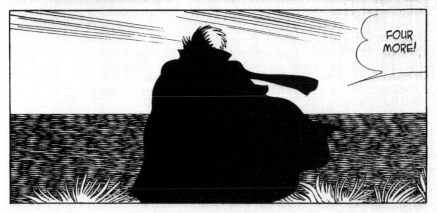

MOTHER
...

YOUNGER BROTHER

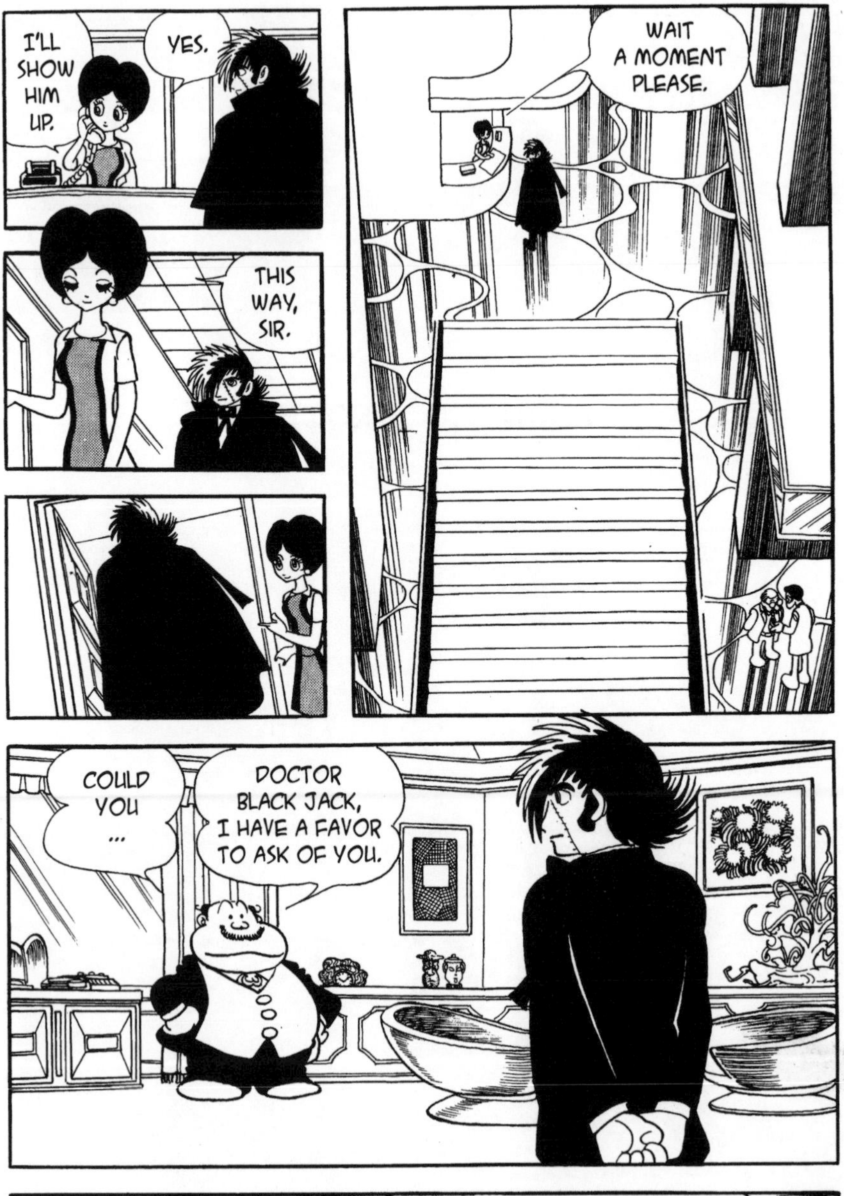
WAIT A MOMENT PLEASE.
YES.
I'LL SHOW HIM UP.
THIS WAY, SIR.
DOCTOR BLACK JACK, I HAVE A FAVOR TO ASK OF YOU.
COULD YOU ...
BECOME MY SON FOR A YEAR?
IF YOU MAY?

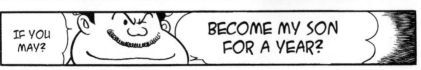

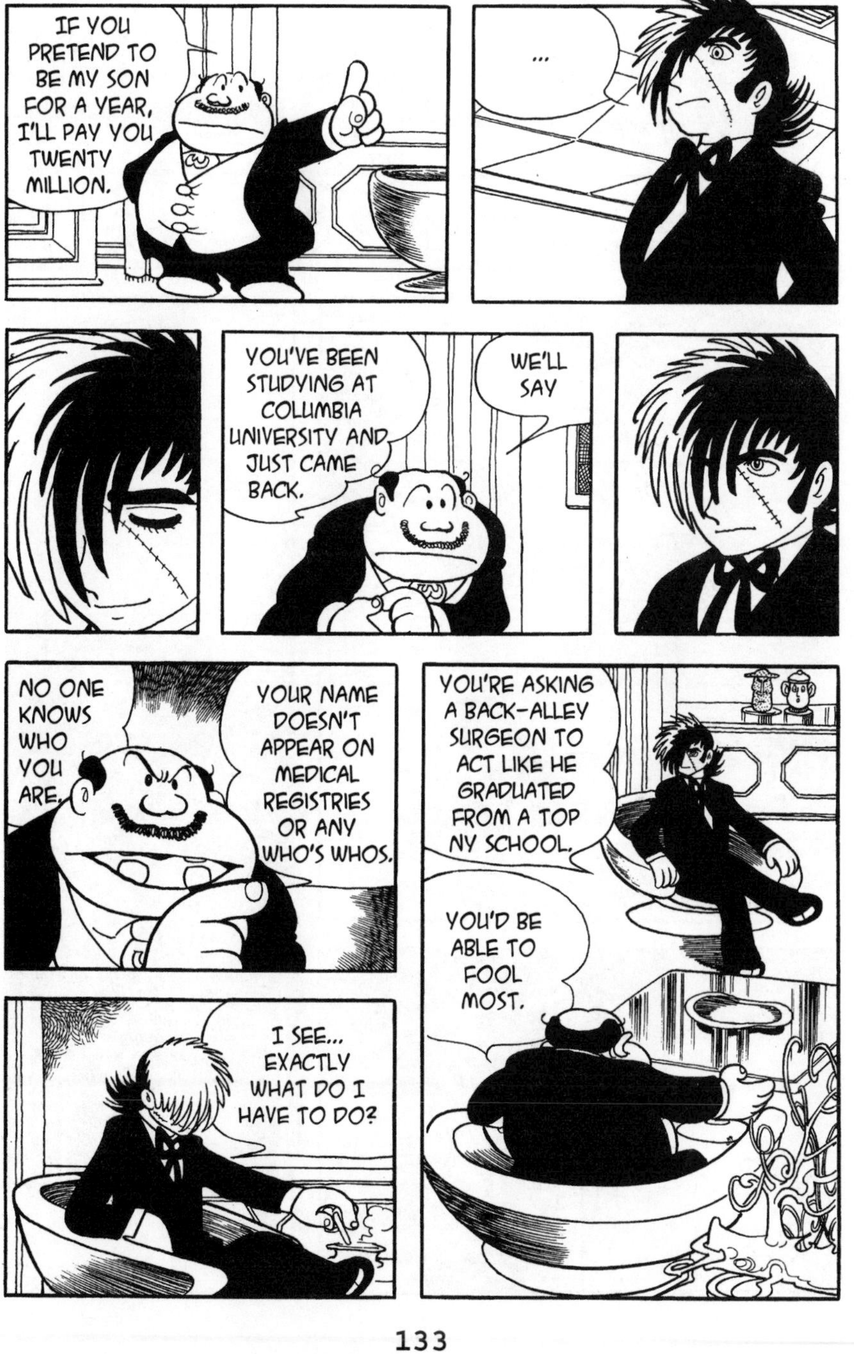
...
IF YOU PRETEND TO BE MY SON FOR A YEAR, I'LL PAY YOU TWENTY MILLION.
WE'LL SAY
YOU'VE BEEN STUDYING AT COLUMBIA UNIVERSITY AND JUST CAME BACK.
YOU'RE ASKING A BACK-ALLEY SURGEON TO ACT LIKE HE GRADUATED FROM A TOP NY SCHOOL.
YOU'D BE ABLE TO FOOL MOST.
YOUR NAME DOESN'T APPEAR ON MEDICAL REGISTRIES OR ANY WHO'S WHOS.
NO ONE KNOWS WHO YOU ARE.
I SEE... EXACTLY WHAT DO I HAVE TO DO?

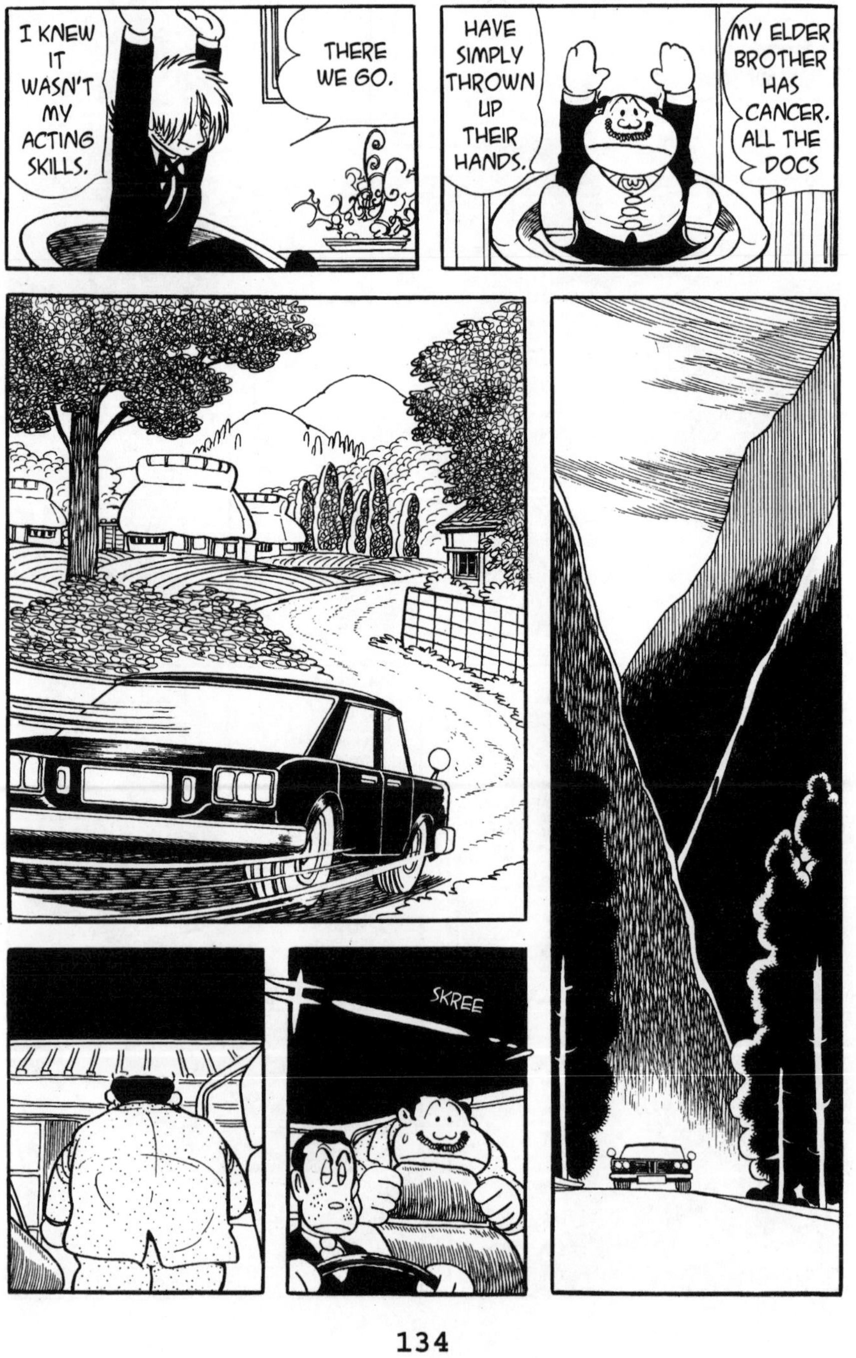
MY ELDER BROTHER HAS CANCER. ALL THE DOCS
HAVE SIMPLY THROWN UP THEIR HANDS.
THERE WE GO.
I KNEW IT WASN'T MY ACTING SKILLS.
SKREE

SISTER, LONG TIME NO SEE.
WHY, IF IT ISN'T EIZO!
HON, GUESS WHO'S HERE?
WHAT, EIZO?! I WON'T SEE HIM! TELL HIM TO GET LOST.
BUT IT'S BEEN TEN YEARS...
SISTER, HOW IS HE DOING?
HE'S ONLY BEEN GETTING WORSE, DESPITE TWO OPERATIONS.
EIZO! HOW DARE YOU SHOW YOUR FACE?
I'VE HEARD YOU AREN'T WELL.
WHAT'S THAT GOT TO DO WITH YOU?

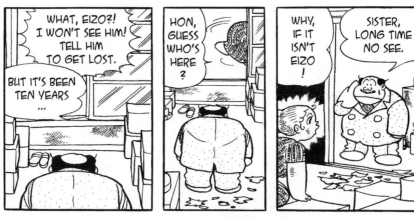

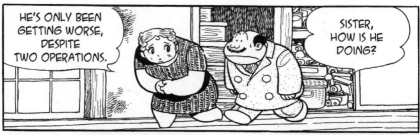

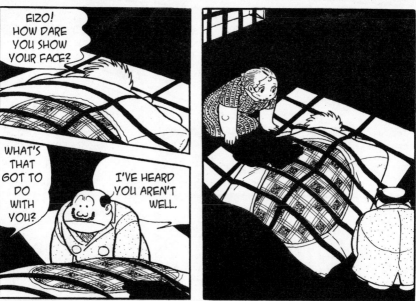

NOTE: IT IS COMMON ETIQUETTE IN JAPAN TO ADDRESS AN ELDER SIBLING'S SPOUSE AS "SISTER/BROTHER."

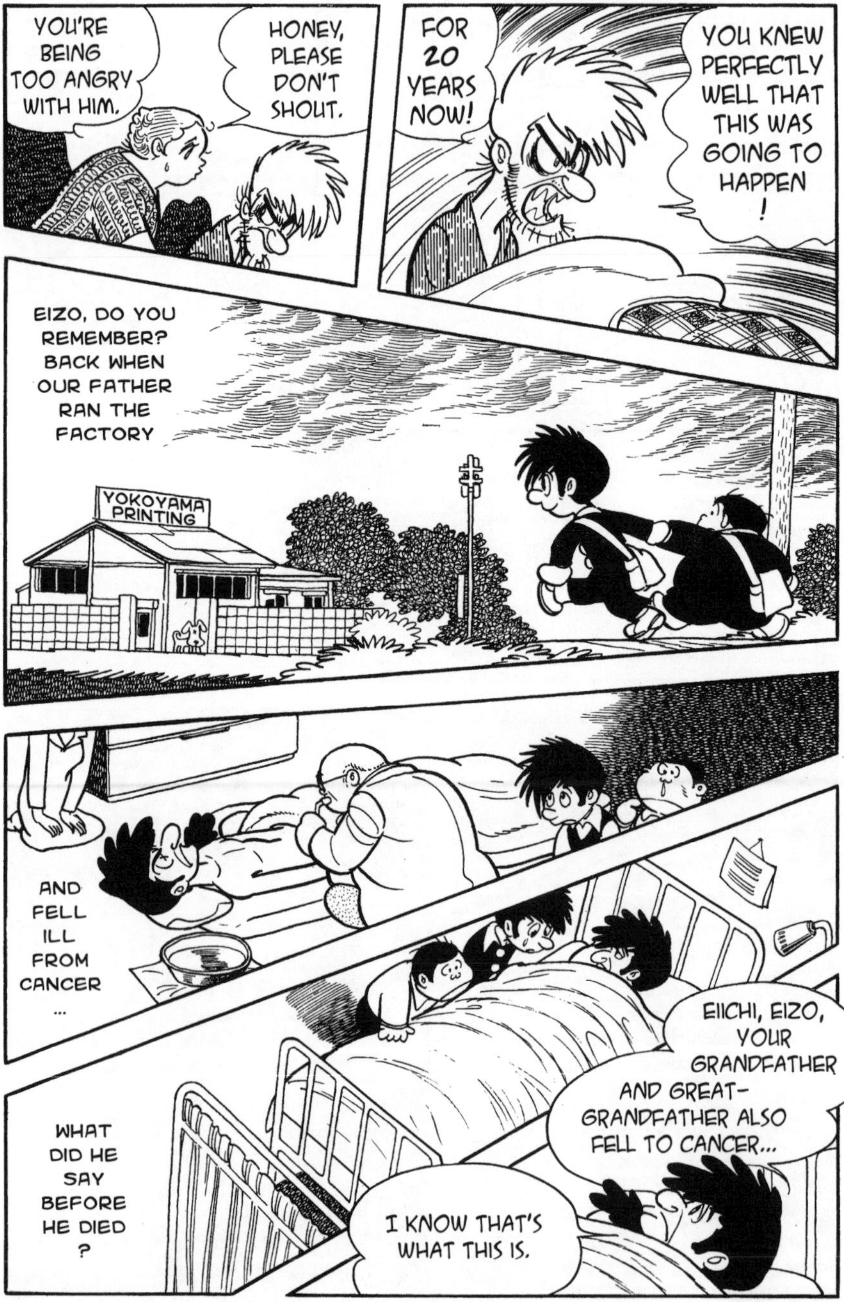
YOU KNEW PERFECTLY WELL THAT THIS WAS GOING TO HAPPEN !
FOR 20 YEARS NOW!
HONEY, PLEASE DON'T SHOUT.
YOU'RE BEING TOO ANGRY WITH HIM.
EIZO, DO YOU REMEMBER? BACK WHEN OUR FATHER RAN THE FACTORY
YOKOYAMA PRINTING
AND FELL ILL FROM CANCER ...
EIICHI, EIZO, YOUR GRANDFATHER AND GREAT-GRANDFATHER ALSO FELL TO CANCER...
I KNOW THAT'S WHAT THIS IS.
WHAT DID HE SAY BEFORE HE DIED ?

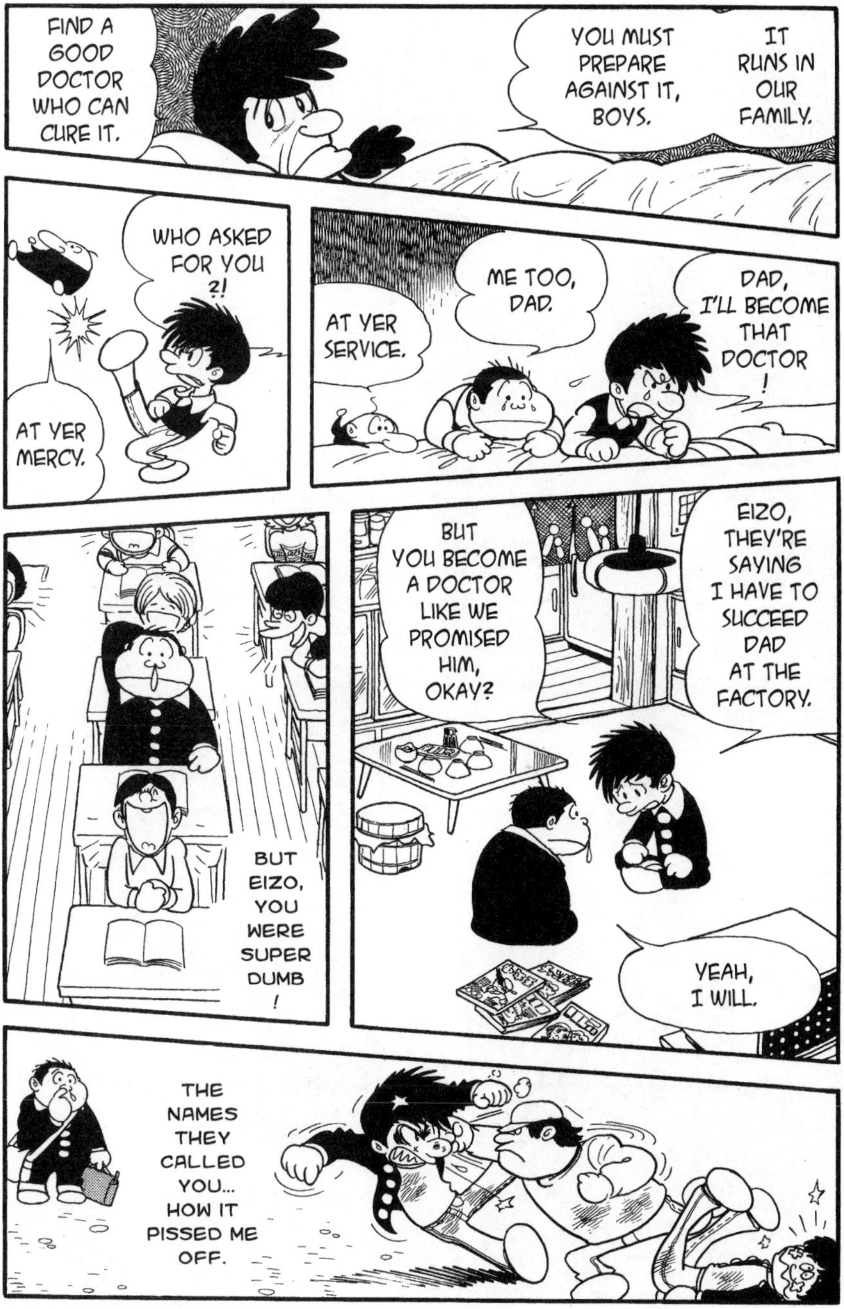
IT RUNS IN OUR FAMILY.
YOU MUST PREPARE AGAINST IT, BOYS.
FIND A GOOD DOCTOR WHO CAN CURE IT.
DAD, I'LL BECOME THAT DOCTOR!
ME TOO, DAD.
AT YER SERVICE.
WHO ASKED FOR YOU?!
AT YER MERCY.
EIZO, THEY'RE SAYING I HAVE TO SUCCEED DAD AT THE FACTORY.
BUT YOU BECOME A DOCTOR LIKE WE PROMISED HIM, OKAY?
YEAH, I WILL.
BUT EIZO, YOU WERE SUPER DUMB!
THE NAMES THEY CALLED YOU... HOW IT PISSED ME OFF.

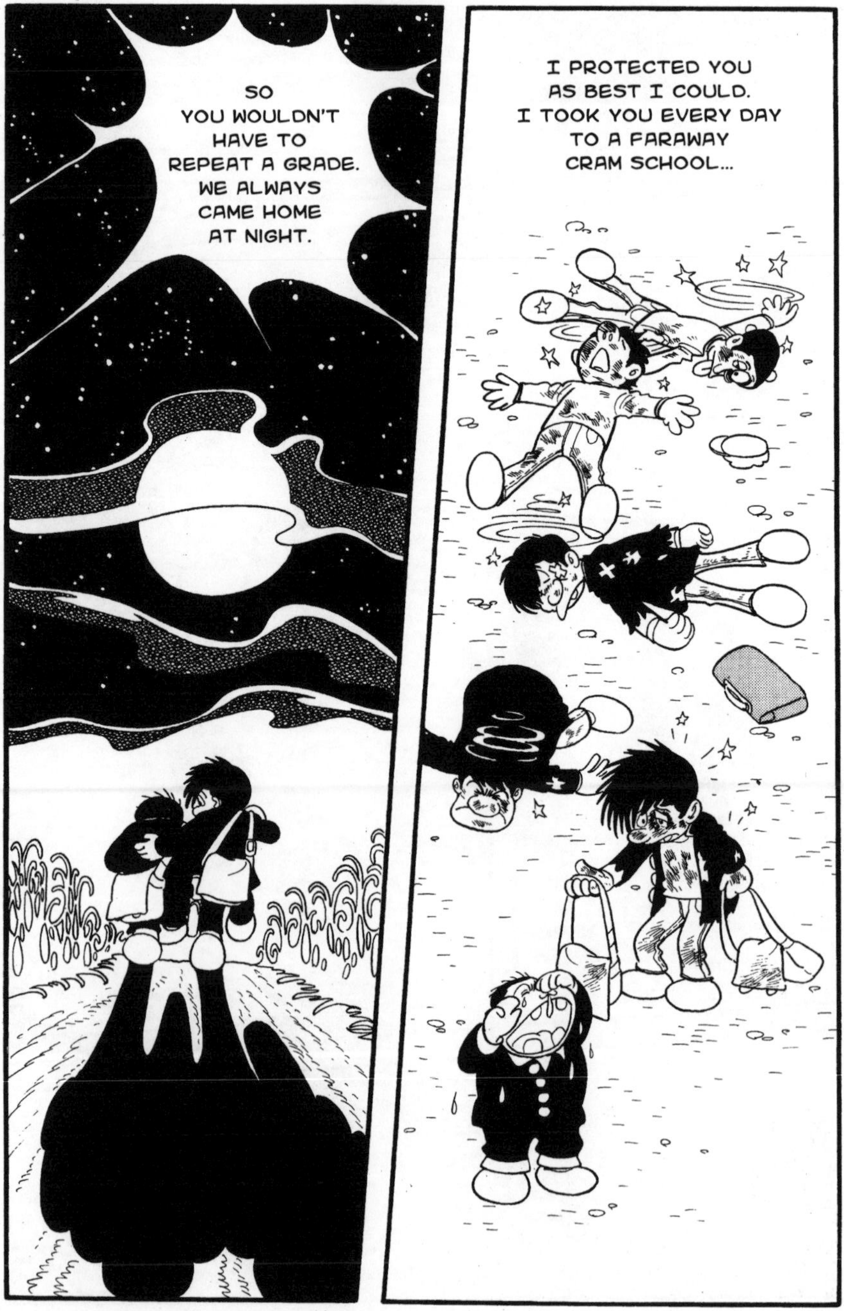
I PROTECTED YOU AS BEST I COULD. I TOOK YOU EVERY DAY TO A FARAWAY CRAM SCHOOL...
SO YOU WOULDN'T HAVE TO REPEAT A GRADE. WE ALWAYS CAME HOME AT NIGHT.

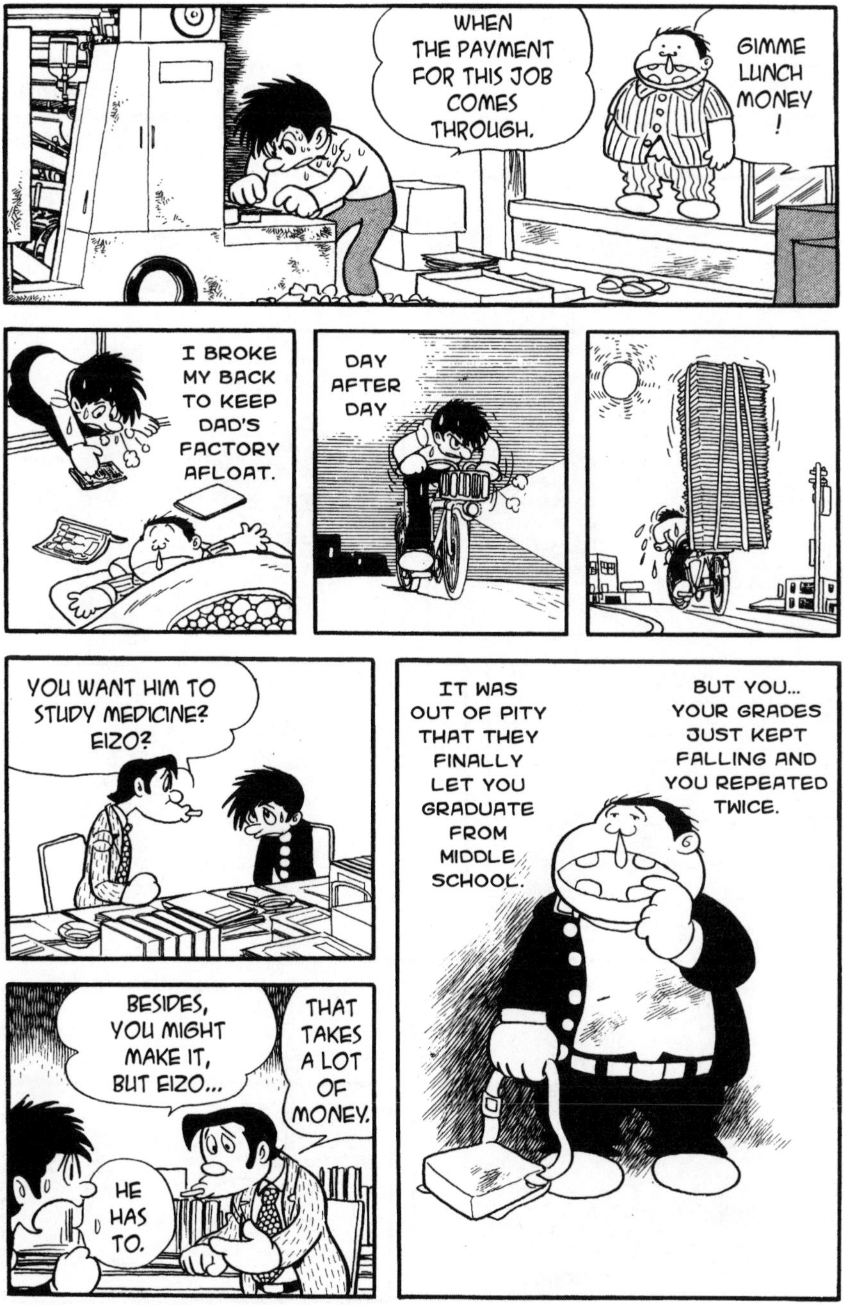
GIMME LUNCH MONEY!
WHEN THE PAYMENT FOR THIS JOB COMES THROUGH.
DAY AFTER DAY
I BROKE MY BACK TO KEEP DAD'S FACTORY AFLOAT.
BUT YOU... YOUR GRADES JUST KEPT FALLING AND YOU REPEATED TWICE.
IT WAS OUT OF PITY THAT THEY FINALLY LET YOU GRADUATE FROM MIDDLE SCHOOL.
YOU WANT HIM TO STUDY MEDICINE? EIZO?
THAT TAKES A LOT OF MONEY.
BESIDES, YOU MIGHT MAKE IT, BUT EIZO...
HE HAS TO.

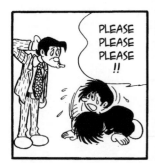

EIZO WILL BECOME A DOCTOR!
WE SWORE TO MY DAD!
PLEASE HELP HIM, SENSEI!
PLEASE PLEASE PLEASE!!
YOU'RE A HIGH SCHOOLER NOW, SO BUST YOUR ASS!
IF YOU CAN'T
SCORE A 10
THEN GO FOR AN 8!
I GOT AN 8
OUT OF 100.
PLEASE GIVE HIM PRIVATE LESSONS!
FOR THIS MUCH.
MAY I USE THE BATHROOM?
YOUR BROTHER SURE LOVES MY BATHROOM...
I'VE HARDLY TALKED TO HIM.

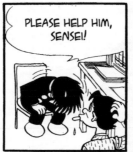

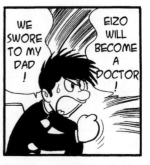

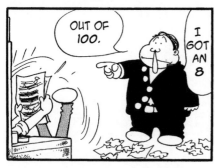

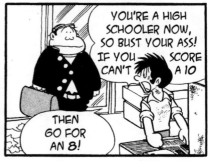

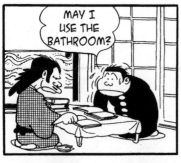

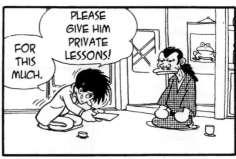

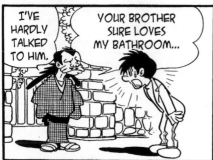

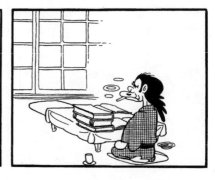

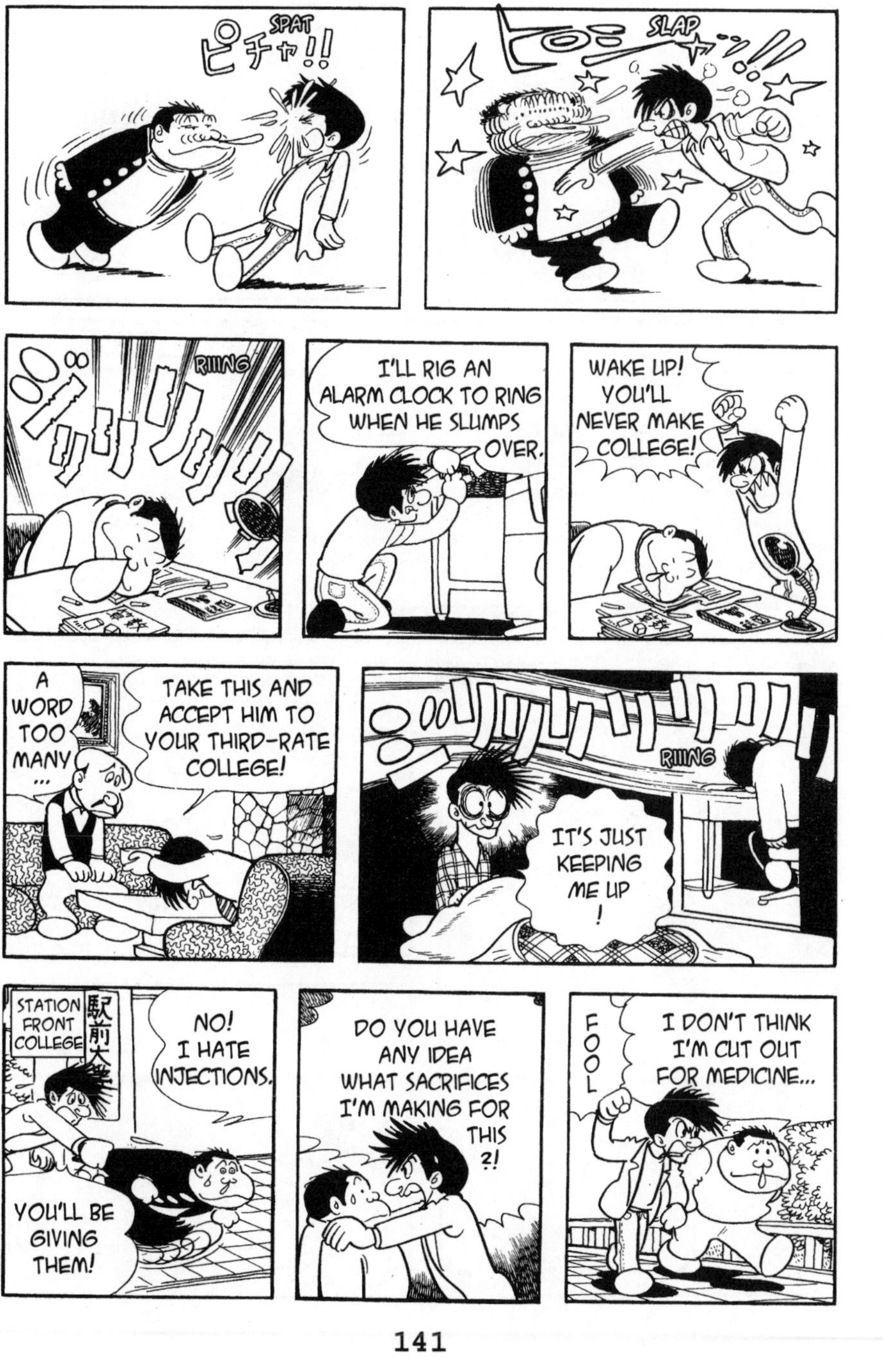
SLAP
SPAT
ピチャ!!
WAKE UP! YOU'LL NEVER MAKE COLLEGE!
I'LL RIG AN ALARM CLOCK TO RING WHEN HE SLUMPS OVER.
RIIING
RIIING
IT'S JUST KEEPING ME UP!
TAKE THIS AND ACCEPT HIM TO YOUR THIRD-RATE COLLEGE!
A WORD TOO MANY...
I DON'T THINK I'M CUT OUT FOR MEDICINE...
FOOL
DO YOU HAVE ANY IDEA WHAT SACRIFICES I'M MAKING FOR THIS?!
NO! I HATE INJECTIONS.
STATION FRONT COLLEGE
YOU'LL BE GIVING THEM!

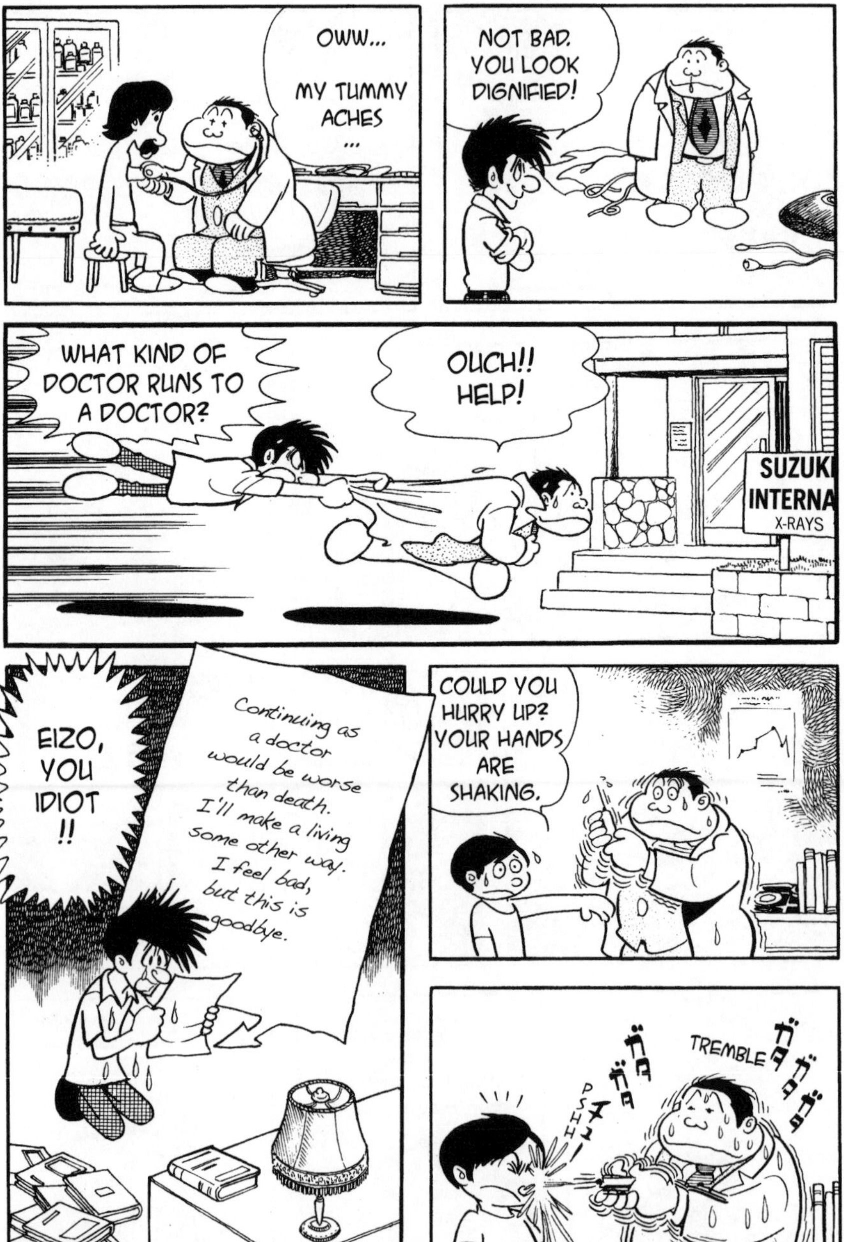
NOT BAD. YOU LOOK DIGNIFIED!
OWW... MY TUMMY ACHES ...
OUCH!! HELP!
WHAT KIND OF DOCTOR RUNS TO A DOCTOR?
SUZUKI INTERNA
X-RAYS
COULD YOU HURRY UP? YOUR HANDS ARE SHAKING.
TREMBLE
ガタガタガタ
ガタガタ
PSHH!
EIZO, YOU IDIOT !!
Continuing as a doctor would be worse than death. I'll make a living some other way. I feel bad, but this is goodbye.

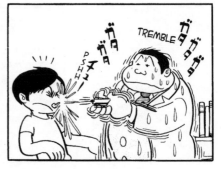

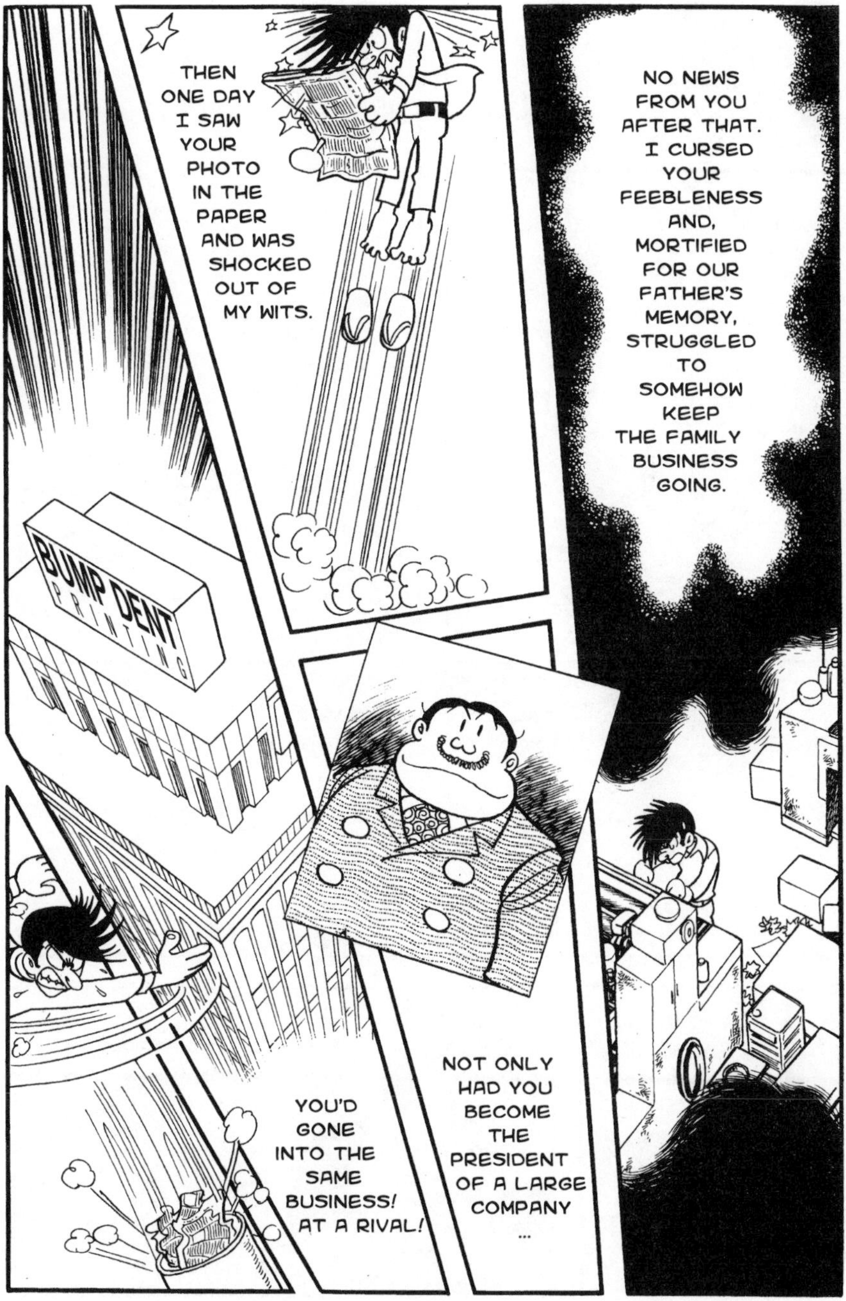
NO NEWS FROM YOU AFTER THAT. I CURSED YOUR FEEBLENESS AND, MORTIFIED FOR OUR FATHER'S MEMORY, STRUGGLED TO SOMEHOW KEEP THE FAMILY BUSINESS GOING.
THEN ONE DAY I SAW YOUR PHOTO IN THE PAPER AND WAS SHOCKED OUT OF MY WITS.
BUMP DENT PRINTING
NOT ONLY HAD YOU BECOME THE PRESIDENT OF A LARGE COMPANY ...
YOU'D GONE INTO THE SAME BUSINESS! AT A RIVAL!

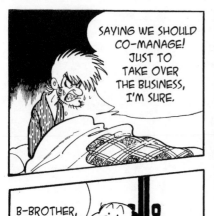

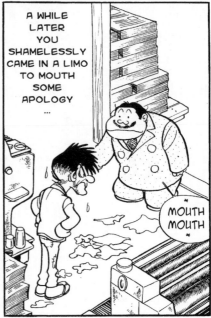

A WHILE LATER YOU SHAMELESSLY CAME IN A LIMO TO MOUTH SOME APOLOGY ...
* MOUTH MOUTH *
SAYING WE SHOULD CO-MANAGE! JUST TO TAKE OVER THE BUSINESS, I'M SURE.
B-BROTHER, THAT'S NOT WHAT I HAD IN MIND ...
MY REPLY IS STILL NO!
IT DOESN'T COMPARE!
THAT'S NOT WHY ...
I'LL PROTECT DAD'S FACTORY IF IT MEANS MY LIFE!
I'M HERE TODAY.
I HEARD YOU'RE SICK.
SO WHAT IF YOU DID?
YOU'RE NOT A DOCTOR, YOU CAN'T CURE ME!
AFTER TWO SURGERIES, I'M STILL DYING!

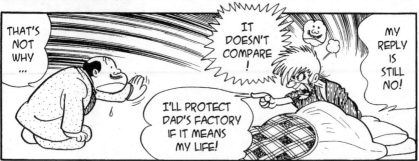

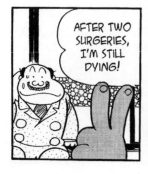

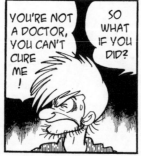

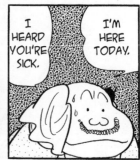

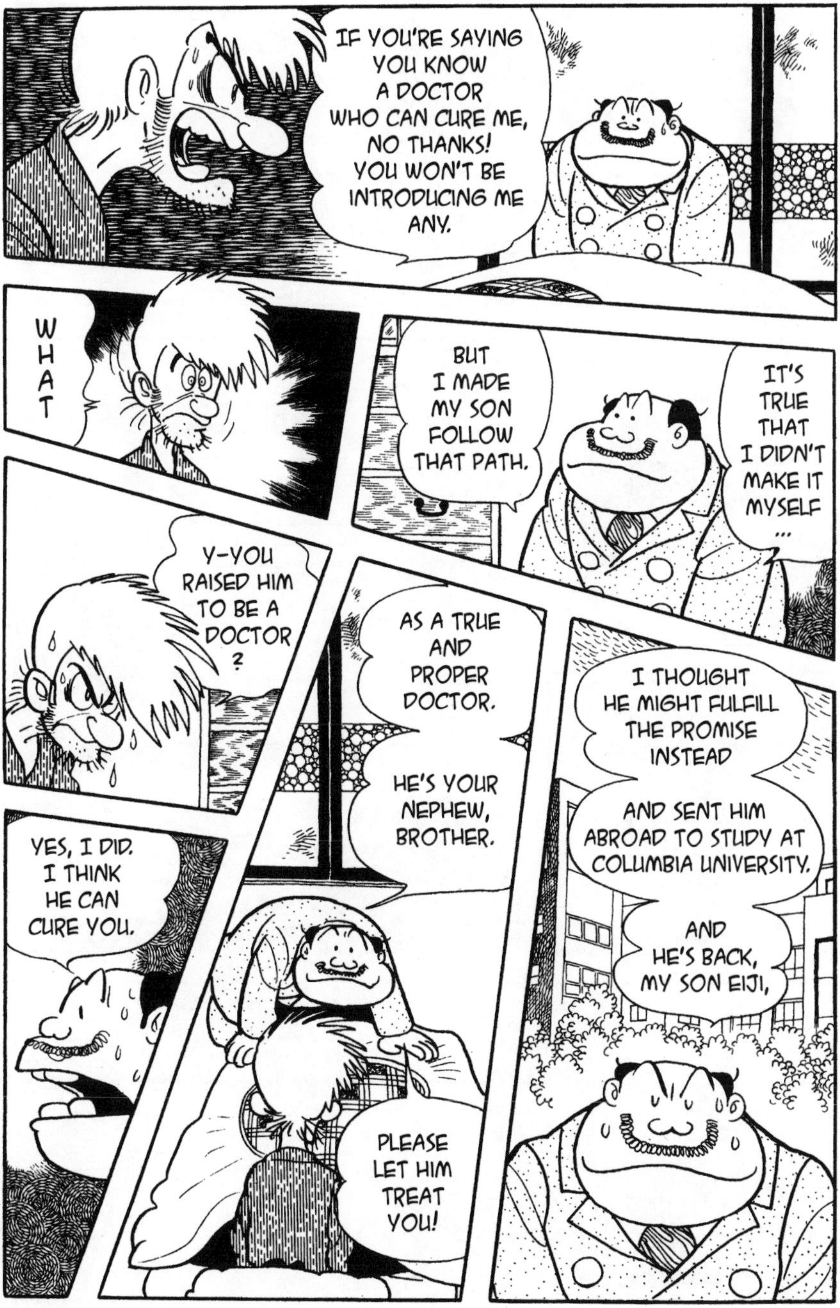

IF YOU'RE SAYING YOU KNOW A DOCTOR WHO CAN CURE ME, NO THANKS! YOU WON'T BE INTRODUCING ME ANY.
IT'S TRUE THAT I DIDN'T MAKE IT MYSELF ...
BUT I MADE MY SON FOLLOW THAT PATH.
WHAT
I THOUGHT HE MIGHT FULFILL THE PROMISE INSTEAD
AND SENT HIM ABROAD TO STUDY AT COLUMBIA UNIVERSITY.
AND HE'S BACK, MY SON EIJI,
AS A TRUE AND PROPER DOCTOR.
HE'S YOUR NEPHEW, BROTHER.
PLEASE LET HIM TREAT YOU!
Y-YOU RAISED HIM TO BE A DOCTOR?
YES, I DID. I THINK HE CAN CURE YOU.

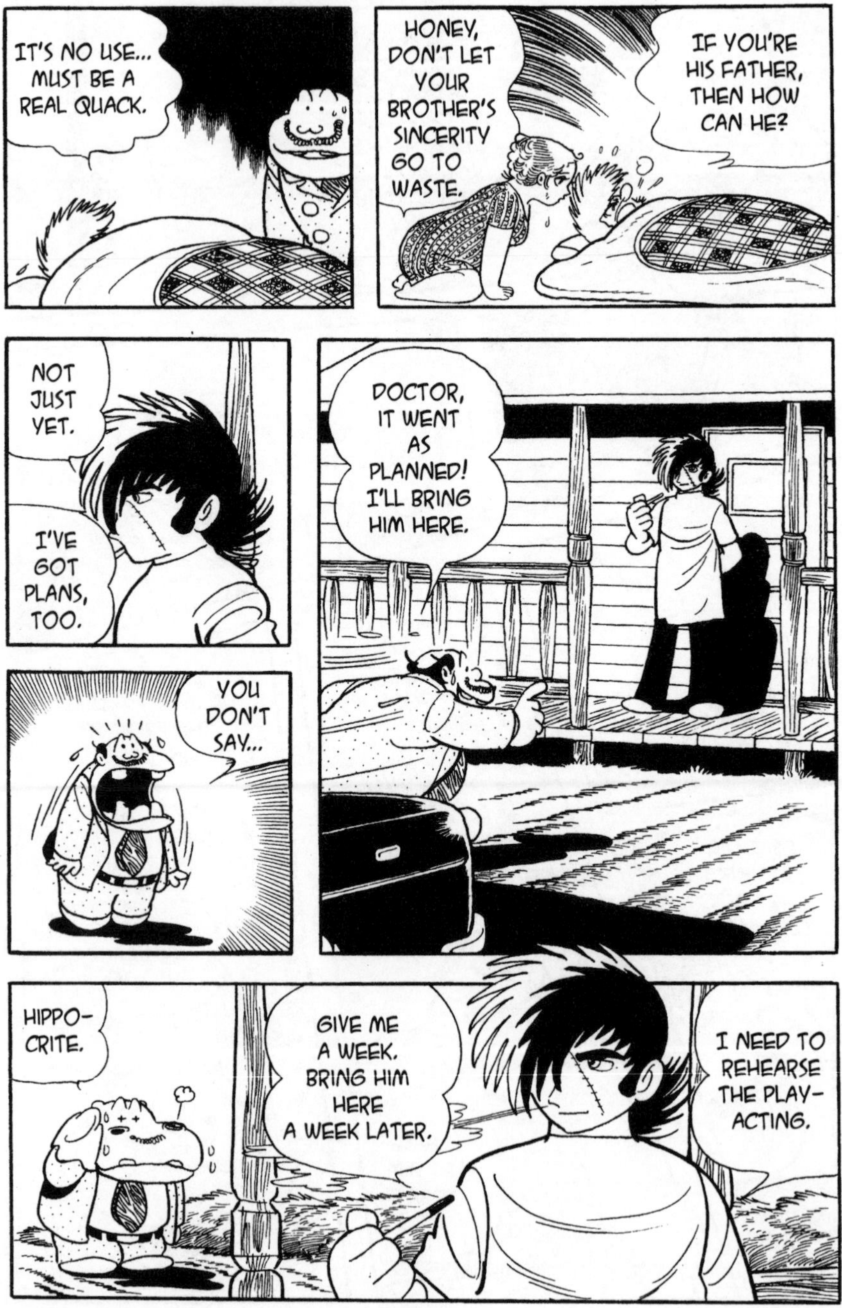
IF YOU'RE HIS FATHER, THEN HOW CAN HE?
HONEY, DON'T LET YOUR BROTHER'S SINCERITY GO TO WASTE.
IT'S NO USE... MUST BE A REAL QUACK.
DOCTOR, IT WENT AS PLANNED! I'LL BRING HIM HERE.
NOT JUST YET.
I'VE GOT PLANS, TOO.
YOU DON'T SAY...
I NEED TO REHEARSE THE PLAY-ACTING.
GIVE ME A WEEK. BRING HIM HERE A WEEK LATER.
HIPPO-CRITE.

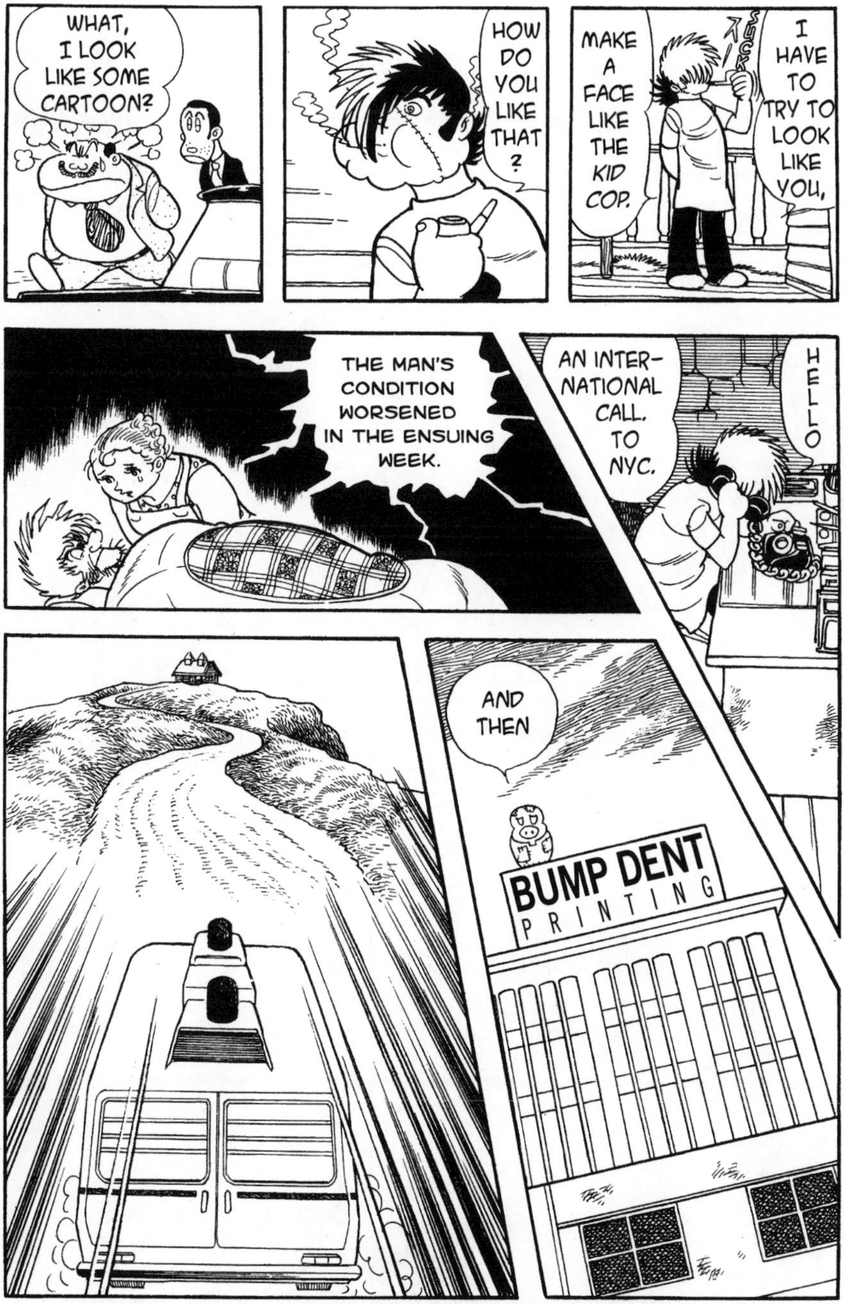
I HAVE TO TRY TO LOOK LIKE YOU,
MAKE A FACE LIKE THE KID COP.
SUCK
HOW DO YOU LIKE THAT?
WHAT, I LOOK LIKE SOME CARTOON?
HELLO
AN INTER-NATIONAL CALL. TO NYC.
THE MAN'S CONDITION WORSENED IN THE ENSUING WEEK.
AND THEN
BUMP DENT PRINTING

NOTE: "GAKI DEKA" (OR KID COP) WAS THE HERO OF AN EPONYMOUS GAG MANGA BY TATSUHIKO YAMAGAMI THAT RAN CONCURRENTLY IN *WEEKLY CHAMPION*.

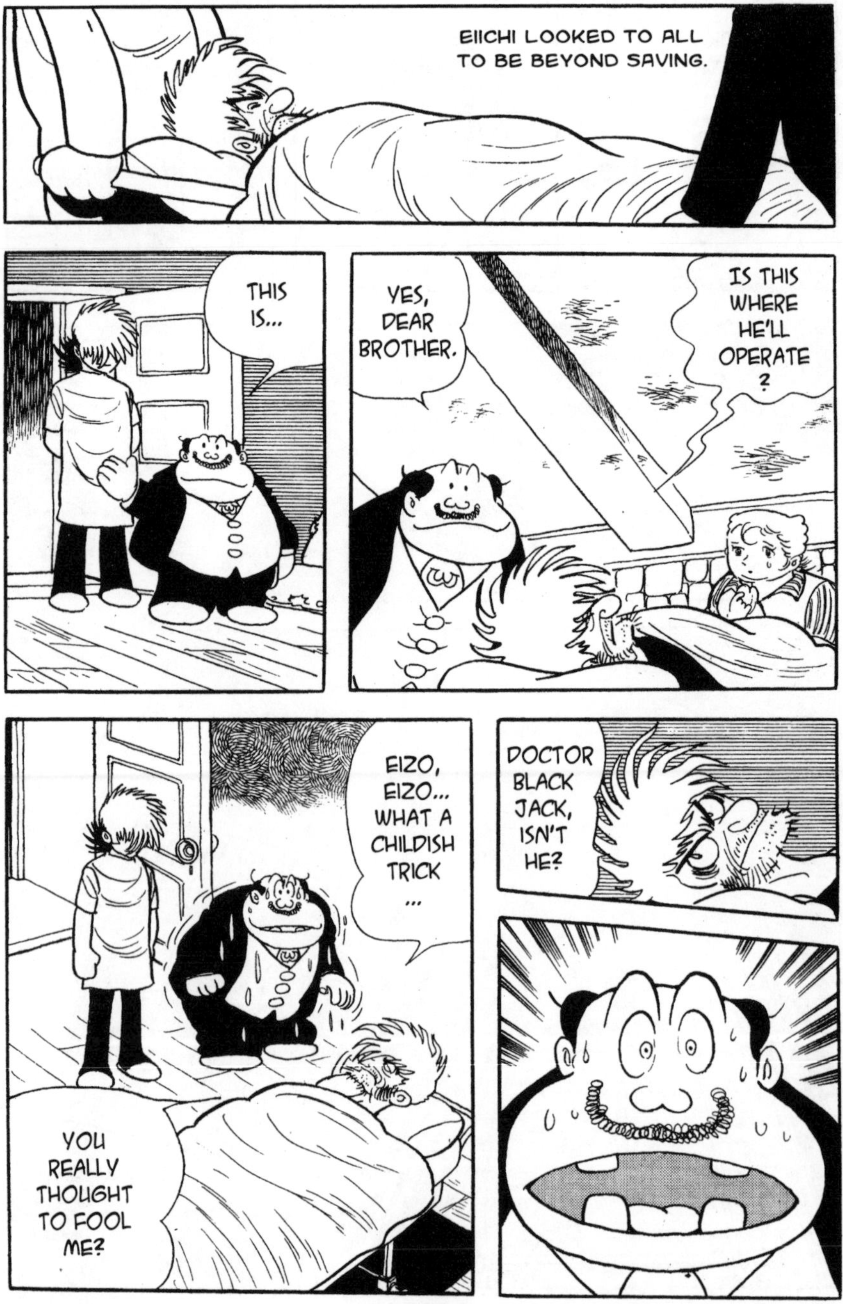
EIICHI LOOKED TO ALL TO BE BEYOND SAVING.
IS THIS WHERE HE'LL OPERATE ?
YES, DEAR BROTHER.
THIS IS...
DOCTOR BLACK JACK, ISN'T HE?
EIZO, EIZO... WHAT A CHILDISH TRICK ...
YOU REALLY THOUGHT TO FOOL ME?

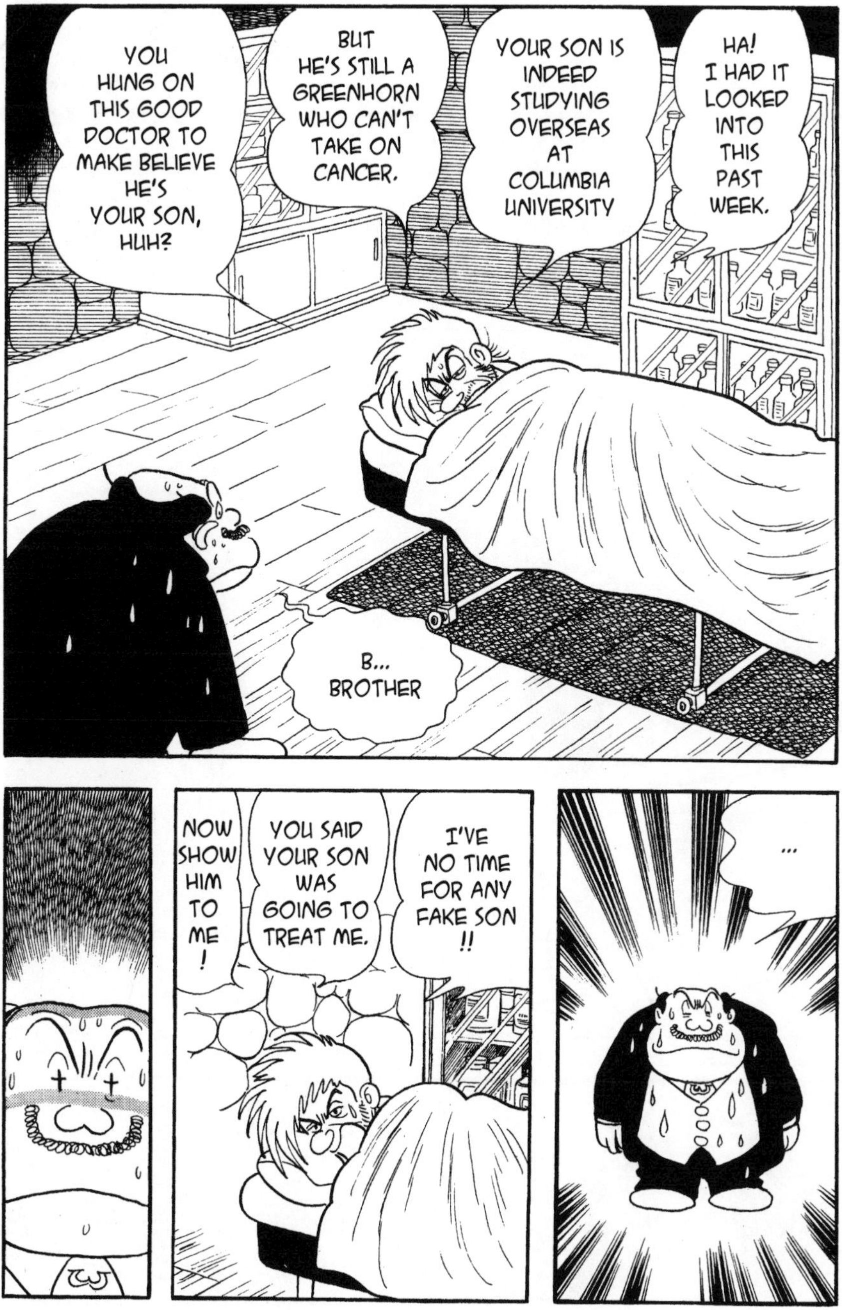
HA! I HAD IT LOOKED INTO THIS PAST WEEK.
YOUR SON IS INDEED STUDYING OVERSEAS AT COLUMBIA UNIVERSITY
BUT HE'S STILL A GREENHORN WHO CAN'T TAKE ON CANCER.
YOU HUNG ON THIS GOOD DOCTOR TO MAKE BELIEVE HE'S YOUR SON, HUH?
B... BROTHER
...
I'VE NO TIME FOR ANY FAKE SON !!
YOU SAID YOUR SON WAS GOING TO TREAT ME.
NOW SHOW HIM TO ME !

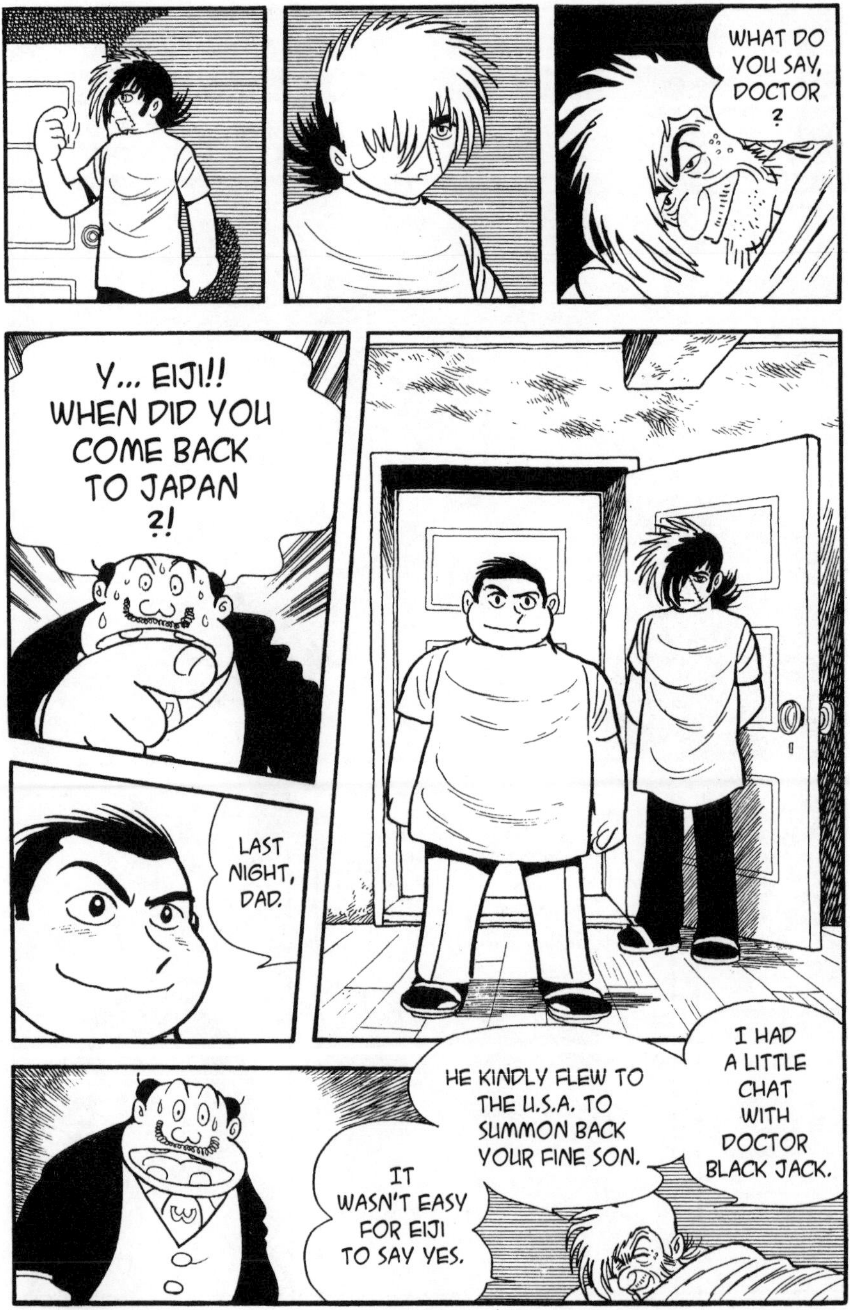
WHAT DO YOU SAY, DOCTOR ?
Y... EIJI!! WHEN DID YOU COME BACK TO JAPAN ?!
LAST NIGHT, DAD.
I HAD A LITTLE CHAT WITH DOCTOR BLACK JACK.
HE KINDLY FLEW TO THE U.S.A. TO SUMMON BACK YOUR FINE SON.
IT WASN'T EASY FOR EIJI TO SAY YES.

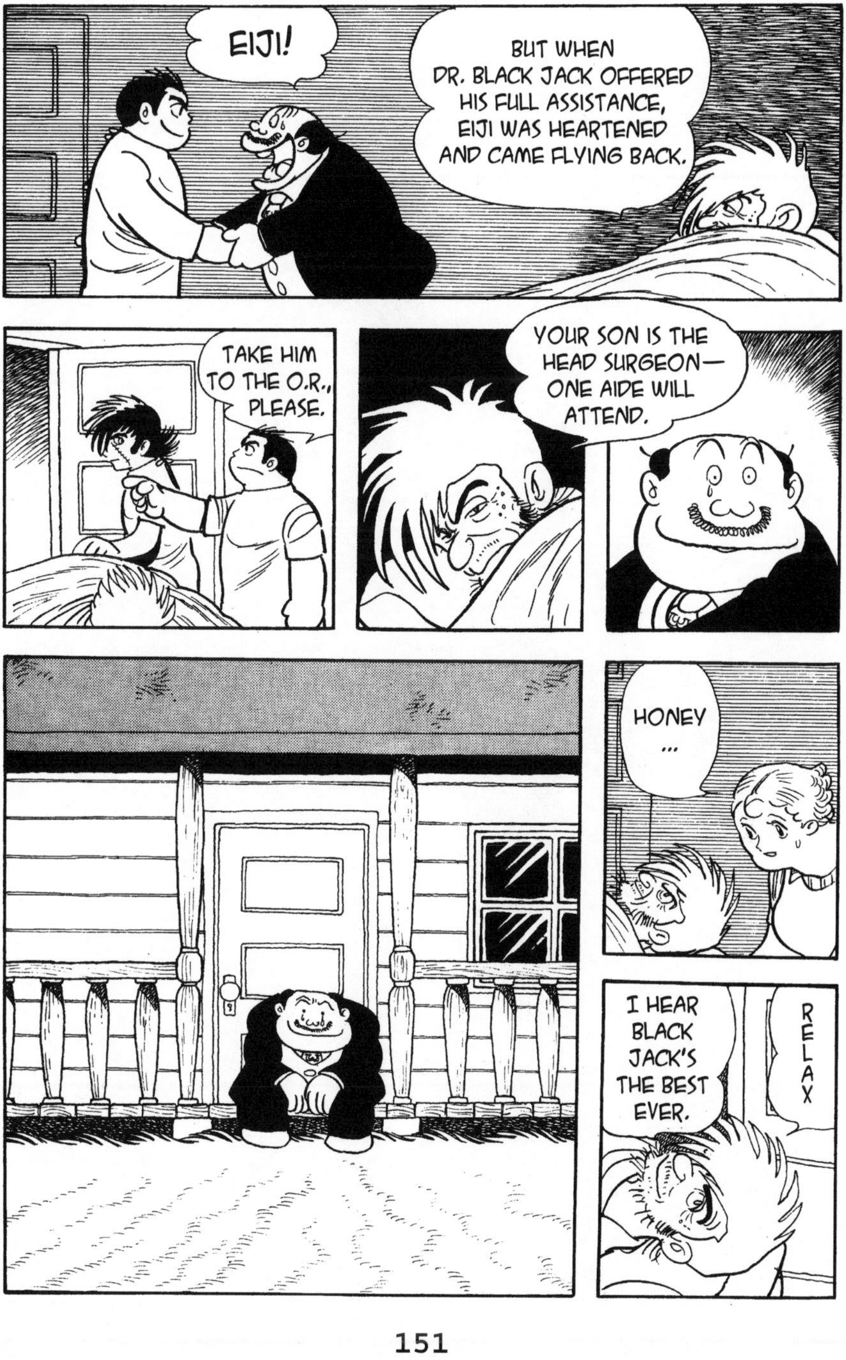
BUT WHEN DR. BLACK JACK OFFERED HIS FULL ASSISTANCE, EIJI WAS HEARTENED AND CAME FLYING BACK.
EIJI!
YOUR SON IS THE HEAD SURGEON— ONE AIDE WILL ATTEND.
TAKE HIM TO THE O.R., PLEASE.
HONEY ...
RELAX
I HEAR BLACK JACK'S THE BEST EVER.

HIGH AND LOW

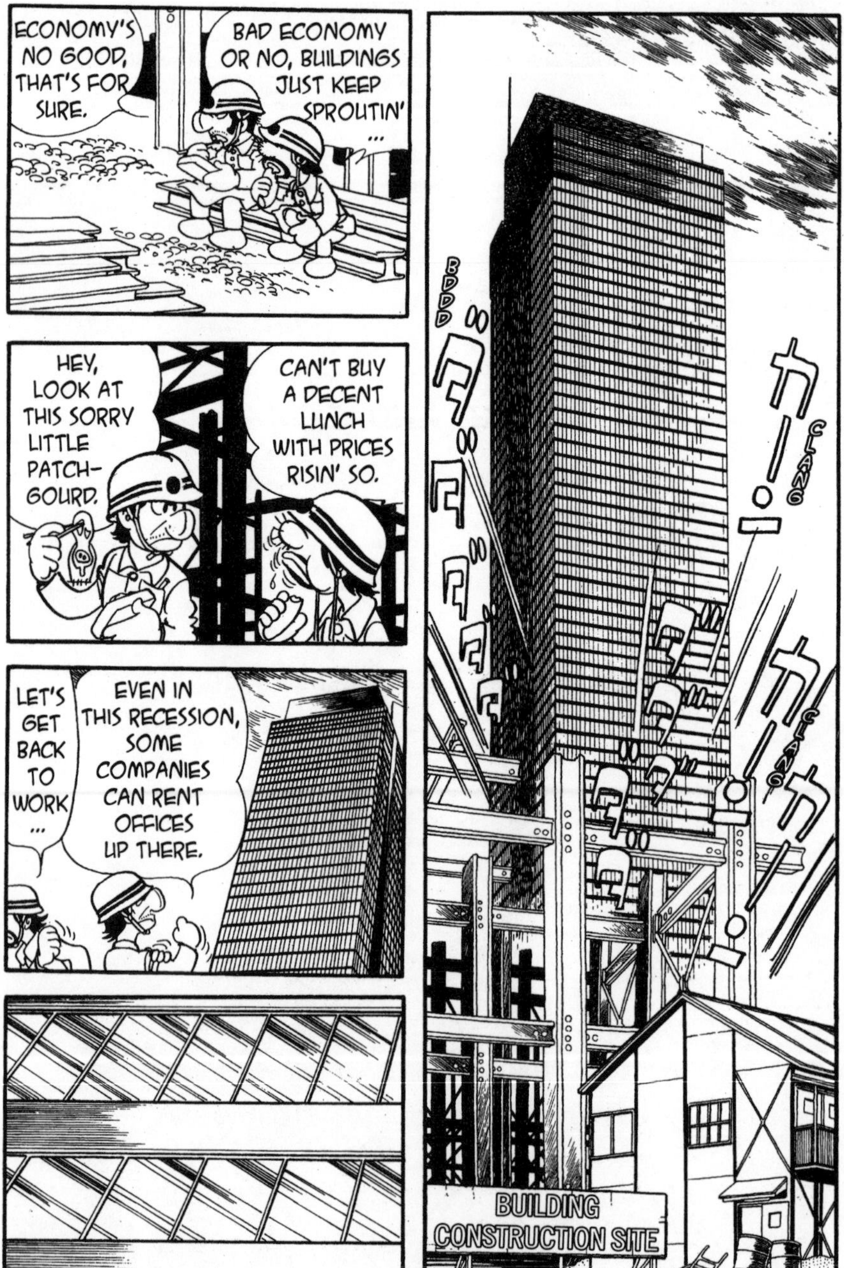
BDDD
CLANG
CLANG
BUILDING CONSTRUCTION SITE
BAD ECONOMY OR NO, BUILDINGS JUST KEEP SPROUTIN' ...
ECONOMY'S NO GOOD, THAT'S FOR SURE.
CAN'T BUY A DECENT LUNCH WITH PRICES RISIN' SO.
HEY, LOOK AT THIS SORRY LITTLE PATCH-GOURD.
EVEN IN THIS RECESSION, SOME COMPANIES CAN RENT OFFICES UP THERE.
LET'S GET BACK TO WORK ...

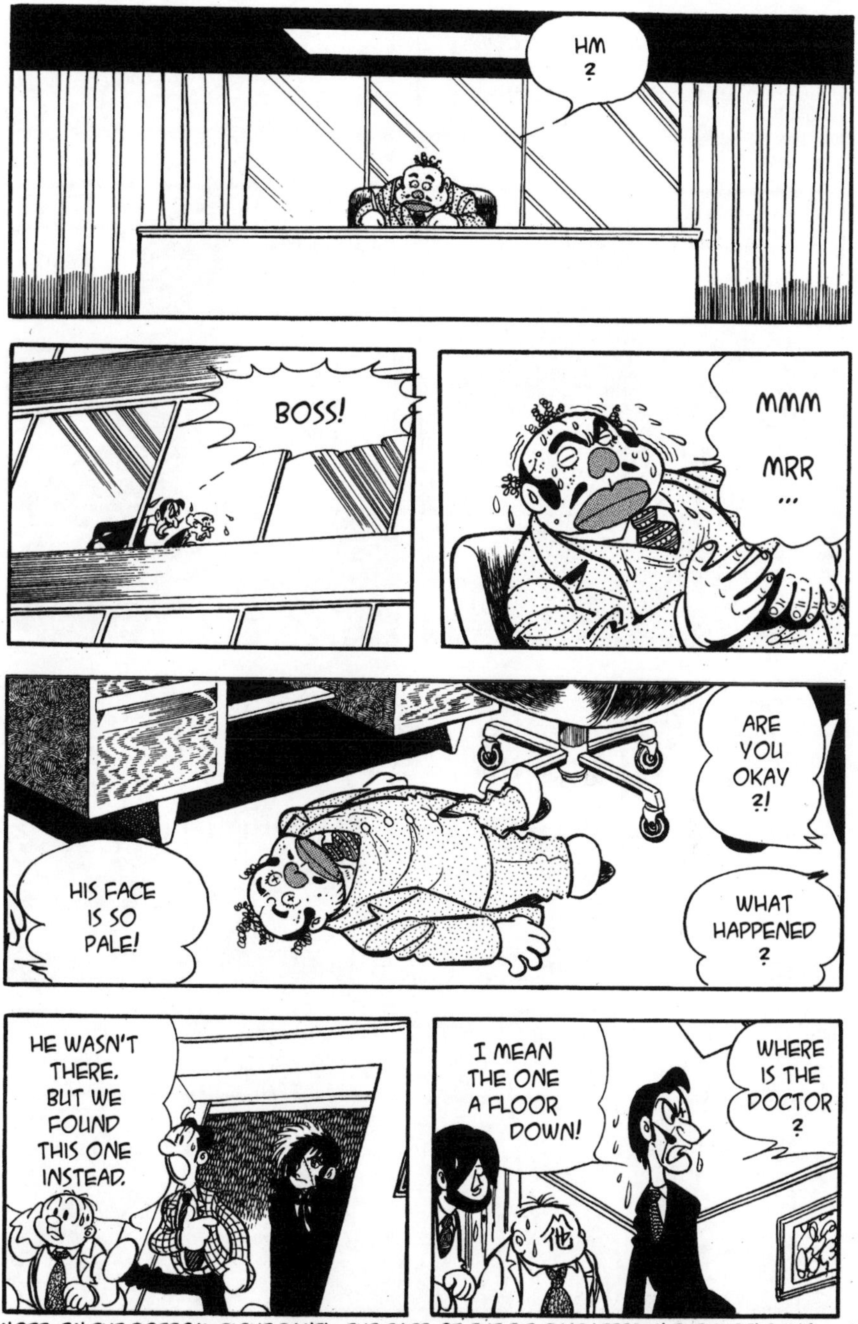
HM ?
MMM MRR ...
BOSS!
ARE YOU OKAY ?!
WHAT HAPPENED ?
HIS FACE IS SO PALE!
WHERE IS THE DOCTOR ?
I MEAN THE ONE A FLOOR DOWN!
HE WASN'T THERE. BUT WE FOUND THIS ONE INSTEAD.

NOTE: IN THE BOTTOM-RIGHT PANEL, THE FACE OF THE BIT CHARACTER IN THE MIDDLE HAS THE IDEOGRAM "TA" OR OTHER UNDERNEATH AN ICON FOR "YAMA" OR *MOUNTAIN*. THUS, DESPITE THE UNUSUAL WAY IT'S RENDERED, HIS NAME IS THE VERY COMMON "YAMADA."

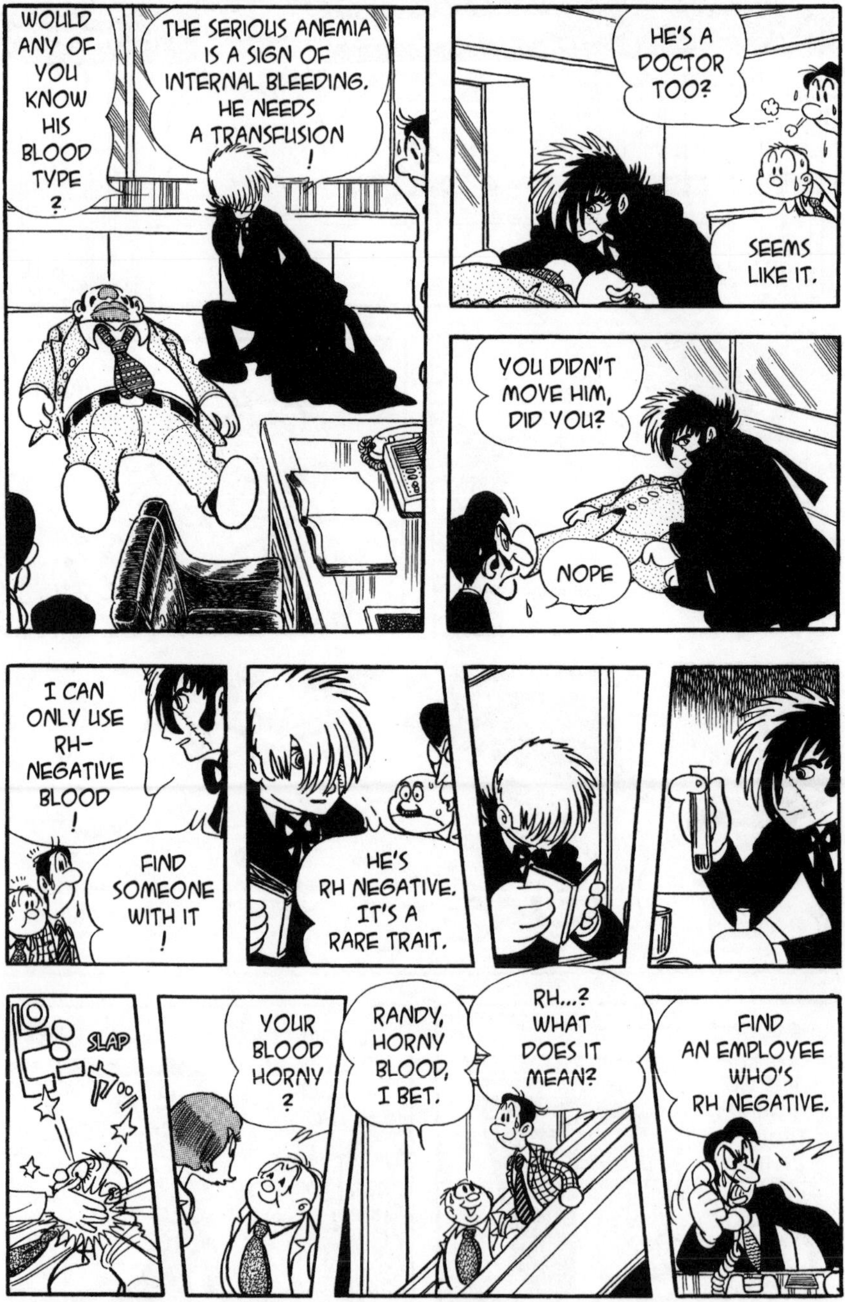
HE'S A DOCTOR TOO?
SEEMS LIKE IT.
YOU DIDN'T MOVE HIM, DID YOU?
NOPE
THE SERIOUS ANEMIA IS A SIGN OF INTERNAL BLEEDING. HE NEEDS A TRANSFUSION!
WOULD ANY OF YOU KNOW HIS BLOOD TYPE?
HE'S RH NEGATIVE. IT'S A RARE TRAIT.
I CAN ONLY USE RH-NEGATIVE BLOOD!
FIND SOMEONE WITH IT!
FIND AN EMPLOYEE WHO'S RH NEGATIVE.
RH...? WHAT DOES IT MEAN?
RANDY, HORNY BLOOD, I BET.
YOUR BLOOD HORNY?
SLAP

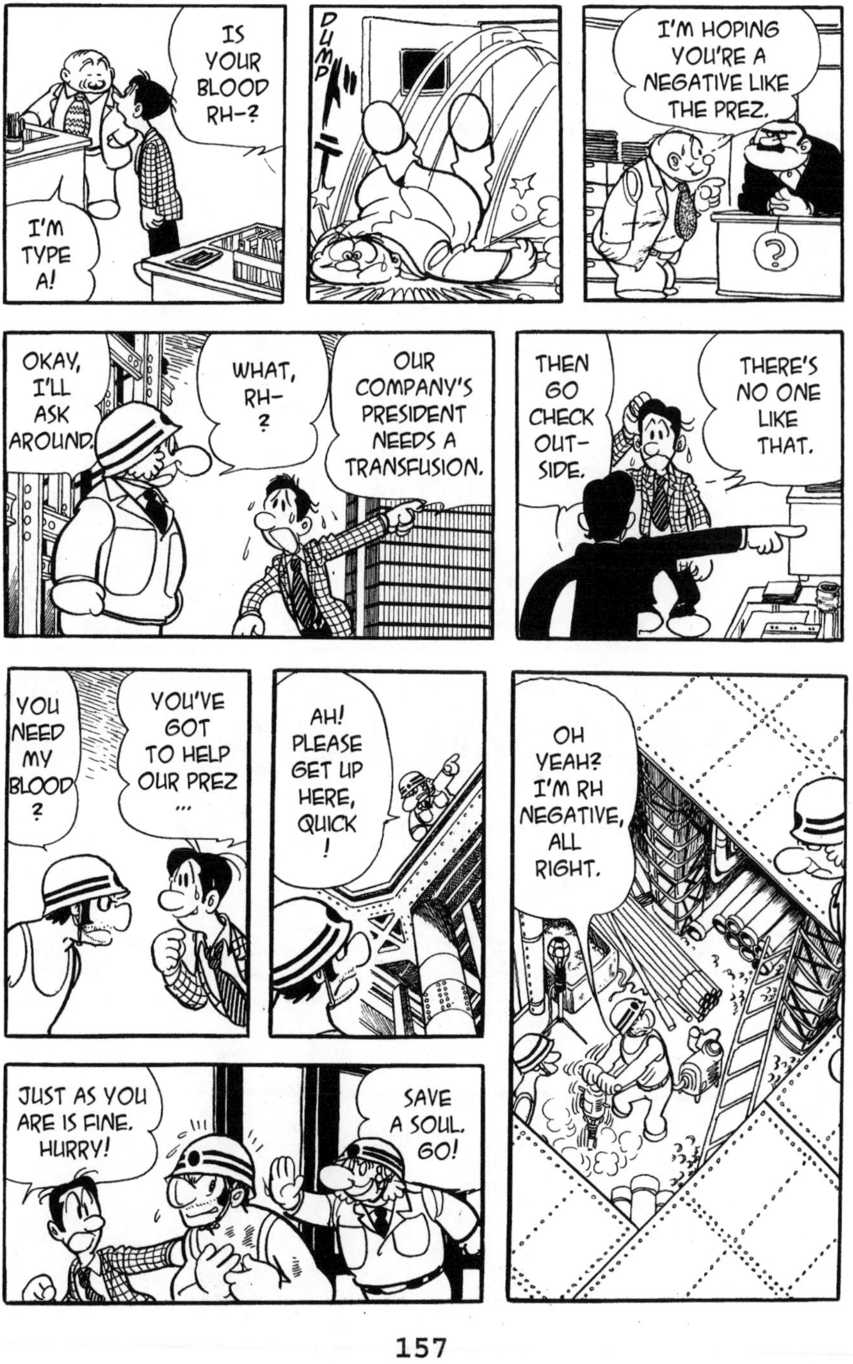
I'M HOPING YOU'RE A NEGATIVE LIKE THE PREZ.
DUMP
IS YOUR BLOOD RH-?
I'M TYPE A!
THERE'S NO ONE LIKE THAT.
THEN GO CHECK OUT-SIDE.
OUR COMPANY'S PRESIDENT NEEDS A TRANSFUSION.
WHAT, RH-?
OKAY, I'LL ASK AROUND.
OH YEAH? I'M RH NEGATIVE, ALL RIGHT.
AH! PLEASE GET UP HERE, QUICK!
YOU'VE GOT TO HELP OUR PREZ ...
YOU NEED MY BLOOD?
SAVE A SOUL. GO!
JUST AS YOU ARE IS FINE. HURRY!

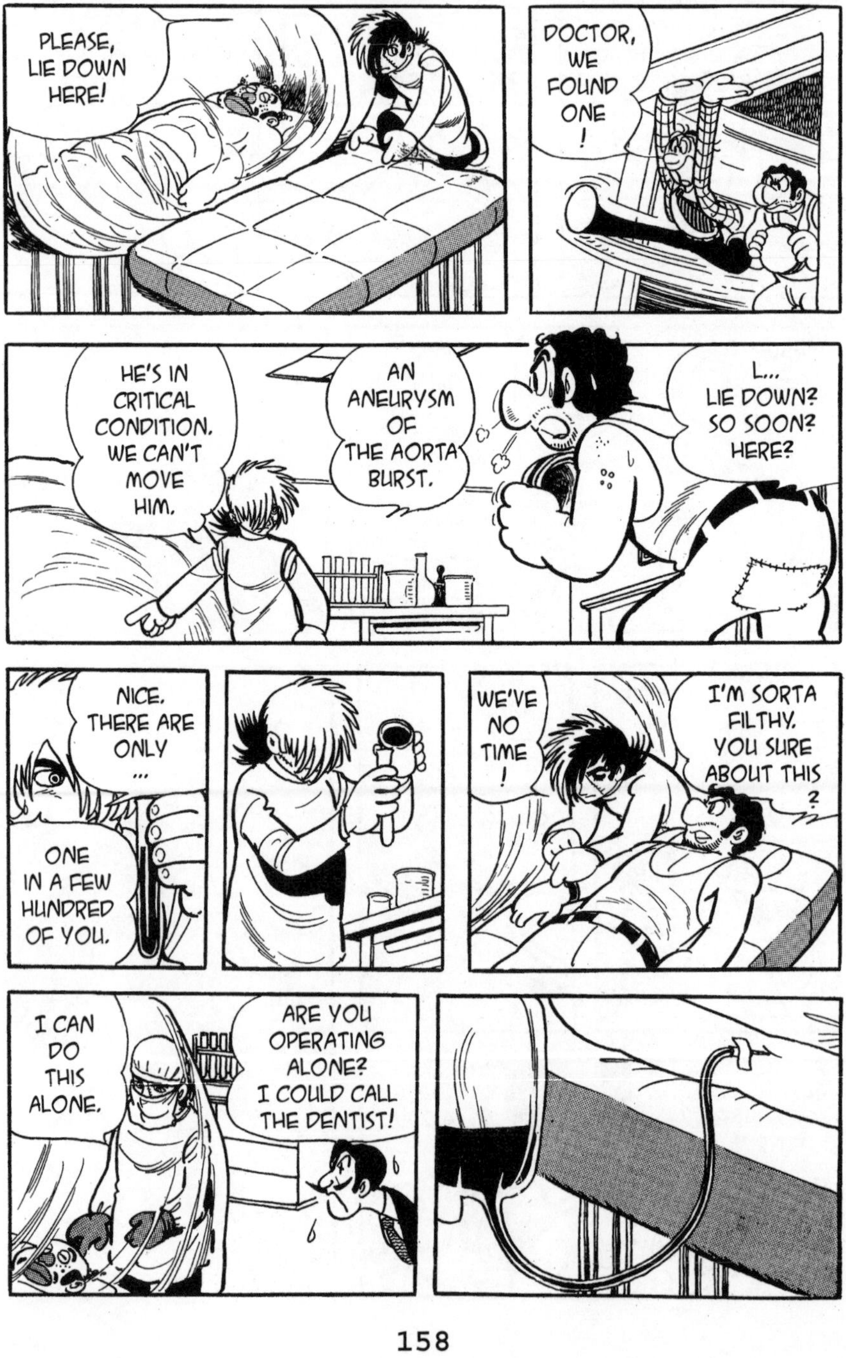
DOCTOR, WE FOUND ONE!
PLEASE, LIE DOWN HERE!
L... LIE DOWN? SO SOON? HERE?
AN ANEURYSM OF THE AORTA BURST.
HE'S IN CRITICAL CONDITION. WE CAN'T MOVE HIM.
I'M SORTA FILTHY. YOU SURE ABOUT THIS?
WE'VE NO TIME!
NICE. THERE ARE ONLY ...
ONE IN A FEW HUNDRED OF YOU.
ARE YOU OPERATING ALONE? I COULD CALL THE DENTIST!
I CAN DO THIS ALONE.

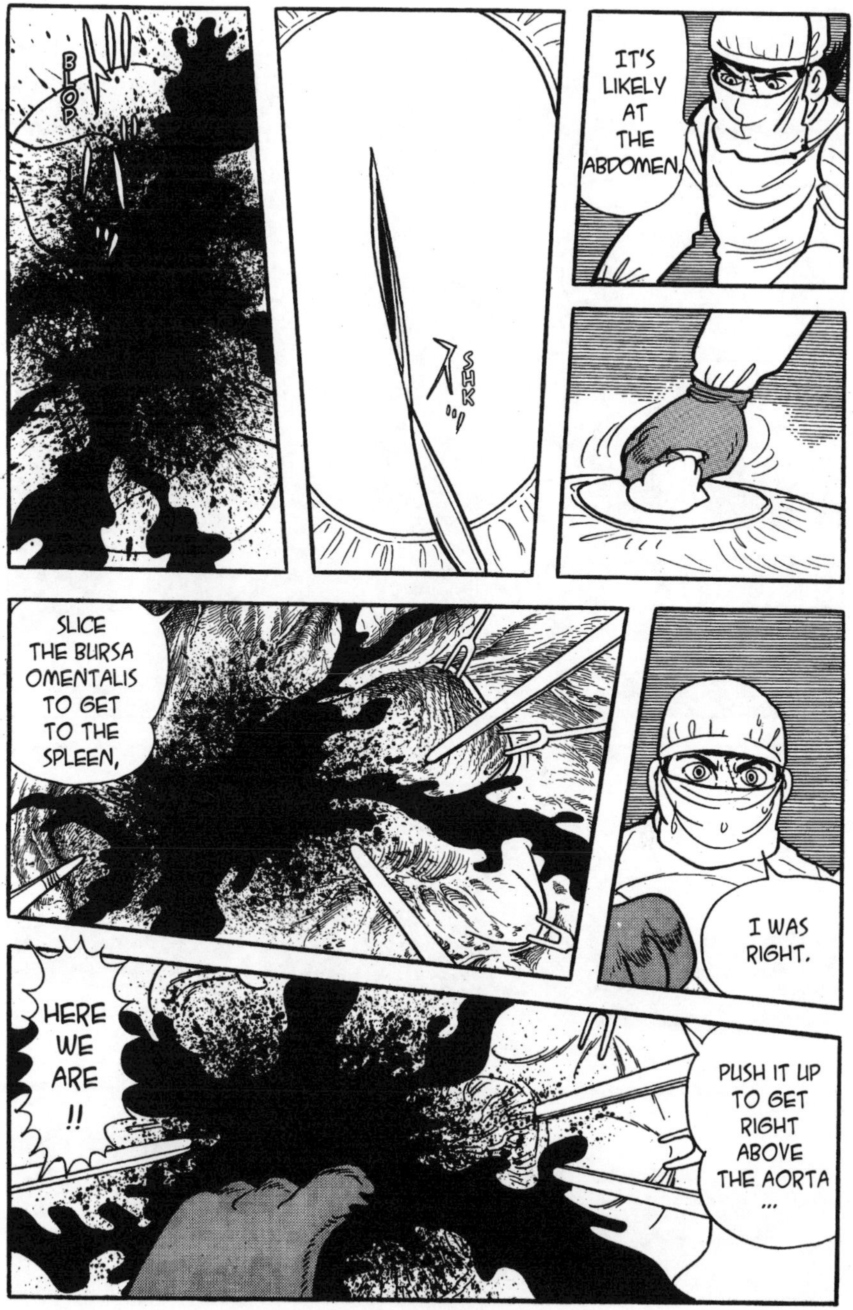
IT'S LIKELY AT THE ABDOMEN,
SHK
BLOP
I WAS RIGHT.
SLICE THE BURSA OMENTALIS TO GET TO THE SPLEEN,
PUSH IT UP TO GET RIGHT ABOVE THE AORTA ...
HERE WE ARE !!

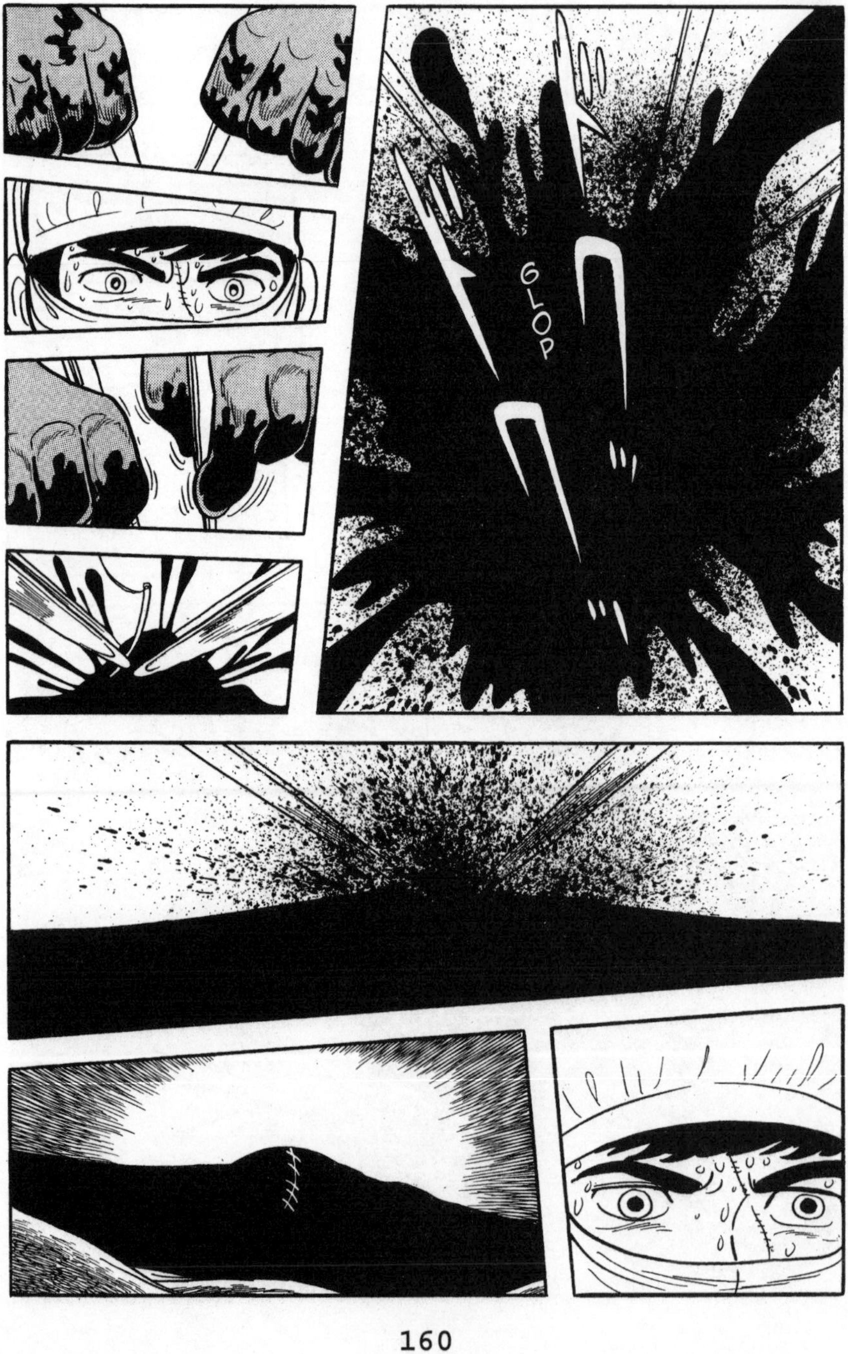
GLOP

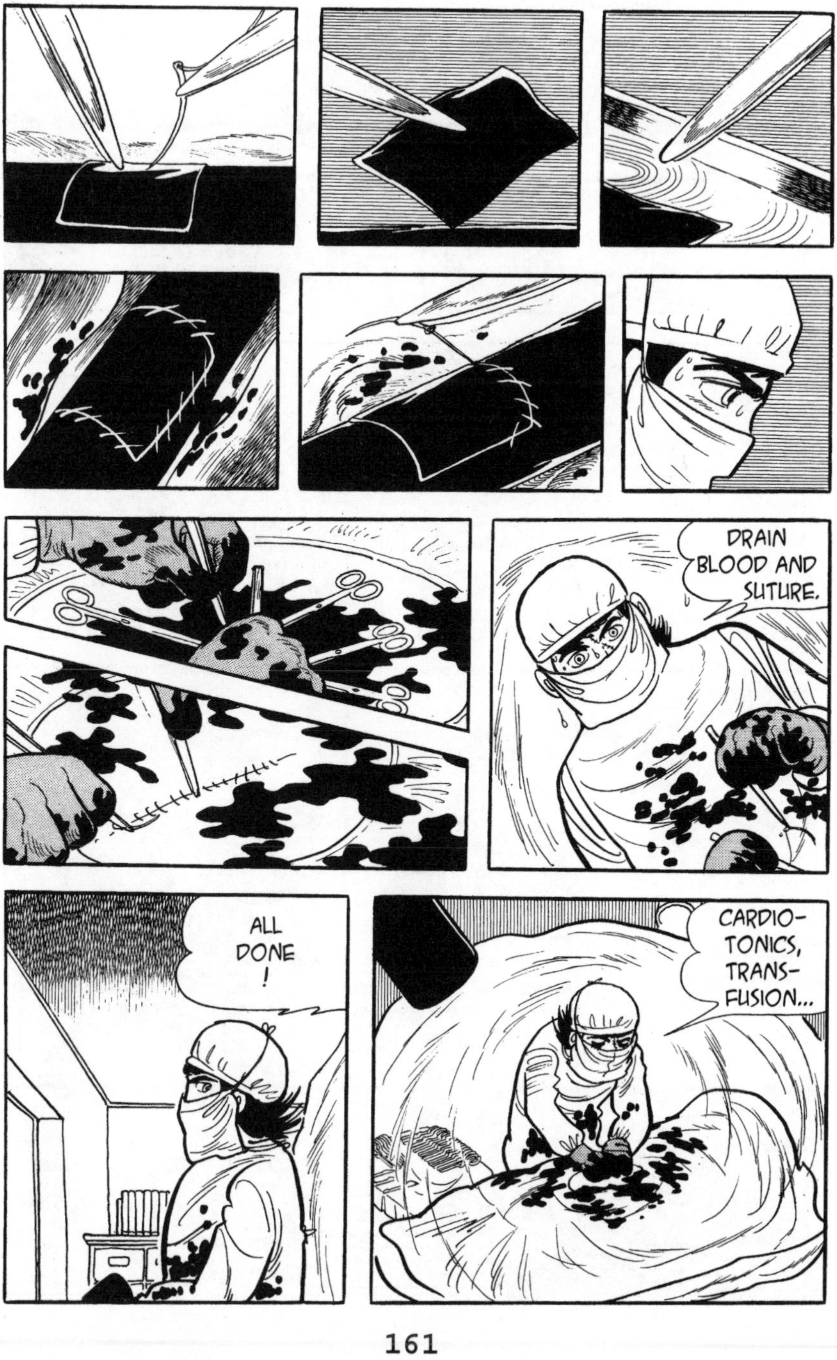
DRAIN BLOOD AND SUTURE.
CARDIO-TONICS, TRANS-FUSION...
ALL DONE!

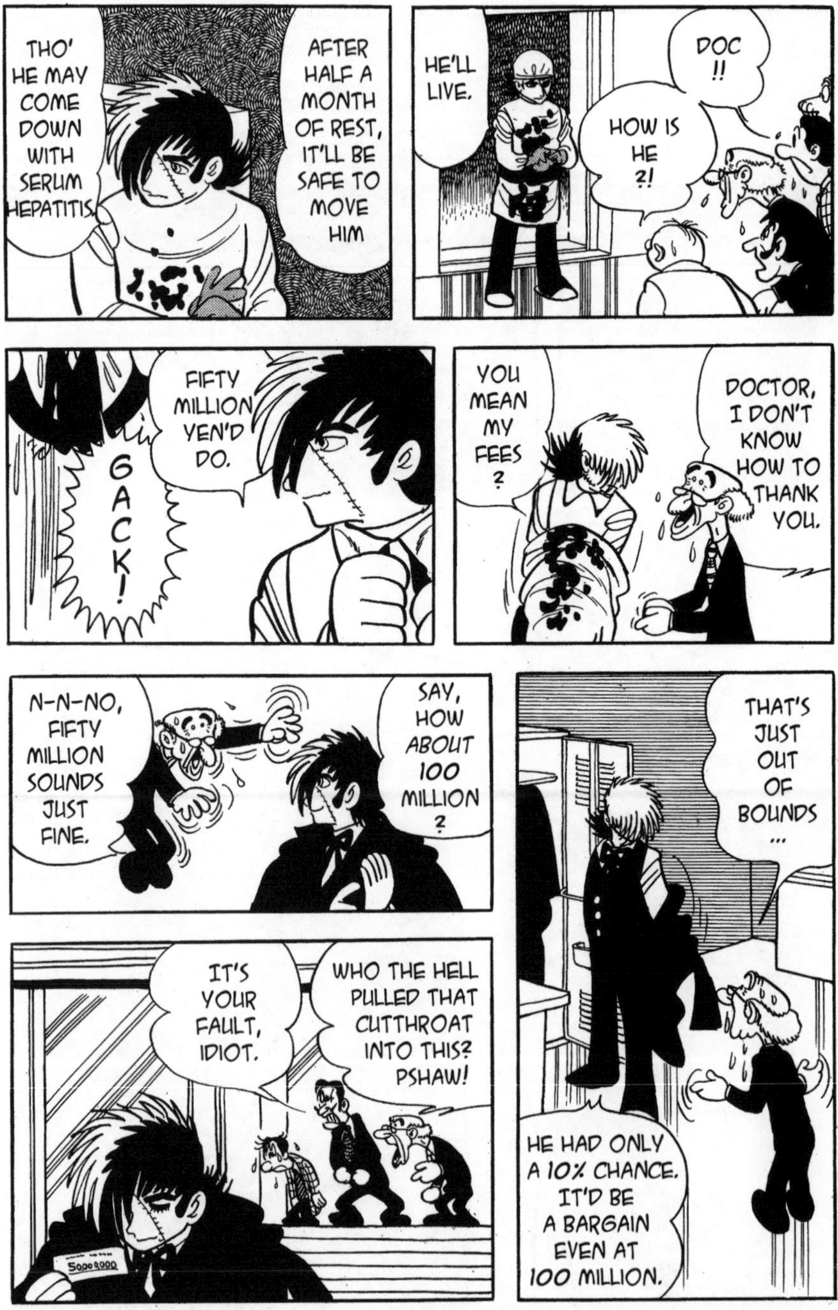
DOC !!
HOW IS HE ?!
HE'LL LIVE.
AFTER HALF A MONTH OF REST, IT'LL BE SAFE TO MOVE HIM
THO' HE MAY COME DOWN WITH SERUM HEPATITIS.
DOCTOR, I DON'T KNOW HOW TO THANK YOU.
YOU MEAN MY FEES ?
FIFTY MILLION YEN'D DO.
GACK!
THAT'S JUST OUT OF BOUNDS ...
HE HAD ONLY A 10% CHANCE. IT'D BE A BARGAIN EVEN AT 100 MILLION.
SAY, HOW ABOUT 100 MILLION ?
N-N-NO, FIFTY MILLION SOUNDS JUST FINE.
WHO THE HELL PULLED THAT CUTTHROAT INTO THIS? PSHAW!
IT'S YOUR FAULT, IDIOT.

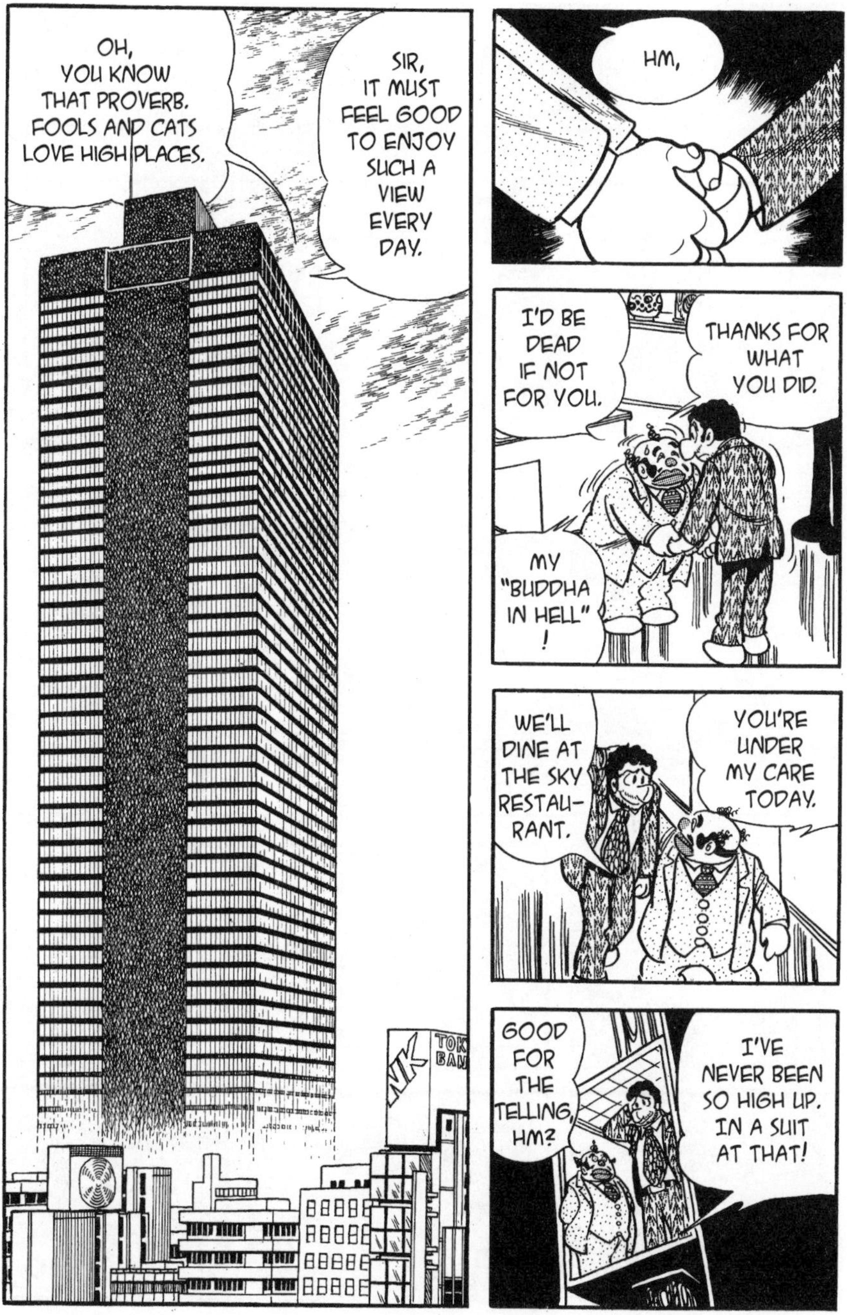
HM,
THANKS FOR WHAT YOU DID.
I'D BE DEAD IF NOT FOR YOU.
MY "BUDDHA IN HELL"!
YOU'RE UNDER MY CARE TODAY.
WE'LL DINE AT THE SKY RESTAU-RANT.
I'VE NEVER BEEN SO HIGH UP. IN A SUIT AT THAT!
GOOD FOR THE TELLING, HM?
SIR, IT MUST FEEL GOOD TO ENJOY SUCH A VIEW EVERY DAY.
OH, YOU KNOW THAT PROVERB. FOOLS AND CATS LOVE HIGH PLACES.

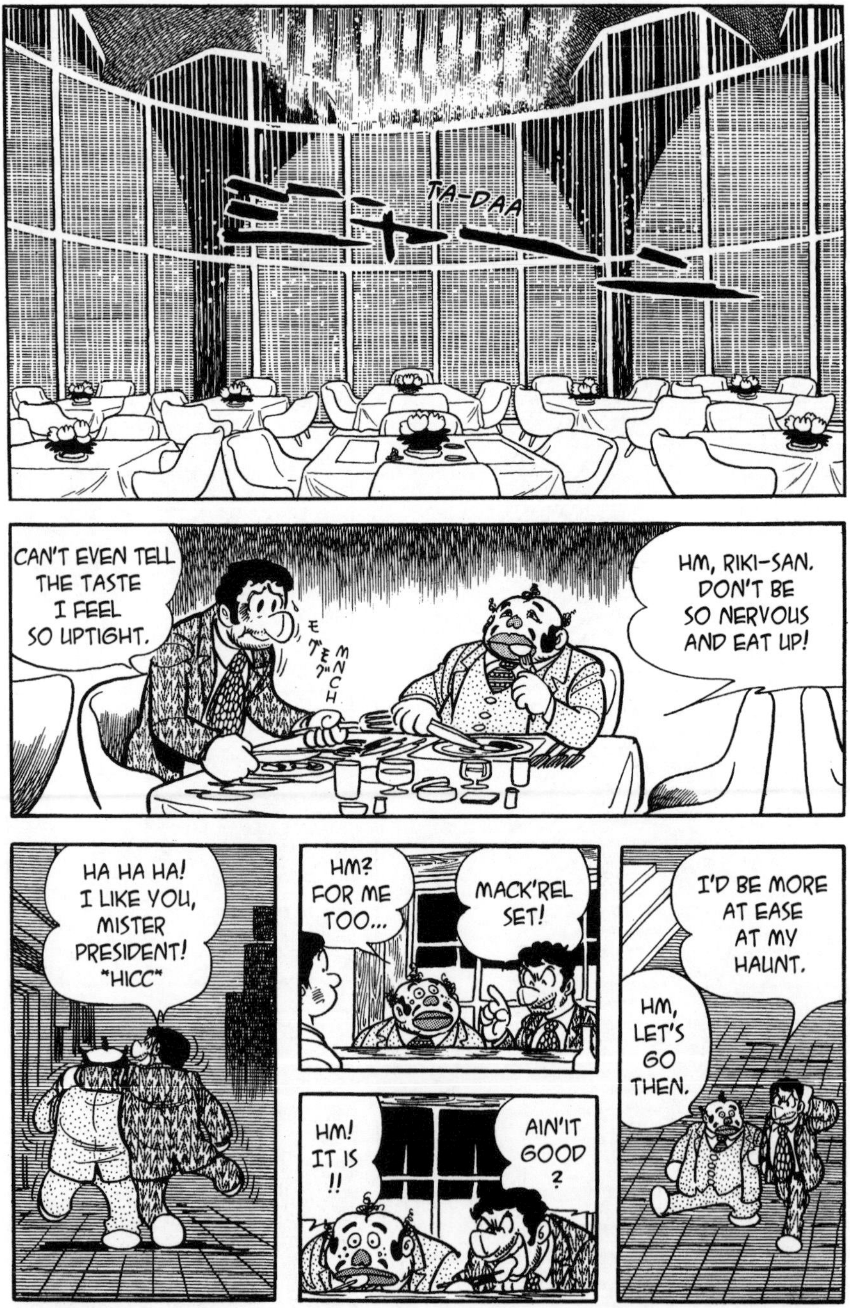
TA-DAA
HM, RIKI-SAN. DON'T BE SO NERVOUS AND EAT UP!
MNCH
CAN'T EVEN TELL THE TASTE I FEEL SO UPTIGHT.
I'D BE MORE AT EASE AT MY HAUNT.
HM, LET'S GO THEN.
MACK'REL SET!
HM? FOR ME TOO...
AIN'IT GOOD ?
HM! IT IS !!
HA HA HA! I LIKE YOU, MISTER PRESIDENT! *HICC*

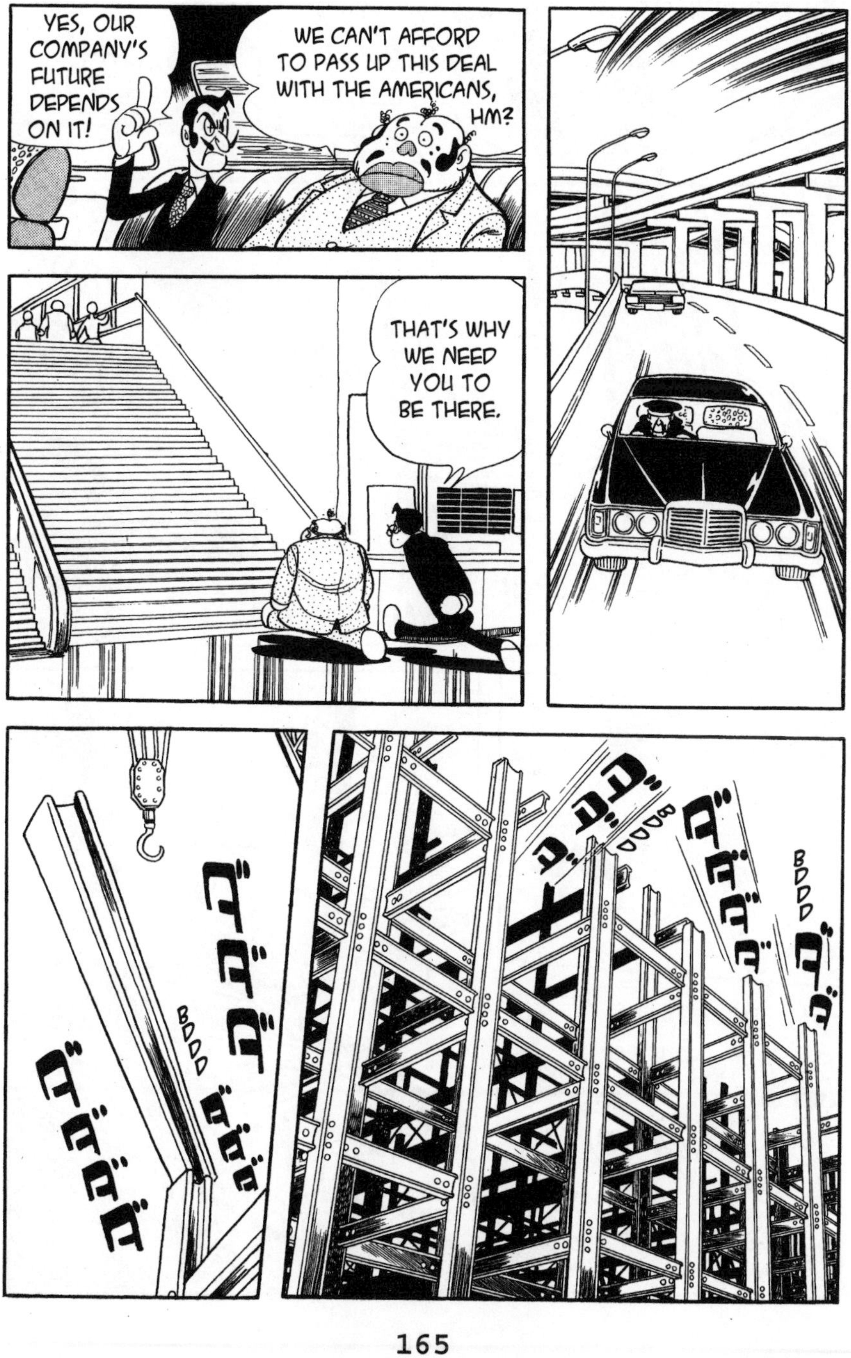
WE CAN'T AFFORD TO PASS UP THIS DEAL WITH THE AMERICANS, HM?
YES, OUR COMPANY'S FUTURE DEPENDS ON IT!
THAT'S WHY WE NEED YOU TO BE THERE.
BDDD
BDDD
BDDD

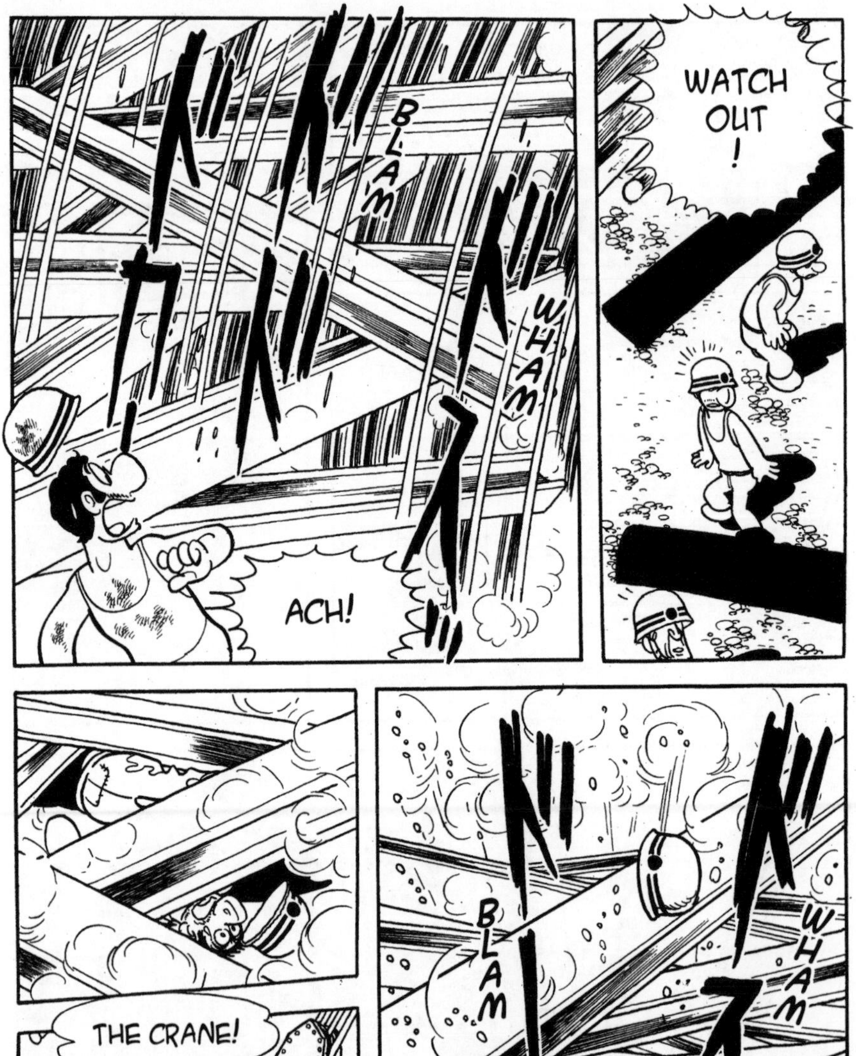
WATCH OUT!
BLAM
WHAM
ACH!
BLAM
WHAM
THE CRANE!

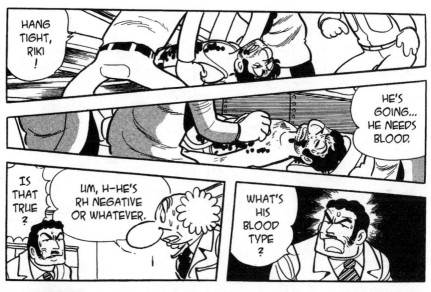

HANG TIGHT, RIKI!
HE'S GOING... HE NEEDS BLOOD.
WHAT'S HIS BLOOD TYPE?
UM, H-HE'S RH NEGATIVE OR WHATEVER.
IS THAT TRUE?
RH-NEGATIVE BLOOD IS QUITE RARE. THANK GOD YOU TOLD ME THAT.
ANYONE HERE WITH THE SAME FACTOR BLOOD?
THE PRESIDENT OF THE COMPANY IN THAT BUILDING!

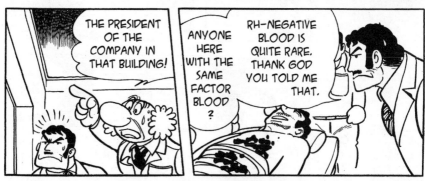

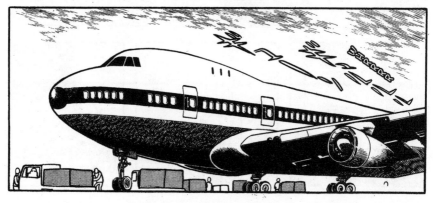

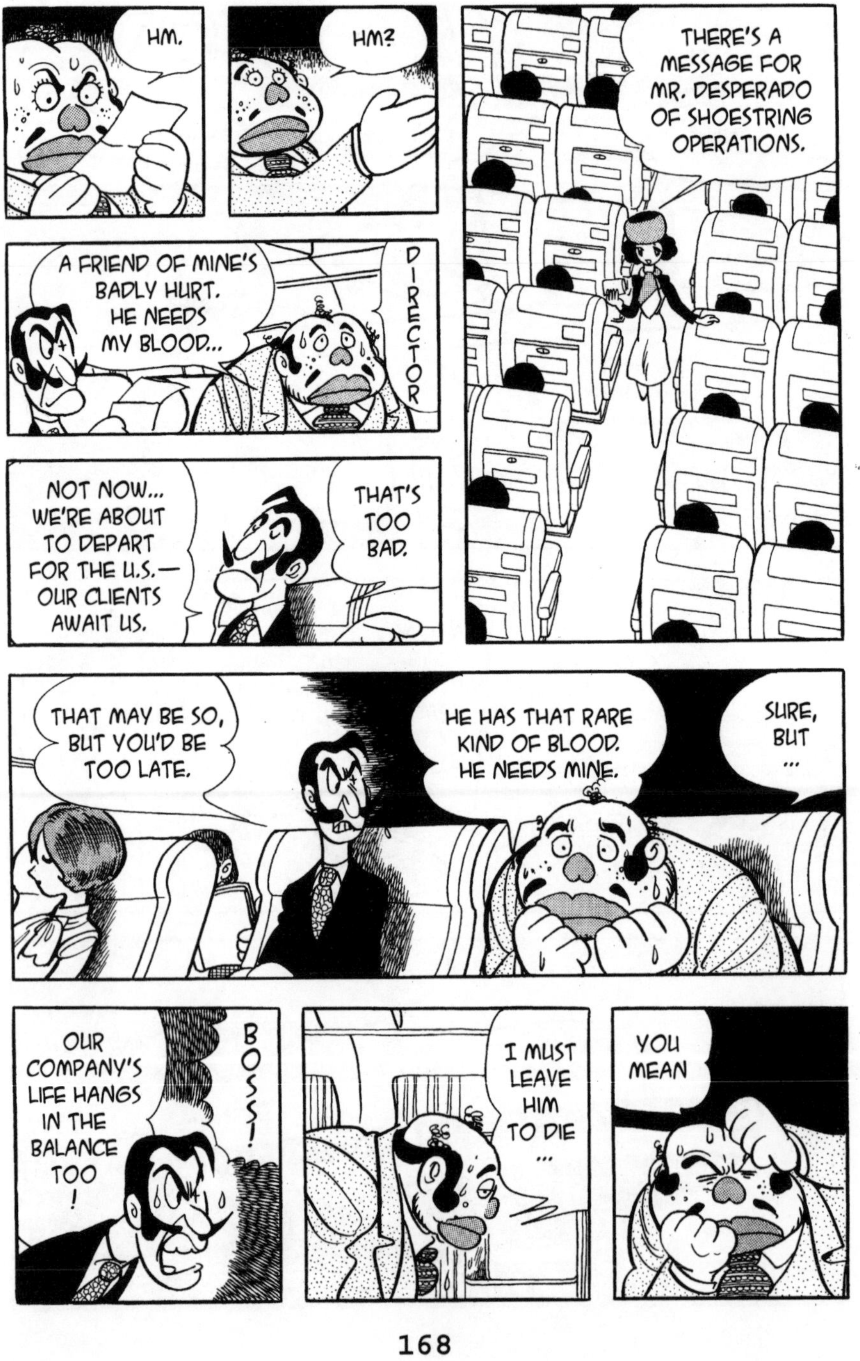
THERE'S A MESSAGE FOR MR. DESPERADO OF SHOESTRING OPERATIONS.
HM?
HM.
DIRECTOR
A FRIEND OF MINE'S BADLY HURT. HE NEEDS MY BLOOD...
THAT'S TOO BAD.
NOT NOW... WE'RE ABOUT TO DEPART FOR THE U.S.— OUR CLIENTS AWAIT US.
SURE, BUT ...
HE HAS THAT RARE KIND OF BLOOD. HE NEEDS MINE.
THAT MAY BE SO, BUT YOU'D BE TOO LATE.
YOU MEAN
I MUST LEAVE HIM TO DIE ...
BOSS!
OUR COMPANY'S LIFE HANGS IN THE BALANCE TOO !

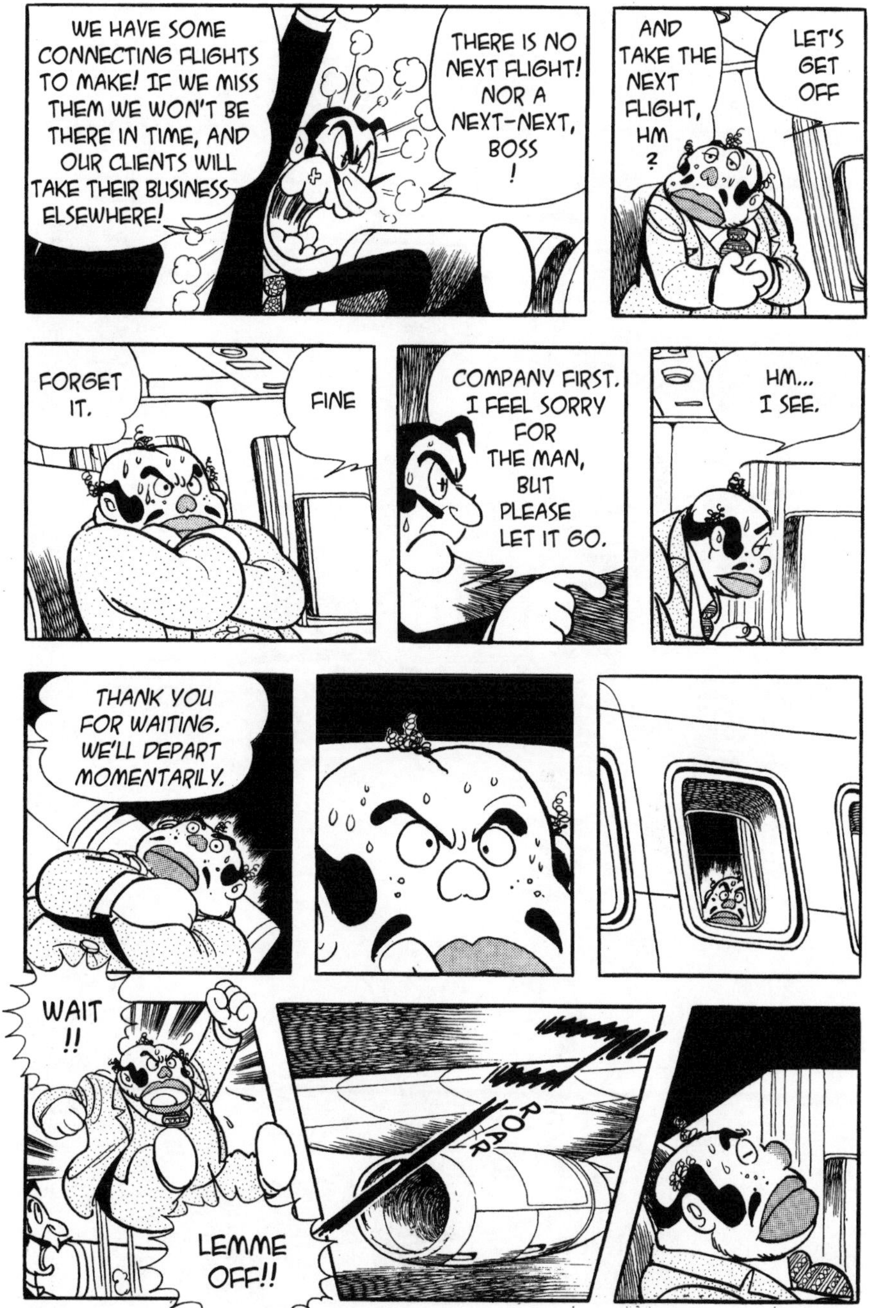
LET'S GET OFF
AND TAKE THE NEXT FLIGHT, HM ?
THERE IS NO NEXT FLIGHT! NOR A NEXT-NEXT, BOSS !
WE HAVE SOME CONNECTING FLIGHTS TO MAKE! IF WE MISS THEM WE WON'T BE THERE IN TIME, AND OUR CLIENTS WILL TAKE THEIR BUSINESS ELSEWHERE!
HM... I SEE.
COMPANY FIRST. I FEEL SORRY FOR THE MAN, BUT PLEASE LET IT GO.
FINE
FORGET IT.
THANK YOU FOR WAITING. WE'LL DEPART MOMENTARILY.
ROAR
WAIT !!
LEMME OFF!!

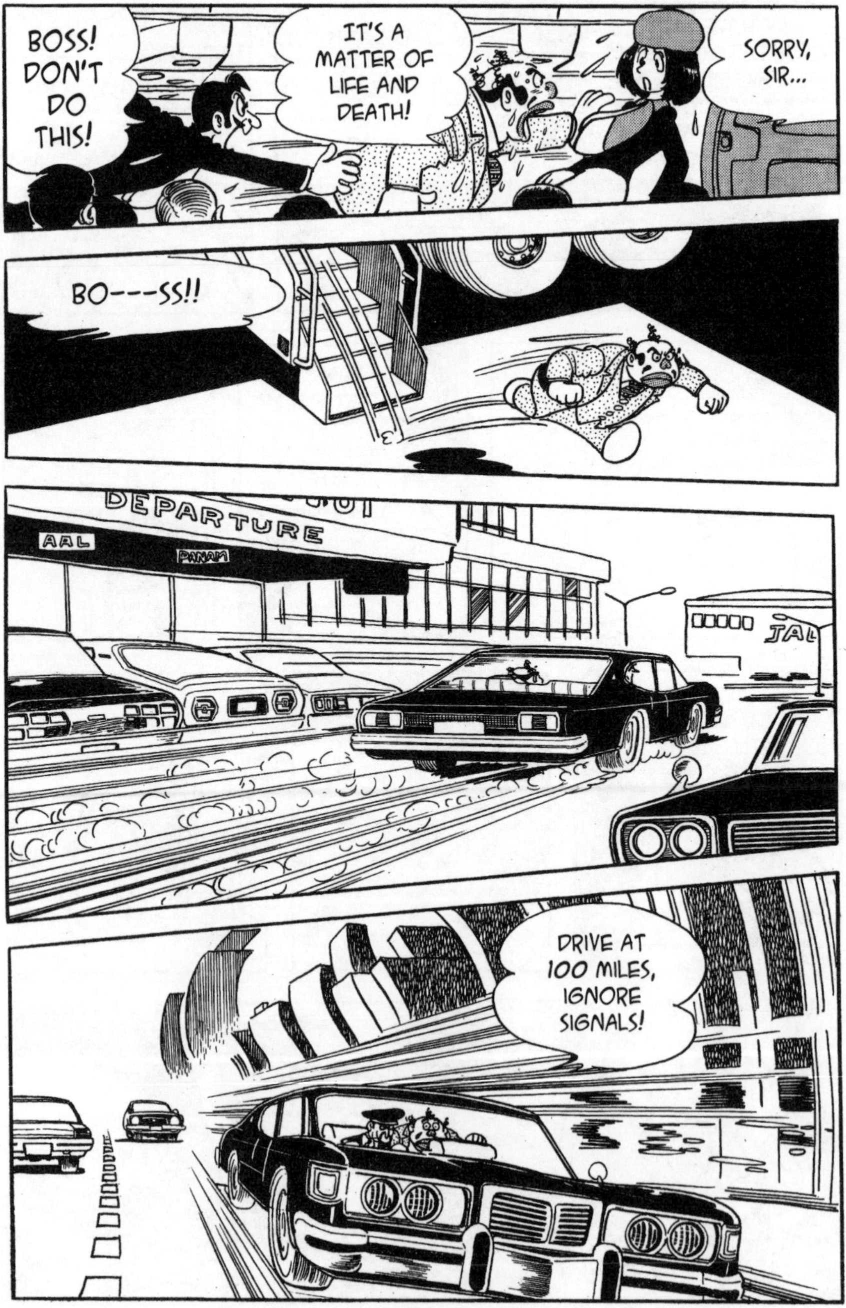
SORRY, SIR...
IT'S A MATTER OF LIFE AND DEATH!
BOSS! DON'T DO THIS!
BO---SS!!
DEPARTURE
AAL
PANAM
JAL
DRIVE AT 100 MILES, IGNORE SIGNALS!

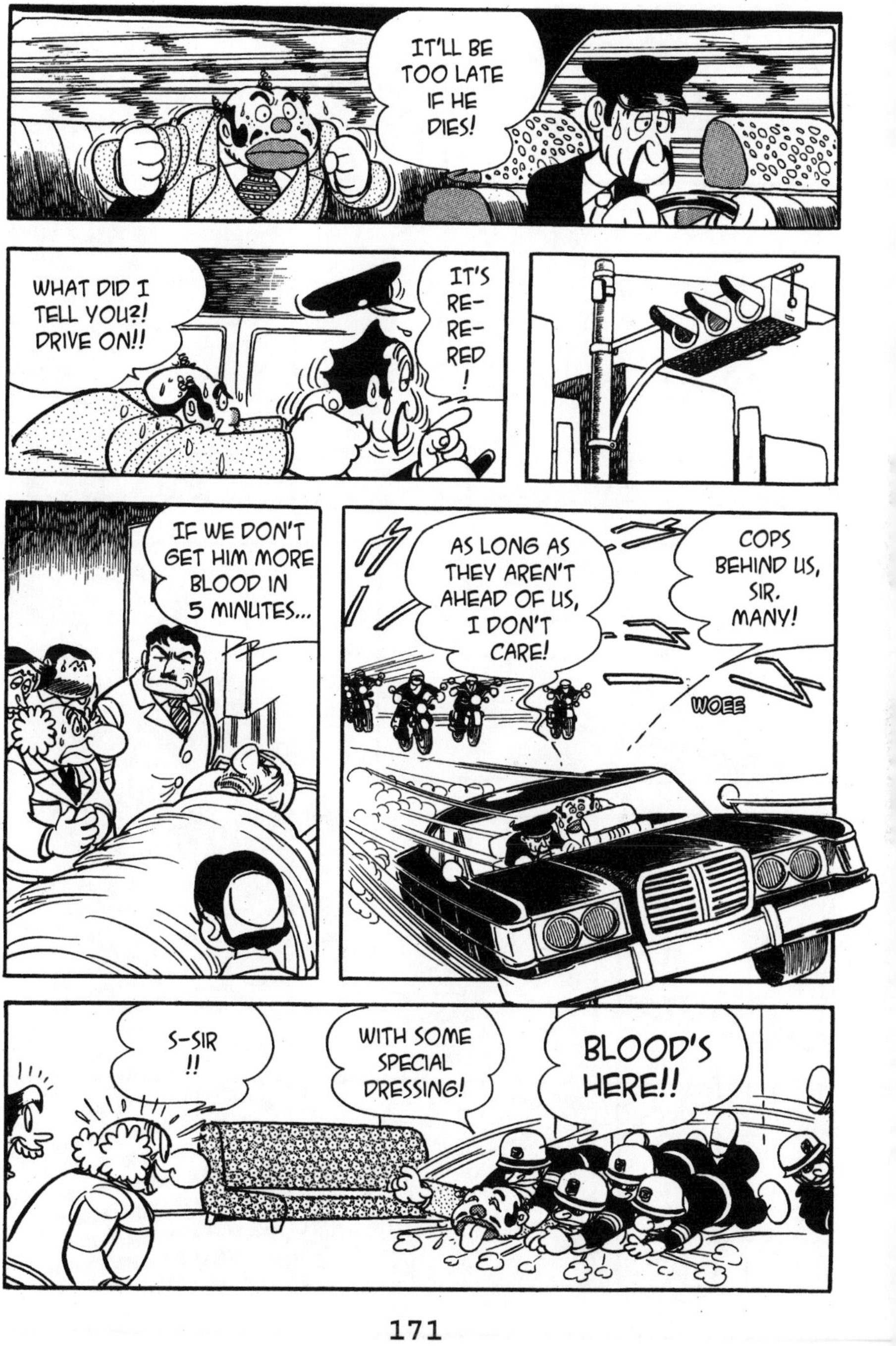
IT'LL BE TOO LATE IF HE DIES!
IT'S RE-RE-RE-RED!
WHAT DID I TELL YOU?! DRIVE ON!!
COPS BEHIND US, SIR. MANY!
AS LONG AS THEY AREN'T AHEAD OF US, I DON'T CARE!
WOEE
IF WE DON'T GET HIM MORE BLOOD IN 5 MINUTES...
BLOOD'S HERE!!
WITH SOME SPECIAL DRESSING!
S-SIR !!

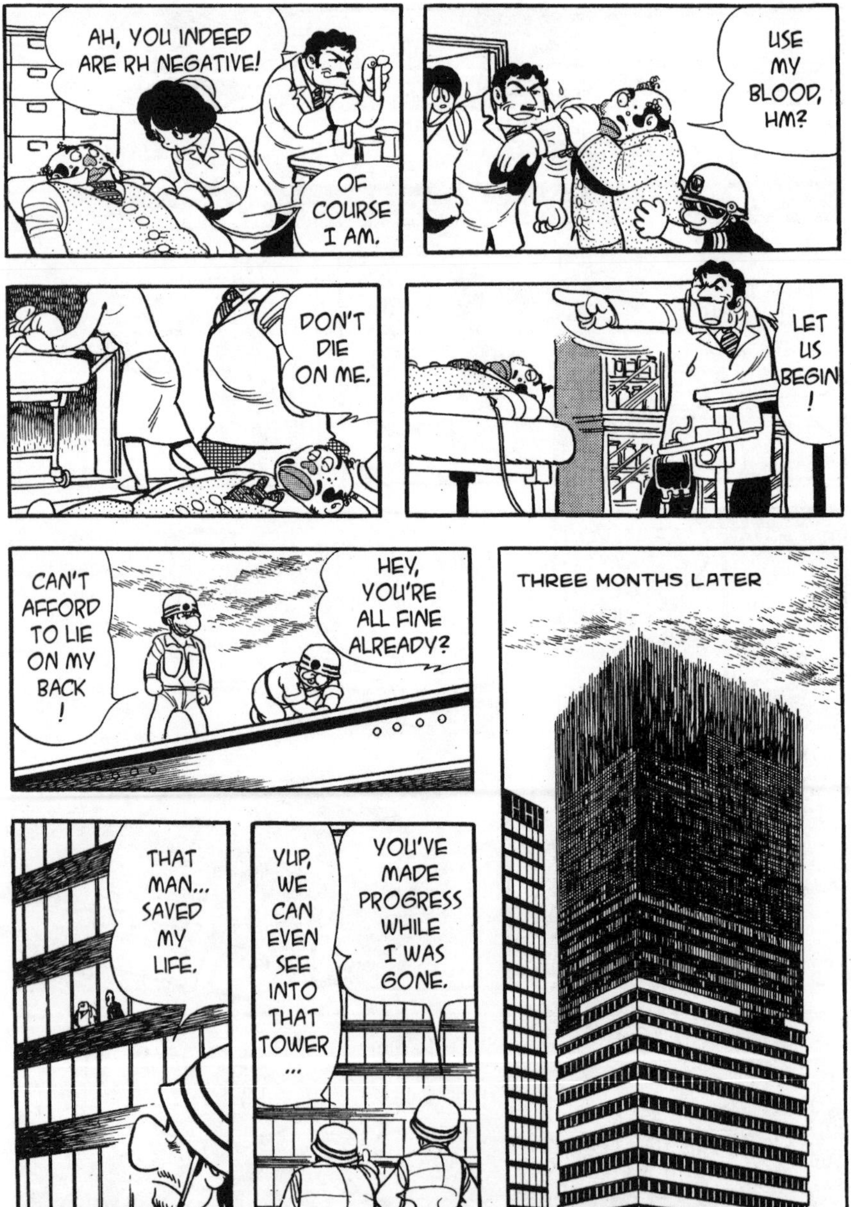
USE MY BLOOD, HM?
AH, YOU INDEED ARE RH NEGATIVE!
OF COURSE I AM.
LET US BEGIN!
DON'T DIE ON ME.
THREE MONTHS LATER
HEY, YOU'RE ALL FINE ALREADY?
CAN'T AFFORD TO LIE ON MY BACK!
YOU'VE MADE PROGRESS WHILE I WAS GONE.
YUP, WE CAN EVEN SEE INTO THAT TOWER ...
THAT MAN... SAVED MY LIFE.

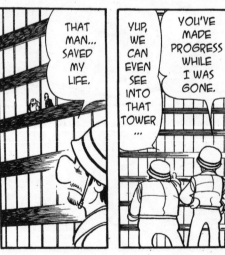

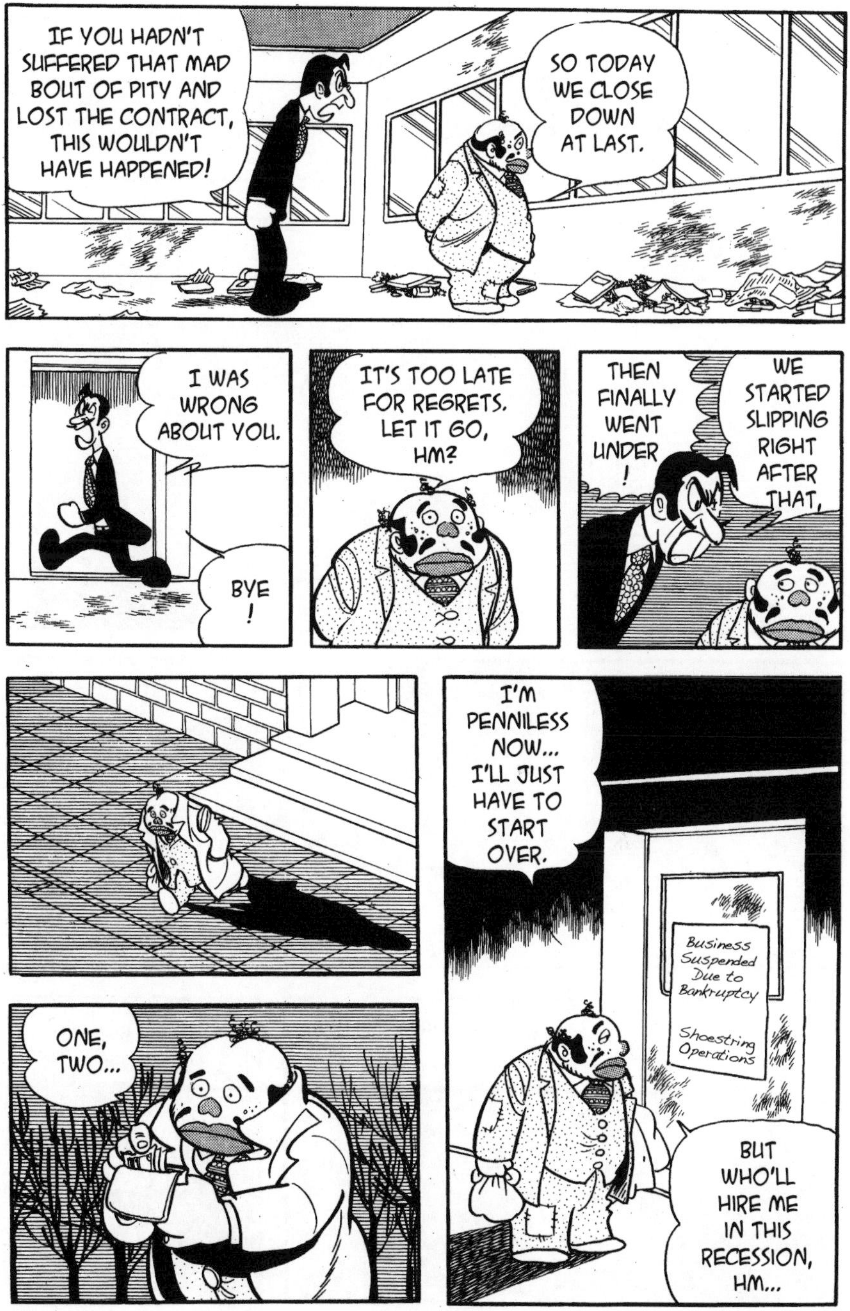
SO TODAY WE CLOSE DOWN AT LAST.
IF YOU HADN'T SUFFERED THAT MAD BOUT OF PITY AND LOST THE CONTRACT, THIS WOULDN'T HAVE HAPPENED!
WE STARTED SLIPPING RIGHT AFTER THAT,
THEN FINALLY WENT UNDER!
IT'S TOO LATE FOR REGRETS. LET IT GO, HM?
I WAS WRONG ABOUT YOU.
BYE!
I'M PENNILESS NOW... I'LL JUST HAVE TO START OVER.
Business Suspended Due to Bankruptcy
Shoestring Operations
BUT WHO'LL HIRE ME IN THIS RECESSION, HM...
ONE, TWO...

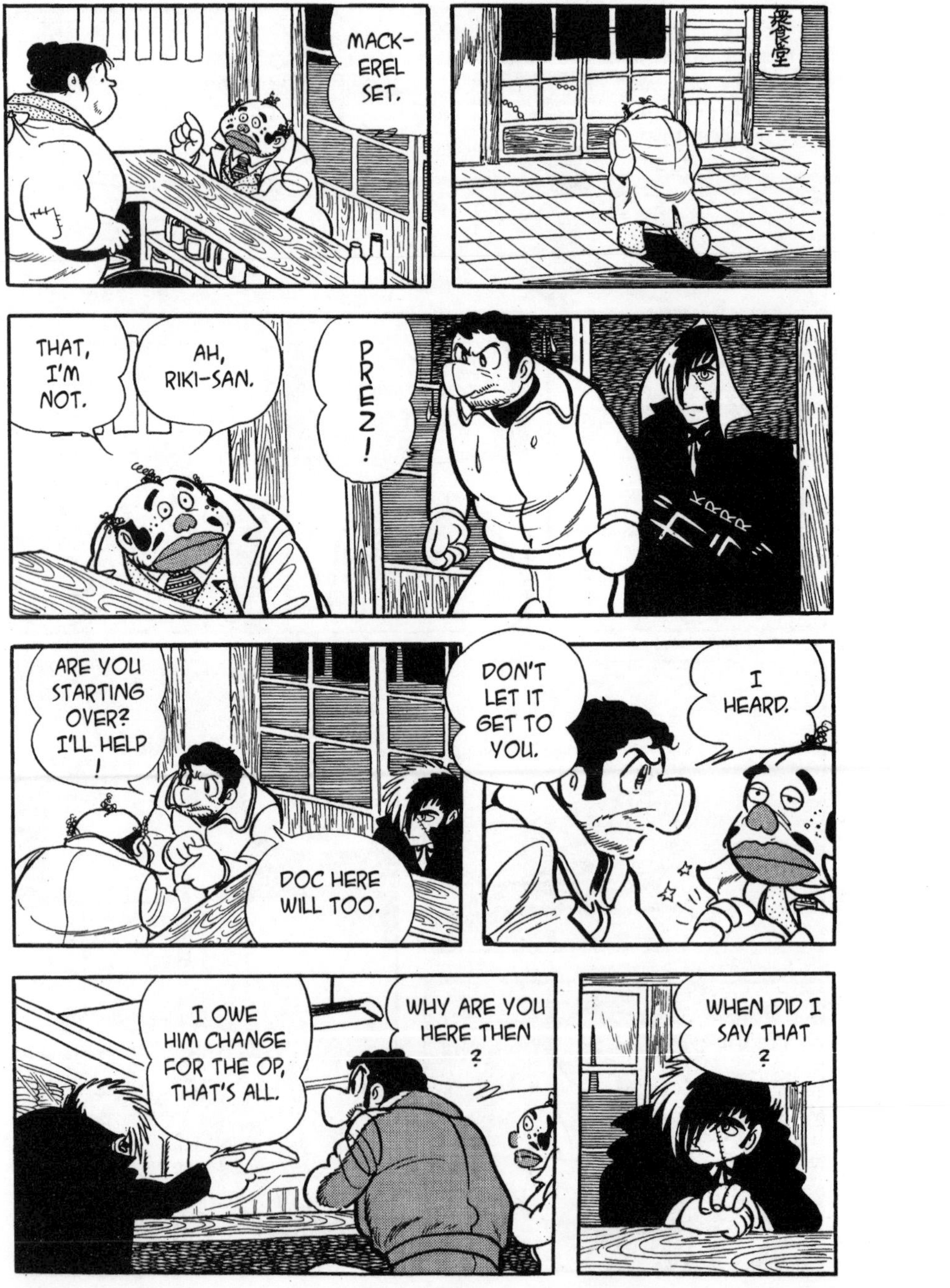
MACKEREL SET.
PREZ!
KRRR
AH, RIKI-SAN.
THAT, I'M NOT.
I HEARD.
DON'T LET IT GET TO YOU.
ARE YOU STARTING OVER? I'LL HELP!
DOC HERE WILL TOO.
WHEN DID I SAY THAT?
WHY ARE YOU HERE THEN?
I OWE HIM CHANGE FOR THE OP, THAT'S ALL.

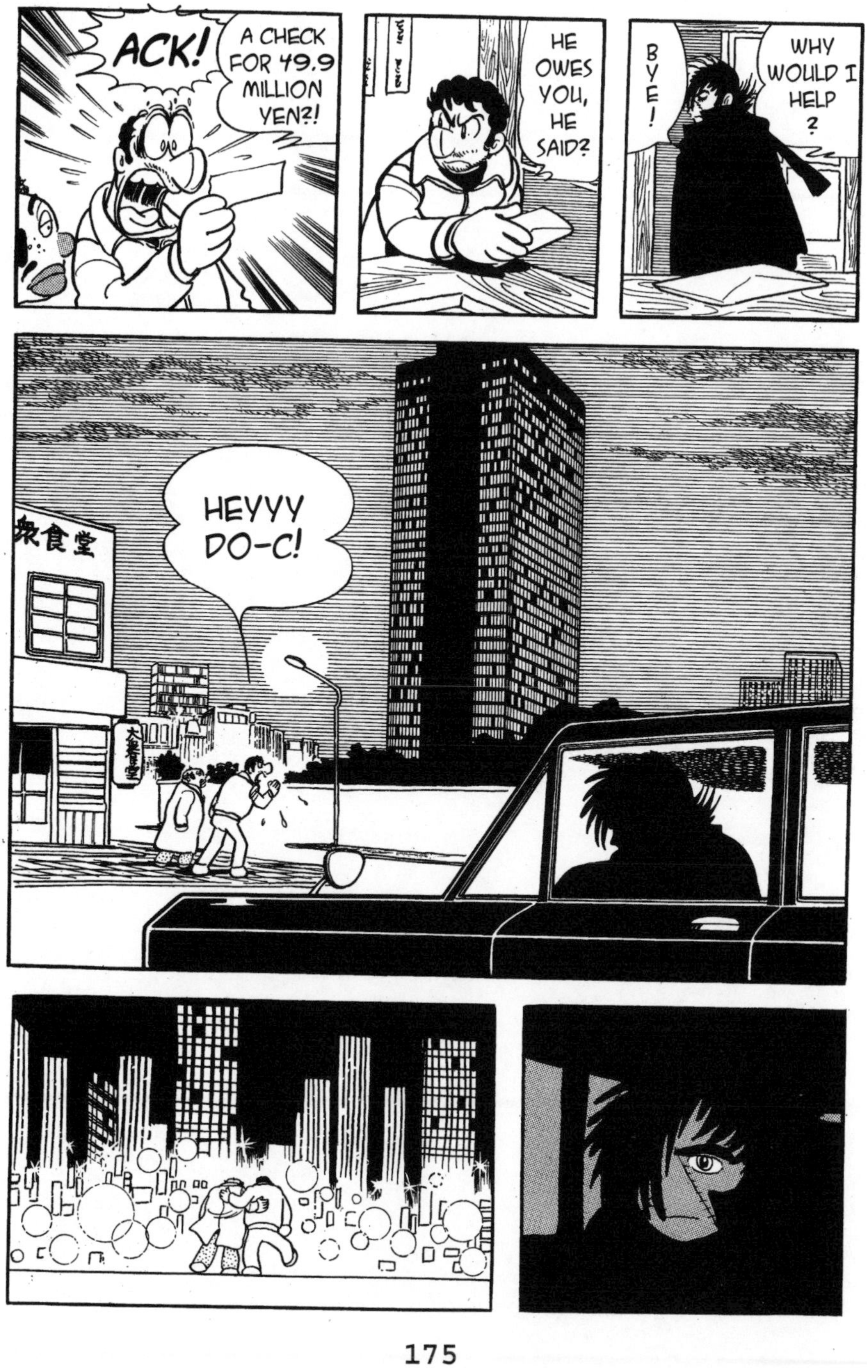
WHY WOULD I HELP?
BYE!
HE OWES YOU, HE SAID?
A CHECK FOR 49.9 MILLION YEN?!
ACK!
衆食堂
HEYYY DO-C!

GORIBEI OF SENJOGAHARA

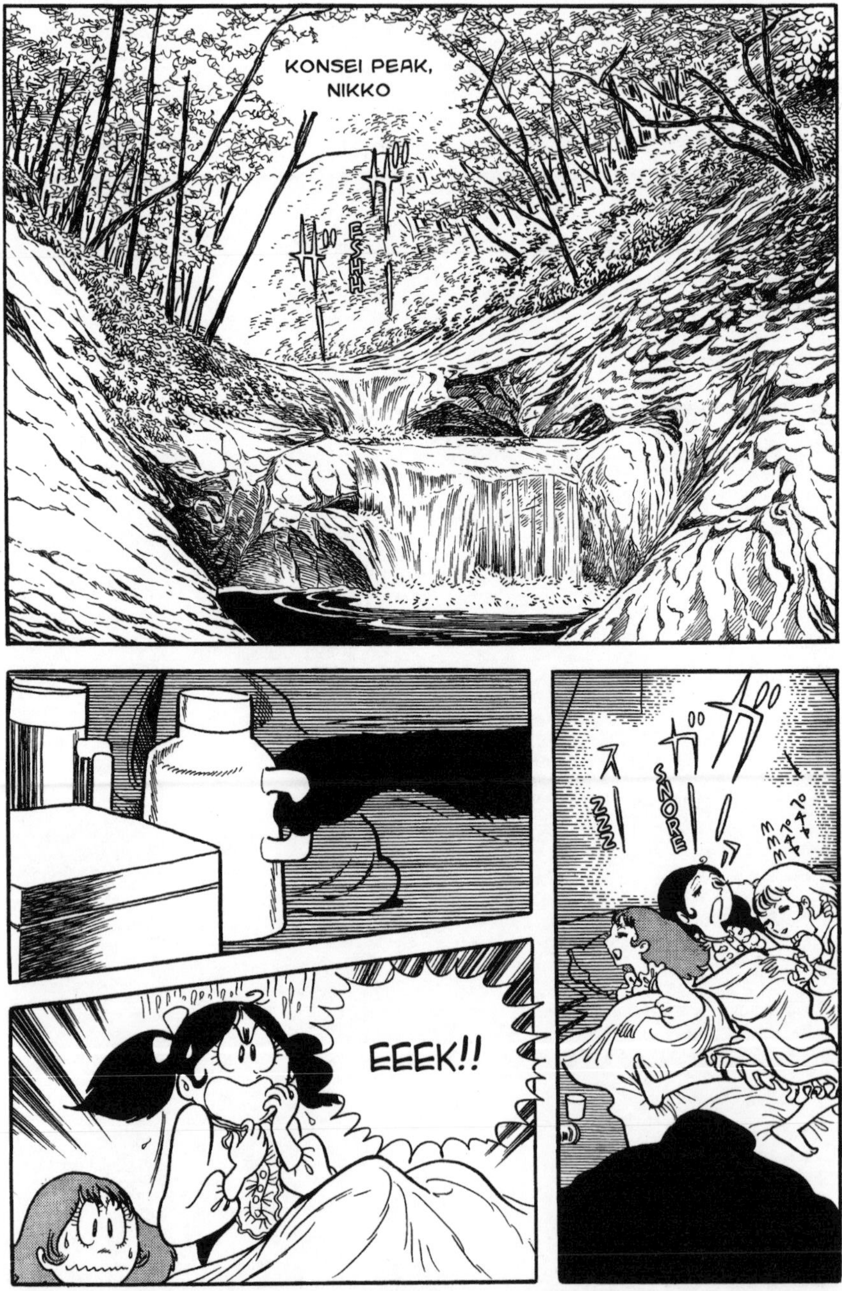
KONSEI PEAK, NIKKO
FSHH
SNORE
ZZZ
MMM
EEEK!!

NOTE: A BUDDHIST AND SHINTO SPIRITUAL CENTER AND POPULAR TOURIST DESTINATION SINCE PRE-MODERN TIMES, NIKKO IS LOCATED IN TOCHIGI PREFECTURE. KONSEI PEAK (2000M) BOASTS A SHRINE DEDICATED TO A PHALLUS.

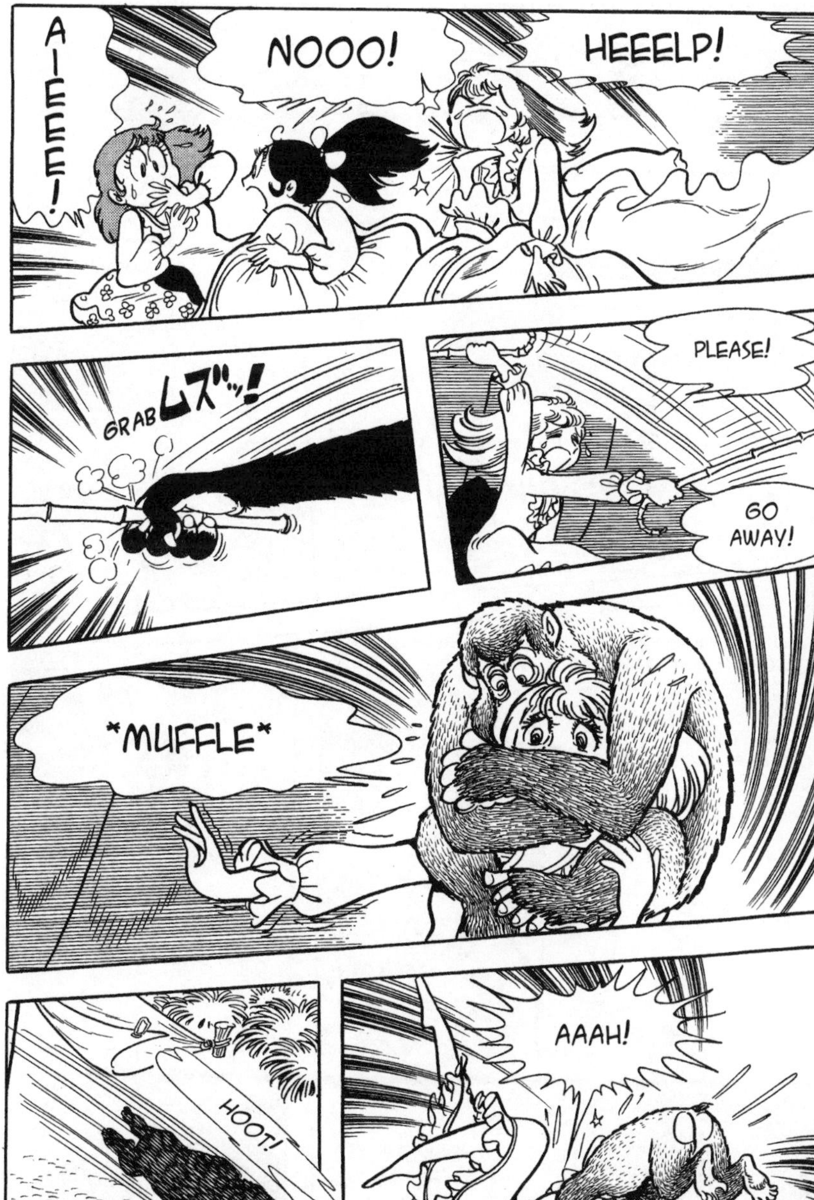
HEEELP!
NOOO!
AIEEEE!
PLEASE!
GO AWAY!
GRAB ムズッ!
MUFFLE
AAAH!
HOOT!

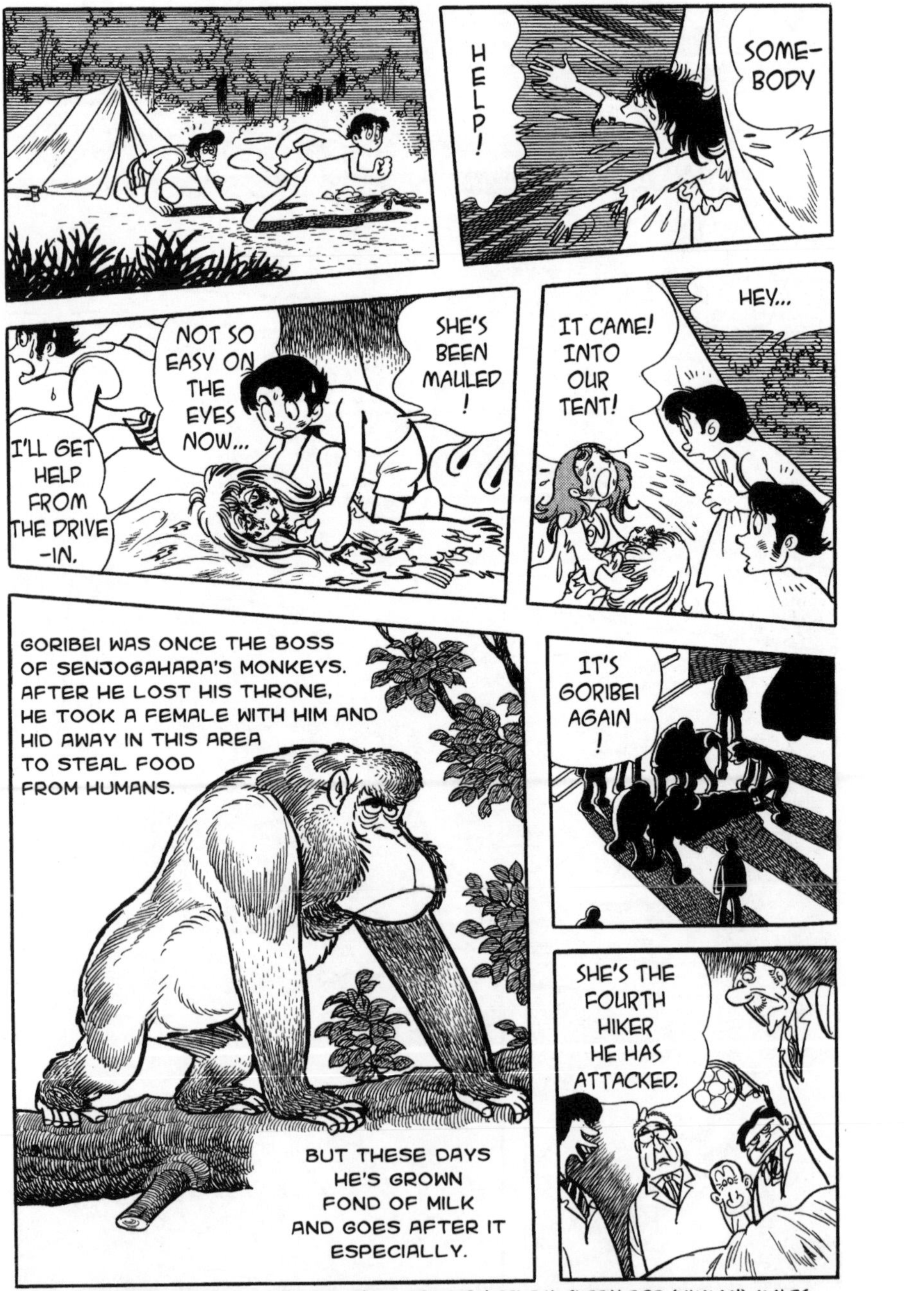
SOME-BODY
HELP!
HEY...
IT CAME! INTO OUR TENT!
SHE'S BEEN MAULED!
NOT SO EASY ON THE EYES NOW...
I'LL GET HELP FROM THE DRIVE-IN.
IT'S GORIBEI AGAIN!
SHE'S THE FOURTH HIKER HE HAS ATTACKED.
GORIBEI WAS ONCE THE BOSS OF SENJOGAHARA'S MONKEYS. AFTER HE LOST HIS THRONE, HE TOOK A FEMALE WITH HIM AND HID AWAY IN THIS AREA TO STEAL FOOD FROM HUMANS.
BUT THESE DAYS HE'S GROWN FOND OF MILK AND GOES AFTER IT ESPECIALLY.

NOTE: "GORIBEI" COMBINES *GORILLA* AND A COMMON FEUDAL SUFFIX FOR (HUMAN) MALES. "SENJOGAHARA," WHICH MEANS *BATTLEFIELD*, IS SO NAMED AFTER A LEGENDARY DUEL BETWEEN TWO MOUNTAIN GODS WHO SUPPOSEDLY FOUGHT THERE IN ANIMAL FORM.

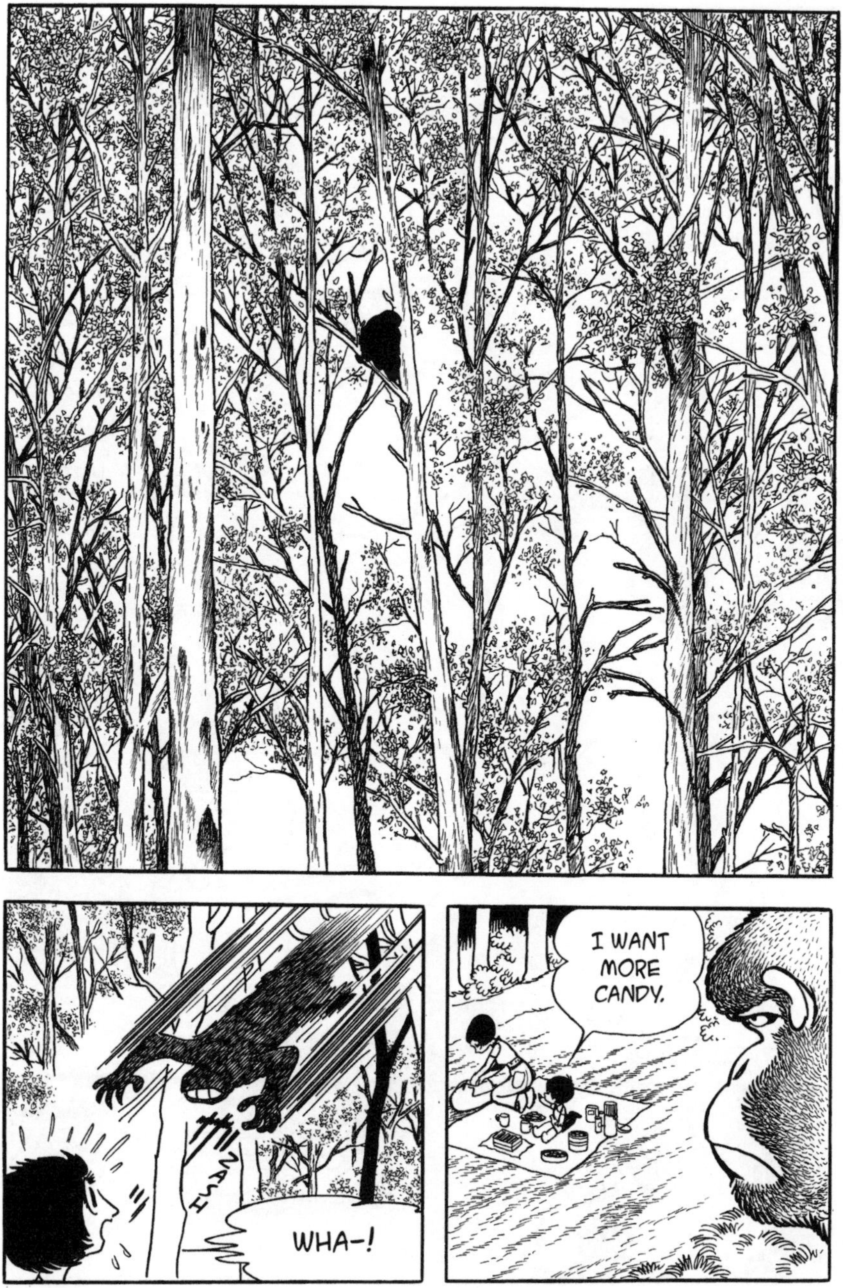
I WANT MORE CANDY.
WHA-!

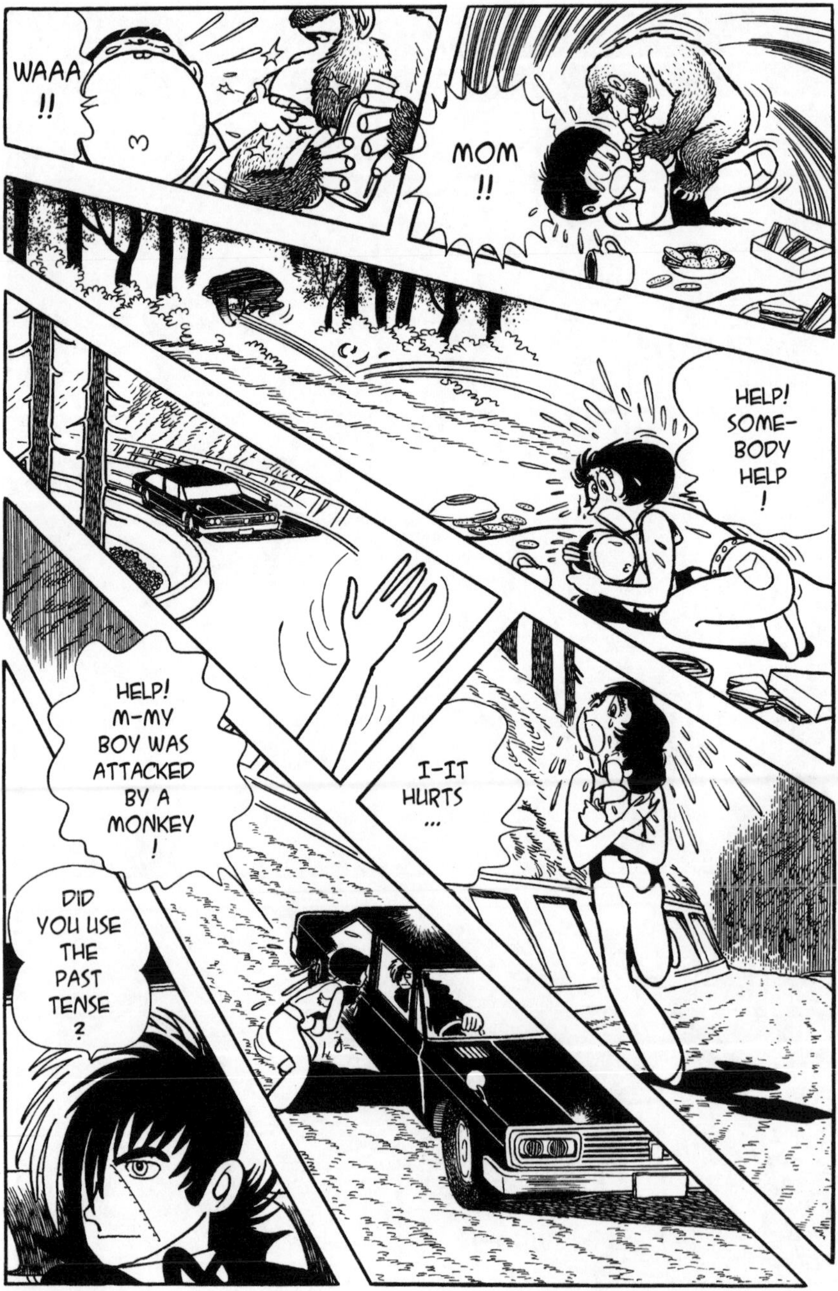
MOM !!
WAAA !!
HELP! SOMEBODY HELP !
I-IT HURTS ...
HELP! M-MY BOY WAS ATTACKED BY A MONKEY !
DID YOU USE THE PAST TENSE ?

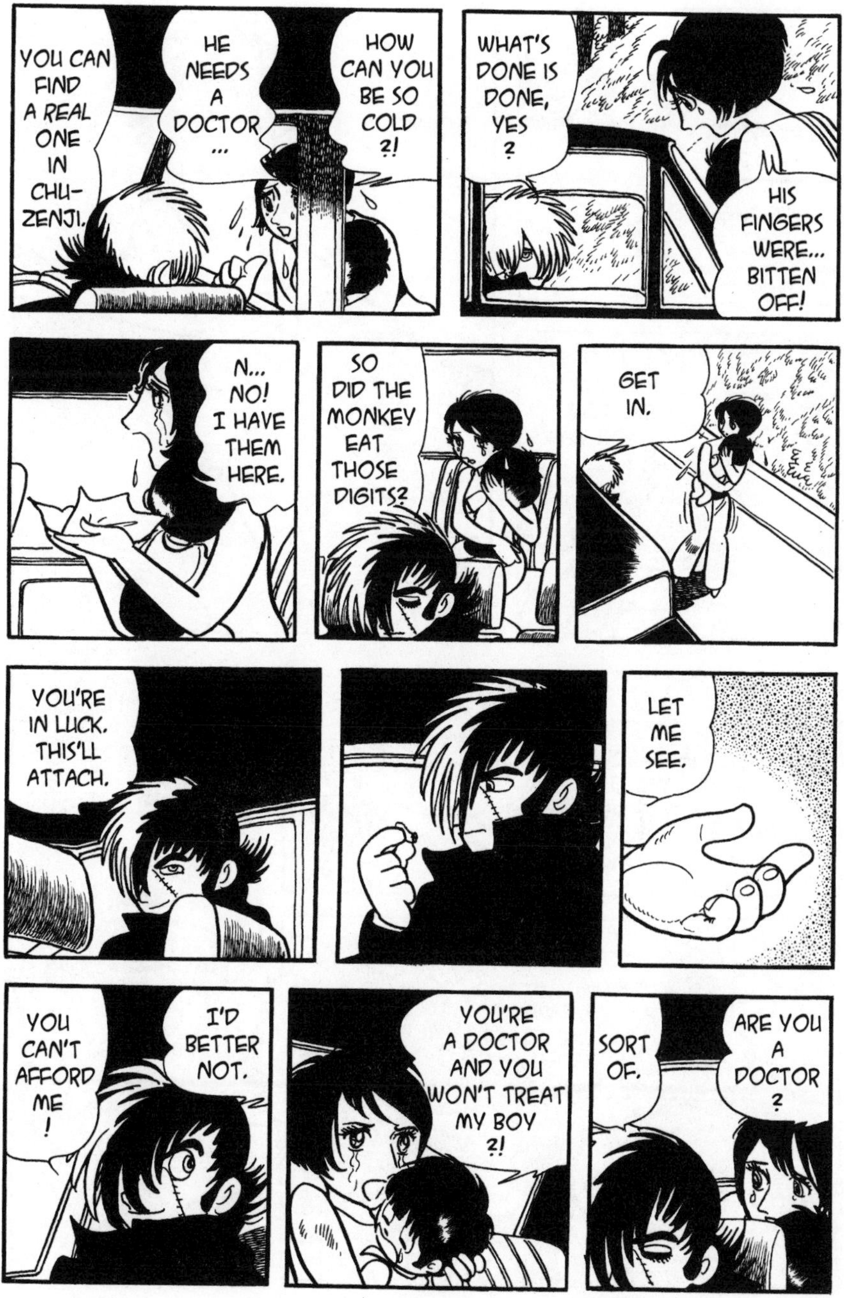
HIS FINGERS WERE... BITTEN OFF!
WHAT'S DONE IS DONE, YES?
HOW CAN YOU BE SO COLD?!
HE NEEDS A DOCTOR...
YOU CAN FIND A REAL ONE IN CHUZENJI.
GET IN.
SO DID THE MONKEY EAT THOSE DIGITS?
N... NO! I HAVE THEM HERE.
LET ME SEE.
YOU'RE IN LUCK. THIS'LL ATTACH.
ARE YOU A DOCTOR?
SORT OF.
YOU'RE A DOCTOR AND YOU WON'T TREAT MY BOY?!
I'D BETTER NOT.
YOU CAN'T AFFORD ME!

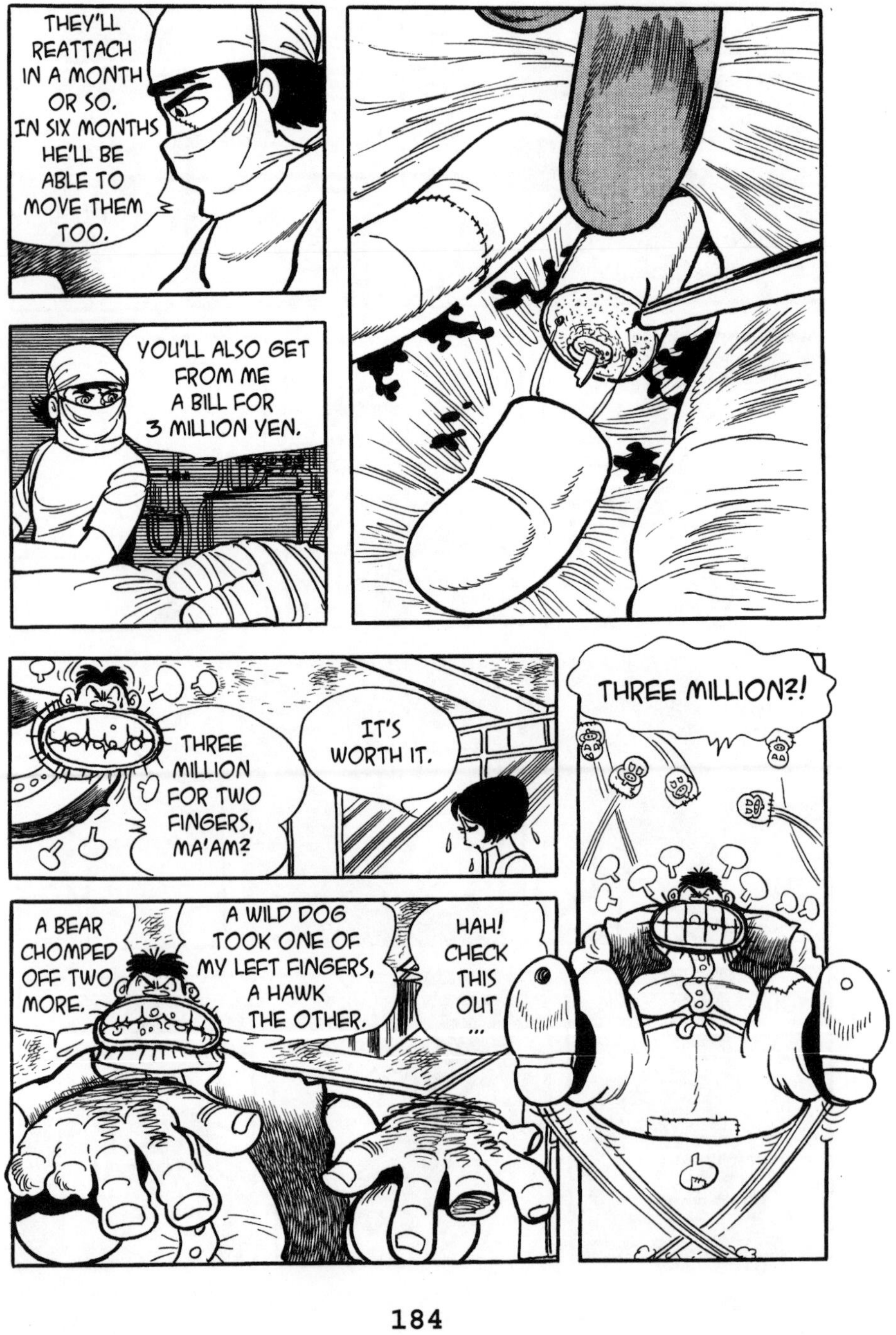
THEY'LL REATTACH IN A MONTH OR SO. IN SIX MONTHS HE'LL BE ABLE TO MOVE THEM TOO.
YOU'LL ALSO GET FROM ME A BILL FOR 3 MILLION YEN.
THREE MILLION?!
IT'S WORTH IT.
THREE MILLION FOR TWO FINGERS, MA'AM?
HAH! CHECK THIS OUT ...
A WILD DOG TOOK ONE OF MY LEFT FINGERS, A HAWK THE OTHER.
A BEAR CHOMPED OFF TWO MORE.

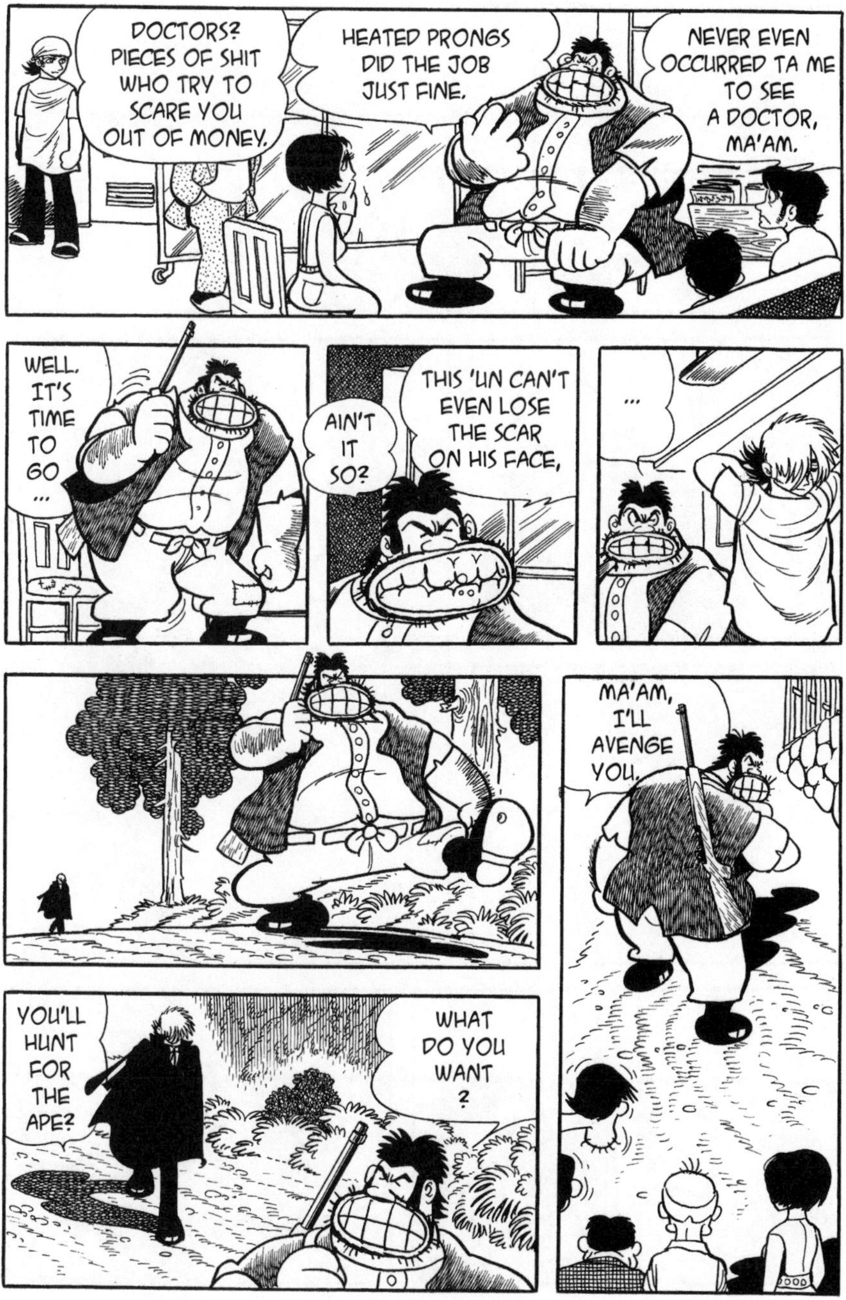
NEVER EVEN OCCURRED TA ME TO SEE A DOCTOR, MA'AM.
HEATED PRONGS DID THE JOB JUST FINE.
DOCTORS? PIECES OF SHIT WHO TRY TO SCARE YOU OUT OF MONEY.
...
THIS 'UN CAN'T EVEN LOSE THE SCAR ON HIS FACE,
AIN'T IT SO?
WELL. IT'S TIME TO GO ...
MA'AM, I'LL AVENGE YOU.
WHAT DO YOU WANT ?
YOU'LL HUNT FOR THE APE?

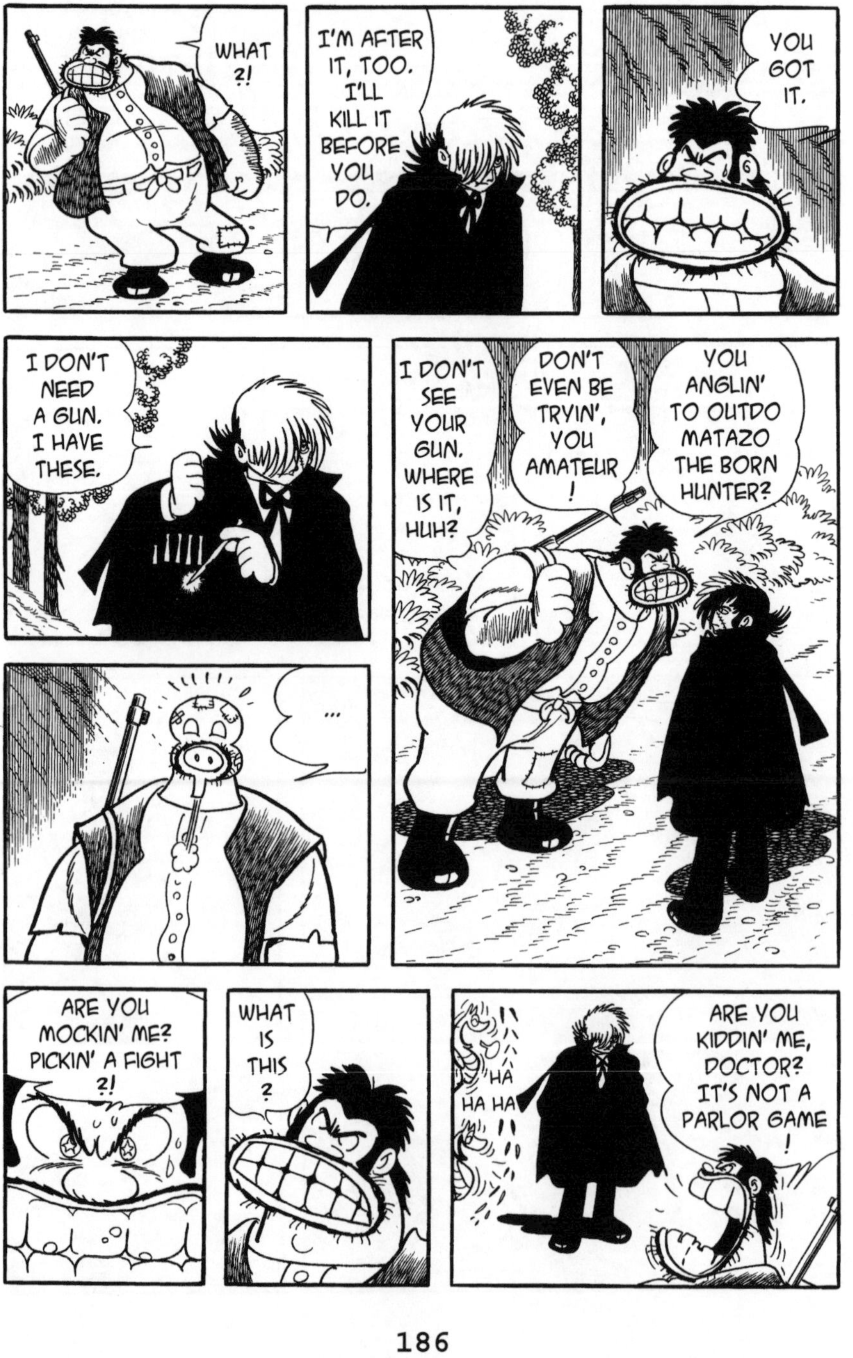
YOU GOT IT.
I'M AFTER IT, TOO. I'LL KILL IT BEFORE YOU DO.
WHAT ?!
YOU ANGLIN' TO OUTDO MATAZO THE BORN HUNTER?
DON'T EVEN BE TRYIN', YOU AMATEUR !
I DON'T SEE YOUR GUN. WHERE IS IT, HUH?
I DON'T NEED A GUN. I HAVE THESE.
...
ARE YOU KIDDIN' ME, DOCTOR? IT'S NOT A PARLOR GAME !
HA HA HA
WHAT IS THIS ?
ARE YOU MOCKIN' ME? PICKIN' A FIGHT ?!

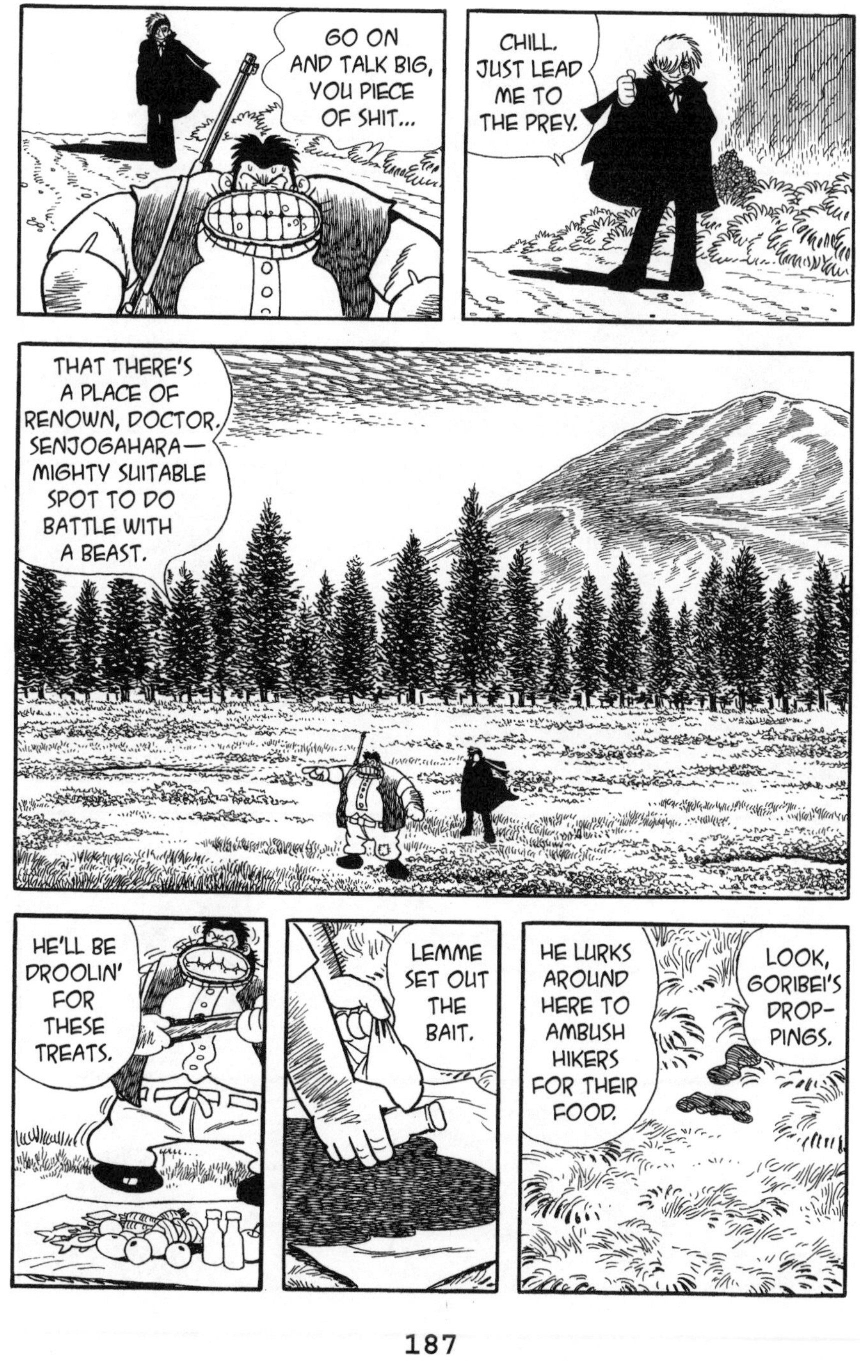
CHILL. JUST LEAD ME TO THE PREY.
GO ON AND TALK BIG, YOU PIECE OF SHIT...
THAT THERE'S A PLACE OF RENOWN, DOCTOR. SENJOGAHARA—MIGHTY SUITABLE SPOT TO DO BATTLE WITH A BEAST.
LOOK, GORIBEI'S DROP-PINGS.
HE LURKS AROUND HERE TO AMBUSH HIKERS FOR THEIR FOOD.
LEMME SET OUT THE BAIT.
HE'LL BE DROOLIN' FOR THESE TREATS.

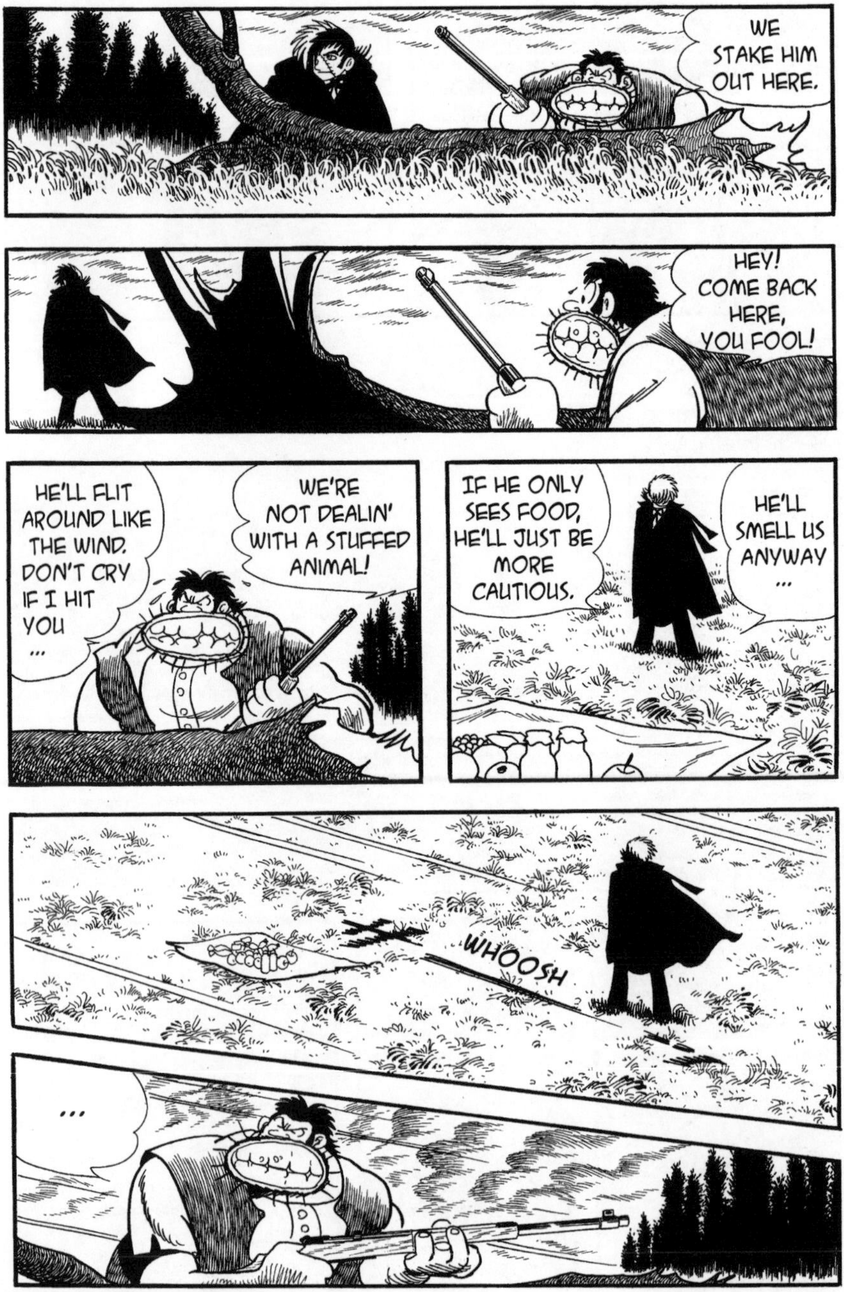
WE STAKE HIM OUT HERE.
HEY! COME BACK HERE, YOU FOOL!
HE'LL SMELL US ANYWAY ...
IF HE ONLY SEES FOOD, HE'LL JUST BE MORE CAUTIOUS.
WE'RE NOT DEALIN' WITH A STUFFED ANIMAL!
HE'LL FLIT AROUND LIKE THE WIND. DON'T CRY IF I HIT YOU ...
WHOOSH
...

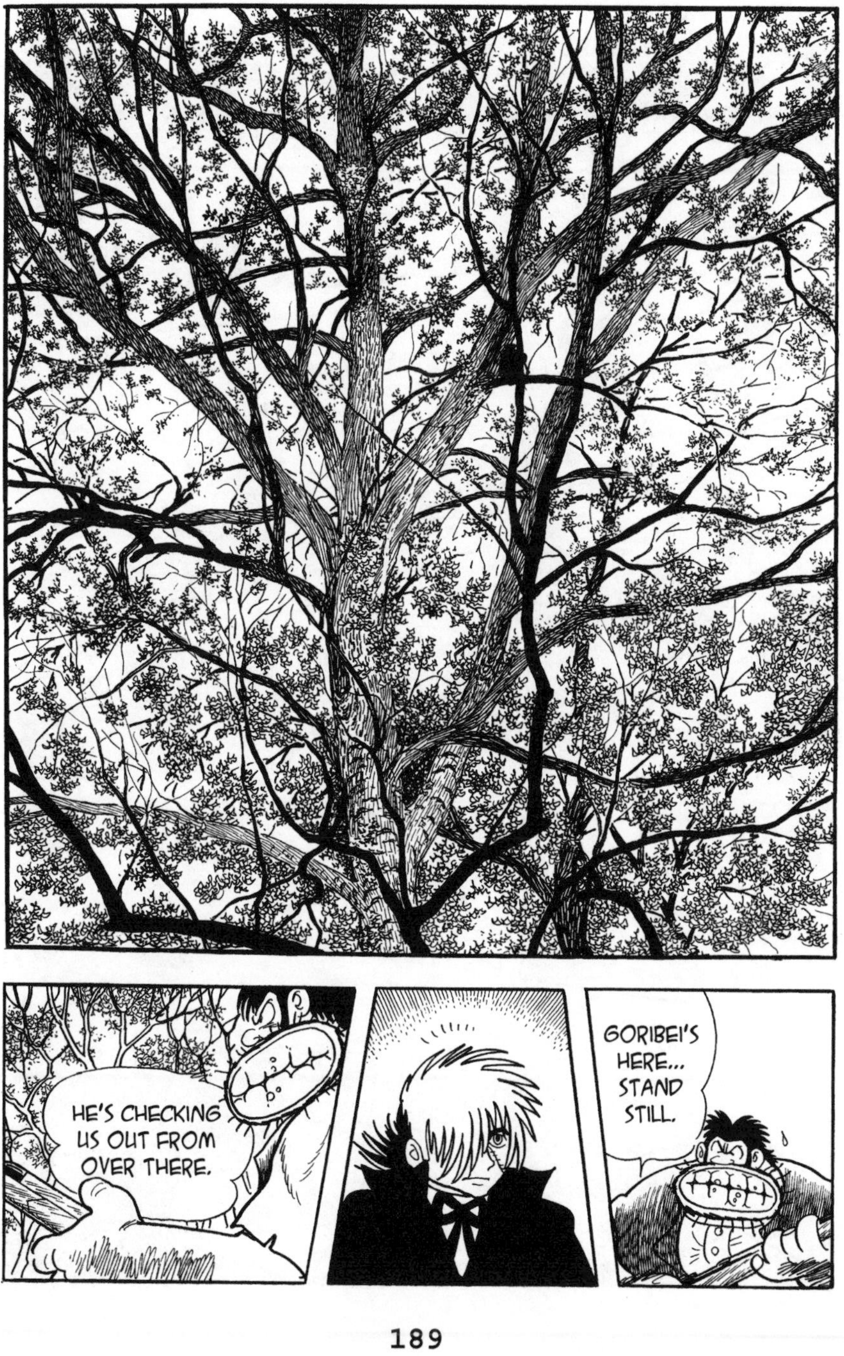
GORIBEI'S HERE... STAND STILL.
HE'S CHECKING US OUT FROM OVER THERE.

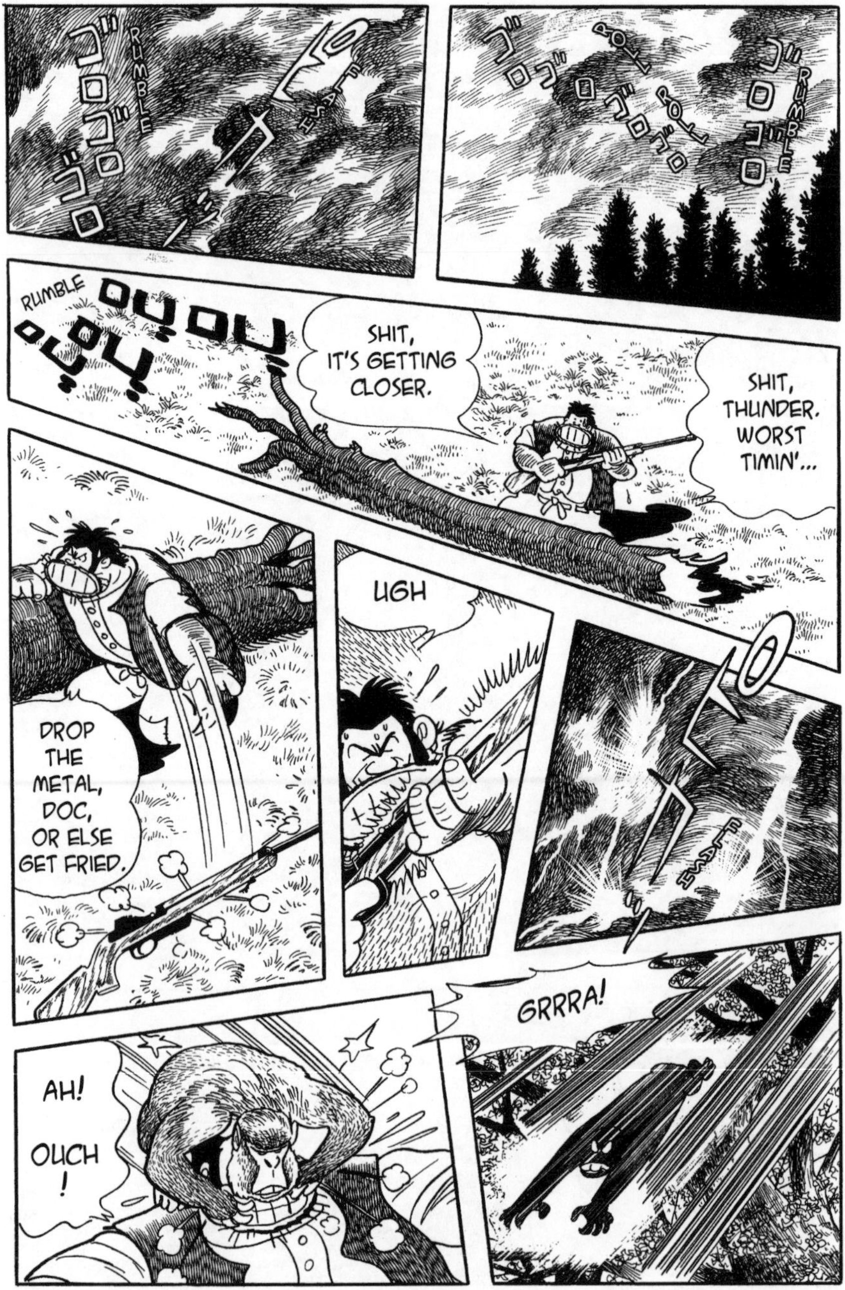
ROLL ROLL
RUMBLE
FLASH
RUMBLE
SHIT, THUNDER. WORST TIMIN'...
SHIT, IT'S GETTING CLOSER.
RUMBLE
FLASH
UGH
DROP THE METAL, DOC, OR ELSE GET FRIED.
GRRRA!
AH!
OUCH!

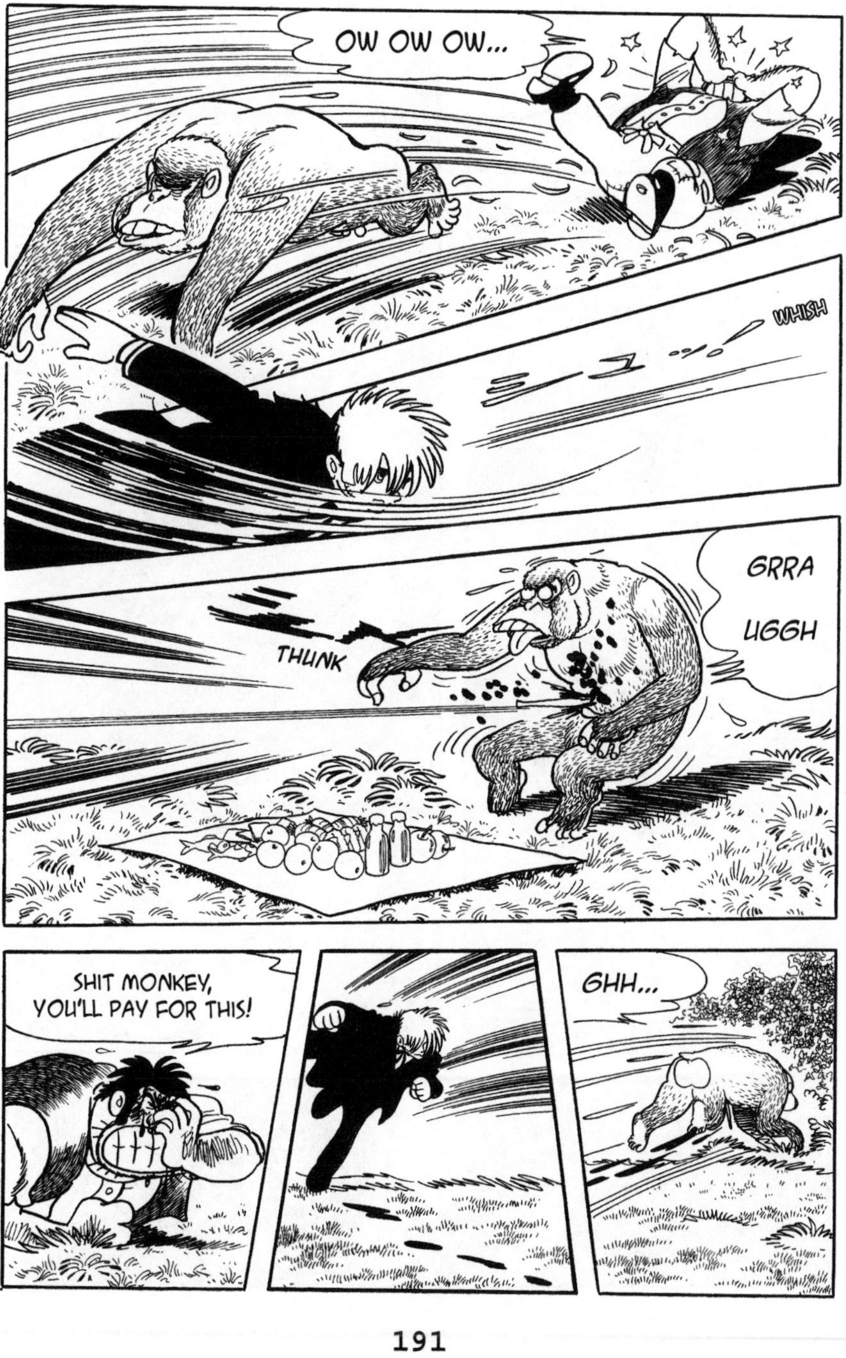
OW OW OW...
WHISH
GRRA UGGH
THUNK
GHH...
SHIT MONKEY, YOU'LL PAY FOR THIS!

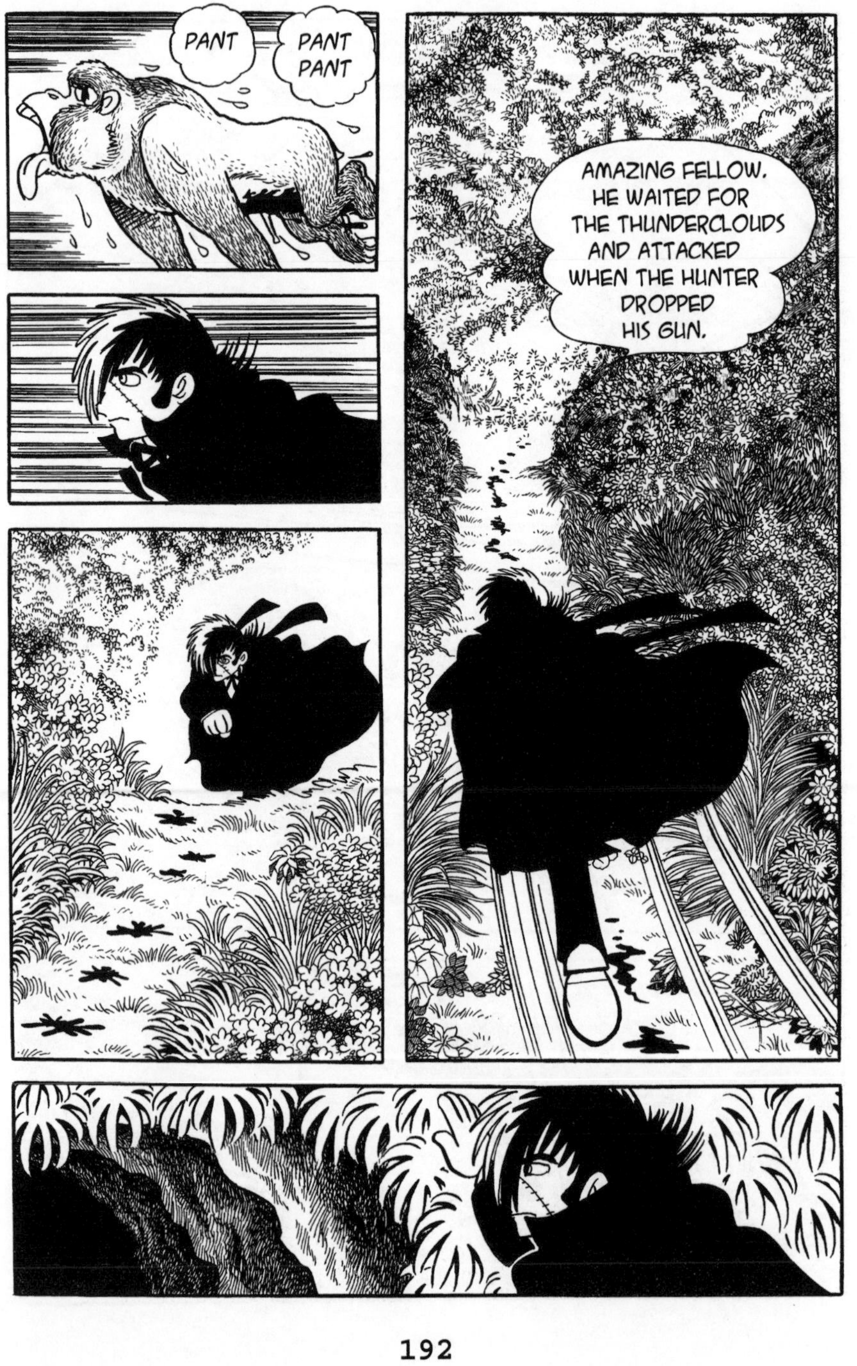
AMAZING FELLOW. HE WAITED FOR THE THUNDERCLOUDS AND ATTACKED WHEN THE HUNTER DROPPED HIS GUN.
PANT PANT
PANT

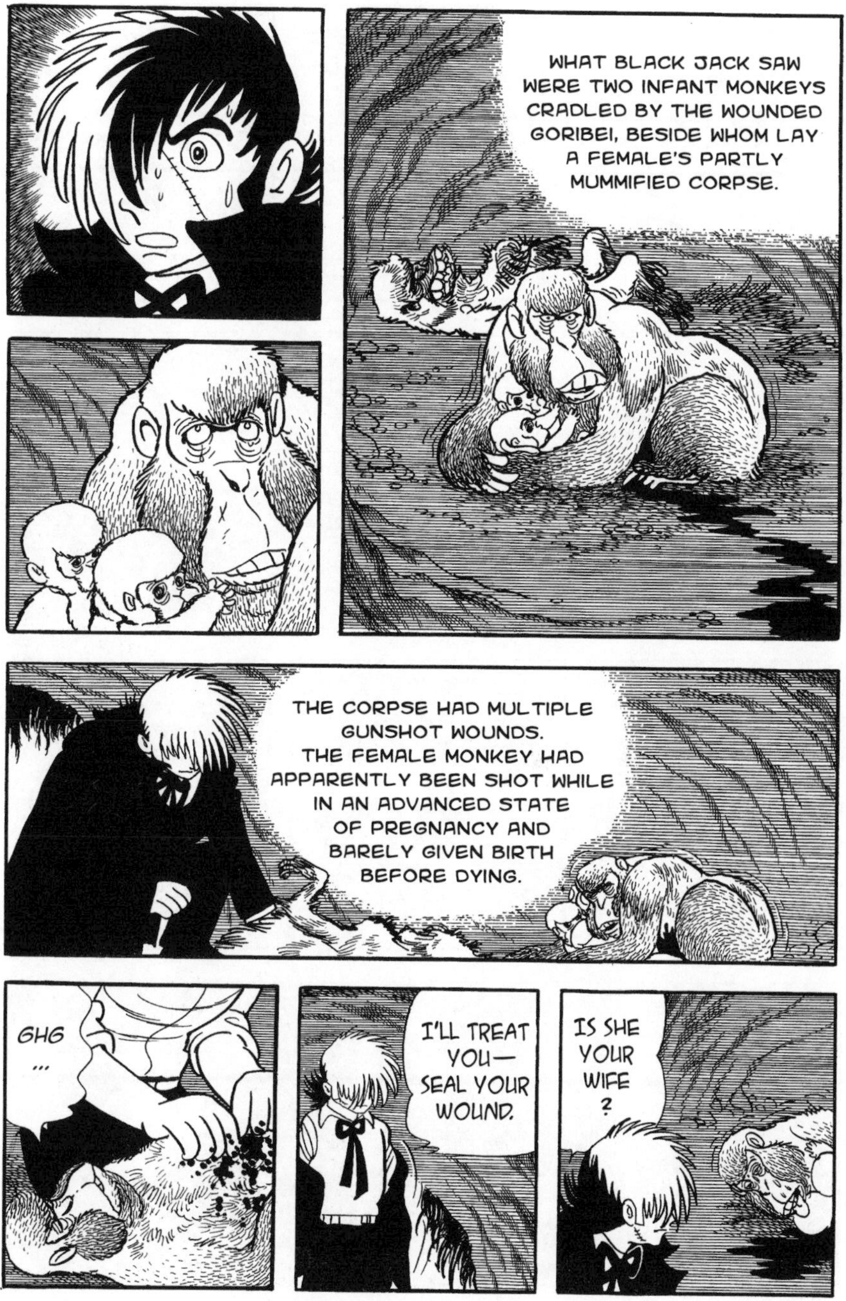
WHAT BLACK JACK SAW WERE TWO INFANT MONKEYS CRADLED BY THE WOUNDED GORIBEI, BESIDE WHOM LAY A FEMALE'S PARTLY MUMMIFIED CORPSE.
THE CORPSE HAD MULTIPLE GUNSHOT WOUNDS. THE FEMALE MONKEY HAD APPARENTLY BEEN SHOT WHILE IN AN ADVANCED STATE OF PREGNANCY AND BARELY GIVEN BIRTH BEFORE DYING.
IS SHE YOUR WIFE ?
I'LL TREAT YOU— SEAL YOUR WOUND.
GHG ...

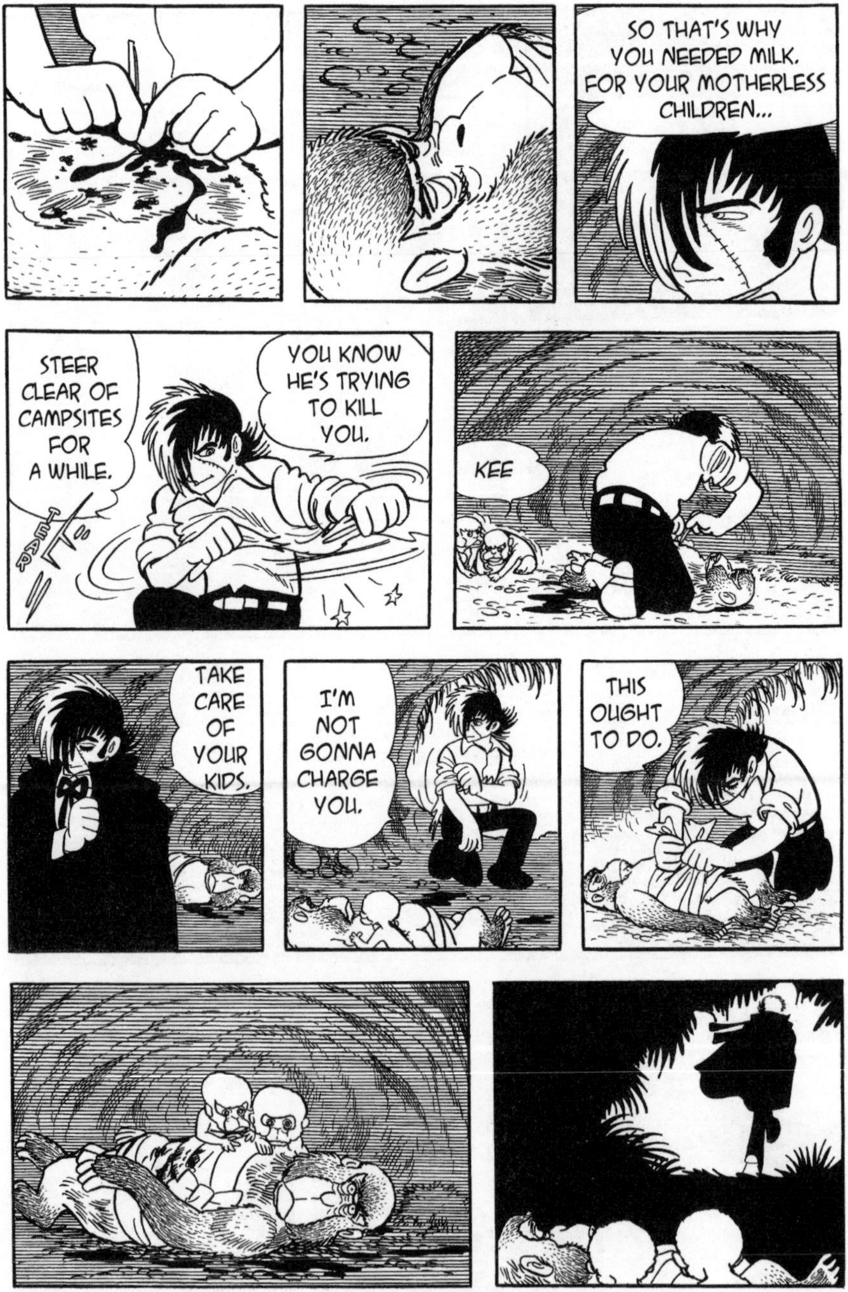
SO THAT'S WHY YOU NEEDED MILK. FOR YOUR MOTHERLESS CHILDREN...
KEE
YOU KNOW HE'S TRYING TO KILL YOU.
STEER CLEAR OF CAMPSITES FOR A WHILE.
TEAR
THIS OUGHT TO DO.
I'M NOT GONNA CHARGE YOU.
TAKE CARE OF YOUR KIDS.

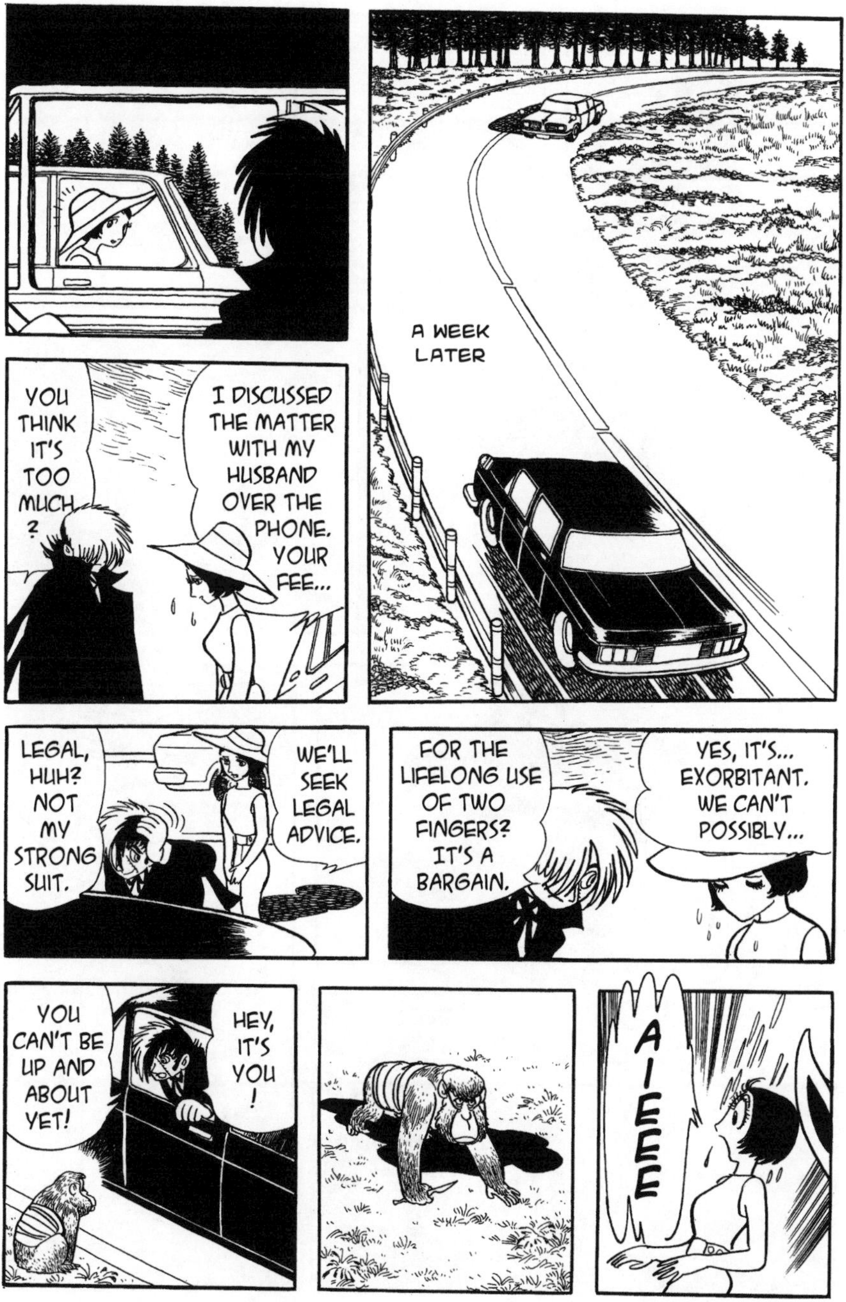
A WEEK LATER
I DISCUSSED THE MATTER WITH MY HUSBAND OVER THE PHONE. YOUR FEE...
YOU THINK IT'S TOO MUCH?
YES, IT'S... EXORBITANT. WE CAN'T POSSIBLY...
FOR THE LIFELONG USE OF TWO FINGERS? IT'S A BARGAIN.
WE'LL SEEK LEGAL ADVICE.
LEGAL, HUH? NOT MY STRONG SUIT.
AIEEE
HEY, IT'S YOU!
YOU CAN'T BE UP AND ABOUT YET!

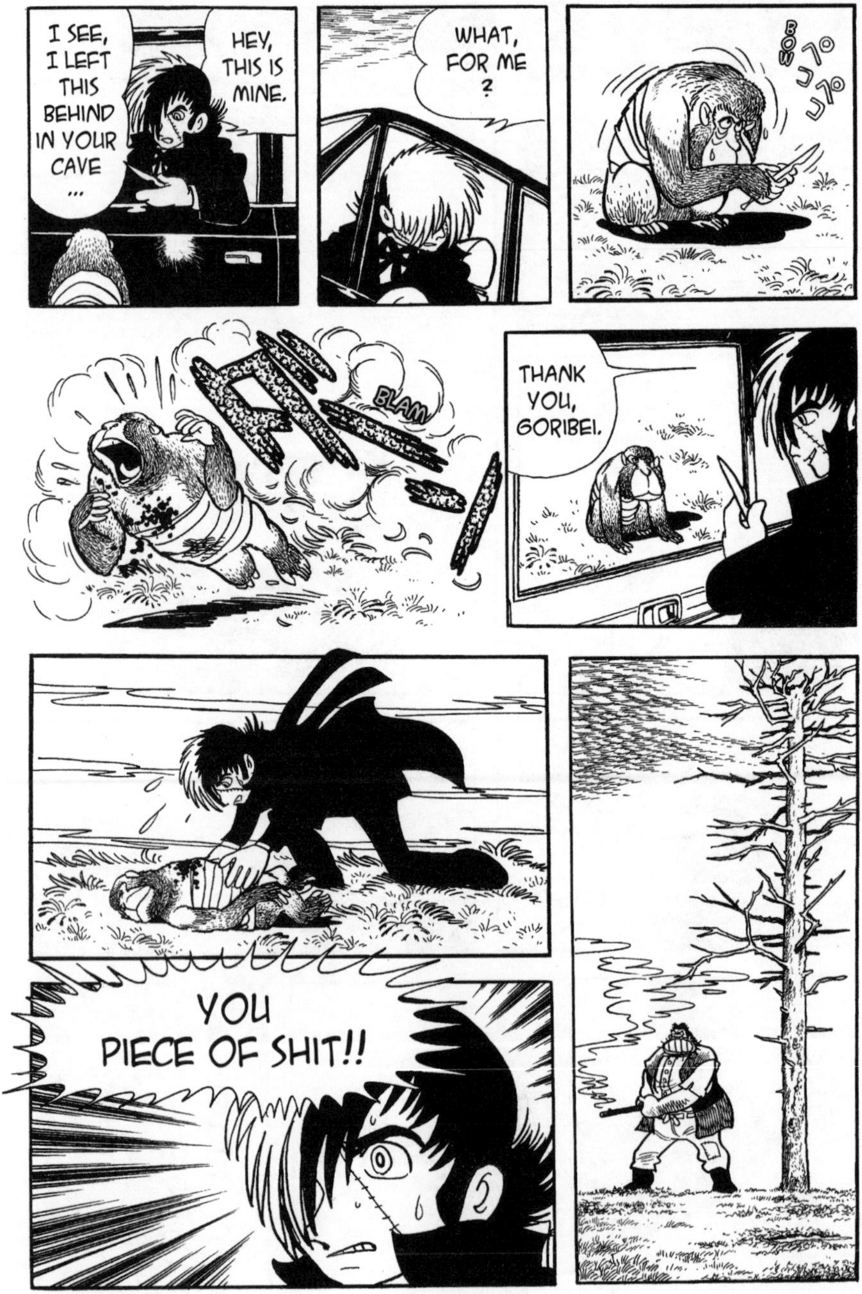
BOW
WHAT, FOR ME ?
HEY, THIS IS MINE.
I SEE, I LEFT THIS BEHIND IN YOUR CAVE ...
THANK YOU, GORIBEI.
BLAM
YOU PIECE OF SHIT!!

THE *KUROSHIO*: A MEMOIR

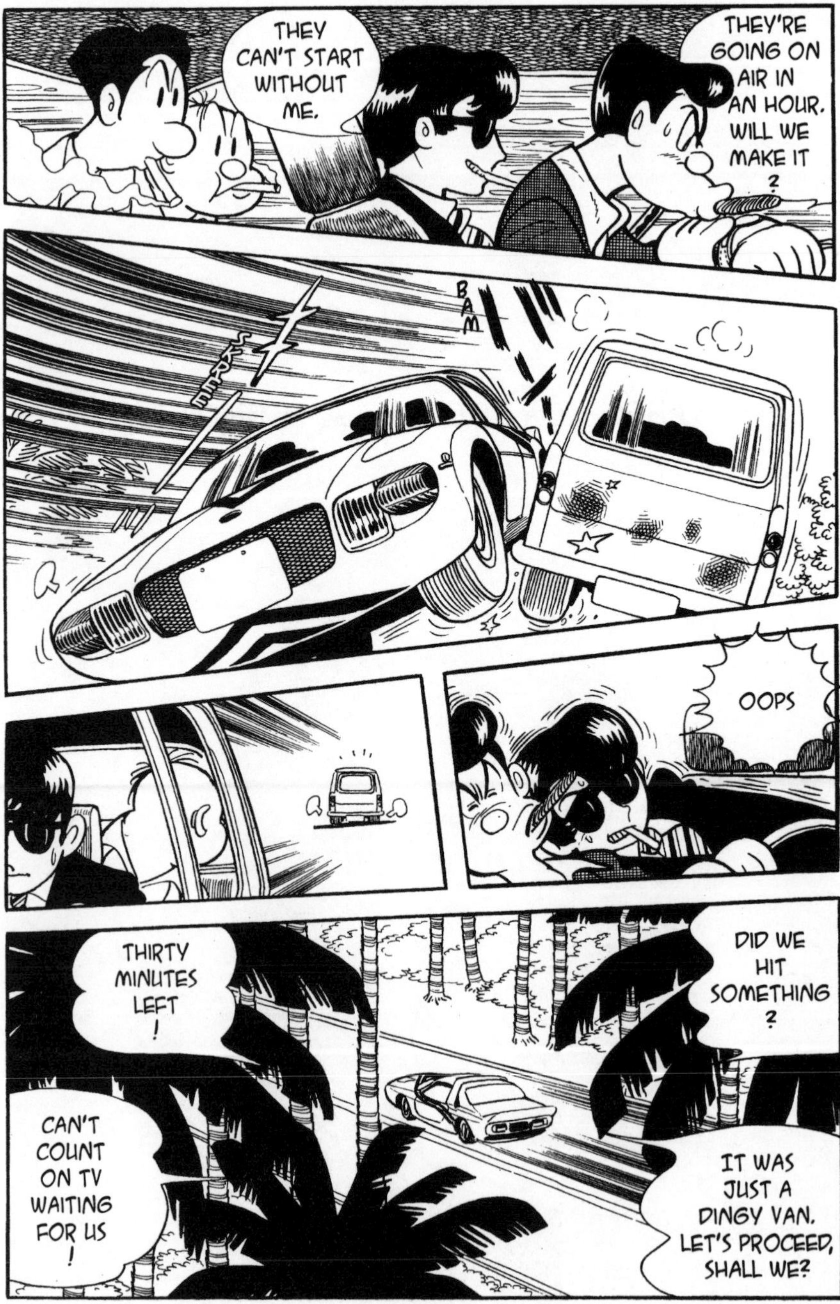
THEY'RE GOING ON AIR IN AN HOUR. WILL WE MAKE IT?
THEY CAN'T START WITHOUT ME.
BAM
SKREE
OOPS
DID WE HIT SOMETHING?
IT WAS JUST A DINGY VAN. LET'S PROCEED, SHALL WE?
THIRTY MINUTES LEFT!
CAN'T COUNT ON TV WAITING FOR US!

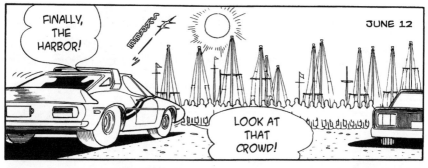

JUNE 12
FINALLY, THE HARBOR!
LOOK AT THAT CROWD!
ROKKU HANMURA IS HERE!
THE HERO OF THIS GREAT ADVENTURE, ROKKU HANMURA!
CLAP
CLAP
AS YOU ALL KNOW, MR. HANMURA IS RESPONSIBLE FOR BESTSELLERS BOTH AS AN AUTHOR AND PUBLISHER. A SUPERMAN, HE HAS RECENTLY PRODUCED AND ACTED IN FILMS AS WELL!
MR. HANMURA'S LATEST CHALLENGE IS TO NAVIGATE THE KUROSHIO CURRENT ALONE BY CANOE FROM MANILA, PHILIPPINES TO KAGOSHIMA, JAPAN!
WHAT IS THE PURPOSE OF THIS SOLO CANOE TRIP?
THE ANCESTORS OF THE JAPANESE MUST HAVE INCLUDED...

NOTE: THE KUROSHIO, LITERALLY *BLACK TIDE*, IS THE GULF STREAM OF THE WESTERN PACIFIC AND OWES ITS DARK HUE TO A PAUCITY OF PLANKTON.

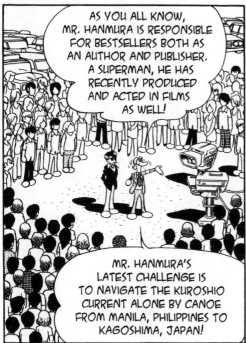

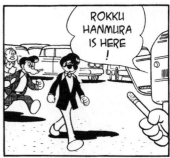

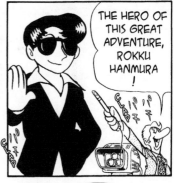

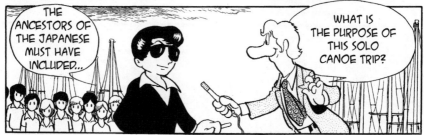

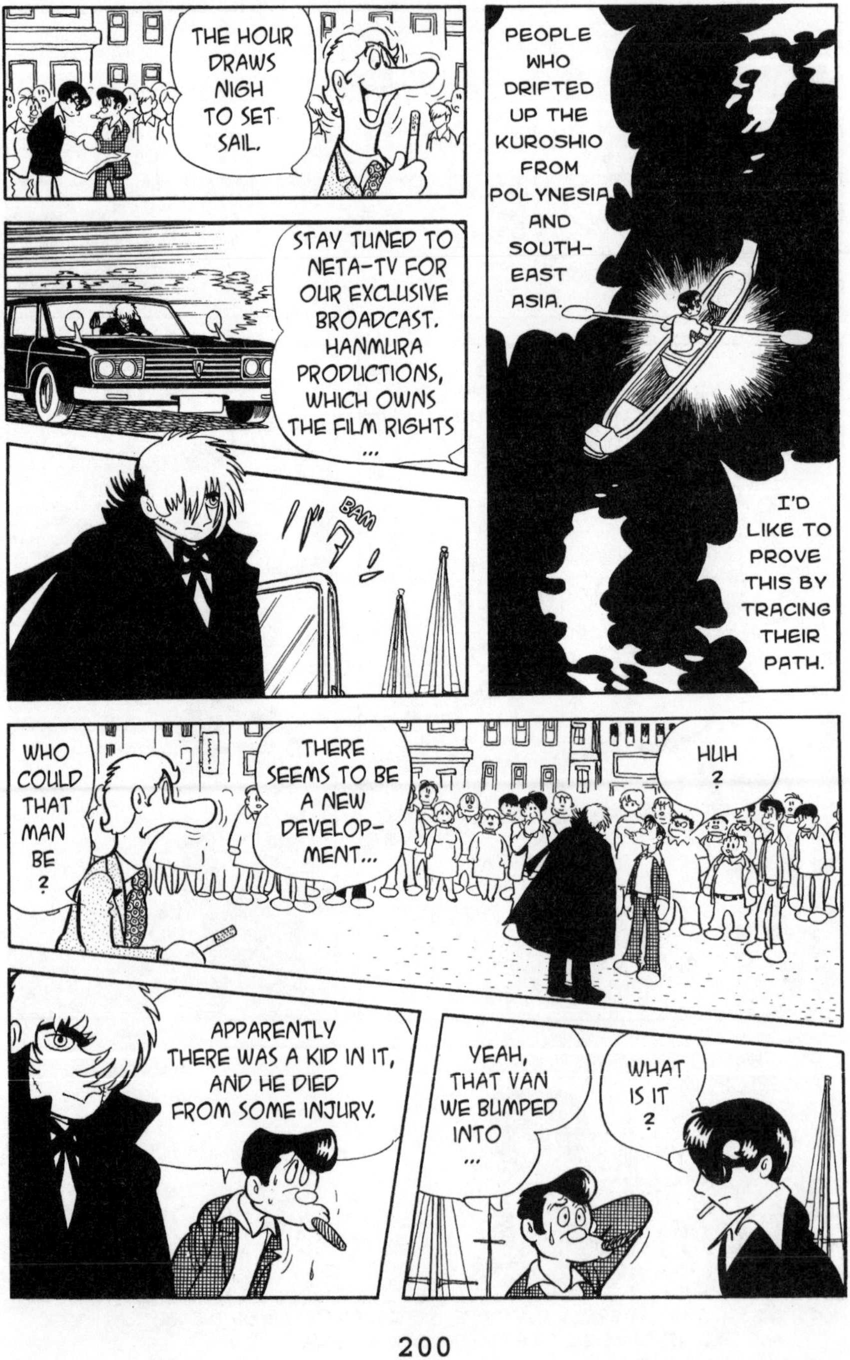
PEOPLE WHO DRIFTED UP THE KUROSHIO FROM POLYNESIA AND SOUTH-EAST ASIA.
I'D LIKE TO PROVE THIS BY TRACING THEIR PATH.
THE HOUR DRAWS NIGH TO SET SAIL.
STAY TUNED TO NETA-TV FOR OUR EXCLUSIVE BROADCAST. HANMURA PRODUCTIONS, WHICH OWNS THE FILM RIGHTS ...
BAM
HUH ?
THERE SEEMS TO BE A NEW DEVELOPMENT...
WHO COULD THAT MAN BE ?
WHAT IS IT ?
YEAH, THAT VAN WE BUMPED INTO ...
APPARENTLY THERE WAS A KID IN IT, AND HE DIED FROM SOME INJURY.

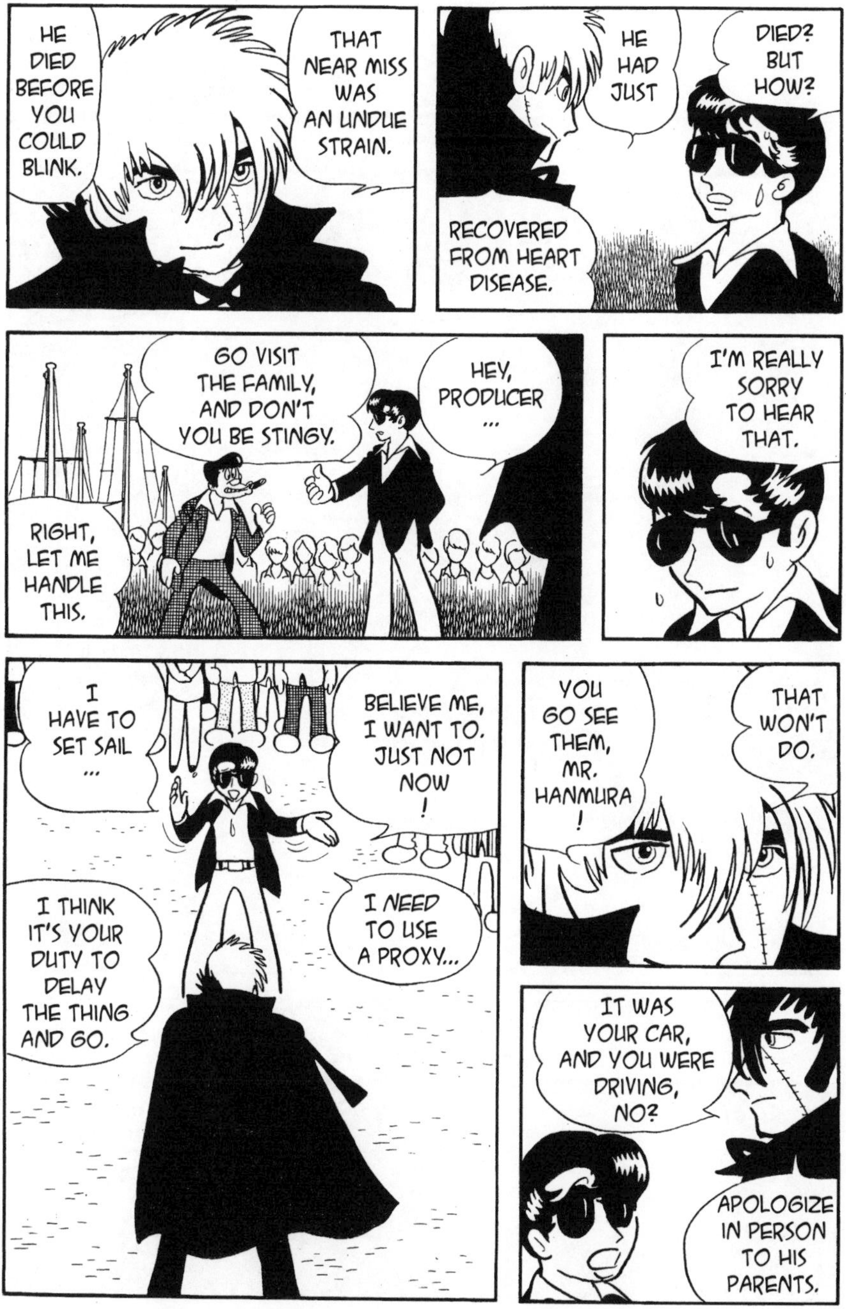
DIED? BUT HOW?
HE HAD JUST
RECOVERED FROM HEART DISEASE.
THAT NEAR MISS WAS AN UNDUE STRAIN.
HE DIED BEFORE YOU COULD BLINK.
I'M REALLY SORRY TO HEAR THAT.
HEY, PRODUCER ...
GO VISIT THE FAMILY, AND DON'T YOU BE STINGY.
RIGHT, LET ME HANDLE THIS.
THAT WON'T DO.
YOU GO SEE THEM, MR. HANMURA!
IT WAS YOUR CAR, AND YOU WERE DRIVING, NO?
APOLOGIZE IN PERSON TO HIS PARENTS.
BELIEVE ME, I WANT TO. JUST NOT NOW!
I HAVE TO SET SAIL ...
I NEED TO USE A PROXY...
I THINK IT'S YOUR DUTY TO DELAY THE THING AND GO.

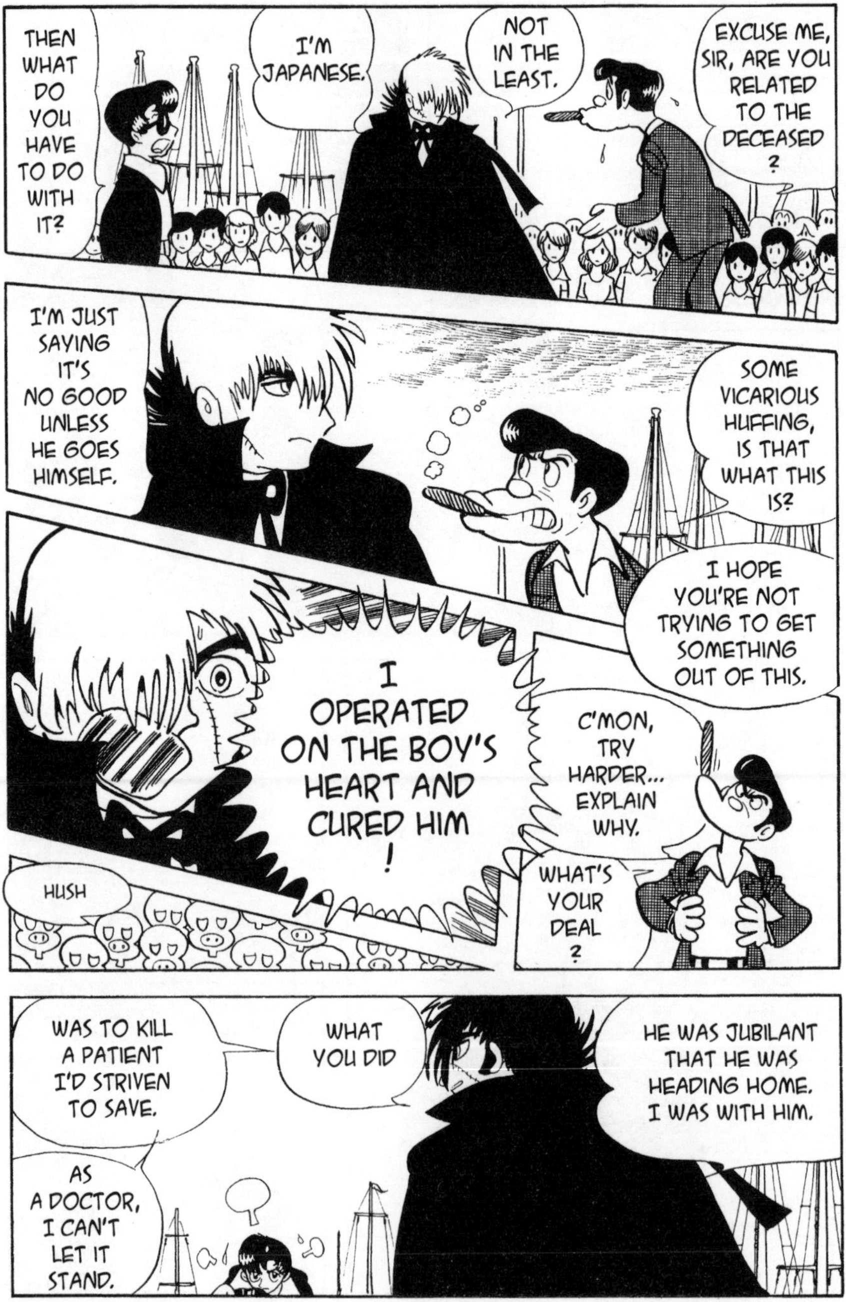
EXCUSE ME, SIR, ARE YOU RELATED TO THE DECEASED?
NOT IN THE LEAST.
I'M JAPANESE.
THEN WHAT DO YOU HAVE TO DO WITH IT?
SOME VICARIOUS HUFFING, IS THAT WHAT THIS IS?
I'M JUST SAYING IT'S NO GOOD UNLESS HE GOES HIMSELF.
I HOPE YOU'RE NOT TRYING TO GET SOMETHING OUT OF THIS.
C'MON, TRY HARDER... EXPLAIN WHY.
WHAT'S YOUR DEAL?
I OPERATED ON THE BOY'S HEART AND CURED HIM!
HUSH
HE WAS JUBILANT THAT HE WAS HEADING HOME. I WAS WITH HIM.
WHAT YOU DID
WAS TO KILL A PATIENT I'D STRIVEN TO SAVE.
AS A DOCTOR, I CAN'T LET IT STAND.

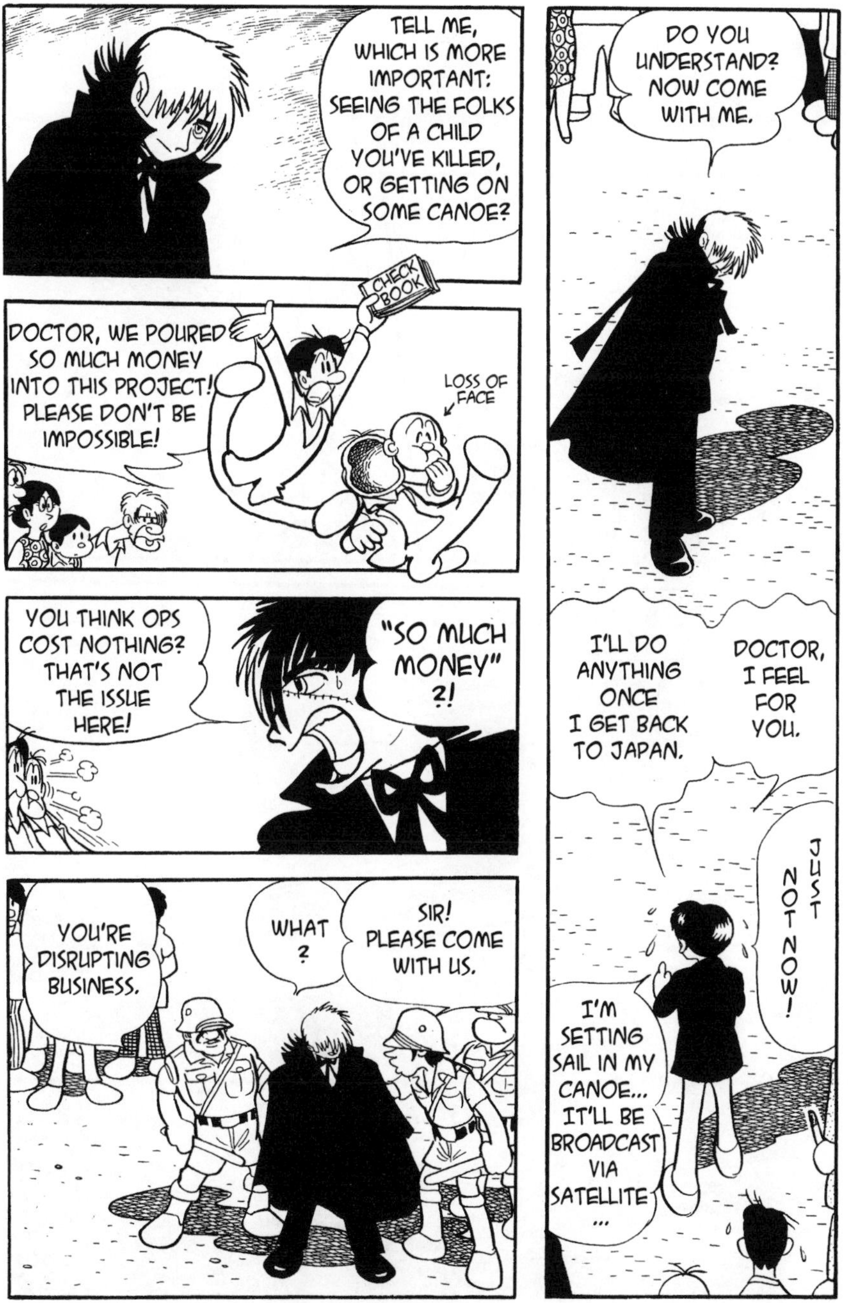
DO YOU UNDERSTAND? NOW COME WITH ME.
DOCTOR, I FEEL FOR YOU.
I'LL DO ANYTHING ONCE I GET BACK TO JAPAN.
JUST NOT NOW!
I'M SETTING SAIL IN MY CANOE... IT'LL BE BROADCAST VIA SATELLITE ...
TELL ME, WHICH IS MORE IMPORTANT: SEEING THE FOLKS OF A CHILD YOU'VE KILLED, OR GETTING ON SOME CANOE?
CHECK BOOK
LOSS OF FACE
DOCTOR, WE POURED SO MUCH MONEY INTO THIS PROJECT! PLEASE DON'T BE IMPOSSIBLE!
"SO MUCH MONEY" ?!
YOU THINK OPS COST NOTHING? THAT'S NOT THE ISSUE HERE!
SIR! PLEASE COME WITH US.
WHAT ?
YOU'RE DISRUPTING BUSINESS.

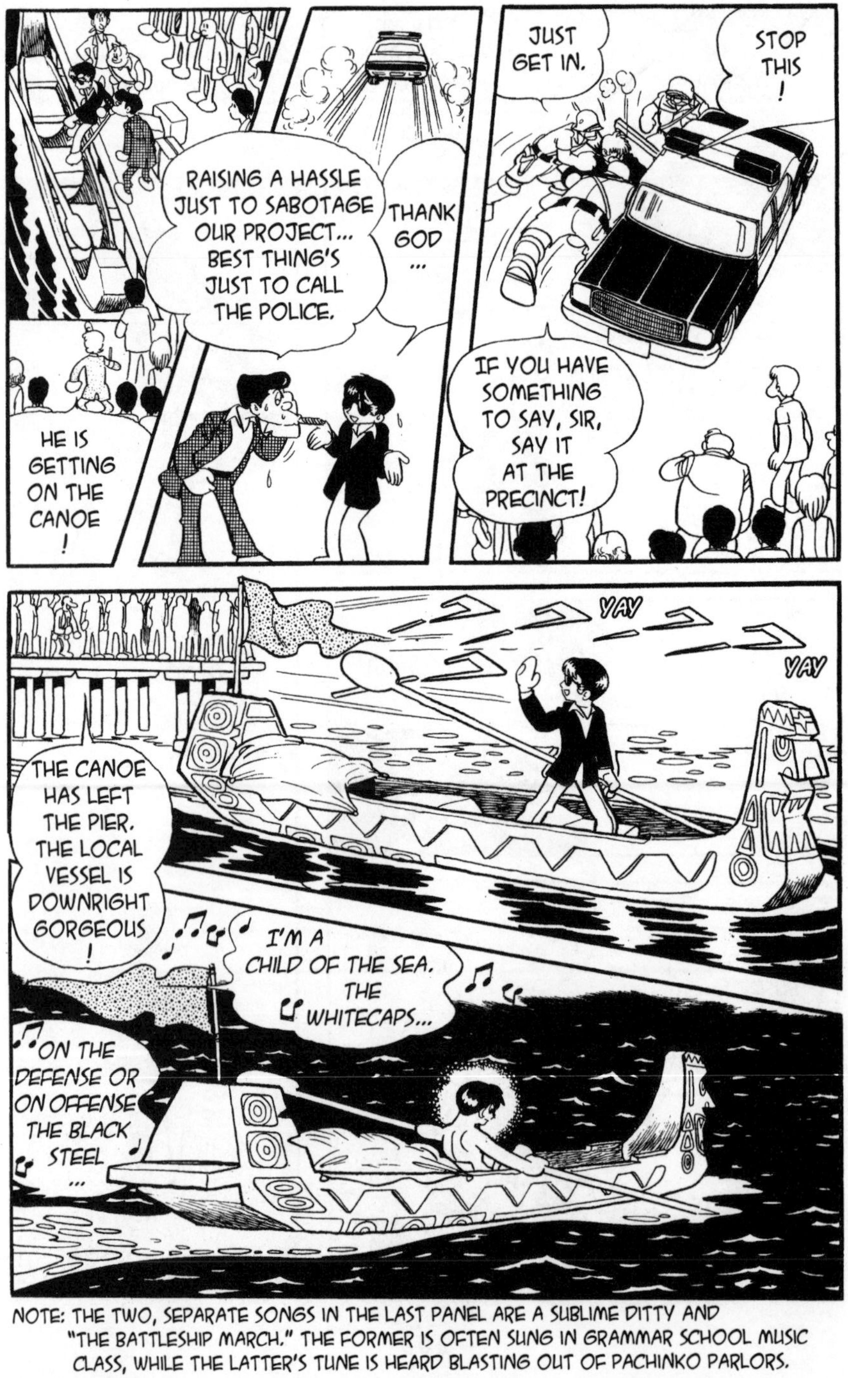
STOP THIS !
JUST GET IN.
IF YOU HAVE SOMETHING TO SAY, SIR, SAY IT AT THE PRECINCT!
RAISING A HASSLE JUST TO SABOTAGE OUR PROJECT... BEST THING'S JUST TO CALL THE POLICE.
THANK GOD ...
HE IS GETTING ON THE CANOE !
YAY
YAY
THE CANOE HAS LEFT THE PIER. THE LOCAL VESSEL IS DOWNRIGHT GORGEOUS !
I'M A CHILD OF THE SEA. THE WHITECAPS...
ON THE DEFENSE OR ON OFFENSE THE BLACK STEEL ...

NOTE: THE TWO, SEPARATE SONGS IN THE LAST PANEL ARE A SUBLIME DITTY AND "THE BATTLESHIP MARCH." THE FORMER IS OFTEN SUNG IN GRAMMAR SCHOOL MUSIC CLASS, WHILE THE LATTER'S TUNE IS HEARD BLASTING OUT OF PACHINKO PARLORS.

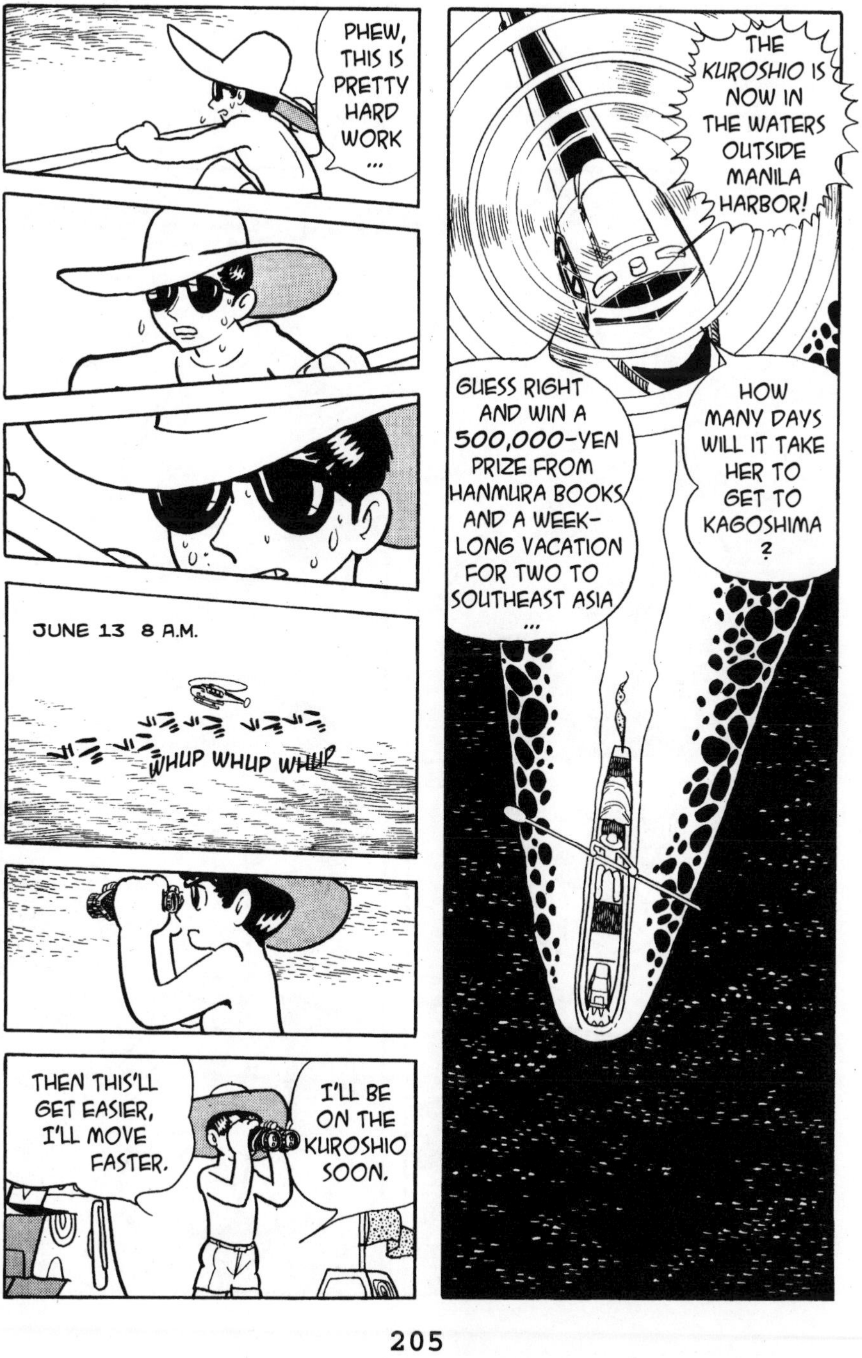
THE KUROSHIO IS NOW IN THE WATERS OUTSIDE MANILA HARBOR!
HOW MANY DAYS WILL IT TAKE HER TO GET TO KAGOSHIMA ?
GUESS RIGHT AND WIN A 500,000-YEN PRIZE FROM HANMURA BOOKS AND A WEEK-LONG VACATION FOR TWO TO SOUTHEAST ASIA ...
PHEW, THIS IS PRETTY HARD WORK ...
JUNE 13 8 A.M.
WHUP WHUP WHUP
I'LL BE ON THE KUROSHIO SOON.
THEN THIS'LL GET EASIER, I'LL MOVE FASTER.

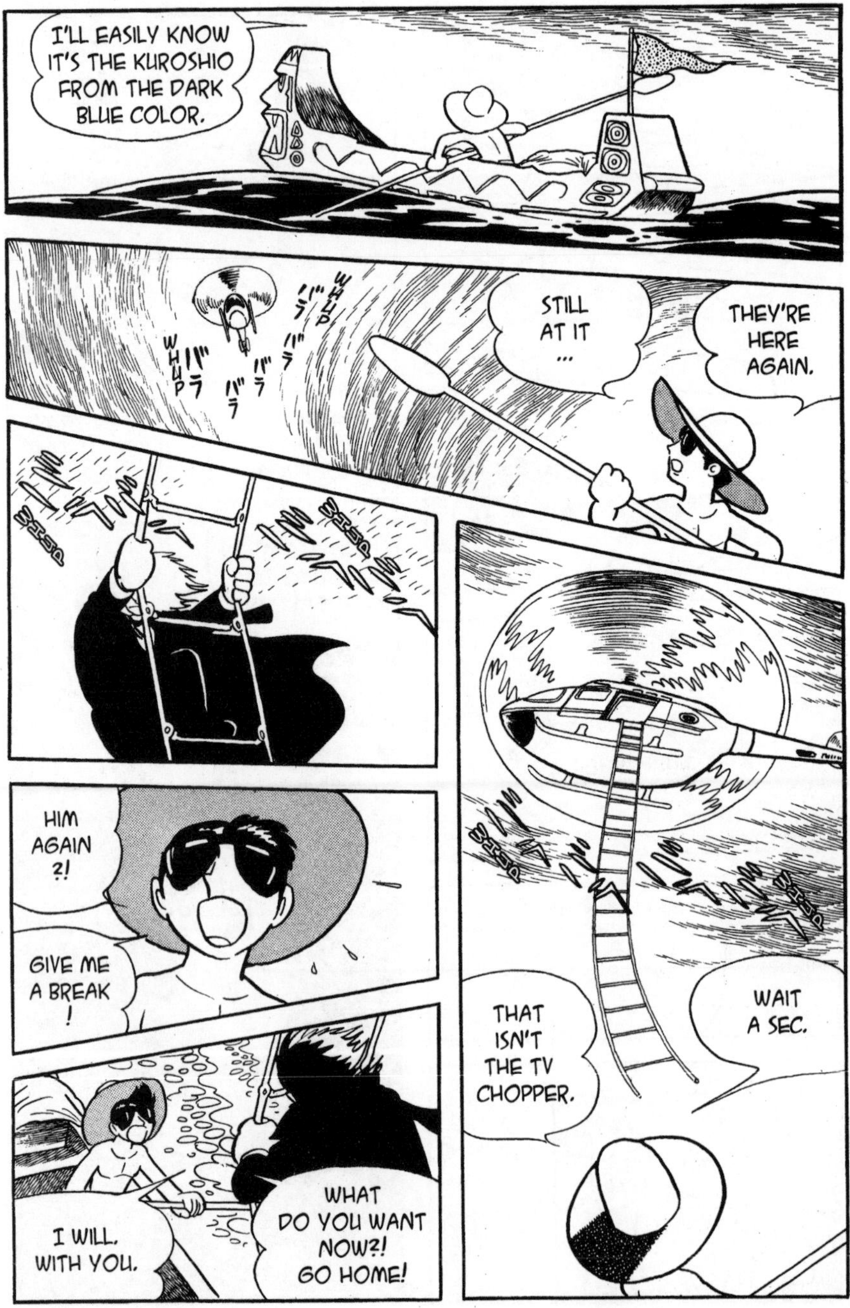
I'LL EASILY KNOW IT'S THE KUROSHIO FROM THE DARK BLUE COLOR.
THEY'RE HERE AGAIN.
STILL AT IT ...
WHUP
バラ バラ
WHUP
バラ バラ
WAIT A SEC.
THAT ISN'T THE TV CHOPPER.
HIM AGAIN ?!
GIVE ME A BREAK !
WHAT DO YOU WANT NOW?! GO HOME!
I WILL. WITH YOU.

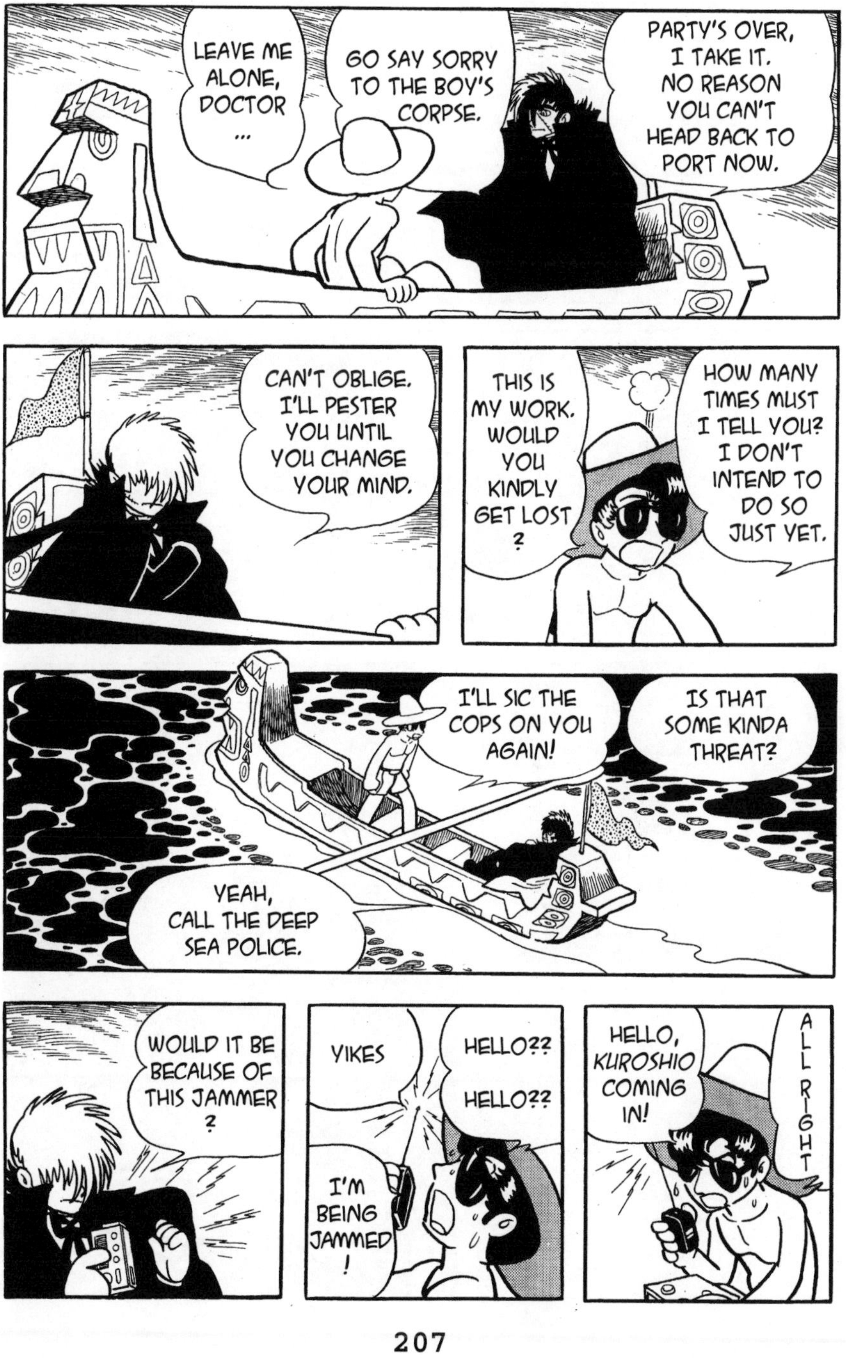
PARTY'S OVER, I TAKE IT. NO REASON YOU CAN'T HEAD BACK TO PORT NOW.
GO SAY SORRY TO THE BOY'S CORPSE.
LEAVE ME ALONE, DOCTOR ...
HOW MANY TIMES MUST I TELL YOU? I DON'T INTEND TO DO SO JUST YET.
THIS IS MY WORK. WOULD YOU KINDLY GET LOST?
CAN'T OBLIGE. I'LL PESTER YOU UNTIL YOU CHANGE YOUR MIND.
IS THAT SOME KINDA THREAT?
I'LL SIC THE COPS ON YOU AGAIN!
YEAH, CALL THE DEEP SEA POLICE.
ALL RIGHT
HELLO, KUROSHIO COMING IN!
HELLO??
HELLO??
YIKES
I'M BEING JAMMED!
WOULD IT BE BECAUSE OF THIS JAMMER?

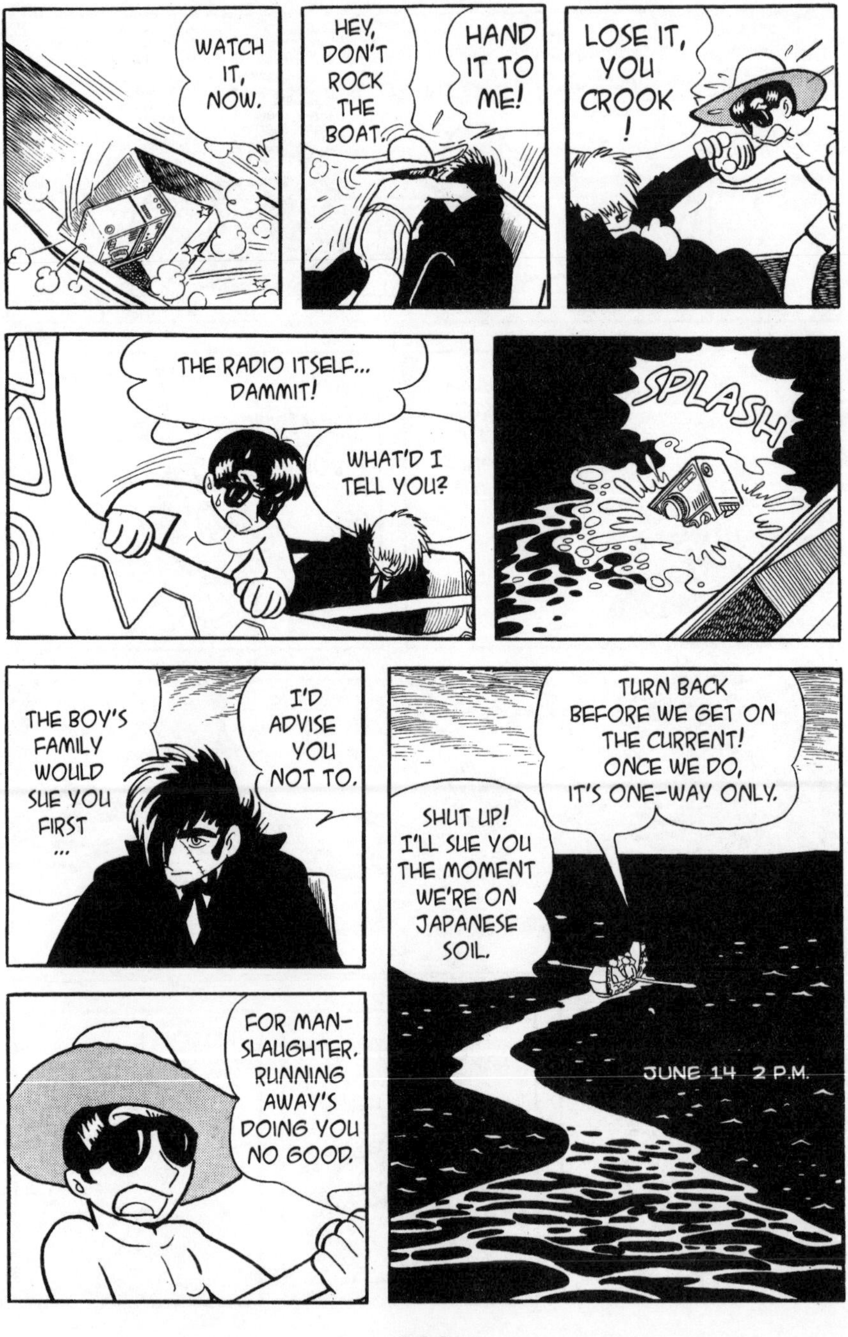

LOSE IT, YOU CROOK!
HAND IT TO ME!
HEY, DON'T ROCK THE BOAT.
WATCH IT, NOW.
SPLASH
THE RADIO ITSELF... DAMMIT!
WHAT'D I TELL YOU?
TURN BACK BEFORE WE GET ON THE CURRENT! ONCE WE DO, IT'S ONE-WAY ONLY.
SHUT UP! I'LL SUE YOU THE MOMENT WE'RE ON JAPANESE SOIL.
JUNE 14 2 P.M.
I'D ADVISE YOU NOT TO.
THE BOY'S FAMILY WOULD SUE YOU FIRST ...
FOR MAN-SLAUGHTER. RUNNING AWAY'S DOING YOU NO GOOD.

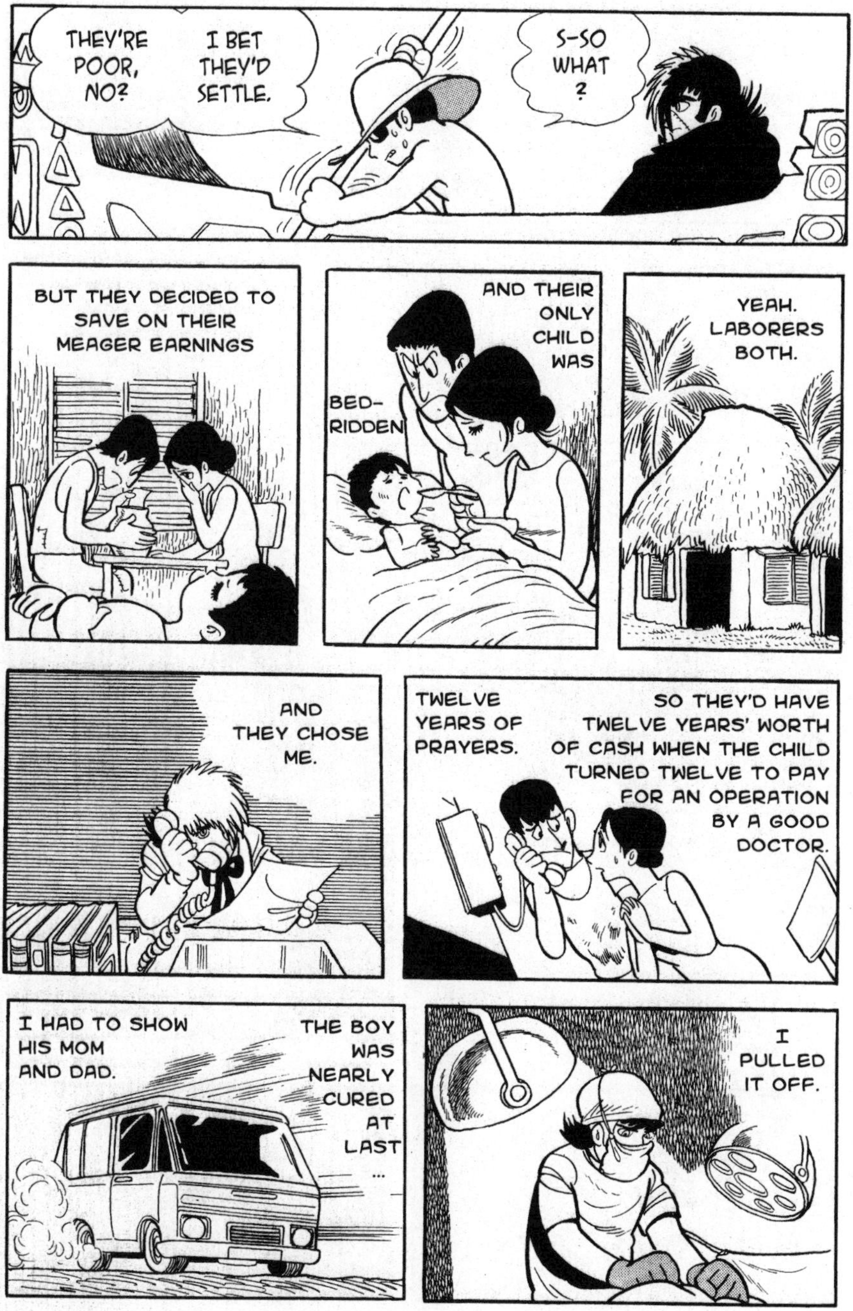
S-SO WHAT?
I BET THEY'D SETTLE.
THEY'RE POOR, NO?
YEAH. LABORERS BOTH.
AND THEIR ONLY CHILD WAS
BED-RIDDEN
BUT THEY DECIDED TO SAVE ON THEIR MEAGER EARNINGS
SO THEY'D HAVE TWELVE YEARS' WORTH OF CASH WHEN THE CHILD TURNED TWELVE TO PAY FOR AN OPERATION BY A GOOD DOCTOR.
TWELVE YEARS OF PRAYERS.
AND THEY CHOSE ME.
I PULLED IT OFF.
THE BOY WAS NEARLY CURED AT LAST ...
I HAD TO SHOW HIS MOM AND DAD.

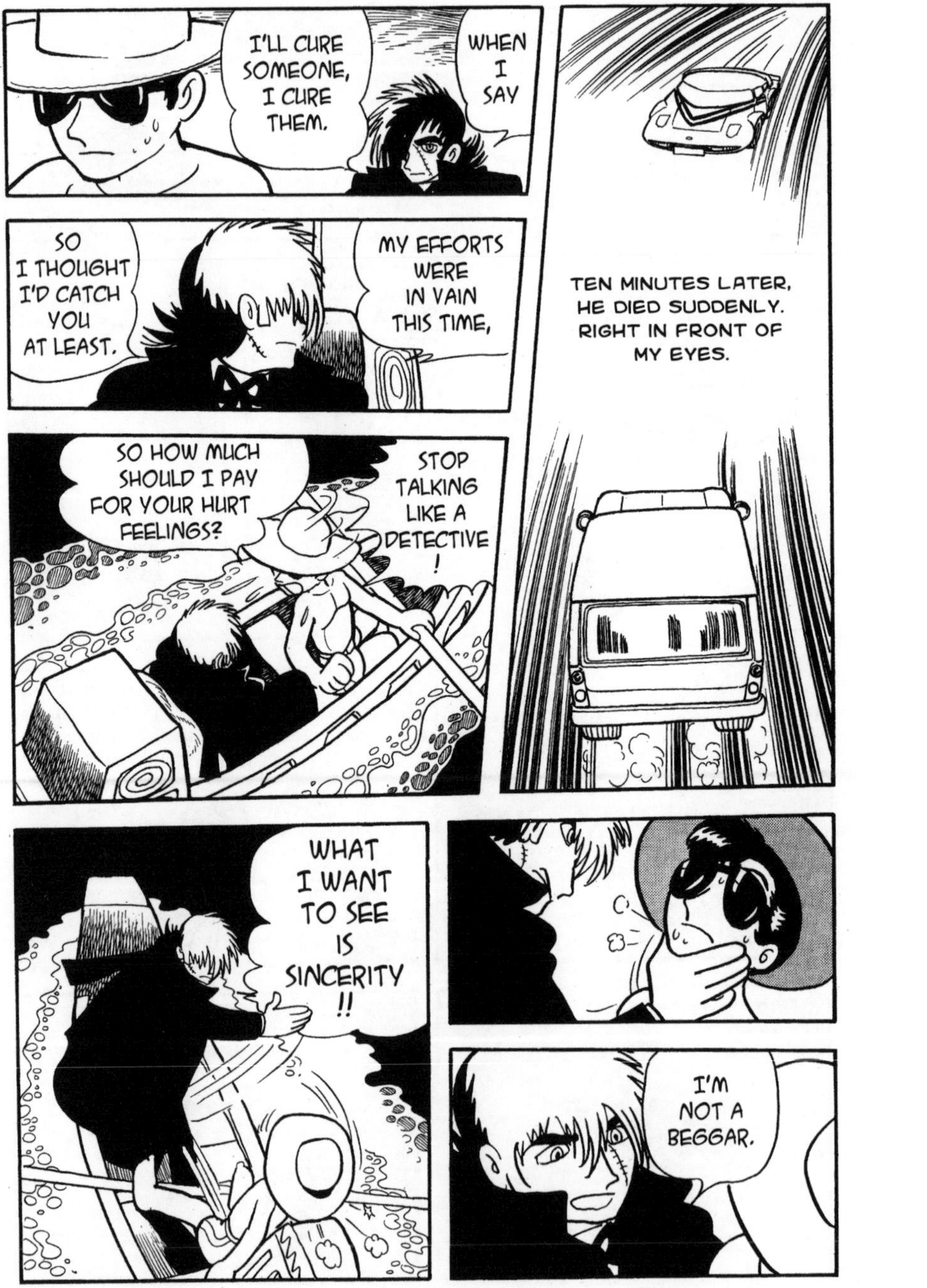
TEN MINUTES LATER, HE DIED SUDDENLY. RIGHT IN FRONT OF MY EYES.
WHEN I SAY
I'LL CURE SOMEONE, I CURE THEM.
MY EFFORTS WERE IN VAIN THIS TIME,
SO I THOUGHT I'D CATCH YOU AT LEAST.
STOP TALKING LIKE A DETECTIVE!
SO HOW MUCH SHOULD I PAY FOR YOUR HURT FEELINGS?
I'M NOT A BEGGAR.
WHAT I WANT TO SEE IS SINCERITY!!

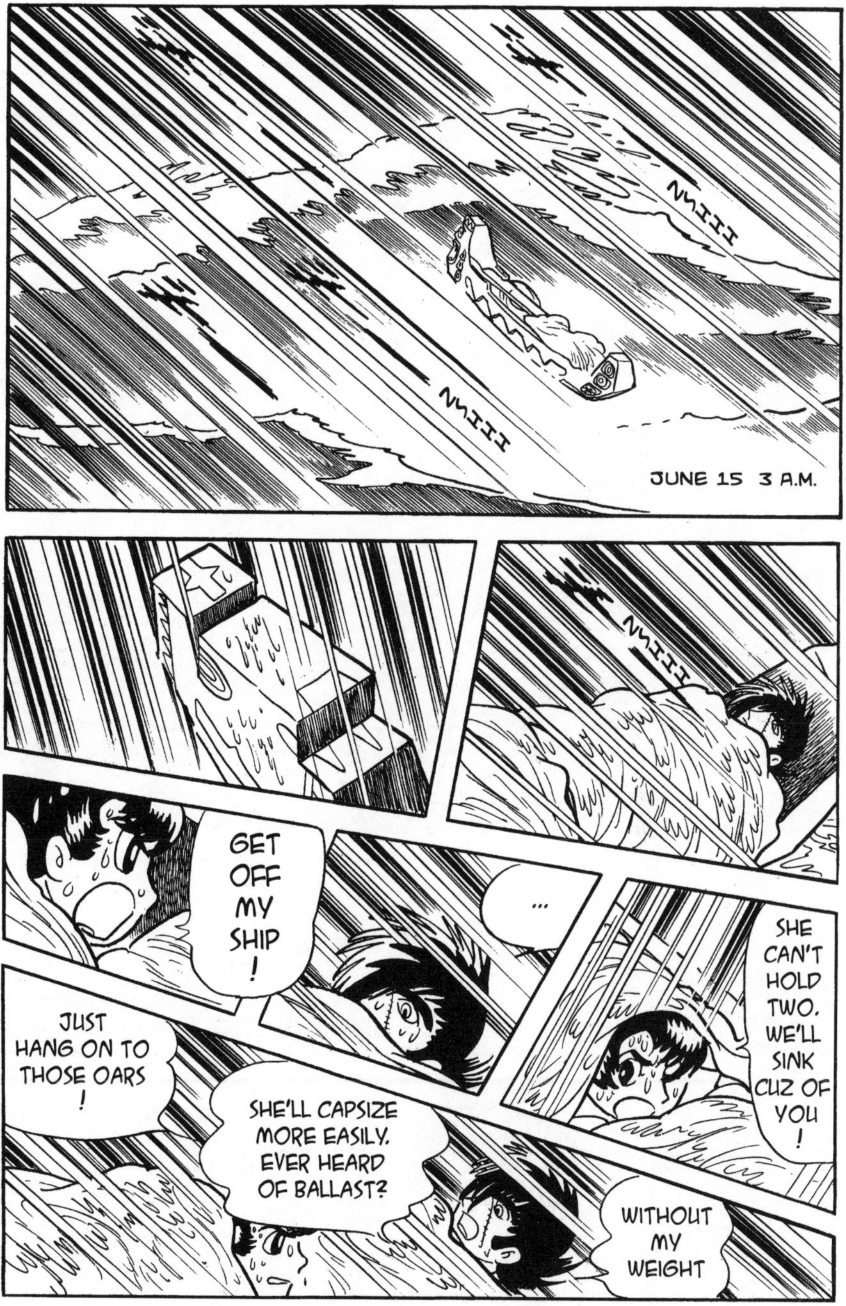
JUNE 15 3 A.M.
SHE CAN'T HOLD TWO. WE'LL SINK CUZ OF YOU!
...
GET OFF MY SHIP!
WITHOUT MY WEIGHT
SHE'LL CAPSIZE MORE EASILY. EVER HEARD OF BALLAST?
JUST HANG ON TO THOSE OARS!

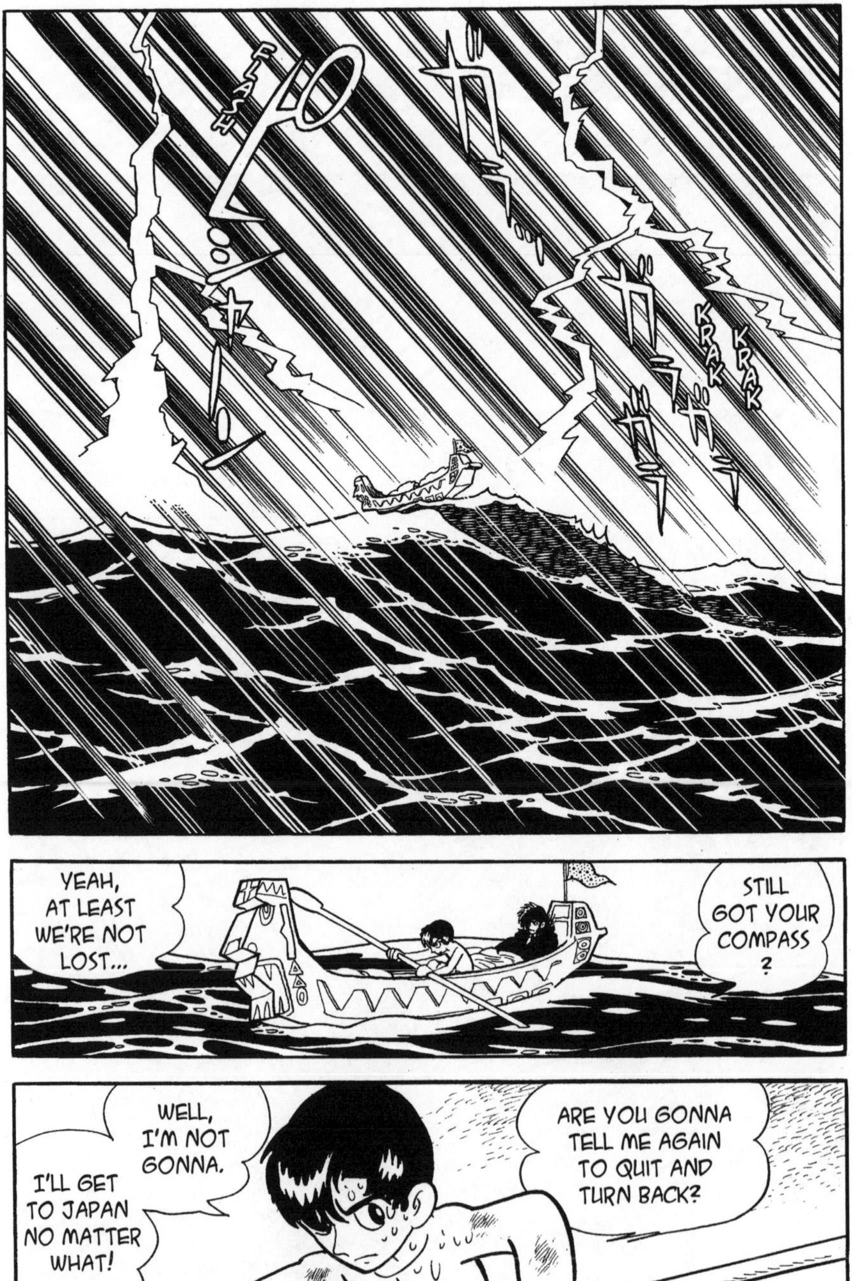
KRAK
KRAK
FLASH
STILL GOT YOUR COMPASS?
YEAH, AT LEAST WE'RE NOT LOST...
ARE YOU GONNA TELL ME AGAIN TO QUIT AND TURN BACK?
WELL, I'M NOT GONNA.
I'LL GET TO JAPAN NO MATTER WHAT!

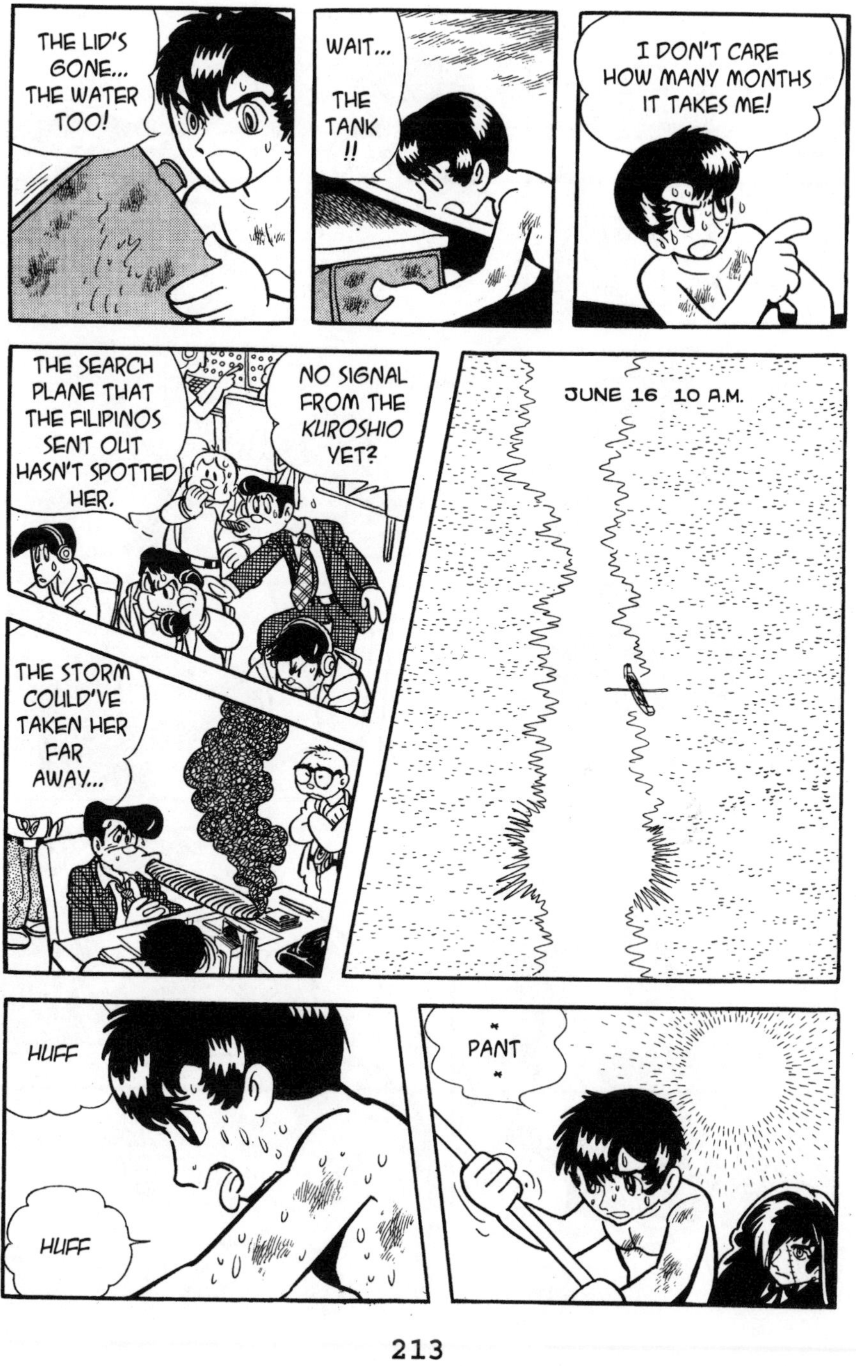
I DON'T CARE HOW MANY MONTHS IT TAKES ME!
WAIT...
THE TANK !!
THE LID'S GONE... THE WATER TOO!
JUNE 16 10 A.M.
NO SIGNAL FROM THE KUROSHIO YET?
THE SEARCH PLANE THAT THE FILIPINOS SENT OUT HASN'T SPOTTED HER.
THE STORM COULD'VE TAKEN HER FAR AWAY...
PANT
HUFF
HUFF

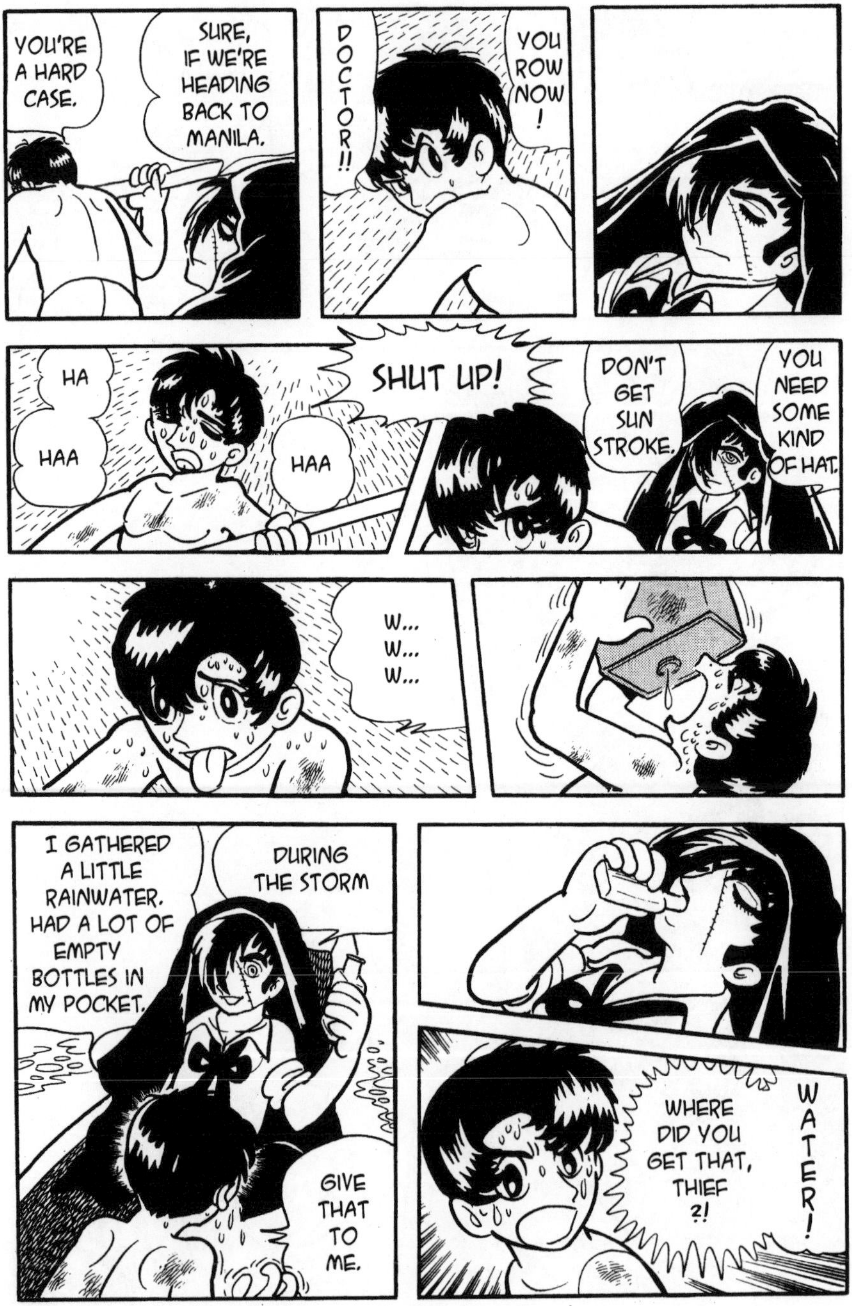
YOU ROW NOW!
DOCTOR!!
SURE, IF WE'RE HEADING BACK TO MANILA.
YOU'RE A HARD CASE.
YOU NEED SOME KIND OF HAT.
DON'T GET SUN STROKE.
SHUT UP!
HA
HAA
HAA
W... W... W...
WATER!
WHERE DID YOU GET THAT, THIEF?!
DURING THE STORM
I GATHERED A LITTLE RAINWATER. HAD A LOT OF EMPTY BOTTLES IN MY POCKET.
GIVE THAT TO ME.

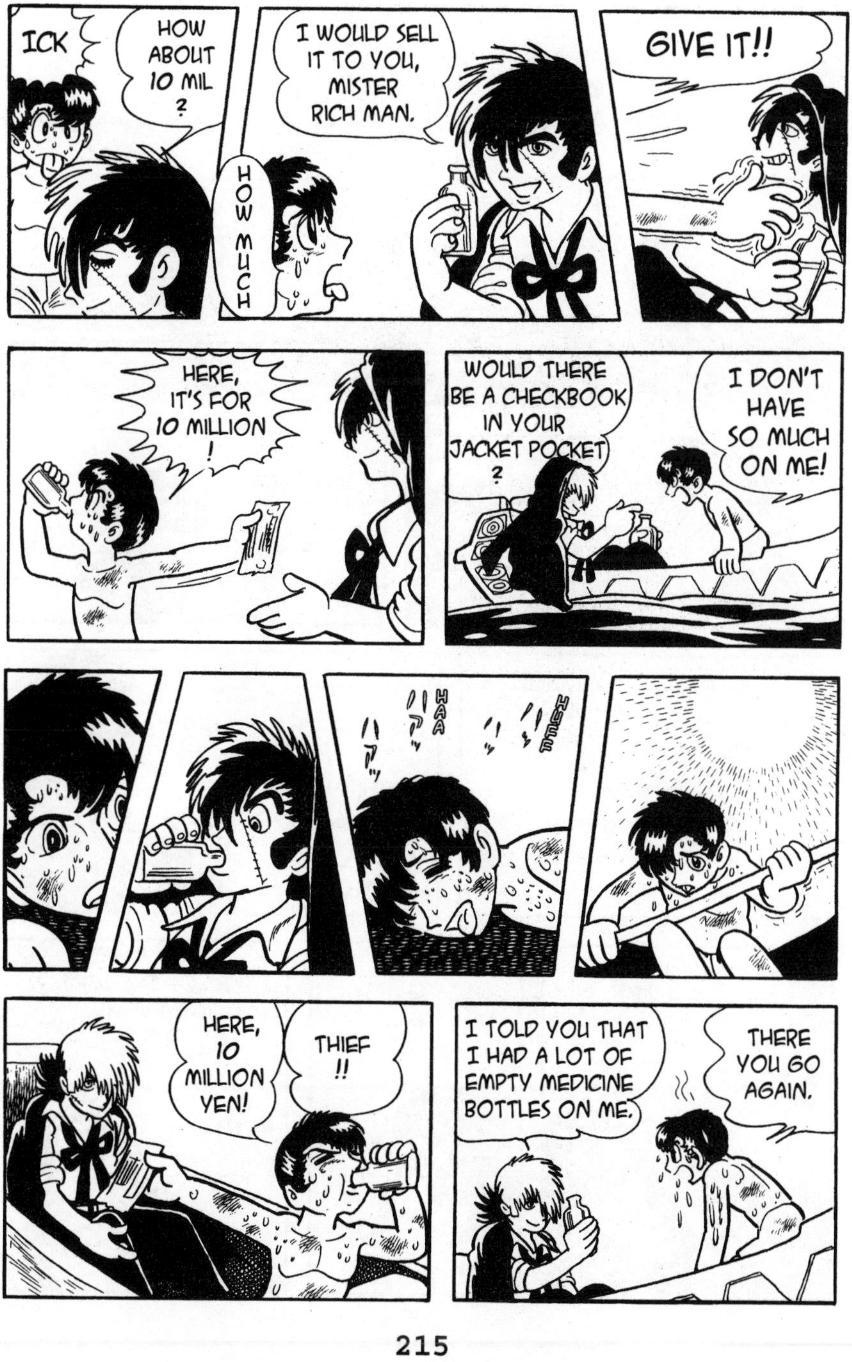
GIVE IT!!
I WOULD SELL IT TO YOU, MISTER RICH MAN.
HOW MUCH
HOW ABOUT 10 MIL ?
ICK
I DON'T HAVE SO MUCH ON ME!
WOULD THERE BE A CHECKBOOK IN YOUR JACKET POCKET ?
HERE, IT'S FOR 10 MILLION !
HUFF
HAA
THERE YOU GO AGAIN.
I TOLD YOU THAT I HAD A LOT OF EMPTY MEDICINE BOTTLES ON ME.
THIEF !!
HERE, 10 MILLION YEN!

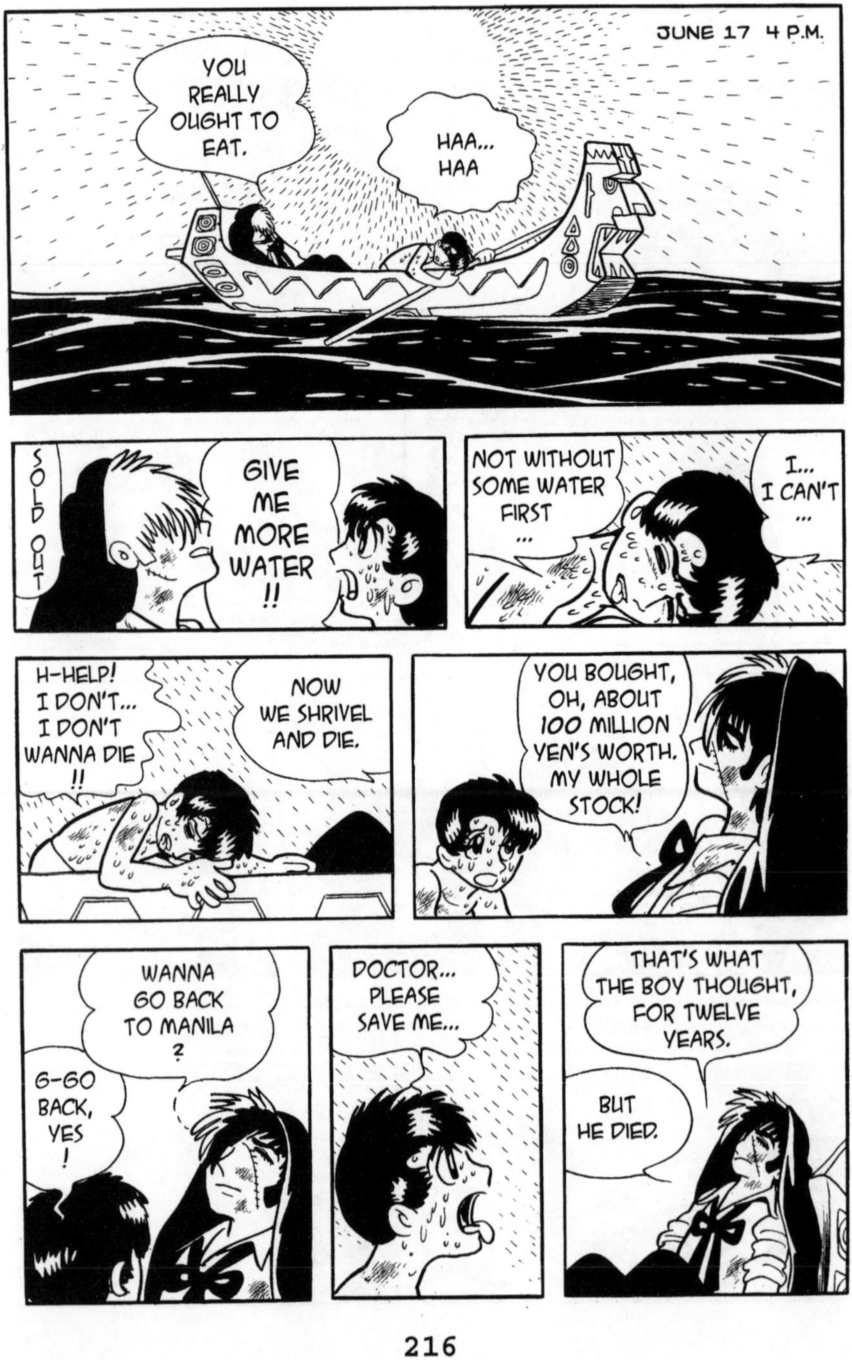
JUNE 17 4 P.M.
HAA... HAA
YOU REALLY OUGHT TO EAT.
I... I CAN'T ...
NOT WITHOUT SOME WATER FIRST ...
GIVE ME MORE WATER !!
SOLD OUT
YOU BOUGHT, OH, ABOUT 100 MILLION YEN'S WORTH. MY WHOLE STOCK!
NOW WE SHRIVEL AND DIE.
H-HELP! I DON'T... I DON'T WANNA DIE !!
THAT'S WHAT THE BOY THOUGHT, FOR TWELVE YEARS.
BUT HE DIED.
DOCTOR... PLEASE SAVE ME...
WANNA GO BACK TO MANILA ?
G-GO BACK, YES !

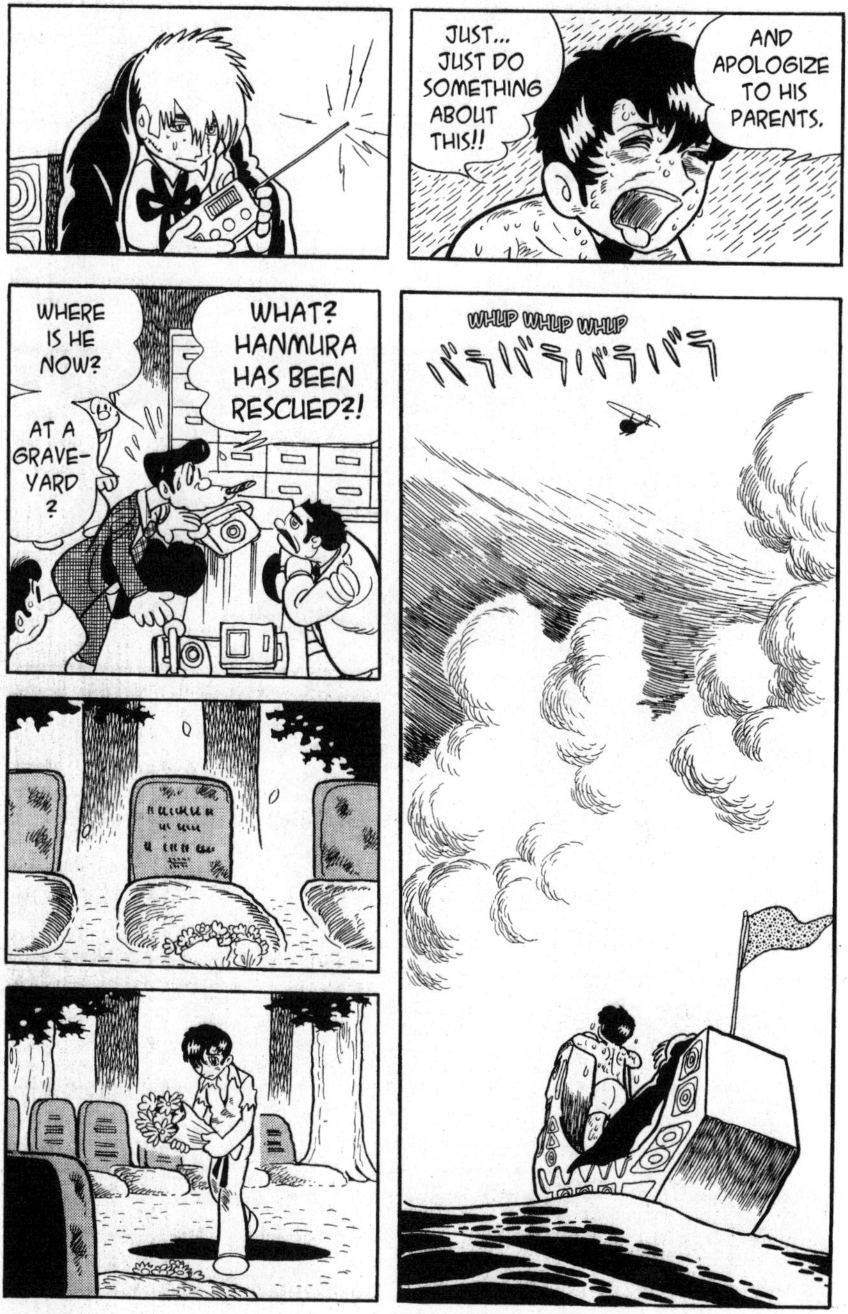
JUST... JUST DO SOMETHING ABOUT THIS!!
AND APOLOGIZE TO HIS PARENTS.
WHLP WHLP WHLP
バラバラバラバラ
WHAT? HANMURA HAS BEEN RESCUED?!
WHERE IS HE NOW?
AT A GRAVE-YARD?

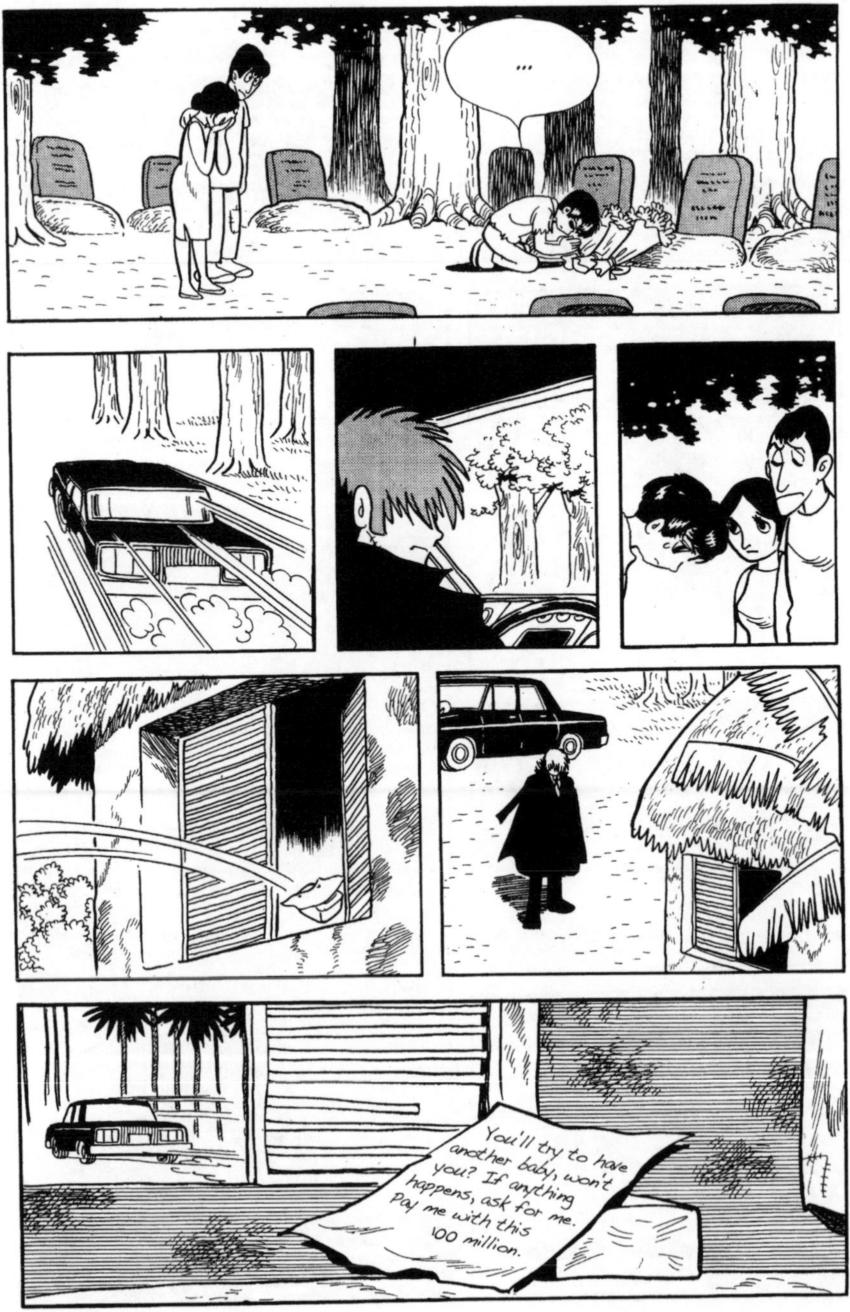
...
You'll try to have another baby, won't you? If anything happens, ask for me. Pay me with this 100 million.

BLACK AND WHITE

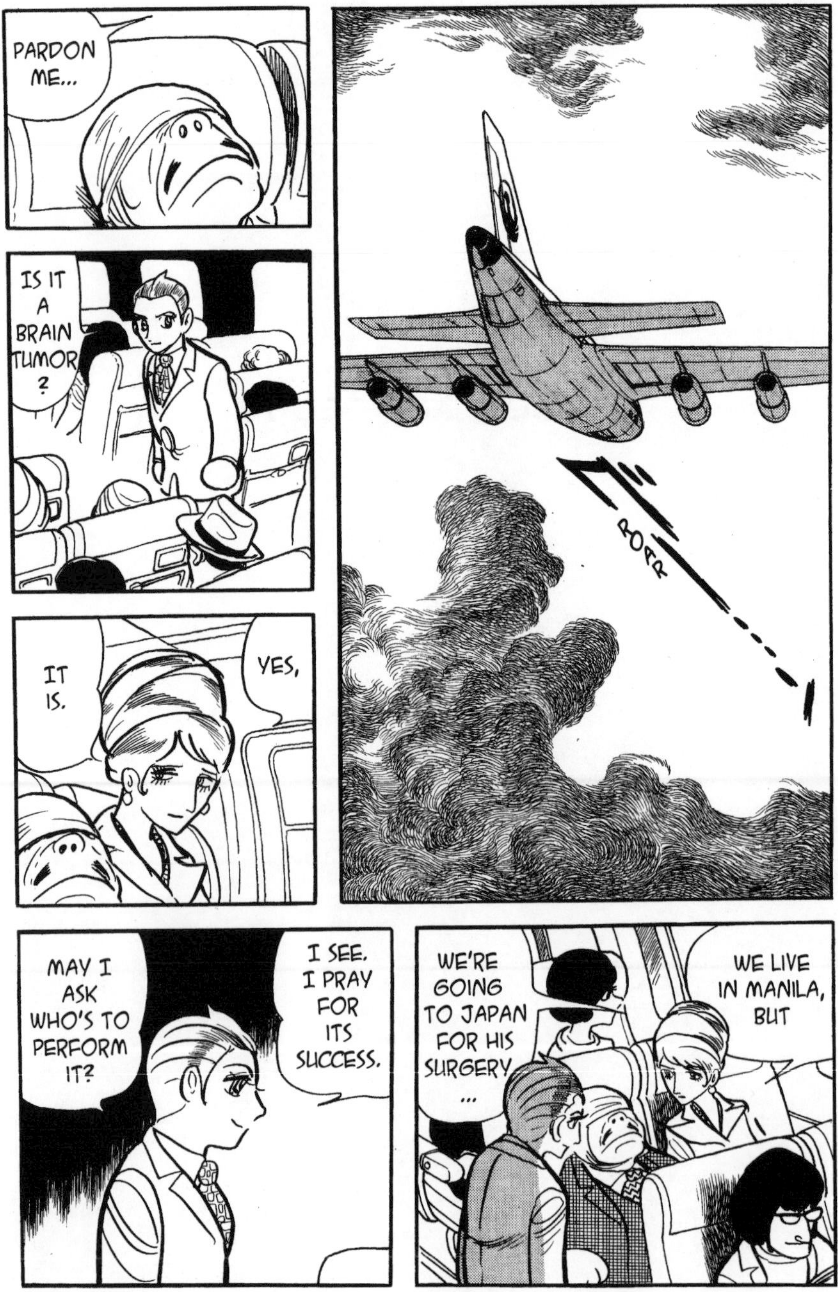
ROAR
PARDON ME...
IS IT A BRAIN TUMOR?
YES,
IT IS.
WE LIVE IN MANILA, BUT
WE'RE GOING TO JAPAN FOR HIS SURGERY...
I SEE. I PRAY FOR ITS SUCCESS.
MAY I ASK WHO'S TO PERFORM IT?

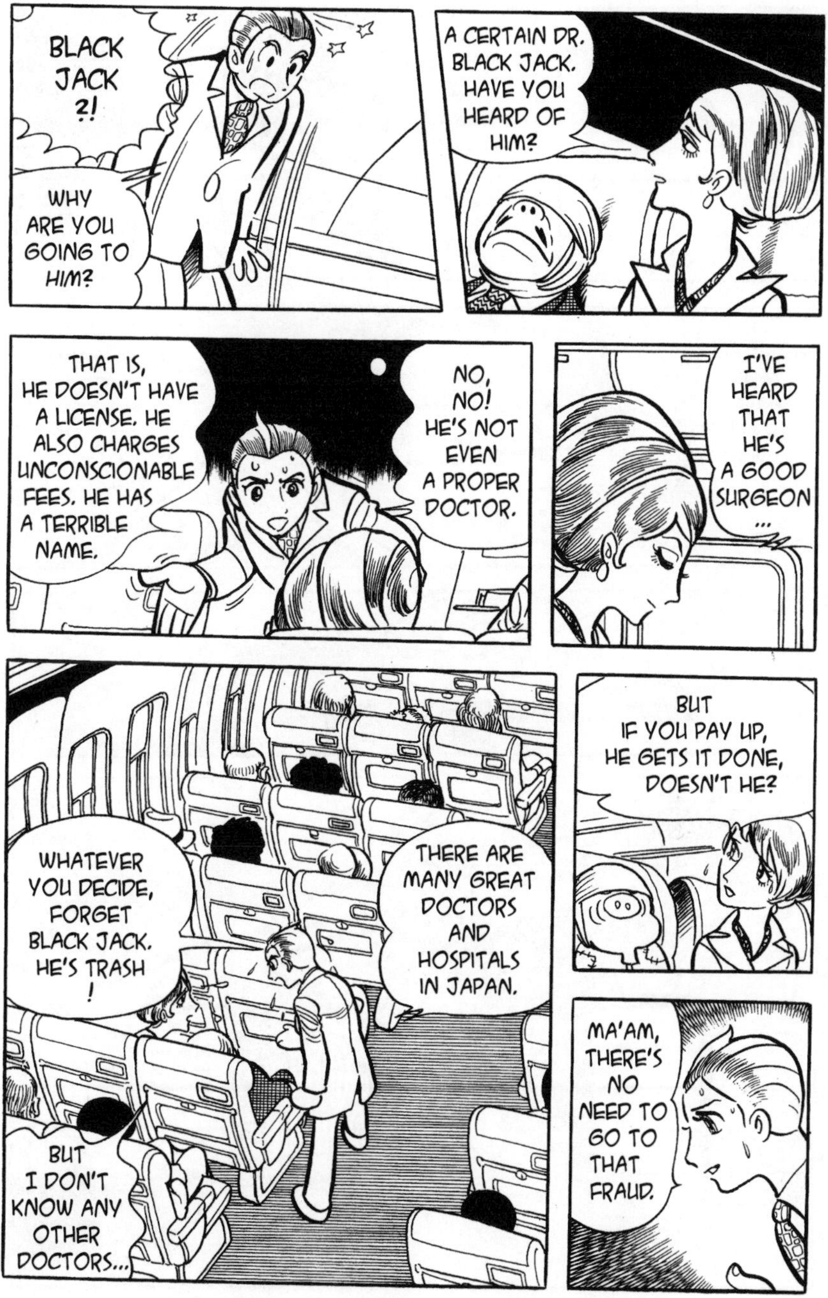
A CERTAIN DR. BLACK JACK. HAVE YOU HEARD OF HIM?
BLACK JACK ?!
WHY ARE YOU GOING TO HIM?
I'VE HEARD THAT HE'S A GOOD SURGEON ...
NO, NO! HE'S NOT EVEN A PROPER DOCTOR.
THAT IS, HE DOESN'T HAVE A LICENSE. HE ALSO CHARGES UNCONSCIONABLE FEES. HE HAS A TERRIBLE NAME.
BUT IF YOU PAY UP, HE GETS IT DONE, DOESN'T HE?
MA'AM, THERE'S NO NEED TO GO TO THAT FRAUD.
THERE ARE MANY GREAT DOCTORS AND HOSPITALS IN JAPAN.
WHATEVER YOU DECIDE, FORGET BLACK JACK. HE'S TRASH !
BUT I DON'T KNOW ANY OTHER DOCTORS...

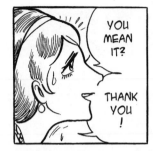

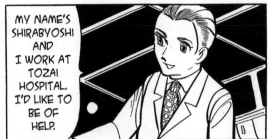

MY NAME'S SHIRABYOSHI AND I WORK AT TOZAI HOSPITAL. I'D LIKE TO BE OF HELP.
YOU MEAN IT?
THANK YOU!
NOT ALL JAPANESE ARE MONEY-GRUBBING ANIMALS.
JAPAN AIR LINES
OUR HOSPITAL CAN PROVE THAT TO YOU!
ギギギ
KREE

NOTE: THE FIRST CHARACTER OF THE NAME "SHIRABYOSHI" MEANS WHITE, IN OBVIOUS CONTRAST TO "BLACK JACK."

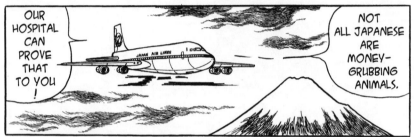

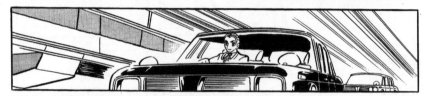

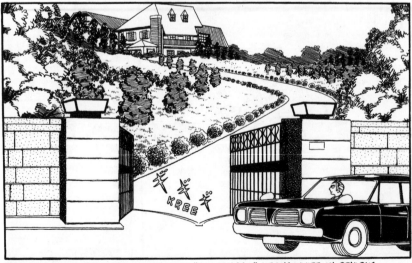

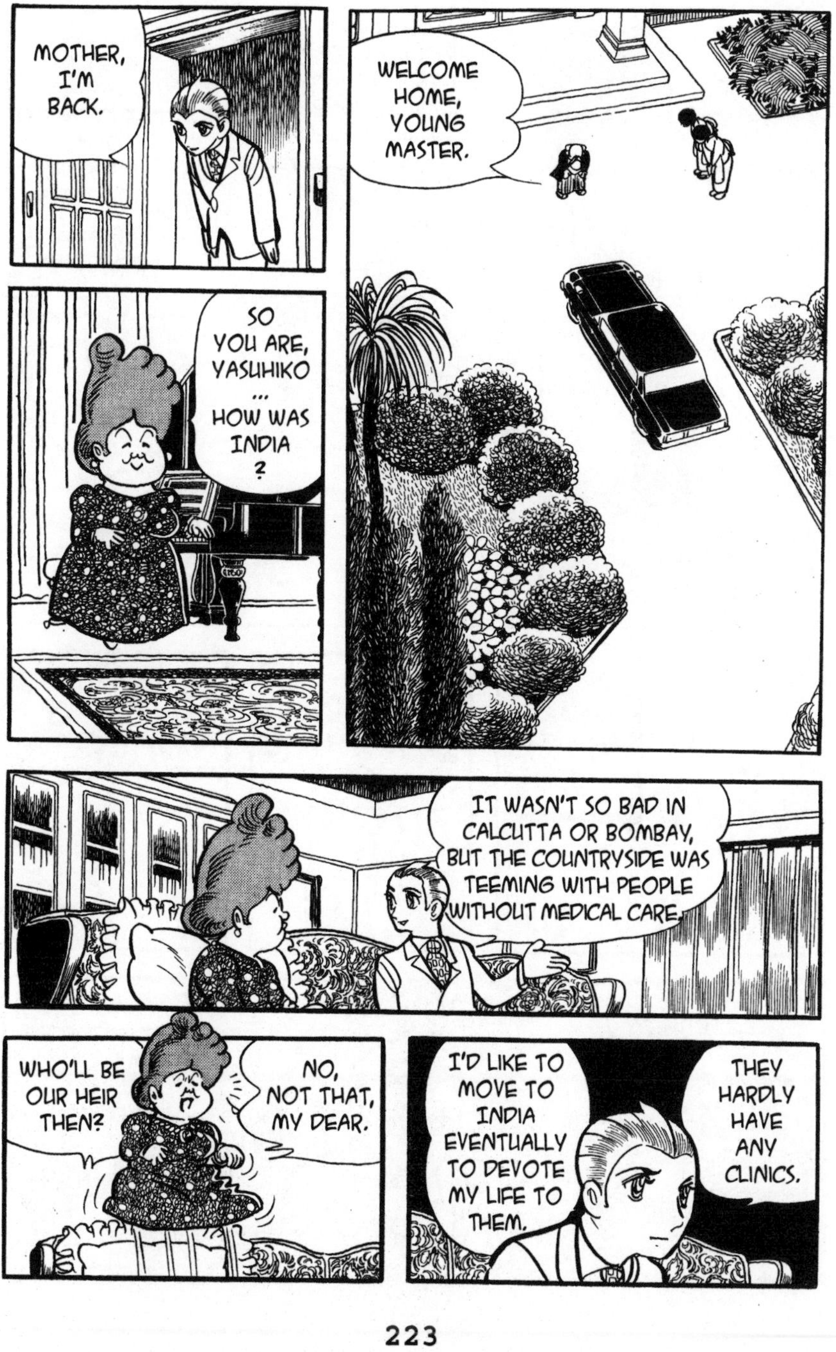
WELCOME HOME, YOUNG MASTER.
MOTHER, I'M BACK.
SO YOU ARE, YASUHIKO ... HOW WAS INDIA ?
IT WASN'T SO BAD IN CALCUTTA OR BOMBAY, BUT THE COUNTRYSIDE WAS TEEMING WITH PEOPLE WITHOUT MEDICAL CARE.
THEY HARDLY HAVE ANY CLINICS.
I'D LIKE TO MOVE TO INDIA EVENTUALLY TO DEVOTE MY LIFE TO THEM.
NO, NOT THAT, MY DEAR.
WHO'LL BE OUR HEIR THEN?

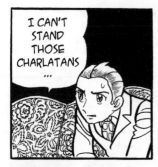

MOTHER, THESE FAITH HEALERS ARE QUITE COMMON IN THE INDIAN INTERIOR EVEN TODAY.
THE TREATMENTS THAT THEY ADMINISTER ARE PREPOSTEROUS. AND YET, SO MANY PEOPLE CHOOSE TO BE SWINDLED BY THEM.
I CAN'T STAND THOSE CHARLATANS ...
WE USED TO HAVE THEM IN JAPAN, TOO.
WE STILL DO.
THERE'S A MAN CALLED BLACK JACK...
HELLO, DR. S?
WHAT IS IT?
WE TOOK AN X-RAY OF THAT PATIENT FROM MANILA THAT YOU HAD CHECKED IN.
AN OBJECT'S LODGED BETWEEN HIS CEREBELLUM AND MEDULLA. NO WAY WE CAN OPERATE.

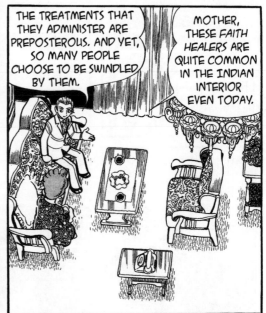

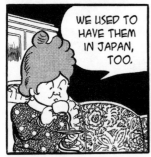

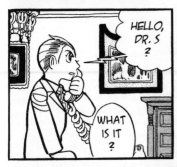

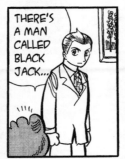

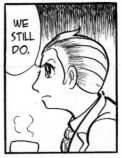

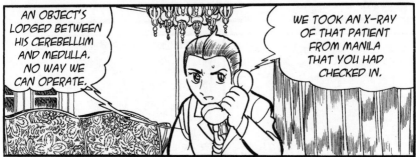

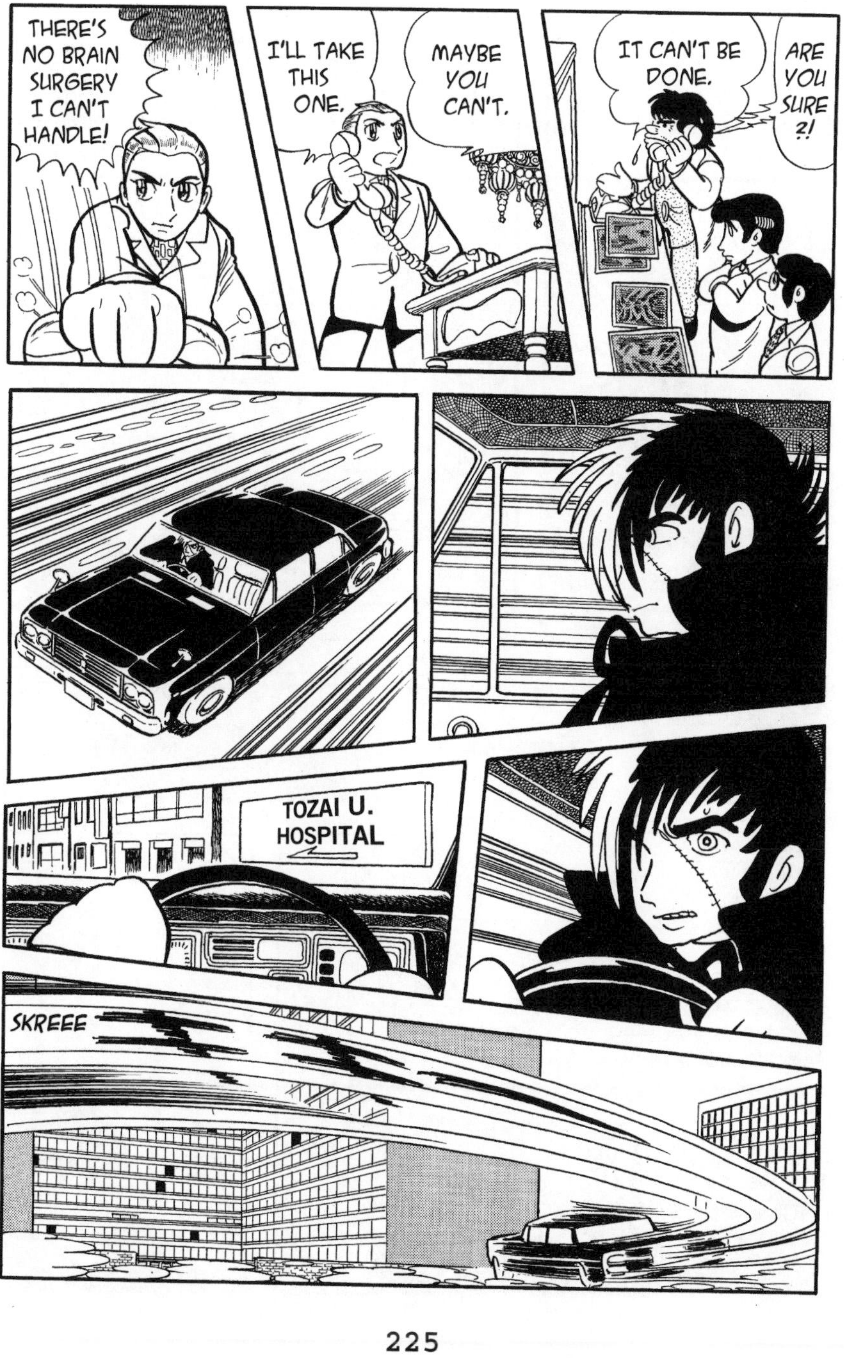
ARE YOU SURE ?!
IT CAN'T BE DONE.
MAYBE YOU CAN'T.
I'LL TAKE THIS ONE.
THERE'S NO BRAIN SURGERY I CAN'T HANDLE!
TOZAI U. HOSPITAL
SKREEE

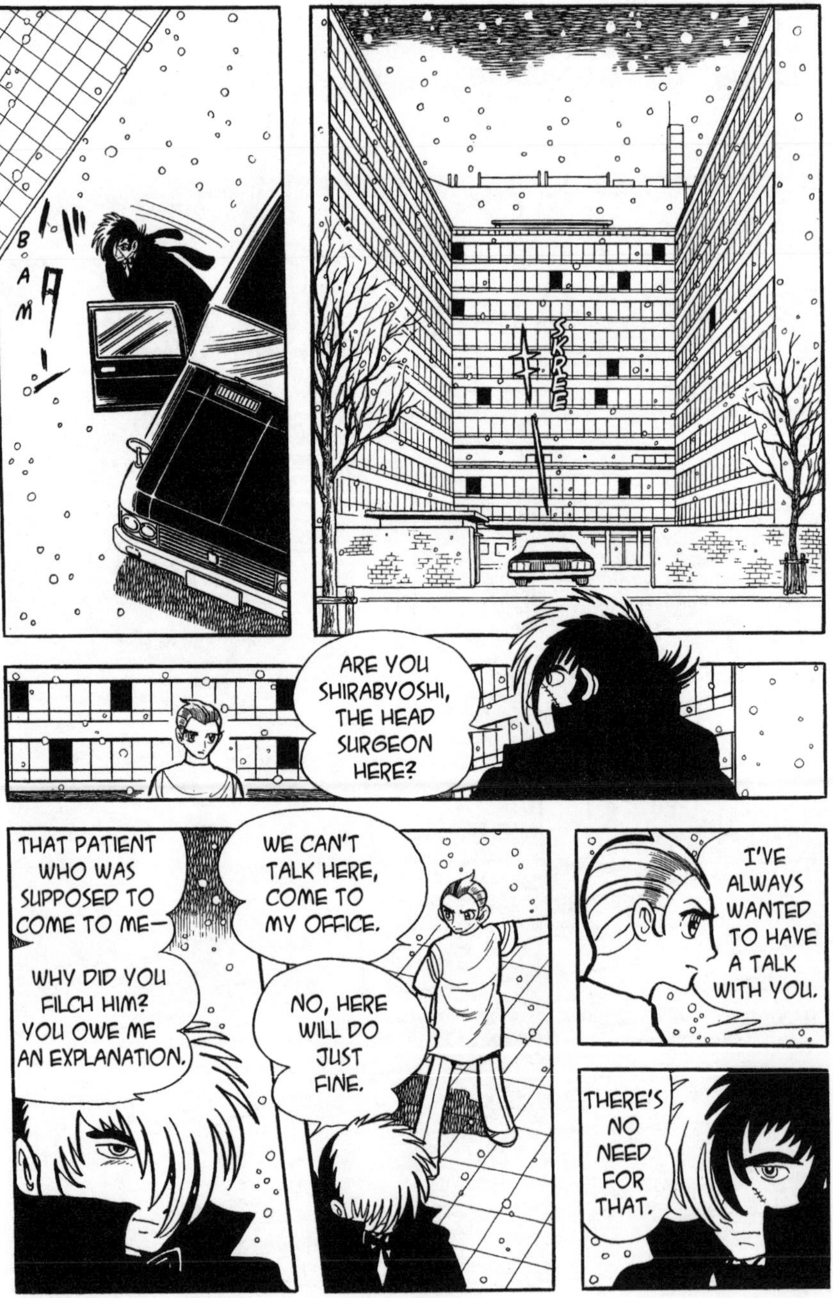
SKREE
BAM!
ARE YOU SHIRABYOSHI, THE HEAD SURGEON HERE?
I'VE ALWAYS WANTED TO HAVE A TALK WITH YOU.
THERE'S NO NEED FOR THAT.
WE CAN'T TALK HERE, COME TO MY OFFICE.
NO, HERE WILL DO JUST FINE.
THAT PATIENT WHO WAS SUPPOSED TO COME TO ME—
WHY DID YOU FILCH HIM? YOU OWE ME AN EXPLANATION.

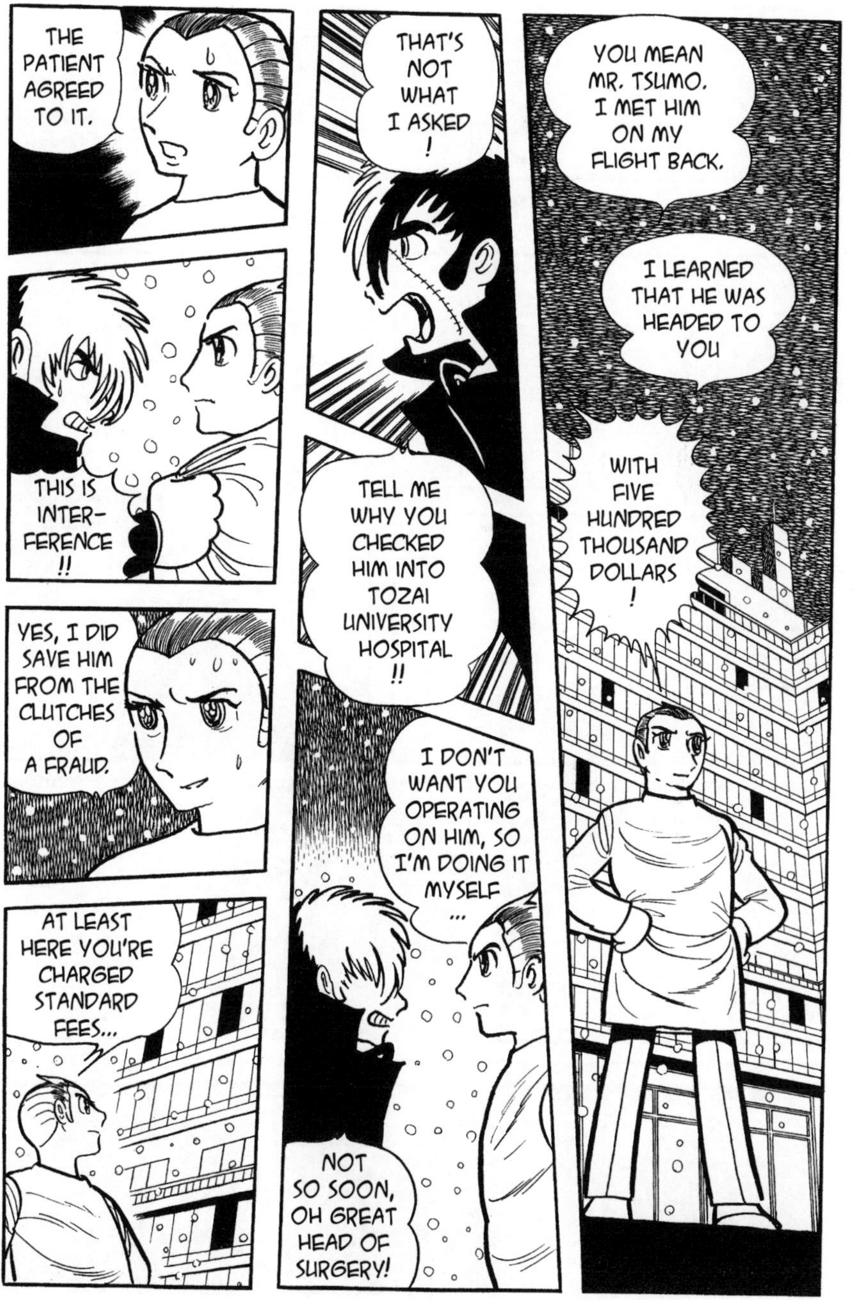
YOU MEAN MR. TSUMO. I MET HIM ON MY FLIGHT BACK.
I LEARNED THAT HE WAS HEADED TO YOU
WITH FIVE HUNDRED THOUSAND DOLLARS!
THAT'S NOT WHAT I ASKED!
TELL ME WHY YOU CHECKED HIM INTO TOZAI UNIVERSITY HOSPITAL!!
I DON'T WANT YOU OPERATING ON HIM, SO I'M DOING IT MYSELF...
NOT SO SOON, OH GREAT HEAD OF SURGERY!
THE PATIENT AGREED TO IT.
THIS IS INTER-FERENCE!!
YES, I DID SAVE HIM FROM THE CLUTCHES OF A FRAUD.
AT LEAST HERE YOU'RE CHARGED STANDARD FEES...

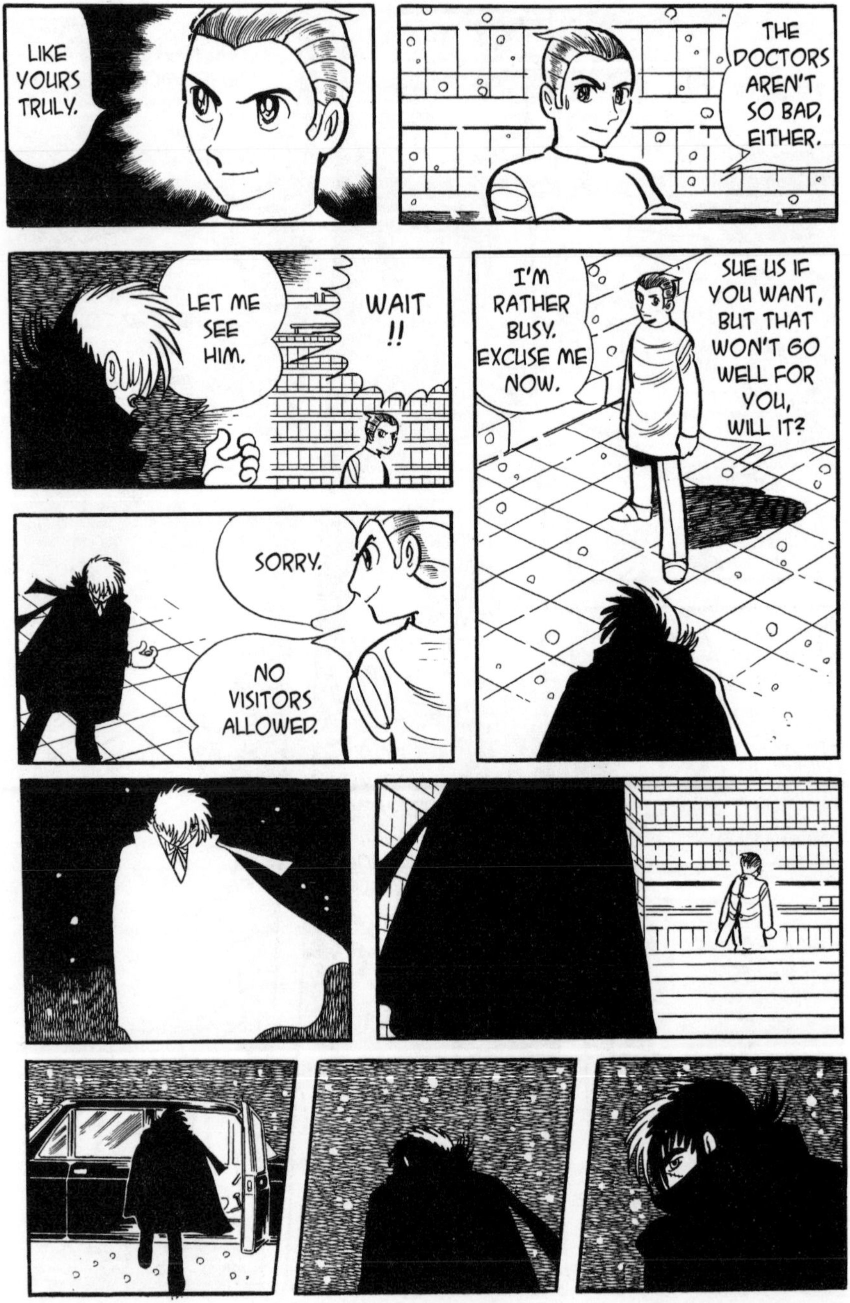
THE DOCTORS AREN'T SO BAD, EITHER.
LIKE YOURS TRULY.
SUE US IF YOU WANT, BUT THAT WON'T GO WELL FOR YOU, WILL IT?
I'M RATHER BUSY. EXCUSE ME NOW.
WAIT !!
LET ME SEE HIM.
SORRY.
NO VISITORS ALLOWED.

AH HA, WELCOME BACK.
HEE HEE
WOULD YOU BE DR. BLACK JACK ?
MR. TSUMO FROM MANILA IS UNDER YOUR CARE, WE TAKE IT?

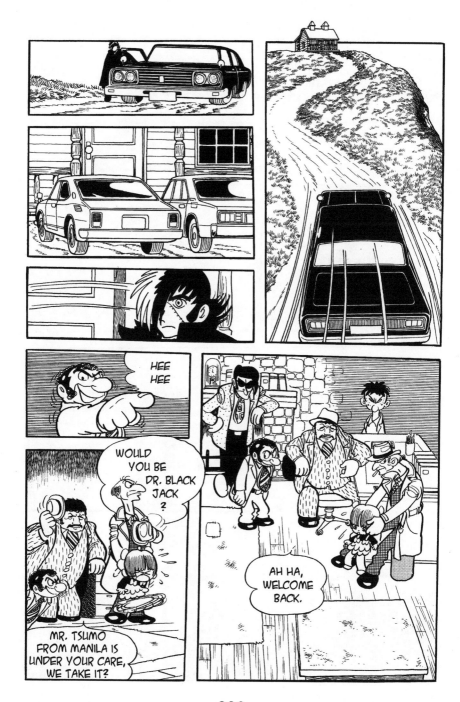

NEVER HEARD OF HIM ...
YOU'RE SUPPOSED TO OPERATE ON HIM.
BETTER FESS UP, DOCTOR.
WE NEED TO FINISH OFF THIS TSUMO. OUR BOSS'S WISH.
TSUMO'S THE RIVAL KINGPIN, YOU SEE.
WE PUT SOME LEAD IN HIM IN MANILA, BUT WHAT A GUY! HE LIVED.
ANYONE WHO TRIES TO HELP TSUMO GETS TREATED THE SAME WAY.
THAT WOULD MEAN YOU, DOC.
HEY, HEY. THAT CALL WILL COST YA.
YOU DON'T WANT THIS GIRL TO BREAK HER NECK, AH?

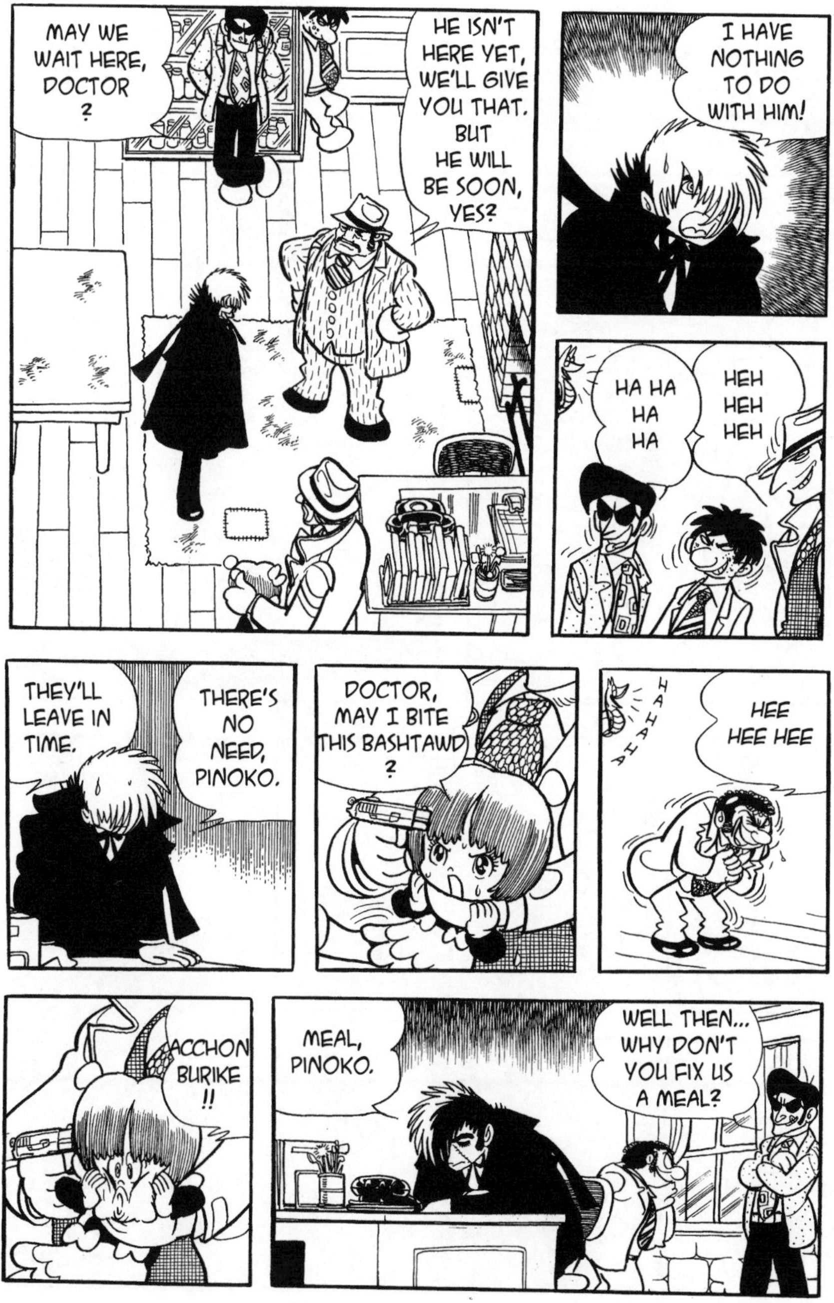
I HAVE NOTHING TO DO WITH HIM!
HEH HEH HEH
HA HA HA HA
HE ISN'T HERE YET, WE'LL GIVE YOU THAT. BUT HE WILL BE SOON, YES?
MAY WE WAIT HERE, DOCTOR?
HEE HEE HEE
HA HA HA HA
DOCTOR, MAY I BITE THIS BASHTAWD?
THERE'S NO NEED, PINOKO.
THEY'LL LEAVE IN TIME.
WELL THEN... WHY DON'T YOU FIX US A MEAL?
MEAL, PINOKO.
ACCHON BURIKE!!

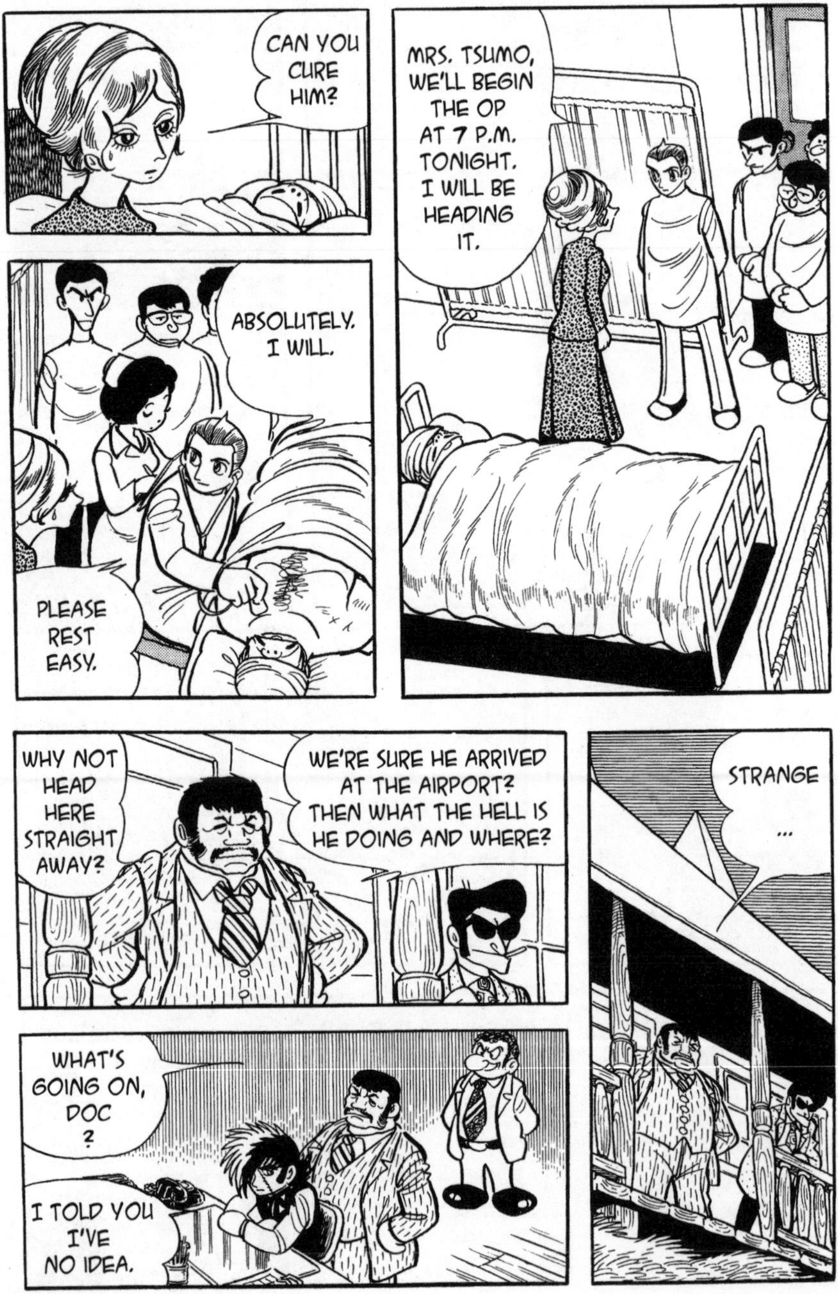
MRS. TSUMO, WE'LL BEGIN THE OP AT 7 P.M. TONIGHT. I WILL BE HEADING IT.
CAN YOU CURE HIM?
ABSOLUTELY. I WILL.
PLEASE REST EASY.
STRANGE ...
WE'RE SURE HE ARRIVED AT THE AIRPORT? THEN WHAT THE HELL IS HE DOING AND WHERE?
WHY NOT HEAD HERE STRAIGHT AWAY?
WHAT'S GOING ON, DOC ?
I TOLD YOU I'VE NO IDEA.

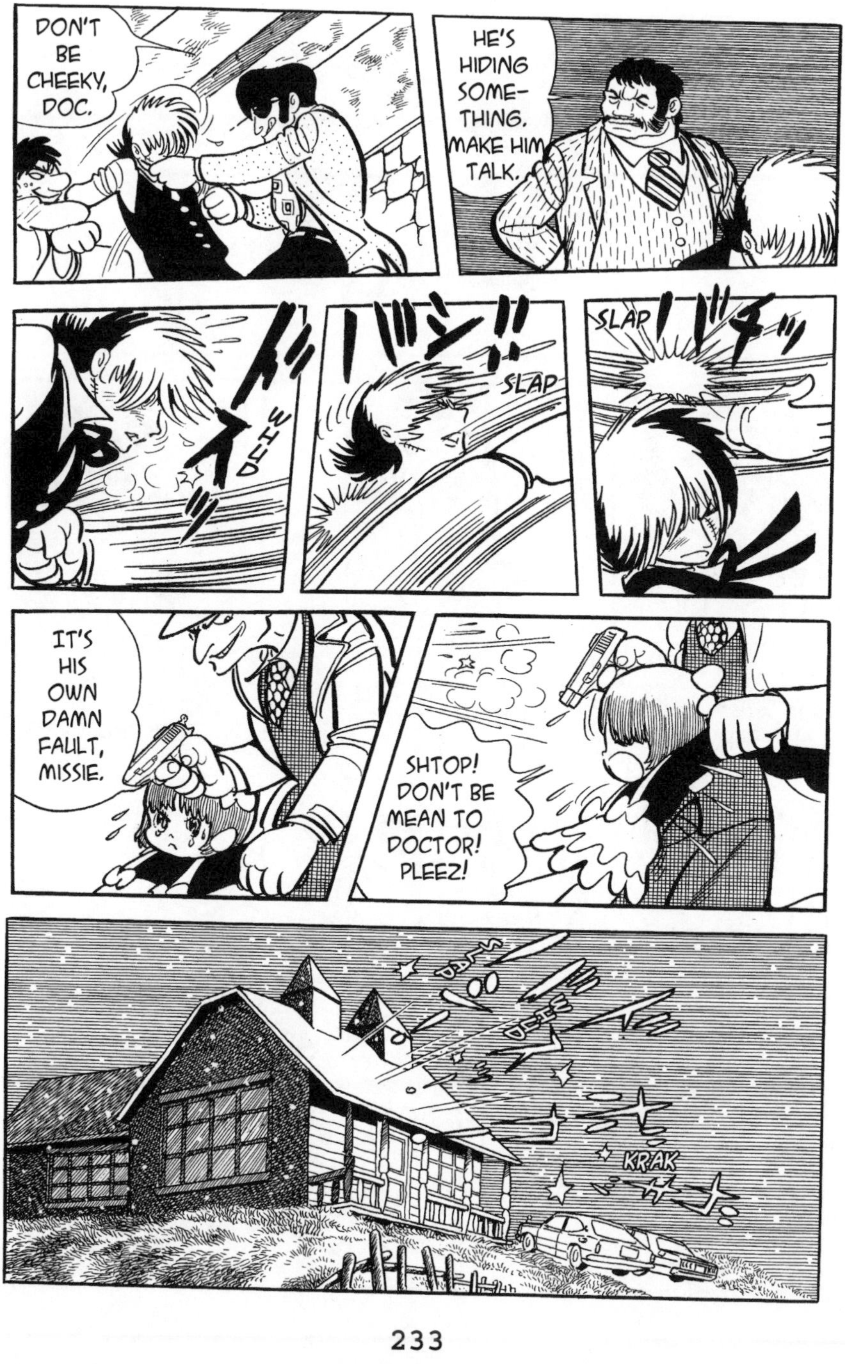
HE'S HIDING SOME-THING. MAKE HIM TALK.
DON'T BE CHEEKY, DOC.
SLAP
SLAP
WHUD
SHTOP! DON'T BE MEAN TO DOCTOR! PLEEZ!
IT'S HIS OWN DAMN FAULT, MISSIE.
KRAK

THOK
TSK... THE GUY'S A REAL CLAM.
KRAK
WAIT, THERE'S A MEMO ON HIS DESK.
IT'S GOT A PHONE NUMBER AND ADDRESS. FOR "TOZAI UNIVERSITY HOSPITAL."
CALL THEM.
HELLO, HELLO? IS THIS THE HOSPITAL? WE'RE LOOKING FOR MR. TSUMO.
AH, HE'S THERE? SURGERY AT 7 ?!
WE'VE FOUND HIM, NOW GO FINISH HIM OFF.
DOCTOR ...

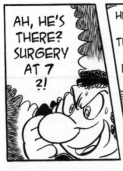

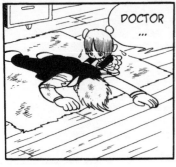

WE'LL ENTER THE CRANIAL CAVITY VIA THE TEMPORAL'S PARS SQUAMOSA AND DEBRIDE AS WE MAKE WAY TO THE COLLICULUS.

HAND A PATIENT OVER TO A ROGUE LIKE BLACK JACK? IT'D BRING SHAME ON JAPANESE MEDICINE!

SCALPEL

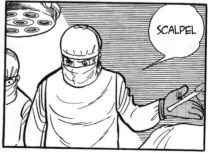

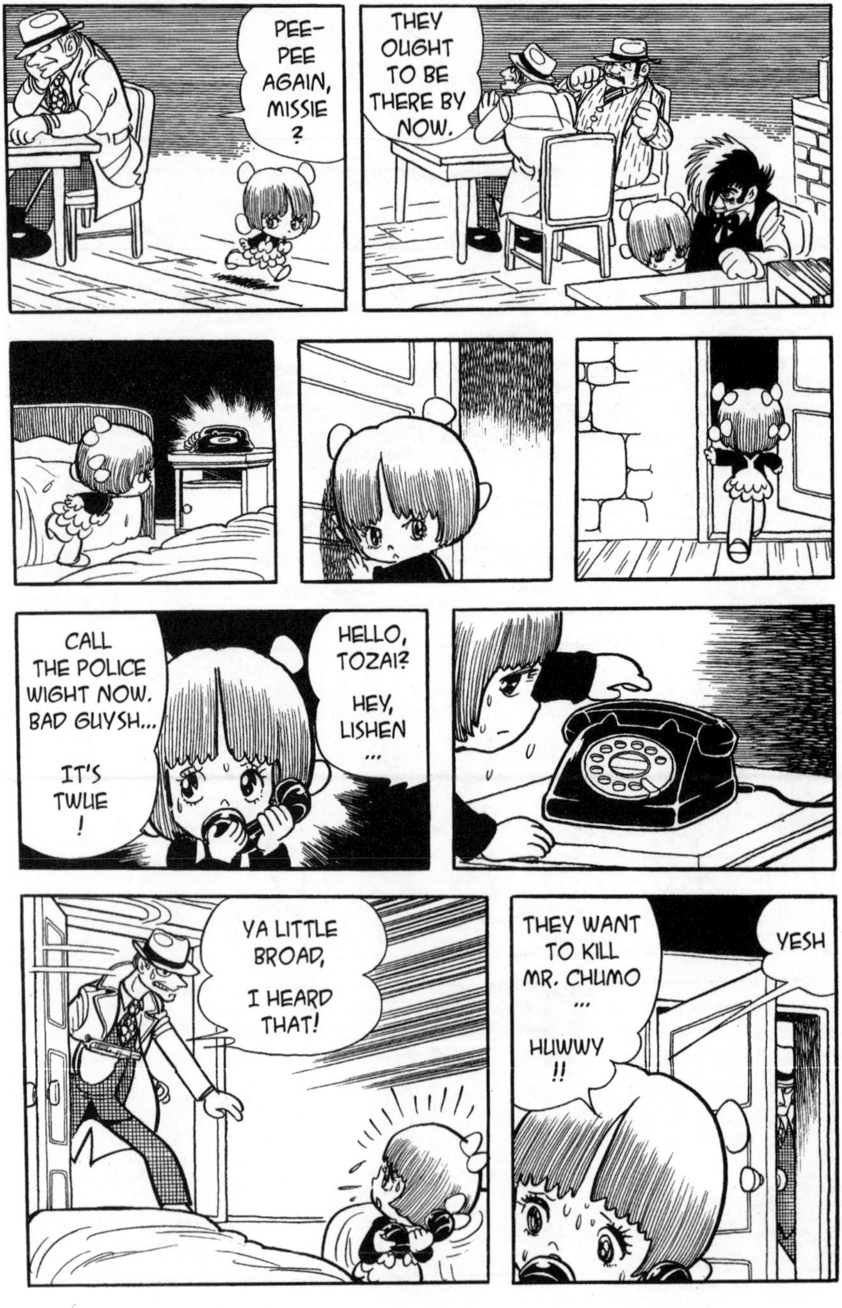
THEY OUGHT TO BE THERE BY NOW.
PEE-PEE AGAIN, MISSIE?
HELLO, TOZAI? HEY, LISHEN ...
CALL THE POLICE WIGHT NOW. BAD GUYSH...
IT'S TWUE!
YESH
THEY WANT TO KILL MR. CHUMO ... HUWWY!!
YA LITTLE BROAD, I HEARD THAT!

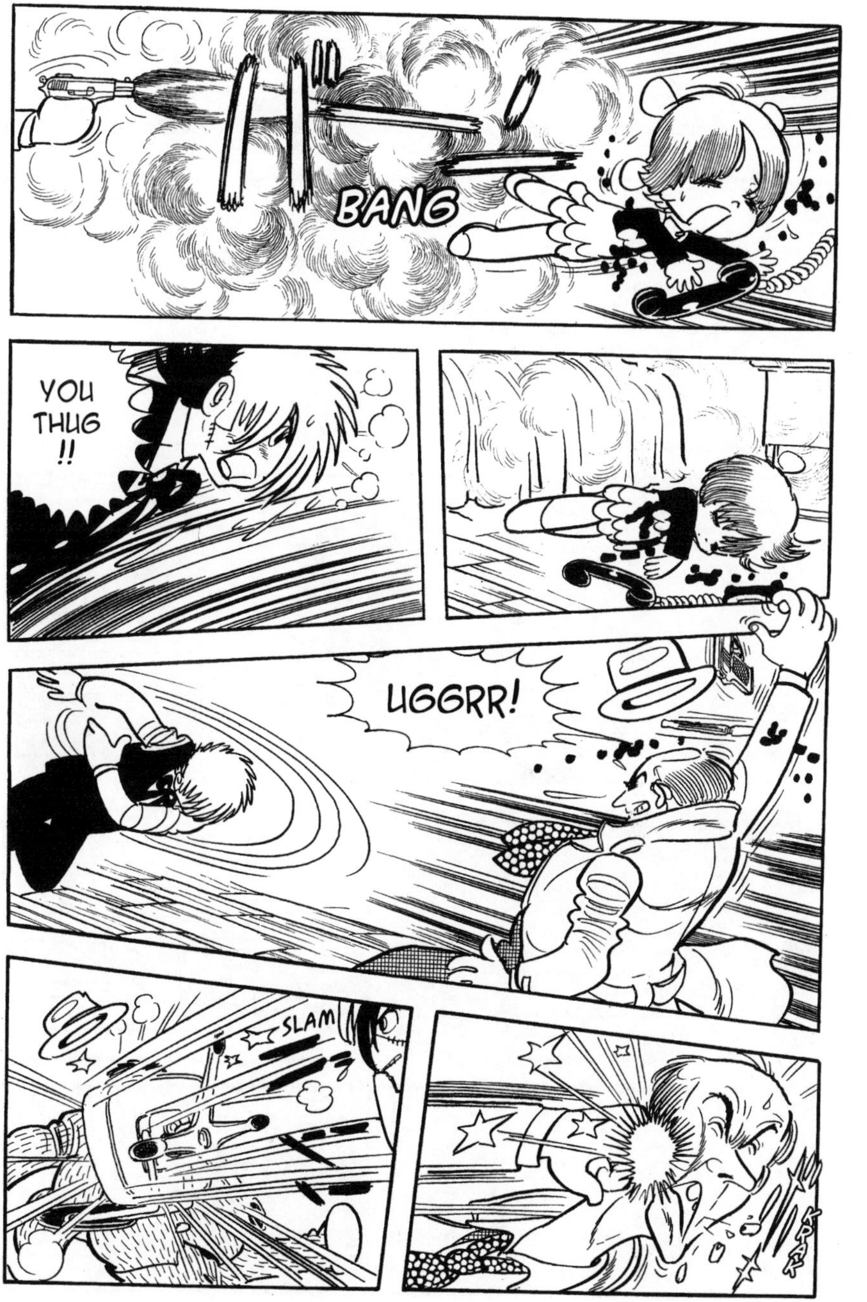
BANG
YOU THUG !!
UGGRR!
KRAK
SLAM

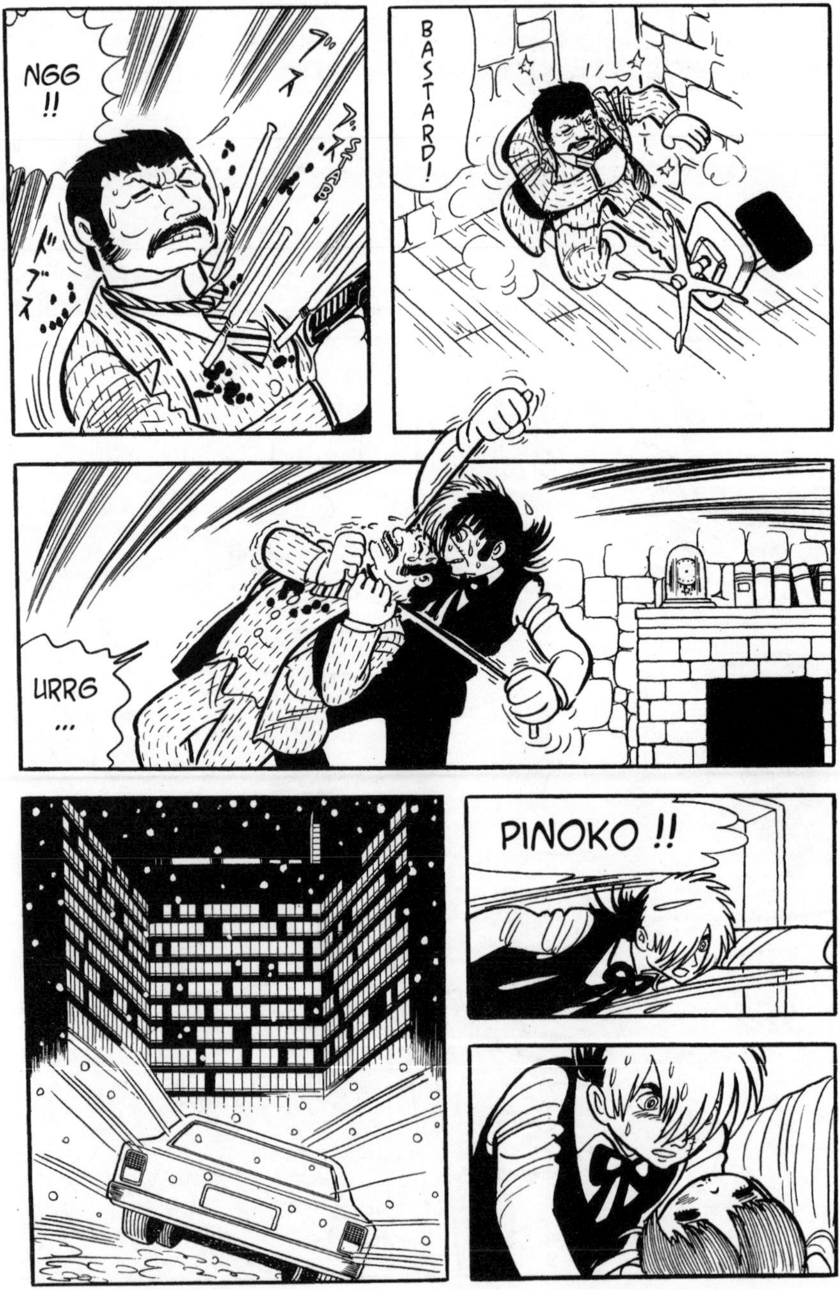
BASTARD!
NGG !!
ブス
ブス STAB
ドブス
URRG ...
PINOKO !!

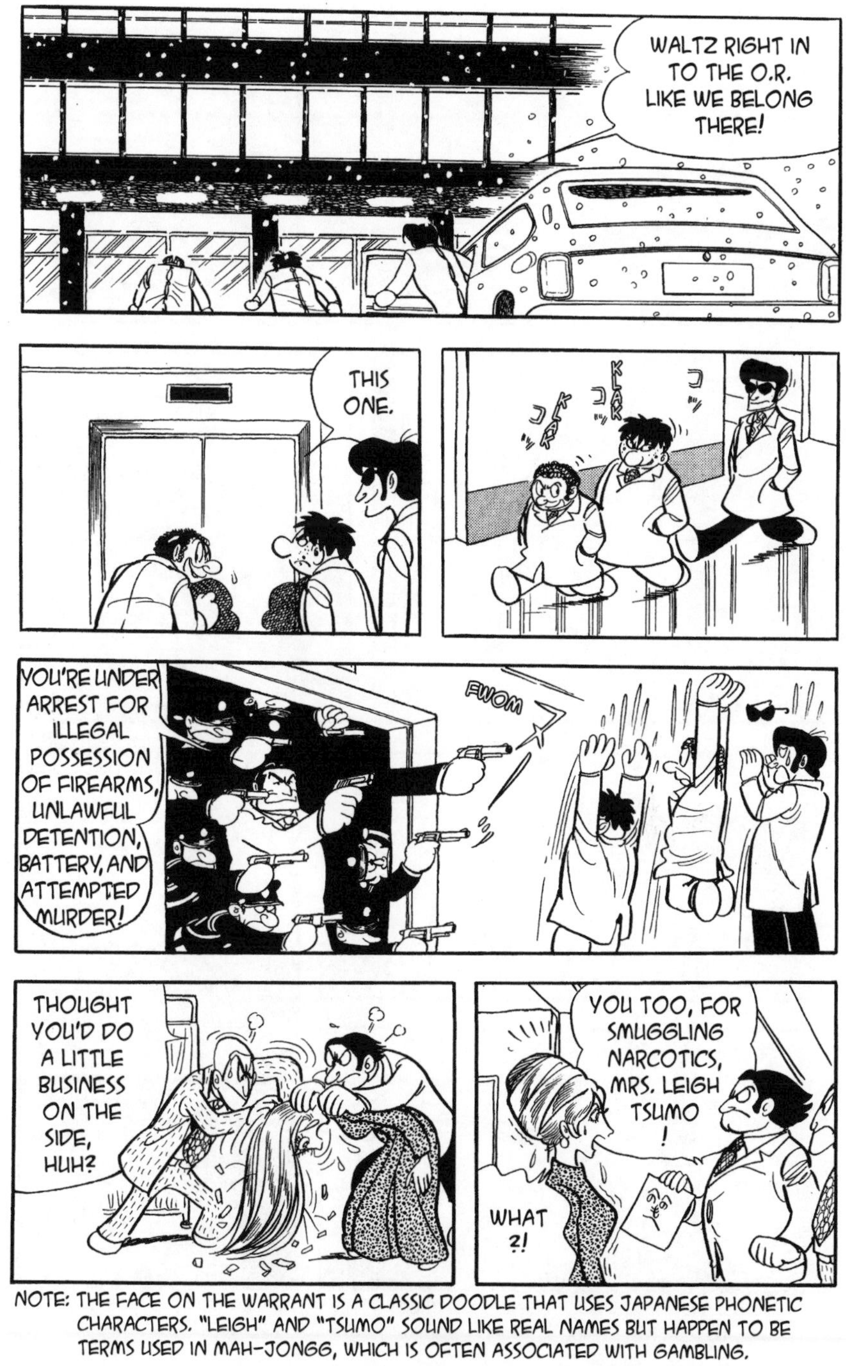
WALTZ RIGHT IN TO THE O.R. LIKE WE BELONG THERE!
KLAK
KLAK
THIS ONE.
FWOM
YOU'RE UNDER ARREST FOR ILLEGAL POSSESSION OF FIREARMS, UNLAWFUL DETENTION, BATTERY, AND ATTEMPTED MURDER!
YOU TOO, FOR SMUGGLING NARCOTICS, MRS. LEIGH TSUMO!
WHAT?!
THOUGHT YOU'D DO A LITTLE BUSINESS ON THE SIDE, HUH?

NOTE: THE FACE ON THE WARRANT IS A CLASSIC DOODLE THAT USES JAPANESE PHONETIC CHARACTERS. "LEIGH" AND "TSUMO" SOUND LIKE REAL NAMES BUT HAPPEN TO BE TERMS USED IN MAH-JONGG, WHICH IS OFTEN ASSOCIATED WITH GAMBLING.

ADIEU L'AMI
...
DO YOU SEE NOW ?
PEOPLE WHO NEED HELP AREN'T ALL GOOD FOLKS.

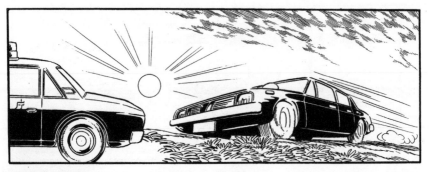

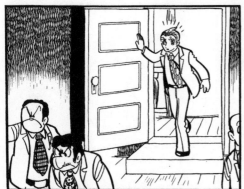

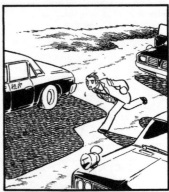

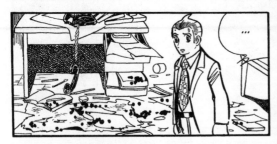

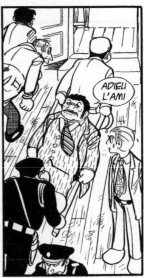

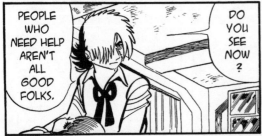

NOTE: ADIEU L'AMI ("FAREWELL, FRIEND") = A 1968 FRENCH THRILLER ABOUT AN EX-FOREIGN LEGIONS DOCTOR STARRING ALAIN DELON AND CHARLES BRONSON

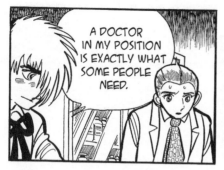

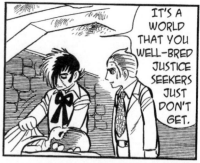

IT'S A WORLD THAT YOU WELL-BRED JUSTICE SEEKERS JUST DON'T GET.
A DOCTOR IN MY POSITION IS EXACTLY WHAT SOME PEOPLE NEED.
IS SHE THE GIRL WHO CALLED US?
YES.
THIS WAS MY FAULT! I'LL SAVE HER IF IT MEANS MY LIFE!
LET ME TAKE HER TO TOZAI!
IS THIS SOME JOKE?
WHAT ELSE DO YOU WANT TO TAKE AWAY FROM ME?
GET LOST NOW!
THIS CHILD IS MINE.

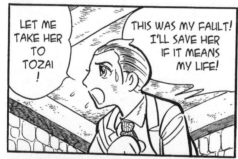

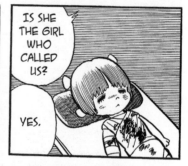

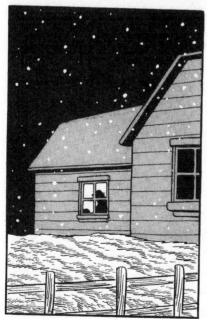

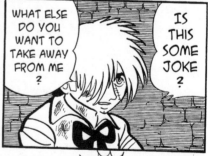

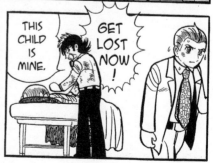

A HILL FOR ONE

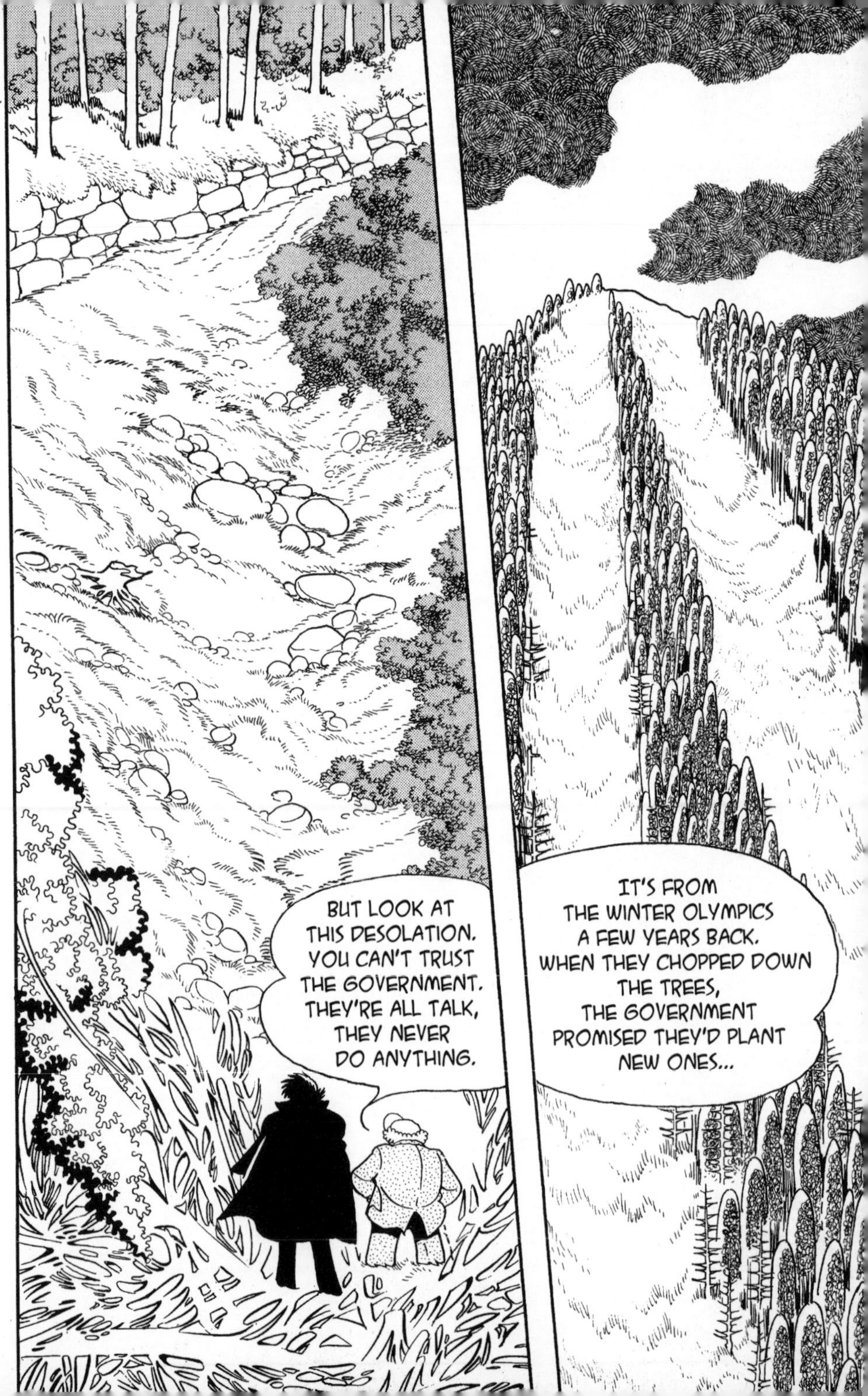
IT'S FROM THE WINTER OLYMPICS A FEW YEARS BACK. WHEN THEY CHOPPED DOWN THE TREES, THE GOVERNMENT PROMISED THEY'D PLANT NEW ONES...
BUT LOOK AT THIS DESOLATION. YOU CAN'T TRUST THE GOVERNMENT. THEY'RE ALL TALK, THEY NEVER DO ANYTHING.

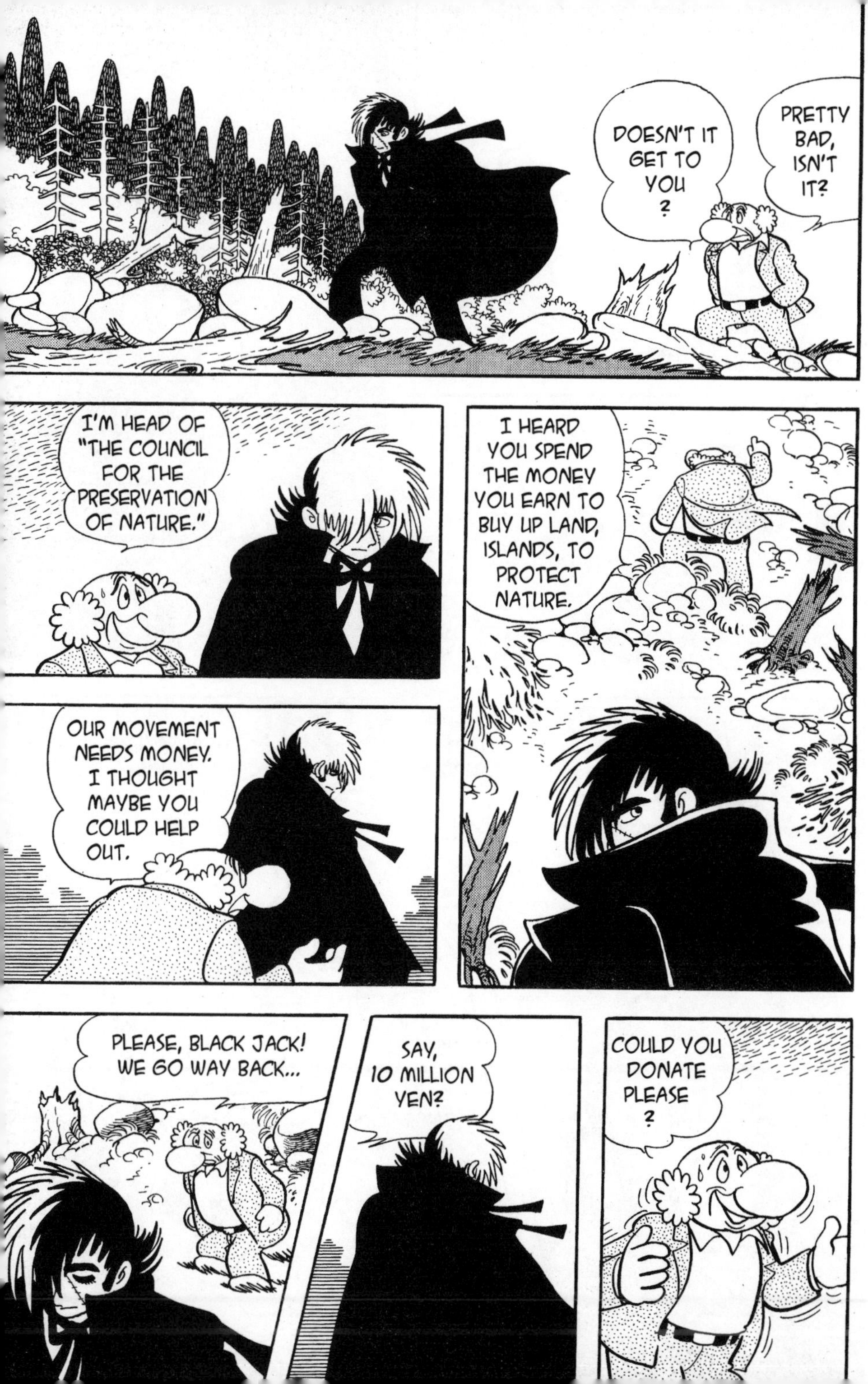
PRETTY BAD, ISN'T IT?
DOESN'T IT GET TO YOU ?
I HEARD YOU SPEND THE MONEY YOU EARN TO BUY UP LAND, ISLANDS, TO PROTECT NATURE.
I'M HEAD OF "THE COUNCIL FOR THE PRESERVATION OF NATURE."
OUR MOVEMENT NEEDS MONEY. I THOUGHT MAYBE YOU COULD HELP OUT.
COULD YOU DONATE PLEASE ?
SAY, 10 MILLION YEN?
PLEASE, BLACK JACK! WE GO WAY BACK...

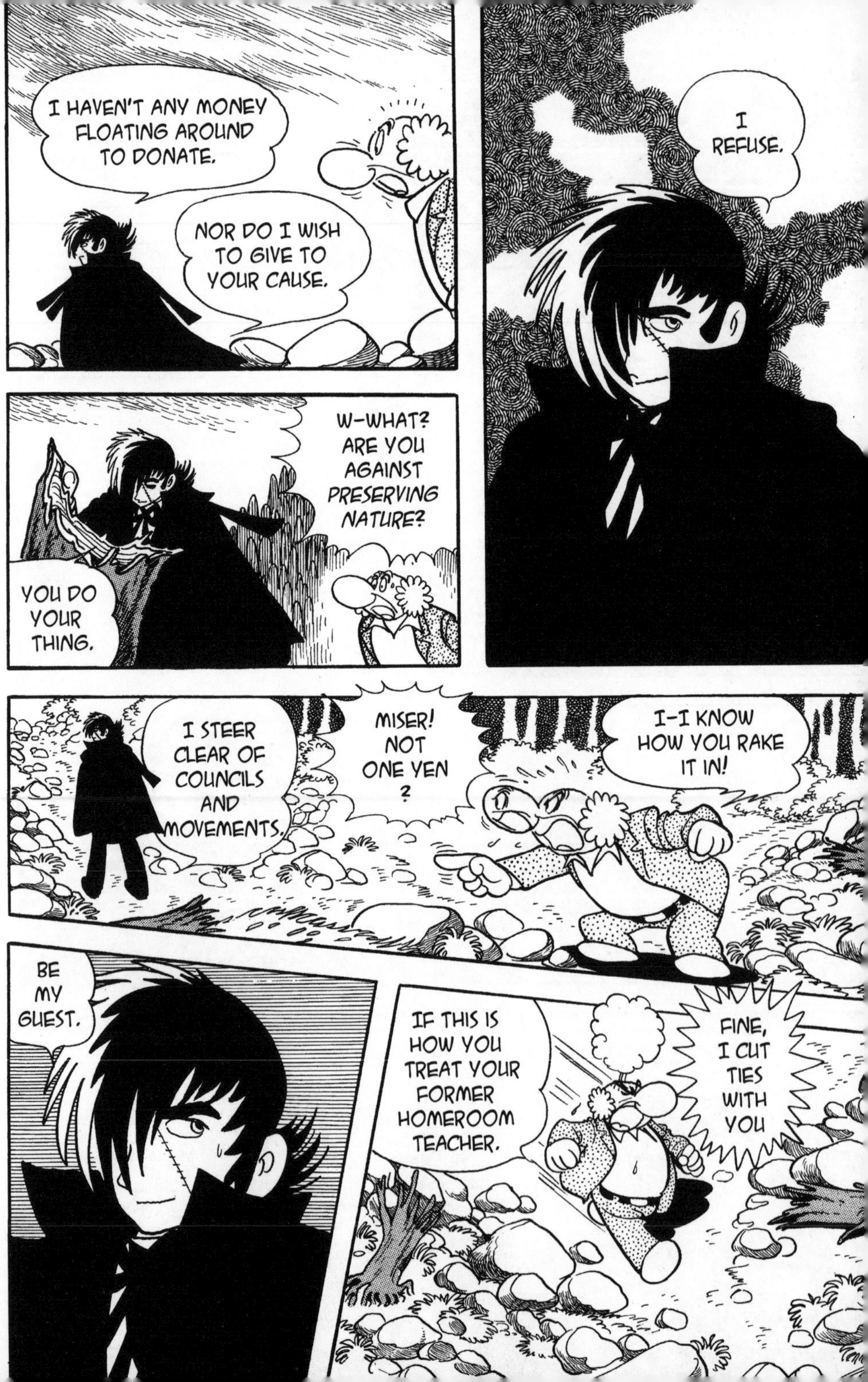
I REFUSE.
I HAVEN'T ANY MONEY FLOATING AROUND TO DONATE.
NOR DO I WISH TO GIVE TO YOUR CAUSE.
W-WHAT? ARE YOU AGAINST PRESERVING NATURE?
YOU DO YOUR THING.
I-I KNOW HOW YOU RAKE IT IN!
MISER! NOT ONE YEN ?
I STEER CLEAR OF COUNCILS AND MOVEMENTS.
FINE, I CUT TIES WITH YOU
IF THIS IS HOW YOU TREAT YOUR FORMER HOMEROOM TEACHER.
BE MY GUEST.

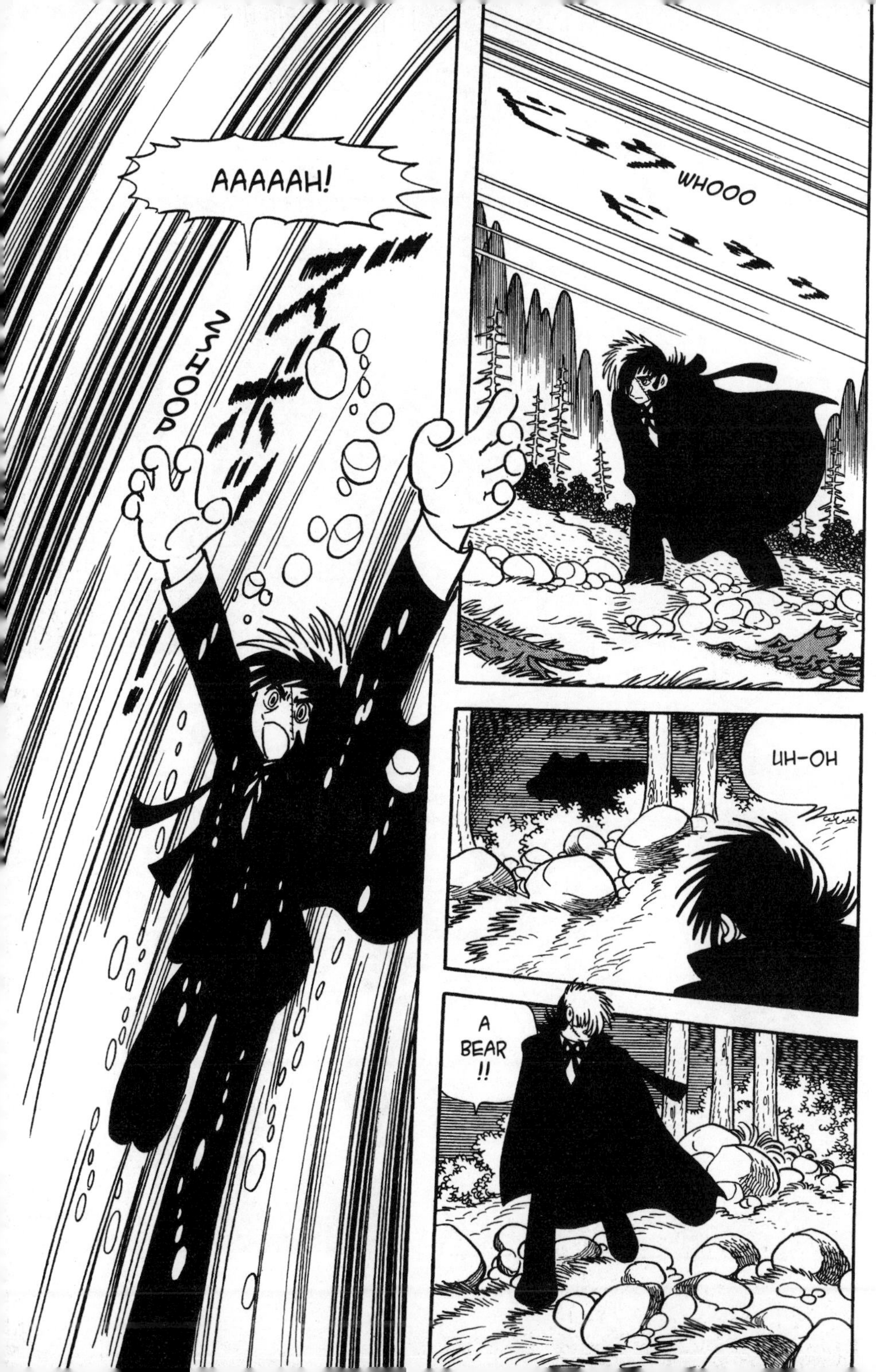
WHOOO
UH-OH
A BEAR !!
AAAAAH!
WHOOOP

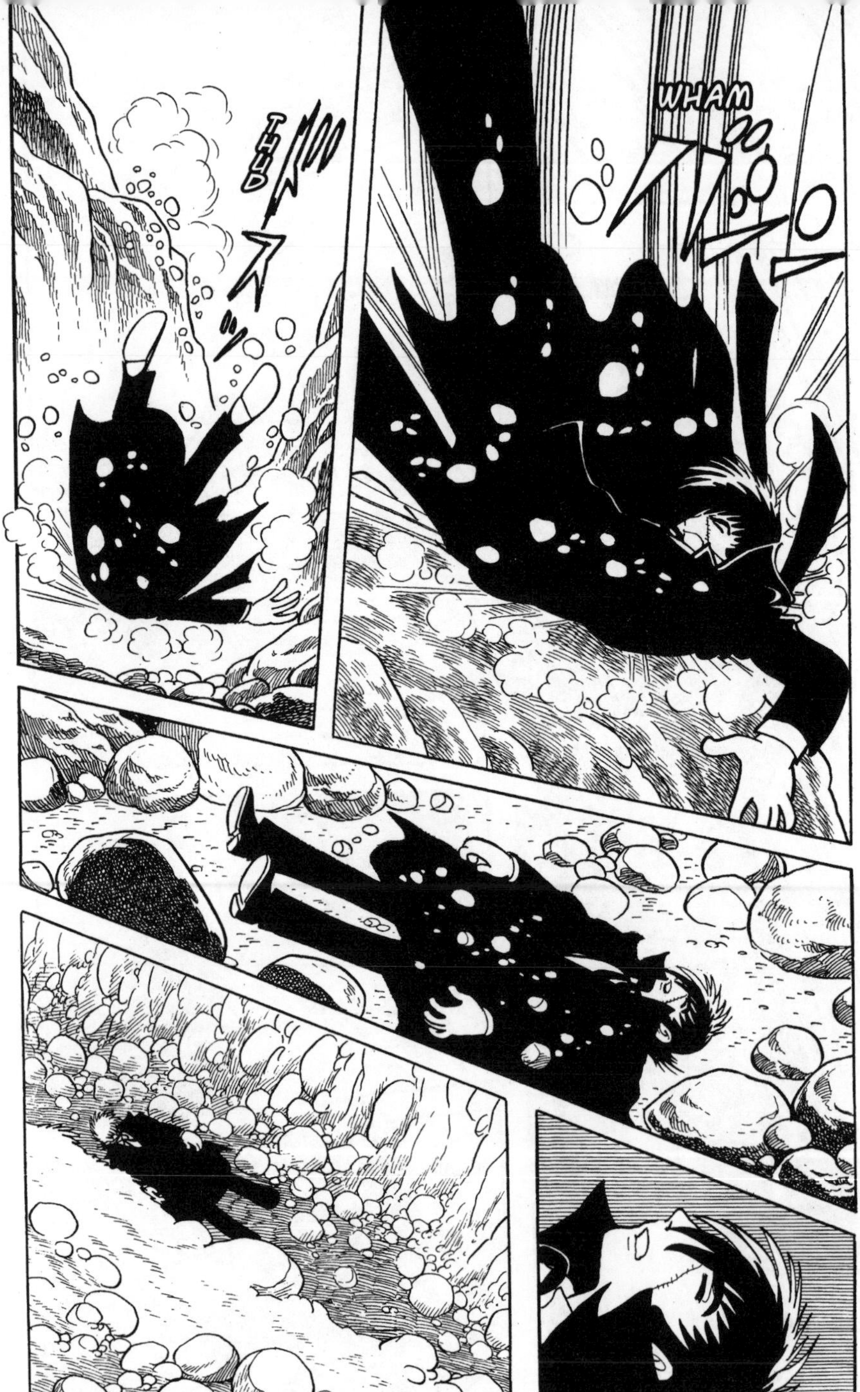
WHAM
THUD

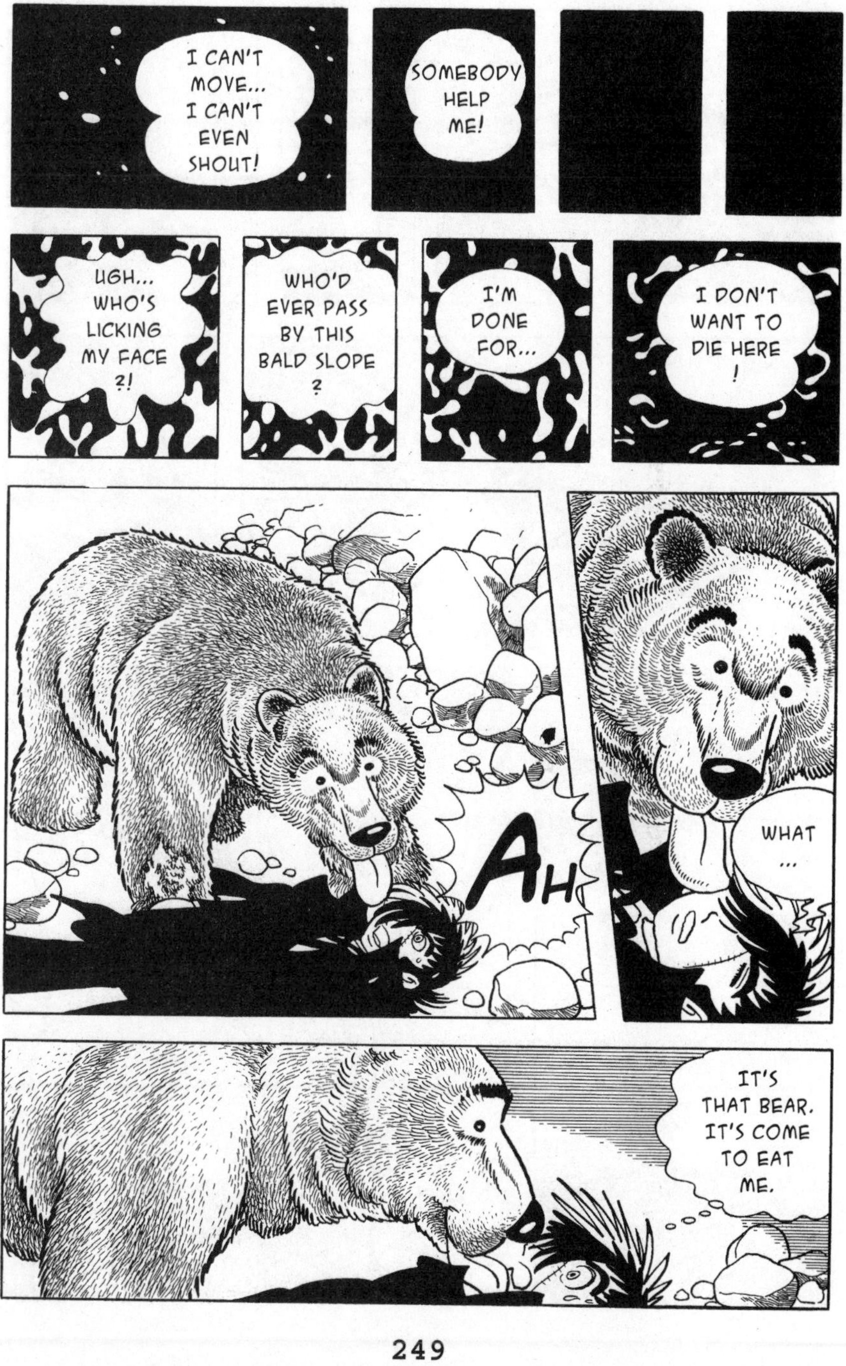
SOMEBODY HELP ME!
I CAN'T MOVE... I CAN'T EVEN SHOUT!
I DON'T WANT TO DIE HERE!
I'M DONE FOR...
WHO'D EVER PASS BY THIS BALD SLOPE?
UGH... WHO'S LICKING MY FACE?!
WHAT ...
AH
IT'S THAT BEAR. IT'S COME TO EAT ME.

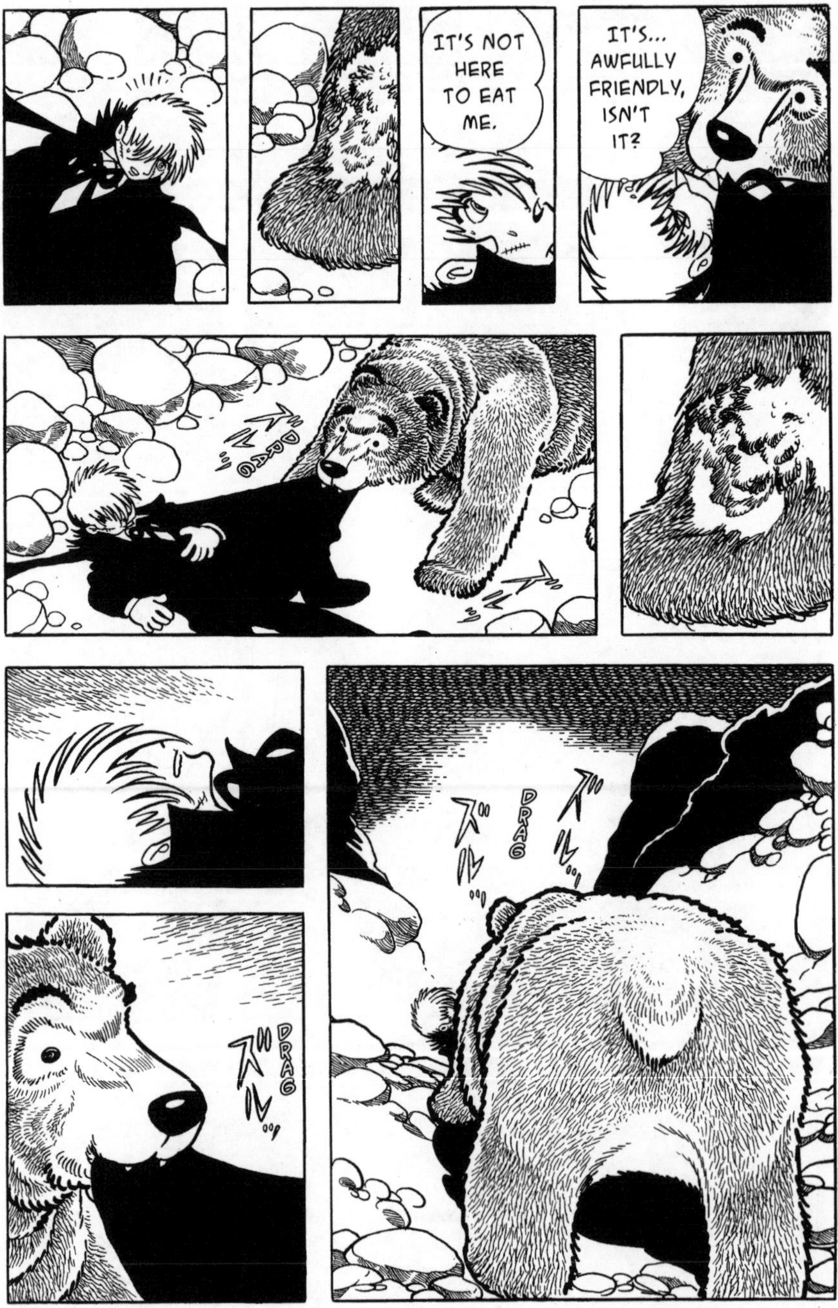
IT'S... AWFULLY FRIENDLY, ISN'T IT?
IT'S NOT HERE TO EAT ME.
DRAG
DRAG
DRAG

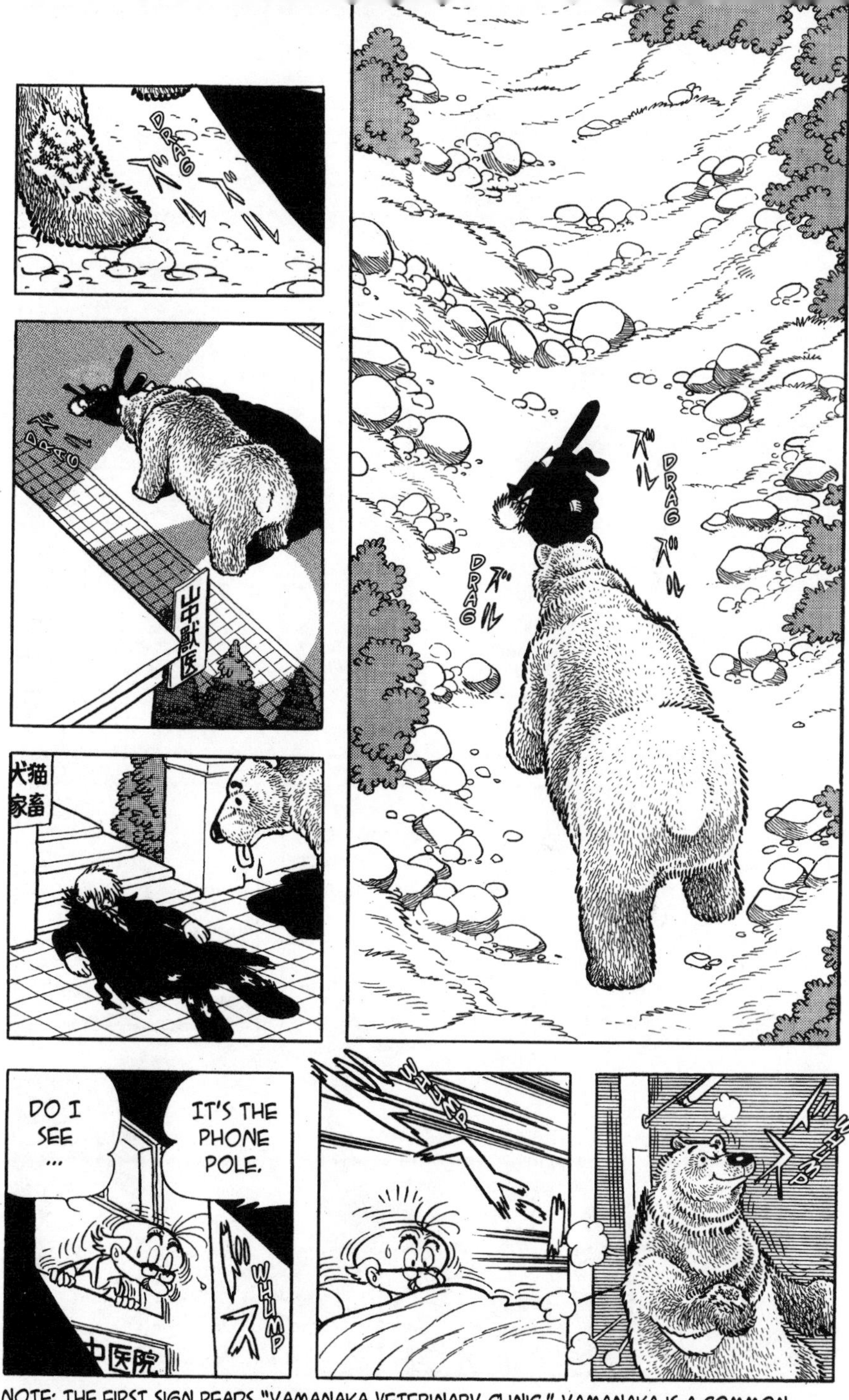
ズル
DRAG
ズル
DRAG
ズル
DRAG
ズル
ズル
DRAG
山中獣医
犬猫
家畜
WHUMP
DO I SEE ...
IT'S THE PHONE POLE.
ズン
WHUMP
中医院

NOTE: THE FIRST SIGN READS "YAMANAKA VETERINARY CLINIC." YAMANAKA IS A COMMON SURNAME WHOSE CHARACTERS MEAN IN THE MOUNTAINS. THE SECOND SIGN READS "DOGS, CATS, LIVESTOCK."

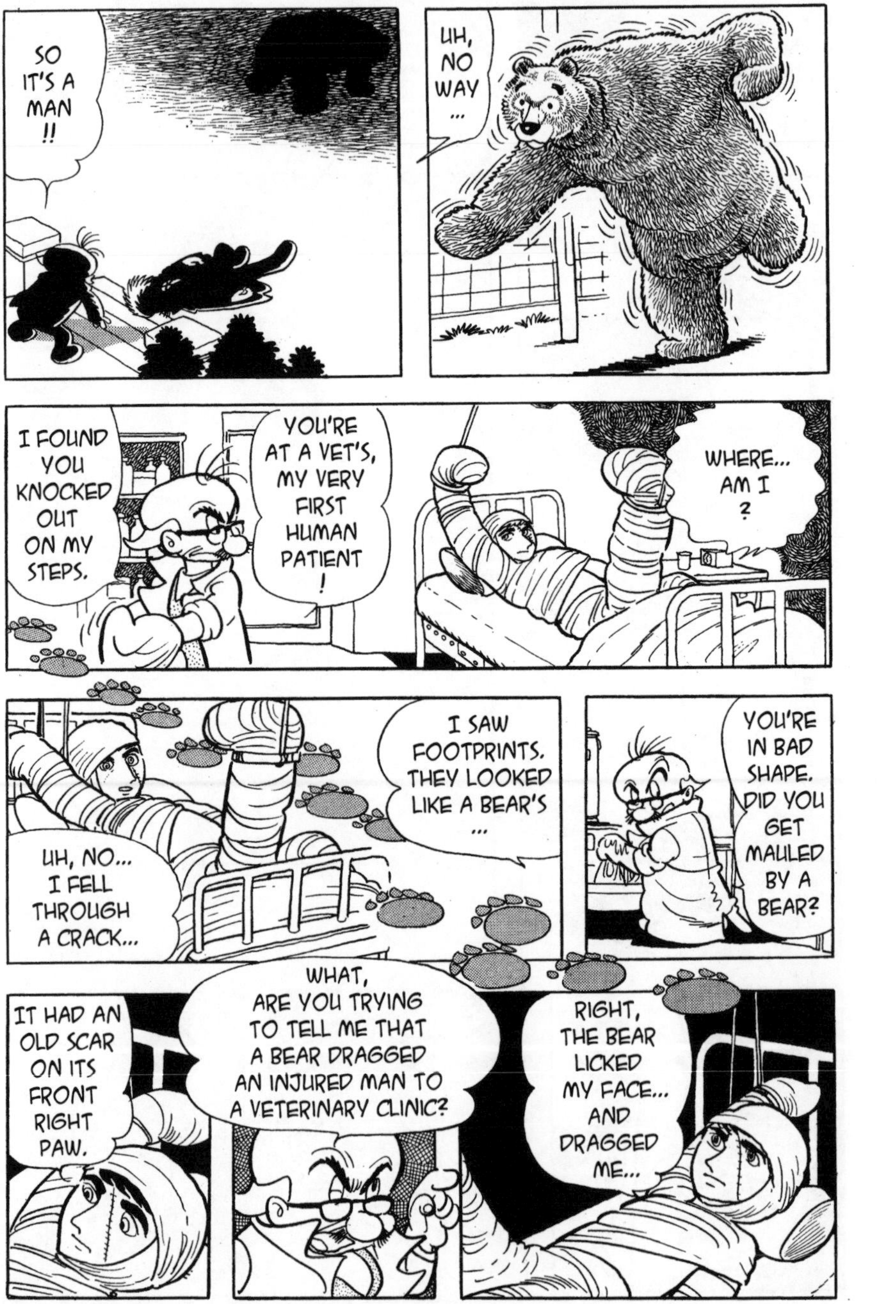
UH, NO WAY ...
SO IT'S A MAN !!
WHERE... AM I ?
YOU'RE AT A VET'S, MY VERY FIRST HUMAN PATIENT !
I FOUND YOU KNOCKED OUT ON MY STEPS.
YOU'RE IN BAD SHAPE. DID YOU GET MAULED BY A BEAR?
I SAW FOOTPRINTS. THEY LOOKED LIKE A BEAR'S ...
UH, NO... I FELL THROUGH A CRACK...
RIGHT, THE BEAR LICKED MY FACE... AND DRAGGED ME...
WHAT, ARE YOU TRYING TO TELL ME THAT A BEAR DRAGGED AN INJURED MAN TO A VETERINARY CLINIC?
IT HAD AN OLD SCAR ON ITS FRONT RIGHT PAW.

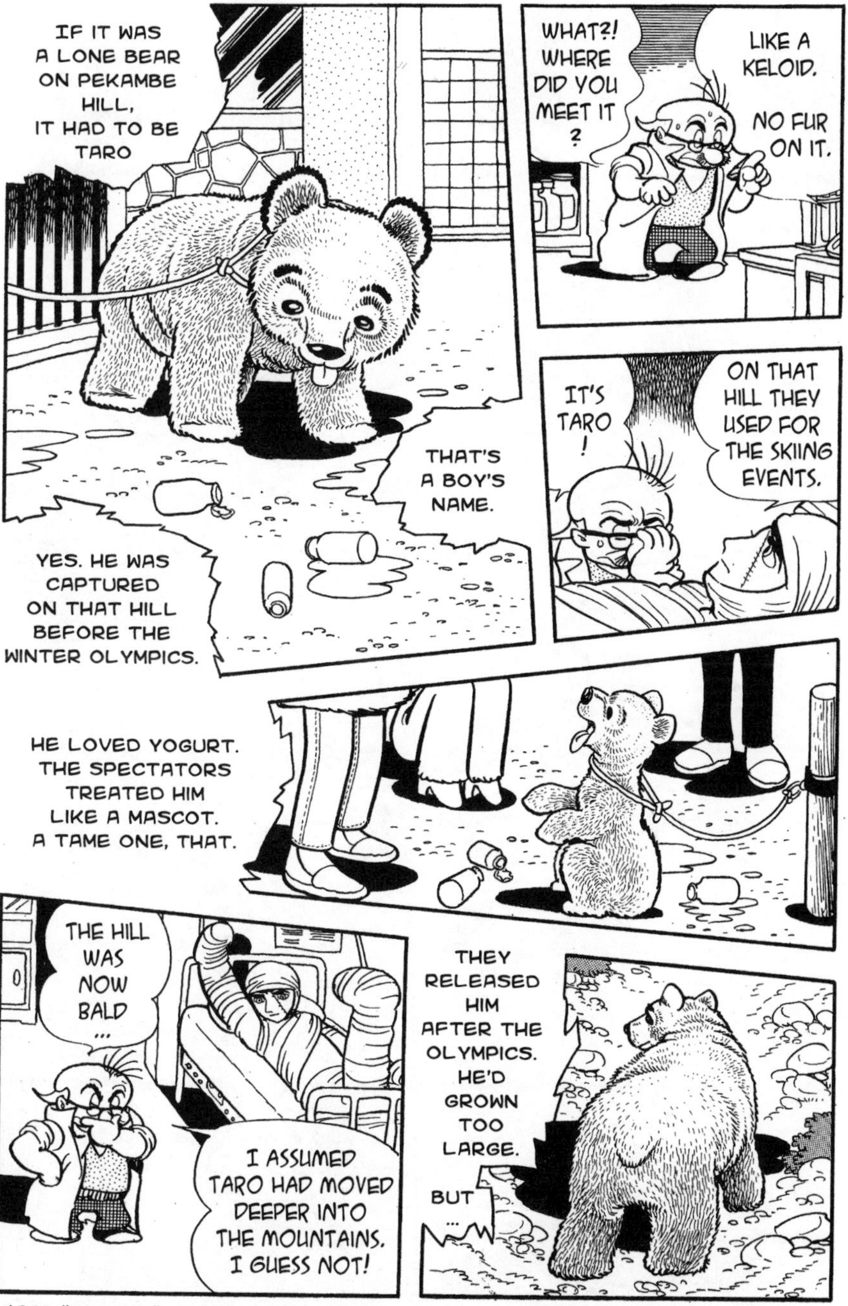
LIKE A KELOID.
NO FUR ON IT.
WHAT?! WHERE DID YOU MEET IT?
ON THAT HILL THEY USED FOR THE SKIING EVENTS.
IT'S TARO!
IF IT WAS A LONE BEAR ON PEKAMBE HILL, IT HAD TO BE TARO
THAT'S A BOY'S NAME.
YES. HE WAS CAPTURED ON THAT HILL BEFORE THE WINTER OLYMPICS.
HE LOVED YOGURT. THE SPECTATORS TREATED HIM LIKE A MASCOT. A TAME ONE, THAT.
THEY RELEASED HIM AFTER THE OLYMPICS. HE'D GROWN TOO LARGE.
BUT ...
THE HILL WAS NOW BALD ...
I ASSUMED TARO HAD MOVED DEEPER INTO THE MOUNTAINS. I GUESS NOT!

NOTE: "PEKAMBE" MEANS *WATER CHESTNUT* IN THE LANGUAGE OF THE INDIGENT AINU OF HOKKAIDO PREFECTURE. THE WINTER OLYMPICS WERE HELD IN SAPPORO, HOKKAIDO, IN 1972.

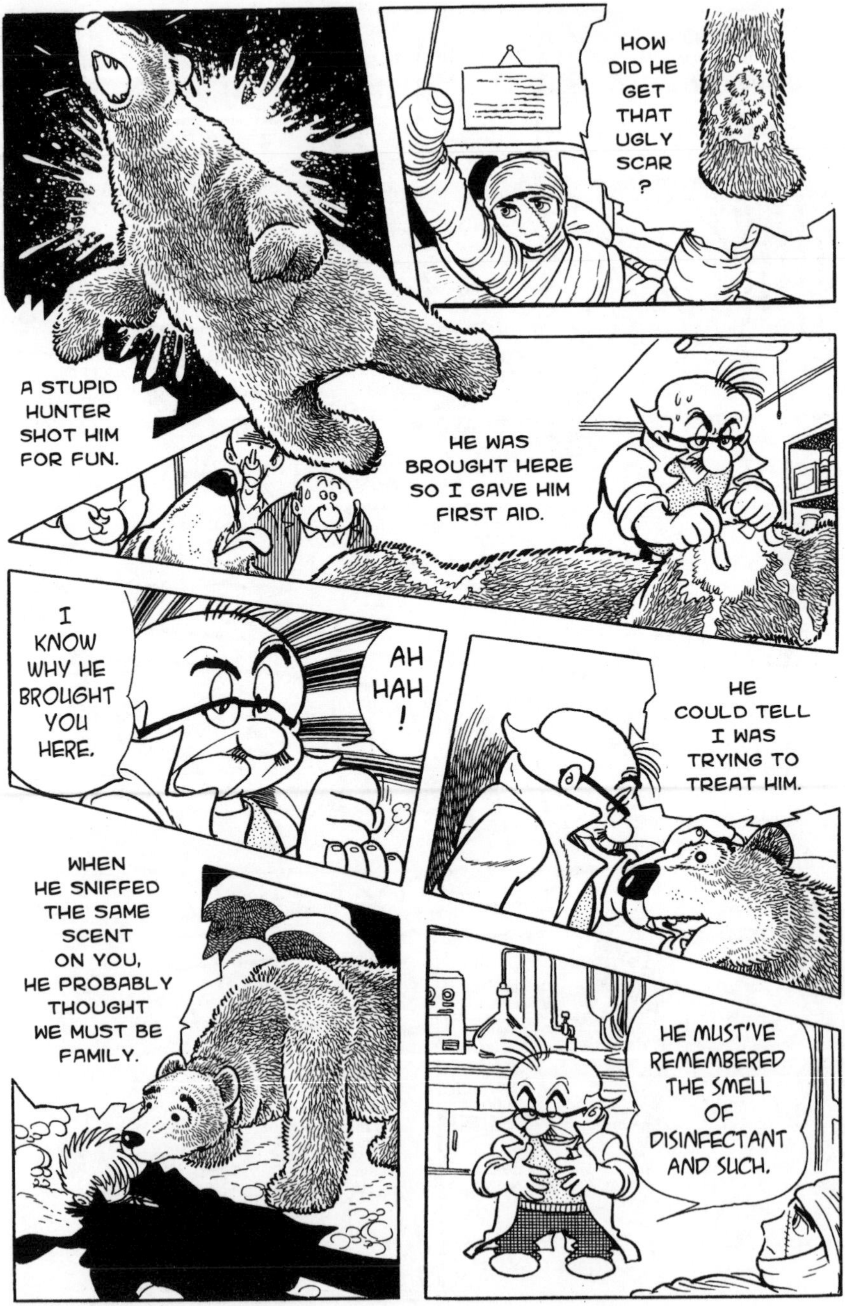

HOW DID HE GET THAT UGLY SCAR?
A STUPID HUNTER SHOT HIM FOR FUN.
HE WAS BROUGHT HERE SO I GAVE HIM FIRST AID.
HE COULD TELL I WAS TRYING TO TREAT HIM.
AH HAH!
I KNOW WHY HE BROUGHT YOU HERE.
HE MUST'VE REMEMBERED THE SMELL OF DISINFECTANT AND SUCH.
WHEN HE SNIFFED THE SAME SCENT ON YOU, HE PROBABLY THOUGHT WE MUST BE FAMILY.

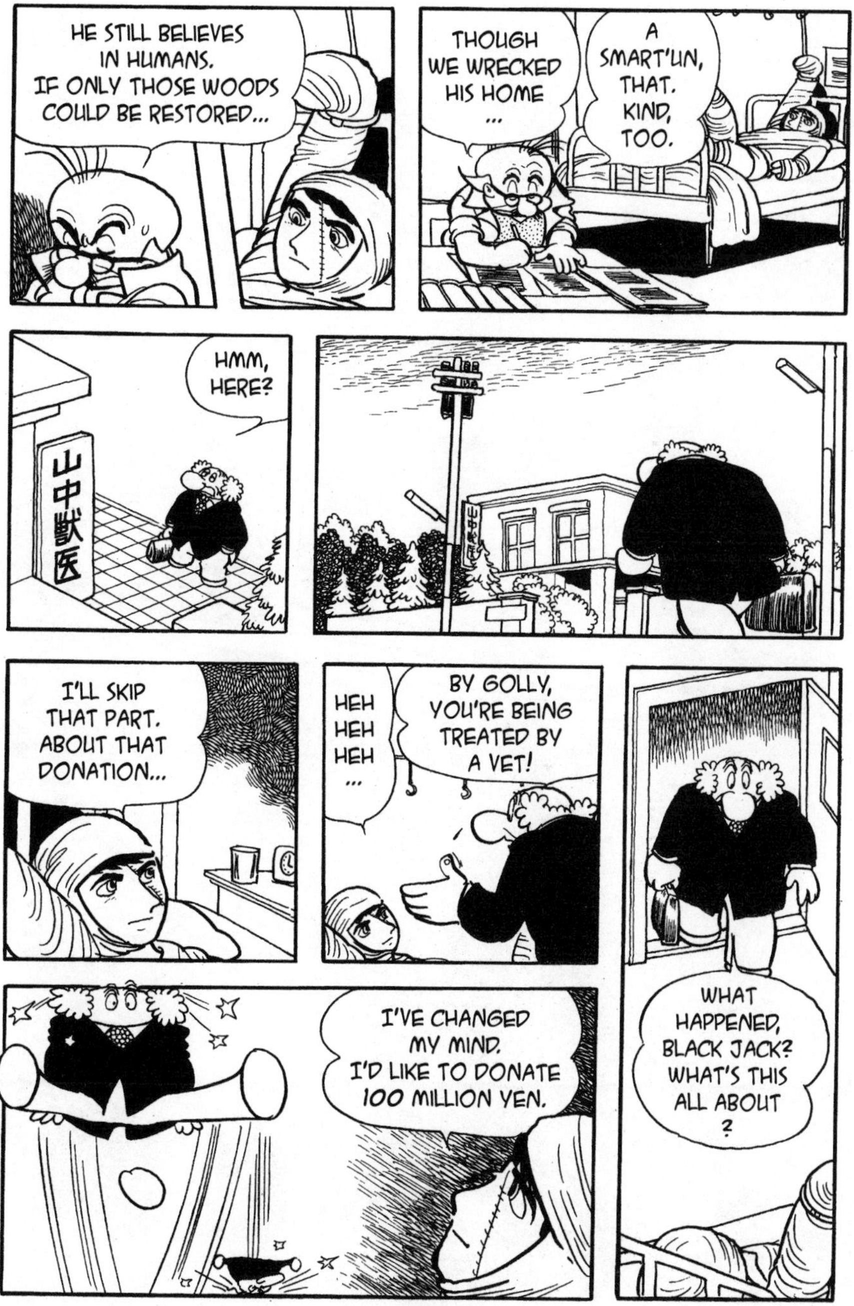
A SMART'UN, THAT. KIND, TOO.
THOUGH WE WRECKED HIS HOME ...
HE STILL BELIEVES IN HUMANS. IF ONLY THOSE WOODS COULD BE RESTORED...
HMM, HERE?
山中獣医
WHAT HAPPENED, BLACK JACK? WHAT'S THIS ALL ABOUT ?
BY GOLLY, YOU'RE BEING TREATED BY A VET!
HEH HEH HEH ...
I'LL SKIP THAT PART. ABOUT THAT DONATION...
I'VE CHANGED MY MIND. I'D LIKE TO DONATE 100 MILLION YEN.

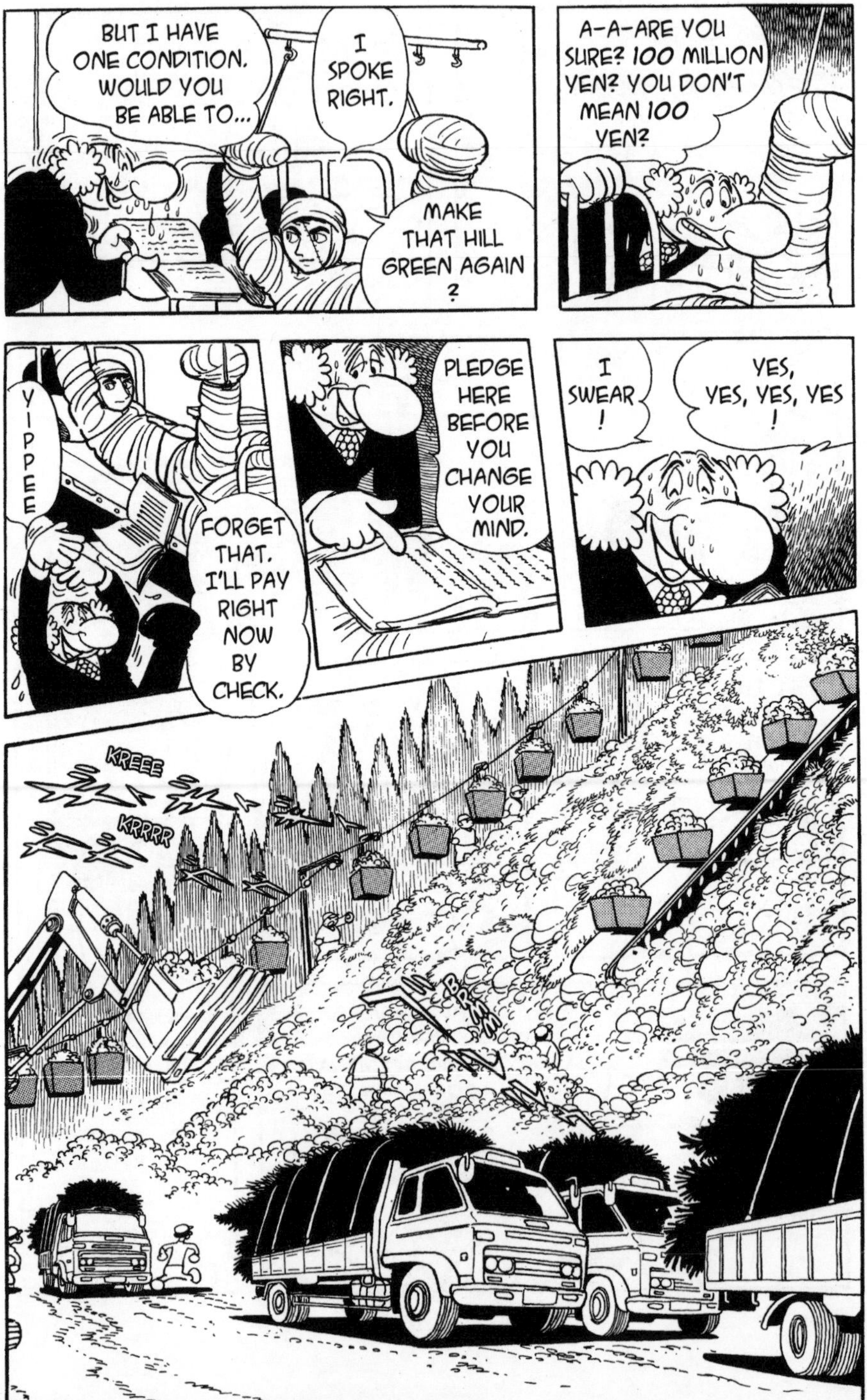
A-A-ARE YOU SURE? 100 MILLION YEN? YOU DON'T MEAN 100 YEN?
I SPOKE RIGHT.
BUT I HAVE ONE CONDITION. WOULD YOU BE ABLE TO...
MAKE THAT HILL GREEN AGAIN?
YES, YES, YES, YES!
I SWEAR!
PLEDGE HERE BEFORE YOU CHANGE YOUR MIND.
FORGET THAT. I'LL PAY RIGHT NOW BY CHECK.
YIPPEE
KREEE
KRRRR
BRMM

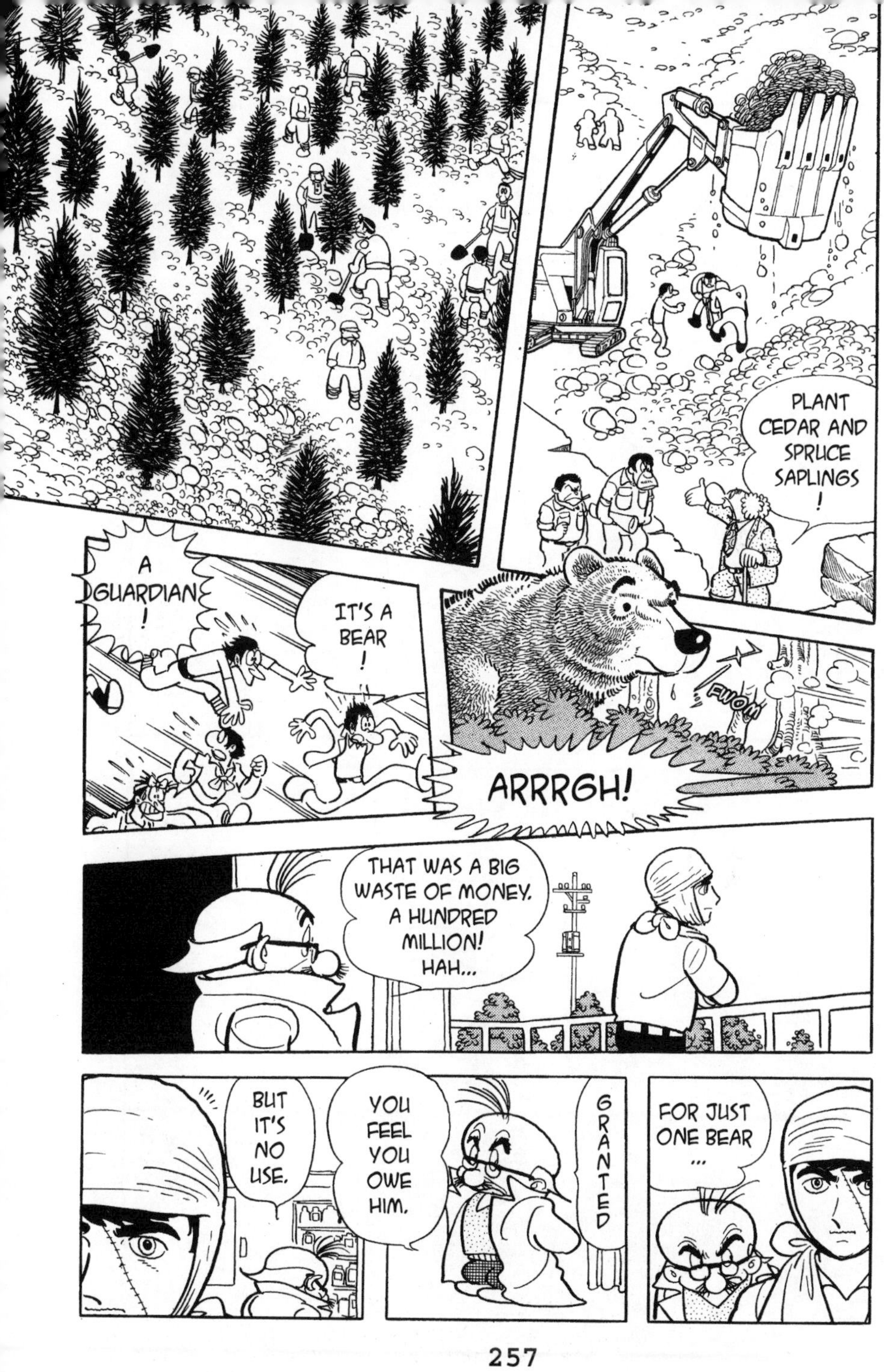
PLANT CEDAR AND SPRUCE SAPLINGS !
FWOM
IT'S A BEAR !
A GUARDIAN !
ARRRGH!
THAT WAS A BIG WASTE OF MONEY. A HUNDRED MILLION! HAH...
FOR JUST ONE BEAR ...
GRANTED
YOU FEEL YOU OWE HIM.
BUT IT'S NO USE.

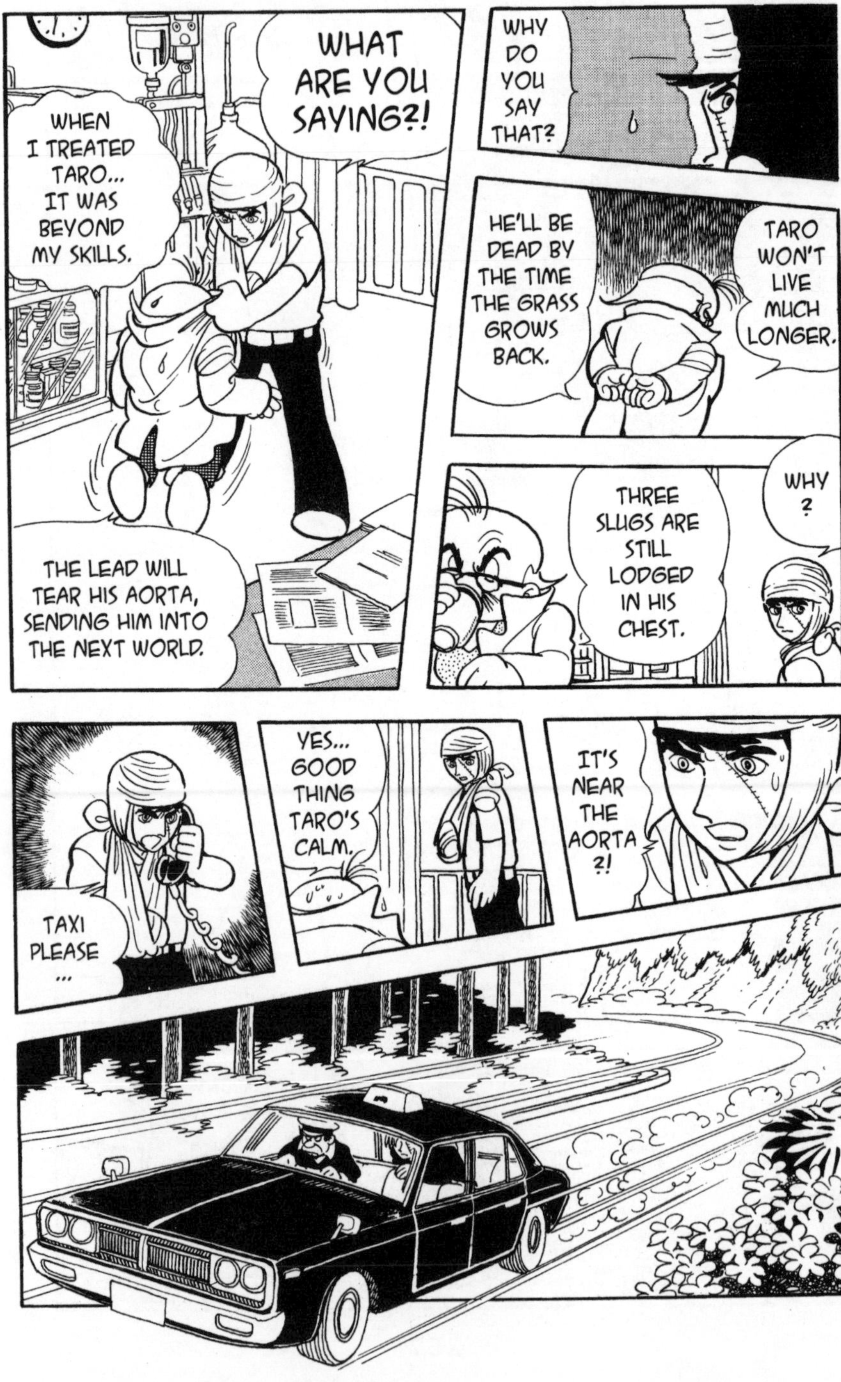
WHY DO YOU SAY THAT?
TARO WON'T LIVE MUCH LONGER.
HE'LL BE DEAD BY THE TIME THE GRASS GROWS BACK.
WHY?
THREE SLUGS ARE STILL LODGED IN HIS CHEST.
WHAT ARE YOU SAYING?!
WHEN I TREATED TARO... IT WAS BEYOND MY SKILLS.
THE LEAD WILL TEAR HIS AORTA, SENDING HIM INTO THE NEXT WORLD.
IT'S NEAR THE AORTA?!
YES... GOOD THING TARO'S CALM.
TAXI PLEASE ...

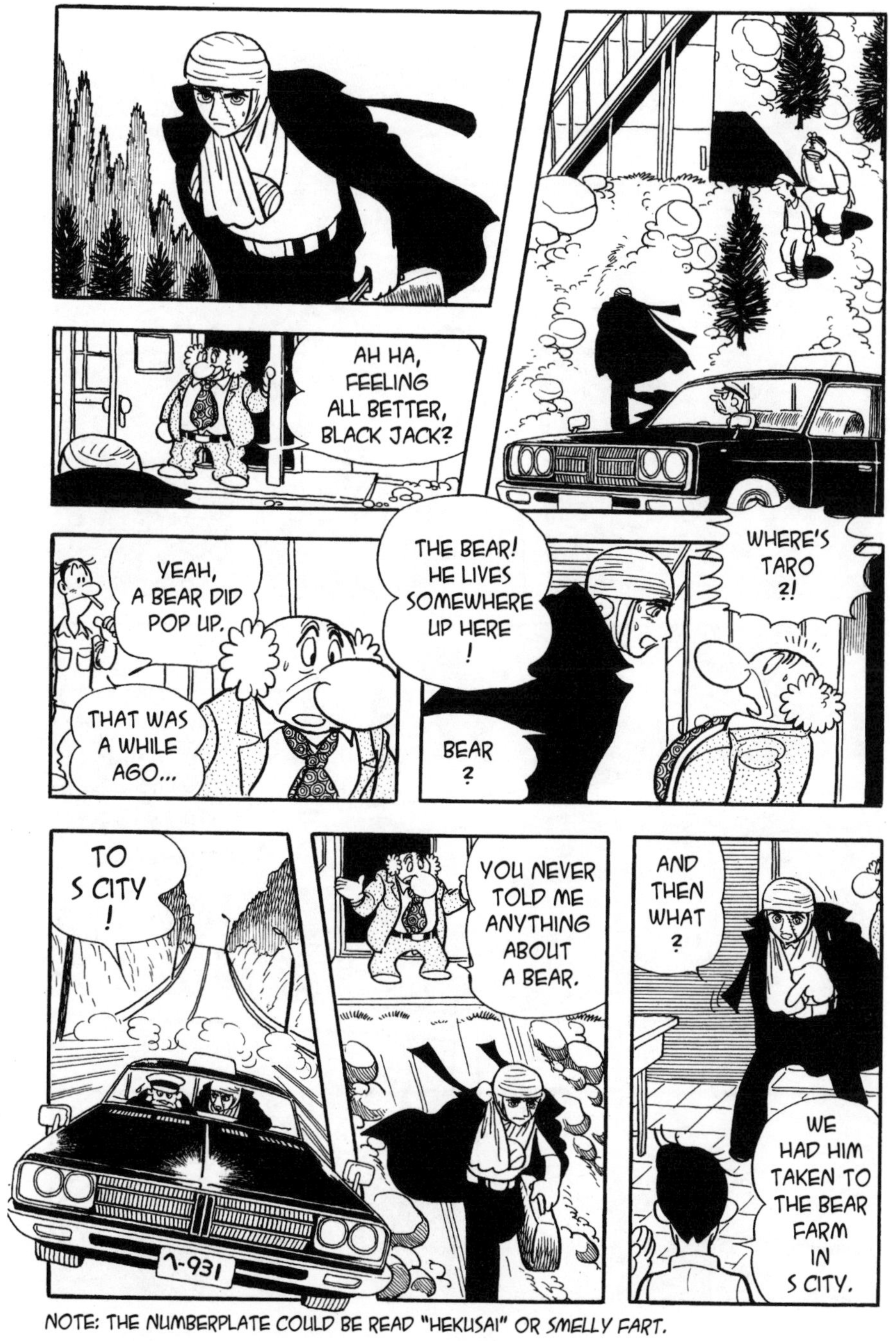
AH HA, FEELING ALL BETTER, BLACK JACK?
WHERE'S TARO ?!
THE BEAR! HE LIVES SOMEWHERE UP HERE !
BEAR ?
YEAH, A BEAR DID POP UP.
THAT WAS A WHILE AGO...
AND THEN WHAT ?
WE HAD HIM TAKEN TO THE BEAR FARM IN S CITY.
YOU NEVER TOLD ME ANYTHING ABOUT A BEAR.
TO S CITY !
ヘ-931

NOTE: THE NUMBERPLATE COULD BE READ "HEKUSAI" OR SMELLY FART.

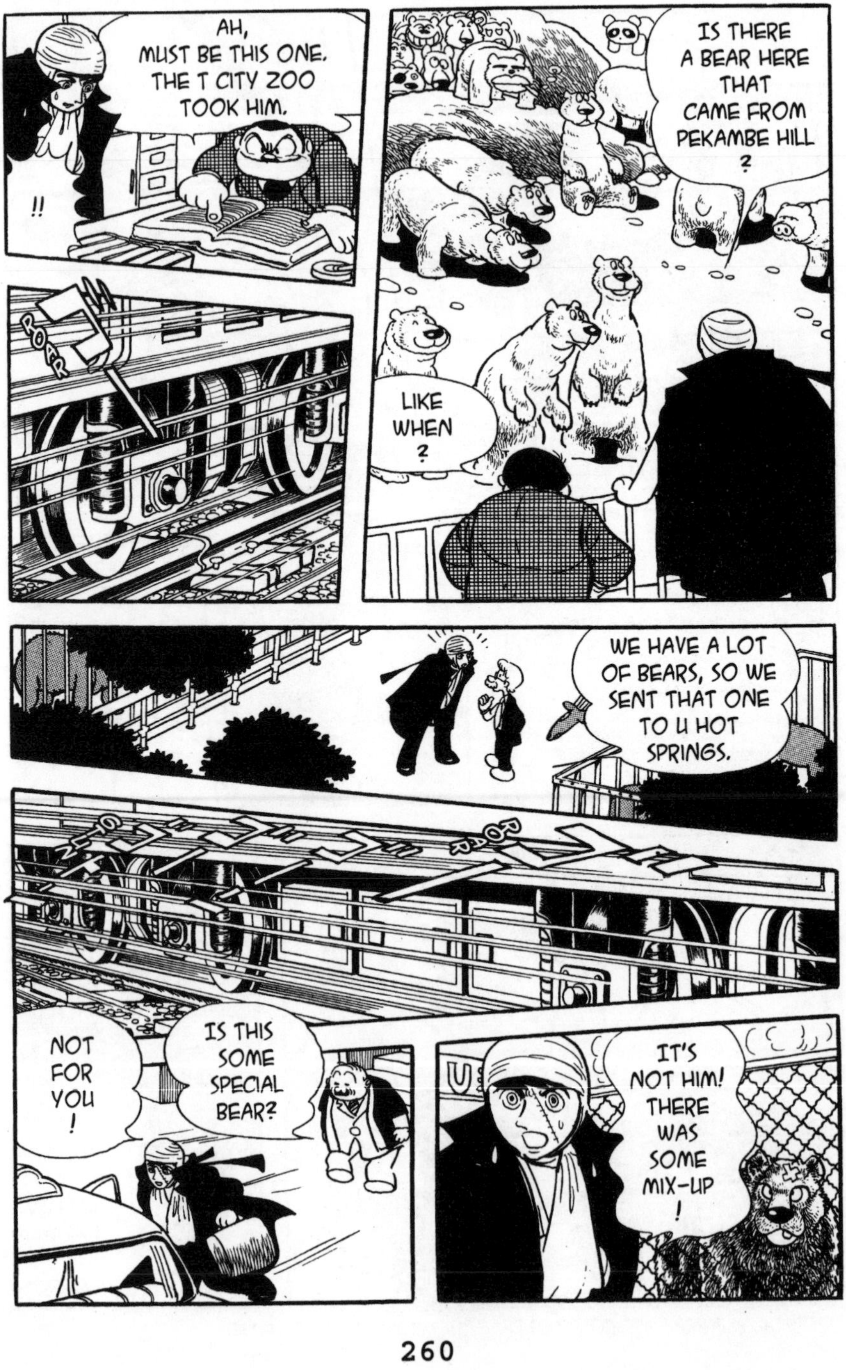
IS THERE A BEAR HERE THAT CAME FROM PEKAMBE HILL?
LIKE WHEN?
AH, MUST BE THIS ONE. THE T CITY ZOO TOOK HIM.
!!
ROAR
WE HAVE A LOT OF BEARS, SO WE SENT THAT ONE TO U HOT SPRINGS.
ROAR
IT'S NOT HIM! THERE WAS SOME MIX-UP!
IS THIS SOME SPECIAL BEAR?
NOT FOR YOU!

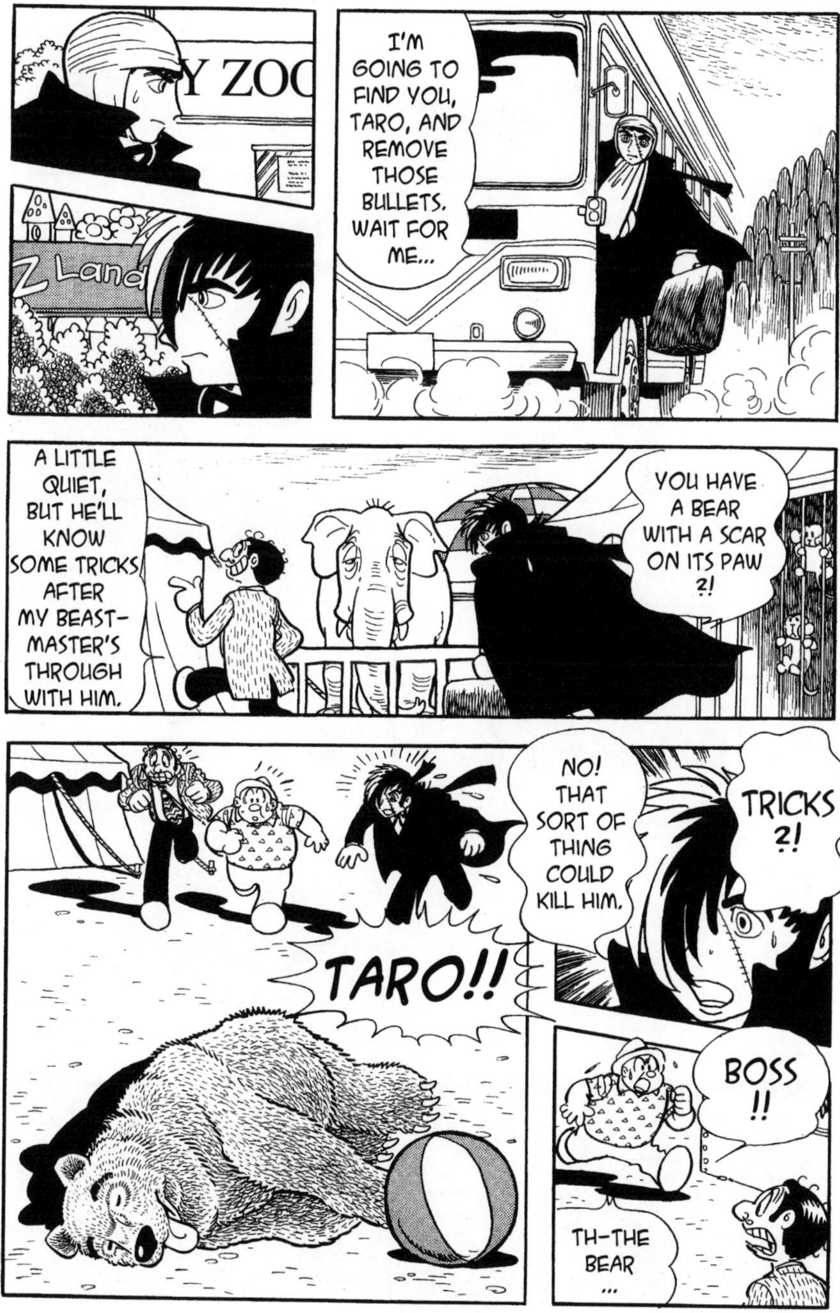
I'M GOING TO FIND YOU, TARO, AND REMOVE THOSE BULLETS. WAIT FOR ME...
Z Land
YOU HAVE A BEAR WITH A SCAR ON ITS PAW ?!
A LITTLE QUIET, BUT HE'LL KNOW SOME TRICKS AFTER MY BEAST-MASTER'S THROUGH WITH HIM.
TRICKS ?!
NO! THAT SORT OF THING COULD KILL HIM.
BOSS !!
TH-THE BEAR ...
TARO!!

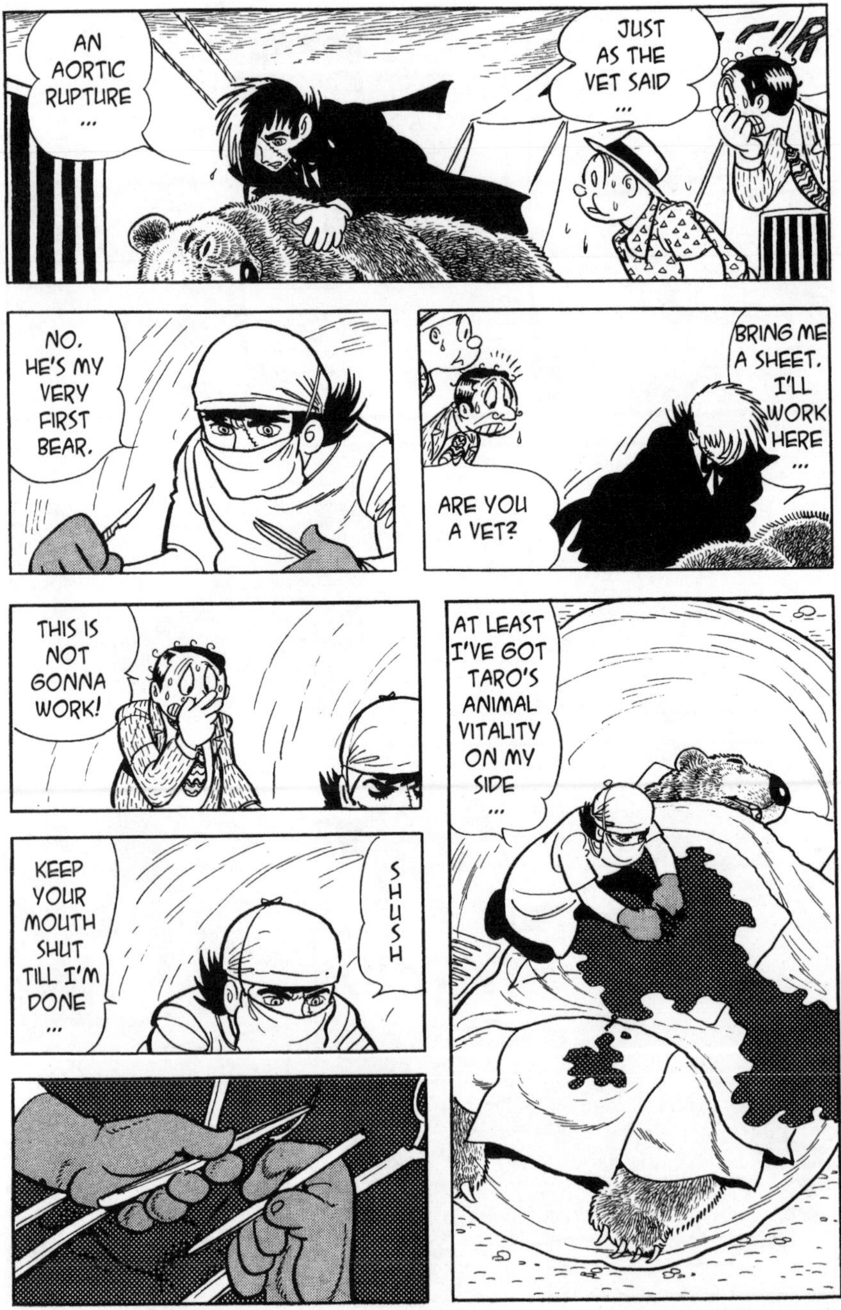
JUST AS THE VET SAID ...
AN AORTIC RUPTURE ...
BRING ME A SHEET. I'LL WORK HERE ...
ARE YOU A VET?
NO. HE'S MY VERY FIRST BEAR.
AT LEAST I'VE GOT TARO'S ANIMAL VITALITY ON MY SIDE ...
THIS IS NOT GONNA WORK!
SHUSH
KEEP YOUR MOUTH SHUT TILL I'M DONE ...

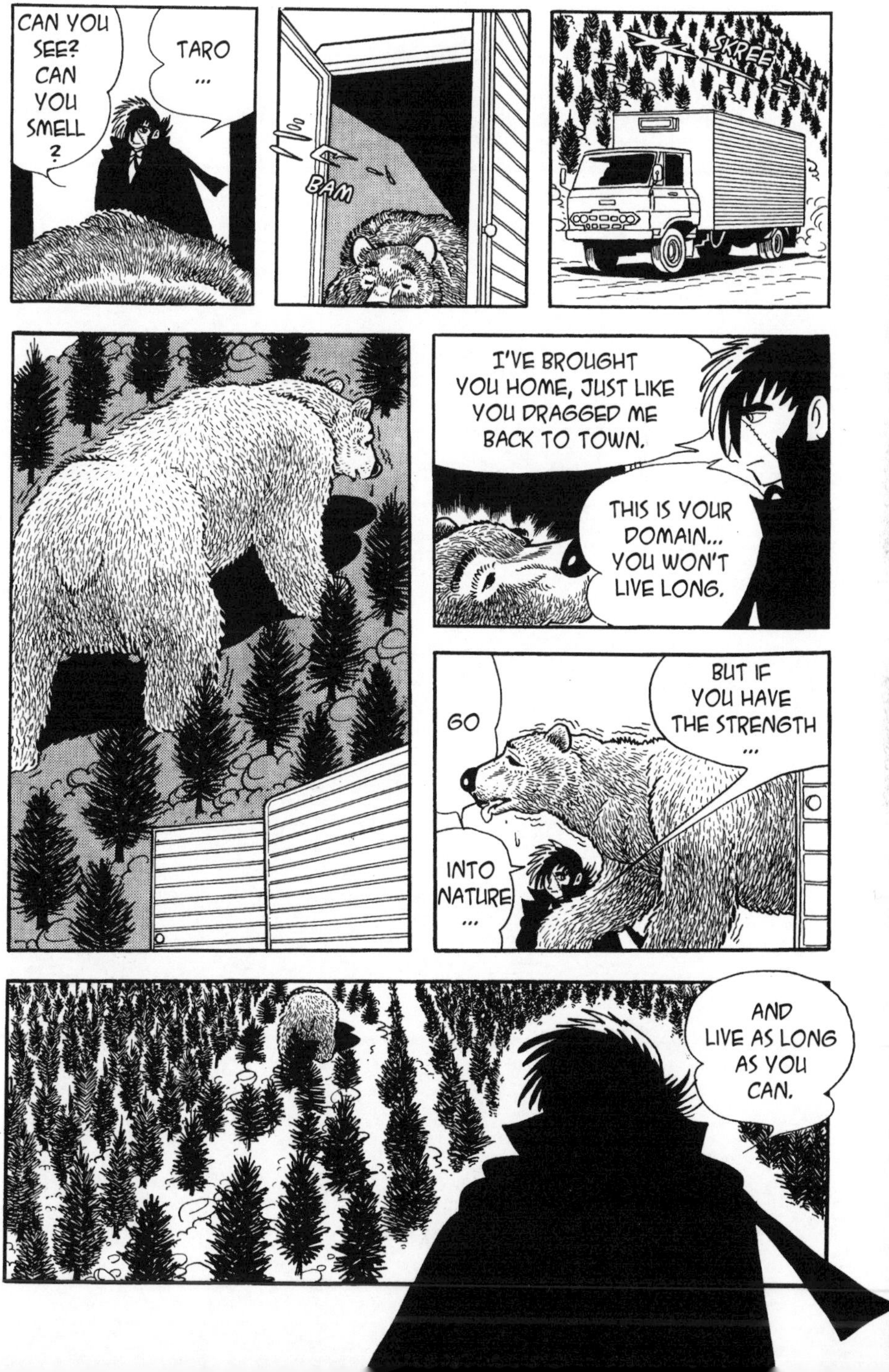
SKREE
BAM
TARO ...
CAN YOU SEE? CAN YOU SMELL ?
I'VE BROUGHT YOU HOME, JUST LIKE YOU DRAGGED ME BACK TO TOWN.
THIS IS YOUR DOMAIN... YOU WON'T LIVE LONG.
BUT IF YOU HAVE THE STRENGTH ...
GO
INTO NATURE ...
AND LIVE AS LONG AS YOU CAN.

CLOUDY, LATER FAIR

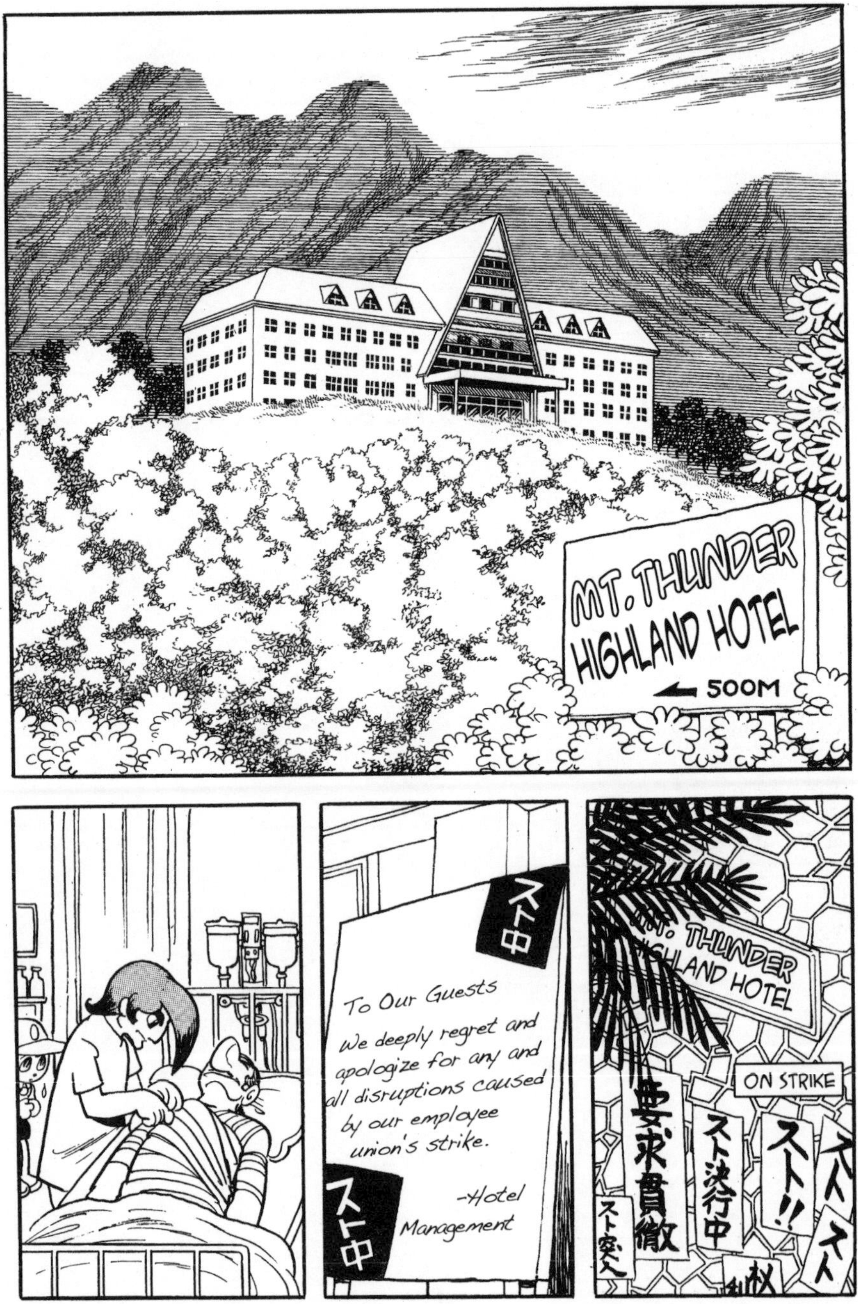
MT. THUNDER
HIGHLAND HOTEL
500M
MT. THUNDER
HIGHLAND HOTEL
ON STRIKE
スト!!
スト決行中
要求貫徹
スト突入
スト中
To Our Guests
We deeply regret and apologize for any and all disruptions caused by our employee union's strike.
-Hotel Management
スト中

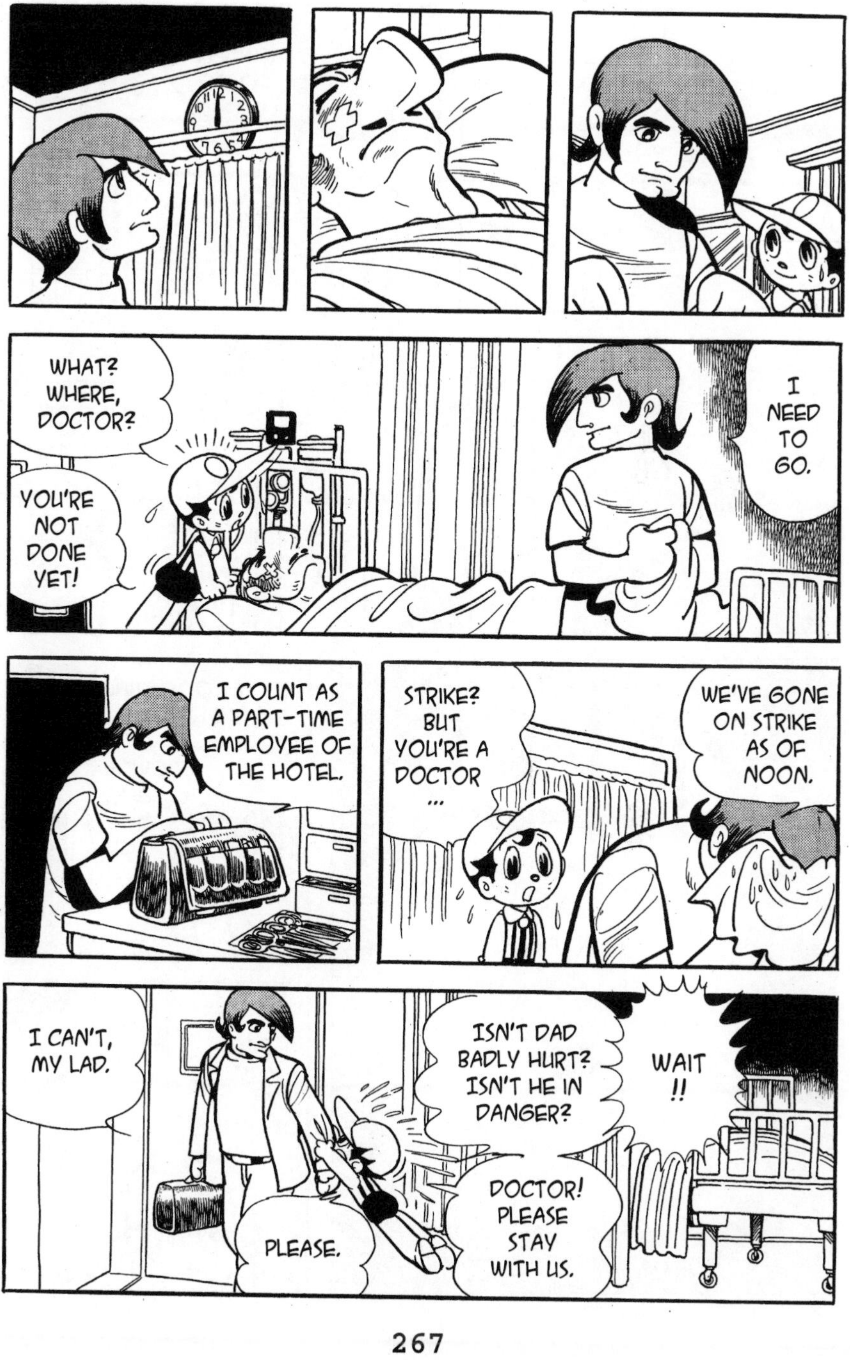
I NEED TO GO.
WHAT? WHERE, DOCTOR?
YOU'RE NOT DONE YET!
WE'VE GONE ON STRIKE AS OF NOON.
STRIKE? BUT YOU'RE A DOCTOR ...
I COUNT AS A PART-TIME EMPLOYEE OF THE HOTEL.
WAIT !!
ISN'T DAD BADLY HURT? ISN'T HE IN DANGER?
DOCTOR! PLEASE STAY WITH US.
PLEASE.
I CAN'T, MY LAD.

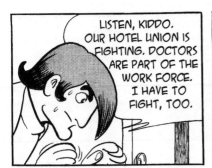

YOU'LL JUST LET HIM DIE?!
MY DAD HAS NOTHING TO DO WITH IT.
LISTEN, KIDDO. OUR HOTEL UNION IS FIGHTING. DOCTORS ARE PART OF THE WORK FORCE. I HAVE TO FIGHT, TOO.
BUT MY DAD IS BADLY HURT!
IF WE RELENT FOR SUCH A THING, WE LOSE.
YOU IDIOT KILLER QUACK !!
YOU'RE TOO YOUNG TO UNDERSTAND THE WORLD OF GROWN-UPS, MY LAD.
DON'T DARE ACCUSE ME AGAIN LIKE THAT.
KILLER

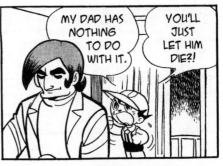

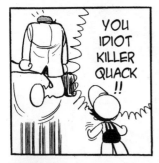

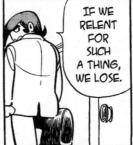

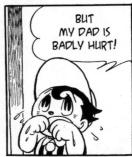

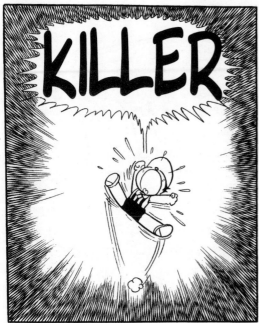

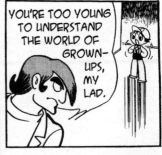

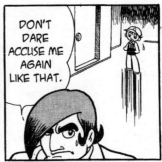

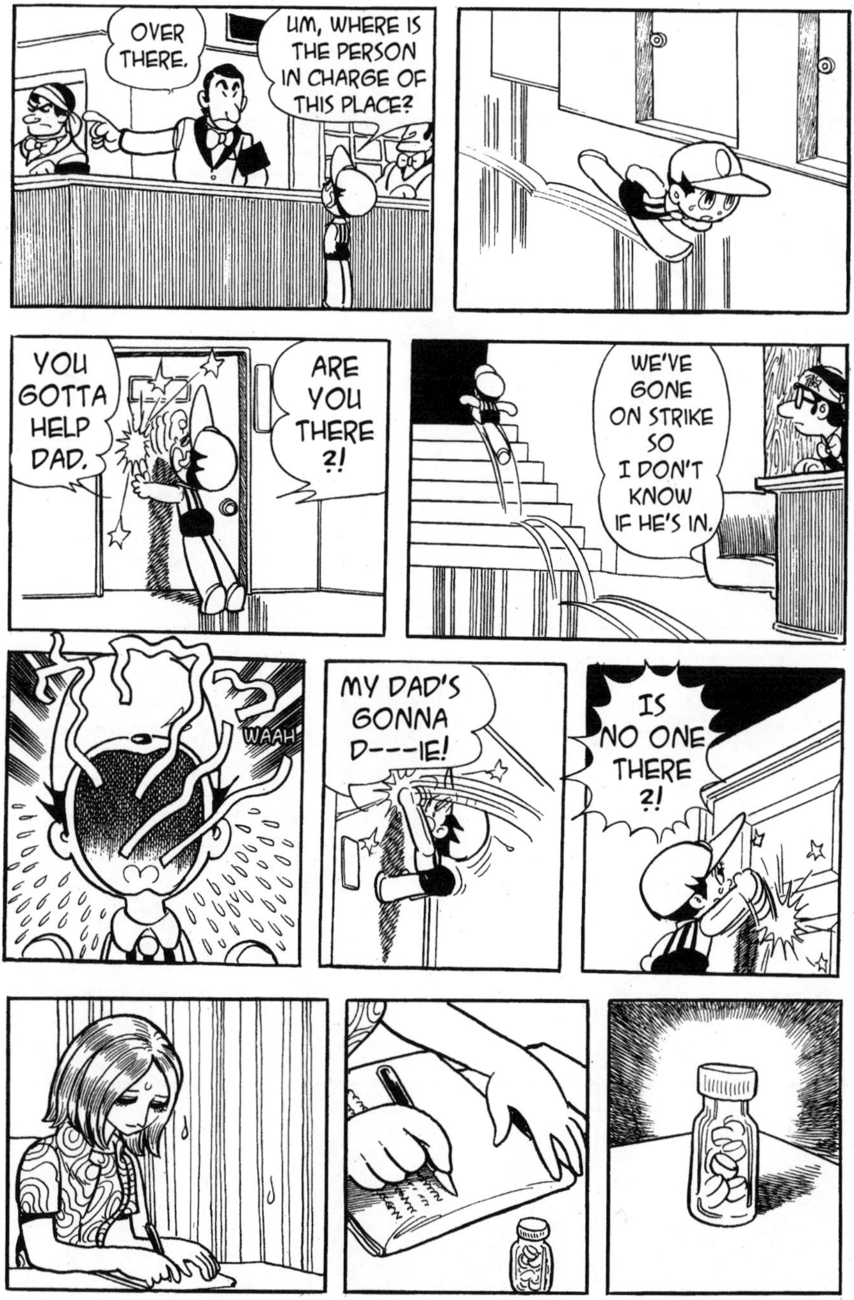
UM, WHERE IS THE PERSON IN CHARGE OF THIS PLACE?
OVER THERE.
WE'VE GONE ON STRIKE SO I DON'T KNOW IF HE'S IN.
ARE YOU THERE ?!
YOU GOTTA HELP DAD.
IS NO ONE THERE ?!
MY DAD'S GONNA D---IE!
WAAH

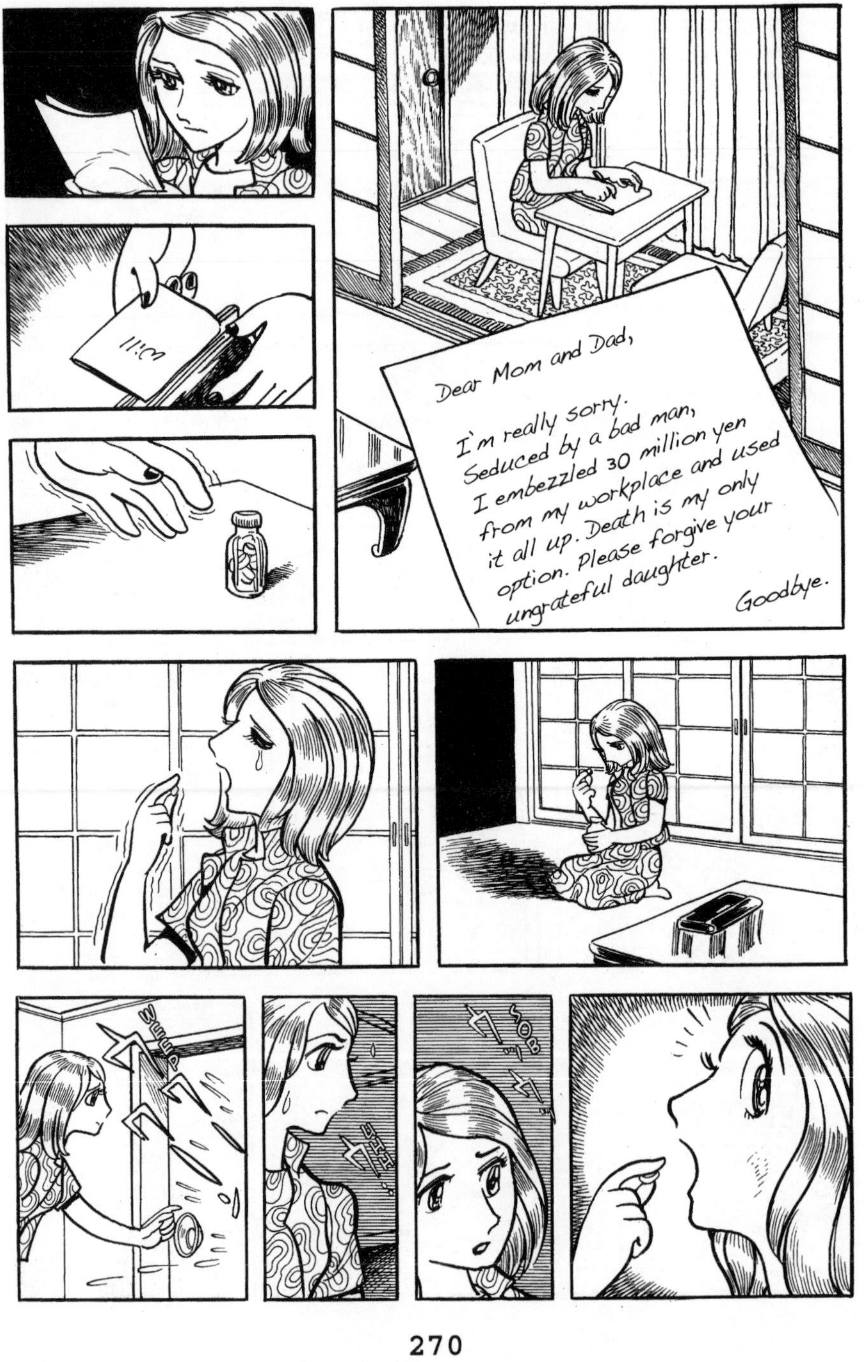
Will
Dear Mom and Dad,
I'm really sorry.
Seduced by a bad man,
I embezzled 30 million yen
from my workplace and used
it all up. Death is my only
option. Please forgive your
ungrateful daughter.
Goodbye.
SOB
SHH
WEEP

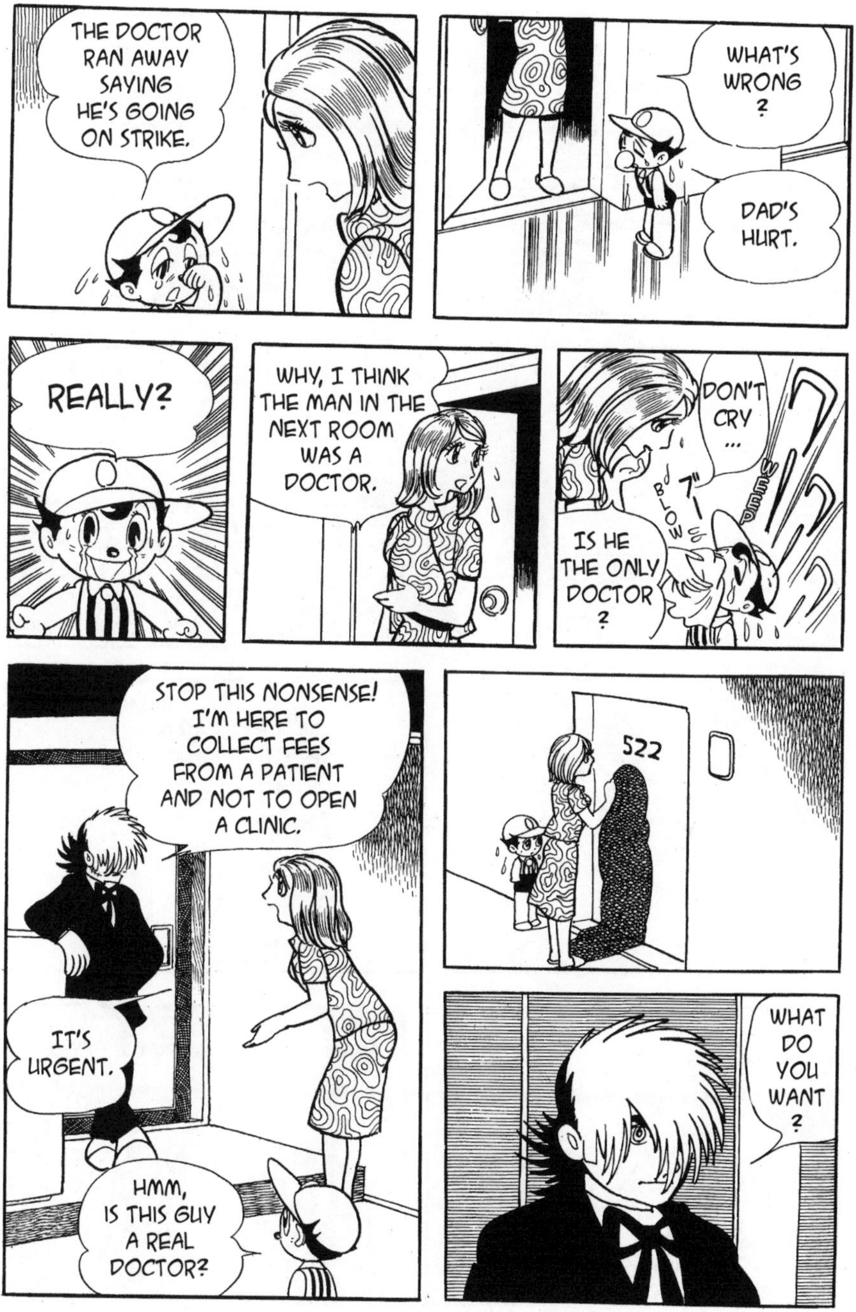
WHAT'S WRONG?
DAD'S HURT.
THE DOCTOR RAN AWAY SAYING HE'S GOING ON STRIKE.
DON'T CRY ...
BLOW
IS HE THE ONLY DOCTOR?
WHY, I THINK THE MAN IN THE NEXT ROOM WAS A DOCTOR.
REALLY?
522
WHAT DO YOU WANT?
IT'S URGENT.
STOP THIS NONSENSE! I'M HERE TO COLLECT FEES FROM A PATIENT AND NOT TO OPEN A CLINIC.
HMM, IS THIS GUY A REAL DOCTOR?

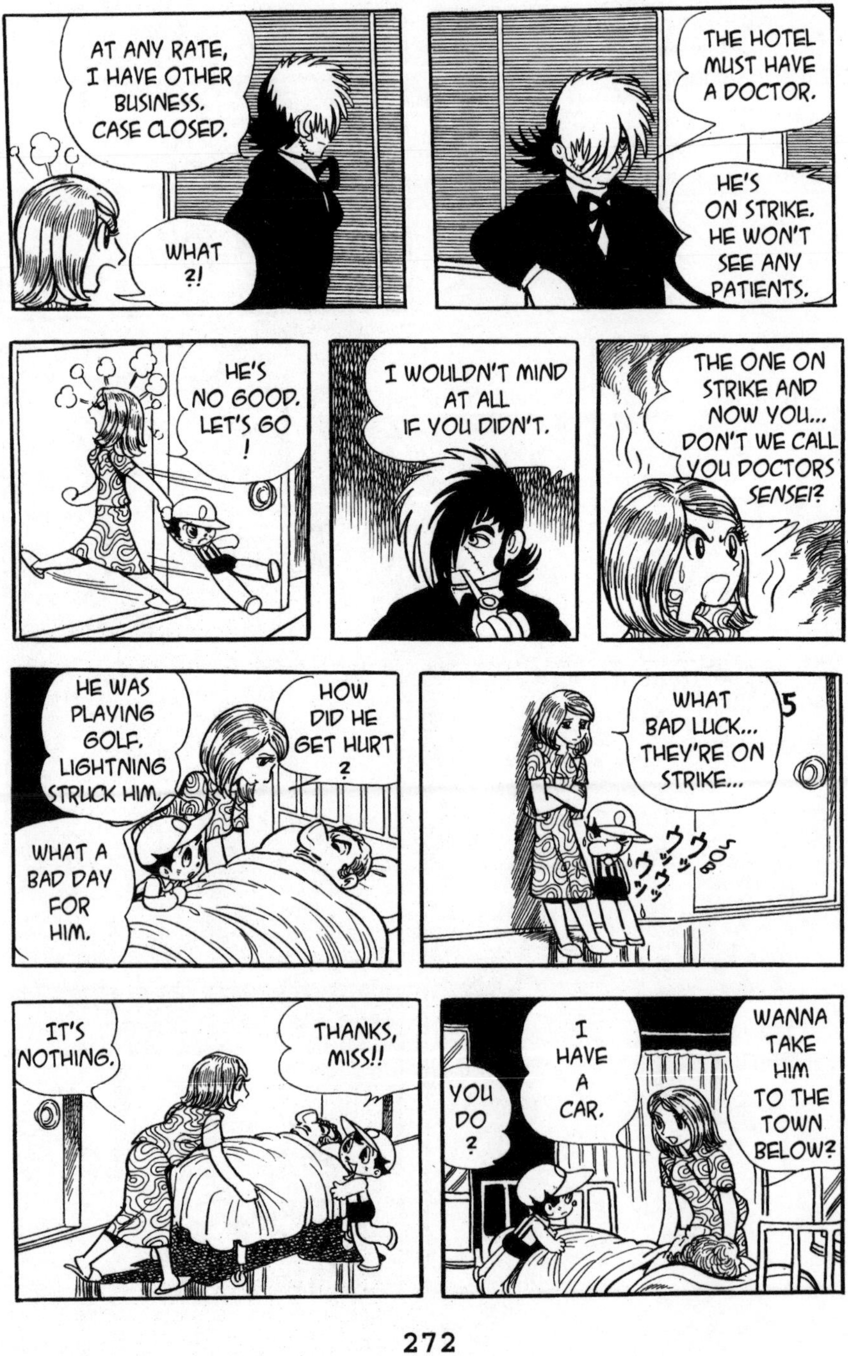
THE HOTEL MUST HAVE A DOCTOR.
HE'S ON STRIKE. HE WON'T SEE ANY PATIENTS.
AT ANY RATE, I HAVE OTHER BUSINESS. CASE CLOSED.
WHAT ?!
THE ONE ON STRIKE AND NOW YOU... DON'T WE CALL YOU DOCTORS SENSEI?
I WOULDN'T MIND AT ALL IF YOU DIDN'T.
HE'S NO GOOD. LET'S GO !
WHAT BAD LUCK... THEY'RE ON STRIKE...
5
ウッウッ ウッウッ
HOW DID HE GET HURT ?
HE WAS PLAYING GOLF. LIGHTNING STRUCK HIM.
WHAT A BAD DAY FOR HIM.
WANNA TAKE HIM TO THE TOWN BELOW?
I HAVE A CAR.
YOU DO ?
THANKS, MISS!!
IT'S NOTHING.

2

CREAK

HUH.

THEY CALL IT MT. THUNDER BECAUSE ACCIDENTS LIKE THAT HAPPEN HERE NOW AND THEN.

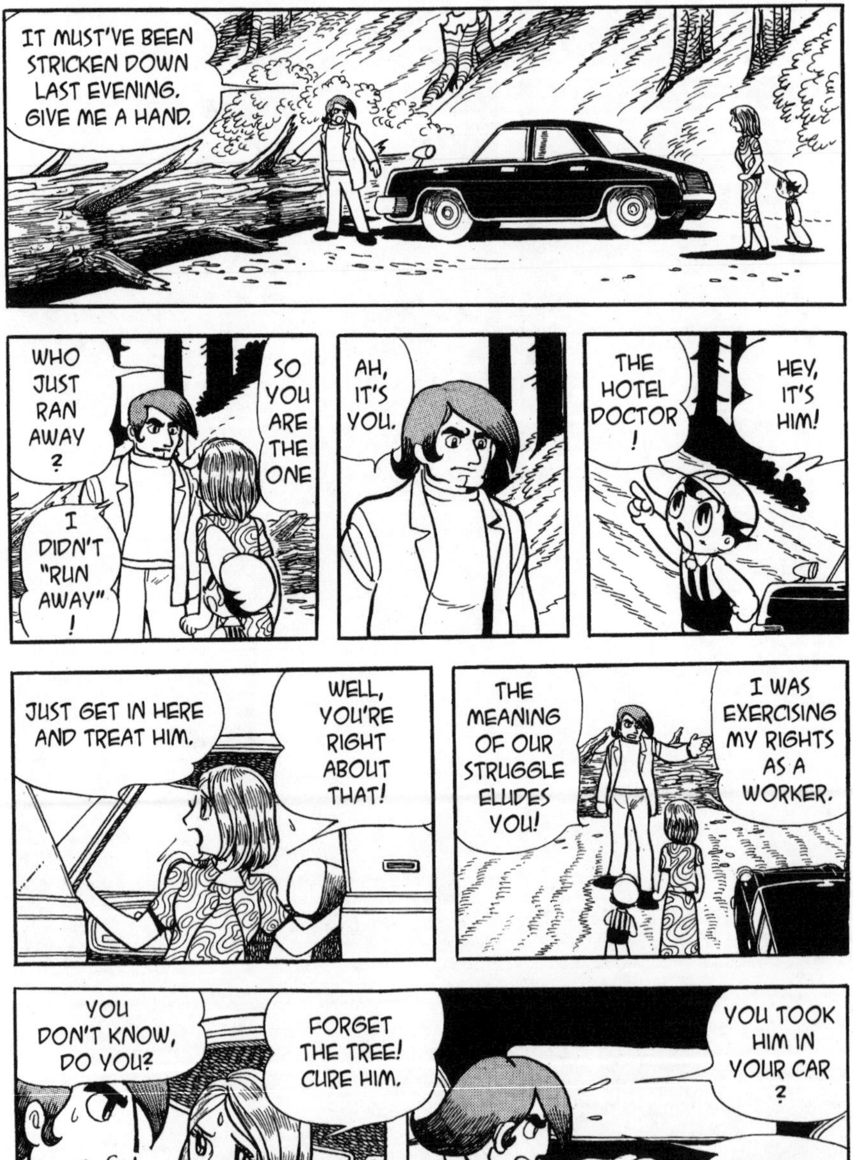
IT MUST'VE BEEN STRICKEN DOWN LAST EVENING. GIVE ME A HAND.
HEY, IT'S HIM!
THE HOTEL DOCTOR!
AH, IT'S YOU.
SO YOU ARE THE ONE
WHO JUST RAN AWAY?
I DIDN'T "RUN AWAY"!
I WAS EXERCISING MY RIGHTS AS A WORKER.
THE MEANING OF OUR STRUGGLE ELUDES YOU!
WELL, YOU'RE RIGHT ABOUT THAT!
JUST GET IN HERE AND TREAT HIM.
YOU TOOK HIM IN YOUR CAR?
WE OUGHT TO MOVE THAT TREE FIRST.
FORGET THE TREE! CURE HIM.
YOU DON'T KNOW, DO YOU?

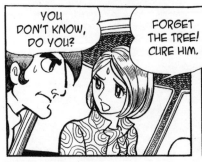

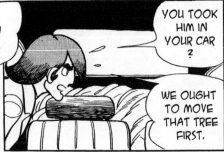

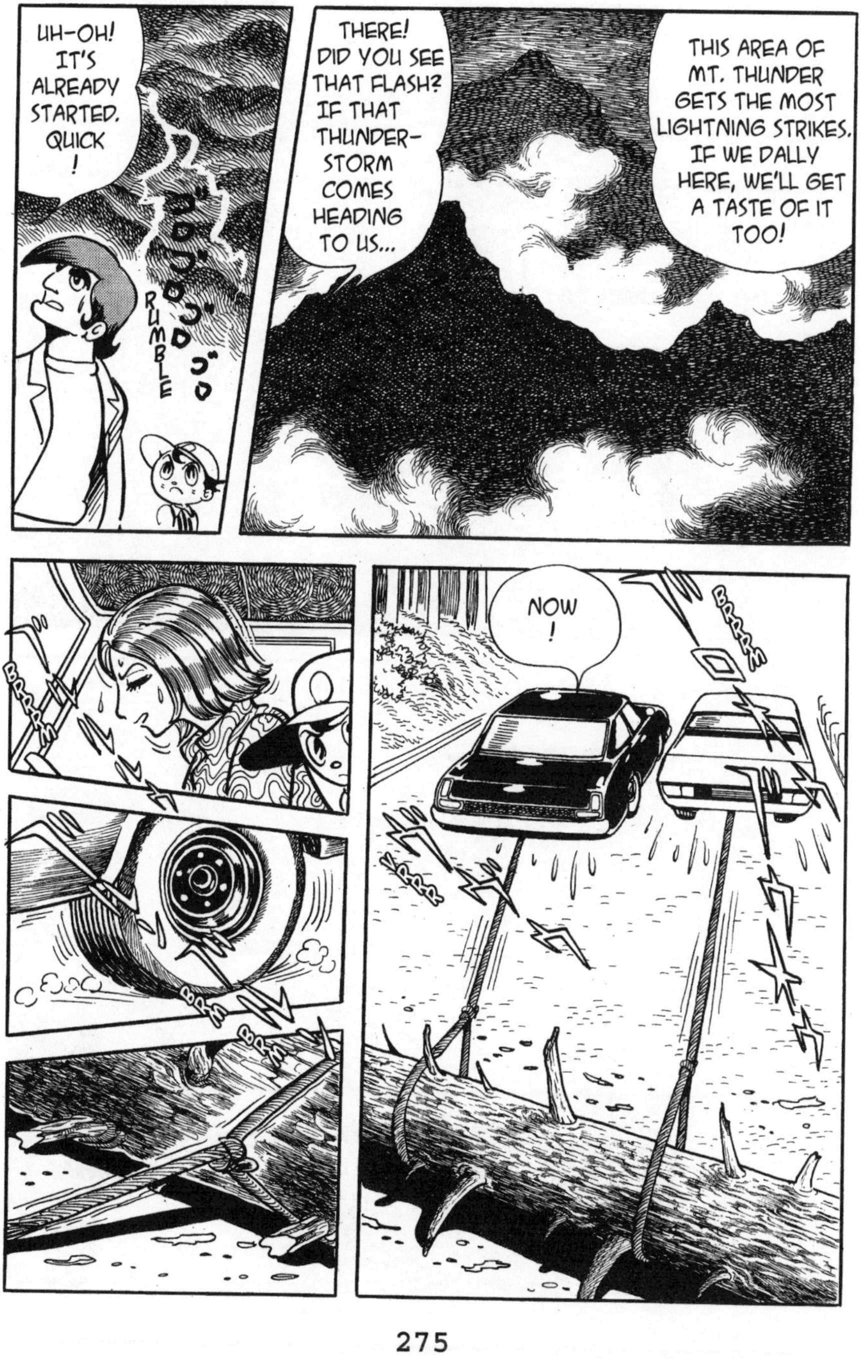
THIS AREA OF MT. THUNDER GETS THE MOST LIGHTNING STRIKES. IF WE DALLY HERE, WE'LL GET A TASTE OF IT TOO!
THERE! DID YOU SEE THAT FLASH? IF THAT THUNDER-STORM COMES HEADING TO US...
UH-OH! IT'S ALREADY STARTED. QUICK!
ゴロゴロゴロ
ゴロ
RUMBLE
BRRRM
NOW!
BRRR
BRRRM

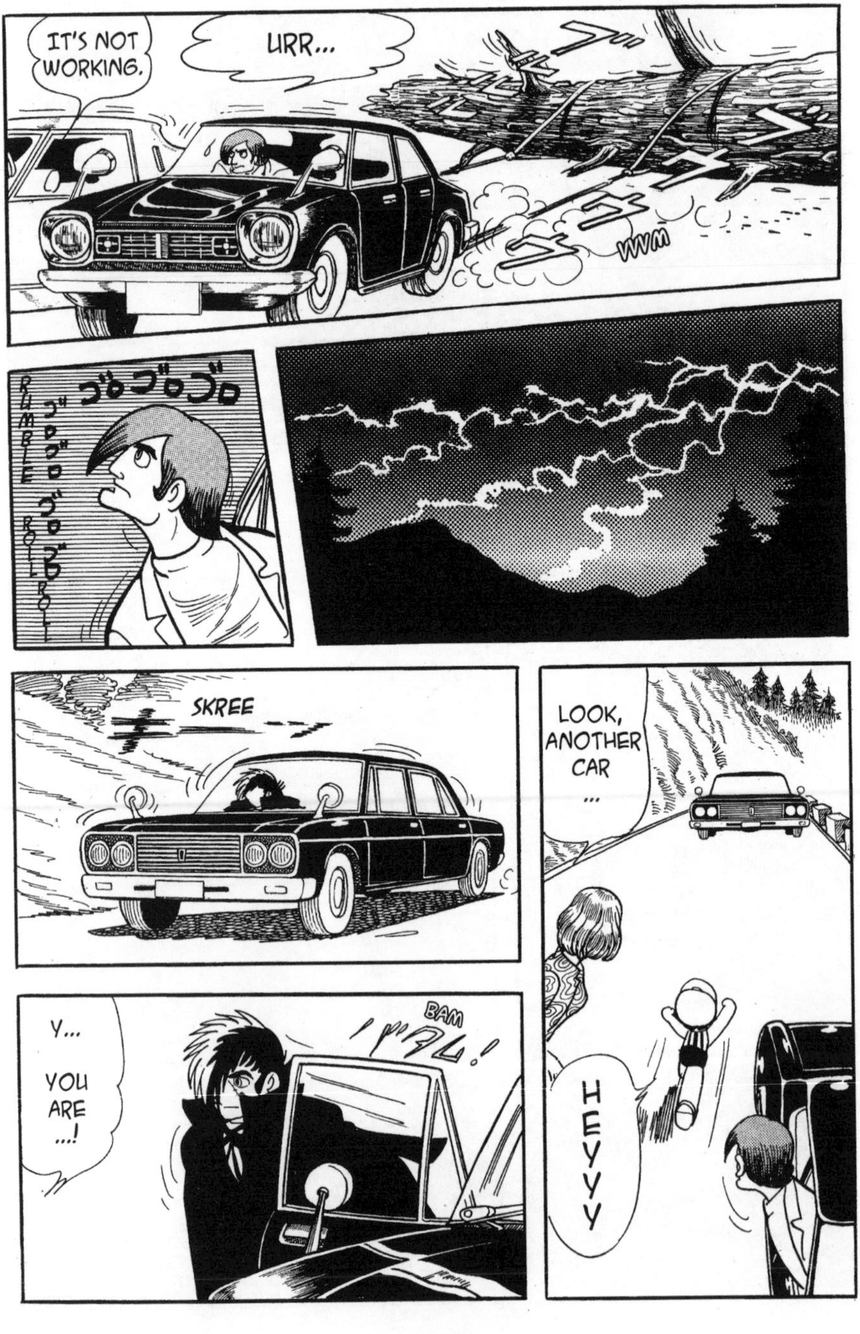
URR...
IT'S NOT WORKING.
WWM
RUMBLE ROLL ROLL
LOOK, ANOTHER CAR ...
HEYYY
SKREE
BAM
Y... YOU ARE ...!

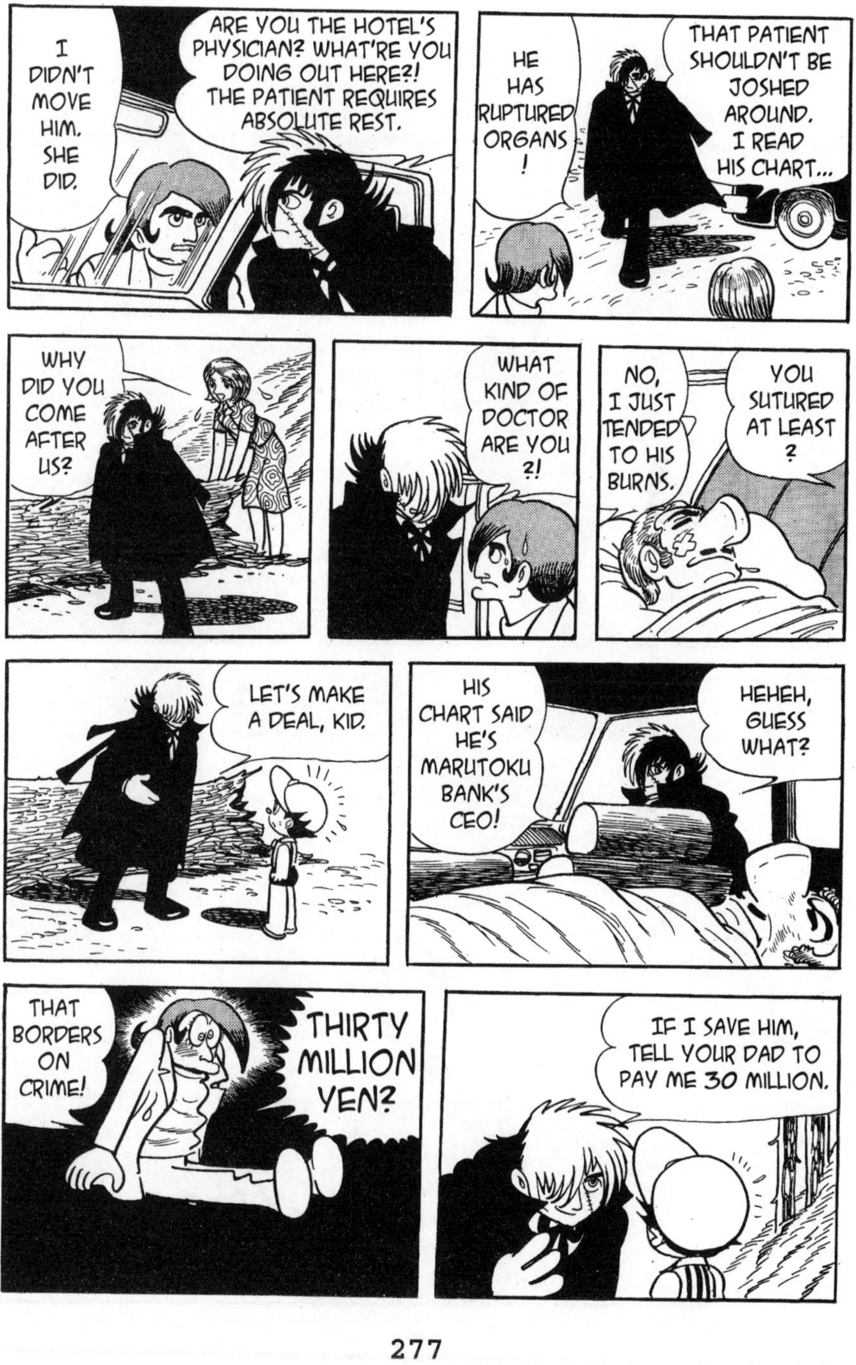
THAT PATIENT SHOULDN'T BE JOSHED AROUND. I READ HIS CHART...
HE HAS RUPTURED ORGANS!
ARE YOU THE HOTEL'S PHYSICIAN? WHAT'RE YOU DOING OUT HERE?! THE PATIENT REQUIRES ABSOLUTE REST.
I DIDN'T MOVE HIM. SHE DID.
YOU SUTURED AT LEAST?
NO, I JUST TENDED TO HIS BURNS.
WHAT KIND OF DOCTOR ARE YOU?!
WHY DID YOU COME AFTER US?
HEHEH, GUESS WHAT?
HIS CHART SAID HE'S MARUTOKU BANK'S CEO!
LET'S MAKE A DEAL, KID.
IF I SAVE HIM, TELL YOUR DAD TO PAY ME 30 MILLION.
THIRTY MILLION YEN?
THAT BORDERS ON CRIME!

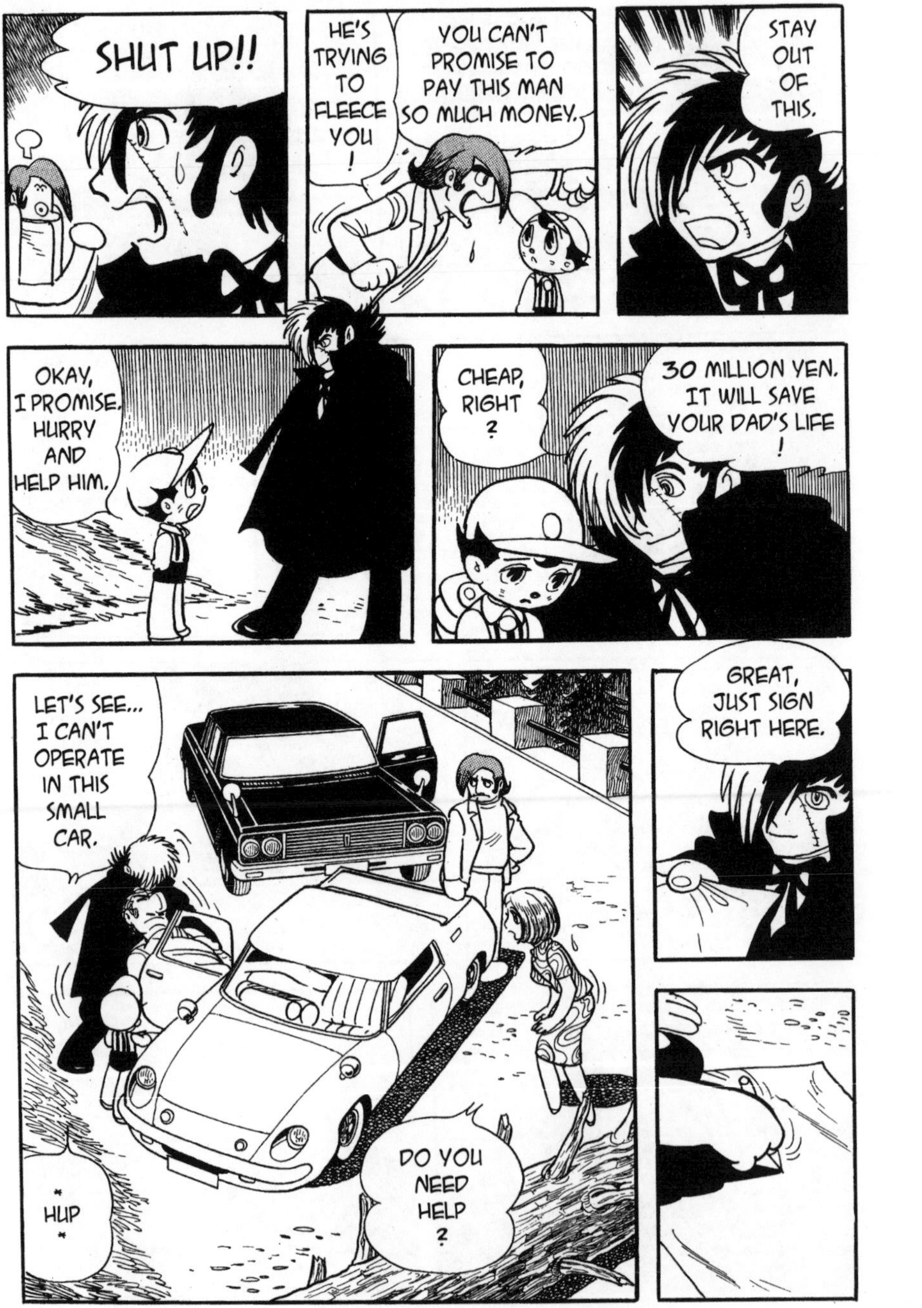
STAY OUT OF THIS.
YOU CAN'T PROMISE TO PAY THIS MAN SO MUCH MONEY.
HE'S TRYING TO FLEECE YOU!
SHUT UP!!
30 MILLION YEN. IT WILL SAVE YOUR DAD'S LIFE!
CHEAP, RIGHT?
OKAY, I PROMISE. HURRY AND HELP HIM.
GREAT, JUST SIGN RIGHT HERE.
LET'S SEE... I CAN'T OPERATE IN THIS SMALL CAR.
DO YOU NEED HELP?
HUP

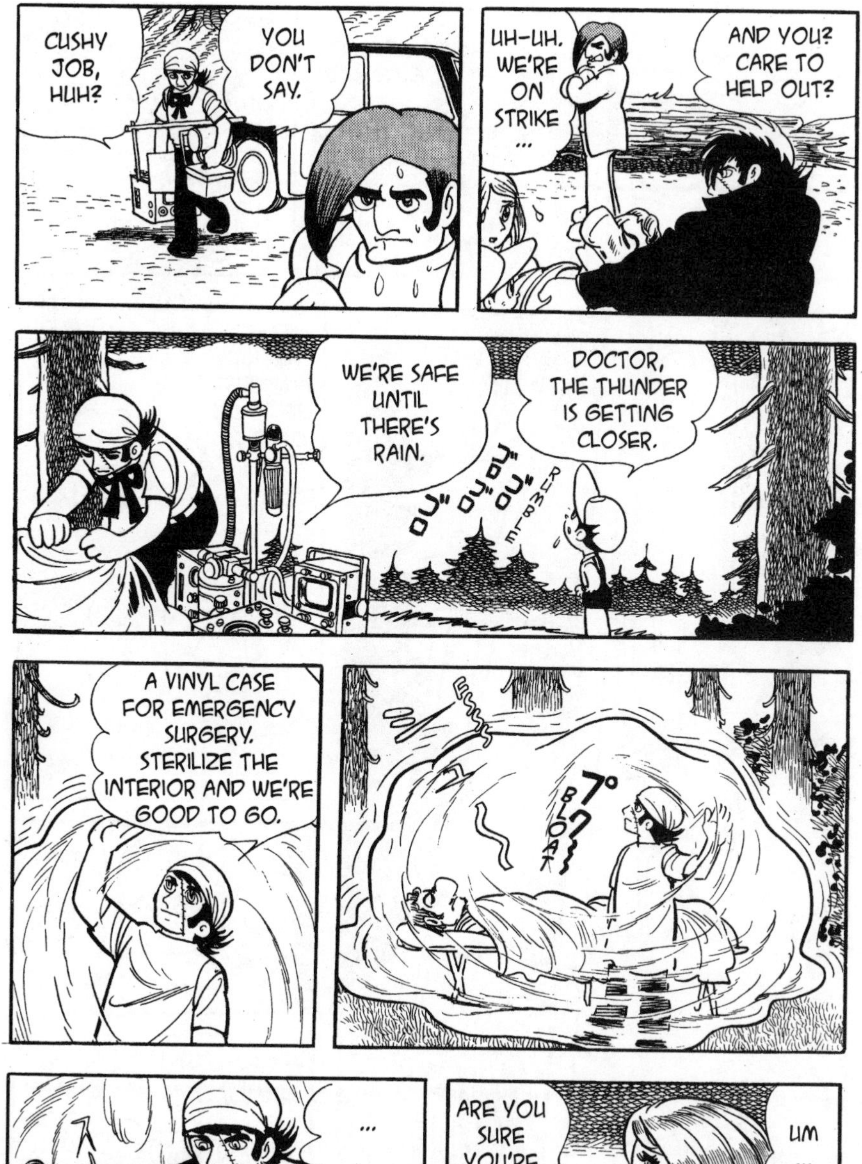
AND YOU? CARE TO HELP OUT?
UH-UH. WE'RE ON STRIKE ...
YOU DON'T SAY.
CUSHY JOB, HUH?
DOCTOR, THE THUNDER IS GETTING CLOSER.
RUMBLE
WE'RE SAFE UNTIL THERE'S RAIN.
BLOAT
A VINYL CASE FOR EMERGENCY SURGERY. STERILIZE THE INTERIOR AND WE'RE GOOD TO GO.
UM ...
ARE YOU SURE YOU'RE SAFE, WITH THE METAL?
...
SUSK

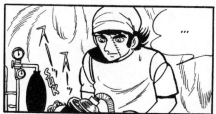

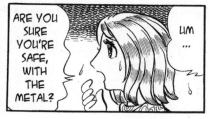

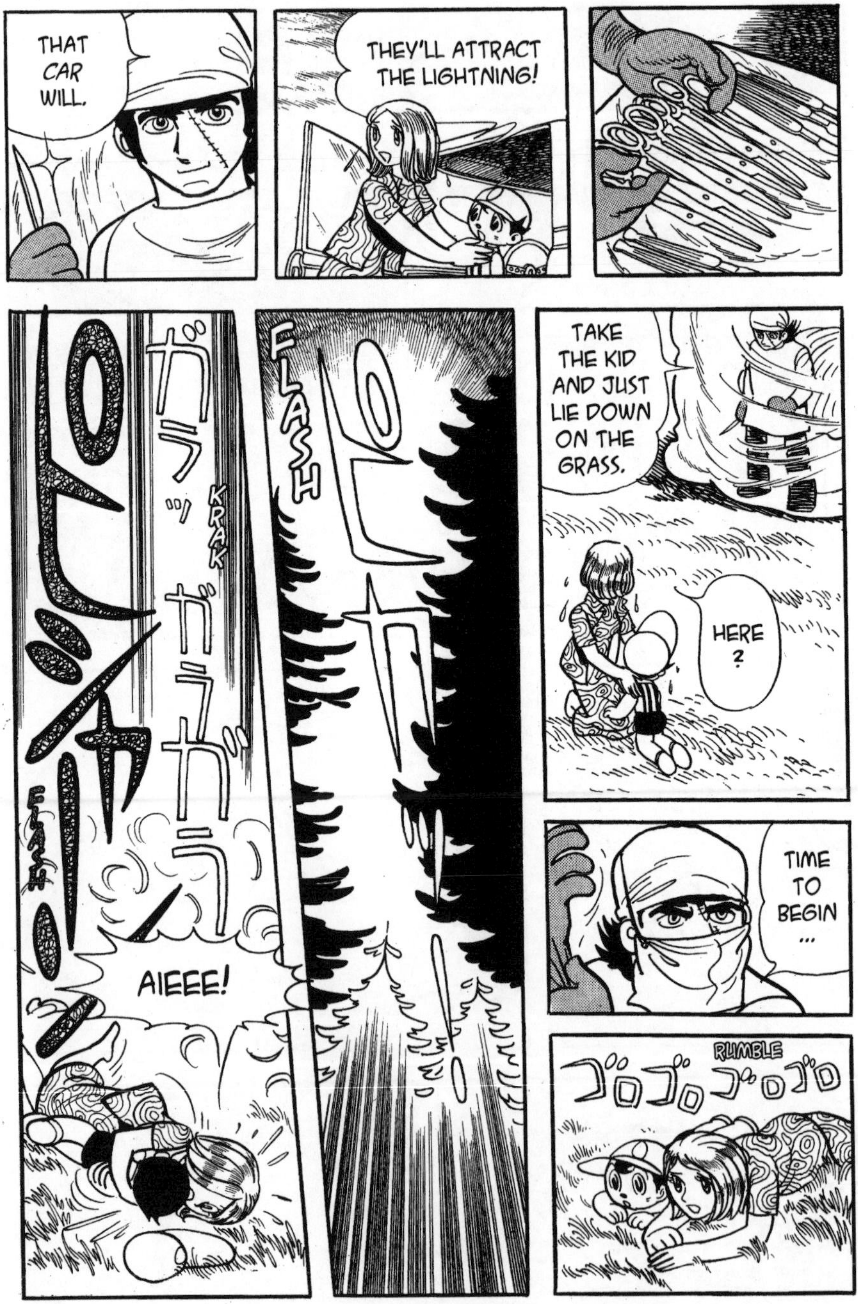
THEY'LL ATTRACT THE LIGHTNING!
THAT CAR WILL.
TAKE THE KID AND JUST LIE DOWN ON THE GRASS.
HERE?
TIME TO BEGIN ...
RUMBLE
ゴロゴロゴロゴロ
FLASH
ガラッ
KRAK
ガラガラ
FLASH
AIEEE!

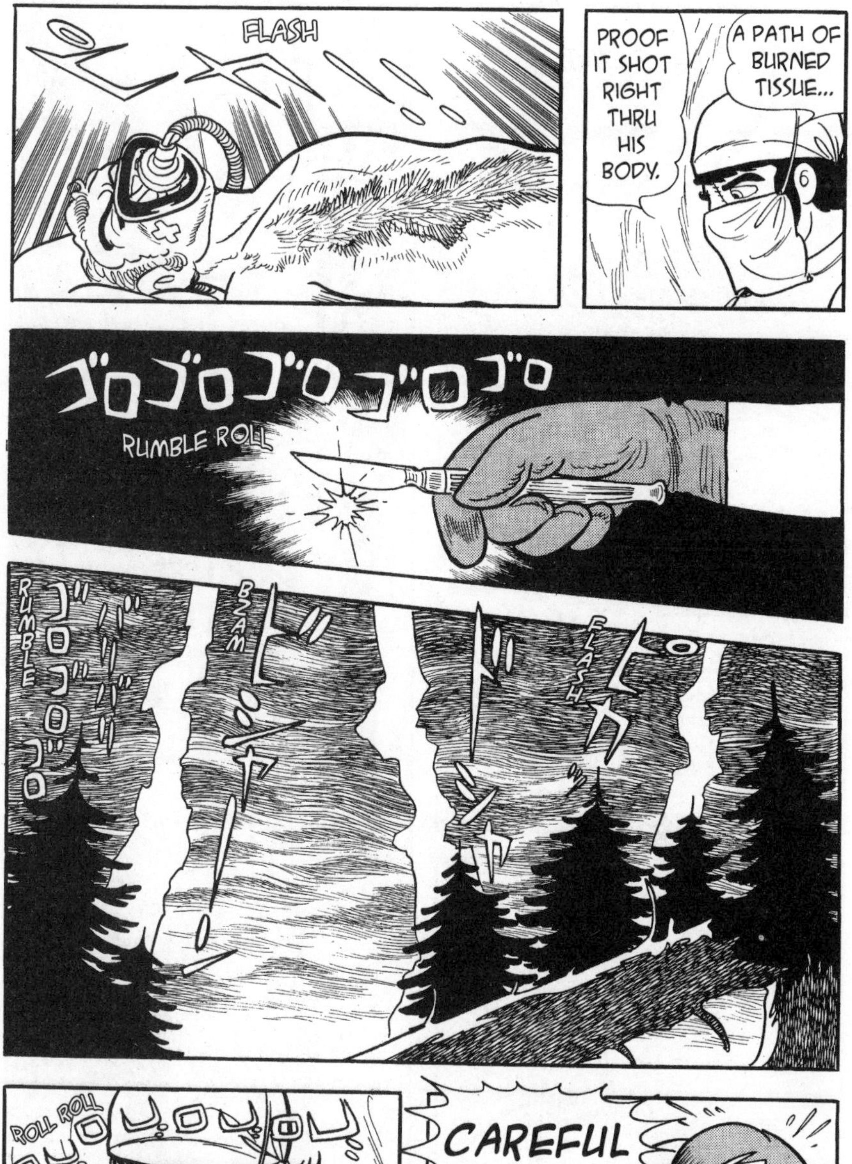
A PATH OF BURNED TISSUE...
PROOF IT SHOT RIGHT THRU HIS BODY.
FLASH
ゴロゴロゴロゴロゴロ
RUMBLE ROLL
FLASH
BZAM
RUMBLE
CAREFUL
ROLL ROLL

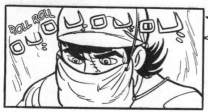

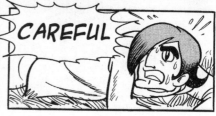

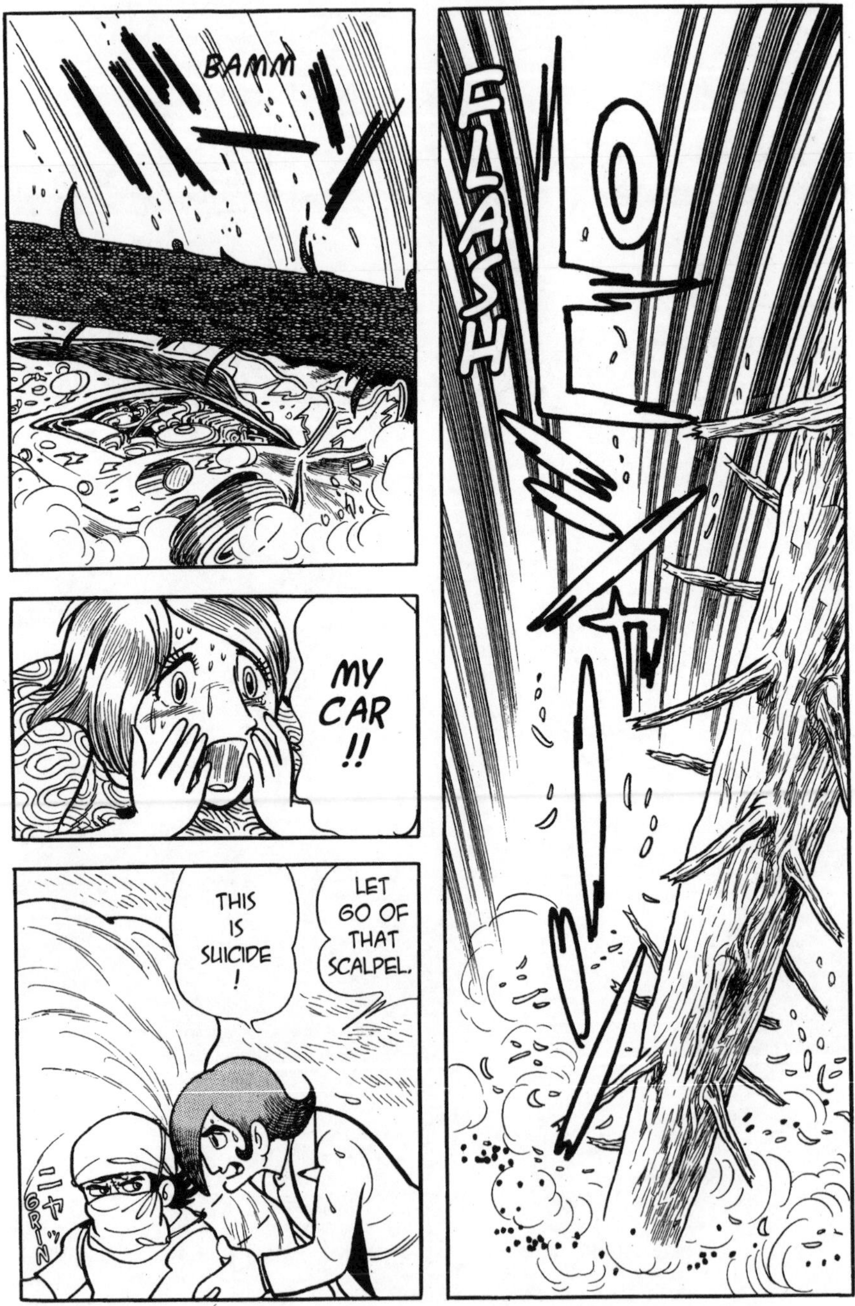
FLASH
BAMM
MY CAR !!
LET GO OF THAT SCALPEL.
THIS IS SUICIDE !
GRIN

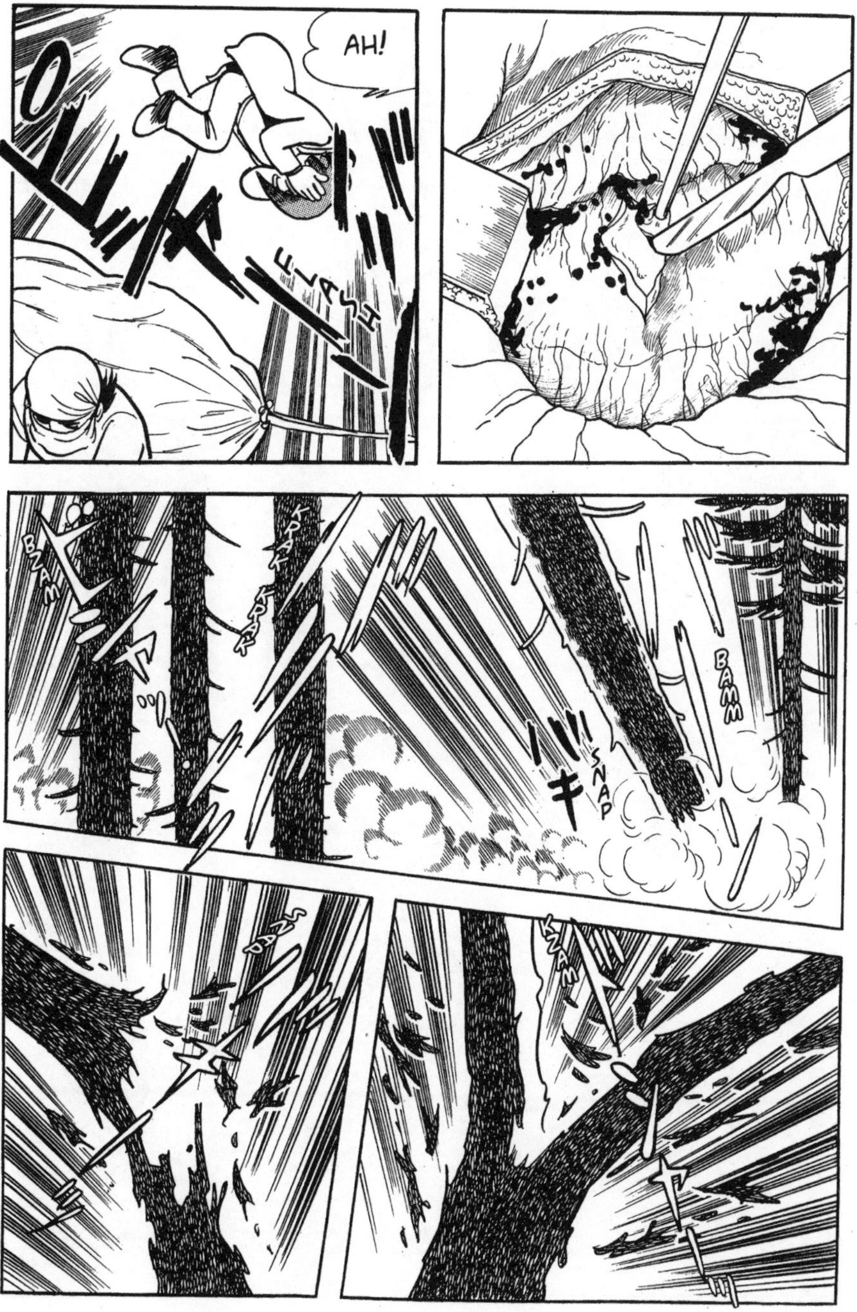
AH!
FLASH
BAMM
SNAP
KRAK KRAK KRAK
BZAM
KZAM
SNAP

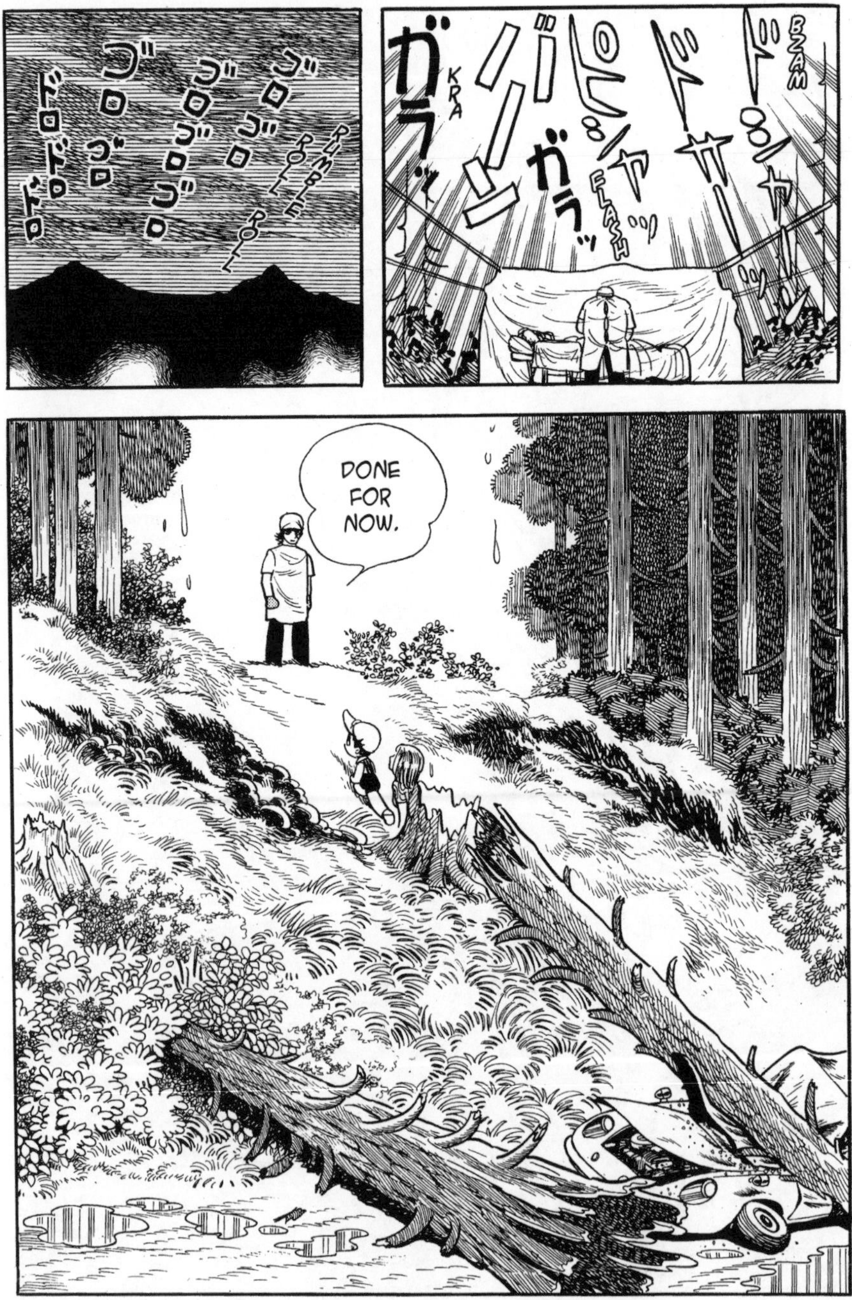
ドシャッ!!
BZAM
ドサーッ
ピシャッ
FLASH
ガラッ
バリーン
ガラッ
KRA
ゴロゴロ
RUMBLE
ゴロゴロゴロ
ROLL ROLL
ゴロゴロ
ドロドロドロ
DONE FOR NOW.

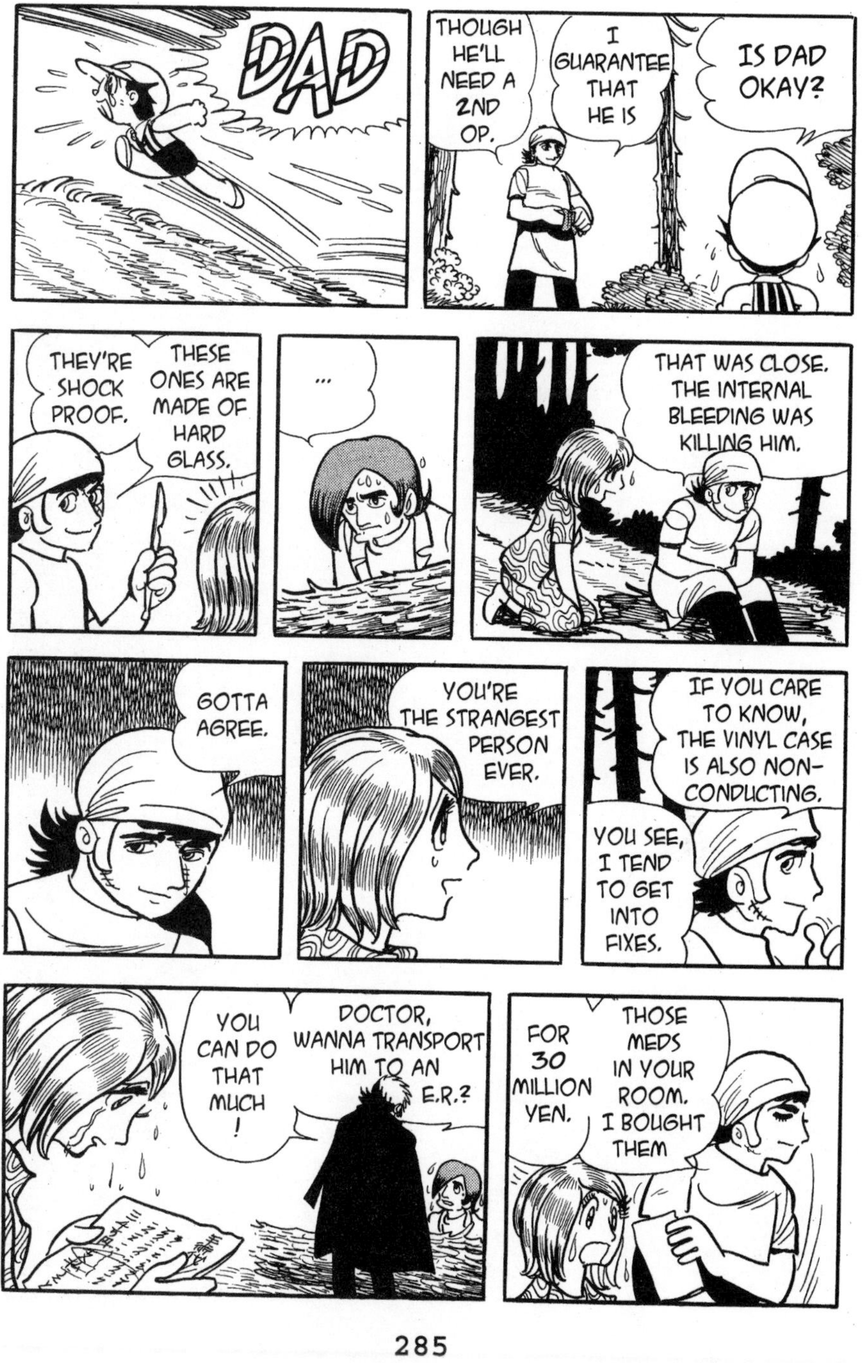
IS DAD OKAY?
I GUARANTEE THAT HE IS
THOUGH HE'LL NEED A 2ND OP.
DAD
THAT WAS CLOSE. THE INTERNAL BLEEDING WAS KILLING HIM.
...
THESE ONES ARE MADE OF HARD GLASS.
THEY'RE SHOCK PROOF.
IF YOU CARE TO KNOW, THE VINYL CASE IS ALSO NON-CONDUCTING.
YOU SEE, I TEND TO GET INTO FIXES.
YOU'RE THE STRANGEST PERSON EVER.
GOTTA AGREE.
THOSE MEDS IN YOUR ROOM. I BOUGHT THEM
FOR 30 MILLION YEN.
DOCTOR, WANNA TRANSPORT HIM TO AN E.R.?
YOU CAN DO THAT MUCH!

HURRICANE

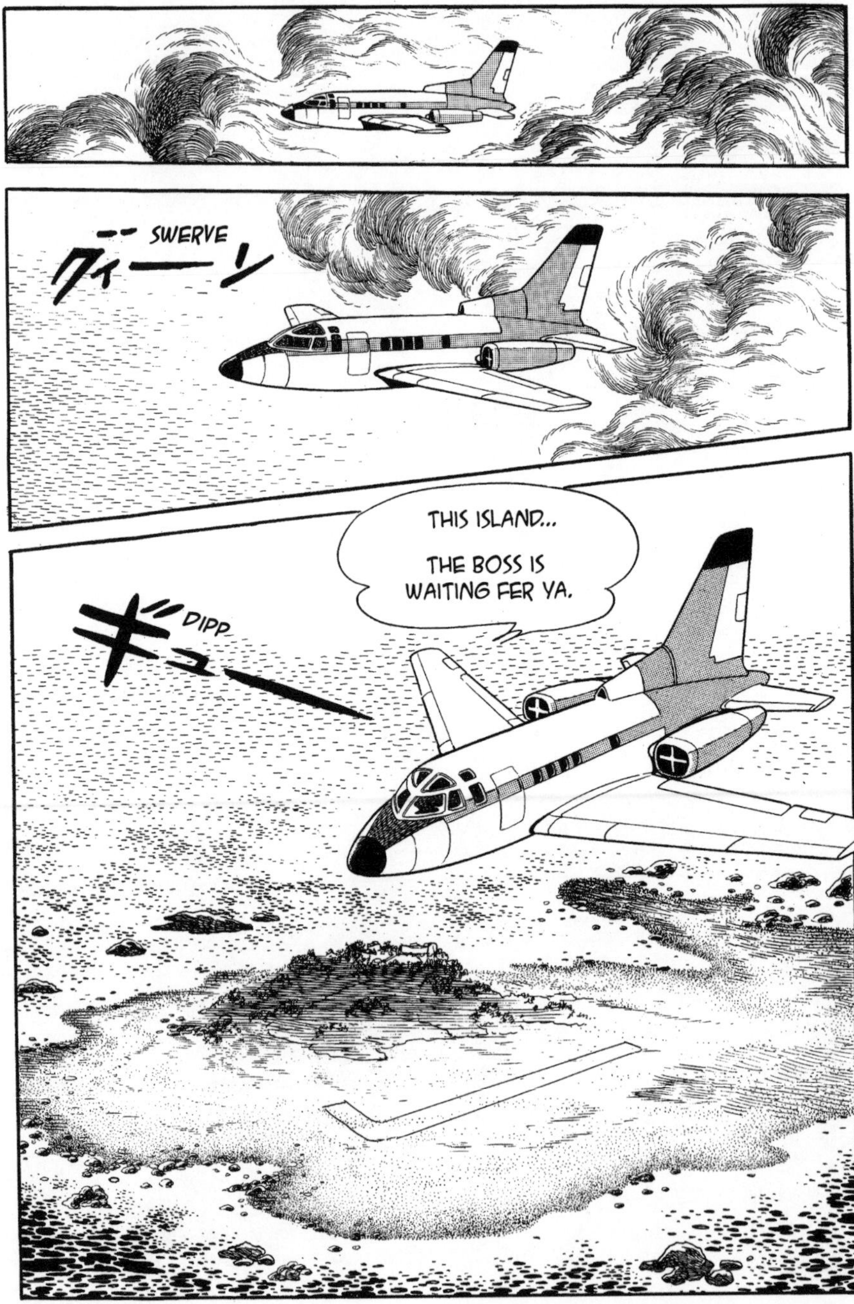
グィーーン
SWERVE
THIS ISLAND...
THE BOSS IS WAITING FER YA.
ギュー
DIPP

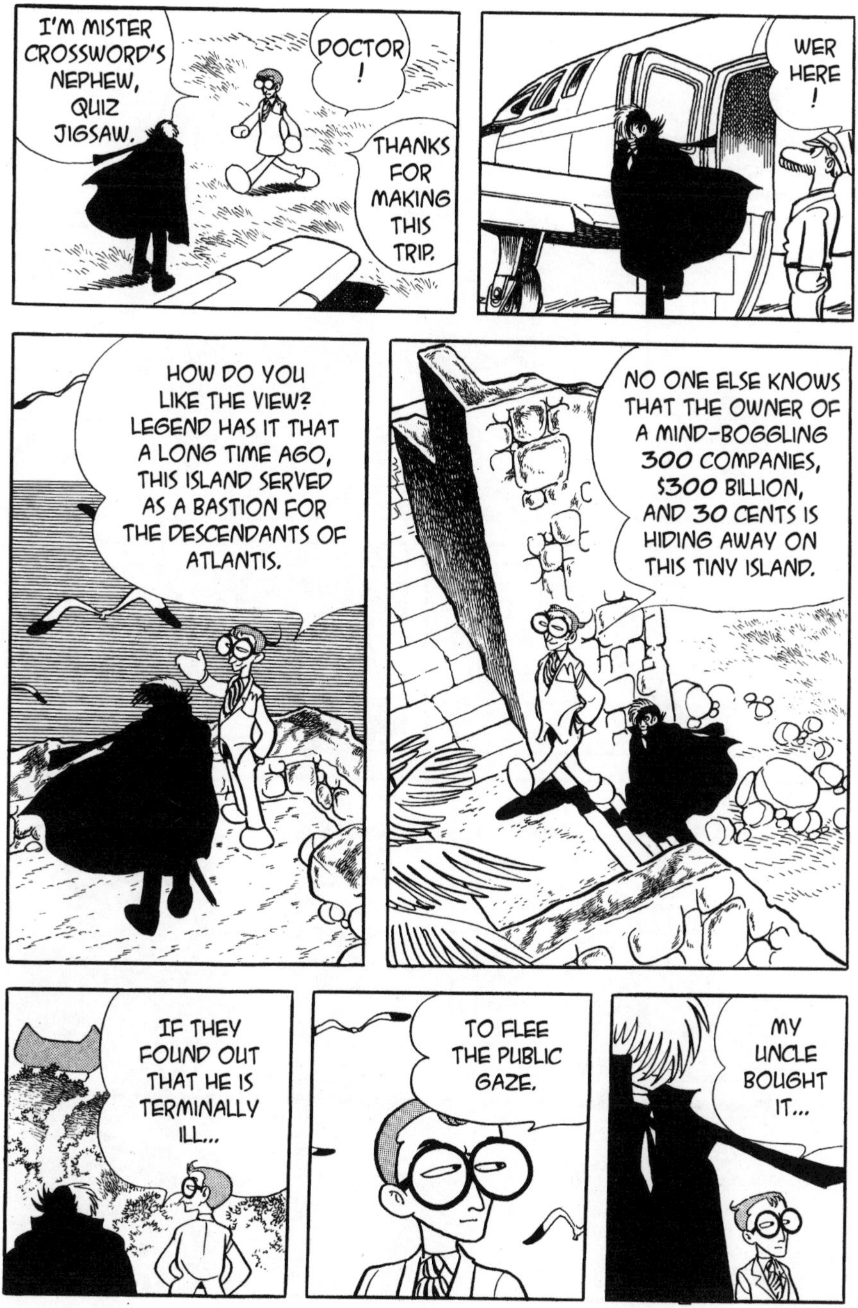
WER HERE!
DOCTOR!
I'M MISTER CROSSWORD'S NEPHEW, QUIZ JIGSAW.
THANKS FOR MAKING THIS TRIP.
NO ONE ELSE KNOWS THAT THE OWNER OF A MIND-BOGGLING 300 COMPANIES, $300 BILLION, AND 30 CENTS IS HIDING AWAY ON THIS TINY ISLAND.
HOW DO YOU LIKE THE VIEW? LEGEND HAS IT THAT A LONG TIME AGO, THIS ISLAND SERVED AS A BASTION FOR THE DESCENDANTS OF ATLANTIS.
MY UNCLE BOUGHT IT...
TO FLEE THE PUBLIC GAZE.
IF THEY FOUND OUT THAT HE IS TERMINALLY ILL...

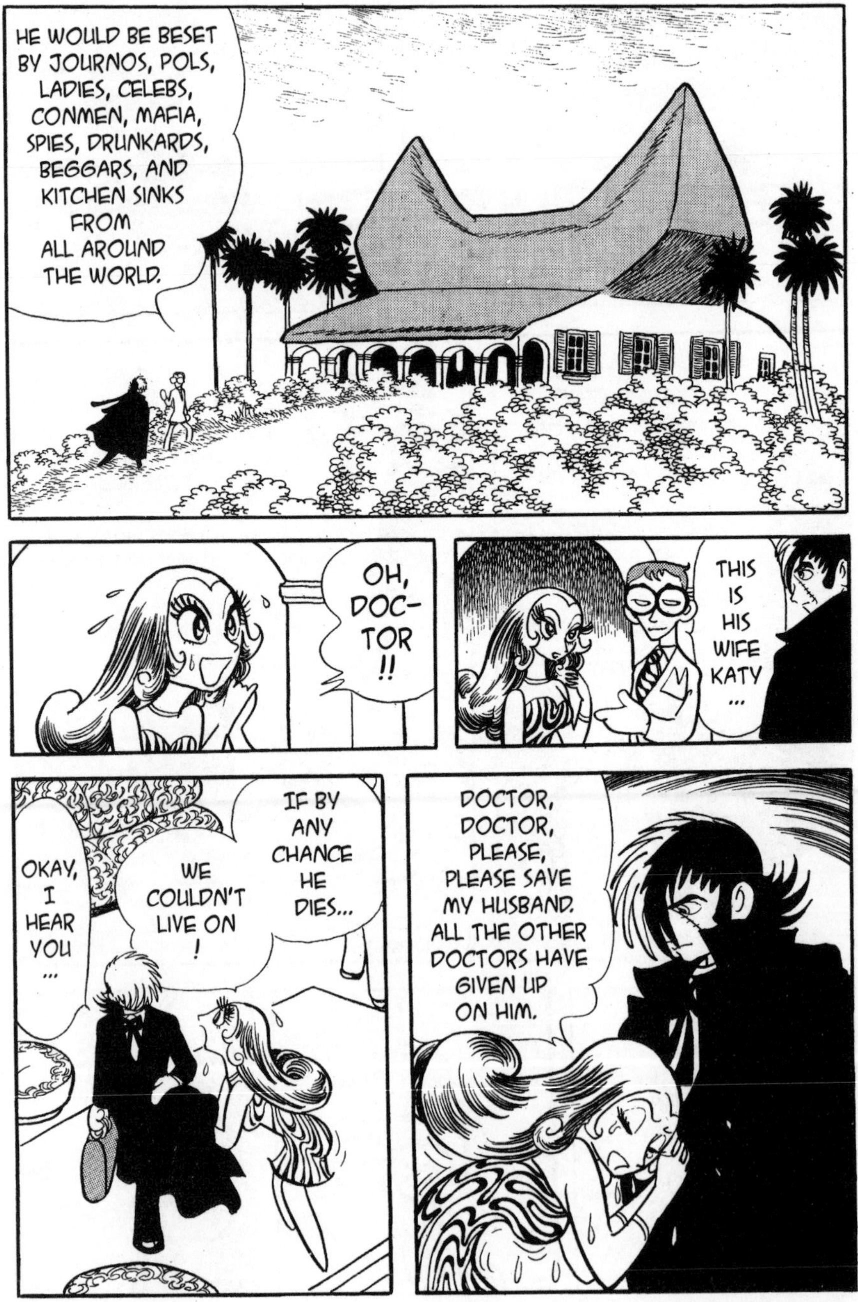
HE WOULD BE BESET BY JOURNOS, POLS, LADIES, CELEBS, CONMEN, MAFIA, SPIES, DRUNKARDS, BEGGARS, AND KITCHEN SINKS FROM ALL AROUND THE WORLD.
THIS IS HIS WIFE KATY ...
OH, DOCTOR !!
DOCTOR, DOCTOR, PLEASE, PLEASE SAVE MY HUSBAND. ALL THE OTHER DOCTORS HAVE GIVEN UP ON HIM.
IF BY ANY CHANCE HE DIES...
WE COULDN'T LIVE ON !
OKAY, I HEAR YOU ...

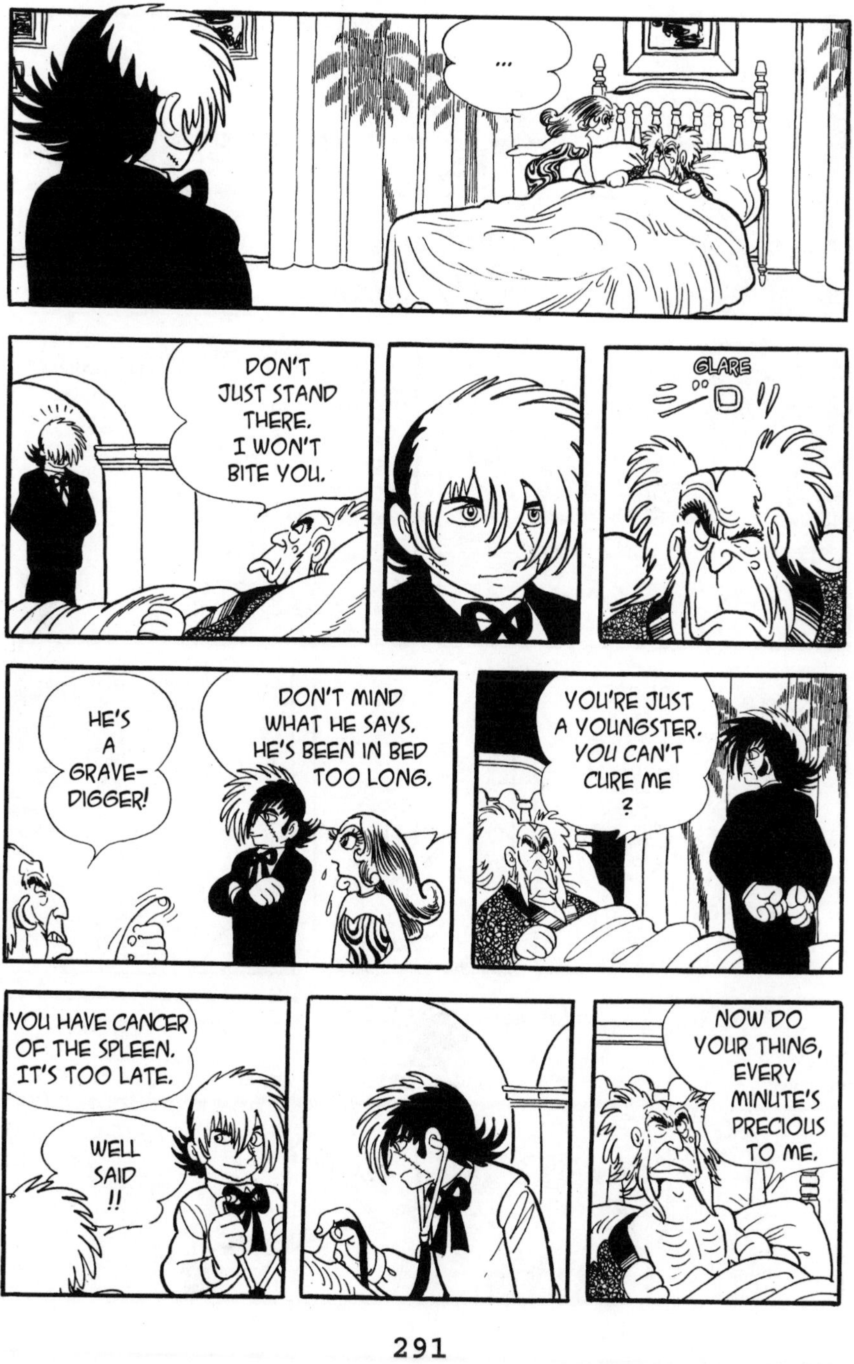
...
GLARE
DON'T JUST STAND THERE. I WON'T BITE YOU.
YOU'RE JUST A YOUNGSTER. YOU CAN'T CURE ME ?
DON'T MIND WHAT HE SAYS. HE'S BEEN IN BED TOO LONG.
HE'S A GRAVE-DIGGER!
NOW DO YOUR THING, EVERY MINUTE'S PRECIOUS TO ME.
YOU HAVE CANCER OF THE SPLEEN. IT'S TOO LATE.
WELL SAID !!

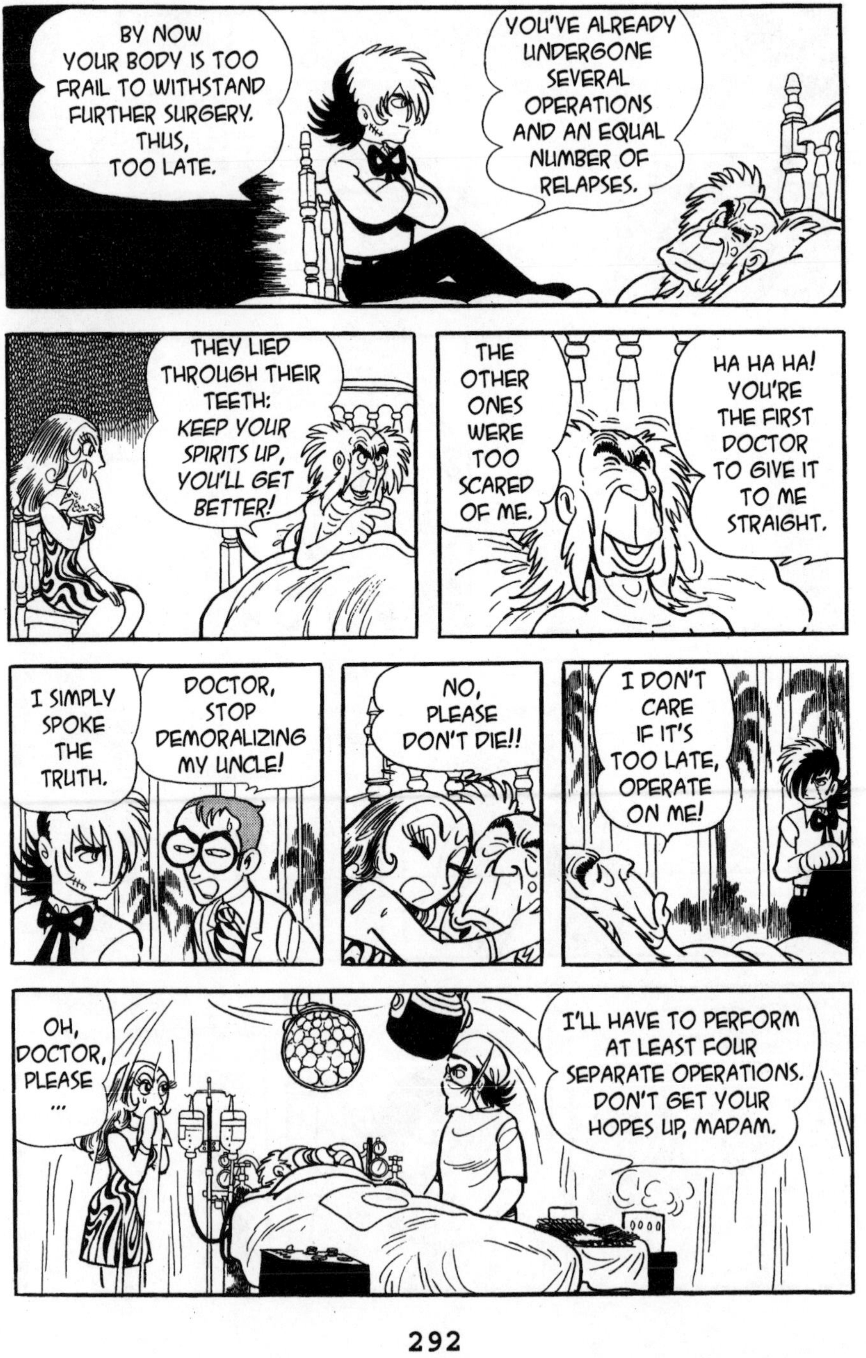
YOU'VE ALREADY UNDERGONE SEVERAL OPERATIONS AND AN EQUAL NUMBER OF RELAPSES.
BY NOW YOUR BODY IS TOO FRAIL TO WITHSTAND FURTHER SURGERY. THUS, TOO LATE.
HA HA HA! YOU'RE THE FIRST DOCTOR TO GIVE IT TO ME STRAIGHT.
THE OTHER ONES WERE TOO SCARED OF ME.
THEY LIED THROUGH THEIR TEETH: KEEP YOUR SPIRITS UP, YOU'LL GET BETTER!
I DON'T CARE IF IT'S TOO LATE, OPERATE ON ME!
NO, PLEASE DON'T DIE!!
DOCTOR, STOP DEMORALIZING MY UNCLE!
I SIMPLY SPOKE THE TRUTH.
I'LL HAVE TO PERFORM AT LEAST FOUR SEPARATE OPERATIONS. DON'T GET YOUR HOPES UP, MADAM.
OH, DOCTOR, PLEASE ...

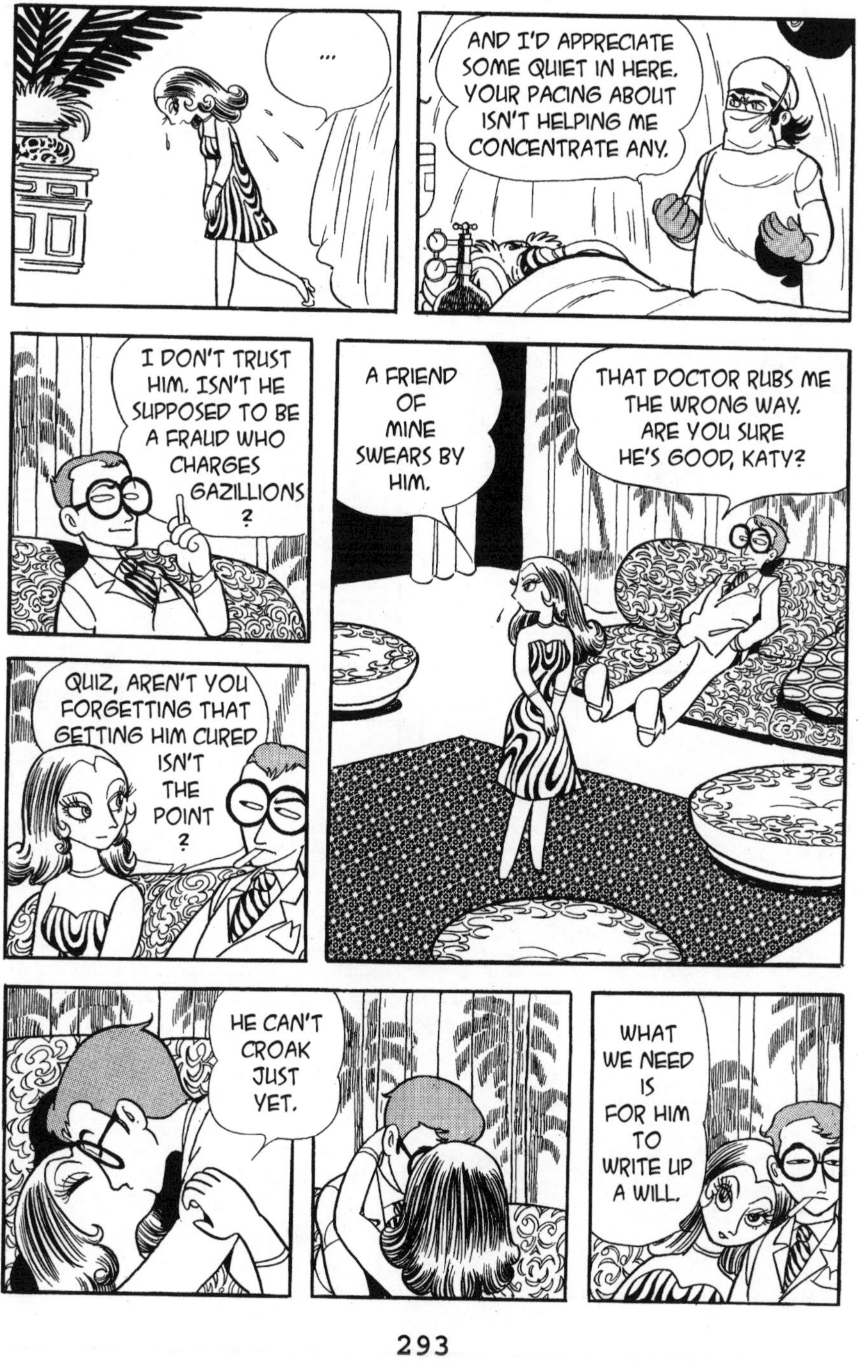
AND I'D APPRECIATE SOME QUIET IN HERE. YOUR PACING ABOUT ISN'T HELPING ME CONCENTRATE ANY.
...
THAT DOCTOR RUBS ME THE WRONG WAY. ARE YOU SURE HE'S GOOD, KATY?
A FRIEND OF MINE SWEARS BY HIM.
I DON'T TRUST HIM. ISN'T HE SUPPOSED TO BE A FRAUD WHO CHARGES GAZILLIONS?
QUIZ, AREN'T YOU FORGETTING THAT GETTING HIM CURED ISN'T THE POINT?
WHAT WE NEED IS FOR HIM TO WRITE UP A WILL.
HE CAN'T CROAK JUST YET.

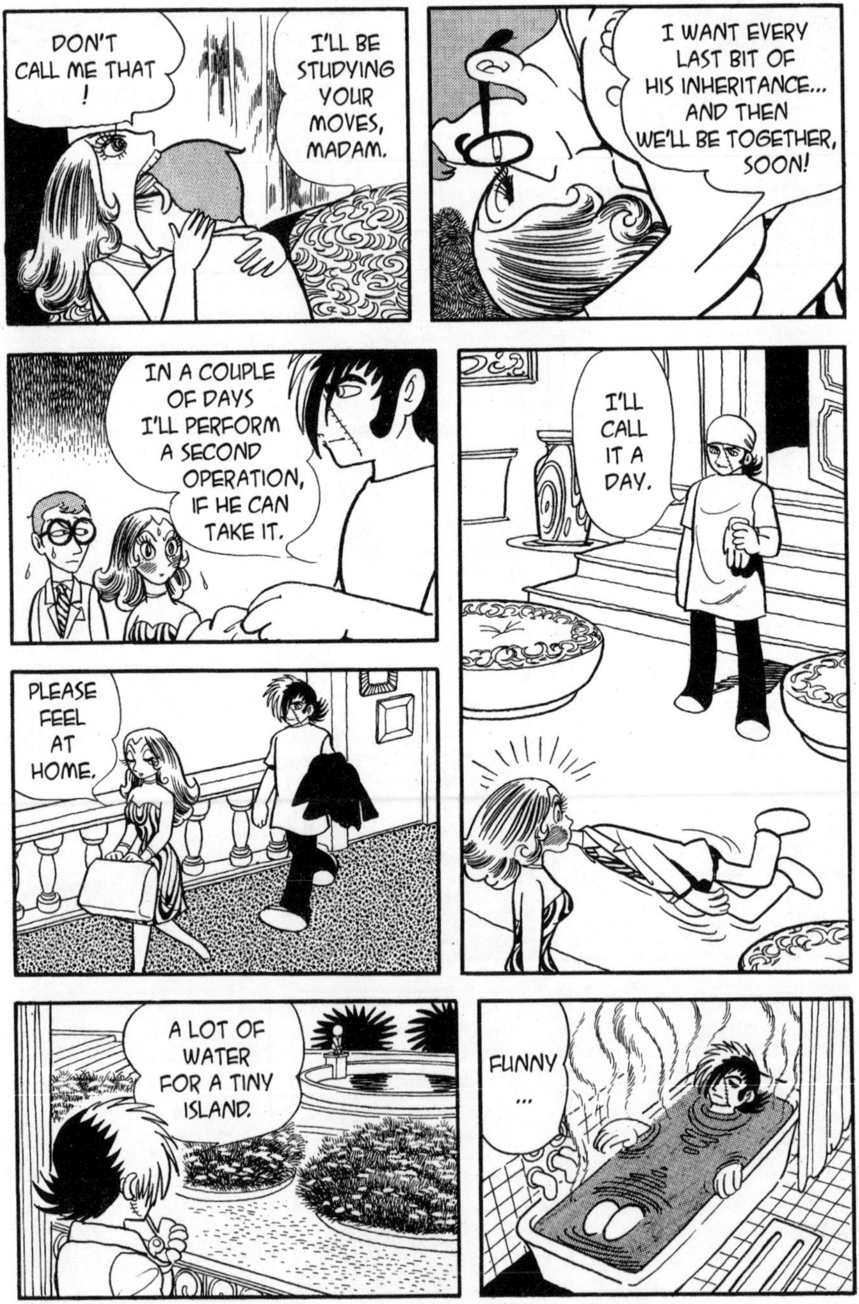
I WANT EVERY LAST BIT OF HIS INHERITANCE... AND THEN WE'LL BE TOGETHER, SOON!
I'LL BE STUDYING YOUR MOVES, MADAM.
DON'T CALL ME THAT!
I'LL CALL IT A DAY.
IN A COUPLE OF DAYS I'LL PERFORM A SECOND OPERATION, IF HE CAN TAKE IT.
PLEASE FEEL AT HOME.
FUNNY ...
A LOT OF WATER FOR A TINY ISLAND.

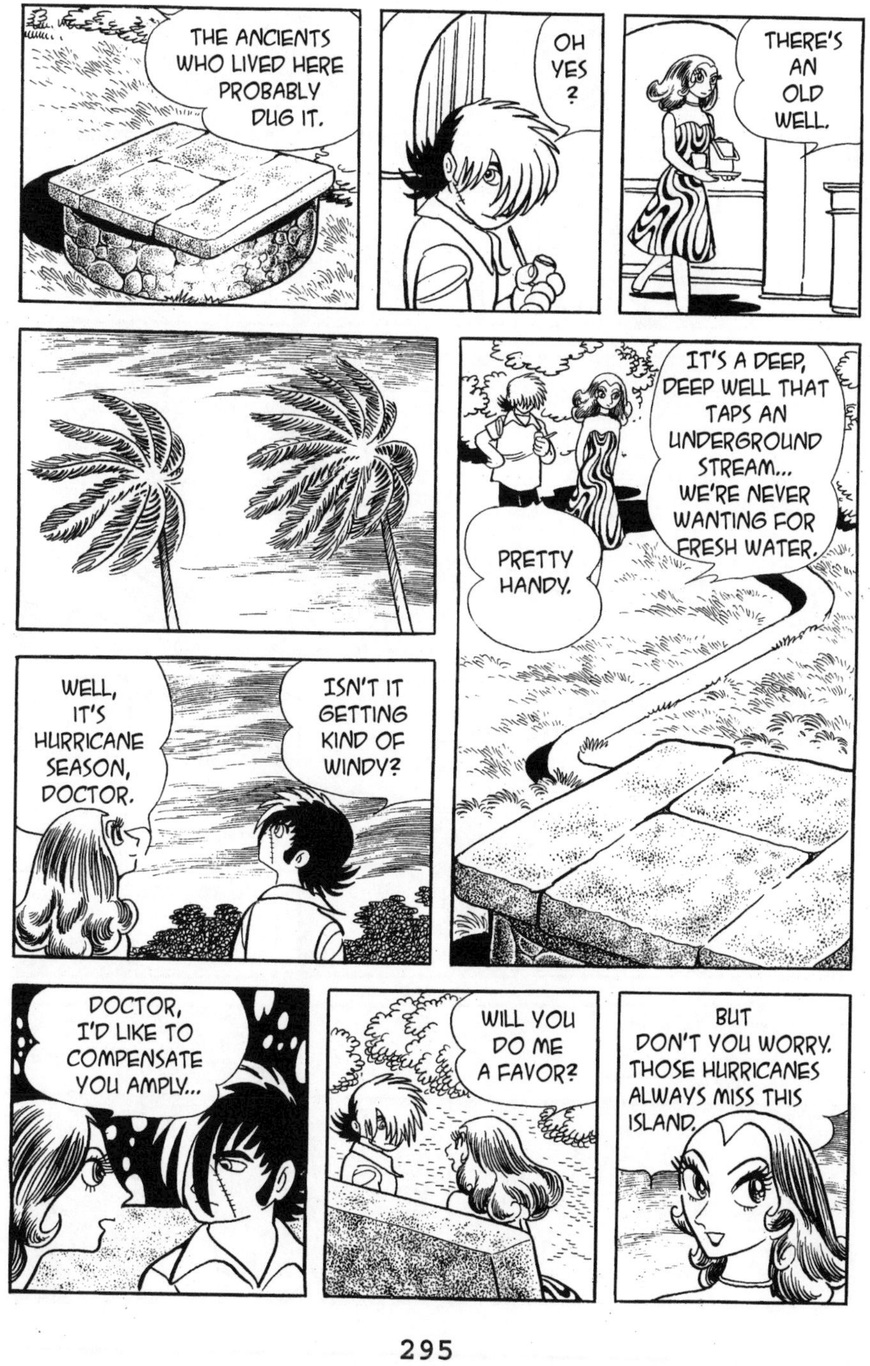
THERE'S AN OLD WELL.
OH YES?
THE ANCIENTS WHO LIVED HERE PROBABLY DUG IT.
IT'S A DEEP, DEEP WELL THAT TAPS AN UNDERGROUND STREAM... WE'RE NEVER WANTING FOR FRESH WATER.
PRETTY HANDY.
ISN'T IT GETTING KIND OF WINDY?
WELL, IT'S HURRICANE SEASON, DOCTOR.
BUT DON'T YOU WORRY. THOSE HURRICANES ALWAYS MISS THIS ISLAND.
WILL YOU DO ME A FAVOR?
DOCTOR, I'D LIKE TO COMPENSATE YOU AMPLY...

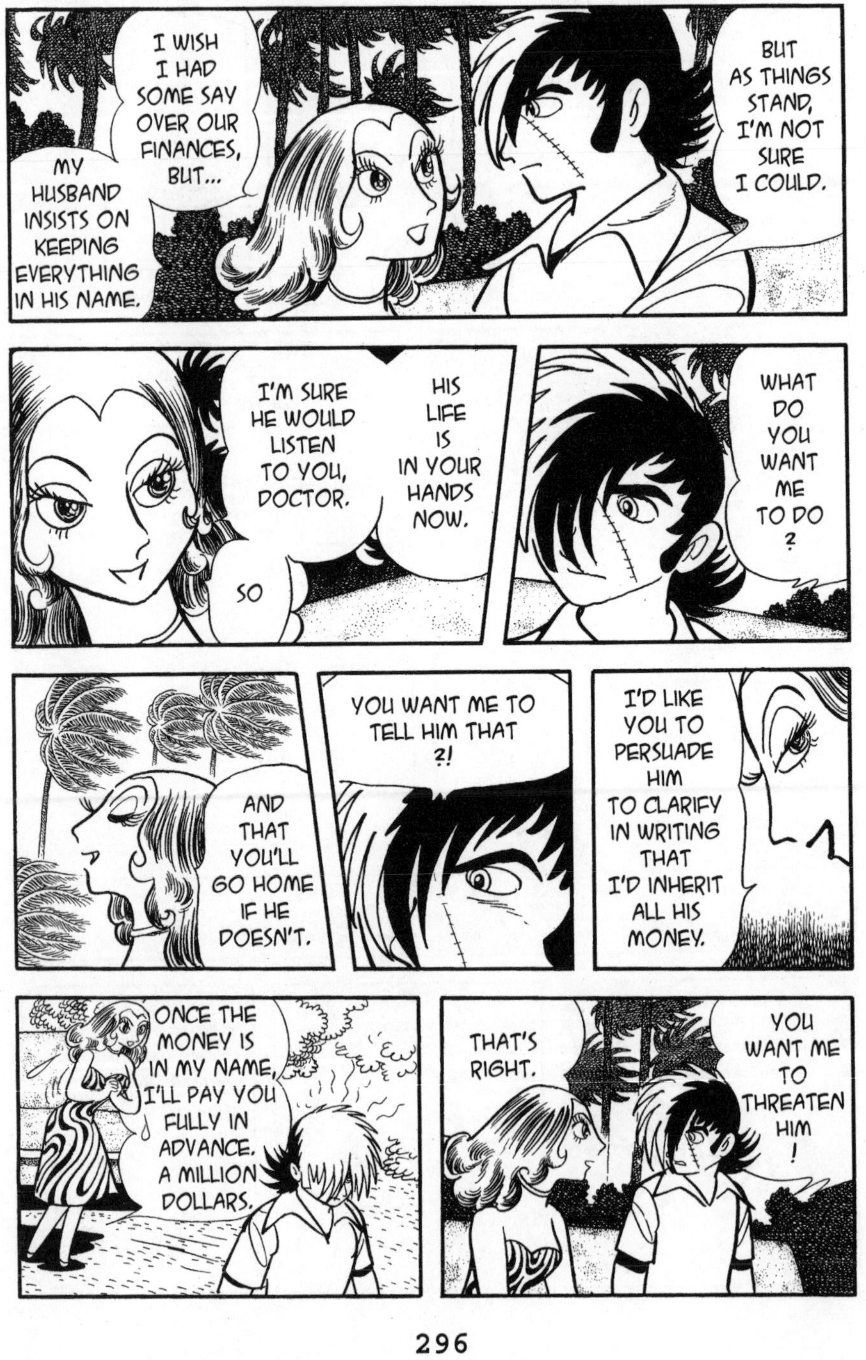

BUT AS THINGS STAND, I'M NOT SURE I COULD.
I WISH I HAD SOME SAY OVER OUR FINANCES, BUT...
MY HUSBAND INSISTS ON KEEPING EVERYTHING IN HIS NAME.
WHAT DO YOU WANT ME TO DO?
HIS LIFE IS IN YOUR HANDS NOW.
I'M SURE HE WOULD LISTEN TO YOU, DOCTOR.
SO
I'D LIKE YOU TO PERSUADE HIM TO CLARIFY IN WRITING THAT I'D INHERIT ALL HIS MONEY.
YOU WANT ME TO TELL HIM THAT ?!
AND THAT YOU'LL GO HOME IF HE DOESN'T.
YOU WANT ME TO THREATEN HIM !
THAT'S RIGHT.
ONCE THE MONEY IS IN MY NAME, I'LL PAY YOU FULLY IN ADVANCE. A MILLION DOLLARS.

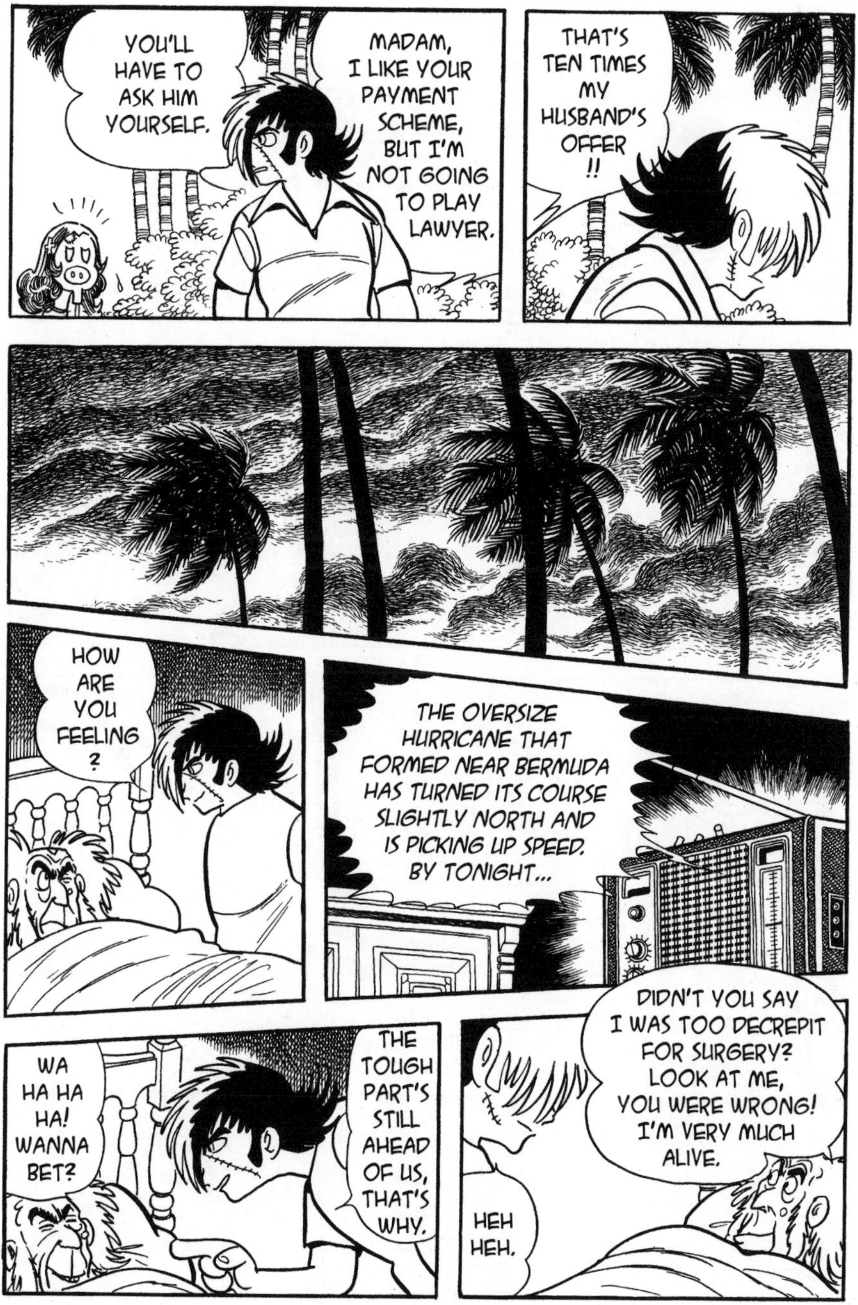
THAT'S TEN TIMES MY HUSBAND'S OFFER !!
MADAM, I LIKE YOUR PAYMENT SCHEME, BUT I'M NOT GOING TO PLAY LAWYER.
YOU'LL HAVE TO ASK HIM YOURSELF.
THE OVERSIZE HURRICANE THAT FORMED NEAR BERMUDA HAS TURNED ITS COURSE SLIGHTLY NORTH AND IS PICKING UP SPEED. BY TONIGHT...
HOW ARE YOU FEELING ?
DIDN'T YOU SAY I WAS TOO DECREPIT FOR SURGERY? LOOK AT ME, YOU WERE WRONG! I'M VERY MUCH ALIVE.
HEH HEH.
THE TOUGH PART'S STILL AHEAD OF US, THAT'S WHY.
WA HA HA HA! WANNA BET?

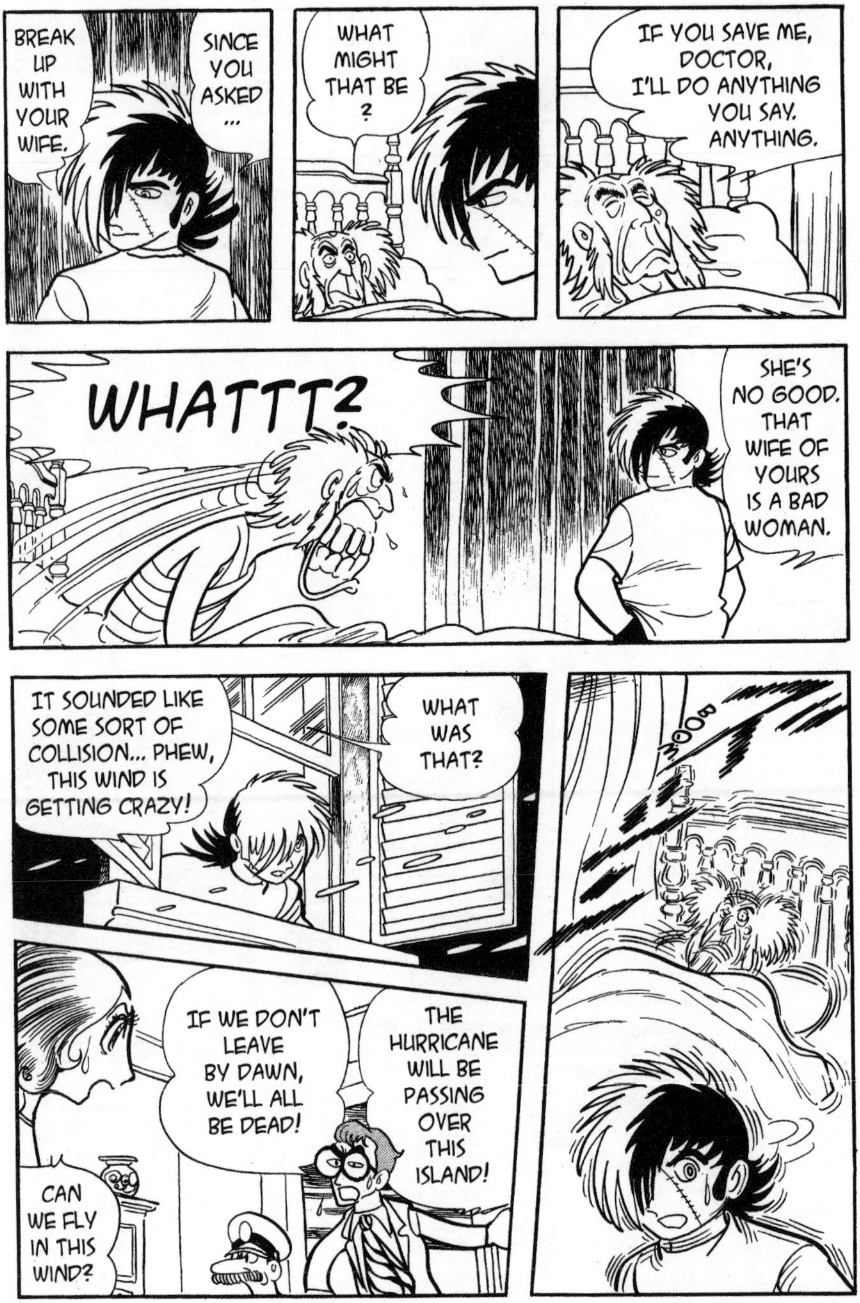
IF YOU SAVE ME, DOCTOR, I'LL DO ANYTHING YOU SAY. ANYTHING.
WHAT MIGHT THAT BE?
SINCE YOU ASKED...
BREAK UP WITH YOUR WIFE.
SHE'S NO GOOD. THAT WIFE OF YOURS IS A BAD WOMAN.
WHATTT?
BOOM
WHAT WAS THAT?
IT SOUNDED LIKE SOME SORT OF COLLISION... PHEW, THIS WIND IS GETTING CRAZY!
THE HURRICANE WILL BE PASSING OVER THIS ISLAND!
IF WE DON'T LEAVE BY DAWN, WE'LL ALL BE DEAD!
CAN WE FLY IN THIS WIND?

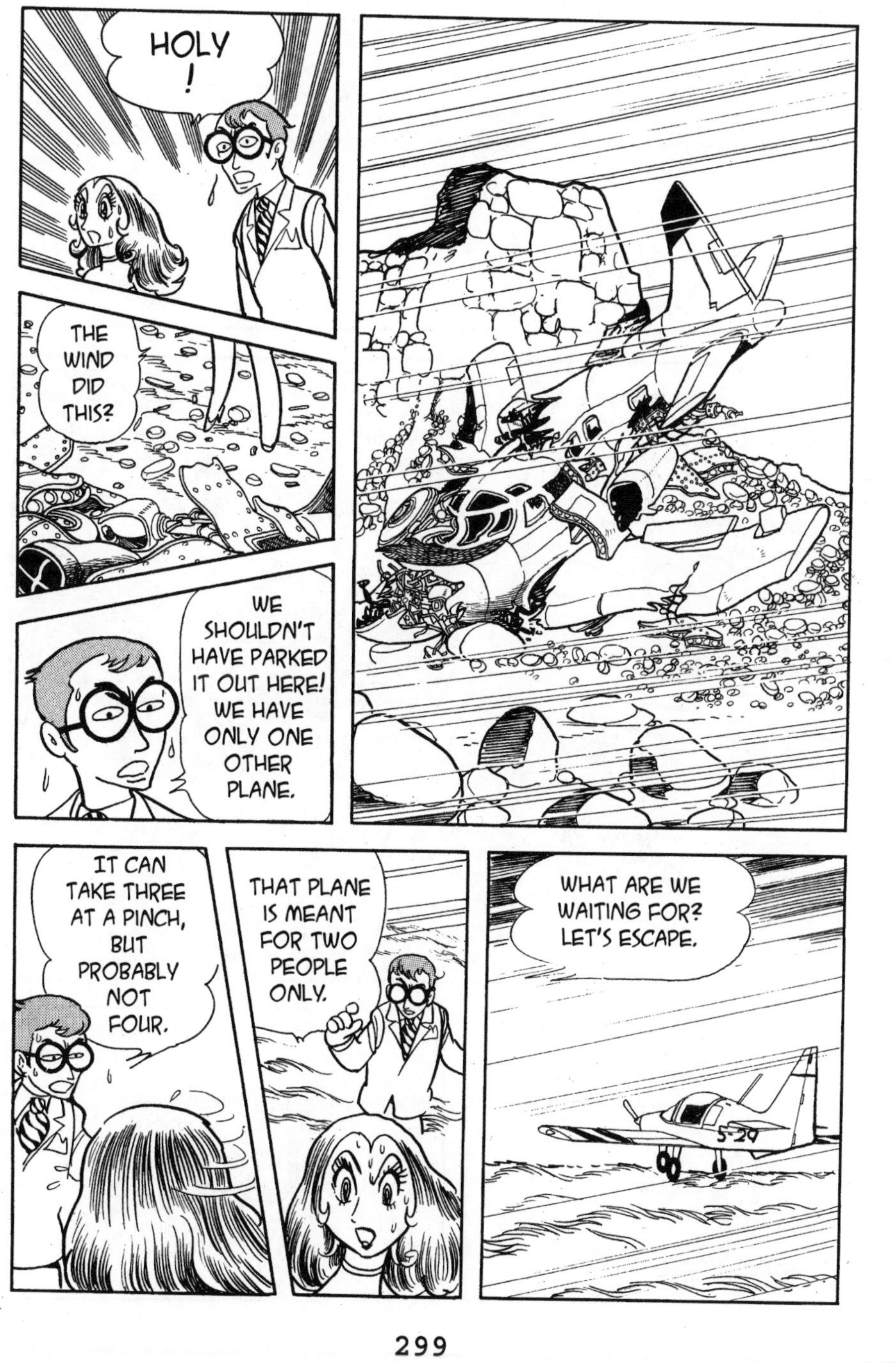
HOLY !
THE WIND DID THIS?
WE SHOULDN'T HAVE PARKED IT OUT HERE! WE HAVE ONLY ONE OTHER PLANE.
WHAT ARE WE WAITING FOR? LET'S ESCAPE.
THAT PLANE IS MEANT FOR TWO PEOPLE ONLY.
IT CAN TAKE THREE AT A PINCH, BUT PROBABLY NOT FOUR.

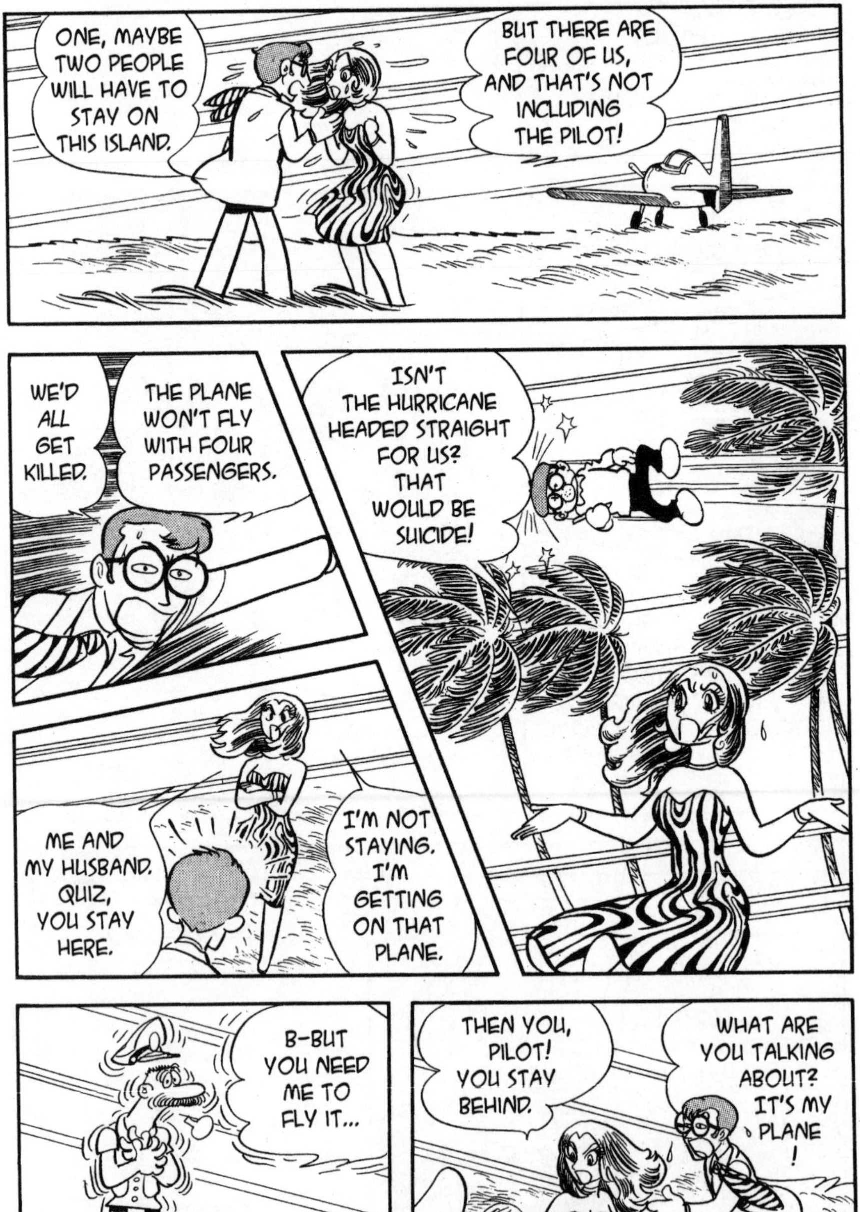
BUT THERE ARE FOUR OF US, AND THAT'S NOT INCLUDING THE PILOT!
ONE, MAYBE TWO PEOPLE WILL HAVE TO STAY ON THIS ISLAND.
ISN'T THE HURRICANE HEADED STRAIGHT FOR US? THAT WOULD BE SUICIDE!
THE PLANE WON'T FLY WITH FOUR PASSENGERS.
WE'D ALL GET KILLED.
I'M NOT STAYING. I'M GETTING ON THAT PLANE.
ME AND MY HUSBAND. QUIZ, YOU STAY HERE.
WHAT ARE YOU TALKING ABOUT? IT'S MY PLANE!
THEN YOU, PILOT! YOU STAY BEHIND.
B-BUT YOU NEED ME TO FLY IT...

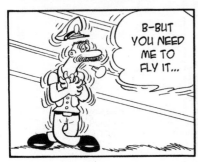

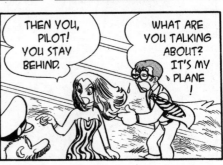

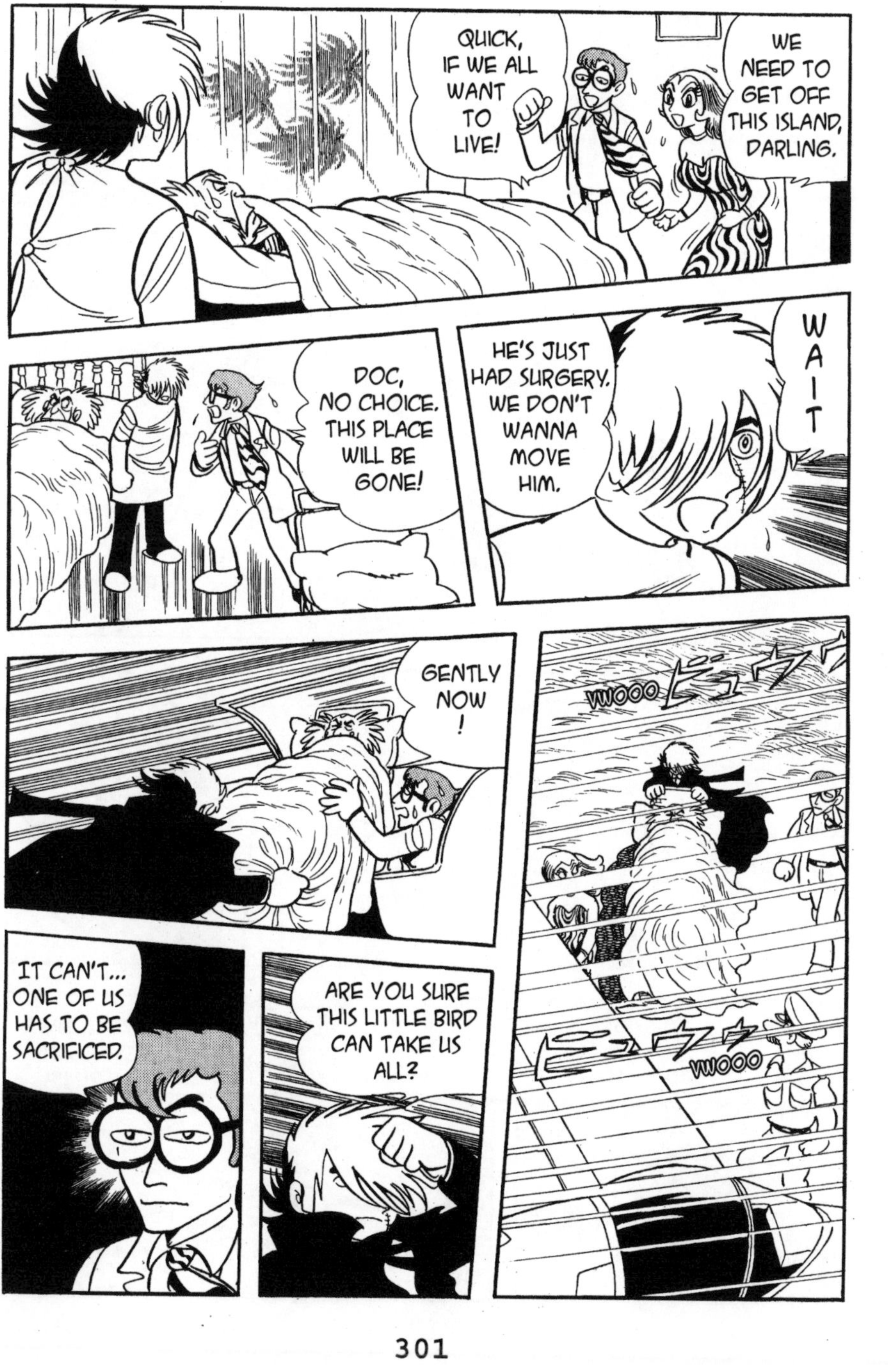
WE NEED TO GET OFF THIS ISLAND, DARLING.
QUICK, IF WE ALL WANT TO LIVE!
WAIT
HE'S JUST HAD SURGERY. WE DON'T WANNA MOVE HIM.
DOC, NO CHOICE. THIS PLACE WILL BE GONE!
VWOOO ビュウウ
ビュウウ VWOOO
GENTLY NOW!
ARE YOU SURE THIS LITTLE BIRD CAN TAKE US ALL?
IT CAN'T... ONE OF US HAS TO BE SACRIFICED.

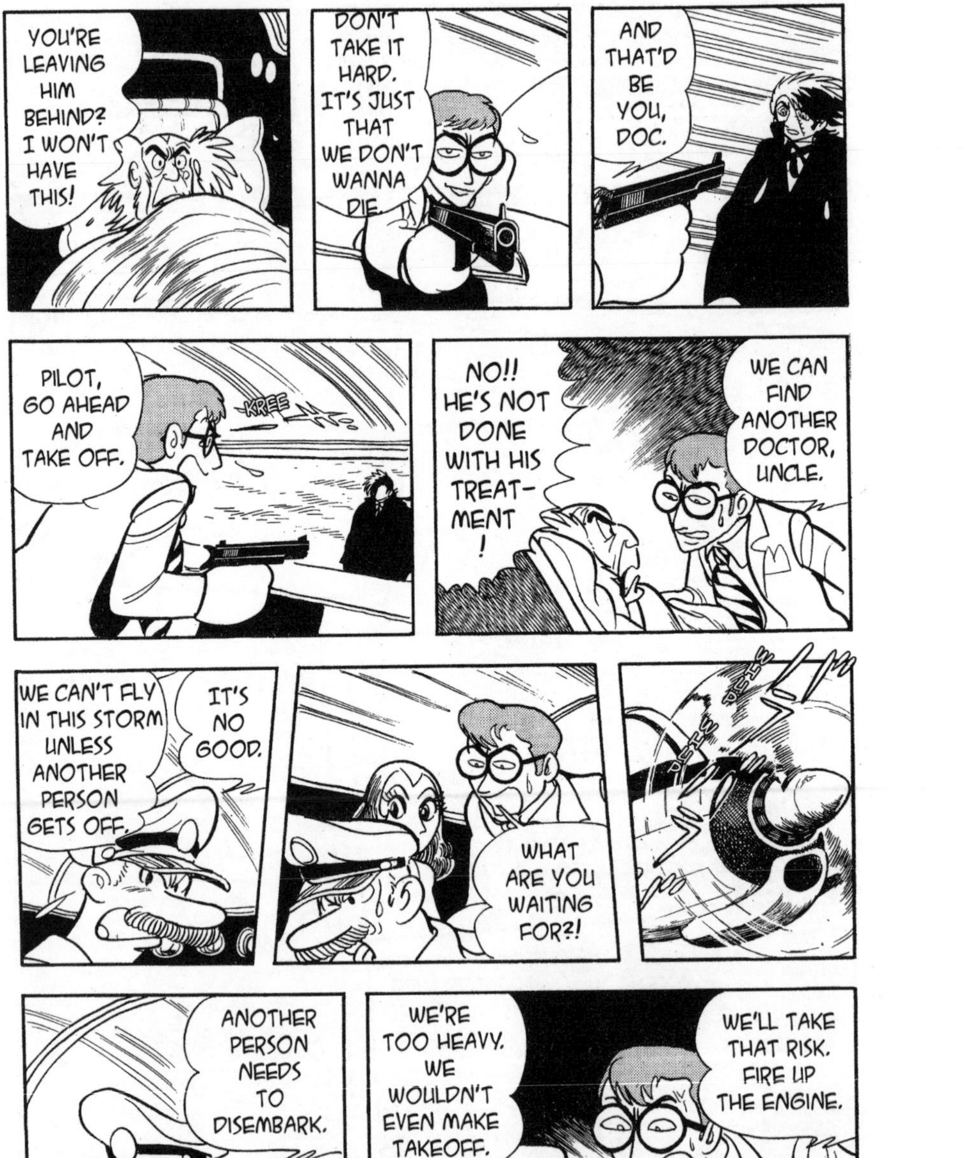

YOU'RE LEAVING HIM BEHIND? I WON'T HAVE THIS!
DON'T TAKE IT HARD. IT'S JUST THAT WE DON'T WANNA DIE.
AND THAT'D BE YOU, DOC.
PILOT, GO AHEAD AND TAKE OFF.
KREE
NO!! HE'S NOT DONE WITH HIS TREAT-MENT!
WE CAN FIND ANOTHER DOCTOR, UNCLE.
WE CAN'T FLY IN THIS STORM UNLESS ANOTHER PERSON GETS OFF.
IT'S NO GOOD.
WHAT ARE YOU WAITING FOR?!
WHUP
WHUP
ANOTHER PERSON NEEDS TO DISEMBARK.
WE'RE TOO HEAVY. WE WOULDN'T EVEN MAKE TAKEOFF.
WE'LL TAKE THAT RISK. FIRE UP THE ENGINE.

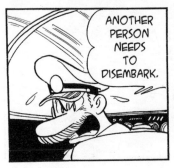

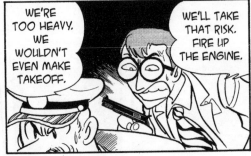

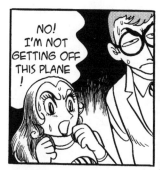

BUT ...!
AND HURRY IT UP, WE'VE NO TIME LEFT !
NO! I'M NOT GETTING OFF THIS PLANE !
THE OLD MAN, THEN.
HEY THERE, CROSSWORD. WANNA REJOIN THE GOOD DOCTOR ?
NO!
WE CAN'T LET HIM DIE. HIS MONEY'S NOT YET MINE.
AWW, SHUT UP !
I WANT TO LIVE.
THE GEEZER'S NOT LONG FOR THIS WORLD ANYWAY.
RUM RUM RUM
BRUM BRUM BRUM BRUM

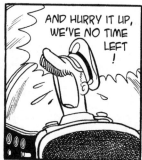

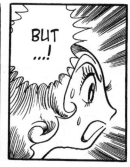

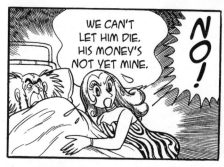

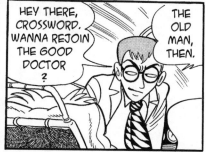

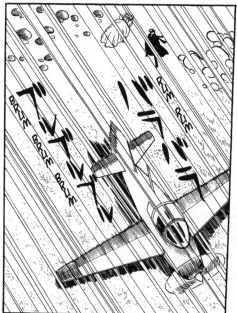

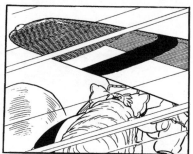

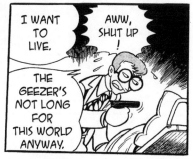

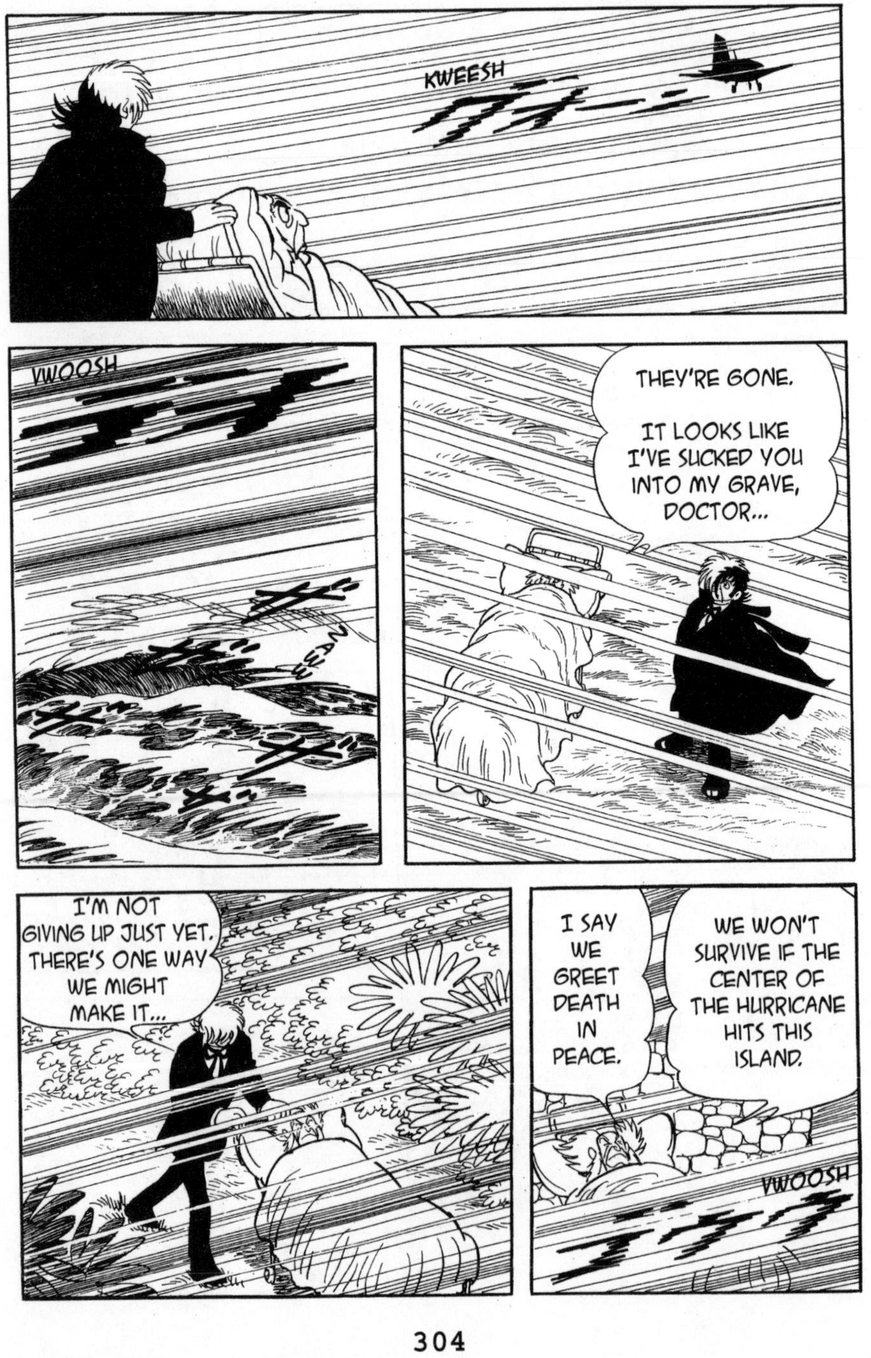
KWEESH
THEY'RE GONE.
IT LOOKS LIKE I'VE SUCKED YOU INTO MY GRAVE, DOCTOR...
VWOOSH
WE WON'T SURVIVE IF THE CENTER OF THE HURRICANE HITS THIS ISLAND.
I SAY WE GREET DEATH IN PEACE.
VWOOSH
I'M NOT GIVING UP JUST YET. THERE'S ONE WAY WE MIGHT MAKE IT...

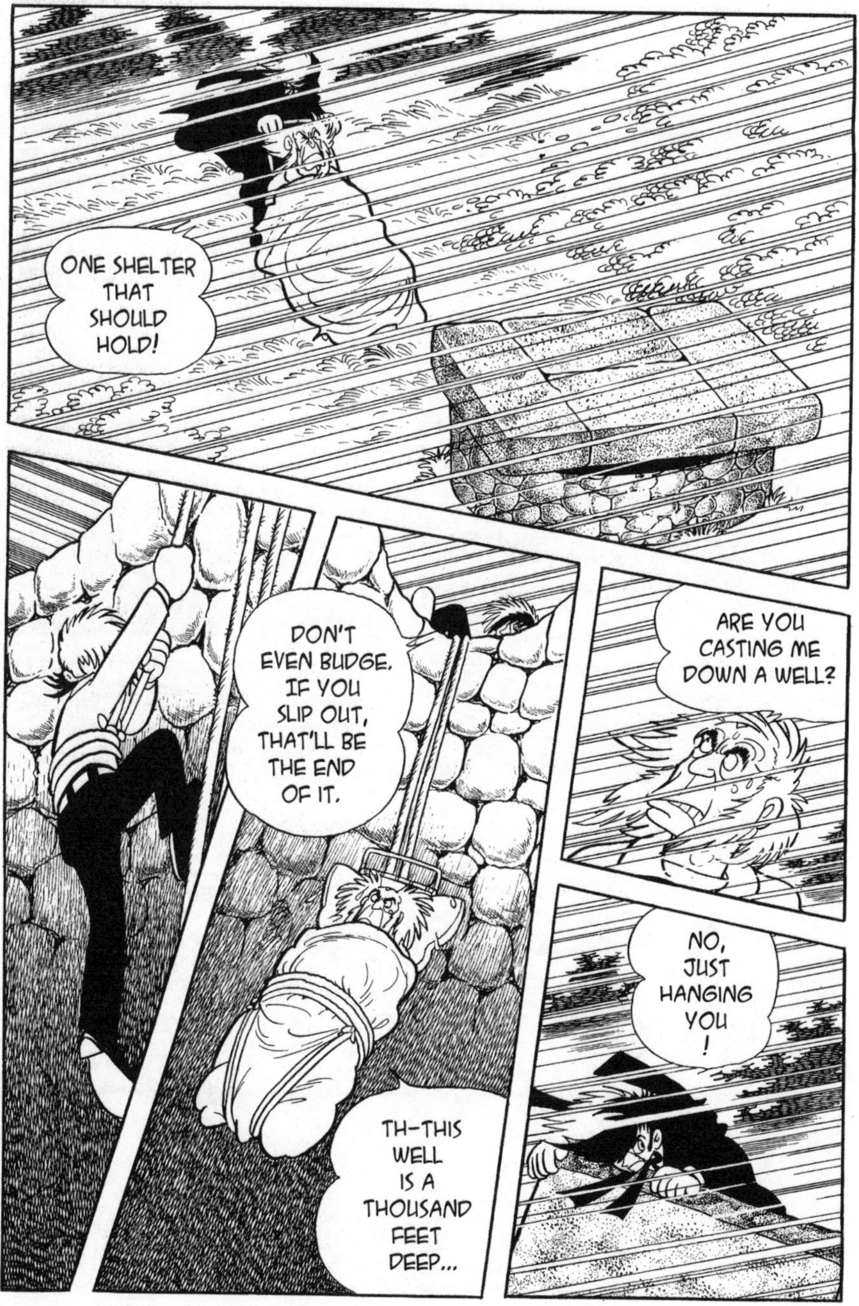
ONE SHELTER THAT SHOULD HOLD!
ARE YOU CASTING ME DOWN A WELL?
NO, JUST HANGING YOU!
DON'T EVEN BUDGE. IF YOU SLIP OUT, THAT'LL BE THE END OF IT.
TH-THIS WELL IS A THOUSAND FEET DEEP...

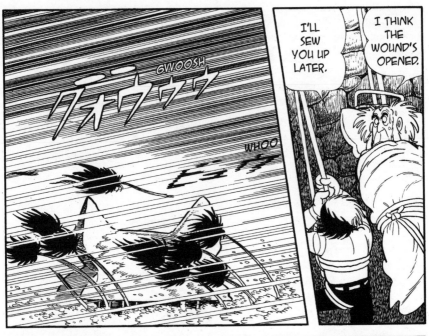

I THINK THE WOUND'S OPENED.
I'LL SEW YOU UP LATER.
GWOOSH
クォウウウウ
WHOO
ZAWW
FIFTY FEET FROM THE MOUTH. THE GALE CAN'T TOUCH US HERE.

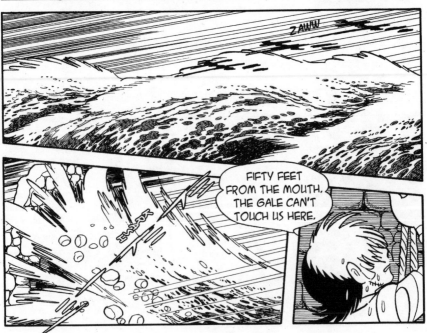

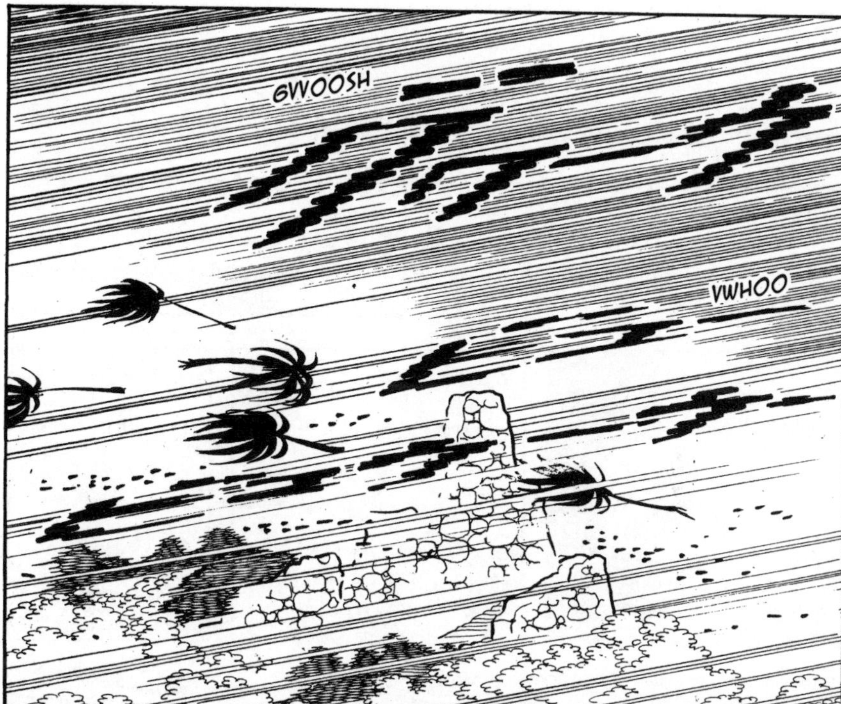
GVVOOSH
VWHOO

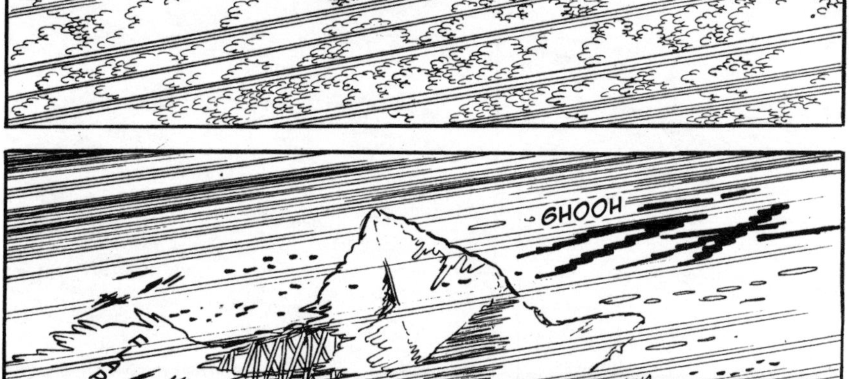
GHOOH
FLAP

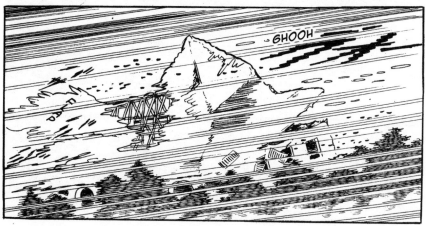

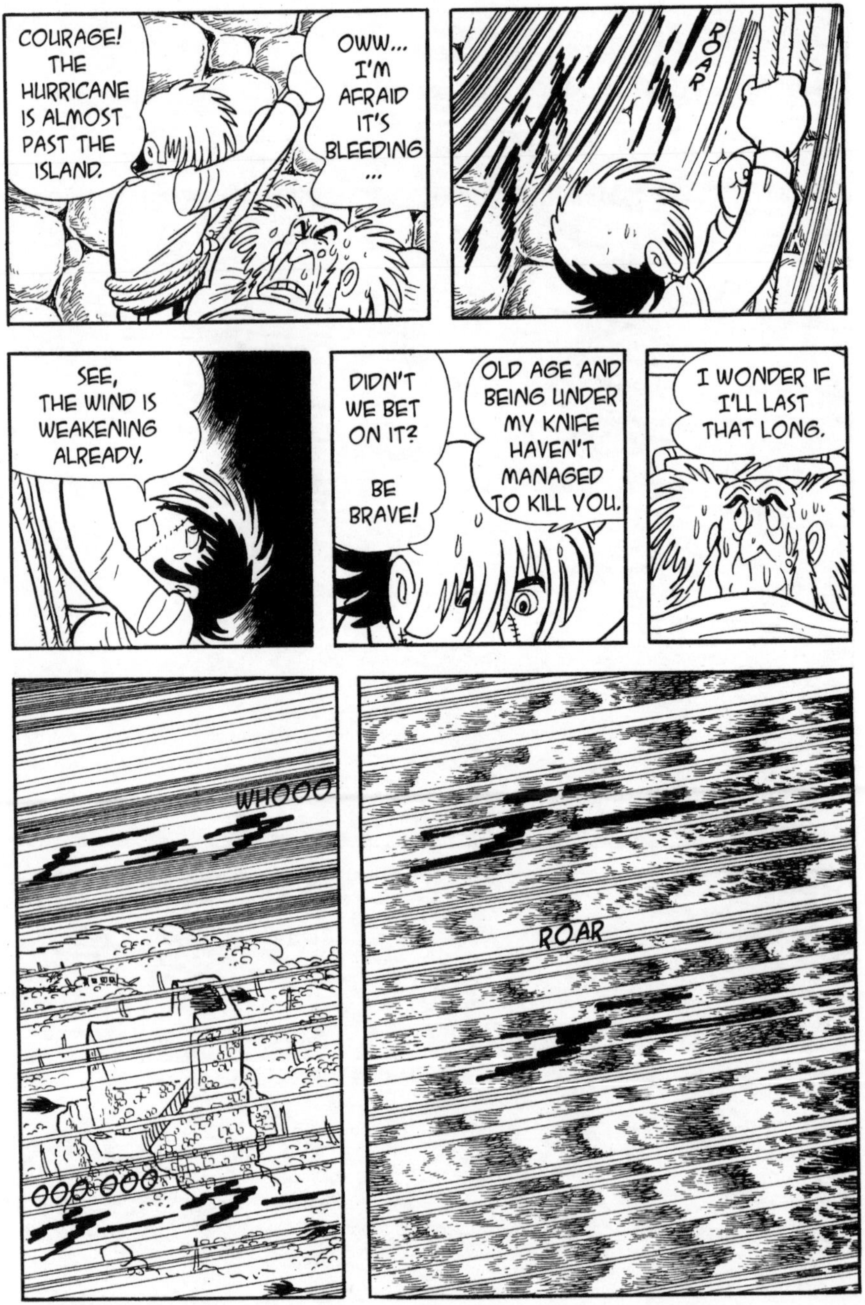
ROAR
OWW... I'M AFRAID IT'S BLEEDING ...
COURAGE! THE HURRICANE IS ALMOST PAST THE ISLAND.
I WONDER IF I'LL LAST THAT LONG.
OLD AGE AND BEING UNDER MY KNIFE HAVEN'T MANAGED TO KILL YOU.
DIDN'T WE BET ON IT?
BE BRAVE!
SEE, THE WIND IS WEAKENING ALREADY.
ROAR
WHOOO
OOO OOO

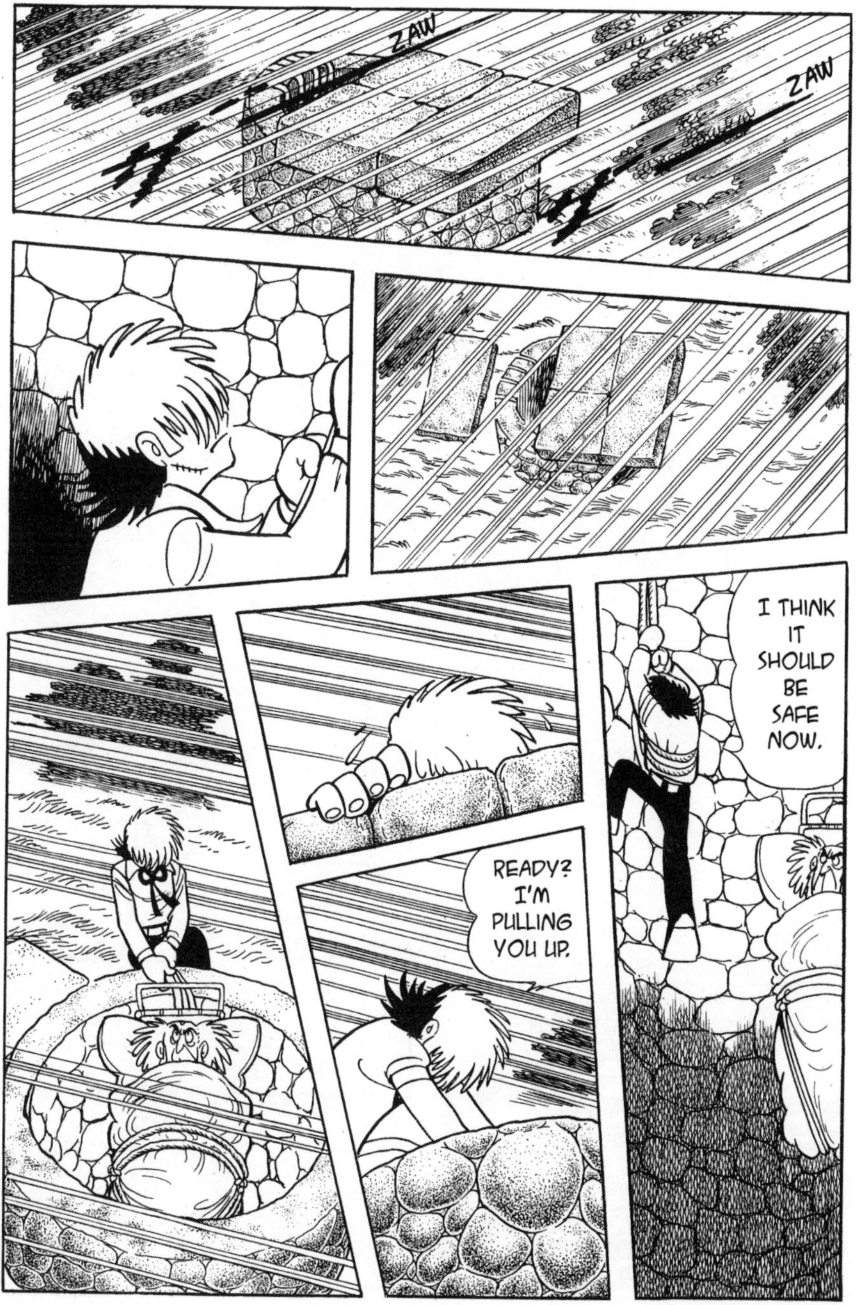
ZAW
ZAW
I THINK IT SHOULD BE SAFE NOW.
READY? I'M PULLING YOU UP.

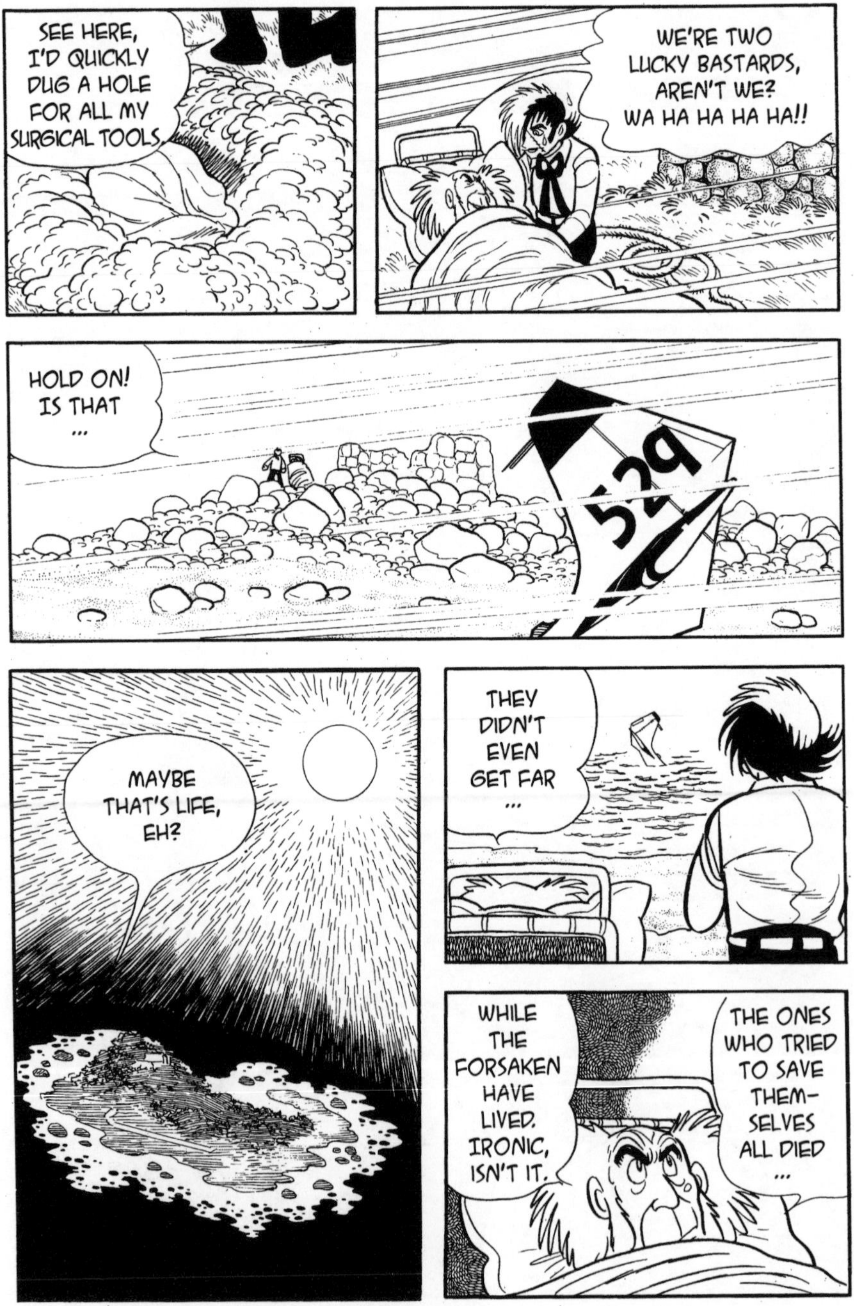
WE'RE TWO LUCKY BASTARDS, AREN'T WE? WA HA HA HA HA!!
SEE HERE, I'D QUICKLY DUG A HOLE FOR ALL MY SURGICAL TOOLS.
HOLD ON! IS THAT ...
529
THEY DIDN'T EVEN GET FAR ...
THE ONES WHO TRIED TO SAVE THEM-SELVES ALL DIED ...
WHILE THE FORSAKEN HAVE LIVED. IRONIC, ISN'T IT.
MAYBE THAT'S LIFE, EH?

TIMEOUT

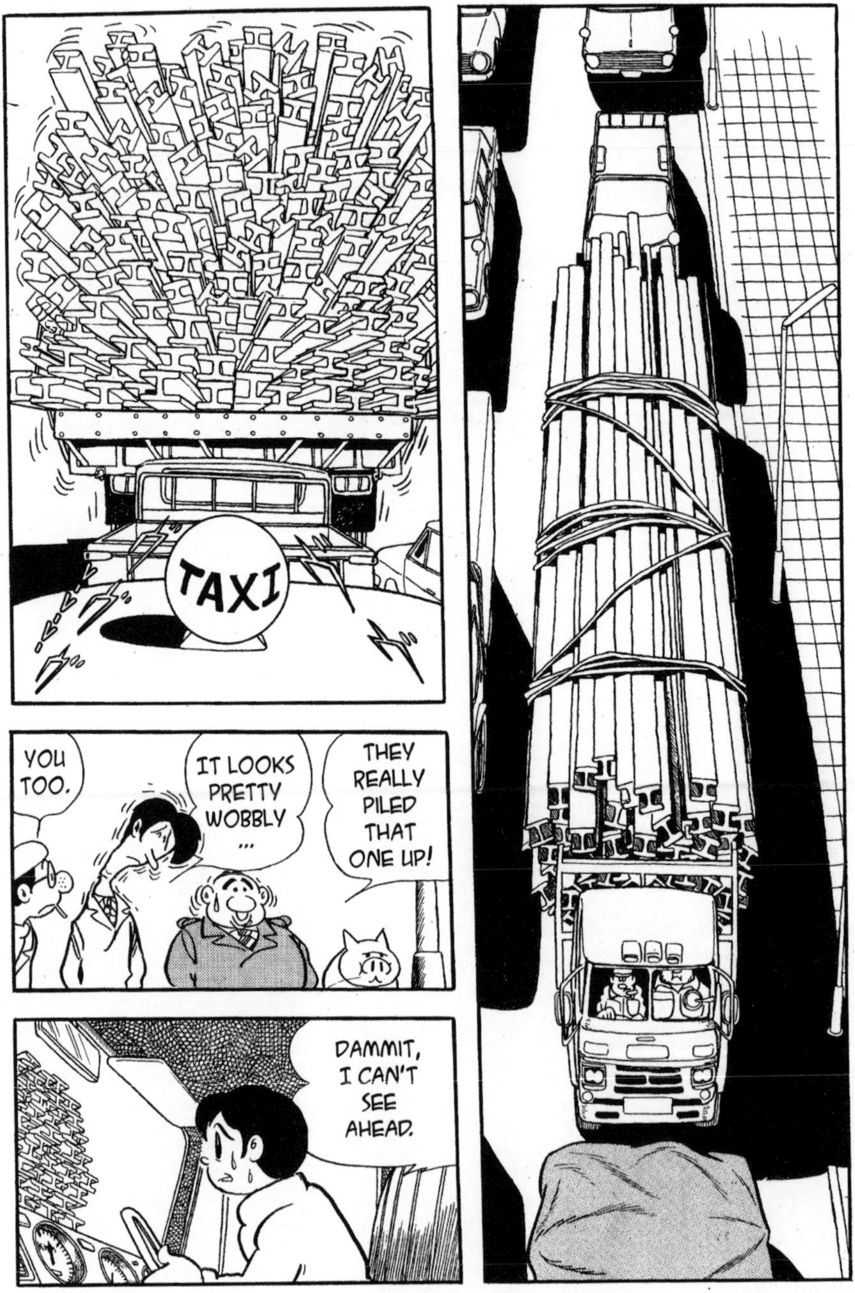
TAXI
THEY REALLY PILED THAT ONE UP!
IT LOOKS PRETTY WOBBLY ...
YOU TOO.
DAMMIT, I CAN'T SEE AHEAD.

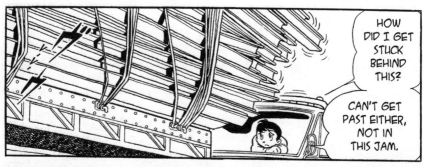

HOW DID I GET STUCK BEHIND THIS?
CAN'T GET PAST EITHER, NOT IN THIS JAM.
BRM
HEY, THEY'VE MOVED UP. STEP ON IT SOME.
CLUNK
HUP
CLUNK
SAY, AIN'T OUR LOAD TOO BIG?
NAH, IT'LL HOLD. THIS IS NOTHING.
LURCH

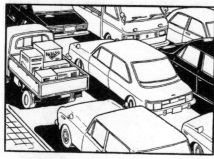

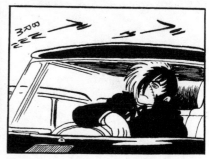

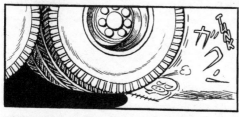

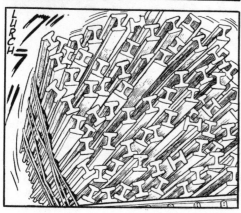

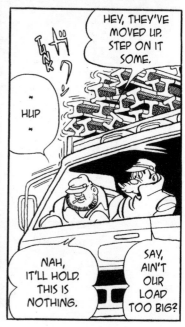

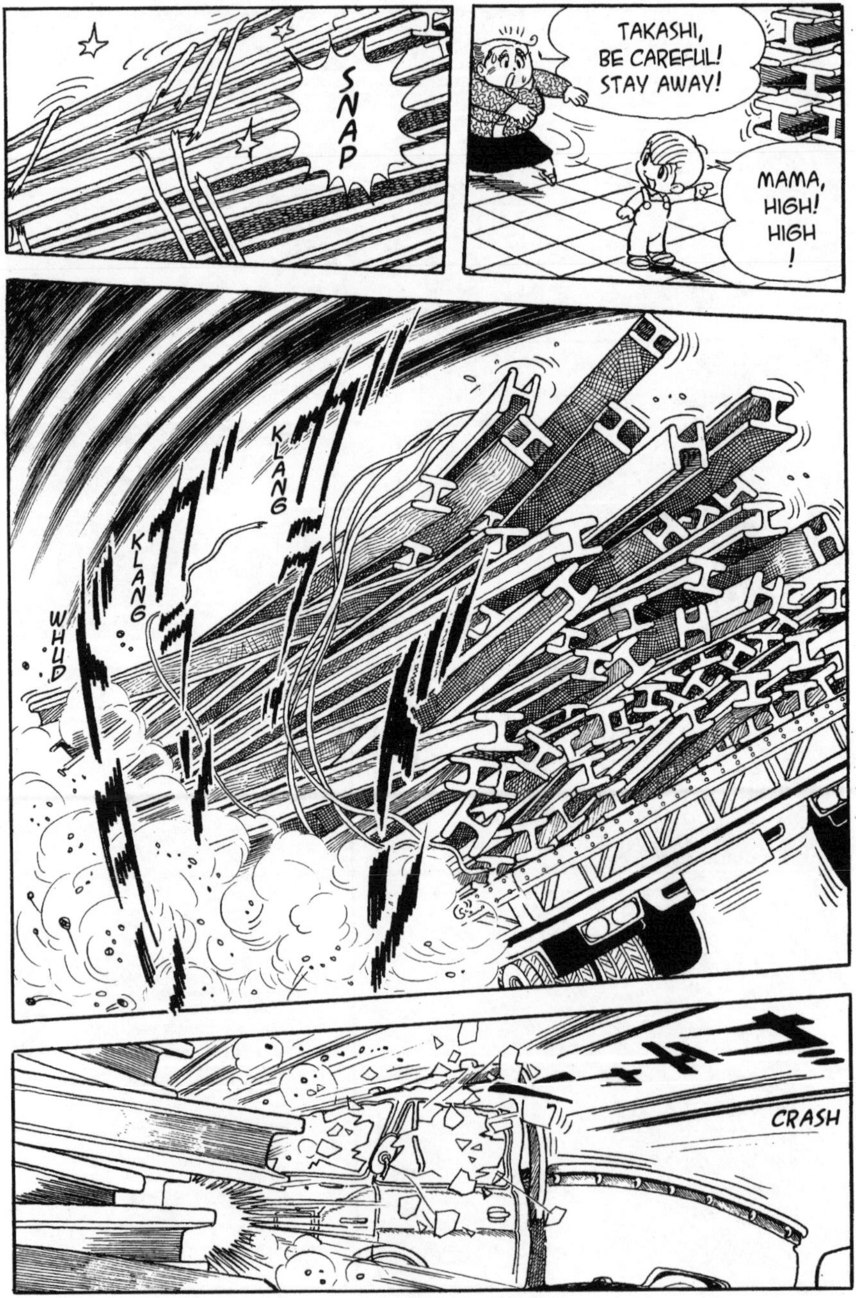
TAKASHI, BE CAREFUL! STAY AWAY!
MAMA, HIGH! HIGH!
SNAP
KLANG
KLANG
WHUD
CRASH

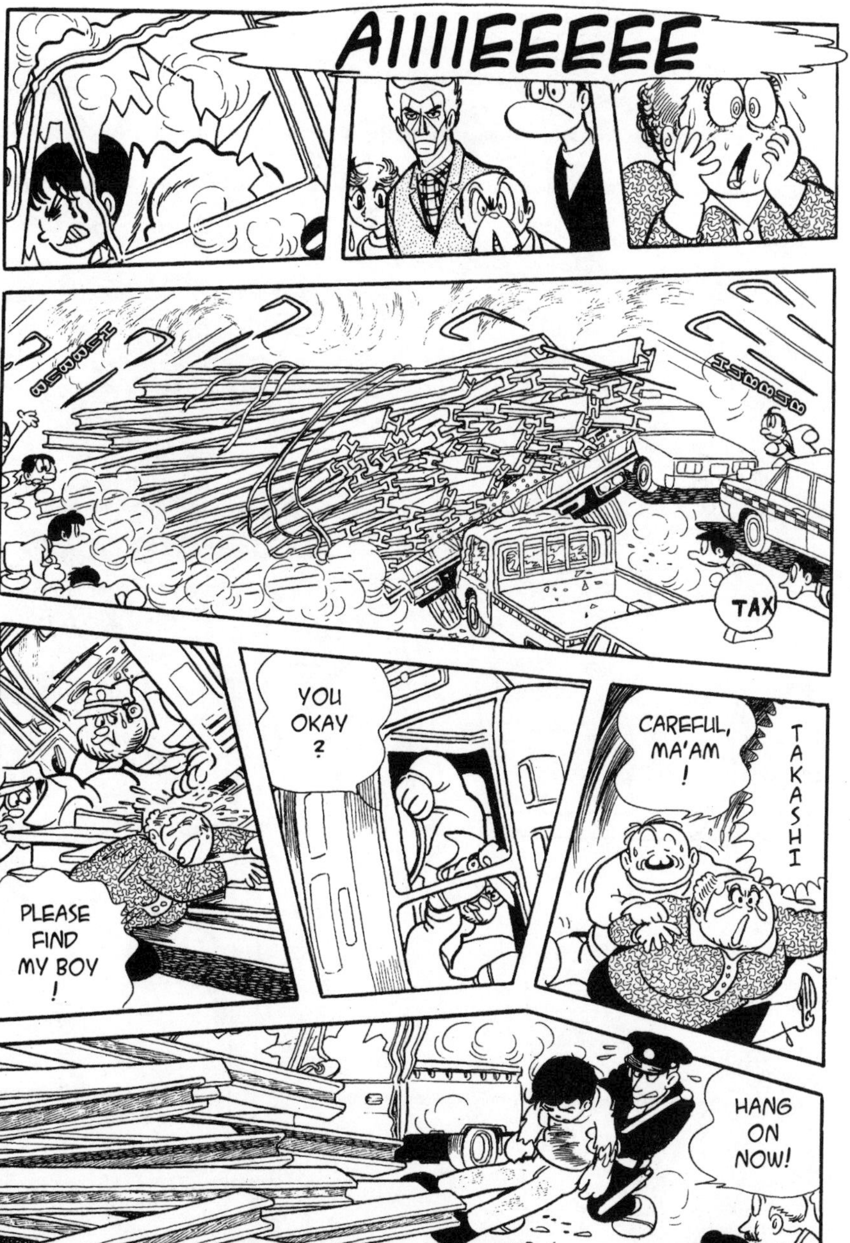
AIIIEEEEE
CAREFUL, MA'AM!
TAKASHI
YOU OKAY?
PLEASE FIND MY BOY!
HANG ON NOW!

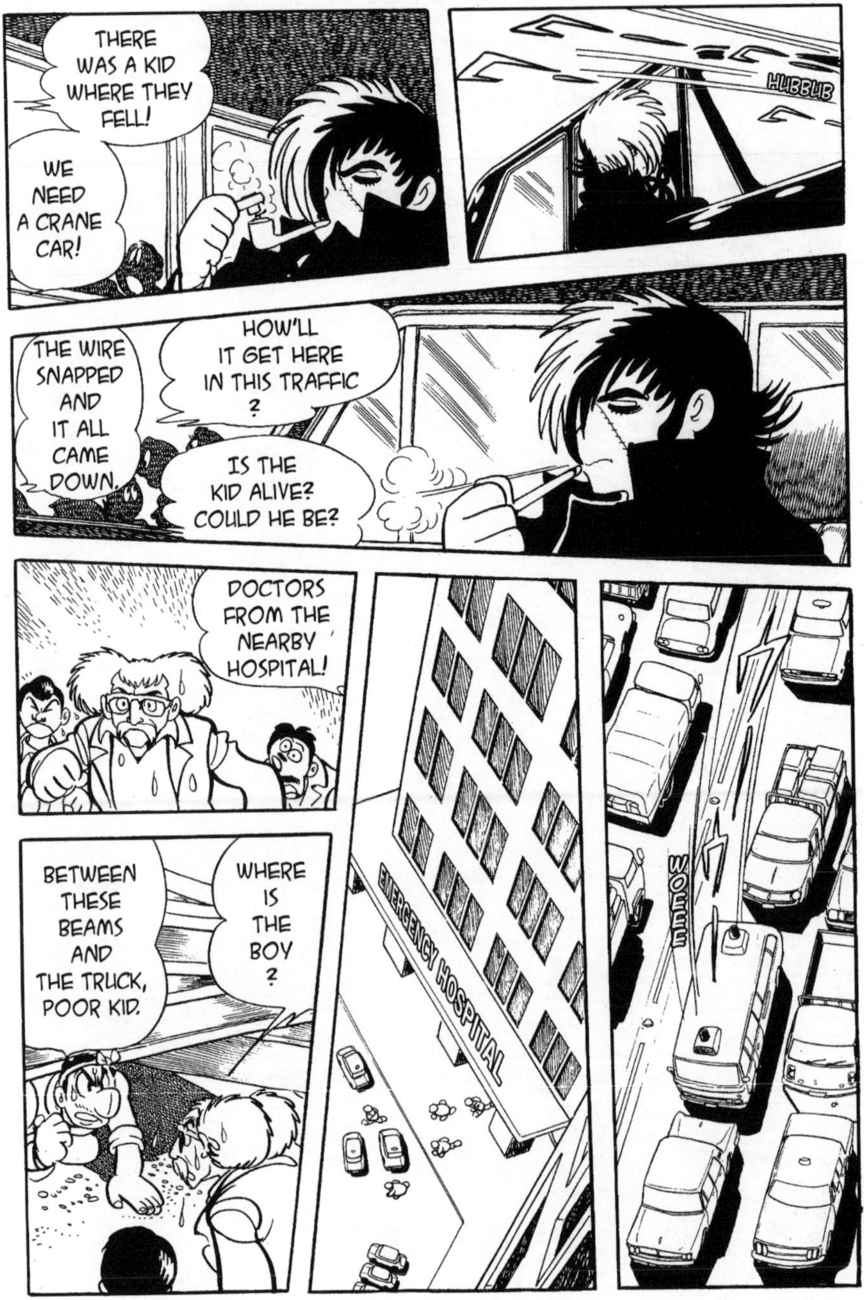
HUBBUB
THERE WAS A KID WHERE THEY FELL!
WE NEED A CRANE CAR!
HOW'LL IT GET HERE IN THIS TRAFFIC?
IS THE KID ALIVE? COULD HE BE?
THE WIRE SNAPPED AND IT ALL CAME DOWN.
WOEEE
EMERGENCY HOSPITAL
DOCTORS FROM THE NEARBY HOSPITAL!
WHERE IS THE BOY?
BETWEEN THESE BEAMS AND THE TRUCK, POOR KID.

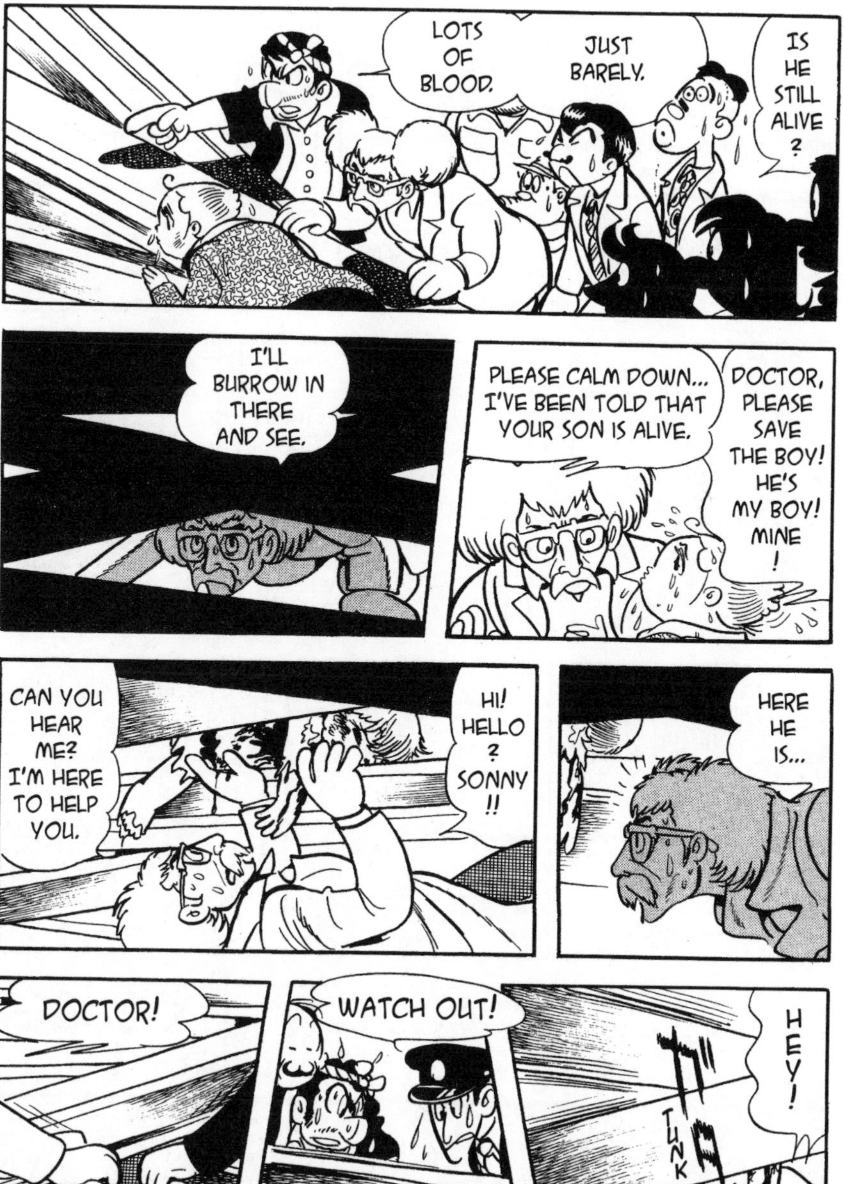
IS HE STILL ALIVE?
JUST BARELY.
LOTS OF BLOOD.
DOCTOR, PLEASE SAVE THE BOY! HE'S MY BOY! MINE!
PLEASE CALM DOWN... I'VE BEEN TOLD THAT YOUR SON IS ALIVE.
I'LL BURROW IN THERE AND SEE.
HERE HE IS...
HI! HELLO? SONNY!!
CAN YOU HEAR ME? I'M HERE TO HELP YOU.
HEY!
TUNK
WATCH OUT!
DOCTOR!

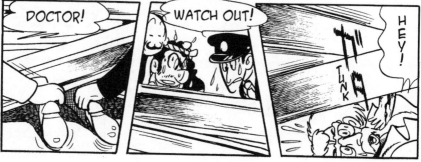

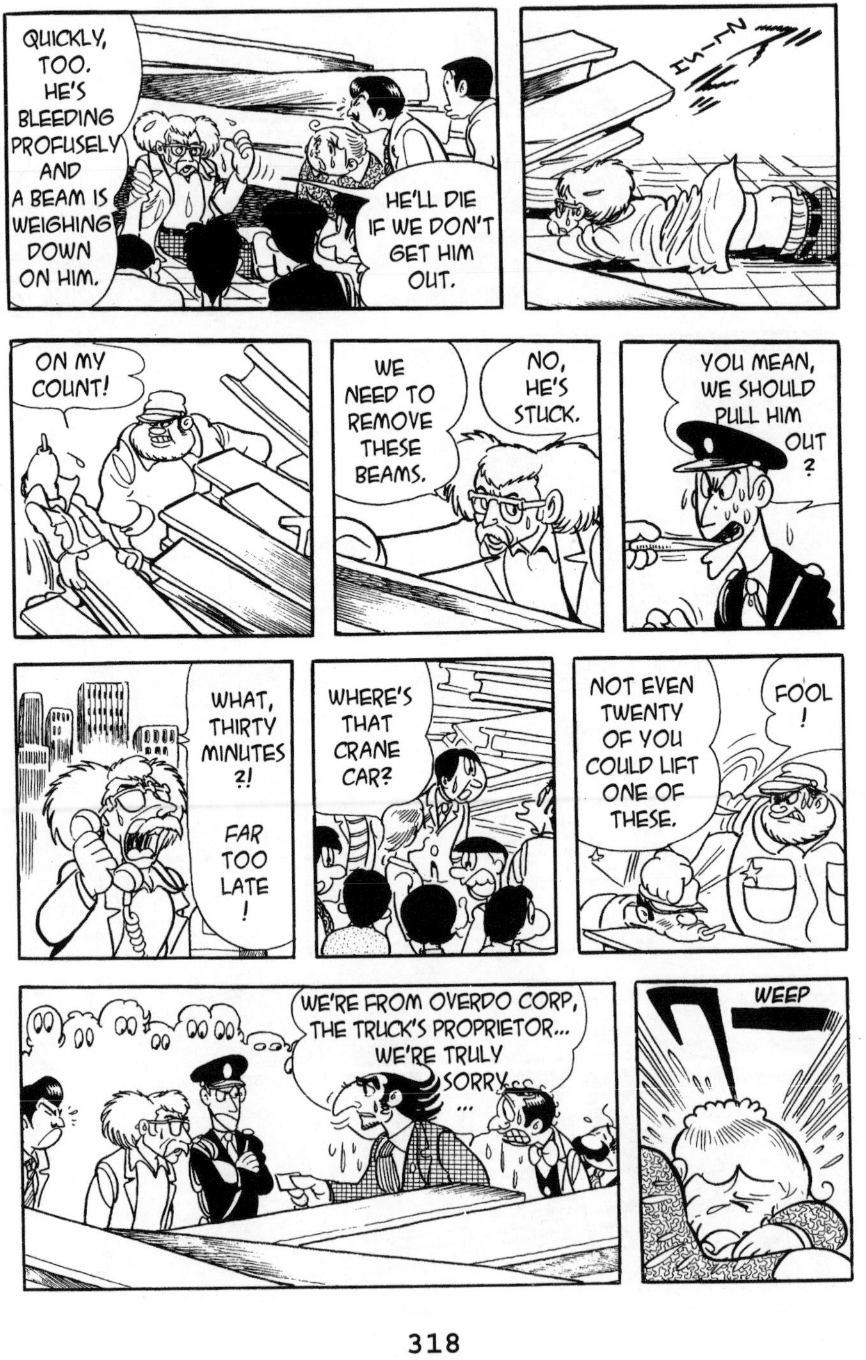
QUICKLY, TOO. HE'S BLEEDING PROFUSELY AND A BEAM IS WEIGHING DOWN ON HIM.
HE'LL DIE IF WE DON'T GET HIM OUT.
YOU MEAN, WE SHOULD PULL HIM OUT?
NO, HE'S STUCK.
WE NEED TO REMOVE THESE BEAMS.
ON MY COUNT!
FOOL!
NOT EVEN TWENTY OF YOU COULD LIFT ONE OF THESE.
WHERE'S THAT CRANE CAR?
WHAT, THIRTY MINUTES?!
FAR TOO LATE!
WEEP
WE'RE FROM OVERDO CORP, THE TRUCK'S PROPRIETOR... WE'RE TRULY SORRY...

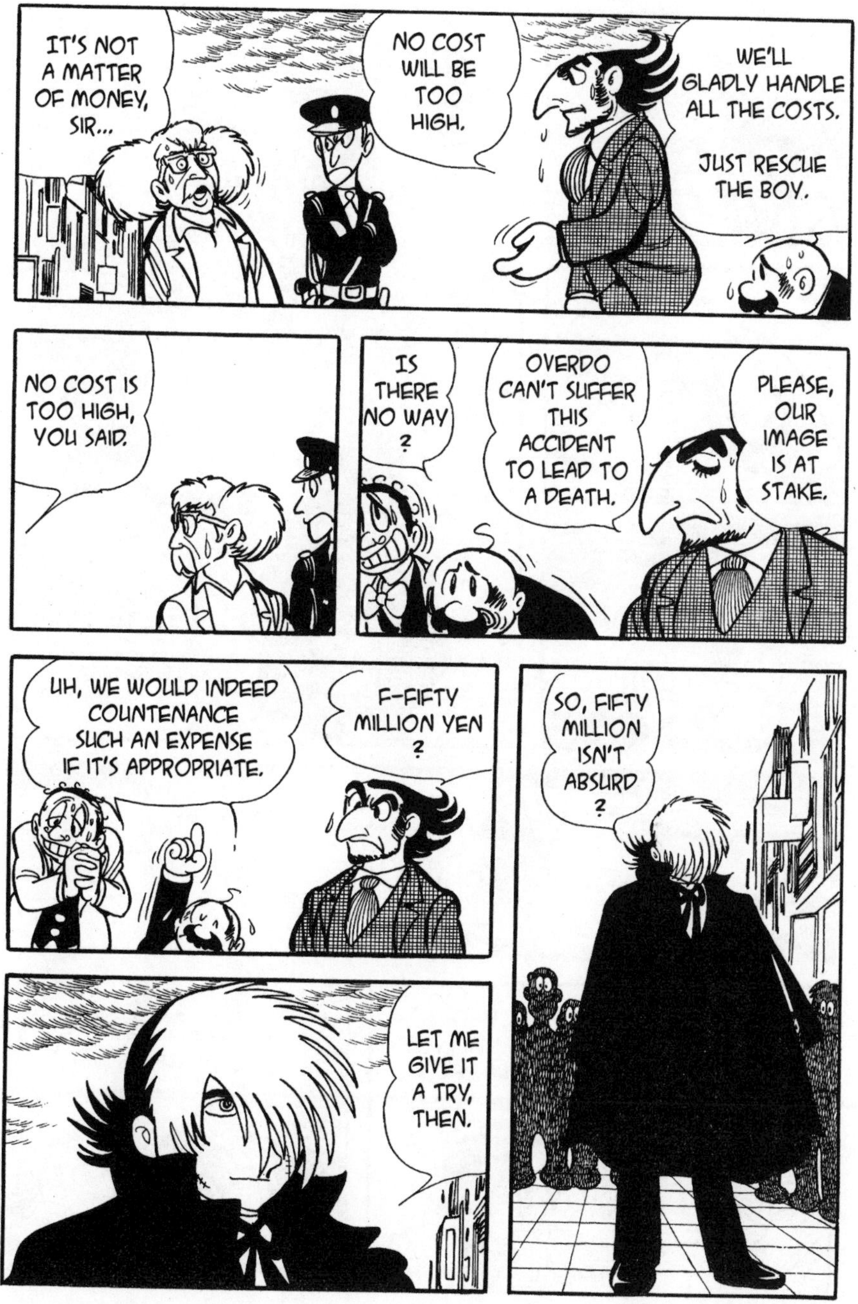
WE'LL GLADLY HANDLE ALL THE COSTS.
JUST RESCUE THE BOY.
NO COST WILL BE TOO HIGH.
IT'S NOT A MATTER OF MONEY, SIR...
PLEASE, OUR IMAGE IS AT STAKE.
OVERDO CAN'T SUFFER THIS ACCIDENT TO LEAD TO A DEATH.
IS THERE NO WAY?
NO COST IS TOO HIGH, YOU SAID.
SO, FIFTY MILLION ISN'T ABSURD?
F-FIFTY MILLION YEN?
UH, WE WOULD INDEED COUNTENANCE SUCH AN EXPENSE IF IT'S APPROPRIATE.
LET ME GIVE IT A TRY, THEN.

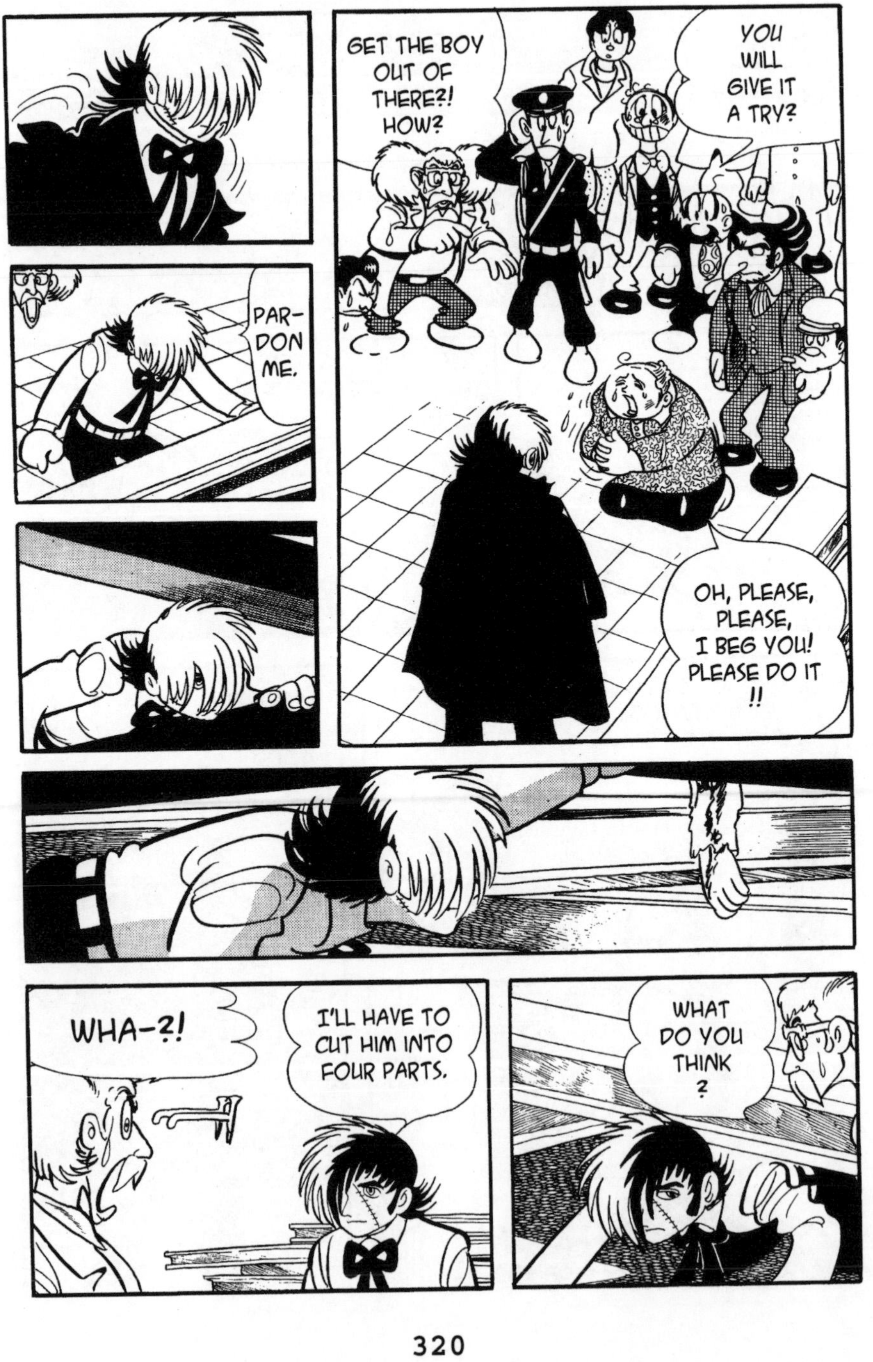
YOU WILL GIVE IT A TRY?
GET THE BOY OUT OF THERE?! HOW?
OH, PLEASE, PLEASE, I BEG YOU! PLEASE DO IT !!
PAR-DON ME.
WHAT DO YOU THINK ?
I'LL HAVE TO CUT HIM INTO FOUR PARTS.
WHA-?!

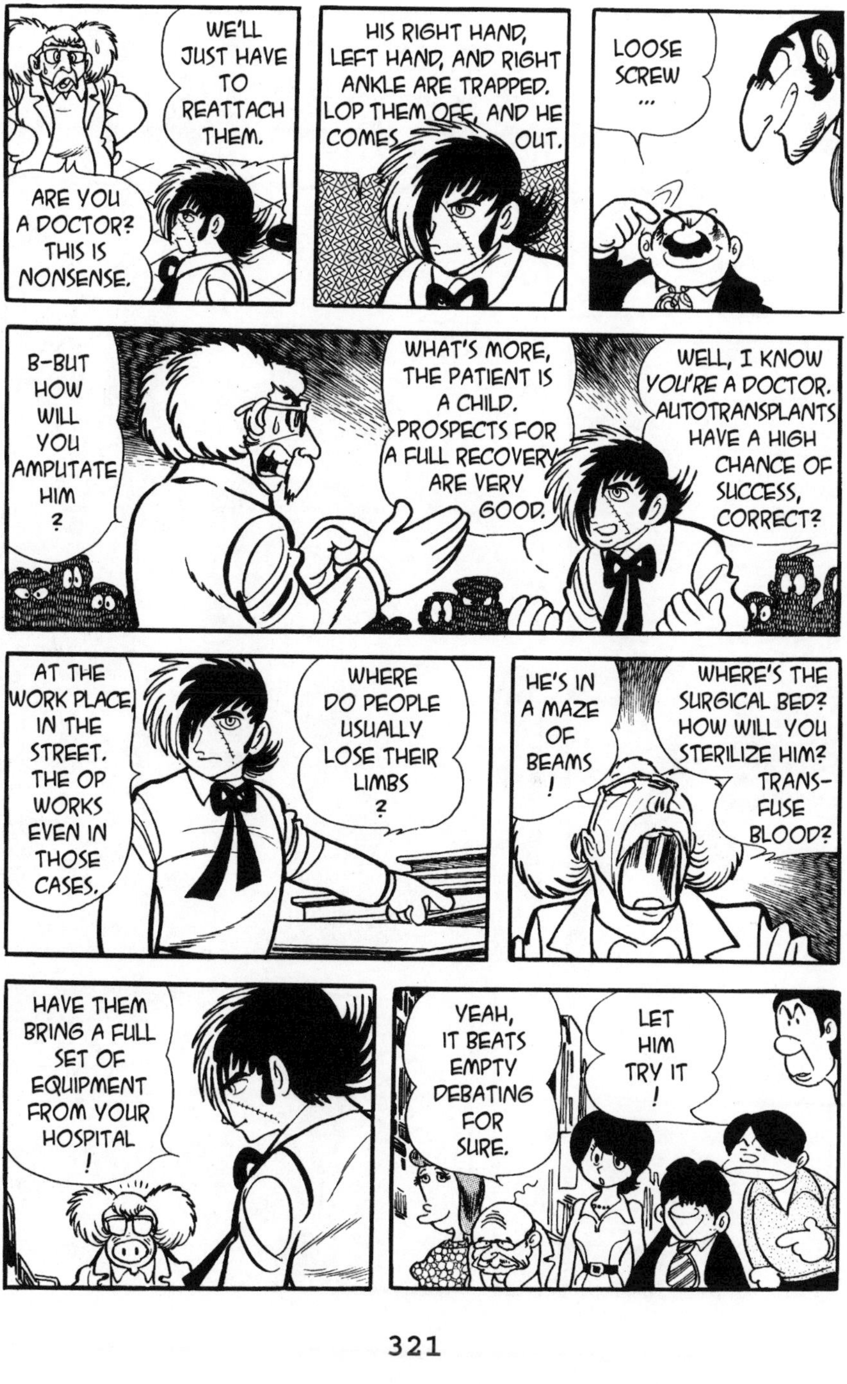
LOOSE SCREW ...
HIS RIGHT HAND, LEFT HAND, AND RIGHT ANKLE ARE TRAPPED. LOP THEM OFF, AND HE COMES OUT.
WE'LL JUST HAVE TO REATTACH THEM.
ARE YOU A DOCTOR? THIS IS NONSENSE.
WELL, I KNOW YOU'RE A DOCTOR. AUTOTRANSPLANTS HAVE A HIGH CHANCE OF SUCCESS, CORRECT?
WHAT'S MORE, THE PATIENT IS A CHILD. PROSPECTS FOR A FULL RECOVERY ARE VERY GOOD.
B-BUT HOW WILL YOU AMPUTATE HIM?
WHERE'S THE SURGICAL BED? HOW WILL YOU STERILIZE HIM? TRANS-FUSE BLOOD?
HE'S IN A MAZE OF BEAMS!
WHERE DO PEOPLE USUALLY LOSE THEIR LIMBS?
AT THE WORK PLACE, IN THE STREET. THE OP WORKS EVEN IN THOSE CASES.
LET HIM TRY IT!
YEAH, IT BEATS EMPTY DEBATING FOR SURE.
HAVE THEM BRING A FULL SET OF EQUIPMENT FROM YOUR HOSPITAL!

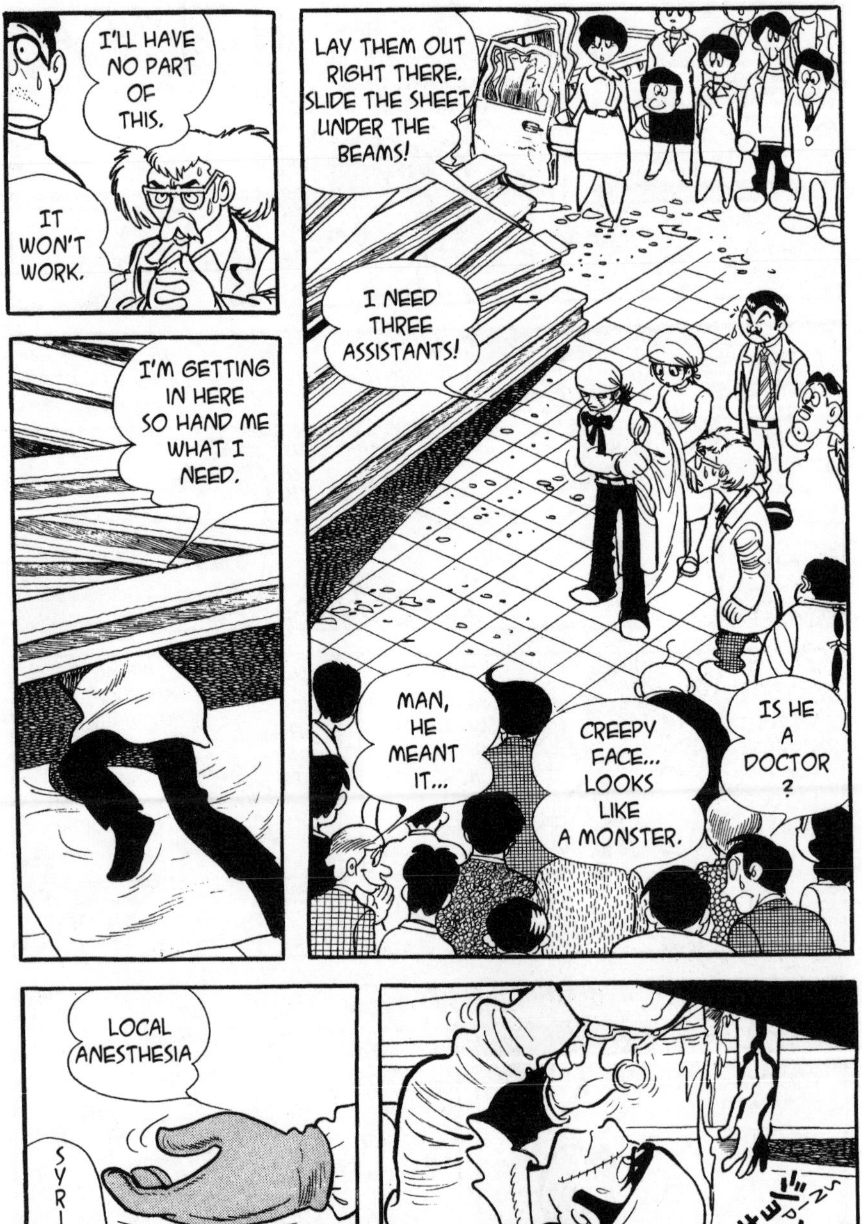
LAY THEM OUT RIGHT THERE. SLIDE THE SHEET UNDER THE BEAMS!
I NEED THREE ASSISTANTS!
IS HE A DOCTOR?
CREEPY FACE... LOOKS LIKE A MONSTER.
MAN, HE MEANT IT...
I'LL HAVE NO PART OF THIS.
IT WON'T WORK.
I'M GETTING IN HERE SO HAND ME WHAT I NEED.
LOCAL ANESTHESIA
SYRINGE

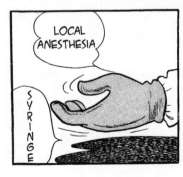

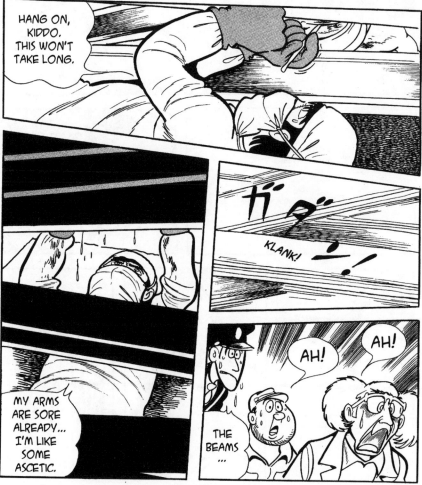

FOR REAL ?!

THIS IS NUTS.

TAMPONADE

HANG ON, KIDDO. THIS WON'T TAKE LONG.

KLANK!

MY ARMS ARE SORE ALREADY... I'M LIKE SOME ASCETIC.

THE BEAMS ...

AH!

AH!

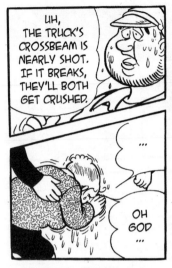

UH, THE TRUCK'S CROSSBEAM IS NEARLY SHOT. IF IT BREAKS, THEY'LL BOTH GET CRUSHED.
...
OH GOD ...
I'VE DISARTICULATED THE RIGHT SHOULDER! HERE, TAKE THE ARM.
RUSH IT TO THE HOSPITAL !
NEXT, THE HIP JOINT ...
THIS WILL BE KINDA TOUGH.
KAERK

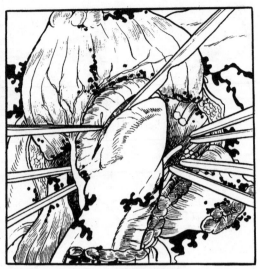

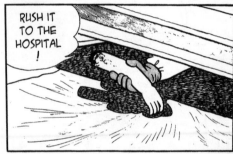

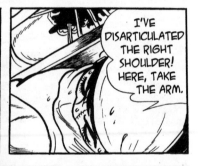

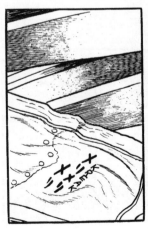

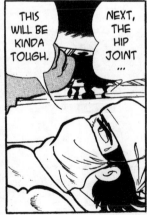

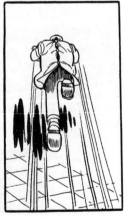

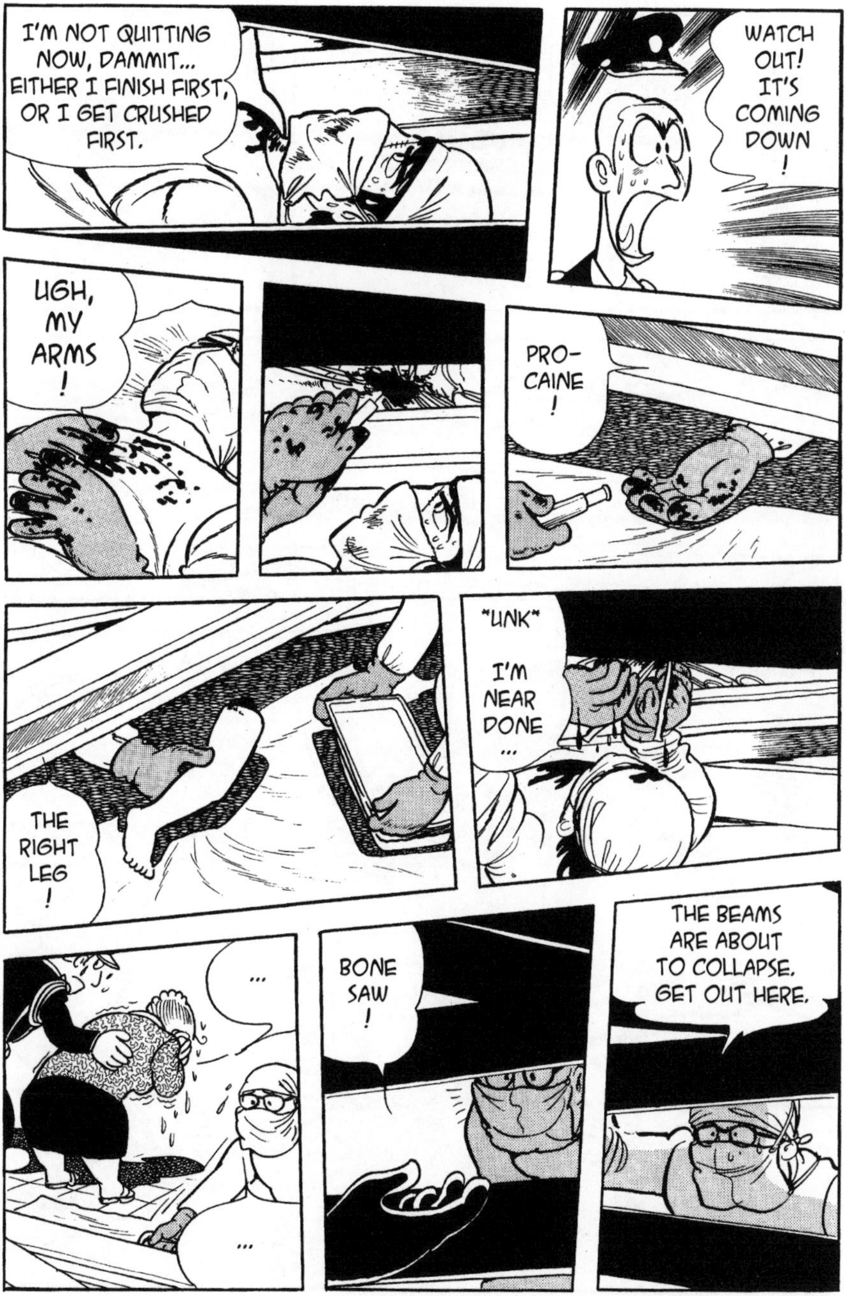
WATCH OUT! IT'S COMING DOWN!
I'M NOT QUITTING NOW, DAMMIT... EITHER I FINISH FIRST, OR I GET CRUSHED FIRST.
PRO-CAINE!
UGH, MY ARMS!
"UNK"
I'M NEAR DONE ...
THE RIGHT LEG!
THE BEAMS ARE ABOUT TO COLLAPSE. GET OUT HERE.
BONE SAW!
...
...

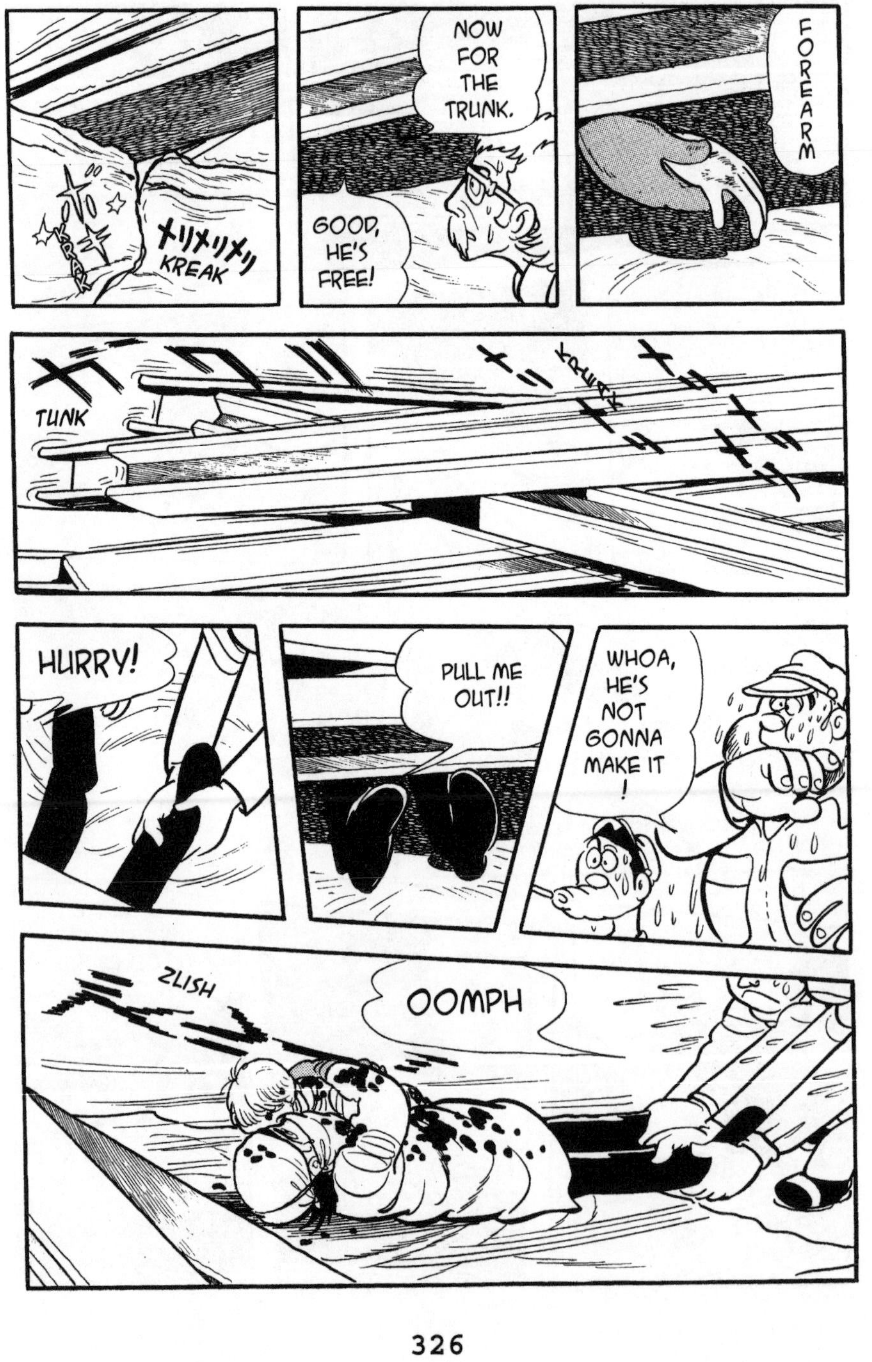
FOREARM
NOW FOR THE TRUNK.
GOOD, HE'S FREE!
メリメリメリ
KREAK
KRAAK
KRWAK
TUNK
WHOA, HE'S NOT GONNA MAKE IT!
PULL ME OUT!!
HURRY!
OOMPH
ZLISH

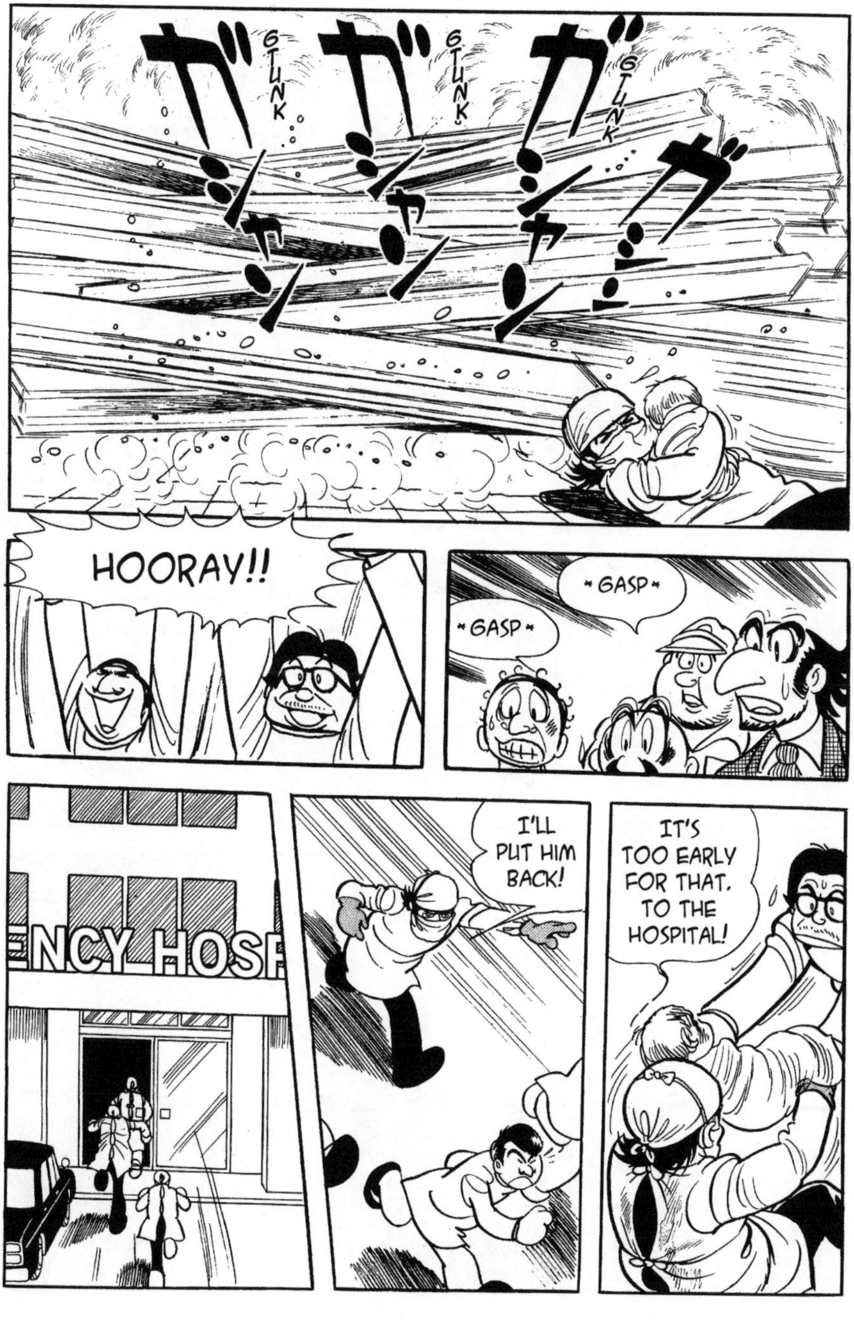
GTUNK
GTUNK
GTUNK
GASP
GASP
HOORAY!!
IT'S TOO EARLY FOR THAT. TO THE HOSPITAL!
I'LL PUT HIM BACK!
ENCY HOSP

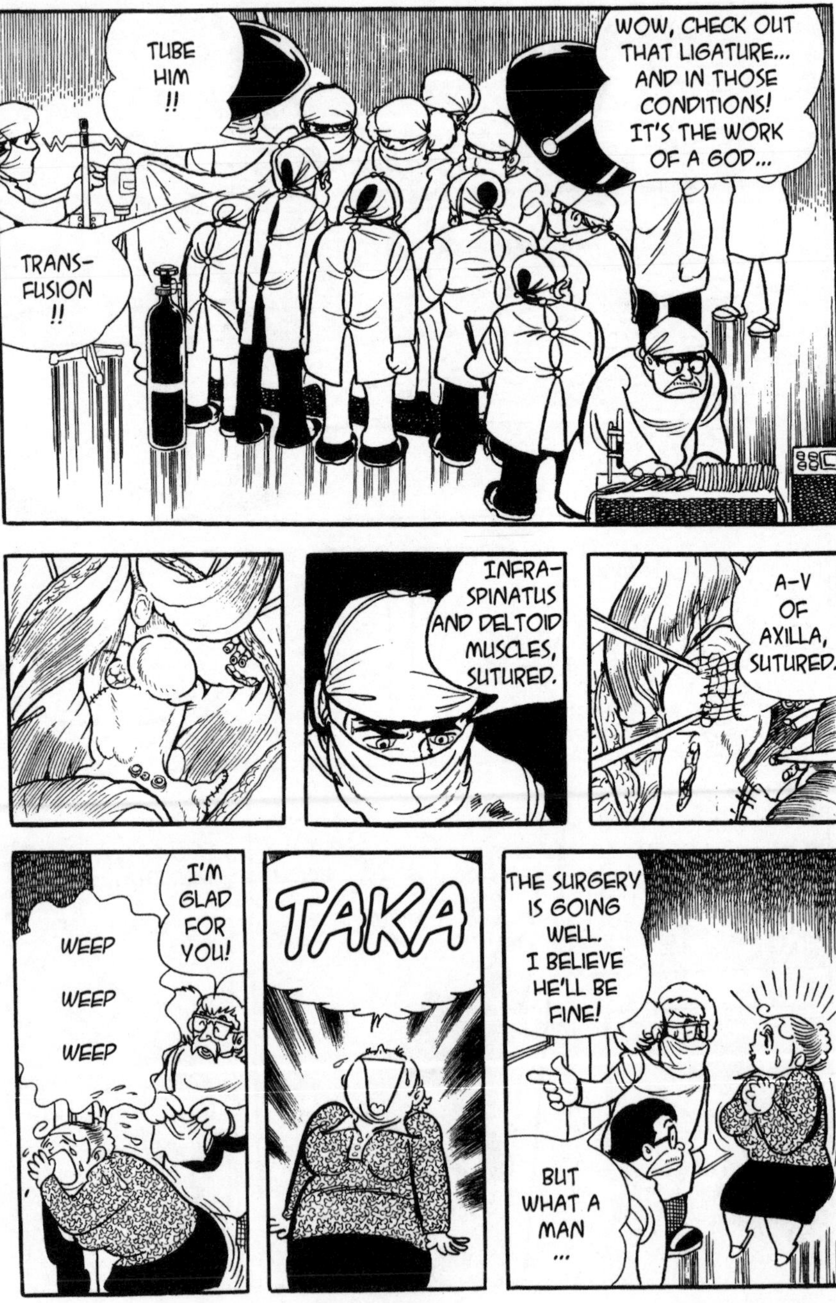
WOW, CHECK OUT THAT LIGATURE... AND IN THOSE CONDITIONS! IT'S THE WORK OF A GOD...
TUBE HIM !!
TRANS-FUSION !!
A-V OF AXILLA, SUTURED.
INFRA-SPINATUS AND DELTOID MUSCLES, SUTURED.
THE SURGERY IS GOING WELL. I BELIEVE HE'LL BE FINE!
BUT WHAT A MAN ...
TAKA
I'M GLAD FOR YOU!
WEEP
WEEP
WEEP

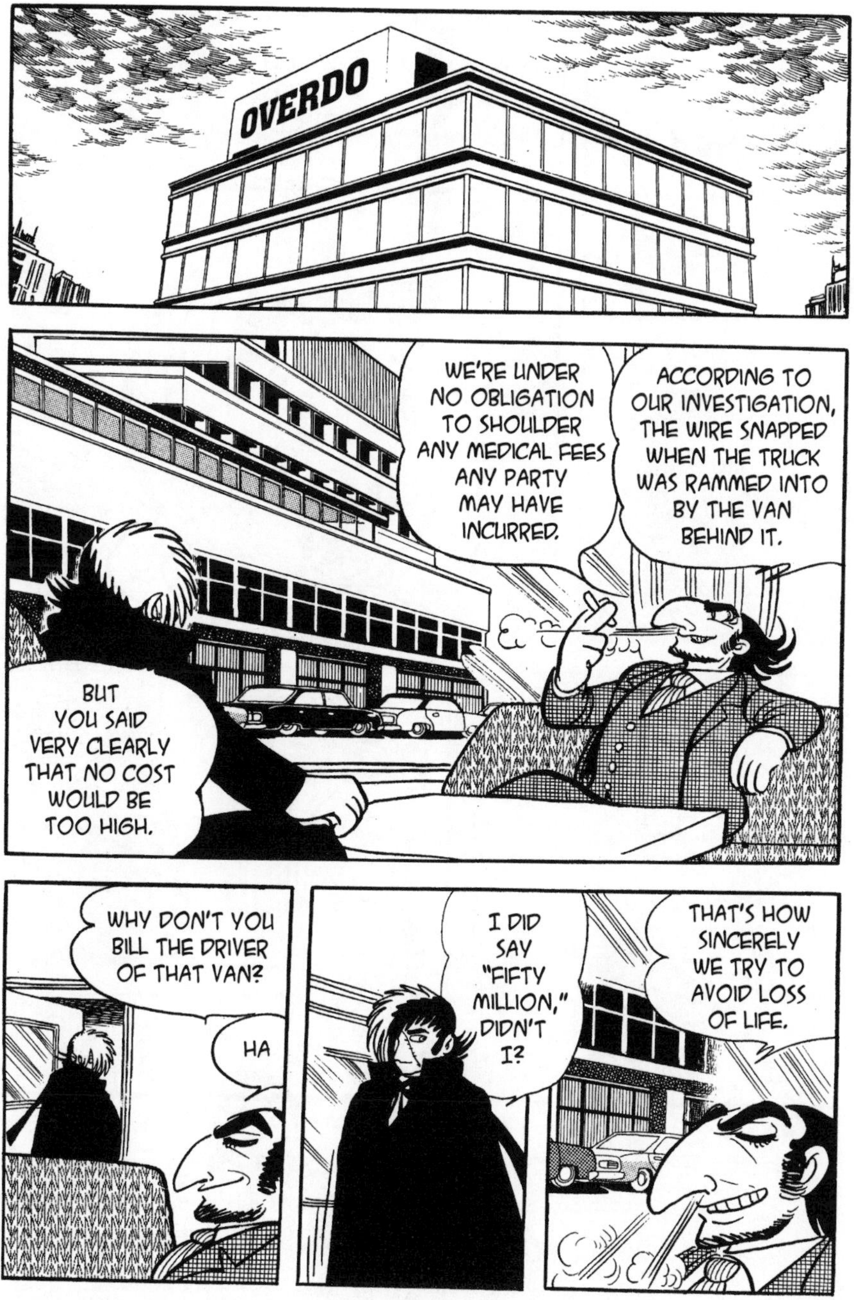
OVERDO
ACCORDING TO OUR INVESTIGATION, THE WIRE SNAPPED WHEN THE TRUCK WAS RAMMED INTO BY THE VAN BEHIND IT.
WE'RE UNDER NO OBLIGATION TO SHOULDER ANY MEDICAL FEES ANY PARTY MAY HAVE INCURRED.
BUT YOU SAID VERY CLEARLY THAT NO COST WOULD BE TOO HIGH.
THAT'S HOW SINCERELY WE TRY TO AVOID LOSS OF LIFE.
I DID SAY "FIFTY MILLION," DIDN'T I?
WHY DON'T YOU BILL THE DRIVER OF THAT VAN?
HA

IT'S A LIE!!
I SAW IT WITH MY OWN EYES! THE WIRE SNAPPED FIRST!
MY CRASH WAS A RESULT!!
OVERDO CORP IS LYING!!
I DON'T HAVE SO MUCH MONEY...
GO TO COURT, THEN.
DOC-TOR!
GIVE YOU!
AH, THIS IS VERY NICE.
WORTH FIFTY MILLION YEN!

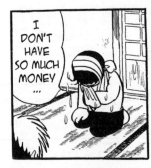

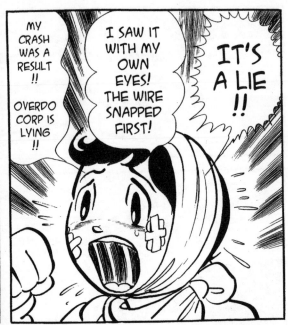

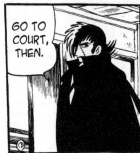

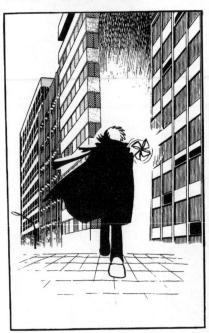

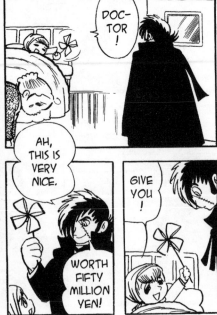

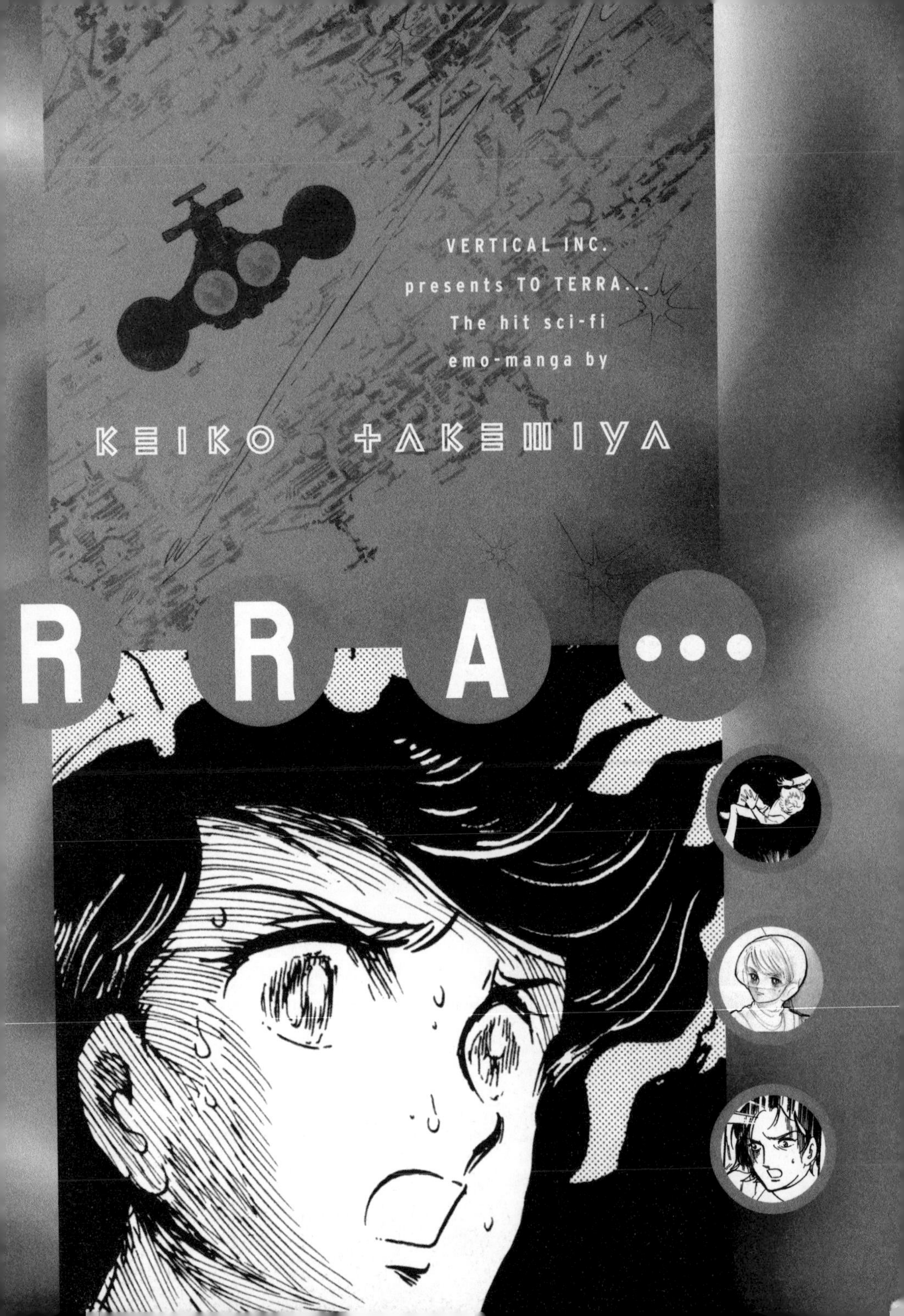
VERTICAL INC.
presents TO TERRA...
The hit sci-fi
emo-manga by
KEIKO TAKEMIYA
RRA...

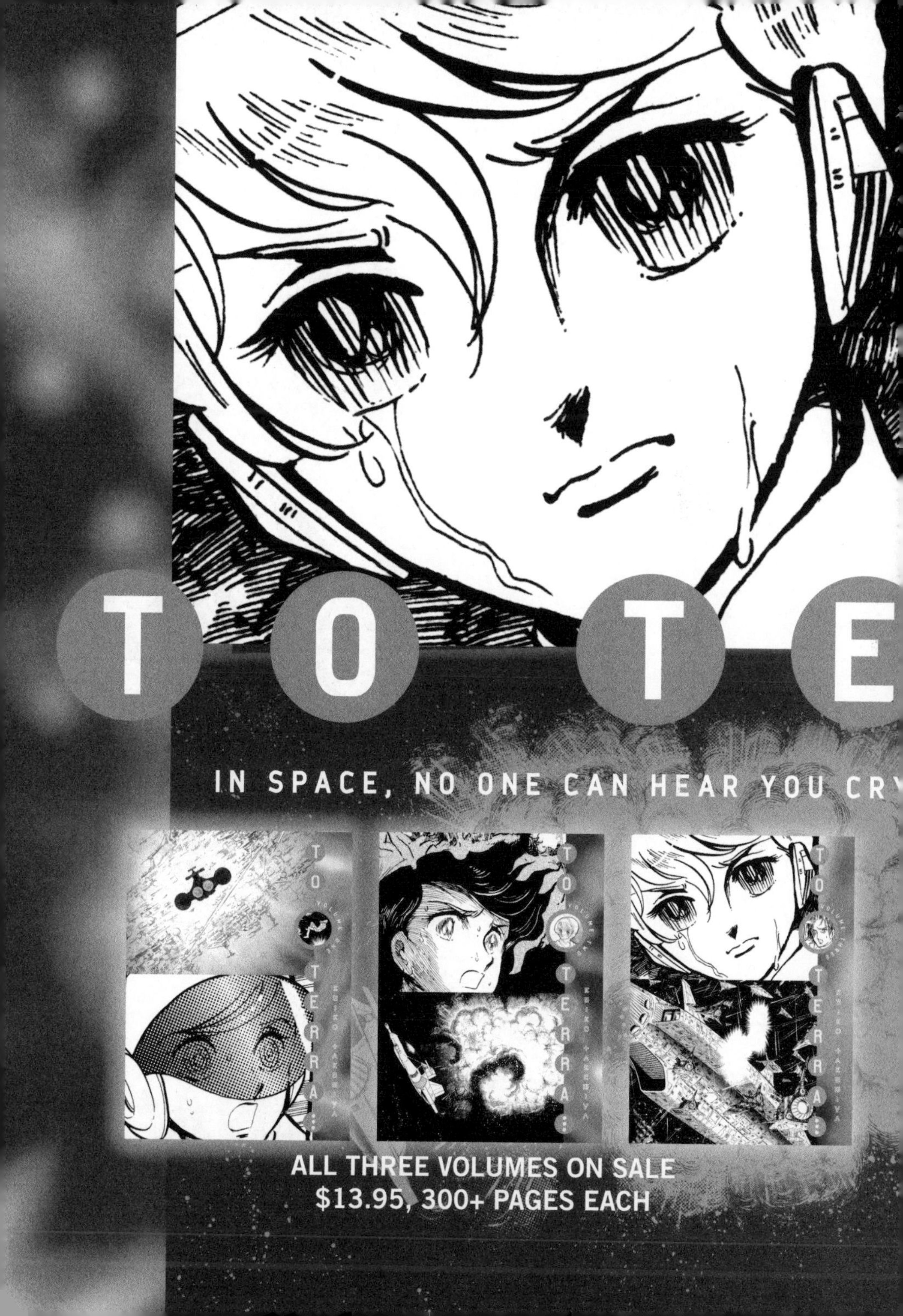

TO TE
IN SPACE, NO ONE CAN HEAR YOU CR
ALL THREE VOLUMES ON SALE
$13.95, 300+ PAGES EACH

PRAISE FOR DORORO:

"**Platinum Award**. Tezuka blends high-adventure plotting with
deep and thoughtful themes in his inimitable style.
It seems a shame it's only all been in Japanese until now."
—*Advanced Media Network*

"**Grade: A**. Osamu Tezuka's ability to immerse
his readers in the lives and hardships of
his characters is staggering. An awesome
action/adventure title with strong characterizations and
a gripping setting." —*Manga Maniac Cafe*

"Tezuka's characters may be big-eyed and cute,
but in *Dororo* they are up to serious business."
—*Daily Yomiuri*

"Tezuka's drawing is as powerful and assured as ever…
and the serious moments of the story
have real power." —*ComicMix*

"A series you will surely see jump from
those 'looking forward to' lists to the
'best of 2008' lists."
—*Mecha Mecha Media*

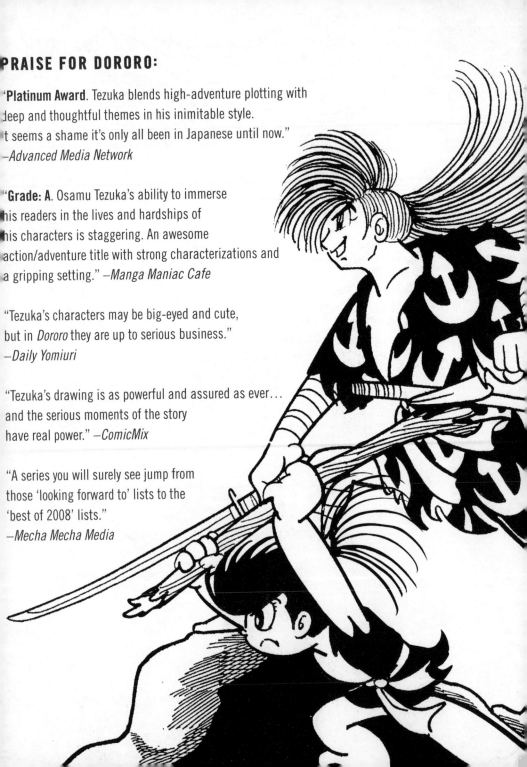